A

# POLITICAL
# ECONOMY
OF THE
# MIDDLE EAST

# A
# POLITICAL ECONOMY
## OF THE
# MIDDLE EAST

State, Class, and
Economic Development

## Alan Richards
UNIVERSITY OF CALIFORNIA–SANTA CRUZ

## John Waterbury
PRINCETON UNIVERSITY

Westview Press
BOULDER, SAN FRANCISCO, AND OXFORD

To the memory of
MALCOLM KERR

Copyright © 1990 by Westview Press, Inc.

Published in 1990 in the United States of America by Westview Press, Inc., 5500 Central Avenue, Boulder, Colorado 80301, and in the United Kingdom by Westview Press, Inc., 36 Lonsdale Road, Summertown, Oxford OX2 7EW

Library of Congress Cataloging-in-Publication Data
Richards, Alan, 1946–
  A political economy of the Middle East : state, class, and
economic development / Alan Richards, John Waterbury.
      p.   cm.
  Includes bibliographical references.
  ISBN 0-8133-0155-6. ISBN 0-8133-0156-4 (pbk.)
    1. Middle East—Economic conditions—1979–    . 2. Middle East—
Economic policy. 3. Working class—Middle East. 4. Middle East—
Politics and government—1979–    . I. Waterbury, John. II. Title.
HC415.15.R53   1990
338.956—dc20                                                                    89-49123
                                                                                         CIP

Printed and bound in the United States of America

⊗  The paper used in this publication meets the requirements
      of the American National Standard for Permanence of Paper
      for Printed Library Materials Z39.48-1984.

10    9    8    7    6    5    4    3    2

# CONTENTS

# TABLES AND ILLUSTRATIONS

# ACRONYMS AND ABBREVIATIONS

| | |
|---|---|
| AAAID | Arab Authority for Agricultural Investment and Development |
| ADLI | agricultural-development-led industrial |
| AMIO | Arab Military Industrialization Organization |
| ANM | Arab National Movement |
| ASU | Arab Socialist Union |
| b/d | barrels per day |
| BNDE | National Economic Development Bank |
| BP | British Petroleum |
| CIA | Central Intelligence Agency |
| CNRA | National Council of the Algerian Revolution |
| D | Tunisian dinars |
| DA | Algerian dinars |
| DC | developed country |
| DISK | Confederation of Progressive Trade Unions |
| EC or EEC | European Community or European Economic Community |
| FAO | Food and Agriculture Organization |
| FDIC | Front for the Defense of Constitutional Institutions |
| FLN | National Liberation Front |
| GDI | gross domestic investment |
| GDP | gross domestic product |
| GNP | gross national product |
| GOBI | growth monitoring, oral rehydration therapy, breast feeding, immunization |
| HYV | higher-yielding varieties |
| IBRD | International Bank for Reconstruction and Development |
| ICOR | incremental capital-to-output ratio |
| ICP | Iraqi Communist party |
| IMF | International Monetary Fund |
| IPC | Iraq Petroleum Company |

| | |
|---|---|
| IRR | internal rate of return |
| ISI | import-substituting industrialization |
| LDC | less-developed country |
| £E | Egyptian pounds |
| LEB | life expectancy at birth |
| MAPAI | Israel Labor party |
| MEB | Military Economic Board |
| MENA | Middle East and North Africa |
| MVA | manufacturing value-added |
| NATO | North Atlantic Treaty Organization |
| NIC | newly industrializing country |
| NLF | National Liberation Front |
| NPC | nominal protection coefficient |
| OCE | Cherifian Foreign Trade Office |
| OCP | Cherifian Phosphates Office |
| OECD | Organization for Economic Cooperation and Development |
| OPEC | Organization of Petroleum Exporting Countries |
| ORT | oral rehydration therapy |
| OYAK | Armed Forces Mutual Assistance Fund |
| PDRY | People's Democratic Republic of Yemen |
| PLO | Palestine Liberation Organization |
| PPA | Algerian People's party |
| PRC | People's Republic of China |
| PRI | Institutional Revolutionary party |
| RCC | Revolutionary Command Council (Iraq, Egypt) |
| ROK | Republic of Korea |
| RPP | Republican People's party |
| SABIC | Saudi Basic Industries Corporation |
| SAVAK | Iranian Security and Intelligence Organization |
| SNS | National Steel Corporation |
| SOE | state-owned enterprise |
| SONACOME | National Corporation for Mechanical Construction |
| SONATRACH | National Corporation for Transport and Marketing of Hydrocarbons |
| TL | Turkish lira |
| UAE | United Arab Emirates |
| UAR | United Arab Republic |
| UGTA | General Confederation of Algerian Workers |
| UGTT | General Confederation of Tunisian Workers |
| UK | United Kingdom |
| UNESCO | United Nations Economic, Scientific, and Cultural Organization |
| UNICEF | United Nations International Children's Emergency Fund |
| USAID | United States Agency for International Development |
| WHO | World Health Organization |
| YAR | Yemen Arab Republic |

# ACKNOWLEDGMENTS

This book is the distillation of over fifty years of the authors' combined experience of living in and studying the Middle East. In that respect it would be impossible to single out individuals who influenced us and helped with this text. Nonetheless, during a five-year period both authors were members of the Joint Committee for the Near and Middle East of the Social Science Research Council, and in the course of our regular meetings we drew on the collective wisdom of that committee's members.

Two individuals merit special mention. Hongqiu Yang could not have anticipated when she came to the United States from the People's Republic of China that she would have to bring order to this text and handle the transcontinental mechanics of putting it together. Her effort was truly prodigious and is greatly appreciated. The second person is Fred Praeger, to whom the idea of this book owes its inception. His patience and encouragement were remarkable. We are grateful to Beijing and Vienna for having produced such superb collaborators.

The authors dedicate this book to the memory of Malcolm Kerr.

*Alan Richards*
Santa Cruz

*John Waterbury*
Princeton

# 1

# INTRODUCTION

There are two great games being played out in the Middle East. One, upon which this book is focused, is a quiet game that seldom makes headlines. It is the game of peoples and governments, states and societies, sometimes in cooperation but more often at odds, trying to advance the prosperity and overall development of the region's nations.

The other is the more conventional great game (see Brown 1984; Walt 1987) in which regional and superpower politics intersect. It has been the unhappy fate of the Middle East to be the stage for an extraordinary amount of conflict, much of it generated within the region itself, and the rest provoked from without. Merely in this century the region has been a major theater in two world wars, and it has witnessed a war for liberation in Turkey and seven years of colonial war in Algeria. There have been four wars between Israel and several of its Arab neighbors, prolonged civil wars in Lebanon and the Sudan, major long-term insurrections in Iraq and the former Spanish Sahara, prolonged violence between Israelis and Palestinians, and until the fall of 1988, one of the two longest conventional wars of this century, between Iraq and Iran (the other being that between Japan and China, 1937–1945).

The Middle East throughout history has always been frontstage in world politics. It has been endlessly fought over, coveted as strategic real estate on the world's major trade routes, and occasionally used as the launching pad for homegrown expansionist powers, the latest of which was the Ottoman Empire. The Middle East will not be left alone; that is its curse and its blessing. Geopolitical significance draws resources and special treatment from outside powers, but it also draws interference, meddling, and occasionally invasion.

These are the events that capture headlines. Over the period in which this book was being written, U.S. planes bombed Libya; Iraq and Iran exchanged missiles and strafed and bombed Arabian/Persian Gulf shipping, the United States downed a civilian Iranian flight with nearly three hundred passengers aboard; planes and ships were hijacked; Israel invaded Lebanon; and there was a major Palestinian uprising in the occupied West Bank.

The above notwithstanding, we premise much of our argument on the assumption that the game of development, no less painful and destructive in some ways than the game of conflict, is of equal if not greater importance. But the two are closely interrelated, as conflict obviously influences the course of development and vice versa. History has made clear, for instance, that regional conflict, even single events, can set in motion processes that destroy resources and disrupt societies, thereby irretrievably altering the political economies of large populations. One need think only of the assassination of the Archduke Ferdinand in Sarajevo, which triggered the events leading to World War I, to realize the extraordinary consequences that small incidents may contain. That act could be seen as a kind of epiphenomenon, in no way part of an ineluctable historical process. Yet it is the case that unresolved conflicts, unsettled scores, grievances unavenged and unforgotten abound to such an extent in the Middle East that events of seeming insignificance may put a spark to the tinder. The June 1967 war could have been avoided—in fact it took some colossal bungling on the part of all parties to launch it. But once launched, it changed not only the military and political landscape of the region, but the economic as well. Much the same could be said of the long war between Iraq and Iran.

In the midst of these tensions and conflicts, rapidly growing populations must be fed, educated, and employed, agricultural productivity increased, industrialization promoted, universities founded and expanded, technology acquired, armed forces trained and equipped, and some semblance of political order maintained. These are the questions with which we are concerned, and we address them through the lenses of political economy. What we have in mind is the formulation of public policies that shape the allocation of resources within societies *and* the political consequences that flow therefrom. Public policy is about choice, alternatives, and opportunity costs. Sometimes it is small groups of leaders who make these choices and then impose them on their societies. Sometimes choices are made that are reflective of the aspirations of major sectors of society, and sometimes choices are made through the elected representatives of society. However the choices may be determined, they always produce relative losses and gains for various sectors of society. Normally we expect those who benefit to try to consolidate their advantages and privileges, whereas those who have fared poorly will try to alter the status quo. Contending groups have various means at their disposal, some legal and some illegal, to try to influence public authorities and public policy in their favor. And as we shall show repeatedly, those authorities, the people who make up the governments and staff the upper echelons of the bureaucracies and public enterprises, frequently constitute an autonomous set of actors and interests in their own right.

Middle Eastern societies range from the very poor, such as North Yemen and the Sudan, to the very rich, such as Kuwait and Saudi Arabia. The highest generalized standards of living are probably to be found in Israel.

Similarly, these societies in political terms run the gamut from authoritarian rule by cliques and juntas to the qualified democracies of Israel,[1] Turkey, and until 1976, Lebanon. No simple generalizations can be made about the economic resources available to Middle Eastern nations, nor about the permissible channels through which Middle Easterners may seek to effect the allocation of those resources. What can be said is that there is a constant dialectic between state actors and various segments of their societies, and that in this century the dialectic has yielded dynamic, constantly changing equilibria. Like the unicorn, the status quo in the Middle East is the figment of fertile imaginations.

In some respects we see our endeavor as unique, but not entirely so. We have plenty of forerunners and sources of inspiration. We have tried to write an integrated, analytic text covering all of the contemporary Middle East. We believe we are the first to have tried to do this in the political economy mode, although Samir Amin's *The Arab Economy Today* (1982) might be seen as a cursory and polemical antecedent. Galal Amin's *The Modernization of Poverty* (1980) is richer and analytically more satisfying.[2] Generally one encounters anthologies in which individual authors contribute country case studies, often descriptive and not necessarily related to any set of analytic themes. Some of these are highly useful, such as Reich and Long (1986) and Ismael (1970), and could nicely accompany the present study.

There have been some notable attempts at synthetic analysis by individuals or coauthors, although none has used political-economic approaches. Halpern's *The Politics of Social Change in the Middle East and North Africa* (1963) is a landmark and although dated is still of great value. Hudson's *Arab Politics* (1977) is also highly recommended, as is Bill and Leiden's *Politics in the Middle East* (1984). Limited to the Maghreb is Moore's *Politics in North Africa* (1970). In other disciplines, there have been illustrious forerunners; in sociology, Berger's *The Arab World Today* (1964) and Lerner's *The Passing of Traditional Society* (1959). The study of North Africa by Hermassi (1972) is one of the rare contemporary contributions to sociological synthesis. In anthropology, Coon's *Caravan* (1958) is excellent but dated. More recently Bates and Rassam (1983) and Eickelman (1981) have provided fine anthropological interpretations of Middle Eastern society. Two economic historians have been unquestionably a source of inspiration for us in that their writings have been explicitly in the political-economy vein: Issawi, *An Economic History of the Middle East and North Africa* (1982), and also his pioneering article "Economic and Social Foundations of Democracy in the Middle East" (1956), and Owen, *The Middle East in the World Economy* (1981).

Finally we come to authors who have used political economy, implicitly or explicitly, in single-country studies. It is no surprise that authors formed in the French tradition of Marxist political economy have played a major role here: Hassan Riad (Samir Amin's nom de plume), *L'Egypte Nassérienne*; Abdel-Malek, *Egypt: Military Society*; and the more recent book by Raffinot and Jacquemot, *Le capitalisme d'état algérien* (1977), are all important. But Anglo-Saxons and anglophones have also made important contributions: O'Brien, *The Revolution in Egypt's Economic System* (1966), Hudson, *The Precarious Republic* (1968), Abdel-Fadil, *The Political Economy of Nasserism* (1980), Bennoune (1988), Hale (1981), Keyder, *State and Class in Turkey* (1987), and Waterbury, *The Egypt of Nasser and Sadat* (1983). In Arabic, works by Khafaji, *The State and the Evolution of Capitalism in Iraq* (1983), and 'Adil Hussein (1982) are noteworthy.

There are many other authors who deserve mention here but who for lack of space will be passed over. It should be clear that the present study has not been assembled in a void. We do claim, however, to have gone beyond country-by-country description, on the one hand, and to have combined analytic approaches derived from politics and economics, on the other, to produce a general understanding of the process of social, political, and economic development in the Middle East today.

There is much that we do not attempt to do in this text, and some analytic approaches that we leave aside are admittedly important. We shall not, for instance, dwell much on psychological variables in explaining political and economic outcomes. We do not deny their importance, and there is a significant literature now that examines psychological factors affecting Middle Eastern leaders and elites: See, inter alia, Brown and Itzkowitz, *Psychological Dimensions of Near Eastern Studies* (1977), Volkan and Itzkowitz, *The Immortal Atatürk* (1984), Zonis, *The Political Elite of Iran* (1971). Muslim fundamentalism as well has stimulated a spate of quasi-psychological explanations, the best of which are Ibrahim, "Anatomy of Egypt's Militant Islamic Groups" (1980), and Mernissi, *Beyond the Veil* (1987). While we shall not explore these dimensions in the heart of this study, let us give a few examples of the kinds of insights psychological analysis might provide. Severe or traumatic experiences shared by a group of leaders or activists may be determinant in shaping their very understanding of politics and society. Political prisoners, whether they are Muslim Brothers jailed by Nasser, Algerian nationalists jailed by the French, or clergy and leftist intellectuals jailed by the shah, undergo torture, physical abuse, and humiliation in degrees that bond them in a common understanding of what must be done. The forces that overthrew the shah, fought the French to a standstill in Algeria, and assassinated Sadat were shaped in prison.

Personal foibles among leaders can lead to momentous changes in the course of events. Shah Mohammed Reza Pahlavi knew he was seriously ill, if not dying, from 1975 on, and that knowledge, as well as the heavy medication he was obliged to take, may have fatally affected his political judgment in the last four years of his reign. Similarly, in 1968, President Bourguiba of Tunisia did not think he had long to live and urged his prime minister to rush through a set of socioeconomic reforms so that Bourguiba would be able to legitimize them. The reforms were a political disaster, Bourguiba recovered his health, and the prime minister was sacked and put on trial.

Anwar al-Sadat's trip to Jerusalem in November 1977 was not the result of a plan carefully worked out with his chief advisers but rather an instinctive leap in the dark made in haste. It was in keeping with what was known of Sadat's personality, a strange blend of sycophancy and riverboat gambler, and it certainly changed the course of Arab-Israeli relations in a major way.

Although psychological variables count, we do not find them consistently useful or powerful in understanding the kinds of policies and processes that are at the center of our study. These variables are most useful in helping understand the leaders' fears, passions, and quirks that occasionally are translated into important decisions. They defy systematic analysis, let alone systematic investigation. We generally learn about them only when a leader has passed from the scene.

Political culture is another important tool in understanding the Middle East but again one that we shall largely pass over. Much has been written about the cultural attributes, political predispositions, and styles of governance in the Middle East. We hear of the quest for martyrdom among Shi'ite Muslims as explaining in part the way in which the Iranian revolution unfolded and the course of war with Iraq. Israel's "Massada Complex" is said to determine the country's outlook toward its adversaries. The docile, wily peasant society of Egypt has been credited with that country's style of government since the pharaohs, and Morocco's tribal past has been invoked to explain contemporary elite behavior (Waterbury 1970). Katouzian (1981, 65), in writing of the constitutional revolution of 1907, captured an understanding of the Iranian psyche that many observers share:

> It was out of the ashes of the most noble, though unrealistic, hopes and aspirations of the Persian Revolution that the various strands of modern Iranian nationalism rose into being. The origins of the exceptionally strong and persistent xenophobia of modern Iran must also be sought in this period: that is, the universal myth—believed by almost every order of urban Iranian society—that any event of the slightest political significance must be the result of a carefully conceived and meticulously executed conspiracy by foreign powers; the unimaginable fatalism which ascribes little or no role to domestic social and economic events, nor the power of ideas and the will of the people in determining social processes, and their change.

In our view, political-culture analysis is potentially a more powerful tool than the psychological analysis of leaders, and we shall refer to political-cultural variables with some frequency. Still, how much they can explain is seldom clear. Let us hypothetically compare Egypt and Iran in terms of tax delinquency. We could hypothesize in political-cultural terms that those in Iran who failed to pay their taxes during the time of the shah did so with a relatively clear conscience, because to Shi'ites awaiting the return of the true Imam, all secular authorities are in some way interlopers and usurpers and hence without legitimacy. In Egypt, by contrast, the tax dodger may be seen as playing an age-old game of manipulating or evading a large, tentacular state whose legitimacy, however, is not at stake. But whatever the cultural explanation of the phenomenon, the end result is the same: tax evasion and decreased government revenues. More important, the means by which to extract more taxes may not vary much at all from one culture to another. Even in those rare instances when we can assess the independent effect of culture on politics and economic life, we must remember that cultures change rapidly too, as the patterns of employment, residence, and life-style themselves change.

In sum, our approach is to focus on major problems in the social and economic transformation of the Middle East, not on specific countries. All the societies of the region face similar problems in extracting and investing resources, building an industrial sector while modernizing agriculture, absorbing an ever-larger proportion of growing populations into cities, all the while trying to maintain political order and to build a credible military establishment. This set of problems confronts all developing countries. What differs are the human and material resources available to the twenty-three countries in the region, and those differences determine in an important way the strategies of resource allocation, the process of class formation, and the political process in each.

We are convinced that in general the process of economic and social change in the Middle East and North Africa (MENA) is not qualitatively different from that in most of the less-developed countries (LDCs). We hasten to add that the differences in levels of overall development, including industrialization, and in standards of living and welfare are as great among the LDCs (compare Brazil, for example, to Rwanda or Nepal) as between the developing and the advanced industrial nations. As we shall see, the variance among Middle Eastern nations is also very great (see especially Chapter 3). Thus we hope that our detailed examination of Middle Eastern experience will contribute to a more general understanding of the development process.

At the same time there are facets of the development process in the Middle East, flowing from its long history of intense and generally adversarial interaction with Europe, that do set this region apart. We try to be attentive to these distinguishing traits and to signal to the reader where and when we think they make a qualitative difference in the processes under scrutiny.

In Chapter 2 we set forth the premises of our analysis, which centers on three vertices: strategies of economic transformation, the state agencies and actors that seek to implement them, and the social actors and classes that react to and are shaped by them. Each of the three vertices entails questions about the nature of the state, the relevance of class analysis, and the effects of various development strategies, questions that should be asked in any developing country. We do not pretend to have definitive answers to any of them, but we do have some strongly held views and, we think, solid evidence to back them.

## NOTES

1. Israeli democracy is the real thing, but only for the country's Jewish citizens. Non-Jews, while enjoying a range of political rights, are nonetheless second-class citizens.

2. To our knowledge, the only other book like this one is Elias Tuma's *Economic and Political Change in the Middle East* (1987). That book was not available to us at the time of writing.

# 2

# THE FRAMEWORK OF
# THE STUDY

The purpose of this chapter is to outline our argument and to provide some examples and illustrations of our perspective. We believe that many of the major problems and questions facing the region today can and should be approached in much the same way that one would approach the problems of any set of LDCs. Accordingly, we shall begin by presenting an implicit "broad brush" model of LDC political economy.

We hold that outcomes in LDC political economy can best be conceptualized as the product of the interaction of three variables: (1) economic growth and structural transformation, (2) state structure and policy, and (3) social class. We shall start with fairly conventional definitions of each of these concepts, discussing major conceptual difficulties, disputes, and so forth, surrounding each as we proceed.

*Economic growth* means simply the increase over time in total output in the economy. Since the concept is often also associated with some idea of increasing welfare for the population, per capita growth is usually also implied. Such growth is almost always quite uneven, however. Some sectors grow faster than others, some groups' wealth and power may increase faster than those of other groups, and in some extreme cases, the absolute standard of living of some (usually poor) individuals and groups may actually decline at some phases of the process. Although the ubiquity or necessity of these outcomes is much disputed, several other features of "unevenness" do appear to be universals: the decline of the percentage of both national output and employment accounted for by the agricultural sector and the increasing proportion of the population that is urban rather than rural. These characteristics of unbalanced sectoral growth are called *structural transformation*. By *state structures and policy* we mean the organization of the monopoly of coercive means within society, the interventions into the economy that such a monopoly makes possible, and the institutions through which intervention is carried out. Finally, by *social class*, we mean groups of people who share a certain set of property rights; i.e., class is

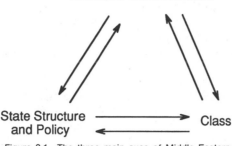

**Structural Transformation**

**State Structure and Policy** ⟶ **Class**

Figure 2.1 The three main axes of Middle Eastern political economy

defined primarily, but not exclusively, by ownership relations rather than by status or political position.

Each of these definitions can be questioned, of course. As noted, economic growth may not be associated with increasing welfare for some groups and/or inequality among social groups may increase. Similarly, there is little agreement on the role of the state in the development process, on its freedom of choice of policy with respect to powerful domestic classes and international actors like the International Monetary Fund (IMF), or the World Bank. And finally, the proprietary concept of class is highly contentious: Some would deny the salience of classes in many Middle Eastern societies, while others would argue that although classes may exist, ownership relations are secondary to relationships of political power.

We do not suffer from the delusion that we can settle such debates or persuade all potential critics. We believe that each of the major concepts is vital for understanding outcomes in the political economy of the region, as we hope to show through the concrete analysis of specific development problems in subsequent chapters. The proof of the pudding will certainly be in the eating.

Before proceeding to a more detailed discussion of each of our three concepts as applied to the Middle East, it is worth emphasizing that all are interdependent. Each one influences and shapes the other; each is therefore both cause and effect, both starting point and outcome. Our model is one of reciprocal causation (Figure 2.1).

We stress that we do not imply any rank ordering of the arrows of Figure 2.1; this is a fully simultaneous model. The meaning of the interconnections may be illustrated as follows.

1. The process of economic growth and structural transformation creates unintended outcomes to which state actors must respond. For example, if the pattern of industrialization is highly capital intensive, the state may then need to respond to a growing employment problem.

2. State policy affects the rate and form of economic growth. Although there is much debate on the precise effect of specific policies, few deny

that state policy influences economic growth through such instruments as fiscal, monetary, and trade policy.

3. Classes mold state policy. Where does policy come from? As a first approximation, interest and pressure groups and, most broadly, proprietary classes seek to protect and promote their own interests through the state. In some cases, the influence of a particular class or classes may be so strong that the state becomes their "instrument."

4. The state shapes, even creates, social classes. We believe that this is generally true throughout the Third World, including the Middle East. If classes are defined primarily with respect to property rights, and if property rights always require enforcement, then it is difficult to see how the concepts of "state" and "class" could *not* be closely linked. In the context of LDCs, the impact of the state on class is especially striking, as the state redistributes property through nationalizations and land reforms.

5. The process of economic growth and structural transformation shapes classes. In some writings, Marx himself argued that classes were as much an *outcome* as a starting point of the accumulation process. After all, a "manufacturing bourgeoisie" emerges only as the result of the growth of industry; the more rapidly industry develops, the stronger that bourgeoisie becomes.

6. Finally, classes affect the rate and form of economic growth, not only indirectly via their impact on state policy, but also directly. For example, an initial concentration of landownership will probably favor a capital-intensive pattern of agricultural growth, with consequences for employment, income distribution, and the growth of different industrial sectors. Similarly, the concentration of rural assets may retard the emergence of a rural domestic market. A highly concentrated distribution of urban income may favor the rapid growth of certain sectors (e.g., consumer durables), rather than of other commodities. We now turn to a more detailed discussion of each major vertex of our triangle and to a more detailed discussion of the interactions among these major variables.

## ECONOMIC GROWTH AND STRUCTURAL TRANSFORMATION

Economic growth is usually measured by gross domestic product (GDP) in a unit of common currency, usually dollars, in order to facilitate international comparisons. GDP is obtained by weighing all outputs by their prices and adding them up. Since output and income are closely related concepts, the measure is also used as a kind of summary statistic for the level of income in the country. When expressed in per capita terms, the number is often employed as a crude indicator of average social welfare.

Several criticisms have been made of this concept. First, GDP per capita offers no evidence on distribution. Therefore one can use increases in GDP as an indicator of increasing social welfare only with great caution. Second, the measure explicitly excludes nonmarketed output; this is a particular problem for evaluating changes over time in the agricultural sector. A shift from home production to market production could, in principle, leave total output unaffected while the measure of output, GDP, would increase. Further, the exclusion of nonmarketed output from the calculation systematically neglects household production. Much of the contribution of women to production thus escapes notice.

Third, the use of official exchange rates as the common denominator for international GDP comparisons introduces further distortions. To say that the average annual income in Egypt is $700 evokes an image of an American buying only $700 worth of goods in a year. In fact, however, an Egyptian with the equivalent of this dollar sum, when converted at the official exchange rate, would be able to buy more goods and services with $700 in her own country than would the American in his. This is because the price of nontraded goods (e.g., housing and haircuts) in relation to that of traded goods (e.g., wheat, cars, textiles) is typically much lower in LDCs than in developed countries (DCs). Using official exchange rates to compare incomes across countries ignores this difference. Even if the Egyptian spent the same percentage of her income on nontraded goods as the American (which is unlikely, given the relative prices), the Egyptian's purchasing power relative to the American's would be understated by using official exchange rates to compare them (Kravis, Heston, and Summers 1978).

Finally, the concept of GDP faces a special difficulty in those countries that derive much revenue from the sale of exhaustible natural resources. Most of this revenue is not income that can be sustained over time. If we are interested in separating "reproducible income" from this kind of revenue, we must make some adjustments. Another way to put it is that some, often most, of GDP in the Gulf is not "income" but "liquidation of capital" (Stauffer 1984).

The distortions introduced by such considerations may be sizable. For example, it has been estimated that if household labor were evaluated at market prices, the GDP of the United States would be some 25% higher than officially reported GDP. Similarly, the use of official exchange rates to convert non-U.S. GDP to dollars understates the "income" of poor countries by as much as 30%. Insofar as the traded-goods sector and/or marketed-goods output expand at the expense of nontraded goods or nonmarketed production, growth rates may be overstated when measured using conventional GDP. Similarly, the use of the conventional measure in oil-exporting countries grossly overstates the level of income that could be sustained without oil. Stauffer estimated that the "reproducible" component of GDP of Saudi Arabia may be as little as one-quarter to one-half of reported GDP.

Despite these problems and issues, we shall use the conventional measure of GDP in this book. Employed with caution, the measure offers us the most comprehensive available set of statistics on national income. The above problems will be taken as precautionary notes about, rather than as devastating criticisms of, the concept of GDP.

Economic growth invariably involves unevenness across sectors, or structural transformation. Despite the wide variation in the patterns of economic growth, rising per capita income is accompanied by a decline in agriculture's share of output and employment and a corresponding increase in the share of industry and services in virtually all countries.

There are numerous interactions among sectors as development proceeds. Since labor productivity, and therefore incomes, are much higher in industry than in agriculture, the transfer of population to industry raises national income. Furthermore, the rate of technological change that raises income per person is typically faster in industry. Consequently, many have thought of industry as the leading sector of development, a sort of engine that pulls the rest of the train behind it. There is much truth to this picture, but neglect of the agricultural sector can be disastrous. The agricultural sector provides not only labor but also food, raw materials for processing, exports, and needed foreign exchange, a domestic market for local industry, and an investable surplus, which may be used to construct industrial facilities. As we shall see, Middle Eastern states, like many LDCs, have neglected or mismanaged the linkages between agriculture and industry. As a result, bottlenecks such as inadequate food supplies, stagnant exports, or feeble domestic markets have undermined structural transformation and economic growth.

The concept of "services" is something of a residual category. It contains activities as diverse as government service and street peddling. Moreover, the mix within the service sector also changes over time, with the proportion of self-employed, typically very poor, service-sector workers declining as national income rises beyond a certain level. The increase in the proportion of the population employed in services may be as much an indicator of economic weakness as of strength, as large numbers of unskilled rural migrants arrive in the cities and engage in a host of small-scale activities that are carried out at low technological levels and that generate paltry incomes. In most cases, however, it seems clear that these people believe that they have improved their lot by migrating, and the available evidence suggests that they know what they are talking about. After all, productivity, technology, and incomes for some agricultural workers may be and often are even lower than those obtainable in the urban informal sector. These issues are taken up in Chapter 10.

The process of economic growth and structural transformation is typically characterized by a variety of distortions and unintended outcomes. Such distortions are both the consequence and the cause of state economic policies. The first distortion is really a final cautionary note on the definition of economic growth and its links to welfare. It is clear that "economic growth" as measured by changes in per capita GDP is not the same as the usual notion of "economic development." The latter concept includes some recognition that improvement in living standards includes especially the meeting of the basic needs (e.g., food, housing, safe drinking water, and education) of all members of a society. It is equally clear that there is only a loose correlation between improvement in basic needs and in the growth of GDP. Some countries with relatively high per capita incomes have quite poor records meeting basic needs (e.g., Brazil), while some with very low per capita incomes appear to have gone very far toward meeting such needs (e.g., Sri Lanka and the People's Republic of China [PRC]).

There is a particular connection between economic development and the development of skills, or "human capital formation." Indeed, by some accounts (e.g., T. W. Schultz 1981) the entire growth process is inconceivable without the improvement of human skills; in this view, education and other types of skill formation are the core of the development process. Technological change, which lies at the core of the process of economic growth, is impossible without an increasingly skilled population. In addition, the very unevenness of economic growth and structural transformation creates numerous disequilibria. Schultz hypothesized that the more educated and trained the population, the more rapidly it can respond to such imbalances, and therefore, the more quickly they are eliminated. Unfortunately, however, the educational standards in many Middle Eastern countries have lagged behind what we might expect, given the rates of growth of incomes.

A second blockage or distortion to the process of economic growth and structural transformation is the problem of foreign exchange. For a variety of reasons, some Middle Eastern governments have found their growth process interrupted by the inadequacy of foreign exchange, for example, Sudan, where growth has been entirely halted, and Tunisia, Morocco, and Turkey in the late 1970s and early 1980s. The Sudan's inability to generate sufficient foreign exchange to provide even the most minimal level of imports, much less to contribute to paying off the $8 billion of foreign debt, has made the country one of Africa's worst cases of the international debt crisis. Turkey's growth in the late 1970s was likewise slowed by the steadily increasing demand for imports at the same time as export revenues lagged. Both external factors (falling terms of trade) and internal policies that encourage imports and discourage exports (overvalued exchange rates, the need to import machinery for industries producing industrial goods for local consumers) created these problems.

These difficulties are endemic in LDCs and are especially associated with import substituting industrialization (ISI). Many Middle Eastern countries have been spared this squeeze, largely because of oil revenues; their regional multipliers, such as investment; and, especially, workers' remittances. However, the experience with such revenues shows that ample foreign exchange is not a panacea for the problems of economic growth and structural transformation. Indeed, the influx of large amounts of foreign exchange can itself cause problems.

The sudden increase in revenues from abroad leads to a phenomenon known as the Dutch Disease, so called because of the experience of the Dutch economy with the large influx of North Sea gas revenues in the

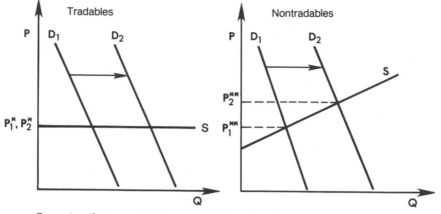

P = price; Q = quantity; S = supply; D = demand

Figure 2.2   Changes in the relative price of traded and nontraded goods. (Assume that both sectors face the same shift in the demand function. The price of traded goods remains the same, the price of nontraded goods rises, and their relative price [P*/P**] falls.)

1970s. Government spending of oil revenues induces labor and capital to shift from traded goods (industry and agriculture) to nontraded goods (services). There are two proposed causal sequences. A "monetarist" version holds that the spending of oil revenues stimulates a rate of inflation that is higher than that of the major (typically Western) trading partners of the oil-exporting country. Since LDC nominal exchange rates are usually fixed, the differential inflation leads to overvaluation of the real exchange rate. Since tradable goods' prices may be denominated in Organization for Economic Cooperation and Development (OECD) currencies (say, the dollar), while nontraded-goods prices are, of course, in local currency, such revaluation of the real exchange rate is the same thing as an increase in the relative price of nontraded goods relative to traded goods.

An alternative version arrives at this same conclusion by a slightly different route. In that version, the spending of government revenue increases demand for both traded and nontraded goods. For most small countries the supply of traded goods is perfectly elastic; that of nontraded goods is not. Therefore, the increased spending will bid up the price of nontraded goods more than traded goods (Figure 2.2). This will be compounded if government spending is concentrated in nontradables, like services and construction, as happened in the oil-exporting countries during the 1970s. Once again, the prices of nontraded relative to traded goods will increase. The advantage of this latter formulation is that it can allow for the fact that some so-called nontradables actually do move in international trade: There are international construction firms, high-level services have inter-

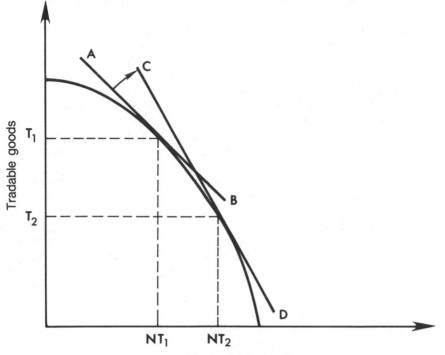

Figure 2.3 Reallocation of resources in response to a shift in the relative price of tradable and nontradable goods. (The shift in relative prices is shown by the change in the price line from AB to CD. Resulting reallocations of labor and capital reduce the equilibrium output of tradables [$T_2 < T_1$] and increase that of nontradables [$NT_2 > NT_1$].)

national markets, foreign teachers may be hired, and so forth. The only question becomes differential supply elasticities, which can in principle be determined empirically rather than simply assumed.

Whatever the causes, these relative-price changes reallocate capital and labor, and shift resources out of the production of traded goods into nontraded goods production (Figure 2.3). This allegedly leads to stagnation of the agricultural and manufacturing sectors, while government and the building industry boom. International competition holds down the prices of, say, food and manufactures, whereas wages and costs in domestic agriculture and industry rise, catching local producers in a profit squeeze. The Dutch Disease contributes to the rural exodus, as farm workers abandon the countryside, seeking construction jobs in the cities. The increase in wage levels thus combines with the overvalued real exchange rate to diminish international competitiveness in agriculture and industry.

There is evidence for such effects in the Middle East and elsewhere, most notably in agriculture. As with any growth-rate comparison, one can obtain quite different results for slightly different time periods. For example, Tunisian agriculture grew at a 4.1% average annual rate from 1970 to 1981, but at only 1.6% from 1973 to 1983. For some oil exporters like Algeria, growth rates of manufacturing and agriculture were greater during the 1973–1983 period than they had been during the previous "cheap oil" decade. The reason for the discrepancy between this evidence and the predictions of the theory was that Middle Eastern and other oil-exporting governments often intervened directly to counteract these relative price shifts, usually by subsidizing their traded-goods sector. Such subsidies, of course, create problems of their own, and no country has solved the problems created by rural emigration. In addition, both the seriousness of the disease and the cure varied considerably from one country to another. The case of the Dutch Disease illustrates the argument that state policy both shapes development and responds to the unintended outcomes of that same process.

The inflow of oil revenues also has important direct political consequences. Oil revenues are rents. *Economic rent* is the difference between the market price of a good or a factor of production and its opportunity cost (the price needed to produce the good or to keep the factor of production in its current use). For example, oil rents in the Gulf are the difference between the market price (say, $14.00 per barrel) and the cost of producing oil there (no more than $1.50). Furthermore, these rents are collected directly by governments, increasing their freedom of maneuver. Oil rents are politically centralizing. However, as the revenues are spent, new domestic actors emerge (as contractors, agents, recipients of subsidies) who then, in turn, begin to limit the freedom of maneuver of the state. This is a very typical pattern: State autonomy may rise in a particular conjuncture but then typically will decline with its exercise over time.

A further effect of oil rents is that they permit the evasion of hard development choices. This is not a problem if the rents are very large or are assumed to be very stable. For many middle-income oil exporters, neither condition holds. Consider the case of Egypt in the early 1980s: With annual oil receipts of some $2.8 billion, along with ample foreign-exchange revenues from workers' remittances (about $3 billion) and from other "locational rents" (tourism, Suez Canal, and U.S. aid), the country was able to avoid a thorough reform of both its highly distorted pricing system and of its structurally imbalanced labor market. The problems of the country have continued to mount, yet because any reform will harm politically powerful groups, decisionmakers have avoided reforms. They can get away with this as long as the rents hold out. Unfortunately, by the time the rents decline and the hour of reckoning is at hand, the problems and their potential solutions will likely be all the more painful (as has been true since 1986).

Such rents also contribute to a further set of difficulties and disequilibria in the process of economic growth and structural transformations: the problem of lagging food supply. The Middle East is now the least food-self-sufficient area in the world. Demand for food has risen by 4 or 5% per year, driven by rapidly rising per capita incomes and by population growth rates surprisingly high given national incomes. Supply has been constrained by nature and by political economy. Drought, urban bias, unequal land-tenure systems, and the Dutch Disease have all contributed to the relatively sluggish supply response. The range of agricultural outcomes in the region is extremely wide, however, extending from the Sudanese famine of 1984 to Turkish net grain exports.

Such agricultural problems impede economic development and create problems for policymakers. Food imports now account for some 20% of all Egyptian imports and some 17% of Moroccan imports. This is perhaps acceptable, provided that the states in question can find other things to sell. So far, foreign exchange has covered food imports. But the difficulties of agricultural transformation, such as the rural exodus toward already bulging cities and the provision of adequate food supplies, are among the most pressing of the disequilibria of economic growth and structural transformation facing the region today.

The pattern of industrial growth has exacerbated the employment problems that rural neglect fosters. The form of industrialization in the Middle East has also created some additional and unique problems. Partly because of a desire to have the most modern technology available, and partly because of distorted price signals, much of the industry installed in the Middle East during the last generation has been capital intensive. Consequently, the amount of investment required to create a job has been very high. Due to managerial inefficiencies and foreign-exchange bottlenecks, these same industrial facilities have been plagued by idle capacity, driving up the amount of investment needed to add to output. Only a few Middle Eastern countries have internationally competitive industries.

Perhaps worst of all, however, these industries have all too often not produced the kinds of simple consumer goods that the bulk of the population wants and can afford. Rather, too often Middle Eastern factories turn out relatively expensive, "top of the line" consumer durables like refrigerators, washing machines, and automobiles. Not only are the production processes for such goods highly capital intensive and characterized by low employment multipliers, but the goods themselves are also disproportionately consumed by the better off. On both demand and supply sides, from both efficiency and equity perspectives, the pattern of industrialization in the Middle East has left much to be desired and has encountered obstacles of its own making, such as the saturation of relatively narrow domestic markets for consumer durables.

Finally, the state itself has often become a drain on resources in the Middle East. This is not to say that the state should not (still less could not) intervene in the development process. In certain conjunctures, however, the state can inhibit the very process that at least officially it seeks to promote. Not only do its interventions often generate misleading price signals for private actors (e.g., undervaluing foreign exchange and local capital), but also its bloated bureaucracies and inefficient state-owned enterprises often absorb resources. One might be tempted to include military spending and the maintenance of large, lethal arsenals and standing armies among the burdens that the state itself creates for the growth process (see Chapter 13). However, foreign aid or grants finance a great deal of Middle Eastern military spending. Although a case for the military as economic drain can be made for some cases (e.g., Israel or Iraq), for others the case is less obvious.

In summary, the course of economic growth and structural change is far from smooth. It is characterized by extensive state intervention, by numerous bottlenecks, and by serious macro- and microeconomic problems. Many of these problems have their origins in state policy; each generates a policy response. It is important to remember, however, that these distortions and problems have rarely been the result of obvious error or stupidity. Hindsight is always 20/20, while future outcomes and unintended consequences are always opaque. Many of the price and other distortions generated by state policy originated in states' attempts to mobilize savings. Agriculture had to be taxed because, for countries like Egypt in the 1950s, there was no alternative source of investable funds. Industry would be capital intensive because planners believed this was necessary to create a modern industrial core. Growth and modernization of production were to take precedence over employment generation and agricultural development because leaders believed that growth itself would automatically provide the latter two. Rapid industrial development under state auspices was also held to be essential to national security. State-led growth was designed to weaken or destroy internal and external enemies. States intervened to accelerate the process of economic growth and to forge a powerful modern nation. Their leaders held certain images of the future, which explicitly included industrialization. But the reality often turned out to be different from the image.

Perhaps no state in the Middle East had formulated a more detailed image of its future than Algeria. By 1969, seven years after independence and a bloody colonial war, Algeria launched a four-year plan that was intended to be the first of several. It was premised on a "big push" strategy of heavy industrialization entirely within the state sector. The crucial element in the strategy was the country's hydrocarbon riches: petroleum and natural gas. Those were to provide, as was to be expected, exports to generate foreign exchange to pay for imported technology, capital goods, and turnkey industries. More important, they were to be the source of energy and basic feedstock for large industrial undertakings in petrochemicals and basic metals.

These industries were in turn to provide a wide range of intermediate and finished goods: fertilizers, butane gas, plastic sheeting and sacking, irrigation pipes, tractors, motors, and consumer durables. It was assumed that the rural sector, under socialist management in the most favored areas, would become the principal consumer of these products, but little attention was paid to issues of agricultural productivity. It was also assumed that given the state-of-the-art technology imported (for instance, gas liquefaction plants), many of these industries would be able to compete in international markets.

In terms of structural transformation, Algeria's technocrats saw the agrarian sector primarily as a customer for the industrial sector, one whose work force would continue to dwindle and whose per capita productivity would rise. The regime was prepared during the big push phase to tolerate high rates of urban unemployment and high levels of worker migration to France. Eventually rising incomes in agriculture and in the new industrial sector would generate substantial demand for goods and services, which would create the jobs necessary to absorb the unemployed. President Houari Boumedienne (1965–1978) saw no reason to worry about Algeria's 3.5% annual population growth rate because the economic growth his plan would provide would yield the prosperity necessary to lower fertility.

The whole strategy became known by the label "industrializing industries" affixed to it by its major foreign architect, G. Destanne de Bernis (1971), of the University of Grenoble. It was an integrated plan, and, for that very reason, when one of its parts failed to conform to the overall strategy, the whole process rather quickly collapsed and the image was shattered. Mismanagement in the socialist agrarian sector and production declines throughout the agricultural sector meant that the latter could not become a reliable customer for industry. The new industries soon faced problems of idle capacity, compounded by the sophistication of their imported technology and inadequate management skills. Seeking external markets, except for some petroleum products, was not a feasible alternative. Unemployment and underemployment mounted while the rural exodus continued. The population continued to grow as broad-based prosperity remained a distant goal. Increasingly large amounts of foreign exchange had to be used to import food and sustain urban standards of living.

By 1976 it had become clear that the big push was in trouble, and after Boumedienne's death in 1978, Algeria's new president, Chadli Benjadid, moved to break up the large state industrial sector into smaller, decentralized units, stimulate the agricultural sector through more favorable prices, and encourage the long-maligned private sector to play a more active role in the country's development (Lawless 1984). The new course is not more assured of success than the old, and in many ways its image of the future is much less certain. These setbacks, we must not forget, occurred in a country blessed with petroleum and gas, ample foreign exchange, and a solid international credit rating. Yet Middle Eastern countries without oil wealth (Turkey, Egypt, Syria, for example) have elaborated images of the future similar to Algeria's and, predictably, fallen further short of realizing them.

One may contrast with Algeria's experience that of another oil-rich country, Iraq, at a much earlier period. In 1950 Iraq was still a monarchy, nominally independent but closely allied to its former imperial master,

Great Britain. In that year royalties paid the Iraqi government on the production and sales of oil increased by 30%, and by 1958 the royalties had grown nearly sixfold to over $200 million. The government, not unwisely, wanted to use these revenues for long-term development purposes. Toward this end an autonomous Development Board was established and 70% of all oil royalties were earmarked for it. The board had the authority and the finances to set Iraq's growth course (Penrose and Penrose 1978, 167–77).

Unlike Algeria, Iraq aimed its big push at agriculture. The Development Board began large hydraulic projects to master floods in the Tigris-Euphrates system, store water, irrigate new lands, improve drainage, and cope with soil salinity. Whereas Algeria's slogan was to sow oil to reap industry, Iraq's was to sow oil to reap agriculture, and that sector was to be the engine of long-term growth.

The flaws in this far-sighted strategy were that it neglected immediate problems of agricultural production, had no particular industrialization program, and devoted no resources to social infrastructure (such as housing and health). The hydraulic projects were not likely to contribute to the economy before several years, if not decades, had gone by. In the meantime, peasants continued to pour into Baghdad and other cities as floods, salinity, and grossly inequitable land distribution impeded increased production. In the cities, neither the urban job market nor the network of social services was adequate to provide a decent standard of living to hundreds of thousands of Iraqis crowded into slums and shantytowns. When elements of the Iraqi armed forces moved to overthrow the monarchy on July 14, 1958, their advancing tank columns were accompanied by masses of denizens from the shantytowns who wanted to assist in the downfall of the regime. With its demise came also that of the Development Board's strategy. The military and their Ba'ath party successors elaborated an entirely new image of the future, not unlike that of Algeria.

## STATE STRUCTURES
## AND DEVELOPMENT POLICY

The interaction of state policy and the process of economic growth and structural change is not merely one of images of the future. Most states of the region have shared a vision of where they would like to go, of how they hope their societies would appear in the future. The problem, of course, is getting there. What strategy will be employed? And who will implement which parts of the strategy? We shall now examine these questions of strategies and agencies.

Without prejudging whether economic-development strategies are "choices" or "sequences," or whether they are politically imposed from within (e.g., by domestic proprietary classes) or from without (e.g., by international financial agencies), we can identify five major routes from predominantly rural, agricultural political economies to urban, industrial ones. These are the paths of agro-exports, of mineral exports, of import-substituting industrialization, of manufactured exports, and agricultural-development-led industrialization. Let us examine these in turn.

## Agro-Export-Led Growth

The usual justification for the agro-export strategy is as follows: At the beginning of the process of structural transformation, most people are by definition rural and agricultural. If there are underexploited land and/or labor resources, these could be used to produce more crops for sale. But because of the poverty of the local population, as well as (perhaps) the relatively small number of people, the domestic market is quite limited. Exports provide the exit from this impasse. The incomes of the farmers may rise, and if some of the profits from such activities are reinvested in increasing productivity and in expanding the productive base of the economy (e.g., by investing in industry), a process of self-sustaining growth may be launched (Lewis 1954; Myint 1959). Further, the process of industrialization requires imports; in the long run, such imports can only be financed by exports. Since such countries may have little to sell except agricultural commodities, developing such exports then provides the foreign exchange needed for structural transformation. Finally, the country may have a strong international comparative advantage in the production of a particular crop, like cotton in the Nile Valley or wine grapes in Algeria.

However, for better or for worse, reliance on agro-exports is commonly associated with colonialism. Historically, of course, the two were closely linked all over the world. The Middle East was no exception: Cotton cultivation for export to Europe was expanded under colonial rule in Egypt and the Sudan, while wine production was introduced and flourished in the settler areas of North Africa. A division of labor between metropole and colony was an integral part of colonial ideology. The agro-export strategy faces several problems besides its historical associations.

*Declining Terms of Trade for Agricultural-Export Products.* Critics of agro-export-led growth strategies have long maintained that there is a long-run necessary tendency for a unit of agro-exports to buy progressively fewer manufactured products. This proposition has been the subject of controversy, from which several points emerge: First, the validity of the proposition is much affected by the choice of beginning and ending year. Because commodity prices show considerable fluctuations over the course of the international business cycle, one can show either a falling trend (peak to trough), a rising trend (trough to peak), or little trend at all. Second, although one might reject the more extreme forms of this proposition on the falling terms of trade, it is nevertheless clear that countries can and have experienced uncomfortably long periods of declining terms of trade (e.g., Sudan 1978–1985). Third, price fluctuations cause problems in their own right, independently of longer-run trends. If commodity export prices fluctuate greatly from year to year, so also will export revenues. Since the point of any agro-export-led growth strategy is to acquire funds for industrialization, and since industrial planning often involves fairly long lead times, such fluctuations can seriously disrupt industrialization efforts.

*Favored Classes.* A second problem with this strategy is that (as with any strategy) certain domestic classes are more favored than others. In particular, many critics of the agro-export approach argue that it strengthens powerful urban commodity-trading interests, who may block further development. If such classes' power derives from the unchallenged economic dominance of their sector, they may especially resent any attempt to impose tariffs on imported domestic goods or to be taxed to provide infrastructure for industry. Such arguments were raised especially by liberal critics of oligarchical rule in Latin America (cf. Hirschman 1963).

The economic, cultural, and political links between metropolitan colonial interests, rural landlords, and urban traders led many nationalists to distrust such intermediaries and the economic growth strategy with which they were associated. This was particularly marked if the growers or traders were culturally distinct from the mass of the local population, whether European settlers in the Maghreb, Syrian traders in Egypt, or Jews, Armenians, and Greeks in the Ottoman Empire.

It is not clear from the historical record of the Middle East that agro-exporters failed to invest, eschewed industrial projects, and generally blocked the rise of "infant industry." The Egyptian case is particularly instructive: Wealthy indigenous Egyptian cotton producers often invested in the agricultural sector and provided the bulk of the capital for the initial industrial endeavors of the Bank Misr in the 1920s (Davis 1983; Tignor 1984). Their loyalty to the nation also seems never to have been seriously in doubt. But it is true that such groups ultimately failed to solve the many pressing domestic political, economic, and social problems facing the country and could not rid the country of the British imperial presence. Their demise as agents of development also spelled the demise of the agro-export-led strategy.

*Excessive Taxation.* A final problem that often arises with agro-exports is the temptation of the government to tax the sector excessively. This problem is the reverse of the previous one. Whereas the argument against "compradors" and oligarchs is based on the political *power* of these classes, the problem of excessive taxation is a result of the political *weakness* of export-crop producers. This situation usually arises if the producers are small peasants whose number, poverty, and geographical dispersion render collective action difficult. Governments are then often tempted to place the burden of growth onto such classes, usually through establishing government control over marketing, input supply, or both. Such an approach is usually self-defeating, however; small peasants shift land, labor, and other inputs out of the controlled-export crops into other noncontrolled ones or resort to smuggling. Exports and state revenues may then grow very sluggishly indeed. The agro-export strategy as a whole may be blamed for these problems, while in reality it is excessive taxation and lack of incentives that are at fault. The Sudan, which in recent years provides a dismal tale along just these lines, is also by now the only country in the region that seriously contemplates an agricultural-export-led growth strategy.

## Mineral-Export-Led Growth

The second principle strategy is also based on the export of natural resources: mineral-export-led growth. In the Middle East, petroleum and phosphates are the major exports of this type. Jordan and, above all, Morocco, have substantial phosphate reserves and large exports. Moroccan phosphate exports are the largest in the world, and reserves (including those of the Western Sahara) are 40% of the world's total. Petroleum, of course, is by far the most valuable and significant natural resource in the region.

One should distinguish between those oil and mineral exporters that have other resources, for example, substantial populations and considerable agricultural potential, and those countries whose economies are entirely dominated by mineral exports. The first group includes Algeria, Morocco, Tunisia, Iraq, and Iran, while the second set consists of Libya and the Gulf States. Saudi Arabia is a unique case because of the size of its petroleum reserves. The officially stated goals of the mineral-based export strategy are quite similar to those of agro-exporters: to acquire revenue from mineral exports to create an industrial base for sustained development after the natural resource is exhausted. This strategy is distinguished from the agro-export-led strategy by the very different pattern of international price developments (for oil but not for phosphates!) and by the exhaustibility of the exported natural source. By using the receipts from a depleting asset, a future without oil can be built.

This is a perfectly reasonable approach for the first group of countries, those that have significant nonpetroleum resources. However, it is much more difficult to see what economic future lies in store for Libya and the Gulf States after their oil runs out. Perhaps sufficient financial assets can be accumulated that can then serve as a reliable source of income. Currently, Kuwait has reached this "pure rentier state" stage, with income from foreign investments now exceeding that from petroleum exports. But such rentier activity leaves a nation very much at the mercy of international political developments; financial assets are fairly easy to seize or impound. But the absence of arable land, water, nonoil mineral resources, and the presence of a small, poorly educated population suggest that the "future without oil" may be bleak.

Let us take the example of Saudi Arabia. The Saudis have about one-fifth of non-Communist petroleum reserves, with new discoveries announced nearly annually. These reserves would last 50 to 250 years, depending on the rate of production. The Saudi strategy of oil-based development has had three major components. First, funds have been used to expand infrastructure, leading to one of the most massive construction booms in economic history. Despite numerous bottlenecks (inevitable given the low level of infrastructure and the size of the projects), roads, schools, hospitals, shopping centers, offices, and other buildings have mushroomed throughout the kingdom. Second, surplus funds—money that could not be spent immediately—were placed in Western financial institutions. The Saudis thereby gained the benefit of the expertise of those institutions in investment. Finally, the Saudis have invested in petroleum-based industry. They have selected industries for expansion that are highly capital and energy intensive and/or use oil or gas as a feedstock. The principal investments have been in petrochemical complexes, fertilizer plants, aluminum smelting, and steel production, using natural gas in a direct reduction process to convert imported iron ore.

It is evident that none of these industrial schemes would be viable without oil; they are in no sense, then, "creating a future without oil." Instead, they are increasing the percentage that remains in Saudi Arabia of the value-added embodied in the final output of petroleum- or energy-intensive industries. Saudi petrochemicals are now so highly competitive internationally that there have been protectionist moves against them in Western Europe and the United States. Despite such problems, the strategy of stretching out the life of their already massive reserves of petroleum makes good sense for Saudi Arabia. However, it is not really a viable strategy for other oil exporters, none of which enjoys reserves on a Saudi scale.

Any mineral-export growth strategy faces two major problems. First, most countries are likely to have only one significant mineral for export. Consequently, their export revenues are highly dependent on price developments for that product or products. This subjects their economies to the problems and difficulties of a sudden fall, or sudden rise, in the price of their export. The collapse of the phosphate price in the mid-1970s has been a major factor in Morocco's severe balance-of-payments and international indebtedness problems. The mid-1980s oil glut and the erosion of real oil prices have forced cutbacks in state spending, in construction projects, and in national incomes throughout the region. And as we saw earlier, the reverse situation creates problems of its own: the difficulties of the Dutch Disease. Second, the existence of large oil revenues combined with political structures and imperatives to create cradle-to-the-grave welfare systems. Although potential human capital is the only nonoil resource that many of these countries have, the incentives to develop it are limited. Why should a Saudi become an engineer if he can more easily become a joint director of a company whose head must always be Saudi? Why should a woman pursue higher education if there will be only a very few interesting job opportunities open for her? Although these problems may be overcome with time, and although the ease of life for the poorer classes of Saudi society may be readily exaggerated, the presence of large oil rents poses problems for the accumulation of human capital.

The situation of the oil exporters is in many ways highly special. The combination of massive reserves, small populations, and few additional resources makes their development strategies and prospects *sui generis*.

Oil exporters of the first group, however, are in a rather different situation. Only Iraq was a capital surplus nation before its invasion of Iran. Countries like Iran, Algeria, and Iraq faced a problem rather similar to that of Egypt after its period of agro-export-led growth: how best to foster the rise of industry. What concrete policies should be adopted to accelerate the process of structural transformation? All of these countries, as well as many nonoil producers, have adopted an import-substituting-industrialization policy approach.

### Import-Substituting Industrialization

Import-substituting industrialization (ISI) has been one of the most tested development strategies among the LDCs. Its logic is compelling. It is designed to move economies traditionally dependent on the export of primary commodities and raw materials to an industrial footing. The new industries would at the same time produce goods that had previously been imported (everything from textiles and shoes to fertilizers and refined sugar) *and* process domestic raw materials (e.g., cotton, minerals, sugarcane, petroleum). The result would be economic diversification and reduced dependency on volatile external markets for primary products and upon high-priced imports.

Through ISI, it was hoped, developing countries could escape the agrarian trap into which imperialist powers or, more anonymously, the international division of labor had thrust them. The place to begin was with known domestic markets. As the process gathered steam and raised revenues for the new workers and managers as well as for the producers of agricultural commodities destined for processing, new markets would develop, and infant industries would achieve economies of scale that would make them profitable and competitive. Eventually the first industries would produce backward linkages, stimulating new enterprises in capital goods, basic metals, machine tools, and the like. In Egypt in the 1960s, when this strategy was pursued with vigor, it was envisaged that the textile sector, using Egyptian cotton and replacing foreign imports, would "link back" to the setting up of an industry to manufacture spinning and weaving machinery, itself utilizing steel from the new iron and steel complex.

Before these linkages could be firmly established and economies of scale achieved, the new industries would have to be protected from foreign competition by high tariff walls. Moreover, given the narrowness of domestic markets, any industry might enjoy, de facto or de jure, a monopoly in its particular sector. Thus, although seen as a temporary phenomenon, ISI implied and frequently meant monopolistic production and marketing at costs higher than similar imports. It also frequently meant lower-quality goods than those that could be imported.

Turkey pioneered among Middle Eastern states in pursuing an ISI strategy. Atatürk's republic, founded at the end of World War I amidst the debris of the Ottoman Empire, was the first fully independent country in the region, and its leader was determined to transform it into an industrial and "Western" nation. During the 1920s, in the absence of a formulated strategy and without any socialist justification, the Turkish state began to launch industries in textiles, cement, and basic metals. With the impact of the Great Depression, Turkey, in 1933, launched its first five-year industrial plan and, with some advice from Soviet planners, entered into a phase of concerted state-led growth. Next door in Iran, Reza Khan, the founder of the Pahlavi dynasty, was moving in similar directions, and throughout the Arab world young men who would lead their countries in the 1950s observed Turkey's experiment closely.

With Algeria's independence in 1962, all major states in the Middle East had won formal sovereignty (the one exception was the former Aden Protectorate, which became the People's Democratic Republic of Yemen in 1969). With rare exceptions, these states pursued, to varying degrees and with different ideological underpinnings, ISI strategies. These made good sense for the larger, more differentiated economies in the region, those with important domestic markets that could sustain large industrial units. They made less sense for the small, undiversified economies of the not-yet-rich oil-exporting countries and for some without oil, such as Lebanon and Jordan. We should note, however, that one large country, the Sudan, only briefly toyed with an ISI strategy, while three large oil-exporting countries, Algeria, Iraq, and Iran, pursued it resolutely.

The most determined efforts to follow in Turkey's footsteps were undertaken by Egypt, Iran, Tunisia, Algeria, Syria, and Iraq. Israel followed the policy mainly with respect to military industries, but given its small population and economic isolation within the Arab world, it could not afford a broad-based ISI strategy. ISI projects tended to fall within the following categories:

1. Consumer durables destined for established middle- and upper-income markets.
2. Textiles, shoes, and other apparel for mass markets.
3. Soft drinks and tobacco products for mass markets.
4. Processing of local agricultural produce: canning, sugar refining, spinning and weaving, alcohol, beer, et cetera.
5. Processing local raw materials: petroleum to fertilizers and plastics, iron ore to iron and steel.

ISI strategies led several states to ignore what neoclassical economists saw as the comparative advantage of these states in world trade: the export of raw materials and unprocessed agricultural produce. But the states' object was precisely to promote economic diversification by building new skills within the work force, to capture for national purposes the value-added in processing that had heretofore accrued to the advanced industrial nations, and to reduce the states' dependency upon unstable world markets for primary produce. ISI has experienced widespread setbacks in the Middle East and elsewhere, but that does not mean that it was conceptually wrong or that it will be unviable in practice in the future.

The setbacks in the ISI strategy stemmed primarily from the degree of protection granted to the infant industries and the proportion of public resources devoted to them at the expense of the agricultural sector. The agricultural sector was taxed through various devices to provide an investable surplus for the new industrial undertakings, while the foreign exchange earned from agricultural exports went to pay for the technologies, capital goods, and raw materials required by the industrial sector. The price of these income transfers was frequently slow or nonexistent agricultural growth. This in turn meant, as we saw in the Algerian case, that the large rural populations could not generate the demand to keep the new industries operating at full capacity. Consequently, idle capacity and production costs rose, but because the industries were protected against cheaper imports by high tariffs and enjoyed sectoral monopolies in domestic markets, they had no incentive to keep costs down. The industries were in general capital intensive and under the best of circumstances not providers of large numbers of jobs. But when operating below capacity, they could only either lay off workers (a rare occurrence) or increase operating costs further by carrying redundant labor. In no way could they meet the challenge of providing jobs for rural workers abandoning a depressed agricultural sector for life and livelihood in the cities.

The net result in many instances was high-cost production destined either for upper-income luxury markets (such as automobiles and refrigerators) or for mass markets where retail prices were subsidized by the government (everything from fertilizers to sugar). The new industries could not, because of their high costs, export their products and earn the foreign exchange needed to pay for imported raw materials and equipment. Thus they contributed to the growing balance-of-payments crises that plagued several ISI experiments. Clearly this was more a problem for the oil-poor, such as Turkey, Egypt, Syria, and Tunisia, than for the oil-rich, such as Iran, Iraq, and Algeria.

In order to lower the price of goods imported for the new industries, most governments maintained overvalued exchange rates for their currencies. These in combination with foreign-exchange-rationing systems that favored the new industries put no pressure upon those industries to reduce the import content in their operations. By contrast, traditional exporters in the agricultural sector in some instances lost their competitive edge in foreign markets because the artificially high exchange rate dampened demand for their commodities.

The need for the government to subsidize the price at which the products of the new industries were sold to consumers, be they other industrial users or buyers at the retail level, contributed significantly to the mounting public deficits and thereby to increasing rates of domestic inflation. Faced with sluggish agricultural performance, industries operating at a loss, large domestic deficits, and growing balance-of-payments difficulties, Middle Eastern governments turned to borrowing abroad to fill these gaps, incurring large foreign debts and heavy servicing requirements (payments of interest and principal).

Not all Middle Eastern countries adopted this strategy, but for many that did, the 1970s brought a far-reaching reappraisal of what they had undertaken. For some, the moment of truth was brought about by the huge increase in their petroleum-import bill after 1973; for countries with abundant oil, the issue seemed to be more one of overheating and structural inefficiencies (namely, Algeria after 1976).

## Manufactured-Export-Led Growth

For Western creditors of heavily indebted Middle Eastern economies, a way out seemed to lie in dramatically increasing manufactured exports to the markets of the OECD countries. South Korea, Taiwan, Singapore, India, Brazil, among others, had to varying degrees succeeded in this domain, earning themselves the epithet of "newly industrializing countries" or NICs. What recommends this strategy is that it addresses two of the main problems arising from ISI. First, it earns the country foreign exchange without sacrificing the goal of industrialization. Second, if it is to have any chance of success, production costs must be lowered so that the exporting industries can compete abroad. Thus the problems of idle capacity, operating losses, and redundant labor would have to be overcome. With world markets as their target, economies of scale can be achieved even for countries with relatively small domestic markets (Hong Kong, Singapore, Honduras, and Costa Rica demonstrate the possibilities).

To sustain the strategy other measures are required. The exchange rate of the national currency may have to be lowered in order to promote exports. Devaluation may stimulate agricultural exports but, by diverting produce to foreign markets, push up the price of agricultural goods in the domestic market. It is also likely that an export-led growth program will involve an effort to restore the market—supply and demand—and make the costs of imported substitutes the determinants of the prices paid domestic producers of primary produce. Thus cotton or sugar growers may receive the equivalent of the international price for their commodities rather than a low price set by a state planning agency and designed to provide cheap inputs to local ISI industries or cheap food to urban consumers. In sum, many of the distortions in resource allocation caused, it is alleged, by the interference of public authorities in the functioning of markets will be put right.

The grandiloquent battle cry of an Egyptian parliamentarian in the mid-1970s, "Export or die!" has echoed around the Middle East. But it is not at all obvious how sound or feasible this strategy really is. Its adoption signals a country's willingness to tie its economic future to the world economy and especially to the fortunes of the advanced industrial nations. In the past decade or so that has been a bad gamble. Even with sustained growth in these economies, it is not clear how many more LDCs could follow in the footsteps of Asia's Little Tigers (South Korea, Taiwan, Singapore, Hong Kong). Three giants have taken large strides along that path: Brazil, India, and, latterly, the People's Republic of China. Is there room in OECD markets, under the best of circumstances, for a number of Middle Eastern exporters? Turkey has had great success in promoting nonagricultural exports to Europe, but uneven growth in Western economies, coupled with substantial protectionism against LDC imports, calls for caution.

There are also daunting domestic challenges to this strategy. "Bad habits" that may have developed during the ISI phase may be dealt with only at high political cost. Some analysts, such as Lipton (1977) and Bates (1981), have suggested the existence in LDCs of an urban or at least nonagrarian alliance consisting of industrial management and capitalists in protected industries, the organized industrial work force, civil servants, and virtually all urban consumers. All have become accustomed to protection—of inefficient management, redundant labor, and consumer and input subsidies. None of this protection can be allowed to endure if export-led growth is to gain momentum. Moreover, devaluation may have a particularly sharp impact on urban consumers, who will see the price of many imported items skyrocket.

A government contemplating this strategy must think carefully of the constituencies it will alienate, some of which are part of the state apparatus itself. The owners and managers of ISI industries may try to sabotage the new experiment, and they will find tacit allies among the workers who risk being laid off as enterprises streamline or who may face relative decreases in salary. All urban constituents may see a sharp rise in cost of living. It is important to remember that the negative effects of the new strategy will be felt immediately, whereas the economic payoffs may be years in coming. No politician likes that sort of bargain.

It is also possible that this strategy will lead to an enclave sector within the national economy, a sector that is charged with generating most exports but that may be linked to the economy as a whole only through its need for cheap labor. It may purchase few raw materials and sell few of its products in domestic markets. Some Middle Eastern countries, especially Egypt, are experimenting with industrial "free zones" (exempted from tariff and customs controls), which bear the seed of what we call elsewhere "disarticulated growth."

Despite the risks, some Middle Eastern countries have moved, haltingly, in this direction. Two of the earliest experiments involve Morocco and Tunisia, both of which negotiated preferential trade agreements with the European Economic Community (EEC or EC) in the late 1960s. Tunisia was moving away from a period of concerted ISI under state auspices, while Morocco sought to diversify its exports beyond its traditional combination of phosphates and citrus. Both hoped to attract light industry from Europe in ready-made apparel, electronics, consumer durable assembly and so forth, or to stimulate their own private sector to move into similar fields. The association initially developed satisfactorily, but the first oil shock of 1973 caused an economic downturn in Europe, accompanied by a revision of the trade agreements. Morocco and Tunisia find themselves today praying for a resurgence in European economic growth and some elusive formula to meet the challenge of the EEC's two most recent members, Greece and Spain.

For nearly two decades Turkey, already a member of the North Atlantic Treaty Organization (NATO), has aspired to full membership in the EEC. Since the early 1970s it has been trying to restructure its economy (after the experiment in ISI launched by Atatürk) so as to be able to compete in European markets. The process took on added urgency in the late 1970s as Turkey, without petroleum deposits, absorbed the full impact of rising international prices for fossil fuels at the same time that European labor markets were closing themselves off to migrant Turkish workers. Balance-of-payments crises, growing external debt, mounting domestic deficits, and inflation produced a situation of political instability and eventual military intervention in 1980. Since then a return to civilian rule has been accompanied by a concerted and partially successful export drive for Turkish manufactures and construction services.

Israel's economy has always been aid and trade dependent. Like Tunisia and Morocco, and well before them, it negotiated a preferential trade agreement with the EEC and has had great success in marketing avocados, citrus, and vegetables in Europe. Its major manufactured export has traditionally been finished industrial diamonds. In the past decade, however, Israel has moved into the export of manufactured metal products and into high-tech electronics exports. These together have eclipsed diamonds. Equally important is Israel's having become a major actor in international arms trade, supporting the scale and sophistication of its own armaments industry by developing foreign markets for its weaponry. Despite its relative success in all export sectors, Israel found itself in the early 1980s facing huge domestic deficits, high labor costs for Israeli workers that limit the areas in which Israel can be competitive internationally, the largest per capita external debt in the world, and a domestic inflation rate in 1985 second only to Bolivia's. Export-led growth has been no panacea for Israel's economic problems.

### Agricultural-Development-Led Growth

A final strategy that has recently received emphasis among political economists is agricultural-development-led growth (e.g., Adelman 1984; Mellor 1976). The strategy is especially aimed at very poor countries with most of their population still in agriculture, without vast mineral resources, and with little prospect of penetrating foreign markets for manufactured goods. It is particularly designed to minimize any conflict between growth and equity in development. The strategy draws on the "basic needs" approach, popular with international agencies during the 1970s, which focused on providing adequate nutrition, health, and education to all people. However, the agricultural-development-led growth approach places more stress on sustaining such human-capital investments by raising productivity, and on the importance of realistic price signals for achieving growth-with-equity. Although no Middle Eastern countries have adopted this strategy, if austerity and sluggish international markets persist, poorer countries like the Yemen Arab Republic (YAR), Morocco, and Sudan could do worse than to try to implement this approach.

Proponents of this strategy are very concerned that the gains of growth be widely shared, and they disbelieve currently fashionable "trickle down" rhetoric. The point of departure for the theoretical framework for this strategy is the simple observation that people's incomes are determined by the assets they own, the number of sales they can make from the services of these assets, and the price of these services. In poor agrarian societies, the principal assets are land and labor (or human capital). The strategy stresses that a redistribution of land *before* the growth process begins will do the most to ensure a widespread sharing of the gains of development. Equity in the distribution of human capital can be best improved by concentrating on achieving universal literacy and by making education as accessible as possible. Once such an equitable distribution has been achieved, the key to growth-with-equity is the number of sales from land and labor that can be made, that is, increasing agricultural production and increasing the demand for labor. Finally, prices are crucial: Any government bias against the services of land and labor will undermine the strategy.

The core of the agricultural-led growth strategy is the expansion of (already highly egalitarian) agriculture. The virtues of such growth are numerous; all revolve around the *labor intensity* of farm production, and the consequent high employment multipliers of agricultural development. Empirical evidence suggests that agriculture is the most labor intensive of any industry; increasing output per unit of land also raises the demand for agricultural labor, usually the poorest people in any country. Furthermore, farmers spend a high proportion of their increased incomes on labor-intensive manufactured goods, like housing, furniture, bicycles. There is therefore a link between increasing agricultural productivity, augmenting farmers' incomes, and raising the demand for industrial labor. Increases in agricultural output can be obtained at a relatively low cost in imported goods (unlike, say, automobile manufacturing where all of the parts may be imported, as was true in Iran under the shah). Finally, improving agricultural infrastructure (roads, irrigation and drainage systems) also are very labor-intensive activities. The strategy tries to take advantage of the agricultural-production function and farmers' tastes to create virtuous circles of increased food production, improved health, steadily growing labor absorption, and relatively equitable rising incomes.

Successful growth-with-equity using this strategy has three requirements: equitable distribution of land, commitment to improving human capital, and prices that do not discriminate against agriculture. If land is unequally distributed, then most gains from agricultural growth will be captured by the already rich. Failure to achieve universal literacy will retard technological change and will prevent the decrease of fertility, a factor that could swamp *any* development strategy. Heavy taxation of farmers and price discrimination against their products will blunt their incentives to produce.

No Middle Eastern country has really implemented such a strategy. None has a farm sector composed of only small owner-operators, as in Taiwan or the Republic of Korea, although Egypt comes the closest. Land reforms have removed major inequities in rural asset ownership, but they have not been the powerful leveling force they were in East Asia. The diffusion of land-yield improving technological change has been disappointing, despite continuous efforts at improving irrigation. Middle Eastern countries' performances in increasing rural literacy, especially of females, has not been impressive. And given the prevalence of import-substituting industrialization in the region, prices have often been biased against farmers. Finally, a potential internal contradiction of the strategy is that, throughout the world, expanding rural education stimulates an exodus of young men and women to the cities.

Nevertheless, some elements of this strategy do seem to have been given greater attention in recent years in the region. Farmers' terms of trade have often improved; education is now spreading rapidly in rural areas; most governments are trying to compensate for their past neglect of agriculture. If oil prices remain low, and if many poorer countries find it difficult to follow the Turkish example and penetrate European markets, some or all of the elements of the agricultural-development-led growth strategy may well become increasingly attractive. Not the least of the attractions of the strategy is its low use of imports, a very important consideration for the many highly indebted countries in the region. At the least, elements of the agricultural-development-led growth strategy could complement other strategies, as, for example, in Sudan, where foreign exchange will continue to come from agro-exports, but where increased attention to poorer farmers could pay important dividends (IFAD 1987).

Indeed, such mixing and combining of strategies is likely to be the norm in the region. For example, ISI and manufactured-export-led growth strategies are not mutually exclusive. It is in fact likely that most of the more developed countries will try to combine elements of both, just as poorer countries may combine agricultural-export-led growth with agro-exports or some modest import substitution. We may find two sectors side by side: one following the ISI pattern perhaps in metals, automobile assembly, fertilizers, and the like, and the other oriented toward external markets in finished textiles, electronic appliances, and instruments. Turkey in the 1980s is pursuing an export-led strategy without totally renouncing its heritage from the years 1930 to 1970 of protected, domestically oriented industries. Other countries have exhibited elements of three strategies: primary exports, ISI, and manufactured exports. Oil exporters such as Iran (at least until 1979) are an example, while Tunisia and Egypt represent countries that have continued traditional exports (cotton, olive oil, and in the 1970s petroleum), maintained an important ISI sector, and sought to promote manufactured exports. This mix of strategies appears to us to minimize the risks arising from each separately and to that extent makes good sense. But mixing is always difficult in practice because each strategy requires different and, sometimes incompatible, stimuli and must be judged by different, sometimes contradictory, performance criteria.

Having described elements of simultaneity in strategy selection, we cannot deny that there may often be sequential elements at stake as well. Put simply, ISI may be adopted as *the* strategy and produce a host of unintended and undesirable consequences, at which point the country shifts to an export-led strategy. There is ample evidence of such sequential shifts in the Middle East—Turkey, Egypt, and Tunisia have all followed this scenario—but it may be that Syria and Algeria are proceeding in similar fashion. In terms of performance, we can easily discern which countries actually implemented an ISI strategy, but, at this point, identifying those that have gone beyond official declarations of intent to promote manufactured exports is not so easy. Turkey, Morocco, and Tunisia appear to have taken action while Egypt remains at the drawing boards. Whether sequential or simultaneous, the state continues to play a preponderant role in shaping the experiment through control of credit, foreign exchange, tax policy, and investment budgets. Stimulating the private sector or honoring the market does not mean abdicating to either. The prominent role of the state in the Korean "miracle" is edifying in this respect.

A final caveat on strategy choice is in order here, to wit, the choice is never unconstrained. It is some set of state actors that makes the choice, and the choice is bounded by a host of factors, some of which are more obvious than others. There are resource constraints: Israel cannot export oil or any other raw material on a significant scale, but it does have a highly skilled work force. The Sudan can export cotton, but it does not have a highly skilled work force. Saudi Arabia can export oil and import a highly skilled work force. ISI, as noted, is ill suited for economies with small markets, and in most instances it does not make sense to establish industries to process resources one does not have.

The choice is also constrained by the relative gains and losses that will be incurred by domestic interests, classes, and ideological factions—this indeed is the primary focus of this book. The choice will be further constrained by the country's regional and international allies, any of which may have its own image of the future and some levers with which to promote it. And the choice will be constrained by international markets and financial flows. The Sudan invested heavily in sugar refining destined for export on the eve of the collapse of world sugar markets. Countries whose external debt is denominated in U.S. dollars found themselves in the early and middle 1980s saddled with huge unanticipated servicing requirements due to the surge in U.S. interest rates and the constant revaluing of the dollar against all other currencies.

Finally, the state cannot implement all elements of a strategy. It must use agencies external to itself, perhaps the local private sector, or the capitalist farming sector, or the multinational corporations. The choice of strategy is, then, constrained by the strengths, weaknesses, and dangers inherent in the agencies available to help implement it.

## The Question of Agencies

There are agencies the state chooses, more or less willingly, to implement its strategy, and there are those that impose themselves, more or less, upon the state. What the state does voluntarily or is forced to do is defined to some extent by its professed ideology. But, one must hasten to add, the professed ideals of the political regime are honored in the breach as often as not.

Most Middle Eastern states have advocated some form of socialism, however vague the content of the label and however insincere the regime's commitment to it. Even Egypt and Tunisia as they moved toward greater reliance on the market, the private sector, and profits as incentives, still spoke of themselves as socialist states. The dominant philosophy in Israel until the advent of the Likud government under Menachem Begin in 1977 was a kind of Zionist hybrid of Fabian socialism. The Sudan, YAR, Syria, Iraq, Libya, and Algeria all claim to be socialist. One has the impression that their socialism, as that of Tunisia and Egypt, consists mainly in a large public-sector and extensive welfare programs. On that score, monarchical Morocco, the Islamic Republic of Iran (as well as the Pahlavi dynasty before it), Turkey, Israel, and all the conservative princedoms of the Gulf and the Kingdom of Saudi Arabia could lay equal claim to socialism. But they do not. Morocco vaunts its political and economic liberalism, while Turkey today speaks mainly of the latter. Israel since 1977 has taken, but not applied, the advice of Milton Friedman of the University of Chicago, and for all the religiously inspired regimes from Iran to Saudi Arabia, socialism is anathema. Still we find the self-proclaimed liberals maintaining large state sectors and interfering in all aspects of market transactions. Similarly, socialist regimes tolerate and sometimes aid and abet private-sector actors in trade, small-scale manufacturing, construction, and farming. By any measure the largest and most dominant state sectors in the Middle East lie in the small oil-exporting countries. The petroleum deposits, the producing and refining companies, and all the proceeds of oil sales are under the control of the state.

With the exception of these same small oil-exporting states, there is a general ideological predisposition to minimize reliance on external actors to implement strategies. This predisposition stems from long periods of colonial domination, economic exploitation, and powerful nationalist movements that cut across left and right ideologies and across religion and secularism. For all the distrust of foreign governments and economic interests, many Middle Eastern countries find themselves thoroughly entangled with foreign powers and interests. The most difficult entanglements to explain away are economic: foreign aid, foreign private investment, servicing the external debt, reform programs negotiated with multilateral donors. Countries of professed liberal persuasion are able to legitimize and openly seek foreign private investment. That is the case in Turkey, Morocco, Tunisia, and Israel.[1] The Egyptian government has sought foreign investment in the past decade but has been accused internally of abandoning its commitment to socialism.

Throughout the Middle East in the 1970s and 1980s Islam has come to play an increasingly important role in shaping ideology and sometimes policy. For the moment we note only that Islam reenforces nationalist suspicions of virtually all outside agencies and nations. The question for Muslims, especially Muslim thinkers, is not one of socialism versus capitalism or public versus private property but rather one of the inherent dangers in dealing with any non-Muslim power. Such dealings can never be neutral or benign but are necessarily conflictual. One may choose among lesser Satans, but the ideal is to make no choice at all.

Many scholars of developing countries have argued that their governments really have no sovereign choice of strategies: These are determined by core capitalist countries, and the nominal differences among strategies are superficial. The international division of labor in this view is not the product of the working of anonymous forces of supply and demand within world markets but rather is a grand design elaborated and implemented by the core capitalist countries to perpetuate their control of the world economy. Thus economic experiments and the choice of strategies in the countries of the periphery must be carefully monitored by the core and oriented in desirable directions. Like any summary of an important body of analysis, the preceding lines do violence to the richness and sophistication of dependency and world systems approaches, but it is fair to say that this line of analysis presumes that the major impulses toward various strategies comes from advanced economies and that the range of choice is, by and large, strictly bounded. Moreover, the core countries have powerful instruments at their disposal with which to engineer their design: multinational corporations, multinational donor and financial institutions such as the IMF and the International Bank for Reconstruction and Development (IBRD), and major private banks that hold much of the aggregate debt of the LDCs. In this view such agencies clearly impose themselves as partners upon LDCs.

As will become clear in several places in this book, we are not comfortable with this line of analysis, particularly with regard to its tendency to deny the possibility of a significant area of sovereign choice for developing countries. The Middle East certainly displays a wide range of experiments and strategies, and while they are constrained by external forces and institutions (one wonders how it could be otherwise under *any* set of international political circumstances), they are not wholly determined by them. ISI as a strategy, for example, was advocated by Latin American economists as a way of breaking or attenuating the dependency of Latin American economies upon the advanced economies of Europe and North America. It was adopted elsewhere, in Turkey for example, in that spirit. One could argue that its widespread failures show that core interests successfully sabotaged it, but one would have expected that given the alleged power of these interests, they would have seen to it that the strategy was never adopted in the first place.

There is no question that when crises in the external accounts of LDCs become manifest—failure to service private external debt and balance-of-payments deficits—then the range of choice available to developing nations narrows significantly. These crises, however, may be exacerbated by but are seldom caused by the functioning of international markets, financial institutions, or multinational corporations. More often than not, the culprits are lagging agricultural production, inefficient industrial production systems, and costly oversized public bureaucracies. However, once the crises become manifest, the agencies of the core gain significant leverage over policy and strategy choice in LDCs. In essence, new lines of credit and the rescheduling of existing debt are traded against structural reforms in the economy of the developing country. Since the mid-1970s scores of developing countries have been driven toward far-reaching and painful structural adjustment programs designed in consultation with the IMF, the IBRD, and Western aid agencies, and the countries in the Middle East have been no exception (see Chapters 8, 9, and 10).

Within the domestic arena, the Middle Eastern state and its leaders have important choices of agencies to make. A central decision is the determination of the relative weights and division of labor between the public and private sectors. If one views the problem from the point of view of conventional class analysis, there may be no real choice involved—a dominant, or would-be dominant class will impose its will on the state and use state resources to service private interests. We argue, by contrast, that Middle Eastern state elites have enjoyed considerable leeway in determining the relative roles of the public and private sectors at specific points in the development process. Clearly, socialist regimes have an ideological bias against the private sector, domestic and foreign, but may encourage those elements within that sector that are defined as nonexploitative and working for the national interest.

One general observation can be made at this juncture, with a much fuller treatment saved for future chapters. ISI strategies have typically relied upon publicly owned enterprises, mainly because the initial investments have usually been very large and beyond the capacity of local entrepreneurial groups, if such groups exist at all. This need not always be the pattern, as Latin American experience with ISI has shown. There, foreign multinational corporations and local private investors undertook important parts of the ISI project. In the Middle East, however, the public sector has dominated the strategy. Conversely, as countries move toward export-led growth programs, there is often an attempt by public authorities to mobilize the private sector to play a significant role in these programs. The foreign donor and creditor community frequently pushes the authorities in this direction, but there may also be an independently formulated expectation that the private sector can adjust more rapidly than the public to the challenge of reducing costs, improving quality, and seeking out customers abroad for the country's products. Ideology is then left to catch up with the new reality.

Much less noted than the so-called Islamic resurgence of recent years has in fact been the resurgence of the private sector in the Middle East; it has become a powerful force in Turkey and has regained legitimacy in Egypt and Tunisia; even the more ideologically socialist countries, Algeria, Syria, and Iraq, have made numerous policy concessions to their private sectors without yet fully revising their ideological charters. The only Middle Eastern country that truly glorified its private sector, Lebanon, after a decade of Hobbesian civil war, barely survives as a state or an economy. We do not care to draw any particular conclusion from that observation.

Whether or not called upon to play an active part in the implementation of strategies, certain interests, strata of the population, and classes will benefit while others will be penalized, depending on the strategy or policies selected. It is the case in general that the rural sector does not benefit from ISI strategies because usually the state turns the domestic terms of trade against it. In an export-led strategy, it may be only capitalist farmers and not the peasantry as a whole that benefits from export incentives. If one looks at urban constituencies affected by ISI, one may see that organized labor in the new industries, managerial strata charged with implementing state-financed projects, and middle- and upper-income consumers may be the major beneficiaries. Large-scale industrialists in the private sector may suffer when state banking institutions and government investment programs favor public-sector enterprise. In contrast, small-scale industrialists may benefit from subcontracting on public-sector projects, especially in the construction sector.

The move toward a manufactured-export-led strategy will likely have an adverse effect on the real incomes of workers, as wages will be allowed to lag behind inflation. Moreover if the strategy is accompanied by devaluation, a shift in the domestic terms of trade in favor of agriculture, and some reduction in consumer subsidies, all citizens in the nonfarm sector, and especially those on fixed incomes, will experience a sharp rise in the cost of living.

At this point we must step back from the question of strategy choice and the winners and losers under different choices in order to introduce a few simple, but nonetheless crucial, propositions on our understanding of class in relation to state actors and structures. Common to both Marxist and liberal schools of analysis is the assumption that forces essentially external to the state are able to control and guide it, using the state to promote or defend their interests. This is an "instrumentalist" view of the state, one that looks, in the liberal tradition, to parties, unions, and interest groups as capturing the state through elections and lobbying or, in the Marxian tradition, to a dominant class, controlling the basic means of production within society, as being in a position to use the state to perpetuate its dominance. We are, for the moment, particularly concerned by this latter view, one that has often prevailed in analyses of the Middle Eastern state.

As will become evident in ensuing chapters, we question the premises of this view. First, the process of structural transformation and the nearly universal shift toward the preponderance of the nonagrarian, urban sector in economic and social terms produces new class actors and undermines the old, with little respect to differing production systems, ideologies, or state formations. Second, at a less macro level, a given development strategy may set in motion a process that virtually creates new class actors. This process should be seen as an unintended by-product of the strategy choice, not conclusive evidence that the state was acting in the interests of a class that had not yet taken shape. The increasing strength of the Turkish private industrial bourgeoisie emerging out of the decades of statist, ISI-oriented politics is a case in point.

Third, in the Middle East, as in most LDCs, class alignments are fluid, class interests ill defined, and class consciousness often amorphous. Powerful landowning groups were often undermined by land reforms. Nowhere have peasantries developed class cohesion. To the extent that capitalist bourgeoisies exist, they have frequently been made up of foreigners of one sort or another and have preferred trade to manufacturing. Because industrialization has come very late to the region, the proletariat is commensurately weak. That leaves a relatively powerful state apparatus, with its legions of civil servants and managers; a relatively powerful military establishment; and a numerically important but organizationally weak stratum of craftsmen, service people, small-scale manufacturers, and myriads of petty tradespeople. For the most part, these classes are not sufficiently coherent and well defined to manipulate the state. It is our contention that the Middle Eastern state, as often as not, is best seen as the instrument of the upper echelons of its own personnel, and that it is in their interests to ensure that the state continues to control as much of the economic resources of the society as possible.

Departing from that premise, we go one step further. Given its relative power and relative autonomy, by class default as it were, the state may be used as a class maker or class creator. That is, the somewhat disembodied politico-military power of the state can be used to allocate resources in the process of structural transformation in such a way that new interests are called forth, establish claims on resources, and eventually develop vested class interests. The policy levers at the disposal of the Middle Eastern state to act in this manner are formidable. It may own and manage the major productive assets in the economy, own and derive revenue from all mineral resources, act as the single largest employer in the economy, control if not own the major banking institutions, regulate and tax economic activities of all kinds, set basic education policy, control prices, and exercise, in Max Weber's terms, the legitimate monopoly of coercive force. Crucial struggles, then, do not occur so much between the state and the forces in civil society that seek to control the state as within the ranks of the state elites themselves.

How the state as class maker works out in practice will be developed throughout this book, but a few examples of what we have in mind are in order here. Agrarian reforms in the Middle East and the implementation of new production strategies in the agricultural sector have frequently resulted in the elimination of large landowners as a major *political* force, the expansion of the ranks of small and middle-sized landowners, a stratum of which is allowed disproportionate access to rural credit and to control rural institutions such as cooperatives and village councils. This stratum is then in a position to take full advantage of unregulated markets for agricultural produce or to lead the way in export drives. This stratum contains the beginnings of a capitalist farmer class.

The groups the state favors need not be of a kind; we should expect a great deal of inconsistency in the doling out of incentives, for the state is not a monolith in its dealings with civil society. For example, in the Sudan, the state and the economy as a whole have long depended on the performance of the Gezira Scheme, one of the world's largest state farms, where the tenants grow cotton for export. The Sudanese state has traditionally sought to extract savings and foreign exchange from this scheme, and in the constant bargaining that goes on between the state and the tenant cultivators the latter have become a powerful interest group—one hesitates to say class—in Sudanese society. At the same time the Sudanese government has encouraged through easy credit and forfeitary land-leasing arrangements the emergence of a sizable group of private commercial farmers undertaking mechanized cultivation of sorghum destined mainly for export to Saudi Arabia. Thus the Sudanese government simultaneously promotes policies to help it extract resources from a huge state farm while it fosters a process of "primitive accumulation" among a growing stratum of capitalist tractor farmers, a stratum that twenty years ago scarcely existed.

Let us look at one final example. Turkey hopes one day to join the European Common Market, which will mean lowering tariff walls and trade barriers in the face of more efficient European producers. Moreover, Turkey is facing immediate debt and balance-of-payments problems, which are to be resolved by greatly increasing Turkey's exports. Toward both goals, the policies of Turkey's prime minister, Turgut Özal, have been to favor the country's large industrial and construction firms through tax incentives and credit policy. If these policies are sustained and successful, we may see the consolidation of a native, capitalist industrial bourgeoisie for the first time in any Middle Eastern society.

For those uninitiated to the debates that rage about how best to understand the state, these propositions may not seem implausible. We simply caution our readers that many scholars would object strenuously to our interpretation: It can be seen as ahistorical, reactionary, insufficiently attuned to constraints upon the state from the world system, and blind to the links between class interests in the core capitalist societies and their allies in the periphery. We are cognizant of our vulnerabilities but will deal with them, if at all, in the complete elaboration of our argument in the following chapters. We do wish to stress, however, that in identifying state autonomy as an important element in understanding the Middle Eastern state, we do not thereby advocate it as a desirable political arrangement.

## CLASS

The final vertex of our theoretical triangle is the concept of class. Not only is the process of class formation important in its own right, but also the other major variables of structural transformation and state policy, we argue, cannot be understood without using this concept. In this final section we shall briefly discuss some competing definitions of the concept of class and then turn to a sketch of the historical process of class formation in the Middle East.

The starting point for any serious discussion of class must be the Marxist definition, of which two major aspects will be stressed. "Class" is defined (1) in relational terms and especially (2) by differential property rights—by the right to exclude others. Marxists conceive of class as *interaction:* landlords and tenants, workers and capitalists, and so forth. (This is to be distinguished from the "orthodox sociological" concept of class as "differences"—the "social stratification" notion of class.) The relational aspect of the Marxist conception derives from the centrality of property ownership in the definition of class: Ownership is the right to exclude others, an inherently relational notion.

This concept must also be distinguished from the usual orthodox conceptions of economics. Such views typically use either the individual or the entire economy as the unit of analysis. The concept of class is evidently an intermediate notion: It recognizes that (1) the ownership of resources creates fundamental, shared interests among subsets of individuals; (2) such interests are typically opposed to the interests of other, similarly defined subsets of actors, (i.e., there is actual or potential conflict between such subsets of people—and, therefore, potential for social change via their differential success in collective action); and (3) such shared interests may be threatened by the unintended outcomes of actions of members of the class itself, again giving rise to collective action and therefore potentially to social change.

The core of the concept of class is access to the means of production. Classes may be further distinguished by their access to political power, their consumption habits, their status in society, by their dress, speech, religious and sexual habits. The Marxist definition of class holds all of these to be fundamentally derivative of the ownership relations. The stress on the distribution and reproduction of access to the means of production, on class relations, constitutes the core of the Marxist definition of class (Richards 1986a).

Two principal criticisms of the proprietary definition of class may be made. First, this definition identifies classes as what Marxists would call "class in itself." That is, classes are defined quite independently of the actual perceptions, beliefs, or political activities of the actors grouped into classes. The notion of "class for itself," of classes acting *as* classes, is certainly a more complicated notion and presumably is the one needed for political analysis. The "for itself" concept includes not only the objective aspects of class in itself (for example, one can usually determine which peasants own which land without asking how they themselves perceive their situation) but also contains elements of ideology, of solutions to the free-rider problems that always emerge in situations characterized by collective action.[2]

The second major criticism of the proprietary definition is that it is insufficient because it (allegedly) neglects power relations. Although the above proprietary definition includes power, as flowing from ownership, critics of this definition assert that it neglects the fact that in the Middle East and North Africa causality often went the other way, as rulers granted and took away with impunity, not only property, but often life itself. There is a strong sense among such critics that power needs to be more central to the definition of class than they believe the Marxist concept permits.

A prominent example of this perspective may be found in an article by Bill (1972a). He started with the Marxist proprietary definition and then attempted to add power explicitly: "Classes are defined as the largest aggregates of individuals united by similar modes of employment and possessing similar power positions to preserve, modify or transform relationships among such aggregates" (424). He proceeded to offer a model, or picture, of class in the Middle East: "In the Middle East these classes traditionally have been the following seven: the ruling class, the bureaucratic middle class, the bourgeois middle class, the cleric middle class, the traditional working class, the peasant class, and the nomadic class. The twentieth century has witnessed the appearance of two new classes: the professional middle class and the industrial working class" (424).

The utility of this critique is its explicit consideration of power as something independent of property rights or ownership. In fact, however, power and the presence of specialized power holders are or should be implicit in any proprietary concept of class. After all, it is difficult to see how one can conceptualize "ownership relations" without including consideration of enforcement mechanisms. If property rights are defined by the right to exclude others, then someone must enforce this exclusion. Given the principle that productivity increases with specialization, we would expect "exclusion specialists" (soldiers, policemen, "enforcers" of all sorts) to emerge. Then, of course, an additional problem arises: Who will exclude the excluders? Consideration of the inevitable interaction of state power and property rights leads us to stress that not only does class influence the state, but, often more obviously, the state makes proprietary classes.

The major difficulty with Bill's formulation is that it presents a rather static picture of class. "New classes" of the twentieth century are simply superimposed on the old in the above statement. This misses the *process* of class formation: the rising and falling of classes, with incipient or proto classes emerging, remnants lingering and so on. But most important, Bill's formulation omits the crucial role of economic growth and structural transformation in the process of class formation. For example, it is not evident that there any longer exists a single "peasant class" in the Middle East. The process of agricultural development and change has led to considerable differentiation of the peasantry and to the emergence of distinct classes (of the "in itself" type), such as rich peasants and landless laborers. Similarly, we argue in Chapters 8–10 that the "bureaucratic middle class" and the "bourgeois middle class" show signs of merging in countries ranging from Algeria to Egypt to Turkey.

Just as the process of economic growth and structural transformation has encountered numerous blockages and unintended outcomes, so too has the process of class formation associated with such growth and structural change been highly uneven. Indeed, in Third World countries, including those in the Middle East, one should expect the coexistence of different class forms and types. Even in highly developed Western societies, which all would agree are class based, not everyone falls into the neat boxes of "capitalists" and "workers." One should expect this to be even more the case in the Middle East and North Africa. Our own approach views class as the outcome of the historical process of growth and structural transformation, including, most prominently, a major role for state actors. Class in our model is endogenously determined by the historical interaction of structural transformation and the state. The nature of classes and state forms inherited from previous eras have had profound, long-lasting effects on this contemporary process. We now turn to a sketch of class as historical process in the Middle East.

## Structural Transformation and Class Formation in Middle East History

Europe's structural transformation over a number of centuries from an agrarian to an industrial-urban base has shaped our general understanding of the process but has not provided a model that will be faithfully replicated in developing countries. The latter may skip some stages by importing technology or telescope others. Developing countries will cope with population growth rates that Europe never confronted. So too, the process of class formation in the Middle East and elsewhere has varied considerably from that of Europe. What, schematically, are the major differences between the Middle Eastern and the European experience in the interaction of class, state, and structural transformation?

The first set of distinctions revolves around the legal institutions of private property, so prominent in European history but relatively absent in Middle Eastern. In the Middle East, India, and China, Marx saw evidence for what he called "the Asiatic mode of production." The elements he saw as crucial to this mode shifted over time in his analysis (see Anderson 1980, 484–85; Islamoğlu and Keyder 1977, 395), but there were some constants that we believe do define a regime peculiar to the Middle East and South Asia. The basic elements were (1) an absence, in the juridical sense, of private property in land and (2) a state that extracted tribute, through appointed intermediaries, from undifferentiated villages that combined agriculture and handicrafts and that displayed few organic linkages among themselves. Marx had difficulty incorporating in his analysis tribalism and nomadism, phenomena that in fact did link villages. This linkage allowed nomads and tribes to compete with the state for the surplus that sedentary populations could produce. Despite this fly in the Marxist ointment, the concept of the Asiatic mode points us in a useful direction.

The Middle Eastern state retained the right (but not always the ability) to dispose of landed property as its rulers saw fit. What it granted were temporary rights to appropriate the produce of the land, that is, usufruct rights. In distinction to European legal institutions, these rights were not permanent and sanctified by law but rather were temporary privileges bestowed upon clients by the ruler: the caliph or sultan and his governors in far-flung regions of the Islamic empires.

Many historians have observed that the state's eminent domain often gave way in practice to what amounted to hereditary access to state-granted land or to the right to collect tribute in the state's name. But the arrival on the scene of a powerful sultan would, and not infrequently did, lead to the revocation of those quasi-hereditary privileges. Likewise, local notables could, in the face of a weak or financially constrained sultan, assert "stable" claims to privilege. The law was indifferent to the outcome of these power struggles; it only endorsed the right of the state to dispose of the public domain as its rulers saw fit.

Between the sultan and his government and the tribute-paying villagers and tribes lay a more or less thick stratum of tax-farmers, tribute gatherers, and rural notables. Some were military figures, like the Ottoman *sipahis*, charged with raising tribute and troops for the sultan in exchange for fieflike estates known as *timar*. Others were tax-farmers pure and simple, granted the right to tax a certain population to whatever extent possible in return for turning over to the sultan a predetermined amount.

The system of *timariots* led some historians to argue for a kind of Middle Eastern feudalism, especially as the privileges associated with the *timar* tended to become hereditary. But the contrasts with European feudalism were, as Issawi has shown (1982, 136–38), major. The elaborate legal, church-sanctified infrastructure of European feudalism was missing or, where it existed, flatly contradicted the principle of an hereditary nobility as much as it contradicted that of inherited vassalage. Indeed, local Middle East power figures had no legal authority over vassals; only the Muslim judge, the *qadi*, had such authority. Second, the privileges of the power figures were legally temporary and often assigned to scattered bits of territory rather than being concentrated geographically, as in Europe. Finally, there were no serfs in the legal sense in the Middle East; peasants were not bound to the land, although all sorts of extralegal pressures might in fact tie them down.

As the Middle East, from the seventeenth century on, was drawn into international trade dominated by the newly industrializing nations of Europe, and Islamic states everywhere (the Ottoman Empire, Persia, Moghul India,

Morocco) dealt with military inferiority vis-à-vis the Europeans, important changes occurred in the relation of these states to their tribute-paying subjects. The need to raise revenues to pay for an enlarged and modernized military establishment pushed the sultans toward conversion of *timar* land into hereditary private land, while tax-farmers (*multazims*) gained heritable and salable rights to their territories. After a time, local notables began to profit from a lucrative agricultural-export trade to Europe and were allowed to establish commercial estates (*çiftliks*) that were tantamount to privately owned commercial farms.

The question of state revenues is crucial in grasping one of the profound differences between European and Middle Eastern patterns of economic change. For the most part, state revenues were drawn from the agrarian sector in the form of taxes in kind or in cash on land, animals, and huts. As much as 80% of state revenues may have been so derived, and as much as 15% of total agricultural production may have been absorbed in tribute (Issawi 1982, 68–69; Owen 1981, 106; Katouzian 1981). These proportions of course varied enormously in time and in place and should be taken only as orders of magnitude. The remaining 20% of state revenues came from taxes on overland trade, excise duties, state monopolies, and taxes on markets and guilds.

The paradox here is that public authorities seldom paid much attention to improving agricultural conditions so as to maximize production and derivatively state revenues. The one *partial* exception may have been the highly productive irrigated agrarian sector of Egypt, where the state on occasion had to concern itself with flood-control projects and the maintenance of the irrigation infrastructure. But even there, the state was mostly concerned with organizing its tribute gatherers and capturing within its net a peasantry that had nowhere to hide.

By and large the attitudes of public authorities toward their major source of revenue conformed to the paradigm that Barrington Moore vividly described as the "predatory state."[3] In its most extreme manifestations, the sultan would dispatch his troops to extract tribute from recalcitrant regions and, if they resisted, destroy their crops and their flocks. Such primitive extraction of course did little to promote long-term investment in the land.

This vicious circle did not always prevail. In the fifteenth and sixteenth centuries the administration of the Ottoman Empire was attentive to the economic well-being of tribute-paying populations, "for only with maximum prosperity could the exchequer be kept full" (Hodgson 1974b, 112). But as the empire expanded, the administration was stretched thin and greater attention was paid "reliable" agricultural zones in the Balkans and Egypt than zones in the "Semitic lands of old Islam." Added to this was the impact of the vast quantities of silver imported by Spain from the New World upon Mediterranean commerce in the seventeenth century. The Ottoman Empire experienced high rates of inflation, debasement of its currency, and a kind of rapacious hunt among the villagers for new revenue.

"Where Occidental observers had earlier commented on how fortunate were the peasants under Ottoman rule, they now found that the peasantry seemed oppressed, the land less well-cultivated, and villages deserted, with their population poured impoverished into the cities" (Hodgson 1974b, 130; see also Islamoğlu and Keyder 1977).

Even had the state been in all epochs more benevolent in its approach to its rural populations, there is reason to doubt that the kinds of locally inspired technological breakthroughs in agriculture that occurred in Europe would have been replicated in the Middle East. The reasons involve the ecology of the region and the existence of large nomadic populations. When we consider the vast extent of the Middle East or even its subregions, its rugged terrain characterized by mountain ranges interspersed with large desert expanses, and the prevailing aridity throughout, we can say that it would have been surprising had the Middle East duplicated European agricultural progress. Take only Saudi Arabia with its 2.2 million square kilometers, or about four-fifths of the Arabian Peninsula. This surface, the equivalent of most of Western Europe including the Iberian Peninsula and Italy, is mainly desert. Whereas European governments dealt with compact areas and generally favorable rain and soil conditions, Middle Eastern states faced staggering distances and hostile terrains that defied centralization, the habits of regular administrative practice, and the consistent maintenance of law and order.

The very ecology of the region produced a social phenomenon, the nomads, that had no counterpart in Western Europe. The nomads in the Middle East, even into the twentieth century, constituted at least 10% of the total population in most areas. Their turf was the "coastal" zones, where the few well-watered areas of sedentary agriculture gave way to the desert proper. It was in these zones that they grazed their animals and pitched their tents. Their self-image was one of warriors, freemen who had only scorn for peasants enslaved to the land. Like the state, the nomads often preyed on the very populations from whom they needed tribute. Not until the twentieth century would distance be conquered, nomads subdued, and the control of the government extended on a permanent basis over all the territories of sedentary population.

What then of the cities and trade as a source of revenue? Urban centers have for millennia been important features on the political and economic landscape of the Middle East. We think first of the ancient cities of Jerusalem, Damascus, Antioch, and Carthage, but in the Muslim Middle Ages major cities stretched from Spain in the west to India in the east: Fez, Cordoba, Tunis, Cairo, Aleppo, Istanbul, Izmir, Tabriz, Tehran, and Baghdad were in size and diversity the rival of anything in Europe. These cities thrived on the long-distance trade linking Europe to the Far East and, to a lesser extent, to Africa. Muslim states were themselves centered in these cities and were able to tax in various ways the commerce passing through them and the crafts and services that were stimulated by overland trade. The cities were the centers as well of Muslim learning and culture.

To some extent, commerce, urban life in general, and high culture were divorced from the sedentary hinterlands of the cities (Amin 1976, 21). But whereas the state might find in the cities and caravan routes a source of income independent of the fluctuating fortunes of agriculture, its approach to urban business was hardly more benign. Writing of Moghul India, Barrington Moore observed (1967, 322): "In general, the attitude of the political authorities . . . toward the merchant seems to have been closer to that of the spider toward the fly than that of the cow herd toward his cow that was widespread in Europe at the same time. Not even Akbar, the most enlightened of the Moguls had a Colbert."

Nonetheless, as Islamoğlu and Keyder argued (1977), merchant groups and merchant capital begin to escape the control of the state in the seventeenth century with the integration of the empire into international trade. Urban merchant capital had, they asserted, served to "articulate" the revenue-gathering stratum with the peasant producers, but the seventeenth-century inflation, the growth in contraband trade, and the expansion of commercial export agriculture put much of urban-financed internal trade beyond the reach of the state and led ultimately to the "disarticulation" of the Asiatic mode of production. Stripped of jargon, what can be said is that by the eighteenth century the Ottoman state faced a momentous fiscal crisis resulting from four factors: (1) the diversion of some overland trade to the new sea routes to the Far East; (2) overextension of the administrative capacity of the empire at the expense of settled agriculture; (3) the quest for new revenues in order to undertake military modernization that resulted in the assignation of land and tax-farming rights of a quasi-hereditary nature; and (4) the consolidation of a rural notability engaged in commercial agriculture for export. The privatization of the state's domain that we usually associate with direct colonial rule was well under way before European powers carved up the Middle East.

If we then look at the class "products" of this historical process, we find a relatively undifferentiated peasantry whose surplus was coveted by both the state and the armed nomadic tribes, urban merchants engaged in both overland and internal trade, urban artisans who produced for upper-income urban consumers, as well as for peasants and tribesmen; and the legal experts of Islam, the *'ulema'* (plural of *'alim,* or one who knows). The *'ulema',* along with the soldiers and the bureaucrats of the state, constituted class actors of a sort, but actors who did not necessarily own or directly control property or means of production. Rather, in the name of the state and of Islam, they exercised the authority and, frequently, the naked power to dispose of property and productive means. Some analysts have suggested that the nomads should be seen as a class, but because they lacked broad-based group cohesion beyond the tribal level and well-defined economic interests, we feel it is best to see them as important actors without class attributes.

## Defensive Modernization and Colonial Transformation

There is no gainsaying that the mid- and late nineteenth century is a watershed in state and class formation in the Middle East. Although processes of monetization, commercialization, and privatization may be discerned prior to that period, they were greatly accelerated thereafter as the increasingly mature industrial societies of Europe contended for geopolitical and economic advantage in the Middle East.

The military threat posed by those societies, as well as by Czarist Russia, had been clear for sometime, and Ottoman sultans and their governors had begun to transform their military establishments along European lines. Large standing armies, modern industries for manufacturing artillery pieces and firearms, road and railroad construction to facilitate the movement of troops and goods, all required expenditures by the state on an unprecedented scale. The search for revenue led Middle Eastern states into new domestic-taxation devices and into external debt to European banks.

By midcentury a so-called reform program (the Tanzimat) was under way throughout the Ottoman Empire and was echoed in Qajar Iran and in Morocco (the *nizam al-jadid,* or new order). The general tendency was to develop the legal infrastructure of private property; the European creditors of the empire argued that stable title to land and wealth would increase productive activity and hence the sultan's tax base. In Egypt the khedive, or Ottoman governor, granted private title to land to all those who would pay five years of agricultural tax in advance. In addition, the collection of taxes in cash become the norm, forcing cultivators into commercial agriculture in order to acquit their obligations. The process was not at all smooth; the Ottoman bey of Tunis in 1857 introduced a head tax in cash (the *majba*), which led to a rural revolt in 1864. The tax, which had produced 50% of the beylical state's revenues, was rescinded, and Tunis then borrowed its way into an unmanageable external debt (Anderson 1986).

The development efforts of the Middle Eastern state thus had as a direct consequence the promotion, if not the creation, of new class interests. The growth of a rural notability through trade and tax-farming was visible everywhere. As land became alienable, it could serve as collateral against loans. This change brought investment into agriculture and began, in parts of the Ottoman Empire, to attract foreign capital to export agriculture. Middlemen proliferated: private moneylenders, real estate banks, buyers and brokers for export crops. Frequently the middlemen were foreigners or from religious minorities that were not subject to Islamic strictures on interest: thus the prominence of Greeks, Armenians, Jews, and Coptic Christians. Increasingly, they linked the new squirearchy of commercial agriculture to foreign markets. The squirearchy itself was mainly indigenous, but we should remember that in Algeria, after the French conquest of

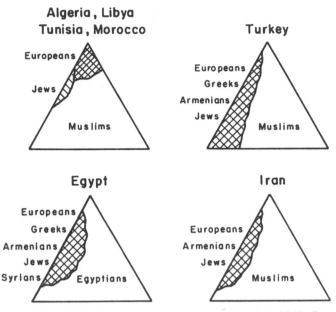

Figure 2.4   European and minority shares in the wealth of the Middle East:
Pre–World War II. *Source:* Charles Issawi, *An Economic History of the Middle
East and North Africa,* New York, Columbia University Press, 1982, p. 9.
Copyright © 1982 by Columbia University Press. Used by permission.

1830, Europeans owned the best lands and dominated the export of wine
to France.

Again, in the effort to stabilize rural revenue sources, the state encouraged
tribal and nomadic chieftains to settle by granting them title to what had
been quasi-communal lands, while state officials, high-ranking military
figures, members of the ruling family or dynasty (such as the Qajar aristocracy
in Iran or the dynasty of Mohammed Ali in Egypt), and even 'aristocratic'
urban families, such as those of the city of Hama in Syria, established
private title to what became veritable latifundia (Iraq, Iran, parts of Syria,
and Eastern Anatolia were particularly affected).

Similar processes were at work in the cities. The public bureaucratic
function increased in importance, as did the bureaucrats themselves; the
military establishment became more elaborate; and a new merchant bourgeoisie, overlapping substantially with the agents of commercial agriculture,
and just as frequently foreign (Figure 2.4), took root (Landes 1958). The
point we wish to stress in all this, one that informs all our analysis, is
that the state authorities can initiate broad-gauged policies in fairly unfettered fashion. Moreover, in the pursuit of specific goals, those authorities
will stimulate processes of economic change whose consequences in the
creation of new class actors and strata are as momentous as they are
unanticipated.

In the late nineteenth and early twentieth centuries, Islamic states collapsed in the face of European imperialism. All areas of the Middle East except Turkey, Iran, and the Arabian Peninsula fell under European rule. The colonial states that were implanted were truly autonomous from the societies they governed. With modern military technology (aircraft, among other things) and administrative practices, they completed the subjugation of territories and peoples that the sultans had begun. Private property, the cash economy, and the tax collector advanced together. The colonial state added two new and vital elements: public education for a limited number of natives and the promotion of a professional civil service. The norms underlying these elements, norms that we now call Weberian, were those of achieved status, that is, position won on the basis of training and competency regardless of factors of birth, blood, or income. Even though Turkey and Iran escaped direct European control, their leaders attempted, more successfully in Turkey than in Iran, to apply these standards to their own bureaucracies.

The colonial state was in general expected by the metropole to be financially self-sufficient. A modern civil service was necessary to manage roads, railroads, ports, and power, to run the mail and telegraph services, to identify and tax the population, to staff all echelons of local administration, to undertake all the intermediate positions between the colonial authorities and the population where mastery of the colonial and the native languages was essential. By the 1930s one finds a new protoclass asserting itself. It was educated, white collar, and salaried. Its status was not dependent upon its ownership of private property—of which it might possess very little—but on its professional attainment. It was bourgeois in aspirations and life-style. It was in embryon what Halpern (1963) was later to call "the new middle class."

The major achievement of the colonial state in class formation consisted in consolidating the position of landowners and in midwifing the birth of the new middle class. The postcolonial state in the Middle East has gone much further than either the Islamic or the colonial state in redrafting the class map of the region. Few postcolonial states had, to begin with, or maintained for long, strong links to wealthy classes in their societies. Syria and Iraq up to 1958, Lebanon, and Morocco were the only major exceptions. The more autonomous states, Turkey, Iran, Egypt, Algeria, and Syria and Iraq after 1958, engaged in far-reaching class engineering. The latifundists, mentioned above, were undermined by agrarian reform, and the merchant bourgeoisie was hemmed in by state regulations, price controls, public trade monopolies, and nationalizations. Foreign and minoritarian commercial groups faced systematic discrimination.

By contrast, varying combinations of agrarian reform and ISI bolstered the ranks of small landowners, left small-scale capitalist farmers at the top of the rural hierarchy, and led to a prodigious growth in the new middle class through mass education and bureaucratic expansion. Meanwhile, the creation and absorption into the public sector of important productive, commercial, and banking assets spawned a new managerial state bourgeoisie.

Two or three decades of state-led growth had brought to a halt or significantly slowed the process of privatization that had begun in the early nineteenth century. But the regional oil shocks of the 1970s coupled with the inefficiencies of state-led ISI appear to have opened up the possibility of a new era of privatization in the 1980s. ISI had tremendous spin-off effects in subcontracting to existing private sectors. They weathered hostile socialist or simply anticapitalist (as in Pahlavi Iran) programs of the state managers. Drawing on state business and credit from public banks, and sheltered behind tariff walls put up to protect the public sector, these private sectors found themselves positioned to respond to a growing mood among public authorities that efficiency would have to take precedence over redistribution if their national economies were to survive. This mood was in no small way sustained, if not produced, by the international donor community. In short, what we may be witnessing is the gradual reduction of the autonomy of the state and its recapture by class actors but, in this instance, class actors that the state had itself created.

As in nearly all aspects of structural transformation and class development with which we are concerned, Turkey serves as bellwether for the region. It is one generation in advance over all its neighbors in the Middle East, having begun in economic policy and state-building in the 1920s what most other countries would not attempt before the 1950s. It now contains a powerful and highly differentiated entrepreneurial bourgeoisie with a well-organized industrial segment. This bourgeoisie developed virtually ex nihilo after 1920. The war for national liberation led by Kemal Atatürk resulted in the mass repatriation to Greece of the most experienced entrepreneurs that Anatolia and Istanbul could offer. During forty years of state-led growth, the infant indigenous bourgeoisie acquired skills and capital and may now be ready, if the international economy is at all hospitable, to consolidate Turkey in the ranks of the NICs and to make the Turkish state its instrument.

## CONCLUSION

The three variables that undergird our analysis—economic growth patterns, state structures and policies, and class—will be treated sequentially in the following chapters. One should not lose sight of the fact that they interact simultaneously and that the sequence in which we approach them implies neither an order of importance nor a line of causality. The next four chapters (3–6) do, however, lay out a broad contextual framework for understanding the rapid social and economic change that has characterized the region in this century. They are a necessary starting point for a full consideration of state and class. We begin with a fuller presentation of our understanding of economic growth and structural change.

## NOTES

1. The justification is all the more compelling in Israel, for every foreign investor that enters that economy must forgo dealings with the Arab world due to the Arab boycott of Israel. Coca Cola Co. is a case in point.

2. The free-rider problem arises when an actor cannot be excluded from the benefits of collective action. Consequently, he may shirk or fail to participate—and still reap the benefits; he gets a "free ride" on the efforts of others.

3. In Moroccan history it is frequently said that the government (the *makhzen*) "ate" a region or a tribe that failed to pay taxes or provide conscripts.

# 3

# OVERVIEW OF ECONOMIC GROWTH AND STRUCTURAL CHANGE

This chapter provides an empirical overview of the varied patterns of economic growth and structural change in the region. We shall inventory the resources of the region, outline the main patterns of growth, and provide some limited commentary on the different rates and forms of growth. The chapter is largely descriptive: We present trends and issues, but with the exception of the petroleum sector, we leave the analysis of these developments to later chapters.

## THE NATURAL RESOURCE BASE

The political economy of the Middle East is dominated by three simple facts: little rain, much oil, and a rapidly growing (and therefore young) population. Most of the Middle East lies in the arid zone of the Eastern Hemisphere, a zone that stretches from Morocco to Mongolia. Much of the region receives less than twenty inches of rain per year, an amount that makes unirrigated agriculture extremely risky (Map 3.1). Precipitation is also highly variable, not only from year to year, but also seasonally. Most of the region experiences distinct wet and dry periods. Even within the rainy season, precipitation is often quite irregular. Annual precipitation figures are often deceptive, since much rain may fall in a short space of time. For example, during 1985–1986, Tunisian rainfall was 150% above normal in March, but little rain fell during the crucial planting months of October to December. With the exception of some highland (e.g., of the YAR) and coastal (e.g., Caspian of Iran) areas, the Middle East lacks the relatively heavy and reliable rainfall of the Asian monsoons, and long, devastating droughts have occurred throughout the region's history.

Only irrigated lands could support a dense population in preindustrial times. Such areas were sharply limited: the Nile Valley of Egypt, parts of the Tigris-Euphrates Valley, and other, more localized areas. All of these irrigation systems underwent extensive changes in their long histories, expanding with stability and peace, contracting with upheaval, war and mismanagement. Irrigation networks also faced (and face) important ecological constraints, like increasing salinity (Hodgson 1974a, 389–91). In more recent times, they have also created international political problems, since most of the major rivers of the region cross national boundaries. The difficult agro-ecology has contributed to the large and growing gap between consumption and domestic production of food in the region, a gap that drives much of the political economy of agriculture.

Because of this limited rainfall and agricultural potential, the region has a low overall population density. Although MENA covers about 11–12% of the world's land area[1] (about one-third larger than the United States), it contains less than 7% of the total world population. The region's overall population density is about 55 persons per square mile (21 per km²), compared with 67 per square mile (26 per km²) in the United States, or 220 persons per square mile (85 per km²) in China and India. However, such an average number is extremely misleading. Because of the aridity, less than 7% of the area is cultivated. There are about 825 Middle Easterners for every square mile (318 per km²) of arable land. The most striking case is that of Egypt. The country contains about 360,000 square miles (932,400 km²)—an area roughly the size of France and Spain combined. But nearly the entire population of about 50 million lives in the approximately 15,000 square miles (38,850 km²) of the Nile River Valley and Delta; the resulting population density of about 3,333 persons per square mile (1,287 per km²) is rivaled only by Java and parts of India and China. The pattern of population distribution is shown in Map 3.2.

The total population of these countries is approximately 300 million (1988), or about 8% of the Third World's population. However, there are about 2 Middle Easterners for every 5 citizens of all of the industrialized market economies; Middle Easterners are more numerous than citizens of either the United States or the Soviet Union. Because of the ecological features of the region, no country supports the huge populations of monsoon Asia. The region contains three countries (Turkey, Iran, and Egypt) with populations exceeding 50 million, comparable to Italy, France, or the United Kingdom. However, the region also contains twelve countries with populations less than 10 million (i.e., less than the population of the greater New York City area), and two more (Saudi Arabia and Syria) with populations just above that number (Table 3.1).

There are now about three times as many Middle Easterners and North Africans as there were in 1950. The region's population is growing at just under 3% per year, which means that it will double in approximately twenty-four years. Within just three generations (of twenty years each), the region's population will have increased *twelvefold!* The current number of Cairo residents is about the same as the total population of Egypt in 1919 (12–13 million). Of major world regions, only the population of sub-

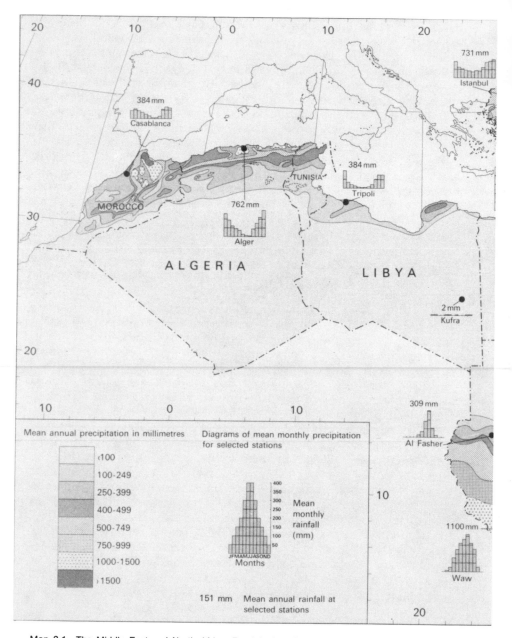

Map 3.1 The Middle East and North Africa: Precipitation. *Source:* Gerald Blake, John Dewdney, and Jonathan Mitchell, *The Cambridge Atlas of the Middle East and North Africa*, Cambridge, Cambridge University Press, 1987, p. 18.

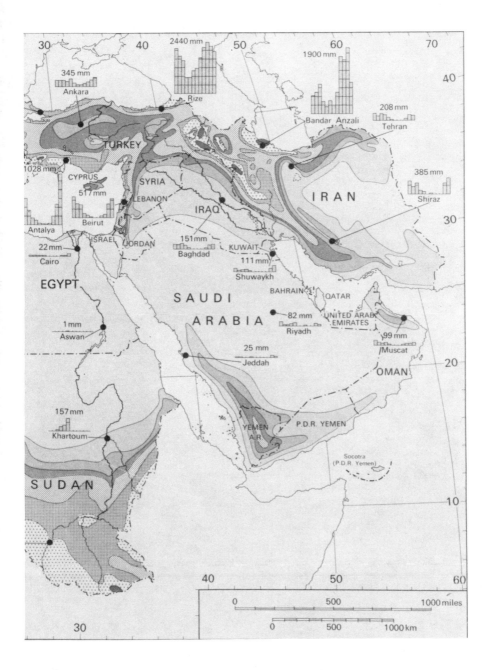

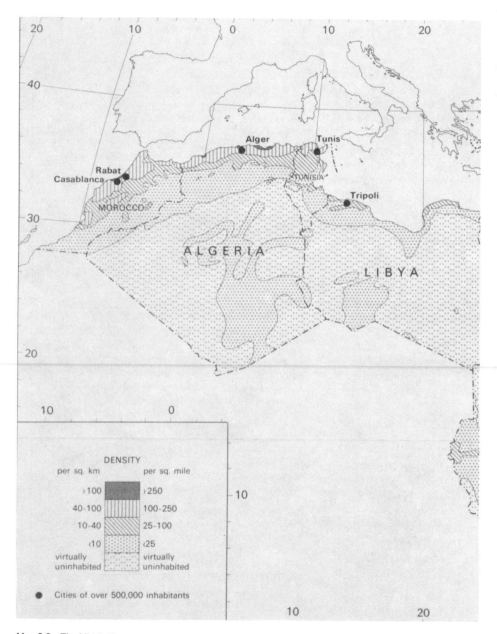

Map 3.2   The Middle East and North Africa: Population density. *Source:* Gerald Blake, John Dewdney, and Jonathan Mitchell, *The Cambridge Atlas of the Middle East and North Africa,* Cambridge, Cambridge University Press, 1987, p. 44.

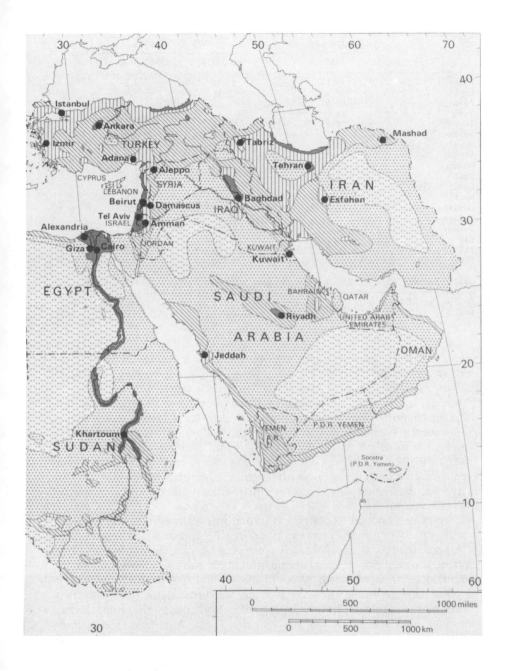

Table 3.1  Population, GNP per Capita, and Average Annual Growth Rate, 1965-1985

|               | Population (millions) | GNP Per Capita | |
|               | 1985 | 1985 U.S.$ | 1965-85 Growth Rate |
|---------------|------|------|------|
| Algeria       | 22.0  | 2,550  | 3.6  |
| Egypt         | 49.0  | 610    | 3.1  |
| Iran          | 45.0  | --     | --   |
| Iraq          | 16.0  | --     | --   |
| Israel        | 4.2   | 4,990  | 2.5  |
| Jordan        | 3.5   | 1,560  | 5.8  |
| Kuwait        | 1.7   | 14,480 | -0.3 |
| Libya         | 3.8   | 7,170  | -1.3 |
| Morocco       | 22.0  | 560    | 2.2  |
| Oman          | 1.2   | 6,730  | 5.7  |
| Saudi Arabia  | 11.5  | 8,850  | 5.3  |
| Sudan         | 22.0  | 300    | 0    |
| Syria         | 10.5  | 1,570  | 4.0  |
| Tunisia       | 7.1   | 1,190  | 4.0  |
| Turkey        | 50.2  | 1,080  | 2.6  |
| UAE           | 1.4   | 19,270 | --   |
| YAR           | 8.0   | 550    | 5.3  |
| PDRY          | 2.1   | 530    | --   |
| United States | 240.0 | 16,690 | 1.7  |

Source: World Bank, World Development Report, New York, Oxford University Press, 1987.

Saharan Africa is growing more rapidly. The rate of growth is now higher than it was in the early 1950s. Because of this rapid rate of population growth, most people in the region are under 20 years old.

A large and growing percentage of these people live in cities. Although different countries use different criteria for defining a "city," which makes cross-country comparisons notoriously unreliable, about half of MENA people live in urban areas, with, again, wide variations among countries (see Table 10.1). Cities were always central to the preindustrial and precolonial social formations in the region. This importance has steadily increased; the region now contains thirty cities with populations greater than 0.5 million.

The region is not particularly rich in nonhydrocarbon mineral resources. A wide variety of minerals are exploited in MENA,[2] but with the exception of Algeria (mercury) and Morocco (phosphate rock), no country's output amounts to even 5% of world production. Most minerals are found in the mountainous areas of North Africa, Turkey, and Iran, with the exception of phosphate deposits. Morocco and the Western Sahara hold over two-thirds of the world's phosphate deposits; Morocco is the third largest producer, after the United States and the USSR. Algeria is the region's leading iron ore producer (ranking only twentieth in the world), with Turkish production about 20% less than Algerian. Only Turkey has significant coal deposits. The 1980s have seen considerable exploration efforts, and significant new finds have occurred. For example, Libya, Egypt, Saudi Arabia, and Algeria have all discovered new iron ore deposits, and Saudi Arabia

Table 3.2  Estimated Oil Reserves, January 1988

| | Reserves (billion [=$10^9$] barrels) |
|---|---|
| Middle East | 364.680 |
| Iran | 92.850 |
| Iraq | 100.000 |
| Kuwait | 91.920 |
| Saudi Arabia | 166.980 |
| Africa | 55.249 |
| Algeria | 8.500 |
| Egypt | 4.300 |
| Libya | 21.000 |
| Western Hemisphere | 146.416 |
| Mexico | 48.610 |
| United States | 25.270 |
| Venezuela | 56.300 |
| Asia-Pacific | 19.350 |
| Western Europe | 22.450 |
| Total non-Communist world | 808.150 |
| USSR | 59.000 |
| Total world | 887.350 |

Source: **Oil and Gas Journal**, December 27, 1987, pp. 36-37.

has discovered gold and coal. Many of these new deposits have been found in remote and isolated areas, which raises the expense of exploiting them (Blake, Dewdney, and Mitchell 1987). All of this is in marked contrast to the region's hydrocarbon resources.

## OIL AND NATURAL GAS

The Middle East and North Africa have most of the world's oil. The usual measure of available oil is "reserves," which in turn are divided into "proved," "probable," "possible," and "speculative." By far the most commonly used measure is "proved reserves"; at the beginning of 1988 the region held approximately 75% of the non-Communist world's "proved reserves" (*Oil and Gas Journal,* December 27, 1987, pp. 36–37) (Table 3.2). "Proved reserves" in the Middle East have increased *twelve times over* since 1950; except for a brief period in the early 1980s, discovery has apparently exceeded production, despite the rapid increase in the latter.

We say "apparently" because the data on "proved reserves" must be treated with caution. The concept is defined as "reserves recoverable with present technology and prices" (*Oil and Gas Journal,* December 28, 1988). Higher oil prices should, in theory, mean higher oil reserves, for three reasons: (1) higher prices should induce further exploration and discovery of new fields; (2) higher prices should stimulate improvements in the technology of recovery from existing fields; and (3) for existing wells, with existing technology, higher prices should make some additional oil recoverable. It is significant that despite rapidly growing world production, world reserves have grown still faster, and the majority of these reserve additions have come from the Middle East.

A more serious problem with the concept of proved reserves is that some countries have been quite secretive about the numbers they release. In 1987 four OPEC countries (Venezuela, United Arab Emirates [UAE], Iran, and Iraq) released data that showed that total world proved reserves had increased by roughly 27%. The new estimate may be credible for Venezuela, where extensive surveys of the Orinoco Basin revealed very large amounts of heavy oil. The increases in Iran (90%) and Iraq (112%) are *very* startling, however. Could these two countries, locked in desparate military struggle, really have devoted the resources to exploration that would have led to such finds? If they had known that they had such oil before the war began (1980), why did they wait until now to announce the fact to the world? The *Oil and Gas Journal,* a leading trade publication, rather gingerly pointed out that these numbers may reflect a belief by the issuing governments that oil production quotas within the Organization of Petroleum Exporting Countries (OPEC) will be allocated on the basis of "proved reserves" (December 27, 1987, pp. 33–34). Whatever the case may be, the episode illustrates the need for caution in using data on reserves.

Nevertheless, there is no doubting the geographical concentration of petroleum deposits in the Middle East; even before the revisions of last year, the region held nearly two-thirds of the non-Communist world's oil reserves. Several other geological facts are important in providing a thumbnail sketch of the political economy of oil. First, more than half of the world's proved reserves come from 33 "supergiant" fields (reserves estimated at greater than 5 billion barrels); of these, 28 are in the Middle East, including 9 of the 10 largest fields. The largest field, the Ghawar field in Saudi Arabia, contains an estimated 60 billion barrels of oil, more than twice the reserves of the *entire* United States, which are about 25.3 billion barrels (Drysdale and Blake 1985, 314–315). Oil reserves are concentrated within the region. Four countries (Saudi Arabia, Iraq, Iran, and Kuwait) have about 75% of the region's oil reserves, and about 50% of all the oil reserves on the planet.

The size of these reserves implies that events in the region will continue to be critical to the international oil market. It is common (although of dubious interest) to point out how long countries' reserves will last at current production rates. We present the most recent figures (1987) in Table 3.3. The numbers are significant for showing the "time horizons" of national governments, a feature that is important for understanding various regional governments' differences over pricing strategies within OPEC: Other things being equal, countries whose oil will last a long time have little interest in large price increases, since these will induce more conservation and discovery of new sources of supply.[3] The numbers are only illustrative, however: Production varies, estimates of reserves change, and patterns of resource use shift dramatically if consumers are given

Table 3.3   Estimated Years of Oil Production Remaining (1988), at Average
Rates for 1972-1987

| | Years of Production Remaining |
|---|---|
| Algeria | 26.0 |
| Egypt | 22.0 |
| Iran | 69.5 |
| Iraq | 143.0 |
| Kuwait | 154.0 |
| Libya | 37.0 |
| Saudi Arabia | 65.0 |

Source: Calculated from data in Oil and Gas Journal, December 27, 1987, pp. 36-37.

enough time (say, ten to twenty years) to adjust. The differences among countries are dramatic: Kuwait can go on exploiting oil for a century and a half, whereas Egypt's official reserves will last for about one generation at the average rate of production from 1972 to 1987.

More important from an economic point of view, Gulf oil is the cheapest oil in the world to produce. In 1985 the estimated cost of production of a barrel of Gulf oil was less than $1.00 per barrel. By comparison, oil from Alaska's North Slope cost about $7.00 per barrel to produce, while North Sea oil cost about $8.00 per barrel (Drysdale and Blake 1985, 315). These low costs have had profound implications for Middle Eastern oil economics and development. In particular, they create the basis for the massive economic rents that were transferred to the oil states and that fueled economic expansion and change throughout the region for over a decade.

Economic rents from oil production in the Middle East are *very* large.[4] If the opportunity cost of producing a barrel of Saudi Arabian light is approximately $0.75, and the price of that barrel is roughly $18.00, the economic rent is $17.25. When the price was around $33.00 per barrel, the economic rent was $32.25. Even in late July 1986, when oil prices were at their post-1973 nadir of about $8.00 per barrel, over 95% of the price of that barrel was still economic rent. Oil revenues of the Gulf States are almost exclusively composed of rent on a depletable natural resource.

The minimum price is given by the cost of production, but what determines the maximum price? How high can prices go? In theory, the "price ceiling" is determined by the cost of production of the closest available substitute, often called the "backstop technology." Because crude oil has so many different uses, this price ceiling varies with the uses to which the crude will be put. Some estimates of the costs of "backstop technologies" made in the early 1980s are shown in Table 3.4. These price ceilings are likely to decline with time and are themselves partly a function of price: We would expect that if the price of crude oil approaches the rent ceiling, and if entrepreneurs believe this price will persist, there would be greater research and development into these alternative technologies.

Table 3.4  Some Estimates of the Costs of "Backstop" Technologies, 1981

| Pricing Dreams into Reality | | Comparative Costs of Fuel Production | |
| --- | --- | --- | --- |
| Production Cost $/Barrel of Oil Equivalent | Fuel Technologies | Generation Cost in Cents per Kwh | Electricity Technology |
| 86 and above | ▪ Corn to ethanol<br>▪ Wood to high-BTU gas<br>▪ Manure to high-BTU gas | 8.1 and above | ▪ Solar, thermal<br>▪ Wind<br>▪ Ocean thermal energy conversion<br>▪ Solar photovoltaic |
| 56-85 | ▪ Coal to methanol<br>▪ Coal gasification, high-BTU gas | 6.6-8.0 | ▪ Biomass (wood chip)<br>▪ Combined cycle, integrated coal gasification |
| 31-55 | ▪ Sugar to alcohol<br>▪ Wood to ethanol<br>▪ Coal gasification, medium-BTU gas<br>▪ Coal liquefaction<br>▪ Wood to methanol<br>▪ Light Arabian crude | 4.1-6.5 | ▪ Conventional oil-fired plant<br>▪ Breeder reactor<br>▪ Fluidized bed combustion |
| 30 and under | ▪ Liquefied natural gas<br>▪ Oil sands and shales<br>▪ Natural gas<br>▪ Coal | 4.0 and under | ▪ Hydroelectricity<br>▪ Conventional natural-gas-fired plant<br>▪ Geothermal, steam<br>▪ Nuclear, light water reactor |

* Includes all investment requirements and operation and maintenance costs, including rate of return (1980 prices).

Source: Economist, December 26, 1981, p. 77.

Such activity should lower the cost of these technologies, pushing down the "rent ceiling."

Of course, the *actual* price of crude oil is determined by supply and demand. The course of these prices is shown in Figure 3.1. Small libraries have been written on why prices rose and fell; we will sketch only the main elements of an explanation.[5]

Demand-side forces played a crucial role both in pushing prices to unprecedented heights in the 1970s and in provoking the crash of prices in 1986. In the 1950s and 1960s, the relative price of oil was both low and declining; the major industrialized countries increasingly switched from energy sources such as coal to oil. In 1950 oil accounted for 40% (U.S.), 14% (Western Europe), and 5% (Japan) of industrial nations' energy use; by 1973 those shares (of a vastly larger total) had risen to 47% (U.S.), 60% (Western Europe), and 76% (Japan) (Stobaugh and Yergin 1979). For both Western Europe and Japan, such a switch meant an increased dependence on imports, especially imports from the Middle East. For the

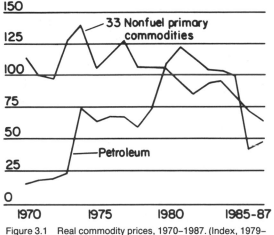

Figure 3.1 Real commodity prices, 1970–1987. (Index, 1979–1981 = 100.) *Source:* World Bank, *World Development Report,* New York, Oxford University Press, 1988, p. 25.

Japanese, with no indigenous oil and with little coal, there was (and is) little alternative to such imports: Even today, about 70% of Japanese energy comes from oil, all of which is imported and 70% of which comes from the Middle East. Western European dependence on Middle Eastern oil also increased during the 1950s and 1960s, as conservative governments sought greater independence from coal miners and as social democrats tried to improve environmental quality. All were drawn to the lower direct cost of oil.

The United States also became increasingly dependent on oil imports. Domestic oil producers had succeeded in restricting imports of (much cheaper) foreign oil in 1958. Until the mid-1960s, the United States retained considerable surplus capacity, which made it (and its friends) considerably less vulnerable to threats of embargoes or to sudden price shocks. This was an unintended outcome of the system to protect domestic producers: The so-called pro-rationing system, whereby state regulatory agencies regulated, and reduced, oil production. In the late 1960s and early 1970s, however, the growth of demand for energy outpaced the expansion of domestic energy supplies. Price controls inhibited the development of natural gas, and little new oil that was competitive at current prices was discovered. By 1973 the United States had no spare capacity; indeed, domestic oil production fell at a rate of 3% per year from 1970 to 1973 (Schneider 1983, 195). Oil imports, including Middle Eastern oil, supplied a steadily increasing percentage of U.S. energy needs, reaching 38% by 1974.

On the supply side, there were two interrelated dynamics, "cash and control" (Rustow and Mugno 1976). "Cash" refers to producing countries attempts to get a higher percentage of the oil rents; the contest for "control" was between the nation-states and the oil companies. One might say that the history of the oil business has been that of repeated attempts to create a cartel, and then the erosion and demise of that cartel. The eight major international oil companies[6] had managed by 1953 to control 95% of non-U.S. non-Communist reserves, 90% of production, 75% of refining capacity, and 74% of product sales (Blair 1976). Interrelations among these companies were extensive: long-term (e.g., twenty-year) supply contracts and joint ventures being the most prominent mechanisms. Perhaps the high-water mark of the oil company cartel's control of world oil came in 1953 when the cartel countered Mohammed Mossadegh's nationalization of British Petroleum's (BP's) Iranian oil facilities by simply refusing to refine or market Iranian oil. When Mossadegh was overthrown and the Pahlavi shah reinstated, another joint venture was established in which nearly all of the major oil companies were represented.

Even with the low prices of the 1950s and 1960s, costs of production were so low and demand was growing so steadily that there were numerous incentives for so-called independent, or smaller, oil companies to enter the market and attempt to wrest a piece of it away from the "majors." Such developments were actively encouraged by governments of some European countries, especially Italy. Some Middle Eastern countries—the most important, Libya under King Idris—had the wisdom to cede oil concessions to a wide variety of oil companies, especially independents. This had very important consequences for developments in the early 1970s.

In one of the ironies so typical of the region, the crushing Israeli defeat of Arab armies in 1967 set the stage for the explosion of oil prices that triggered the flood of rent into the region. The war closed the Suez Canal, requiring Gulf crude to be transported around the Cape of Good Hope, a journey that both raised the cost and provoked a tanker shortage. Western European nations increased their reliance on cheaper oil from west of Suez, and from Libya in particular.[7] Libyan oil also had a lower sulphur content and was therefore favored on environmental grounds. The new government of Mu'ammar Qaddhafi (who took power in 1969) immediately demanded an increase in the "posted price" of oil.[8] Although the larger oil companies refused, the independent oil companies were more vulnerable to pressure. Libya prevailed through a classic divide-and-rule policy. Its success prompted the Gulf producers to follow suit, and nominal oil prices began to move upward.[9]

Of course, the completion of the shift of both cash and control from consumers and companies on the one hand to producing governments on the other was precipitated by the October War of 1973. The decision of the Nixon administration first to resupply the Israelis (October 13), and then to give them $2.2 billion of military assistance (October 19), prompted the Saudi embargo of the United States and the Netherlands on October 20. Oil companies cushioned the impact of this embargo on those two countries by reallocating world supply. However, the embargo created an atmosphere of panic buying on the spot (or open) market; the shah of

Iran in particular took the opportunity to hold an auction in order to see what price his oil might fetch. The answer was between $9.00 and $17.34 per barrel (Schneider 1983, 236), while the Rotterdam spot price hit $26.00 per barrel (Danielson 1982, 172).

It is significant that the final price that OPEC agreed to charge customers on the "marker crude"[10] was $11.65; it was a *negotiated* price, with the "price doves," led by Saudi Arabia, compromising with the "price hawks," led by Iran. This is to be expected, given the huge gap between the cost of production and the rent ceiling on the one hand, and the very low short-run elasticity of demand for oil on the other. With nearly all excess capacity inside the OPEC countries, and with few short-run alternatives, consuming countries had little choice but to pay any price below the rent ceiling.

The resulting transfer of resources was massive (Table 3.5). The dramatically higher payments for oil contributed to the phenomenon of "stagflation" (recession combined with inflation) in the developed world. Inflation, in turn, slowly eroded the real gains of 1974, while recession weakened demand; real oil prices in 1978 were slightly below those of 1974. Europe and Japan responded to the change not only by passing on prices to their consumers but also by increasing tax rates on oil and by fostering the development of alternative energy supplies (e.g., North Sea oil and gas and nuclear power). However, the world's largest consumer, the United States, did little. Accordingly, U.S. imports of OPEC oil continued to grow from 38% of consumption in 1974 to 47% in 1979. OPEC's market share dropped only slightly, from about 66% of non-Communist oil production in 1974 to about 62% in 1978. The stage was set for the second oil shock of 1979.

Once again, political events opened the next act in the oil-price drama. The Iranian revolution removed about 2 million barrels a day from production; although the Saudis at first tried to make up the shortfall, they had been producing close to capacity already in an attempt to restrain further price increases, which they (correctly) believed were not in their medium- and long-term economic interest. Furthermore, the conclusion of the Camp David Accords, with their neglect of the Palestinian issue, angered the Saudis considerably. In response, they actually *reduced* production in the immediate aftermath of Camp David, setting the stage for another round of panic buying on the spot market. The resulting record-breaking market price helped the OPEC hawks to carry the day, and the OPEC reference price leapt first to $17.26 in 1979, then to $28.67 in 1980.

The resulting price hike was lower in proportional terms than that of 1973–1974, but considerably greater in absolute dollar value. The increase in revenues was truly prodigious (Table 3.5). Governments launched even more massive development projects than before, with consequences that we shall discuss in detail in later chapters. Never had so much been paid by so many to so few: Never before in human history had such an enormous amount of wealth been transferred in such a short amount of time, accruing

Table 3.5 Government Oil Revenue, 1974-1986 (million U.S.$)

| | 1974 | 1975 | 1976 | 1977 | 1978 | 1979 | 1980 | 1981 | 1982 | 1983 | 1984 | 1985 | 1986 |
|---|---|---|---|---|---|---|---|---|---|---|---|---|---|
| Algeria | 3,500 | 4,000 | 4,500 | 5,000 | 5,400 | 7,500 | 11,700 | 10,800 | 8,500 | 9,700 | -- | -- | 8,000 |
| Iran | 22,000 | 20,500 | 22,000 | 23,000 | 20,900 | 18,800 | 11,600 | 8,500 | 19,000 | 21,700 | -- | 14,000 | -- |
| Iraq | 6,000 | 8,000 | 8,500 | 9,500 | 11,600 | 21,200 | 26,500 | 10,400 | 9,500 | 8,400 | -- | 12,000 | -- |
| Kuwait | 8,000 | 7,500 | 8,500 | 8,500 | 9,500 | 16,300 | 18,300 | 14,800 | 10,000 | 9,900 | -- | 10,000 | -- |
| Libya | 6,000 | 6,000 | 7,500 | 9,400 | 9,300 | 15,200 | 23,200 | 15,700 | 14,000 | 11,200 | -- | 10,400 | -- |
| Qatar | 1,650 | 1,700 | 2,000 | 1,900 | 2,200 | 3,100 | 5,200 | 5,300 | 4,200 | 3,000 | -- | 4,400 | -- |
| S/Arabia | 29,000 | 27,000 | 33,500 | 38,000 | 36,700 | 59,200 | 104,200 | 113,300 | 76,000 | 46,000 | -- | 43,700 | 17,500 |
| UAE | 5,500 | 6,000 | 7,000 | 8,000 | 8,700 | 13,000 | 19,200 | 18,700 | 16,000 | 12,800 | -- | 13,000 | -- |

Note: Revenue includes income from refined products and natural gas liquids.

Source: Oil and Gas Journal, December 27, 1987, pp. 20-21.

to governments with such (typically) small populations.[11] As we shall see, however, the wealth *was* shared widely, albeit indirectly, in the Middle East and North Africa through labor migration.

But booms are not forever. Although it was not immediately apparent, OPEC overreached itself in 1979–1980. A comparison of the 1980 price with the figures in Table 3.4 shows that for some uses, the 1980 price exceeded the rent ceiling. In any case, the incentives for conservation in the consuming countries were now dramatically enhanced, especially once the United States decontrolled petroleum prices. OPEC soon fell afoul of both the "external" and the "internal" cartel problem. The external problem refers to the simple fact that if prices are very high, consumers and producers have incentives to change their behavior. The demand for oil is a derived demand: We want oil not for its own sake but because we want to move around, heat our homes, light our lamps, and so forth. With high oil prices, consumers had every incentive to find ways of using less oil to accomplish these ends and also (during the recession of the early 1980s) to make do with less transportation, heating, electricity. In short, conservation was greatly stimulated. By the mid-1980s, the industrial countries were using less than 70% as much oil per unit of output as they had been in 1973. Non-OPEC producers compounded the external cartel problem. Such producers had strong incentives, often reinforced by consuming governments, to seek, find, and exploit new sources of petroleum and of alternative energy sources. Alaskan, North Sea, and Mexican oil became especially important new sources of oil, and OPEC's share of the non-Communist world's oil production fell from 63% in 1979 to 38% in 1983 (*Economist,* March 5, 1983, p. 75).

These developments aggravated the internal cartel problem, the fact that it is in the interests of cartel members to cheat on production quotas. Actually, OPEC lacked formal production quotas until very recently, and even now these are often openly ignored (e.g., by Iraq and Iran). In practice, just as OPEC was the "residual supplier" to the world market, Saudi Arabia was the "residual supplier" within OPEC. Only the Saudis could play this role: They could vary their production from a low of just above 2 million barrels per day (2.2 in August 1985) to a high of nearly 10 million barrels a day. (By way of comparison, their *low* figure exceeds the current production figure of any Middle Eastern country except Iran and is only slightly lower than total Mexican production.) The Saudis had long demanded that other oil producers agree to production quotas, and had long argued that the post-1979 prices were too high. They argued in vain in OPEC counsels: Quota agreements, first established in March 1982, were violated almost as soon as they were drafted. The Saudis saw their own market share steadily erode from 21% in 1980 to 8.5% in 1985 (*Oil and Gas Journal,* December 27, 1987). Saudi government revenues also declined, even as it had made extensive commitments to development expenditures and projects.

It appears that the Saudis finally decided to send a message to other oil producers. In July and August 1986, they opened the taps, producing about 6 million barrels per day; in late August, they were producing at a rate of about 7 million barrels per day. (*Oil and Gas Journal,* December 30, 1985, p. 65). Prices collapsed, falling to under $10.00 in late summer of 1986. The Saudis had sent a signal to fellow–OPEC members ("Quit cheating; we can take losses better than you can"), to non-OPEC producers ("Let's make a deal; your production costs are much higher than ours"), and to investors in conservation technology ("We can push the price down and put you out of business"). Only the last message seems to have been received. Although OPEC has now begun to try to fix production quotas, enforcement mechanisms are weak and cheating remains rife. Britain has refused to cooperate with OPEC, and although prices rebounded to around $18.00 per barrel and hovered there until the end of the 1980s, the future of oil prices remains highly uncertain. The only thing that can be said with safety is that Middle Eastern producers, and especially Saudi Arabia, will continue to play a major role in determining the future path of oil prices.

## ECONOMIC GROWTH AND STRUCTURAL CHANGE

Economic growth and structural change have proceeded briskly in the region during the past generation. In assessing the numbers in the following tables, several items should be kept in mind. First, the data are often simply the best guesses of informed observers; for some of the least developed and poorest countries, the data are of very poor quality. For all countries, they should be taken as indicating orders of magnitude, rather than precise "truth." Second, it is important to remember that many countries of the region have started the process from a *very* low base; in some cases (YAR, Oman), the process of modern economic growth began less than one generation ago.

The range of wealth in the region is extremely wide; indeed, it is probably fair to say that no major area of the world shows a higher variance in per capita incomes across nation-states (Table 3.1). The region boasts two very wealthy countries, Kuwait and the UAE, whose subjects enjoy a material standard of living that rivals that in the developed countries. Israel remains classified by the World Bank as a "less-developed country" more for political than economic reasons; its per capita gross national product (GNP) exceeds that of three members of the EC (Spain, Ireland, and Greece), and, unlike the high-income oil exporters, the country possesses a diversified economic and industrial structure and levels of health and literacy that rival those in Southern Europe. At the same time, the average Sudanese lives in a poverty far more similar to the rest of sub-Saharan Africa than to the prosperity of the Gulf, while millions of Egyptians and Moroccans live very close to subsistence. (See Tables 6.13 and 10.7 for estimates of the extent of absolute poverty in the region.)

The diversity of experience with economic growth and structural change is just as wide. At one extreme, MENA contains not only essentially

Table 3.6 Structure of Production: Sectoral Shares of GDP, 1960 and 1985
(percentages)

| | Agriculture | | Industry | | Manufacturing | | Services | |
|---|---|---|---|---|---|---|---|---|
| | 1960 | 1985 | 1960 | 1985 | 1960 | 1985 | 1960 | 1985 |
| Algeria | 16 | 8 | 35 | 48 | 8 | 11 | 49 | 43 |
| Egypt | 30 | 20 | 24 | 31 | 20 | -- | 46 | 49 |
| Iran | 29 | -- | 33 | -- | 11 | -- | 38 | -- |
| Iraq | 17 | -- | 51 | -- | 10 | -- | 32 | -- |
| Israel | 11 | -- | 32 | -- | 23 | -- | 57 | -- |
| Jordan | -- | 8 | -- | 28 | -- | 12 | -- | 64 |
| Kuwait | 20* | 1 | 73* | 58 | 3* | 8 | 27* | 41 |
| Libya | 5* | 4 | 63* | 57 | 3* | 5 | 32 | 39 |
| Morocco | 23 | 18 | 26 | 32 | 16 | 17 | 51 | 50 |
| Oman | 74 | 3 | 8 | 59 | 1 | 3 | 18 | 38 |
| Saudi Arabia | 8* | 3 | 60* | 56 | 9* | 8 | 32* | 41 |
| Sudan | 54 | 26 | 9* | 18 | 4* | 9 | 37* | 57 |
| Syria | 29 | 22 | 22 | 21 | -- | -- | 49 | 57 |
| Tunisia | 24 | 17 | 18 | 34 | 8 | 14 | 58 | 49 |
| Turkey | 41 | 19 | 21 | 35 | 13 | 25 | 38 | 46 |
| UAE | -- | 1 | -- | 67 | -- | 10 | -- | 32 |
| YAR | -- | 34 | -- | 16 | -- | 7 | -- | 50 |
| PDRY | -- | -- | -- | -- | -- | -- | -- | -- |

* 1963.

Sources: World Bank, <u>World Development Report</u>, New York, Oxford University Press, 1980, p. 193; 1987, p. 225.

industrialized and developed Israel but also Turkey, formerly the heartland of one of history's greatest empires and a pioneer in industrialization outside of Europe and Japan. Manufacturing accounts for 25% of all output in Turkey (Table 3.6), a percentage equal to that of France and above the average both for all OECD countries or for the United States. In contrast, the region also contains Oman, whose former sultan hermetically sealed the country in medieval poverty until his son deposed him in 1970. Some less colorful distinctions are found in the rates of growth and structural transformation, the size, efficiency, and diversity of industrial production, agricultural-production experience, and composition of international trade. These are shown in subsequent tables.

Overall growth rates of GDP for 1960 to 1985 are shown in Table 3.7. Unsurprisingly, given the impact of the oil boom, the per capita output in the region has grown more rapidly than the average for LDCs. Some countries (Jordan, Saudi Arabia, Oman, Syria, Tunisia, and the YAR) grew faster than 4.0% per year, slightly more than doubling per capita incomes during the past two decades. Only Israel, Sudan, and Morocco have grown more slowly than the average for countries of their income group,[12] while Turkish growth has been roughly equal to the group average. Other nations, notably hapless Sudan and quixotic Libya, have stagnated.

Growth has, of course, been uneven over time (Table 3.7). Growth for many countries accelerated in the 1970s with the oil-price revolution and then declined in the 1980s. The collapse of oil prices was not the only

Table 3.7   Growth of GDP, 1960-1985 (percent per year)

|              | 1960-70 | 1970-80 | 1980-85 |
|--------------|---------|---------|---------|
| Algeria      | 4.3     | 7.0     | 4.9     |
| Egypt        | 4.3     | 7.4     | 5.2     |
| Iran         | 11.3    | 2.5     | --      |
| Iraq         | 6.1     | 12.1    | --      |
| Israel       | 8.1     | 4.1     | 1.7     |
| Jordan       | --      | --      | 4.1     |
| Kuwait       | 5.7     | 2.5     | 0.3     |
| Libya        | 24.4    | 2.2     | -6.1    |
| Morocco      | 4.4     | 5.6     | 3.0     |
| Oman         | 19.5    | 6.5*    | 4.0     |
| Saudi Arabia | --      | 10.6    | -2.1    |
| Sudan        | 0.7     | 4.4     | -0.7    |
| Syria        | 4.6     | 10.0    | 1.5     |
| Tunisia      | 4.7     | 7.5     | 4.1     |
| Turkey       | 6.0     | 5.9     | 4.5     |
| UAE          | --      | --      | -2.8    |
| YAR          | --      | 9.2     | 4.5     |
| PDRY         | --      | --      | 1.6     |

* 1973-83.

Sources: World Bank, World Development Report, New York, Oxford
University Press, 1982, p. 196; 1987, p. 223.

brake on growth; structural adjustment and rising indebtedness have also
made their contribution.

Growth was also uneven across sectors; this is the essence of "structural
transformation." Country data are displayed in Table 3.8. The share of
agriculture has declined in all countries. Two groups of countries have
seen rapid rates of growth of manufacturing: oil exporters like Algeria,
Libya, Saudi Arabia, and the UAE, all of which started in 1965 with very
little industry, and those countries with a longer industrial history like
Turkey, Iran, and Egypt. Tunisia, which also had little industry at independence and which exports very modest amounts of oil, also registered
a high rate of growth of manufacturing output. The resulting patterns of
structural change are shown in Table 3.6. As usual, the residual category
of "services" accounts for one-third to over one-half of output; the percentage
share of "industry" in national product for most countries is either the
same or slightly below what we would expect on the basis of their per
capita incomes. Although Algeria and Oman have a much higher percentage
of output from industry than the average for upper-middle-income countries,
this is deceptive, since "industry" includes the petroleum sector.

A better picture of industrialization levels (and as argued in Chapter
2, "sustainable" structural change) is given by the percentage of output
that comes from manufacturing, or by the size and growth of manufacturing
value-added (MVA) (Tables 3.9 and 3.10). Total MVA in the region is
approximately equal to that of Brazil. It is instructive to compare MVA for
Turkey and Iran with that of Italy, which has roughly the same number

Table 3.8  Sectoral Rates of Growth, 1965-1985 (annual percentage growth rate)

| | Agriculture | | Industry | | (Manufacturing) | | Services | |
|---|---|---|---|---|---|---|---|---|
| | 1965-80 | 1980-85 | 1965-80 | 1980-85 | 1965-80 | 1980-85 | 1965-80 | 1980-85 |
| Algeria | 5.8 | 2.1 | 8.1 | 5.3 | 9.5 | 9.0 | 7.1 | 4.9 |
| Egypt | 2.8 | 1.9 | 7.0 | 7.0 | -- | -- | 9.5 | 5.1 |
| Iran | 4.5 | -- | 2.4 | -- | 10.0 | -- | 13.3 | -- |
| Iraq | -- | -- | -- | -- | -- | -- | -- | -- |
| Israel | -- | -- | -- | -- | -- | -- | -- | -- |
| Jordan | -- | 6.4 | -- | 4.0 | -- | 5.6 | -- | 3.8 |
| Kuwait | -- | -- | -- | -- | -- | -- | -- | -- |
| Libya | 10.7 | 7.3 | 1.2 | -8.8 | 13.7 | 11.5 | 15.5 | -3.7 |
| Morocco | 2.2 | 1.0 | 6.1 | 1.3 | 5.9 | 0.7 | 6.5 | 4.3 |
| Oman | -- | -- | -- | -- | -- | -- | -- | -- |
| Saudi Arabia | 4.1 | 8.0 | 11.6 | -9.7 | 8.1 | 7.7 | 10.5 | 7.3 |
| Sudan | 2.9 | -5.5 | 3.1 | 4.3 | -- | -- | 4.9 | 0.6 |
| Syria | 4.8 | -1.4 | 12.2 | 0.6 | -- | -- | 9.0 | 2.9 |
| Tunisia | 5.5 | 4.2 | 7.4 | 3.8 | 9.9 | 6.7 | 6.5 | 4.3 |
| Turkey | 3.2 | 2.6 | 7.2 | 6.0 | 7.5 | 7.9 | 7.6 | 4.5 |
| UAE | -- | 13.3 | -- | -6.1 | -- | 20.2 | -- | 5.9 |
| YAR | -- | 0.2 | -- | 8.3 | -- | 16.5 | -- | 5.2 |
| PDRY | -- | -- | -- | -- | -- | -- | -- | -- |

Sources: Calculated from data in World Bank, World Development Report, New York, Oxford University Press, 1982, p. 186; 1987, p. 228.

Table 3.9  Manufacturing Value-added: Total and Regional Distribution, 1985

|  | Total ($10$^6$) | % Required Total |
|---|---|---|
| Algeria | 4,631 | 7.3 |
| Egypt | 4,292 | 6.8 |
| Iran | 11,817 | 18.7 |
| Iraq | 1,929 | 3.0 |
| Israel | 3,865 | 6.1 |
| Jordan | 479 | 1.0 |
| Kuwait | 1,932 | 3.1 |
| Libya | 972 | 1.5 |
| Morocco | 3,299 | 5.2 |
| Saudi Arabia | 8,648 | 13.7 |
| Sudan | 671 | 1.1 |
| Syria | --* | 1.0 |
| Tunisia | 1,530 | 2.4 |
| Turkey | 18,542 | 29.3 |
| YAR | -- | -- |
| PDRY | 110 | -- |
| MENA Total | 63,343 | |
| Republic of Korea | 26,031 | |
| Mexico | 46,044 | |
| Italy | 110,788 | |
| Brazil | 65,785 | |

* 626 in 1980.

Source: UNIDO, Industry and Development: Global Report, 1987, Vienna, 1987.

Table 3.10  Value-added in Manufacturing, 1970 and 1984 (percentages)

|  | Growth | Food & Agr. | | Clothing & Textile | | Machinery | | Chemicals | | Other | |
|---|---|---|---|---|---|---|---|---|---|---|---|
|  | 1970-84 | 1970 | 1984 | 1970 | 1984 | 1970 | 1984 | 1970 | 1984 | 1970 | 1984 |
| Algeria | 8.5 | 33 | 18 | 29 | 26 | 5 | 7 | 4 | 3 | 29 | 47 |
| Egypt | 7.5* | 22 | 24 | 35 | 29 | 5 | 13 | 7 | 8 | 32 | 26 |
| Iran | 4.3* | 25 | 11 | 18 | 19 | 8 | 18 | 7 | 5 | 42 | 48 |
| Iraq | 6.4* | 19 | -- | 24 | -- | 18 | -- | 4 | -- | 35 | -- |
| Israel | 2.4* | 10 | 13 | 12 | 10 | 20 | 25 | 7 | 8 | 51 | 44 |
| Jordan | 12.5 | 26 | 26 | -- | -- | -- | -- | 2 | 4 | 72 | 71 |
| Kuwait | 6.7 | 3 | 8 | -- | -- | -- | -- | 3 | 7 | 94 | 95 |
| Libya | 12.1 | -- | -- | -- | -- | -- | -- | -- | -- | -- | -- |
| Morocco | 4.0 | 28 | 35 | 27 | 21 | 9 | 4 | 6 | 10 | 30 | 30 |
| Saudi Arabia | 7.2 | 7 | 10 | -- | -- | -- | -- | -- | -- | 93 | 90 |
| Sudan | 0.5* | 30 | 38 | 24 | -- | 2 | 3 | 2 | 4 | 42 | 56 |
| Syria | -- | 27 | 33 | 38 | 31 | 1 | 2 | 6 | 7 | 28 | 27 |
| Tunisia | 9.7 | 26 | 24 | 28 | 21 | 3 | 8 | 10 | 10 | 33 | 37 |
| Turkey | 5.8 | 16 | 21 | 27 | 16 | 12 | 16 | 8 | 11 | 38 | 37 |

Note: 1970-1984 growth--Republic of Korea: 16.8; Brazil: 11.4; Spain: 9.8; India: 6.7; PRC: 7.0.

Sources: World Bank, World Development Report, New York, Oxford University Press, 1987, p. 228;  * 1975-85: UNIDO, Industry and Development: Global Report, 1987, Vienna, 1987.

of people: Italy's MVA is more than five times that of Turkey, and roughly ten times that of Iran. Those two countries of the "northern tier" of MENA together account for just under half (48%) of all manufacturing in the entire region. Two oil exporters, Algeria and Saudi Arabia, account for another fifth. The addition of Egypt brings the total share of manufacturing for the five countries with the largest manufacturing sectors to over two-thirds of the total. Manufacturing in MENA is geographically concentrated.

Growth rates of MVA and its subsectoral distribution are shown in Table 3.10. Growth rates of MVA have been respectable, but not spectacular; the region boasts no star performers like the Republic of Korea (MVA growth rate = 16.8% per year, 1965–1985), or Brazil (MVA growth rate = 11.4% per year).[13] Tunisia's industrial growth was approximately the same as Spain's, while growth rates in Algeria, Egypt, and Saudi Arabia exceeded those of the PRC (7.0%). These are all reputable performances. But as we shall see, industrial growth has been hampered by numerous political and economic problems; the search for their solution is a key to the political economy of the more industrialized countries of the area.

The pattern of distribution of MVA holds few surprises. Many countries' industries process agricultural outputs or produce textiles. Because of the labor intensity and relatively well-established technology of such industries, most countries concentrate on them initially. The more industrialized countries have gone far beyond this stage, producing significant quantities of machinery, chemicals, and a host of other products. The most industrialized diversified countries are Israel and Turkey; the political economy of the drive to create a competitive manufacturing sector in the latter country is examined in Chapters 7–9.

Trends in the distribution of the labor force are shown in Table 3.11. A number of features stand out. First, the percentage of the labor force in agriculture has declined considerably in all countries (except Kuwait), even in (stagnant and still mainly agricultural) Sudan. Whereas in 1950 between two-thirds to one-half of the work force was in agriculture, the sector's share of total employment had fallen to less than a third by 1980 in many countries. Three notable exceptions were Egypt, Morocco, and Turkey—where 40% of the region's people live: Farmers and farm workers were just under half of the labor force in the first two countries, and, surprisingly, given the longevity, size, and diversity of its industrial sector, agriculturalists were over half of the Turkish labor force. The relatively slow decline of the Turkish farm labor force has multiple causes; we shall see that unlike policy in many countries of the region, Turkish policy has been favorable toward agriculture ever since peasants got the vote in 1950. Note also that the *absolute size* of the farm work force may continue to grow even if its *share* declines (see Table 6.12).

Although industry now often employs between one-fourth and one-third of the labor force in many MENA countries, often well over half of these workers are in small establishments, which employ fewer than twenty people. The growth in "service" employment is often in the so-called

Table 3.11 Sectoral Distribution of the Labor Force, 1950-1980 (percentages)

| | Agriculture | | | | Industry | | | | Services | | | |
|---|---|---|---|---|---|---|---|---|---|---|---|---|
| | 1950 | 1960 | 1970 | 1980 | 1950 | 1960 | 1970 | 1980 | 1950 | 1960 | 1970 | 1980 |
| Algeria | 79 | 67 | 61 | 31 | 9 | 12 | 15 | 27 | 12 | 21 | 24 | 42 |
| Egypt | 60 | 58 | 54 | 46 | 12 | 12 | 19 | 20 | 28 | 30 | 27 | 34 |
| Iran | 61 | 54 | 46 | 36 | 19 | 23 | 28 | 33 | 20 | 23 | 26 | 31 |
| Iraq | 58 | 53 | 47 | 31 | 16 | 18 | 22 | 22 | 26 | 29 | 31 | 48 |
| Israel | 19 | 14 | 10 | 6 | 33 | 35 | 35 | 32 | 48 | 51 | 55 | 62 |
| Jordan | 52 | 44 | 34 | 10 | 22 | 26 | 33 | 26 | 26 | 30 | 33 | 64 |
| Kuwait | 2 | 2 | 2 | 2 | 34 | 34 | 34 | 33 | 64 | 64 | 64 | 65 |
| Lebanon | 55 | 38 | 20 | -- | 20 | 23 | 25 | -- | 25 | 39 | 55 | -- |
| Libya | 75 | 53 | 32 | 18 | 9 | 17 | 22 | 30 | 16 | 30 | 46 | 52 |
| Morocco | 63 | 62* | 57 | 46 | 13 | 14 | 17 | 25 | 24 | 24 | 26 | 29 |
| Oman | -- | -- | -- | 50 | -- | 15* | -- | 22 | -- | 22* | -- | 28 |
| Saudi Arabia | 76 | 71 | 66 | 49 | 9 | 10 | 11 | 14 | 15 | 19 | 23 | 37 |
| Sudan | 90 | 86 | 82 | 71 | 4 | 6 | 8 | 7 | 6 | 8 | 10 | 22 |
| Syria | 58 | 54 | 51 | 32 | 18 | 19 | 21 | 32 | 24 | 27 | 28 | 36 |
| Tunisia | 68 | 56 | 50 | 35 | 14 | 18 | 21 | 36 | 18 | 26 | 29 | 29 |
| Turkey | 87 | 78 | 68 | 58 | 7 | 11 | 12 | 17 | 6 | 11 | 20 | 25 |
| UAE | -- | 20* | -- | 5 | -- | 33* | -- | 38 | -- | 47* | -- | 57 |
| YAR | 86 | 83 | 80 | 69 | 6 | 7 | 9 | 9 | 8 | 10 | 11 | 22 |
| PDRY | 75 | 70 | 65 | 41 | 12 | 15 | 18 | 18 | 13 | 15 | 17 | 41 |

* 1965.

Sources: World Bank, World Development Report 1986, New York, Oxford University Press, 1986; FAO, "World-Wide Estimates and Projections of the Agricultural and Non-Agricultural Population Segments, 1950-2025," Statistical Division, Economic and Social Policy Department, Rome, December 1986.

Table 3.12  Incremental Capital-to-Output Ratios, 1950-1985

|              | 1950-60 | 1960-70 | 1970-80 | 1980-85 |
|--------------|---------|---------|---------|---------|
| Algeria      | 5.0     | 7.0     | 6.2     | 7.7     |
| Bahrain      | --      | --      | 5.1     | --      |
| Egypt        | 3.5     | 2.9     | 3.7     | 9.3     |
| Iran         | 2.6     | 1.6     | 3.7[a]  | --      |
| Iraq         | 2.0     | 2.6     | 2.5[b]  | --      |
| Israel       | 2.5     | 3.2     | 5.5     | 11.8    |
| Jordan       | --      | --      | 5.0     | 9.7     |
| Kuwait       | --      | 2.9     | 7.3     | 64.4    |
| Libya        | --      | 1.0[c]  | 10.4    | -4.3    |
| Morocco      | 5.9     | 2.8     | 4.6     | 4.3     |
| Oman         | --      | 0.7     | 5.1     | --      |
| Saudi Arabia | --      | 1.7     | 2.3     | -13.8   |
| Sudan        | 1.3     | 24.4    | 2.7     | -17.6   |
| Syria        | --      | 2.7     | 2.8     | 16.0    |
| Tunisia      | --      | 4.9     | 3.8     | 6.7     |
| Turkey       | 2.4     | 2.9     | 4.8     | 5.0     |
| UAE          | --      | --      | 2.7[d]  | -10.6   |
| YAR          | --      | --      | 3.9     | 7.5     |

[a] 1970-77.
[b] 1970-79.
[c] 1962-70.
[d] 1973-80.

Note: ICOR: Incremental Capital-to-Output Ratio, or investment per $ increase in output.

Calculated as: $I/\Delta Q = \dfrac{GDI}{GDP} \Big/ \dfrac{\Delta GDP}{GDP}$.

Sources: World Bank, World Development Report, New York, Oxford University Press, 1979, p. 192; 1982, pp. 196-97; 1987, p. 223.

informal sector, inhabited by firms with very low capitalization, selling in easily entered markets, and offering low-paying, insecure jobs. The rate and pattern of industrial growth has failed to provide enough decent jobs for all members of the rapidly growing labor force. This gap between labor-force growth and job creation is one of the central issues facing policymakers throughout the region.

The problem of insufficient job creation has not been caused by too little investment. In general, MENA countries have invested as high a proportion of national output as other LDCs (see Table 8.1). The Algerian case is instructive here: After Algeria relentlessly invested over one-third of output for a generation (one of the highest investment rates in history), in the mid-1980s nearly one in five workers was unemployed! A clue to the problem may be found in Table 3.12, which displays incremental capital-to-output ratios, or ICORs. These show, roughly, the amount of investment required per unit of additional output. For LDCs with scarce capital and abundant labor, a lower ICOR (and therefore higher growth and employment creation) can be achieved by selecting relatively labor-intensive techniques. However, if policy creates biases toward capital intensity, a given amount

Table 3.13  Growth of Merchandise Trade, 1965-1985

| | Exports | Imports | Growth Rates | | | |
|---|---|---|---|---|---|---|
| | | | Exports | | Imports | |
| | 1985 (000s) | 1985 (000s) | 1965-80 | 1980-85 | 1965-80 | 1980-85 |
| Algeria | 13,034 | 9,061 | 1.6 | 0.9 | 13.1 | -0.2 |
| Egypt | 4,150 | 11,200 | 2.0 | 3.9 | 6.0 | 8.0 |
| Iran | 13,186 | 11,658 | -- | -- | -- | -- |
| Iraq | 9,050 | 9,780 | -- | -- | -- | -- |
| Israel | 6,601 | 10,163 | 8.9 | 5.0 | 6.2 | 3.8 |
| Jordan | 789 | 2,733 | 13.5 | 8.3 | 9.8 | 3.1 |
| Kuwait | 10,992 | 6,614 | -1.9 | -9.2 | 11.8 | 3.8 |
| Libya | 10,841 | 6,186 | -2.1 | -9.1 | 15.0 | -8.9 |
| Morocco | 2,156 | 3,885 | 3.6 | 3.5 | 6.6 | 0.3 |
| Oman | 4,962 | 3,153 | -- | -- | -- | -- |
| Saudi Arabia | 27,403 | 23,697 | 8.8 | -24.0 | 25.9 | -0.1 |
| Sudan | 374 | 771 | -0.3 | 6.1 | 2.4 | -8.9 |
| Syria | 1,640 | 3,844 | 11.4 | 0.4 | 8.6 | -0.9 |
| Tunisia | 1,738 | 2,757 | 8.5 | -1.8 | 10.4 | -2.8 |
| Turkey | 8,255 | 11,035 | 5.5 | 25.3 | 7.8 | 10.1 |
| UAE | 14,337 | 7,590 | 10.9 | -3.9 | 20.2 | -0.1 |
| YAR | 10 | 1,360 | -0.3 | 1.8 | 25.2 | -3.0 |
| PDRY | 645 | 1,543 | -13.6 | 1.3 | -7.3 | 3.7 |

Source: World Bank, **World Development Report**, New York, Oxford University Press, 1987, pp. 199, 200.

of investment will foster less growth and create fewer jobs. Algeria's ICOR during the 1970s was nearly twice as high as that in the labor-intensive, rapidly growing South Korean economy.[14]

Few of the non–oil exporters of the region have escaped the typical LDC problem of a balance-of-trade deficit (Table 3.13). Development economists usually argue that such deficits are perfectly appropriate for a developing country, *as long as exports grow.* In theory, capital *should* flow from capital-abundant developed countries to capital-scarce LDCs. However, if exports fail to grow, then the trade gap becomes a debt trap. We shall see in Chapter 8 that this has become a serious problem for many countries.

Finally, the commodity composition of trade is shown in Tables 3.14 and 3.15. Of course, petroleum exports dominate the trade (and entire economies!) of many countries of the region. As discussed in Chapter 2, the region has one agro-exporter, Sudan, and three countries that export mainly manufactured goods: Turkey, Israel, and Jordan. We shall see that countries like Egypt, YAR, and Jordan have also relied heavily on the export of human beings (international labor migration) for foreign exchange. A notable feature of the commodity composition of imports is the high percentage of food imports in countries like Egypt, Morocco, and Algeria. Imports of fuel for countries without oil and imports of capital goods (machinery) for the more industrialized countries are also evident.

Table 3.14  Structure of Merchandise Exports, 1965 and 1985 (percentages)

| | Fuels & Minerals | | Other Primary Goods | | Machinery | | Other Manuf. | | (Textiles) | |
|---|---|---|---|---|---|---|---|---|---|---|
| | 1965 | 1985 | 1965 | 1985 | 1965 | 1985 | 1965 | 1985 | 1965 | 1985 |
| Algeria | 57 | 98 | 39 | 0 | 2 | 0 | 2 | 2 | 0 | 0 |
| Egypt | 8 | 72 | 71 | 18 | 0 | 0 | 20 | 10 | 15 | 8 |
| Iran | 88 | 98 | 8 | 1 | 0 | 0 | 4 | 1 | 4 | 1 |
| Iraq | 95 | 99 | 4 | 1 | 0 | 0 | 1 | 0 | 0 | 0 |
| Israel | 6 | 3 | 28 | 14 | 2 | 21 | 63 | 63 | 9 | 6 |
| Jordan | 27 | 32 | 54 | 16 | 11 | 14 | 7 | 38 | 1 | 7 |
| Kuwait | 98 | 95 | 1 | 0 | 1 | 1 | 0 | 3 | 0 | 0 |
| Libya | 99 | 98 | 1 | 0 | 1 | 1 | 0 | 1 | 0 | 0 |
| Morocco | 40 | 32 | 55 | 28 | 0 | 1 | 5 | 39 | 1 | 14 |
| Oman | 0 | 92 | 0 | 1 | 0 | 5 | 0 | 2 | 0 | 0 |
| Saudi Arabia | 98 | 98 | 1 | 0 | 1 | 1 | 0 | 1 | 0 | 0 |
| Sudan | 1 | 2 | 98 | 94 | 1 | 1 | 0 | 3 | 0 | 1 |
| Syria | 1 | 65 | 89 | 22 | 1 | 1 | 9 | 12 | 7 | 8 |
| Tunisia | 31 | 47 | 51 | 11 | 0 | 5 | 19 | 37 | 2 | 18 |
| Turkey | 9 | 10 | 89 | 36 | 0 | 5 | 2 | 49 | 1 | 32 |
| UAE | 99 | 95 | 1 | 1 | 0 | 1 | 0 | 0 | 0 | 0 |
| YAR | -- | -- | -- | -- | -- | -- | -- | -- | -- | -- |
| PDRY | 79 | 94 | 15 | 4 | 2 | 1 | 4 | 1 | 2 | 0 |

Note: Textiles is a subcategory of "Other Manufactures."

Source: World Bank, World Development Report, New York, Oxford University Press, 1987, p. 198.

Table 3.15  Structure of Merchandise Imports, 1965 and 1985 (percentages)

| | Food | | Fuel | | Other Primary Goods | | Machinery | | Other Manuf. | |
|---|---|---|---|---|---|---|---|---|---|---|
| | 1965 | 1985 | 1965 | 1985 | 1965 | 1985 | 1965 | 1985 | 1965 | 1985 |
| Algeria | 27 | 19 | 0 | 2 | 6 | 6 | 15 | 32 | 52 | 41 |
| Egypt | 26 | 25 | 7 | 4 | 12 | 10 | 23 | 25 | 31 | 36 |
| Iran | 16 | 12 | 0 | 5 | 6 | 6 | 36 | 39 | 42 | 38 |
| Iraq | 24 | 15 | 0 | 1 | 7 | 2 | 25 | 45 | 44 | 37 |
| Israel | 16 | 9 | 6 | 16 | 12 | 6 | 28 | 27 | 38 | 42 |
| Jordan | 28 | 19 | 6 | 22 | 6 | 4 | 18 | 20 | 42 | 35 |
| Kuwait | 22 | 10 | 1 | 5 | 7 | 3 | 32 | 44 | 39 | 38 |
| Libya | 13 | 10 | 4 | 10 | 3 | 3 | 36 | 36 | 43 | 40 |
| Morocco | 36 | 17 | 5 | 28 | 10 | 13 | 18 | 18 | 31 | 24 |
| Oman | -- | 14 | -- | 2 | -- | 2 | -- | 41 | -- | 41 |
| Saudi Arabia | 30 | 10 | 1 | 1 | 5 | 3 | 27 | 45 | 37 | 41 |
| Sudan | 23 | 11 | 5 | 21 | 4 | 3 | 21 | 31 | 47 | 33 |
| Syria | 22 | 18 | 10 | 34 | 9 | 4 | 16 | 19 | 43 | 24 |
| Tunisia | 16 | 15 | 6 | 11 | 7 | 10 | 31 | 31 | 41 | 33 |
| Turkey | 6 | 5 | 10 | 36 | 10 | 7 | 37 | 25 | 37 | 26 |
| PDRY | 19 | 23 | 39 | 37 | 5 | 3 | 10 | 19 | 26 | 17 |

Source: World Bank, World Development Report, New York, Oxford University Press, 1987, p. 231.

## CONCLUSION

It is possible to discern certain patterns in the midst of all the diversity of detail in the region. We offer a taxonomy of national economic growth and structural change patterns, dividing the countries into five groups. The categories are a mixture of actual past performance and what the authors believe are potentially viable strategies. Needless to say, performance within any of these groups often varies considerably.

1. "The Coupon Clippers": Libya, Kuwait, Oman, UAE, Bahrain, Qatar. These states have much oil, and little of anything else, including people. They have been, and will continue to be, almost entirely dependent upon oil and any money earned from overseas investments. Kuwait, which is the only country in the world earning most of its income from overseas investment, is the most successful of these.

2. "The Oil Industrializers": Iraq, Iran, Algeria, and Saudi Arabia. These countries enjoy substantial oil exports and revenues as well as large enough populations and/or other resources to make industrialization a real option. They should really be divided into two subgroups. The first three states share the main features of large oil exports, a substantial population, other natural resources, and a chance to create industrial and agricultural sectors that will be sustainable over the long run. Its massive oil reserves place Saudi Arabia, the world's largest rentier state, in a class by itself. Although it lacks the other resources of the first three countries, its current and future petroleum resources and access to capital are so enormous that it, too, can contemplate specializing in capital- and energy-intensive industry.

3. "The Watchmakers": Israel, Jordan, Tunisia, and Syria. These four small countries have limited natural resources and must therefore concentrate on investing in human capital and on exporting skill-intensive manufactures. We shall see in Chapter 5 that they have all made major efforts to educate their people; manufactured goods now account for 84% of Israeli, 52% of Jordanian, and 42% of Tunisian exports. Although Syria lags behind on both counts, we believe that this path is the most logical one for the country to follow over the long haul. The same would be true for any future Palestinian state.

4. "The NICs": Turkey, Egypt, and Morocco. These countries either have no oil (Turkey and Morocco) or not enough to provide the basis for any long-run growth strategy (Egypt). In regional terms they have relatively large populations, relatively good agricultural land or potential, and a long experience with industrial production. Turkey is clearly a full-fledged NIC, more similar to countries like Mexico than to many countries of the region. The current regime has opted for a manufactured-export-led growth strategy; we will examine the chances for its success below. Students of the Egyptian economy have been saying that the country had no choice but to industrialize for over a generation; they are still right. The country must continue to improve its already very productive agriculture, but 360,000 square miles (932,400 km²) alone cannot support 50 million people. The country has

the largest skilled labor force and pool of technical talent in the Arab world. Morocco may fit rather poorly here, in some ways belonging to the next category. Nevertheless, its industry produced 17% of GDP, employed 25% of its work force, and generated 40% of its exports in 1985. Despite serious ecological problems, its agricultural potential remains impressive. Continued industrialization, linked to agricultural development, could increase both the welfare of its people and its stature as an NIC.

5. "The Agro-Poor": Sudan and the Yemens. These are the poorest countries of the region and ones where the agricultural-development-led industrialization (ADLI) growth strategy seems to offer the best hope. The Sudan has great agricultural potential but also enormous political, social, ecological, and infrastructural problems. Its growth performance has been the worst in the region; its immediate prospects are grim. Like the Alpine regions of Europe during that continent's industrialization, the Yemens have remained agricultural while increasingly depending on emigration and remittances. Such a path, of course, ties them in very strongly with the health of their neighboring Oil Industrializers and Coupon Clippers. The lack of natural resources and paucity of human capital make industrialization a distant hope.

This taxonomy is meant only to be suggestive; its boundaries are porous. For example, Egypt and Tunisia are partly oil industrializers, and the recent discovery of oil may yet turn the YAR into a coupon clipper. Unless important new discoveries are found soon, dwindling Algerian oil reserves will turn that country into an NIC in a generation. Syria and Egypt collect "rents" on their strategic location, and Morocco shares some features with the agro-poor. Like any taxonomy, its aim is to help organize our thoughts. One might object that all this is simply "closet modernization theory": the argument that all of the world will reenact the history of Europe and its overseas offspring (United States, Canada, Australia). We certainly *do* believe that the process of economic growth includes structural change; the data given above amply demonstrate the declining weight of agriculture in the economies of the region and the increase in a *kind* of industry in most cases. This process was, of course, also true of the now-developed countries. If this be modernization theory, make the most of it!

However, we certainly do *not* believe that the process of economic growth is smooth; it is uneven over time, over space, and over people: There are losers, and some of the winners do rather better than others. Furthermore, as we argued in Chapter 2, we believe that the process of economic growth and structural change is replete with unintended outcomes. And we do not believe that all (even any) of the MENA countries can or will "look like" the industrialized West or Japan, even economically. It is implicitly understood in the chapters that follow that economic growth in the region has many crucial differences from those found in the history of any now-developed country, if for no other reason than the critical role that rents have played in regional growth. And still less do we think that Middle Eastern and North African countries will resemble the West politically or (most absurd of all) culturally. We simply argue that the course of politics cannot be understood without an understanding of the process of economic growth and structural change, a process that has a logic of its own.

Finally, we must add one more cautionary note. It is possible that "development" of the usual kind is simply not possible for the world as a whole. Ecological constraints must be taken seriously. The apparent scientific consensus on the greenhouse effect suggests that we may already have unleashed forces whose long-term effects are frightening to contemplate. Increased heat and aridity would undermine *any* development strategy in the Middle East and North Africa. If the droughts of the recent past become more frequent, the region (and the world) will face a human and ecological disaster. Understanding how such tragedies might occur, and what might be done to prevent them, will surely require first an understanding of the interaction of economic growth, state policies, and class action. Even if the earth does not warm up, the continued pressure of population on scarce resources poses serious problems for the region. We turn to the political economy of population growth in the next chapter.

## NOTES

1. Excluding Antarctica.

2. The more significant are antimony, chromite, copper, iron ore, lead, lignite coal, manganese, mercury, phosphate rock, and silver.

3. Other things are usually *not* equal, however: Iran and Iraq have been consistent "price hawks" because the size of their populations and their development (not to mention military) needs have induced their political leaders to opt for short-run revenue gains.

4. Recall from Chapter 2 that "economic rent" is the difference between price and the opportunity cost of production, that is, the amount of resources required to keep a factor (or factors) of production in its current use.

5. For more details, see, inter alia, Danielson 1982, Stork 1975, Sampson 1975, Mosley 1974, Stobaugh and Yergin 1979, Blair 1976, Rustow and Mugno 1976, Schneider 1983, and Griffin and Teece 1982).

6. The so-called Seven Sisters: British Petroleum (BP), Texaco, Exxon, Royal Dutch Shell, Mobil, Standard Oil of California (Chevron), and Gulf Oil, plus the state-owned Compagnie Française de Petrol (CFP).

7. Nigerian oil shipments were disrupted by the civil war that broke out in 1967.

8. The "posted price" was the price on which the companies agreed to pay royalties to the countries, as opposed to the market price, which could fluctuate.

9. However, *real* oil prices were roughly constant from 1970 to 1974; most of the nominal increases simply kept pace with the accelerating inflation in the industrialized countries.

10. "Marker crude" is Saudi Arabian Light crude oil. The price of other oils was determined by various markups or discounts from the price of Saudi Arabian Light.

11. The only competitor would be the Spanish plundering of the Americas of precious metals in the sixteenth century.

12. Measured by using the World Bank classification: "low income": below $400 per capita gross national product (GNP); "lower-middle income": from $400 to $1,600; "upper-middle income": over $1,600 to $7,000; "high-income oil exporters," a category composed entirely of MENA states: Libya, Saudi Arabia, Kuwait, and the UAE. (Countries at the upper end of the upper-middle-income category, like Singapore, Hong Kong, or Israel, often have higher incomes and as diversified an economic structure as those at the bottom of the category "industrial market economy," like Spain and Ireland.)

13. Two exceptions are Jordan and Libya, whose measured MVA growth rates slightly exceeded that of Brazil. Both countries started from *very* low levels, however.

14. However, one should be cautious in using Table 3.12. The methodology is quite crude and is used only for illustrative purposes. There is little evidence that cross-country variance in ICOR within the region can be plausibly explained by the extent of price distortions. Furthermore, countries with low or moderate ICOR like Tunisia and Morocco have also faced severe job-creation problems.

# 4

# THE IMPACT OF RAPID POPULATION GROWTH

For good or ill, the peoples of the Middle East are multiplying rapidly. Only sub-Saharan Africa has a higher rate of population growth than the Middle East and North Africa. Although fertility rates have fallen during the past generation, the decline in the death rate has been swifter, accelerating population growth during the past ten years. At current rates of growth, there will be roughly half again as many Middle Easterners and North Africans by the year 2000 as are now (1989) alive. Since the women who will bear these children are now living, governments can at best slow their countries' population growth.

Such rates of growth may be viewed as catastrophic, problematical, or even as occasions for rejoicing. The old debates on the political economy of population, first incarnated as "Malthus versus Marx," have lost none of their vigor. Some neo-Malthusians believe that rapid population growth dooms any attempts at development to failure; in this view, population growth is *the* cause of underdevelopment (e.g., Ehrlich 1968). Some Marxists exactly reverse this causality, maintaining that poverty and underdevelopment cause rapid population growth (e.g., Mamdani 1972). They may, however, agree that rapid population growth may be undesirable. Finally, neo-Panglossians such as Simon (1982) aver that population growth is an unalloyed blessing, arguing that "the mind is greater than the stomach": The more talented, energetic people there are, the better off the human race will be. For them, economies of scale, accelerating human-capital formation, and rapid technological and institutional innovation put humanity on a continual upward path of progress as its numbers steadily expand.

We reject each of these extreme views. We agree with the majority of modern demographers who argue that (1) population growth is at least partially the result of social conditions and economic incentives (i.e., crude Malthusian "population determinism" is silly); (2) population growth is not *solely* determined by economic conditions (and therefore, family-planning programs are likely to have some effect quite independently of

*82*

Table 4.1  Demographic Indicators, 1965-1985

| | Population Growth Rate | | Crude Birth Rate* | | Crude Death Rate* | | TFR** | |
|---|---|---|---|---|---|---|---|---|
| | 1965-80 | 1980-85 | 1965 | 1985 | 1965 | 1985 | 1965 | 1985 |
| Algeria | 3.0 | 3.3 | 50 | 41 | 18 | 10 | 6.3 | 4.2 |
| Egypt | 2.4 | 2.8 | 43 | 36 | 19 | 10 | 4.7 | 3.3 |
| Iran | 3.2 | 2.9 | 50 | 41 | 17 | 11 | 5.6 | 4.3 |
| Iraq | 3.4 | 3.6 | 49 | 44 | 18 | 8 | 6.7 | 5.2 |
| Israel | 2.8 | 1.8 | 26 | 23 | 6 | 7 | 2.9 | 2.3 |
| Jordan | 2.6 | 3.7 | -- | 39 | 17 | 7 | 6.2 | 3.9 |
| Kuwait | 7.0 | 4.5 | 48 | 34 | 7 | 3 | 5.2 | 3.0 |
| Lebanon | 1.6 | -- | 40 | -- | 12 | -- | -- | -- |
| Libya | 4.5 | 3.9 | 49 | 45 | 17 | 10 | 7.2 | 5.5 |
| Morocco | 2.5 | 2.5 | 49 | 36 | 18 | 11 | 4.9 | 3.6 |
| Oman | 3.6 | 4.8 | 50 | 44 | 24 | 13 | 6.7 | 4.6 |
| Saudi Arabia | 4.6 | 4.2 | 48 | 42 | 20 | 8 | 7.1 | 5.7 |
| Sudan | 3.0 | 2.7 | 47 | 45 | 24 | 17 | 6.6 | 5.5 |
| Syria | 3.4 | 3.6 | 48 | 44 | 16 | 8 | 6.7 | 4.1 |
| Tunisia | 2.1 | 2.3 | 44 | 32 | 16 | 9 | 4.6 | 3.1 |
| Turkey | 2.4 | 2.5 | 41 | 30 | 14 | 8 | 3.9 | 2.7 |
| UAE | 15.9 | 6.2 | 41 | 30 | 14 | 4 | 5.9 | 3.7 |
| YAR | 2.8 | 2.5 | 49 | 48 | 27 | 21 | 6.8 | 5.8 |
| PDRY | 2.0 | 2.6 | 50 | 46 | 26 | 19 | 6.0 | 4.4 |

*  per thousand.
** total fertility rate.

Source: World Bank, World Development Report, New York, Oxford University Press, 1987, p. 215.

other development progress); and (3) population growth exacerbates certain development problems, particularly those of educating the young and providing sufficient employment opportunities. In short, our position is that rapid population growth complicates the development process and generates political problems. Policymakers must confront both of these difficulties. They can respond both directly by promoting family planning programs and indirectly by altering the incentives for couples to have children. However, both sorts of instruments are often highly charged politically.

## COMPARATIVE DEMOGRAPHIC PATTERNS OF THE MIDDLE EAST

The numbers in Table 4.1 show demographic developments in the region during the past generation. Several facts deserve emphasis.

Population growth has accelerated in the region as a whole. In 1950–1955, the rate of population growth, at 2.64% per year, was the second highest of the major cultural-economic regions of the world. In 1980–1985, the rate had risen to 2.98, still the second highest in the world. Such a rate implies a doubling of population in twenty-four years, or in roughly one generation. In this section we shall explore the causes of this rapid growth rate and then turn to its economic and political consequences in the subsequent sections. In the simplest terms, population growth accelerated because the birthrate declined more slowly than the death rate. Since no one advocates population control by raising the death rate, population policy analysis focuses on the birthrate.

The key to population issues in the region is the stubbornly slow decline in fertility. The region has always had a very high birthrate: In 1950–1955, the regional crude birthrate was the highest in the world, 50.5 per 1,000. The crude birthrate (defined as the quotient of the number of births and the total population) fell between 1950–1955 and 1980–1985, but in percentage terms, the decline was only about one-half of the decline for the LDCs as a whole, leaving only sub-Saharan Africa with a higher crude birthrate. The crude birthrate for the region is above the average for lower-middle-income countries (37), for upper-middle-income countries (31), and is only slightly below the average for the world's poorest countries (44) (National Research Council 1986, 3).

The denominator—the total population—in the crude-birthrate quotient includes men, prepubescent girls, and postmenopausal women. A more revealing statistic is the total fertility rate, which tells us roughly how many children the "average woman" will have during her fertile period.[1] By this measure, Middle Eastern women were the most fecund in the world in the early 1950s and were second only to sub-Saharan African women by the early 1980s, when Middle Eastern women were each still bearing an average of six children (National Research Council 1986). Although the fertility rate for LDCs as a whole fell by about 33% during the past generation, the rate fell by less than half that percentage in MENA. There can be little doubt that MENA fertility rates are high in international comparative terms.

Middle Eastern fertility rates are also high in relation to incomes. It is well established that, in general, fertility falls with increases in per capita incomes; the relationship between fertility and incomes for 94 developing countries is shown in Figure 4.1. The relationship is not, of course, a simple one. Indeed, if everything else remains the same, higher incomes may lead to more children, since poor health at low income levels may constrain the number of children that women can have. The inverse relationship may be thought of as the outcome of a highly complex social process, in which new attitudes, new preferences, new habits are generated. Or one may have recourse to the theories of economic demography, which hold, in effect, that parents start to substitute "child quality" for "child quantity" as they become richer (e.g., T. W. Schultz 1981). But for both the sociological and the economic theory of fertility, increased incomes *alone* are unlikely to reduce fertility; additional socioeconomic change is required.

The MENA evidence (Figure 4.1) confirms such a perspective: Fertility rates exceed what would be "expected" given per capita incomes for every

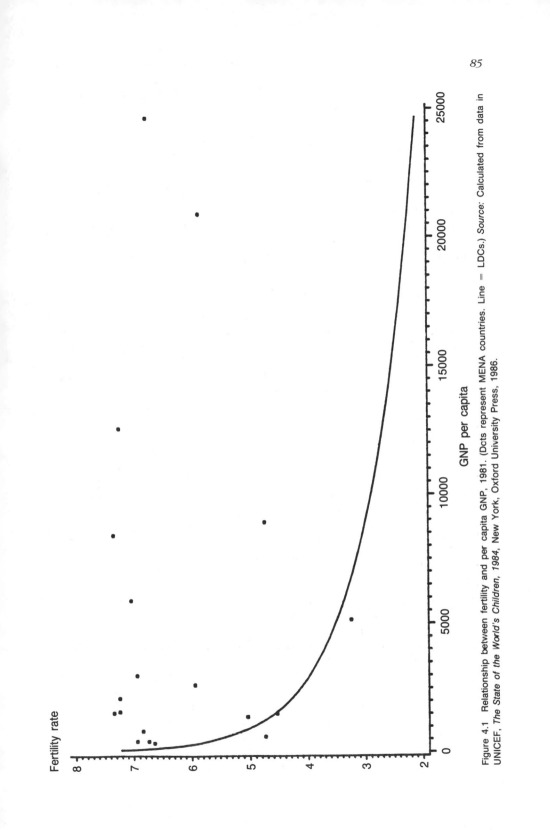

85

Figure 4.1 Relationship between fertility and per capita GNP, 1981. (Dcts represent MENA countries. Line = LDCs.) *Source:* Calculated from data in UNICEF, *The State of the World's Children, 1984*, New York, Oxford University Press, 1986.

country in the region except Egypt, Tunisia, and Turkey. The disparity becomes most notable for major oil-exporting countries: Despite income levels roughly comparable to those of many Western European countries, fertility rates in Saudi Arabia and Libya are as high as those in the poorest African countries, whose per capita incomes are less than one-tenth those of the Gulf States. The *regional* total fertility rate of 6.1 is roughly the same as the *average* rate for all *low-income* countries in the World Bank. The relatively weak relationship between higher incomes and reduced fertility in the region is not confined to oil exporters: Both Syria and Jordan have fertility rates much above what would be expected given their incomes. We need to explain not only why regional fertility rates are high relative to other regions of the world but also why they have remained so high despite the sustained economic growth of the decade of the oil boom.

Here we encounter a difficulty: Modern demographers do not agree on the precise determinants of fertility. All concur that economic conditions play some role; all agree that the social position of women is highly significant; all concede that high infant mortality is correlated with high fertility rates. But different analysts accord quite different weights to these and to other factors. This is not very surprising: The decision to have a child is so complex and the quality of available data so open to various interpretations that dogmatic positions are out of place. Accordingly, we will survey some of the plausible explantions for high fertility in the Middle East without offering a firm conclusion (inappropriate at current states of knowledge). We do believe that the social position of women and choices by national political leaders are central to any satisfactory explanation of why MENA fertility rates are "high."

One hypothesis is that poor health conditions raise fertility rates. Most demographers agree that infant mortality is an important determinant of fertility. Parents are interested in *surviving* children, for a combination of economic and emotional reasons. If many infants die, people will, on average, tend to have more children to compensate. The health experience of the region is discussed in more detail in the next chapter. Here it suffices to note that infant-mortality figures are high in the region, whether by cross-regional or by income-level standards (see Table 5.1). Such high rates contribute to an explanation of the high fertility rates so common in the region. However, they do not provide anything like a complete explanation of fertility behavior; for example, Turkey has a notably higher infant-mortality rate than does Syria, yet fertility in the latter country is well above that of its northern neighbor.

Economic analysis provides a useful perspective on fertility. Although, of course, any couple's decision to have a child is a complex outcome of social norms and personal psychology, some insights can be gained if one treats the decision in the same light as any other economic decision, as a balancing of "costs" and "benefits," recognizing from the outset that neither of these will be exclusively monetary. This view suggests that since most people like children, they will tend to have *more* of them as they become richer, just as they buy more clothes, meat, radios, entertainment. How, then, to explain the observed correlation between higher incomes and lower fertility? Economic analysts of demography argue that the key is the rising opportunity cost of having children as family incomes rise. In turn, these rising costs have two major components: (1) the increased amount of money that parents wish to spend on each child; and (2) the higher opportunity cost of parents' time. If rising incomes do not also generate such changes, increased wealth may do little to reduce fertility.

An important component of the opportunity cost of having children is the economic activity of children: The earlier a child can perform productive labor, the sooner his or her net contribution to the family budget will be positive. In most peasant societies, including those of the Middle East, children can and do perform numerous tasks, ranging from caring for younger children to harvesting cotton. In general, the more child labor performed in agriculture, the lower the opportunity cost of having many children, and therefore, the higher the fertility rate. It has been observed that in Egypt peasant families with more land to work and more cotton to pick tend to have more children than other peasant families. Some have even suggested that one of the major social benefits of farm mechanization is that it removes the incentive to have children simply to do farm work (Kelley, Khalifa, and El-Khorayaty 1982). This aspect of the "low levels of development engender high fertility" argument is certainly reasonable and is confirmed by evidence from the region. In this regard, the Middle East is little different from most of the peasant societies of the Third World.

Clearly, a critical component of the economic analysis of fertility is the opportunity cost of *women's* time, since it is certainly still the case throughout the Third World (and elsewhere) that women have primary responsibility for child care. If women are illiterate and if they are more or less systematically excluded from alternative employment, the opportunity cost of their time will be low. When such considerations are combined with and reinforced by social pressures on women to have many children, the result is likely to be a high fertility rate.

Such an analysis suggests that the socioeconomic status of women may be *the* critical determinant of fertility rates. Here we can find a clue to our puzzle of regional fertility rates exceeding what we would expect given both income levels and rates of infant and child mortality. The adult literacy figures for women in the Middle East are dismally low (Table 4.2). Although many Middle Eastern rural women do participate extensively in crop and livestock production, such work is typically integrated with child care and thus creates little pressure to reduce fertility. But women's participation in work that is more directly competitive with child rearing is, with a few exceptions, extremely low in the region: In 1985 only about one in eight nonfarm workers was female (FAO 1986).[2] Female illiteracy and the absence of nonfarm, nonhousehold job opportunities for women foster the region's rapid population growth.

These considerations raise the question of how "culture" contributes to the outcome of high fertility and, in particular, what, if any, role Islam

Table 4.2   Adult Female Literacy Rates, 1970 and 1980 (percentages)

|              | 1970 | 1980 |
|--------------|------|------|
| Algeria      | 11   | 24   |
| Egypt        | 20   | 28   |
| Iran         | 17   | 30   |
| Iraq         | 18   | 32   |
| Jordan       | 29   | 53   |
| Kuwait       | 42   | 54   |
| Libya        | 13   | 36   |
| Morocco      | 11   | 18   |
| Saudi Arabia | 2    | 12   |
| Sudan        | 6    | 14   |
| Syria        | 21   | 35   |
| Tunisia      | 17   | 34   |
| Turkey       | 35   | 50   |
| UAE          | 7    | 19   |
| YAR          | 1    | 2    |
| PDRY         | 9    | 16   |

Source: UNICEF, The State of the World's Children, 1984, New York, Oxford University Press, 1986, pp. 120-21.

plays in promoting population growth. It should be obvious that the answer to the broadly stated question, Does culture affect fertility? must be, Of course! The social norms regulating the sexual division of labor and, indeed, all aspects of relations between the sexes powerfully shape individual actions. Specifying the precise ways in which culture influences reproductive behavior is extremely difficult. However, we can offer a few general points. It is important to remember that most MENA countries are (or have been until very recently) largely peasant or herder societies. There are *no* peasant societies in which women are treated equally with men; everywhere the norm has been women's "social marginalization and economic centrality" (Meillasoux 1981). The importance of family life, the social and economic pressures to bear sons, and the strict control of women's sexuality are found in most peasant societies, whether Muslim or non-Muslim. Therefore, at least part of the subordination of women (and consequent high fertility rates) may be due to their position as peasants, rather than as Muslims.

But this can hardly be the whole story. After all, China is still overwhelmingly a peasant society, yet its fertility rate has plummeted over the past generation. Furthermore, to an outsider, Muslim societies seem especially socially restrictive for women. There are stringent practices of female seclusion and segregation of the sexes. Islamic law defines women as juridical minors; men can easily divorce women, whereas the reverse is not true; the father, not the mother, typically gets custody of the children. Some Muslim women try to have large families as a kind of "insurance policy" against divorce: A man might be more reluctant to divorce the mother of six than the mother of an only daughter.

However, several additional points on the issue of Islam, women's status, and fertility are in order. First, Islam is a living religion; its content is in part defined by how its adherents interpret their own tradition. There is much debate in the Muslim world over personal-status questions. Many Muslim scholars believe that many of the practices that Westerners label "Islamic" are in fact corruptions of Islam, derived from other sources, such as *'urf,* or "customary law." They are horrified by practices such as clitoridectomy (also widely practiced in non-Muslim Africa and rarely in West Asia) and denounce them regularly. To outsiders, some of this debate may seem forced, but it is critical: Only internal change that is consistent with people's beliefs has any chance of affecting such deeply personal issues as the regulation of family life. When we say that "Islam" promotes the subordinate status of women and thus high fertility, we mean "Islam— as currently practiced by Muslims."

A second, complimentary point to remember is that all great cultures are flexible; they can accommodate wide-ranging changes in economic, political, and social life. For example, one might summarize the above discussion by saying that Islam places great stress on family life and considers that women's primary place is in the home. But then, of how many cultures could one say otherwise? After all, few would try to argue that family life is marginal in Chinese culture, yet fertility rates in China have declined more rapidly than anywhere else in the world over the past twenty years. The status of women in Chinese society was lower than in the poorest Muslim society: A married Chinese woman could own no property distinct from her husband's, divorce was even easier for men than in Muslim societies, and women were essentially the property of their husbands. Yet governments as diverse as that of the PRC, Taiwan, and Singapore have all succeeded in educating women, raising their legal status, and dramatically lowering fertility rates. "Culture" is not immutable.

The question is not whether "culture" or "belief systems" affect behavior. The issue is whether these belief systems would continue to produce high fertility *even after* substantial changes elsewhere in social and economic life. For example, it is clear that early marriage contributes to higher fertility. Few children are born outside of marriage in the Middle East; if couples are formed early in life, fertility will be higher. Indeed, recent research has shown that postponing the age of marriage was the principal mechanism for limiting fertility in preindustrial Europe and Japan (Mosk 1983; Wrigley and Schofield 1981; World Bank 1984). The practice of early marriage is common in Islamic countries and receives social sanction and reinforcement. On average, about one young woman out of three is married before her nineteenth birthday (Lapham 1983). There is considerable variation across nations, as the data on Table 4.3 indicate. Government family-planning policies can also affect such practices. The change was most dramatic in Tunisia, where the percentage of teenage women who were married fell from 42% in 1956 to only 6% in 1975. Similar, although less dramatic, declines occurred in Egypt and Turkey.

This underscores a fundamental point: State policy affects fertility rates. It is hardly an accident that the three countries that have somewhat lower fertility than per capita incomes would lead us to expect have family-

Table 4.3  Percentage of Women Married at Least Once, Selected Countries, 1980

|                | Age: 15-19 Years | Age: 20-24 Years |
|----------------|------------------|------------------|
| Egypt          | 21.8             | 61.1             |
| Iran           | 34.3             | 78.6             |
| Iraq           | 33.0             | 67.2             |
| Israel         | 7.5              | 54.1             |
| Kuwait         | 29.2             | 71.0             |
| Libya          | 39.6             | 88.0             |
| Sudan          | 43.1             | 85.0             |
| Tunisia        | 10.6             | 54.5             |
| Turkey         | 21.7             | 72.9             |
| UAE            | 56.5             | 87.8             |
| United States  | 8.0              | 46.6             |

Source: United Nations, U.N. Demographic Yearbook, New York, 1982, Table 24, pp. 496-501.

planning programs. These programs date from the mid-1960s: 1964 in Tunisia and 1965 in Egypt and Turkey. Morocco also began such a program in 1966. Policymakers elsewhere in the region have largely avoided family planning; if they have also neglected the education of women, ignored their employment discrimination, and refused to alter their legally subordinate position, we should hardly be surprised at high fertility rates and rapid population growth. There are several determinants of such policy neglect. First, and probably most important, the benefits of reduced population growth accrue in the future. We shall see repeatedly in this book that myopia characterizes most government economic policy. Second, some governments do not believe that rapid population growth is a problem; these "pronatalist" countries (e.g., Sudan until 1984 and Iraq) *want* more people. To evaluate this position one must consider the economic consequences of population growth and the politics of ethnic differences in population growth (see below). Third, many believe that only changing economic conditions, not family planning, reduce population growth. Such arguments, sometimes buttressed by appeals to Marx, are both hypocritical and false. They are hypocritical because, as we shall see in the next chapter, the regional performance in changing the "basic needs" indicators like health and women's education that are so crucial for fertility reduction has hardly been spectacular. They are false because by now there is considerable evidence that the availability of family planning exerts an independent, negative pressure on fertility rates.

Perhaps the critical point here is not whether governments can affect fertility (they can) but, rather, how hard do they have to try, what does it "cost" them politically? We should also ask what the role of religion is in such costs. The legal age of marriage is still only 15 in countries like Morocco and Turkey; raising it encounters opposition from Islamic revivalists. It is probably not accidental that Moroccan television did not begin showing family-planning information until 1982, when economic crisis left little choice. Only if the government places a great deal of weight on the need to reduce population growth would a regime already hard-pressed by an Islamic opposition risk major family-planning drives. The weakness of family-planning policy thus becomes merely symptomatic of wider weakness by regional states. It is difficult not to conclude that high fertility levels are the result of political, not cultural, failure in the Middle East.

## THE ECONOMIC CONSEQUENCES
## OF RAPID POPULATION GROWTH

Does rapid population growth matter for economic development? Although most social scientists would answer in the affirmative, there is a minority that holds that population growth is a good thing. Members of this minority can point out that in the Middle East, for example, the standard of living and life prospects of the more than 50 million Egyptians alive today far exceed those of their 10 million grandparents in 1900. They also note that some of the development problems of the Sudan are the result of a highly dispersed population. One could accept such arguments without necessarily swallowing the more-is-better line whole. But one does need to specify exactly just how high fertility and rapid population growth will affect national economies.

A critical feature of the demography of Middle Eastern countries is the high number of young people in proportion to the total population. A comparison of age pyramids for a few countries in the region with that of the United States is instructive (Figure 4.2). Most Middle Easterners are less than 20 years old; rapidly growing populations are young populations. It is worth noting, however, that the age pyramid for the Middle East in the nineteenth century, before rapid population growth began, would have looked quite similar. This is because declines in mortality, which drive increases in population growth, affect the survival not only of the young but also of the old: The relative percentage of young people does not shift much when the death rate falls. By contrast, a sharp fall in the fertility rate quickly reduces the proportions of young people in the population, while continued improvements in health prolong old age, further reducing the percentage of the young in the total population. However, the *scale* of the problem today is entirely different; the absolute numbers of young people now, rather than their proportion to the rest of the population, make the critically important difference.

There are both economic and political consequences of the youthfulness of MENA populations. The political impact is considered in the next section. The principal economic effects are the implications for the quality of education and the consequences for labor markets. First, there is something approaching consensus among demographers that the amount of money spent per pupil is reduced by rapid population growth (see the discussion in National Research Council 1986). This usually takes the form of reduced teacher salaries and high pupil-teacher ratios. However, as we shall see in the next chapter, there is little evidence that the latter is a problem in

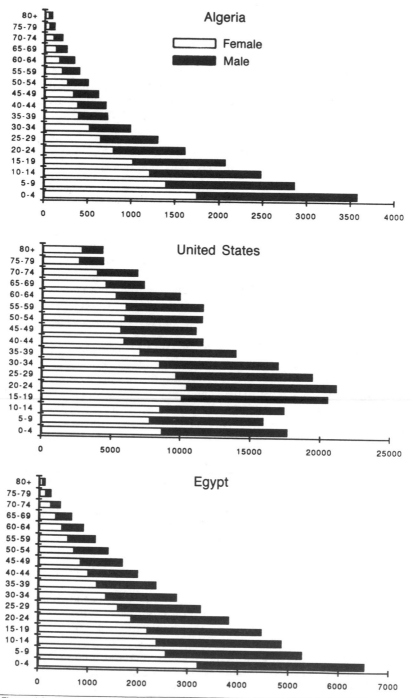

Figure 4.2  Distribution of population by age and sex in Algeria, the United States, and Egypt, 1980 (in thousands)

Table 4.4  Rates of Growth of Labor Force, 1965-2000 (percent per year)

|              | 1965-1980 | 1980-1985 | 1985-2000* |
|--------------|-----------|-----------|------------|
| Algeria      | 2.2       | 3.6       | 3.7        |
| Egypt        | 2.2       | 2.6       | 2.7        |
| Iran         | 3.2       | 3.3       | 3.2        |
| Iraq         | 3.6       | 3.7       | 4.0        |
| Israel       | 3.0       | 2.2       | 2.1        |
| Jordan       | 1.7       | 4.4       | 4.2        |
| Kuwait       | 6.9       | 6.2       | 3.5        |
| Lebanon      | 1.7       | --        | --         |
| Libya        | 3.6       | 3.7       | 3.5        |
| Morocco      | 2.9       | 3.3       | 3.1        |
| Oman         | 3.8       | 5.2       | 2.7        |
| Saudi Arabia | 4.9       | 4.4       | 3.5        |
| Sudan        | 2.4       | 2.8       | 3.1        |
| Syria        | 3.3       | 3.5       | 4.0        |
| Tunisia      | 2.8       | 3.1       | 2.8        |
| Turkey       | 1.7       | 2.3       | 2.0        |
| UAE          | --        | 5.2       | 2.1        |
| YAR          | 0.7       | 2.6       | 3.4        |
| PDRY         | 1.6       | 2.8       | 3.1        |

* estimated.

Source: World Bank, **World Development Report**, New York, Oxford University Press, 1987, p. 221.

the region; most countries try very hard to spend money on education. However, it is obviously true that a country starting to educate its children will find it more difficult to offer primary education to all of them if their numbers are growing rapidly. For example, although the total number of Algerian children enrolled in primary school nearly quadrupled from 1962 to 1978, there were still more than 1 million school-age children not in school in 1978 (Bennoune 1988). Rapid population growth swamps even the most determined attempts to diffuse basic education.

But the problems that a burgeoning number of young people create for society are not limited to educational difficulties. The impact on the job market is equally profound. Rates of growth of national labor forces are given in Table 4.4. A rapidly expanding labor force compels the diversion of investment to providing jobs with a given amount of capital per worker. Since increasing the amount of capital per worker is typically necessary to raise worker productivity and therefore incomes, rapid population increase slows the growth of per capita incomes, ceteris paribus. Rapid population growth means that money must be spent just to create jobs, rather than to improve those that already exist or to create more productive ones. It is particularly difficult to create the entry-level jobs that the (very young) labor force requires, especially when skilled older workers are so scarce. Since for nonoil (and increasingly for oil-exporting) states, funds for investment are very scarce, rapid population growth slows the pace of growth and development.[3]

Rapid population growth exacerbates other development problems in the region. Investable funds are diverted not merely from "capital deepening" but from *any* form of job creation to social-overhead investment (e.g., housing, sewage and water systems). Some investment may be necessary simply to repair the damage caused by population growth, as in the funds now being used to try to rehabilitate ecologically degraded areas of the Sudan. Rapid population increase contributes to the very rapid growth of cities, which are expanding at roughly twice the rate of the overall population in the region. Cairo's population of 12–13 million could double in twelve years—hardly a comforting thought to planners struggling with infrastructure that was originally planned and installed for a city of 1.5 million. Not only does such rapid urban-population growth divert investment funds, but it also strains administrative capacities of governments and fosters political problems. Rapid population growth contributes to a soaring demand for food in the region, thus adding to the "food security" problem. Finally, by increasing the supply of labor relative to capital, and by raising the ratio of unskilled to skilled labor, rapid population growth probably worsens the distribution of income.

It should be noted that population growth is neither exogenous nor a "monocause" of development problems. It is merely one (albeit important) variable in the ensemble of relationships in the political economy. But the rapid growth of population does exacerbate important economic development difficulties in the region. It also poses political problems, to which we now turn.


## THE POLITICS OF YOUNG POPULATIONS

In countries with moderate or low population growth rates, political leadership is generally drawn from an age pool that contains a significant proportion, if not the majority, of the population. In North America, Western and Eastern Europe, the Soviet Union, and Japan, not only are most citizens legal adults (68% of the U.S. population is 20 years old or older), but also the populations as a whole are aging. There is, in these countries, a much more profound sharing of experience between leaders and their major constituencies than is to be found in societies experiencing rapid population growth.

Political generations are often depicted as having been shaped by national crisis—for example, Churchill, Roosevelt, Truman, Stalin, and de Gaulle all spoke for a generation that shared the trauma of the world depression and World War II. Similarly, in 1980 there were 57 million Americans, or 26% of the entire population of the United States, who were born before 1925, grew up during the depression, and were at least teenagers during World War II. That experience provided them and their elected leaders a common language and a set of symbols that were drawn from their own lives.

The situation in the Middle East is entirely different. When we note that in 1980, 60% of the Algerian population was under 19 years old, we can see startling political implications. First, only 40% of the population are adults in the legal sense, entitled to vote and stand for election. Also, two-thirds of all living Algerians were born *since* independence in 1962. They know nothing directly of the French colonial presence, nor of seven years of war and devastation. By contrast, all three of Algeria's presidents since 1962—Ahmad Ben Bella (1962–1965), Houari Boumedienne (1965–1978), and Chadli Benjadid (1979–  )—were leading figures in the revolutionary war, as were most members of the Algerian political elite. The legitimacy of that elite is in no small measure dependent upon its role in the struggle against France, but for most Algerians that struggle is history, not a living memory or a shared experience. In 1980 only 17% of the population was old enough to have been 15 at the outbreak of the war in 1954.

Equally striking is the phenomenon of the Ayatollah Khomeini of Iran, a man born at the turn of the century. He lived through the demise of the Qajar dynasty, the constitutional struggles of the 1920s, the consolidation of the autocratic regime of Reza Shah, the postwar confrontation between Reza Shah's son and the nationalist prime minister, Mohammed Mossadegh, and, finally, the shah's launching of the White Revolution in 1963. It was Khomeini's virulent opposition to various measures contained in that revolution that forced him into an exile that ended in 1979 with the deposition of the shah and Khomeini's triumphant return to an Islamic and republican Iran.

The majority of all Iranians have been born since Khomeini went into exile. They did not live through the effervescence and occasional violence of the shah's White Revolution, which consisted of a series of measures involving land reform, female suffrage, the right of non-Muslims to stand as candidates, and the creation of a literacy corps. They did not hear or witness Khomeini's denunciations of some of these measures or his opposition to the special legal status granted U.S. personnel at that time. Even rarer are those Iranians old enough to have participated in the events of 1953 when Prime Minister Mossadegh nationalized British oil interests and drove the young shah, Mohammed Reza Pahlavi, into brief exile.

One could go on with examples of the enormous disparities in age and experience of leaders and followers in the Middle East: Habib Bourguiba, born in 1903 and president of Tunisia from 1956 to 1987, or the septuagenarians that led Lebanon for years (Camille Chamoun, Suleiman Frangieh, Kemal Jumblatt, Pierre Jamayyel) are cases in point. The youngest of all Middle Eastern leaders, Mu'ammar Qaddhafi of Libya, in his mid-40s, can no longer be seen as embodying the youthful élan of the bulk of the Libyan population.

There may yet be enough deference paid to age in the Middle East so that the youthful majorities of the region will not reject or confront their relatively aged leaders. Khomeini's prestige among all Iranians appeared undiminished, at least until the cease-fire with Iraq in the summer of 1988, and hundreds of thousands of young Iranians died in the name of an anti-Iraqi crusade that he insisted on pursuing. In Lebanon by contrast, after years of civil war, leadership has passed out of the hands of venerable *zu'ama* (confessional bosses) and into those of much younger militia chieftains and street fighters. Elsewhere, however, the young have not yet insisted on a role in the political arena proportionate to their numbers.


## THE POLITICS OF DIFFERENTIAL FERTILITY

In defining the rights and obligations of citizens, the constitutions of most Middle Eastern states are blind to their ethnic or religious origins. Nonetheless, in a de facto sense, the relative weights of religious and ethnic communities weigh heavily in the political calculus of each state's leadership. There is an unstated expectation that the flows of public patronage will reflect communal weights. If income distribution patterns, particularly the locus of poverty, correspond closely to ethnic or religious boundaries, then a potentially explosive situation may develop. The violent assertion of Shi'ite demands in Lebanon is a dramatic example.

The only way to know how many there are of what communities is through the national census. Censuses are carried out under the control of the national authority and can be doctored to reflect its interests. In Turkey, where, since the 1920s, there have been sporadic outbursts of Kurdish separatism in Eastern Anatolia, the national census provides no head count of the ethnic Kurds. In Iraq, where ethnicity (Kurd-Arab) cuts across religious sect (Sunni-Shi'i Muslim), the regime has typically been dominated by Sunni Arabs. Periodically there is talk of autonomy for regions in which Kurds predominate, but to delimit these regions requires a census. While negotiating over conducting a census, the regime has resettled Arabs in Kurdish areas, and Kurds, who are Sunni Muslims, in Shi'ite areas. The Iraqi example illustrates the moving of people to achieve a desired census outcome. In Egypt the problem is one of adjusting census results. The Coptic Christian minority there has always protested that it has been undercounted by some 50% in Egypt's national census.

The two countries of the region in which the problem of ethnic and sectarian head counting is most acute are Lebanon and Israel. The system of political representation in Lebanon, cobbled together by the French after World War I, was founded on sectarian communities. Representatives in parliament competed for seats that were allocated in proportion to the numerical strength of each religious group in the population. The basic ratio is that for every five Muslim seats in parliament, there are six Christian seats.

This formula resulted from Lebanon's last official census in 1932. At that time the total population was 793,000. The Maronite Christians alone constituted 29% of the population, while Greek Orthodox, Armenians, Greek Catholics, and others gave the Christians a narrow but absolute majority of the population. The second-largest religious group was the Sunni Muslims, with 21% of the population. The Shi'ites were, in 1932, 18% of the population.

Table 4.5  Lebanon's Estimated Population, by Sect, 1932-1983

|  | 1932 | | 1983 | | 1983 | |
|---|---|---|---|---|---|---|
|  | Pop. | % | Pop. | % | Pop. | % |
| Total Christians | 410,246 | 51.7 | 1,525,000 | 42.6 | 965,000 | 36.6 |
| Maronites | 226,378 | 28.6 | 900,000 | 25.0 | 580,000 | 21.0 |
| Greek Orthodox | 76,522 | 9.6 | 250,000 | 7.0 | 185,000 | 6.8 |
| Greek Catholic | 45,999 | 5.8 | 150,000 | 4.2 | 115,000 | 4.2 |
| Armenians | 31,156 | 3.9 | 175,000 | 4.9 | 70,000 | 2.6 |
| Others* | 30,191 | 3.8 | 50,000 | 1.4 | 40,000 | 1.5 |
| Total Muslims and Druze | 383,180 | 48.3 | 2,050,000 | 57.3 | 1,435,000 | 60.2 |
| Sunnis | 175,925 | 22.2 | 750,000 | 21.0 | 600,000 | 25.0 |
| Shi'ites | 154,208 | 19.4 | 1,100,000 | 31.0 | 665,000 | 27.5 |
| Druze | 53,047 | 6.7 | 200,000 | 5.6 | 180,000 | 7.7 |
| Total | 793,426 | 100.0 | 3,575,000 | 100.0 | 2,400,000 | 100.0 |

* Includes Jews.

Sources: The first and last columns are from Arnon Soffer, "Lebanon--Where Demography Is the Core of Politics and Life," Middle Eastern Studies 22, 2 (April 1980), p. 199. The middle column is from Lebanon: A Conflict of Minorities, London, Minority Rights Group, November 1983, as cited in Middle East, March 1986, p. 41.

It was clear to everyone that the natural rate of increase of the Muslim populations was more rapid than that of the Christians. Moreover, the rate of long-term migration outside of Lebanon was higher among Christians than among Muslims. There was little doubt that a post–World War II census would show that the Christians had become a minority in Lebanon. Following the logic of the confessional system of apportionment, they would have lost the presidency and the majority of the seats in parliament. The result: No official census has been taken in Lebanon since 1932. President Amin Jamayyel (1982–1988) was a Maronite Christian, as is his unelected successor, Gen. Michel Aoun, and the majority of seats in the now-moribund parliament are still occupied by Christians. In the last few decades there have been several informal attempts to measure the Lebanese population (Hudson 1968, 54–60). They all show that the Shi'ites have become the single largest religious group in Lebanon. Neither the Christians nor the Sunni Muslims wish to concede this fact officially.

Current estimates vary widely (Table 4.5). The two 1983 columns reveal a discrepancy of over 1 million people. Only Soffer explained the derivation of his figures, which assume 80,000 dead in the civil war and the emigration of 400,000 Lebanese, half of whom were Maronite. He also put the foreign population of Lebanon at 220,000 Palestinians and 80,000 others. The Shi'ites are the poorest of all the religious sects. They are concentrated in the impoverished southern agricultural area bordering on Israel, with large pockets of relatively poor migrants in Sidon and Beirut. Their resentment at years of neglect has taken violent form. Their prominent role in the civil war in recent years is in large part motivated by their determination to win economic and political rewards commensurate with their numbers.

In Israel questions of ethnic and religious numbers are equally sensitive. And as in Lebanon, communal boundaries correspond to differential socioeconomic status. However, in Israel censuses have been taken regularly and accurately. That very fact has produced data that alarm the Israeli establishment. The question is not so simple as how many Jews and non-Jews there are in Israel. The Jews themselves divide between the Ashkenazim, of Eastern European origin, and the Sephardim (or more accurately the Oriental Jews), of Middle Eastern and Spanish origin. Israel's political establishment has been dominated since independence by the Ashkenazim. As a group they are highly educated, relatively wealthy, and have small families. The Oriental Jews, by contrast, occupy lower socioeconomic positions in Israeli society and are seen as more traditional (read "backward"). Birthrates among the Oriental Jews are higher than among the Ashkenazim, and the former and their Israeli-born offspring have become a majority of the Jewish population. They have yet to inherit the political kingdom.

Far more crucial is the question of Israeli-Arab birthrates. Over the period 1950–1968, the Israeli-Arab community grew at the extraordinary rate of 4% per annum, or from 160,000 to 406,000 out of a total population of 2.9 million. Non-Jews thus represented 14% of the population. Even with significant migration from abroad, the Israeli Jewish population over the period 1952–1968 grew by only 3.1% per annum. In the past two decades Jewish rates of natural increase and of immigration have been declining (Ben-Porath 1972, 503–39).

Since the June War of 1967, Israel has occupied the West Bank, formerly under Jordanian control, and Gaza, formerly under Egyptian control, and has annexed East Jerusalem and the Golan Heights. In 1988, out of a total population of 4.5 million in Israel (including the annexed areas), there were 817,000 Arabs (including Druze), or 18% of the total population. The Druze had been absorbed after 1948 and, like other Israeli Arabs, enjoy Israeli citizenship. In addition, in the early 1980s, there were 1.2 million Arabs resident in the West Bank, Gaza, and Golan, who were not and are not Israeli citizens. Israel's dilemma is twofold. First, if present trends continue, Israeli citizens of Arab origin will come to constitute as much as a quarter or a third of the entire population. A minority of that size, if not fully reconciled to the Israeli state, could destroy it, or at least its democratic system. Second, if Israel decides, for security or religious reasons, to annex the West Bank, that would immediately raise the proportion of non-Jews in Israel to well over one-third. Then, with their high birthrates, the Arabs of Israel could plausibly expect to become an absolute majority within the country. On political grounds alone, few Jewish Israelis would be prepared to accept that. In a more profound sense it would be the abandonment of the Zionist quest for a Jewish state. Demographic trends will not stand still while the Israelis wrestle with this dilemma.

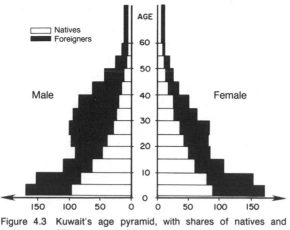

Figure 4.3  Kuwait's age pyramid, with shares of natives and foreigners, 1975 (in thousands)

Although the problem has been seemingly less acute, it is the case that Kuwait, the United Arab Emirates, Qatar, and Saudi Arabia face politically perilous demographic situations. Like Israel, they domicile large numbers of residents without citizenship. For the most part they are migrant workers and professionals from the oil-poor countries of the region, as well as from India, Pakistan, and points further east. In Kuwait there is also a substantial community of Palestinian refugees. In these countries not only is most of the work force foreign but nearly half the resident population may also be foreign. Moreover, because they are worker-migrants, they are adults and preponderantly male (Figure 4.3). While the economic life of these countries is dependent upon their presence, they have been excluded from political life. To date they have not exploited their strategic economic position to express political demands, but the fact that they might do so is sufficiently alarming that all the host states are actively pursuing policies to diminish their presence.

Nearly every country in the Middle East is to some extent affected by the issues of counting various minorities and the different rates at which their numbers grow. In policy terms the ideal of the homogenous nation-state in which every citizen is equal to every other is something of a myth. In that sense, the national census becomes the instrument both for determining relative weights and for giving or denying formal recognition to specific minorities.

## RAPID POPULATION GROWTH AND
## THE WOULD-BE MIDDLE CLASS

Twenty-five years ago Halpern (1963, 62–66) wrote of the new middle class and the would-be middle class. He had in mind those educated

Middle Easterners who had moved into the white-collar ranks of the civil service and the professions, as well as the educated Middle Easterners who aspired to those ranks but could find no room in them. Part of the risk Halpern foresaw was the formation of a kind of intellectual proletariat made up of upwardly mobile but frustrated young men. It must be stressed that it is only very recently that educated Middle Eastern women have entered the job market in appreciable numbers.

Over the past two decades, the structural problem Halpern sketched has become far more acute. In the mid-1980s there were roughly 75 million Middle Easterners between the ages of 15 and 25 out of a total population of around 270 million. Most of the males among them had some education—probably some 8 million had at least a secondary school diploma. Until the 1950s that much education would have qualified the recipient for a comfortable if unglamorous white-collar job, a decent standard of living, and a modicum of social prestige.

That is no longer the case. The young Middle Easterners recruited into the civil service and professions twenty to twenty-five years ago are not yet 50 years old. They have enjoyed rapid promotion and some have risen to the top of their administrative hierarchies. They will not retire soon. Yet behind them are new, even larger cohorts of men and women with equal aspirations and sometimes better professional credentials. They are being offered make-work jobs or no jobs, salaries that lag behind inflation, and low social status. Their numbers are growing and will continue to grow for at least a generation. It is hard to see how and where they can be productively absorbed into the work force. Because they are literate and politically aware, denying them material security is potentially dangerous.

It is reasonably clear that this age group contributes significantly to various kinds of radical movements, from the street fighters of Beirut to the Islamic militants of Cairo or Tunis. One would be wrong, however, to attribute common political attitudes to an entire age cohort. Its members are just as likely to be worker migrants to the Gulf States or to be following conventional career paths in the bureaucracy or service sector as they are to be political activists. Yet the opportunities for them to achieve their aspirations will narrow as their numbers increase. It is not likely that they will be passive in the face of such a situation.

Middle Eastern regimes have experimented with an array of policies to contain the menace, from the creation of redundant civil service jobs to the encouragement of migration abroad. Until the rate at which jobs can be created comes into equilibrium with the rate at which this generation grows, these young people will constitute one of if not the most important source of political instability in the Middle East. The Middle East is not at all unique in this respect. Much the same analysis could be applied to India or Mexico or a host of other developing countries. In the Middle East, however, the problem is more acute because, as a result of very high birthrates in the 1960s, the relative numbers of new job-seekers is also higher.

## CONCLUSION

The approaches to population growth and control in developing countries have taken some peculiar twists. In the 1950s and 1960s the United States and other developed nations urged the LDCs to adopt national programs of family planning and population control. Many in the developing world saw these urgings as racist in nature, the fear of whites of the rising tide of blacks, browns, and yellows. Moreover, it was an era of grandiose development plans and optimism in the Third World. High rates of economic growth suggested that ever-larger numbers of people would be provided for and employed. It was assumed that larger cohorts of the young could be educated and trained so as to contribute to the growth effort rather than be a drain upon it. A striking example of this outlook is provided by President Houari Boumedienne, who in one speech (June 19, 1969) squelched a campaign for family planning that had been quietly building in Algeria. Inaugurating a huge steel works at Annaba, he said (as cited in Waterbury 1973a, 18):

> Our goal . . . over the next twenty years is to assure that our people, who will number 25 million souls, will have a standard of living which will be among the highest of the modern peoples of the world of tomorrow. I take this opportunity to say—concerning what is called "galloping demography"— that we are not partisans of false solutions such as the limitation of births. We believe that that is the same as suppressing difficulties instead of searching for adequate solutions. . . . We believe that the real solution to this problem resides in development, even if that demands greater efforts.

There are not many leaders in the Middle East today who would be prepared to make such a statement. Indeed, despite the admonitions of Muslim leaders who tend to see the strength of Islam lying in numbers, secular leaders have come to see the need to lower birthrates. Their belated recognition of the problem contrasts with the revisionist position of the Reagan administration, which, in its concern over issues of abortion and right-to-life, adopted a line not unlike that of Houari Boumedienne in 1969.

We are all well advised, as P. T. Bauer has warned, to avoid confusing the welfare of individuals (more children survive and people live longer) with that of the welfare of nations. The paradox he discerned is that "in statistics of national income the birth of a calf represents an increase in living standards but the birth of child represents a fall" (Bauer 1973, 63). Yet while living is preferable to dying and living long preferable to dying young, there are questions that cannot be overlooked about the quality of individual lives and the ability of national economies to make those lives tolerable if not pleasant. There do seem to be "carrying capacities" in various economic systems, and although they may be elastic, they are not infinitely so. To contribute to economic growth, each Middle Easterner needs good health, education, and some vocational or professional skills, but numbers have to some extent overwhelmed the capacities of economies and administrations to provide these goods. In the next chapter we shall examine the disappointing record of the Middle East in this regard.

## NOTES

1. That is, "the total fertility rate represents the number of children that would be born per woman, assuming that she lives to the end of her childbearing years and bears children at each age in accord with prevailing age-specific fertility rates" (World Bank 1984, p. 282).

2. These numbers are for the "Near East," which excludes the Maghreb. In 1985 women comprised 11.2%, 22.3%, and 23.8% of the nonfarm work force in Algeria, Morocco, and Tunisia, respectively (FAO 1986).

3. This conclusion would be invalidated only if more rapid population growth either increased the domestic savings rates or stimulated additional capital inflows from abroad. There is no evidence to support either conjecture.

# 5

# HUMAN CAPITAL—
# HEALTH AND EDUCATION

Both those who lament and those who rejoice at rapid population growth
can easily agree on one thing: Standards of health and education must
improve if poor counties are to raise their living standards. Perhaps the
one aspect of development on which there is the least dispute is the
necessity to invest in "human capital": to ameliorate health conditions
and to educate people as widely as possible. There are two reasons for
this unusual consensus. First, all agree that good health and universal
literacy are fundamental human rights and, as such, are ends in themselves.
A society that fails to educate its children and to eradicate preventable
disease is a society that stands indicted of gross neglect of the general
welfare. Second, most analysts believe that healthier and better educated
people are more productive. Neoclassical economists point to high "rates
of return on investments in human capital," while Marxists stress the need
for socialist regimes to "liberate the productive potential of the masses."
It is indeed rare in the field of development studies to find such substantively
similar conclusions emanating from such otherwise radically different
perspectives.

Human-capital issues are particularly important for the countries of the
Middle East and North Africa because, with the obvious exception of oil,
the region is relatively poor in natural resources. Many analysts (e.g.,
Amouzegar 1983) therefore argue that development of human resources
should lie at the center of national development plans. Unfortunately the
performance record of these countries is quite mixed. Health standards
have improved during the last generation, but still lag well behind what
we would expect based on per capita income levels alone. Although
educational systems have expanded rapidly, adult illiteracy, especially among
women, remains widespread. Here, as with questions of population growth,
the issue of the status of women is critical: Considerable evidence suggests
that restrictions on women's choices block achieving high health standards.
Furthermore, the type of education that Middle Easterners receive too often

fails to provide them with the skills and training that modern industrial and commercial life requires. Consequently, there is often a mismatch between the demand and the supply of skills; poor educational policy engenders labor-market disequilibria and exacerbates employment problems. But the very expansion of education, coupled with demography, has created a potent political force: secondary and university-level students who often cannot find jobs consistent with their aspirations.

Despite these serious deficiencies, the current situation is nevertheless a considerable improvement over that which prevailed a generation ago. We have a "glass half empty, glass half full" situation: Current levels of health and education are unimpressive when compared with per capita incomes, but the changes during the last generation have been quite rapid in some cases. Starting from extremely low levels of health and literacy, many Middle Eastern nations have made dramatic advances during the past quarter century. They still have much unfinished business, but the achievements are undeniable. Yet, despite these accomplishments, we may fairly accuse some governments of neglecting or misdirecting the "ultimate resource" of the region.

## HEALTH ISSUES IN
## MIDDLE EASTERN DEVELOPMENT

Two points on health in the region stand out: Most countries have made considerable progress in improving health conditions for their citizens, and these conditions still fall well short of aspirations. "Good health" is obviously a multidimensional, complex phenomenon; measuring it is correspondingly difficult. Two indicators are widely used as "summary statements" of health conditions: life expectancy at birth (LEB) and infant mortality. LEB may be the single most robust indicator of national health conditions. Based on age-specific mortality rates, this number simply says how long, on average, a newly born child can expect to live. It summarizes health, nutritional, and other welfare factors into a single, easily understood number. LEB figures for the region are shown in Table 5.1.

Infant mortality is a second key indicator of the overall state of health of a country (Table 5.2). Not only are avoidable infant deaths especially poignant, but they are also symptomatic of wider health problems, such as malnutrition, polluted water, poor infant feeding practices. When just under 1 million infants die in a half-decade, as in Turkey in the late 1970s, we know that much is wrong with the health conditions of the country.[1] Finally, we have seen in the last chapter that high infant mortality fosters high fertility and rapid population growth. From a demographic perspective, as well as from a simple humanitarian one, understanding the causes and remedies for high infant mortality is in order.

Our evelution of Middle Eastern health performance is greatly affected by whether we focus on health *levels* or on *rates of change* in those levels. From the first perspective, the region appears a rather unhealthy place,

Table 5.1  Life Expectancy at Birth, 1965 and 1984

| | Males | | Females | |
|---|---|---|---|---|
| | 1965 | 1984 | 1965 | 1984 |
| Algeria | 49 | 59 | 51 | 62 |
| Egypt | 47 | 59 | 50 | 62 |
| Iran | 52 | 61 | 52 | 61 |
| Iraq | 50 | 58 | 53 | 62 |
| Israel | 70 | 73 | 73 | 77 |
| Jordan | 49 | 62 | 51 | 66 |
| Kuwait | 61 | 69 | 64 | 74 |
| Libya | 48 | 57 | 51 | 61 |
| Morocco | 48 | 57 | 51 | 61 |
| Oman | 40 | 52 | 42 | 55 |
| Saudi Arabia | 47 | 60 | 49 | 64 |
| Sudan | 39 | 46 | 41 | 50 |
| Syria | 51 | 62 | 54 | 65 |
| Tunisia | 50 | 60 | 51 | 64 |
| Turkey | 52 | 61 | 55 | 66 |
| UAE | 57 | 70 | 61 | 74 |
| YAR | 37 | 44 | 38 | 46 |
| PDRY | 37 | 46 | 39 | 48 |
| Sweden | 72 | 74 | 76 | 80 |
| Ind. Mkt. Econ. | 68 | 73 | 74 | 79 |

Source: UNICEF, **The State of the World's Children, 1984**, New York, Oxford University Press, 1986, p. 93.

certainly when compared with the OECD countries. The United Nations International Children's Emergency Fund (UNICEF)—now called the United Nations Children's Fund—for example, classes most Middle Eastern countries' infant mortality rates as either "very high" (over 100 per 1,000) or "high" (over 50 per 1,000). Only the UAE, Lebanon, and Kuwait have "moderate" rates of infant death, while only Israel has a "low" rate (Table 5.2). Some observers believe that even these high recorded numbers are underestimates of the actual situation (Kavalsky 1980). Moreover, these national numbers conceal considerable regional and social class variations. In some rural areas of the Sudan, 2 out of 5 children die before their fifth birthday; rural infant-mortality rates routinely exceed urban throughout the region (Ghonemy 1984). One in 5 children born into poor rural Turkish families die before they reach their first birthday. Class counts in urban areas as well: Infant mortality for lower and lower-middle classes in Damascus in 1976 were 83.7 and 72.8 per 1,000, respectively, compared with 55.5 and 34.4 for upper-middle and upper classes, respectively (Shorter 1985, 67).[2] In the Middle East as elswhere, the poor watch more of their children die than do the rich.

Table 5.2  Infant Mortality Rates, 1960 and 1981 (per thousand live births)

|              | 1960 | 1981 |
|--------------|------|------|
| Algeria      | 170  | 110  |
| Egypt        | 170  | 120  |
| Iran         | 160  | 100  |
| Iraq         | 140  | 80   |
| Israel       | 31   | 16   |
| Jordan       | 140  | 70   |
| Kuwait       | 90   | 33   |
| Lebanon      | 70   | 40   |
| Libya        | 160  | 100  |
| Morocco      | 160  | 100  |
| Oman         | 190  | 130  |
| Saudi Arabia | 190  | 110  |
| Sudan        | 170  | 120  |
| Syria        | 130  | 60   |
| Tunisia      | 110  | 100  |
| Turkey       | 190  | 120  |
| UAE          | 140  | 50   |
| YAR          | 210  | 190  |
| PDRY         | 210  | 140  |
|              |      |      |
| United States| 26   | 12   |
| Japan        | 30   | 7    |

Source: UNICEF, The State of the World's Children, 1984, New York, Oxford
University Press, 1986, p. 93.

At the same time, for many countries of the region, LEB has increased dramatically during the past generation. A Middle Eastern child born in the early 1980s could expect to live more than thirteen years longer than his parents, aunts, or uncles who were born in the early 1950s. Of course, LEB varies widely by country, ranging from a low of 44 years for a North Yemeni male baby to a maximum of 77 years for an Israeli girl (Table 5.1). Infant mortality is also much lower than it was even twenty years ago, although again, performance varies widely by country (Table 5.2).

Improvement has undoubtedly occurred, but assessing these gains requires a comparative perspective. After all, the increase in LEB has been a worldwide phenomenon: Medical advances potentially affect all nations. Taking the region as a whole, the improvements have not been spectacular, but neither have they been notably deficient. Whether measured in terms of absolute change, percentage change, or more sophisticated formulas, Middle Eastern countries' performance in improving health and longevity is somewhat below the overall average for all LDCs. However, the calculation for the whole Third World is population weighted and therefore is strongly affected by the spectacular achievements of the People's Republic of China in improving health. It is also helpful to compare Middle Eastern experience with that of other major regions (Table 5.3). Viewed in this perspective, Middle Eastern performance is neither the best nor the worst in the world.

A second type of comparative perspective can by obtained by comparing the health conditions of Middle Easterners relative to their incomes. Much evidence suggests that economic growth improves health. Visions of car-

Table 5.3  Life Expectancy at Birth (LEB) in Comparative Perspective,
          1950/55-1980/85

| | Years | | Change | | |
|---|---|---|---|---|---|
| | 1950/55 | 1980/85 | Absolute (Yrs.) | % | Sen Index* |
| Sub-Saharan | | | | | |
| Africa | 36.4 | 47.9 | 11.5 | 32 | 30 |
| Latin America | 50.0 | 64.1 | 14.1 | 26 | 42 |
| East Asia | | | | | |
| (excl. Japan) | 41.1 | 64.8 | 23.7 | 58 | 70 |
| South Asia | 39.0 | 51.6 | 12.6 | 33 | 35 |
| MENA | 43.6 | 57.0 | 13.4 | 31 | 43 |
| LDCs | 41.4 | 56.9 | 15.5 | 38 | 46 |

\* Sen Index = Percentage change in "longevity shortfall" (defined as = 75 years
minus actual LEB).

Source: LEB: National Research Council, Population Growth and Economic
Development: Policy Questions, Washington, D.C., National Academy Press, 1986,
p. 26.  Changes: calculated by authors.

cinogenic industry notwithstanding, there is a clear positive correlation
between LEB and per capita income: For a set of over 100 countries,
variations in per capita income "explain" about 45% of the variation in
LEB.[3] Figure 5.1 presents a graphic illustration of these relationships.
Although no other single variable plays so important a role in explanations
of cross-country differences in LEB, over half of the variance remains to
be explained. Less formally, the recent experience of countries like China
and Sri Lanka show that increased income is not a *necessary* condition
for improving health: Both of these countries have LEBs comparable to
advanced industrial countries, although both are classed as "low-income
countries" by the World Bank. Conversely, a highly inegalitarian pattern
of economic growth may reduce infant mortality only very slowly.

Unfortunately, as Figure 5.1 shows, Middle Eastern countries are exceptional in the sense that their LEBs are typically *lower* than what we
would expect, given those countries' per capita incomes. We need to
scrutinize health performance in greater detail to understand why, despite
undeniable progress, most countries of the region have poorer health
conditions than their incomes would warrant.

## EXPLANATIONS FOR POOR
## HEALTH PERFORMANCE IN THE MIDDLE EAST

Why do so many babies and young children die unnecessarily in the
Middle East? Answers to this grim question may be sought by asking two
subsidiary questions: What diseases kill babies (the "proximate" causes of
infant death), and why do they catch these diseases in the first place or
why are they not swiftly cured (the "underlying" causes of mortality)? A
great deal is known about both of these questions. The tragedy of high
infant-mortality rates is that most children in the Third World die from

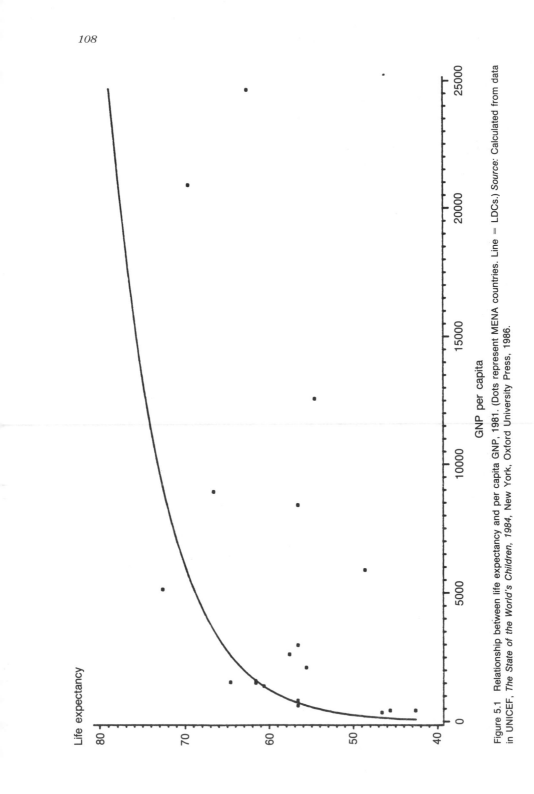

Figure 5.1 Relationship between life expectancy and per capita GNP, 1981. (Dots represent MENA countries. Line = LDCs.) *Source:* Calculated from data in UNICEF, *The State of the World's Children, 1984,* New York, Oxford University Press, 1986.

diseases that can be prevented, often at very low cost. At least 40 percent of all infant deaths are due to diarrhea.[4] Other major child killers are diphtheria, whooping cough, tetanus, measles, poliomyelitis, tuberculosis, and malaria. With the partial exception of malaria, prevention is relatively cheap with proven methods, either by inoculation or by other simple measures, described below.

UNICEF and other international health organizations now stress a package of simple practices (summarized by the acronym GOBI) whose adoption could reduce infant mortality below 50 per 1,000, a level that we have seen has been attained only by Israel and two small oil exporters of the Gulf. The acronym stands for the initials of four separate practices: growth monitoring, oral rehydration therapy, breast-feeding, immunization. Growth monitoring refers to the use of simple weight-for-age and weight-for-height charts in infant and early child care. Use of such charts can help to spot children who are malnourished and therefore susceptible to disease. Although we can all recognize a starving person, like the desperate Ethiopians shown on television in 1984, most of us cannot discern less advanced malnutrition without special training. Many mothers of malnourished children *do not know* that their children are suffering from this condition—until they become sick, when it may be too late to do much about it. But if they bring their children into clinics for regular checkups, they can be weighed and their growth progress monitored using these simple charts, which act as "early warning devices" for malnutrition and disease.

Oral rehydration therapy (ORT) is a simple package combining sugar, salt, and water, which when ingested enables the body to retain the fluids whose loss is the cause of death in fatal cases of diarrhea. The cost of such packets is less than U.S. $.05 apiece, and the mixing requires only a cup and a spoon. This is one of the most important and promising discoveries in infant health care in decades. Breast-feeding is essential for child welfare in the early months of infancy, not only because human milk is the best "formula" for humans, but also because the many antibodies in human milk provide crucial protection for the otherwise highly vulnerable infant. However, after about six months, a diet of human milk alone is inadequate and must be supplemented with other foods. And finally, immunization is strongly recommended to prevent the ravages of the major infant and child killers listed above.

Middle Eastern countries have had a mixed experience with such practices. The problem with growth charts is that their use usually requires mothers to visit clinics. There are typically too few of these in most countries of the region, and the staff is too poorly paid, to avoid significant delays and long waiting times. Consequently, many (especially poorer) residents use them only as a last resort, when the child is already sick and perhaps beyond simple treatment (U.S. Institute of Medicine 1979). In addition, in many countries such clinics are more abundant in urban than in rural areas, while too often the "treatment of patients by doctors is depersonalized and haughty" (U.S. Institute of Medicine 1979, 76). By contrast, in countries like Tunisia, "only in areas of extremely dispersed population was accessibility to some kind of health care a problem" (H. Nelson 1979, 104). But in the countries with the highest infant-mortality rates, like North Yemen and Sudan, rural outpatient clinics are rare indeed. Such deficiencies in facilities makes it difficult to practice growth monitoring, as well as to disseminate ORT.

ORT is spreading in the region, with Syria, Tunisia, Morocco, and Egypt now manufacturing their own packages of salts. There is evidence that use of this simple technique has cut Egyptian infant mortality from diarrhea by over 50% in only a few years (Nyrop 1982; UNICEF 1986). Some early Egyptian experiences with such practices yielded disappointing results, largely because of a failure to involve local community leaders and medical personnel in campaigns (UNICEF 1986), but the responsible authorities appear to have learned from these failures. Although the large majority of Middle Eastern women breast-feed their children, use of substitute infant formulas is spreading in some countries, such as YAR (Mynti 1985). One study found that Yemeni children fed with (often dirty) plastic nipples and bottles were *eight times* as likely to die as breast-fed Yemeni infants (UNICEF 1986). By contrast, breast-feeding until the age of six months appears to be nearly universal in Egypt (U.S. Institute of Medicine 1979). Finally, immunization has lagged in the region: Many children in most countries for which there exist data are *not* immunized against the major child-killing diseases. And finally, all too often, the expansion of irrigation, an agricultural investment priority, also increases the incidence of malaria.[5]

Organizations like UNICEF also stress that three other features are essential for reducing infant mortality, the so-called Three Fs: family spacing, food supplements, and female education. There is a strong correlation between infant health and the length of time between births. Too little time between births weakens the mother, thereby threatening her own health and that of her children. Such problems are clearly the result of the failure to practice contraception (since, unlike in many sub-Saharan African societies, prolonged sexual abstinence after the birth of a child is not common in the region). UNICEF estimates that as many as three out of four infant deaths in Syria could be avoided if at least twenty-four months elapsed between births (UNICEF 1986).

Food supplements are designed to break the synergies between malnutrition and disease. Not only does malnutrition reduce resistance, but also disease can engender malnutrition by impeding the body's ability to absorb or properly to utilize ingested nutrients. Compared to other Third World regions, Middle Eastern countries have done well here. The World Bank estimated that only 10% of the people of the region receive "insufficient calories for an active working life" (i.e., less than 90% of Food and Agriculture Organization/World Health Organization [FAO/WHO]-recommended caloric intake), as compared to 13% in Latin America, 14% in East Asia and the Pacific, 44% in sub-Saharan Africa, and 50% in South Asia (World Bank 1986b, 17).

However, there are important national and intranational variations. For example, as many as one in five Moroccans may be malnourished, and throughout the region, rural areas with scarce land appear to be worse off than urban areas, where extensive food-subsidy systems prevail. There are also significant class biases in nutrition. It is now widely accepted that lack of purchasing power or other access to food, not failures of national (much less global) food supplies, is the main cause of hunger everywhere (Sen 1981a; World Bank 1986b). A nationwide survey conducted in 1978 in Egypt found approximately 50% of children from low-income families suffered from mild-to-moderate protein/calorie malnutrition (U.S. Institute of Medicine 1979). And as elsewhere within disprivileged groups, the members suffering most severely from malnutrition are children and pregnant and lactating women, hence the idea of "food supplements" to bring the supply of nutrients up to the high demands of such groups. Few Middle Eastern governments have supplementary-feeding programs, although most have sharply reduced malnutrition through extensive (and costly) consumer-food-subsidy systems.

The last "F," female education, really brings us to the underlying causes of poor health in the region. A recent study of mortality determinants in developing countries argued that nations with "exceptionally good" performances (China, Sri Lanka, Kerala state in India, and Costa Rica) all had relatively high degrees of "female autonomy" (Caldwell 1986). The author also found that nine of the eleven *worst* performers are Middle Eastern, Muslim countries.[6] Since in all Third World countries women have primary responsibility for child care, it is essential that they be sufficiently well educated *and* accustomed to taking initiatives on their children's behalf. They must recognize early warning signs (such as a child's failure to grow properly), understand disease origins and preventions, and be ready and able to act immediately to seek remedies. All such behavior, of course, presupposes female literacy; Caldwell argued that this kind of basic education is only a necessary, not a sufficient, condition for such autonomy. If a woman is educated, but is not in the habit of venturing out of her home unaccompanied, he asserted, child health will still suffer.[7]

An extremely large number of Middle Eastern mothers cannot read or write. For assessing current health, the key statistic is the enrollment ratio of the 1960s and 1970s, since that is when today's (typically young) Middle Eastern mother was of school age. As the data in Table 5.4 show, in 1960 most Middle Eastern girls were *not* in school. By 1970, over half were enrolled, and by 1985, three of four Arab girls were in school (UNESCO, *Statistical Yearbook* 1987). Although some countries have shown rapid expansion in the proportion of girls enrolled in school, other nations, especially Egypt, Sudan, and Morocco, have progressed much more slowly, and even today fewer than one of five girls attend school in the YAR.

Here, as with questions of fertility, one must ask what, if any, is the role of Islam in generating the outcome of low female literacy and attendant high infant mortality. We argued in Chapter 4 that although people's (culturally derived) attitudes were obviously important, the impact of culture on fertility, child health, and women's education is affected by political systems. Regimes in overwhelmingly Islamic societies have some-

Table 5.4   Primary School Enrollment Ratios, 1960 and 1979/81 (percent of
           age group)

|  | 1960 | | 1979/81 | |
|---|---|---|---|---|
|  | Male | Female | Male | Female |
| Algeria | 55 | 37 | 106 | 81 |
| Egypt | 80 | 52 | 89 | 63 |
| Iran | 56 | 27 | 121* | 80* |
| Iraq | 94 | 36 | 112 | 110 |
| Israel | 99 | 97 | 94 | 96 |
| Jordan | 94 | 59 | 105 | 102 |
| Kuwait | 131 | 102 | 98 | 93 |
| Lebanon | 105 | 99 | 123 | 114 |
| Libya | 92 | 24 | -- | -- |
| Morocco | 67 | 27 | 95 | 58 |
| Oman | -- | -- | 81 | 43 |
| Saudi Arabia | 22 | 2 | 77 | 51 |
| Sudan | 35 | 14 | | |
| Syria | 89 | 39 | 112 | 87 |
| Tunisia | 88 | 43 | 119 | 92 |
| Turkey | 90 | 58 | 110 | 93 |
| UAE | -- | -- | 117 | 115 |
| YAR | 14 | -- | 82 | 12 |
| PDRY | 20 | 5 | 93 | 51 |

* 1977.

Note: Figures include reenrollments and thus may exceed 100.

Source: UNICEF, The State of the World's Children, 1984, New York, Oxford
University Press, 1986, pp. 120-21.

times chosen to promote female literacy and autonomy, and they have
sometimes made considerable progress. The decline in infant mortality
and the increase in enrollments of girls in primary school has been quite
rapid both under regimes espousing a socialist ideology (PDRY, Iraq, Libya,
and Syria) and under more conservative governments (Tunisia, Turkey,
Pahlavi Iran). With the exception of South Yemen, none of these regimes
is officially non-Muslim, while Libya, which has experienced very rapid
change, adheres to an explicitly (self-declared) Islamic political ideology.
It may well be, as Caldwell argued, that Islam makes it *relatively more
difficult* for a regime to foster female education and autonomy. But there
can be little doubt that quite a few regimes dominated by male Muslims
have and are rapidly expanding the enrollment and education of women.
It is plausible to predict that the decline in infant mortality rates in the
region will accelerate as the schoolgirls of the 1980s become the mothers
of the 1990s and 2000s.

## EDUCATIONAL SYSTEMS: AN OVERVIEW

As with health conditions, our assessment of Middle Eastern progress
in education depends upon whether we look at what conditions are or at
how rapidly they have improved. On the one hand, current levels of literacy

Table 5.5   Adult Literacy Rates, 1980 (percentages)

|                | Total | Male | Female |
|----------------|-------|------|--------|
| Algeria        | 42.0  | 60   | 24     |
| Egypt          | 42.0  | 56   | 28     |
| Iran           | 42.5  | 55   | 30     |
| Iraq           | 50.0  | 68   | 32     |
| Israel         | 93.5  | 96   | 91     |
| Jordan         | 65.5  | 78   | 53     |
| Kuwait         | 63.0  | 72   | 54     |
| Lebanon        | 73.5  | 83   | 64     |
| Libya          | 56.0  | 76   | 36     |
| Morocco        | 29.5  | 41   | 18     |
| Saudi Arabia   | 23.5  | 35   | 12     |
| Sudan          | 26.0  | 38   | 14     |
| Syria          | 53.5  | 72   | 35     |
| Tunisia        | 47.5  | 61   | 34     |
| Turkey         | 65.0  | 80   | 50     |
| UAE            | 24.5  | 30   | 19     |
| YAR            | 10.0  | 18   | 2      |
| PDRY           | 32.0  | 48   | 16     |

Source: UNICEF, The State of the World's Children, 1984, New York, Oxford University Press, 1986, p. 133.

in the Middle East are low; on the other hand, most nations have made rapid progress in expanding educational opportunities during the past generation. And again like health, conditions vary considerably not only from one country to another, but also between urban and rural areas, and between social classes. And finally, as stressed above, the education of women has lagged, but has advanced markedly in recent years from a very low starting point.

Overall adult-literacy levels are shown in Table 5.5. Several points stand out. First, in most countries, rates of adult literacy are unjustifiably low: In only two countries (Iraq and Israel) can more than four of five adults read and write. In a second group of countries,[8] two-thirds to three-fourths of the adults are literate. Only 60% of adult Syrians are literate, while about half of those in Algeria, Iran, Tunisia, and Qatar can read and write. In the other countries of the region, the majority of adults is illiterate. Because this last category includes three populous countries (Egypt, Morocco, and Sudan), the *majority* of all adult Middle Easteners are illiterate.

Second, as stressed above, illiteracy is concentrated among women: In only six countries of the region,[9] can a majority of adult women read and write; by contrast, in Latin America, only in Haiti and Guatemala are most women illiterate. Egyptian female literacy is lower than that in Laos and Kampuchea, two of the poorest countries in the world. Third, illiteracy in the Middle East as elsewhere is concentrated in rural areas and among the poor. Although nearly three-quarters of urban Egyptian adult males are literate, less than half of their country cousins can read and write;

roughly two-thirds of rural male Tunisians are illiterate, compared with about one-third of urban men. Although two-thirds of women in Tunisian cities, and roughly one-half of Egyptian urban women, were illiterate in the early 1980s, female illiteracy was much higher in the rural areas, about 93% in Tunisia and 87% in Egypt (Ghonemy 1984). Finally, even in those countries that have devoted large resources to primary education, there are now *more* illiterate people than there were one generation ago: With only a few exceptions, population growth has swamped a generation of efforts to diffuse basic education.

These are unpleasant facts. A comparative perspective affords little comfort. As before, two types of comparison seem apposite—those with other Third World regions and those in terms of per capita incomes. If adult literacy is our standard, the Middle East is a relatively backward region of the globe: Only South Asia has a significantly lower percentage of literate adults (35%) than does the Middle East, whose overall adult-literacy rate of about 43% is approximately the same as the rate for sub-Saharan Africa, where average incomes are far below those in the Middle East. By contrast, adult-literacy rates are *much* below those of Latin America (79%) or East Asia and the Pacific (70%) (National Research Council 1986). As the African comparison suggests, adult-literacy rates in the region are well below what we would predict on the basis of per capita incomes alone (Figure 5.2).

However, a historical perspective partially mitigates this grim picture. It is essential to remember that Middle Eastern countries started their efforts to educate their populations from a very low base. The ancien regimes of the region did essentially nothing to educate most of their people. In some cases, education of the rural poor was actively discouraged, as on the estates of wealthy Egyptians under the Farouk monarchy (Richards 1982; Adams 1986). Arab and Berber children in North Africa were either entirely excluded from education or channeled into segregated schools under French colonial rule.[10] These countries faced severe difficulties in expanding their educational facilities after independence. There was a mass exodus of teachers, nearly all of whom were Europeans: In Algeria, 27,000 of 30,000 teachers left in 1962; only one-fifth of the 20,000 new Algerian teachers were qualified (Bennoune 1988, 220). A glance at literacy rates for 1960 shows how far many countries have come since colonial days (Table 5.5), when two-thirds to three-quarters of the people of the region were illiterate. By way of comparison, when South Korea shifted its development strategy to export-led growth in the early 1960s, over 70% of the population could already read and write.

Not only do levels of literacy vary widely by country, but rates of improvement also show considerable differences. There is some dispute on how best to measure improvements in literacy. The simplest approach is to look at percentage changes in literacy rates. However, analysts like Sen have argued that this approach biases results in favor of countries that begin with low literacy rates.[11] Sen advocated instead looking at the

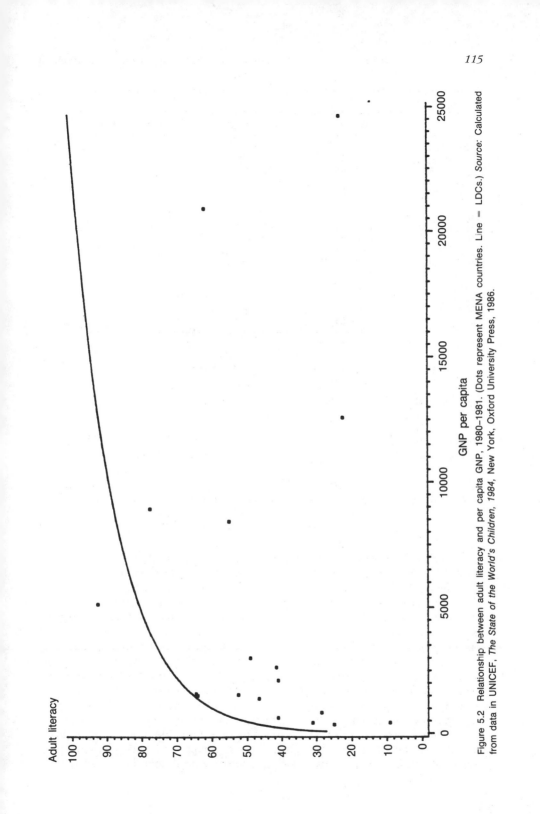

Adult literacy

GNP per capita

Figure 5.2  Relationship between adult literacy and per capita GNP, 1980–1981. (Dots represent MENA countries. Line = LDCs.) *Source:* Calculated from data in UNICEF, *The State of the World's Children, 1984,* New York, Oxford University Press, 1986.

Table 5.6   Percentage Change in "Literacy Shortfall," 1957-1985 (selected
            years)

| | Years | Change in Literacy Shortfall |
|---|---|---|
| Algeria | 1962-85 | 44 |
| Bahrain | 1959-85 | 63 |
| Egypt | 1960-85 | 25 |
| Iran | 1961-85 | 42 |
| Iraq* | 1957-85 | 88 |
| Israel | 1961-85 | 69 |
| Jordan | 1961-85 | 63 |
| Kuwait | 1962-85 | 65 |
| Libya | 1964-85 | 58 |
| Morocco | 1960-85 | 22 |
| Saudi Arabia | 1962-80 | 23 |
| Syria | 1960-85 | 43 |
| Tunisia | 1961-85 | 46 |
| Turkey | 1960-84 | 58 |
| YAR | 1962-85 | 11 |
| PDRY | 1973-85 | 20 |

* Literacy for 15-45 year olds only.

Note: "Literacy Shortfall": 100% minus actual percentage of literate
adults.

Sources: Calculated from UNESCO, Statistical Yearbooks, various years.

"percentage change in literacy shortfall," that is, in the percentage change
in the difference between actual literacy and the goal of 100% literacy
(Sen 1981b). Such a calculation is displayed in Table 5.6. Whatever the
measure, performance varies widely by country. In general, the wealthy
oil-exporting states did very well during the last generation, as did Iraq,
Israel, Jordan, and Turkey.[12] Countries like Tunisia, Syria, Algeria, and Iran
achieved less, while the records of Egypt, Morocco, Saudi Arabia, and the
Yemens are frankly dismal.

Historical legacies alone do not explain persistently high adult illiteracy.
With the exceptions of Iraq, Algeria, and the People's Democratic Republic
of Yemen (PDRY), Middle Eastern countries have largely ignored the
problem of illiterate adults, choosing instead to concentrate resources on
educating children. Here the record is rather more encouraging, although
as before, the countries of the region still have much unfinished business.
Enrollment ratios are shown in Table 5.4. Eleven countries of the region
have achieved nearly universal enrollment of boys; if we use the "percentage
change in enrollment shortfall" method to measure progress, the PDRY
has also done remarkably well, reducing the percentage of unenrolled boys
from 80% to only 7% in twenty years (Table 5.7). Enrollment of girls has
also improved considerably; four countries have all of their girls in school,
while Tunisia, Turkey, and Iran have also recorded notable progress. Change
in other countries, especially North Yemen, Egypt, and Sudan has been
quite slow over the past two decades, while enrollment rates for girls

Table 5.7  Percentage Change in "Enrollment Shortfall," 1960-1980

|  | Boys | Girls |
|---|---|---|
| Algeria* | 100 | 70 |
| Egypt | 45 | 23 |
| Iran | 100 | 84** |
| Iraq* + | 100 | 100 |
| Israel | <0 | <0 |
| Jordan* + | 100 | 100 |
| Kuwait | (undefined) | <0 |
| Lebanon* + | (undefined: no shortfall in 1960 or 1980) | 100 |
| Morocco | 78 | 42 |
| Saudi Arabia | 70 | 47 |
| Sudan | 38 | 34 |
| Syria* | 100 | 79 |
| Tunisia | 100 | 86 |
| Turkey* | 100 | 83 |
| UAE* + | 100 | 100 |
| YAR | 79 | 12 |
| PDRY | 91 | 48 |

\* Countries with all boys enrolled, 1980.
\** 1983.
+ Countries with all girls enrolled, 1980.

Source: Calculated by author, using data from Table 5.4.

actually fell in Kuwait and Israel from nearly universal enrollment. Despite the rather poor performance by populous countries like Egypt and the Sudan, a majority of boys are now in school in all countries, and 90% are enrolled in most nations. Enrollment of girls continues to lag, but this, too, has advanced rapidly in the last twenty years. The total number of children not in school has declined in most countries since 1960, in contrast to the total number of illiterate persons.[13]

Most countries of the region have made strenuous efforts to improve education. Comparisons of national budgets show a relatively high percentage of government expenditure allocated to education. Although the numbers vary considerably across years and among countries, most Middle Eastern governments devoted between 10 and 15% of their spending to education. The Arab countries spent 4.7% of GNP on education in 1983, compared with an average of 4.0 for all developing countries. In the same year Arab states spent over $120 per inhabitant on education, nearly twice as much as was spent in Latin America and nearly four times the average for LDCs (UNESCO, *Statistical Yearbook* 1985).[14] Algeria was devoting nearly 30% of its national budget to education by the mid-1970s (Bennoune 1988). Although there are exceptions (e.g., Sudan, which allocates consistently less than 10% of funds to education), lack of spending is not the major problem with most educational systems in the region.[15]

The real difficulty with most Middle Eastern educational systems is how the money is spent. Literacy rates remain low and children remain out of school because gender, urban, and class biases are rampant in many countries' educational-allocation decisions. By 1980, a higher percentage of boys attended school than the average for middle-income LDCs, while the reverse was true for girls. Nevertheless, as noted above, there have been dramatic changes in female enrollments during the last generation. Rural enrollment rates are consistently lower than urban throughout the region, while drop-out rates are higher. For example, by the late 1970s over 90% of urban Egyptian children were in school, while only 70% of rural Delta children, and 60% of rural Upper Egyptian children, were enrolled (Nyrop 1982). While primary enrollment rates in 1977 in Algiers and Oran were over 85%, in some rural districts (e.g., Djelfa), they were less than 50% (Bennoune 1988).

The reasons for this lie on both the supply and the demand sides. Many widely dispersed rural children are far from any school. Countries that insist on separate schools for girls and boys multiply the costs of schooling. It is especially difficult to attract women teachers to rural areas. At the same time, many rural families see no point in educating all of their children. It is quite common in the region for rural families to make sacrifices to educate at least one son; one study of Turkey found that the highest rates of return to investment in education were obtained by the sons of farmers attending primary school (Özgediz 1980), while observers of rural Egypt often note how peasant families will try to educate at least one son through high school, hoping that he can obtain a very secure government job. However, educating all children and especially all daughters is expensive and has low priority. Children can and do contribute to peasant-family budgets at young ages by tending animals, helping with processing, harvesting cotton, weaving rugs, and so forth. And peasant attitudes toward women's status die hard: Upper Egyptian peasants asserted to one researcher recently that sending girls to school was "shameful" (Adams 1986, 142).

However, it is not simply high costs, peasant attitudes, and home economics that impede universalizing primary education in the region. Only a few countries have made investment in rural and/or female education a top priority of their educational plans; funds go elsewhere. Indeed, many countries of the region display class bias in their educational expenditures and enrollment profiles. Middle Eastern secondary education and, even more so, university training, are overwhelmingly urban, male, and middle class. Although 28.6% of all Third World students were in secondary schools and universities, 34.3% of Arab students were in the higher grades (UNESCO *Statistical Yearbook* 1975, 1980). As usual, there are significant differences among countries: In the Yemens, Algeria, and Tunisia, the rate of growth of secondary enrollments from 1960 to 1976 was typically about 20%, while in Egypt, Jordan, Syria, Iran, Libya, and Kuwait, the corresponding rates usually exceeded 40%. In Morocco during the period 1971–1977, primary enrollment grew at 6% per year, secondary by 10%, while university enrollment tripled (UNESCO *Statistical Yearbook* 1975, 1980).

Such allocations are extremely difficult to justify economically; much evidence suggests that, if educational spending is (properly) treated as an investment, the social rates of return[16] are highest to investment in *primary* education. Calculations in the early 1970s suggested that the social rates of return to primary education were more than twice as high as those to university education. Furthermore, although the private rates of return exceed the social for all educational levels, the divergence increases at the higher grades, rising from a gap of only 4% (29% versus 25%) for primary education to nearly 10% at the university level (22% versus 12%) (Psacharopoulos 1980; Colclough 1982). Politics, not economics, dictates the bias in favor of secondary and, especially, higher education.

The politics of this all-too-common distortion in the allocation of human-capital spending is not hard to understand. First, there is, of course, some complementarity between diffusing primary education and widening more advanced educational opportunities: Someone has to do the teaching, and a growing, industrializing economy needs more advanced skills as well as basic literacy and numeracy. This need is especially acute in countries that inherit little skilled labor from colonialism or the ancien regime and that are eager to defend their independence. Given the "national project" of Arab Socialist, Atatürkist, and other early developmentalist regimes in the region, it is hardly surprising that they vigorously promoted the development of university training.

Second, the urban middle classes had greater influence on policy. Planners themselves typically come from such backgrounds, and regimes sought to open more "room at the top," via greater access to higher education, as a mechanism of income redistribution. And since the private rate of return to higher education remains very high, middle-class families press for space in the universities. Regimes wishing to mollify this social group responded by rapidly expanding secondary and higher education.

Egypt provides perhaps the most striking case of class bias in education.[17] Although the average ratio of enrollments in primary and secondary schools and universities in middle-income LDCs is 10:4:1, in Egypt the corresponding ratio is 10:6:2 (Kavalsky 1980). Such enrollment ratios and such a pattern of educational development in Egypt strongly suggest that the middle and lower-middle classes were favored over the mass of the population: The ratios suggest that in comparison with similar countries, Egypt's educational system is top heavy, with a disproportionate share of students in secondary school and universities. Although less than half of adult Egyptians can read and write, a full generation after Nasser's revolution, the country boasts thirteen universities. Although the number of primary and secondary students tripled between 1952 and 1972, the number of university students quadrupled .The government made university education especially attractive by offering heavy subsidies for students and by guaranteeing a government job to any graduate. Even ignoring the fact that many of these graduates acquired only marginally useful skills, there is little doubt that the country's development would have been better served by shifting resources out of more advanced education toward primary schooling. Recently there have been changes in educational policies, particularly, the cessation of the job guarantee for university graduates and the slowing of enrollment growth: From 1975 to 1980, university enrollments were permitted to grow at only 1.1% per year (Ikram 1981, 129).

Other commonly voiced complaints about Middle Eastern education are that the quality of education is very low, that drop-out rates are high, and that too few students master technical subjects, especially math and science. One in five Algerian primary school students leaves before completing the curriculum (Bennoune 1988). In Morocco, about one-third of university students study technical or scientific studies, 56% study the humanities and social sciences, while the remaining 12% are preparing to be teachers (*Annuaire Statistique du Maroc* 1984). It is very likely that these choices are individually rational; a recent study of Egyptian higher education argued that Middle Eastern students, like their counterparts in the West, select careers with an eye on the job market (Psacharopoulos 1980). Thus although agricultural studies retain their traditionally "low status" in the country, many students enroll in them because of expanding placement opportunities. If students are not developing the proper skills, it is because the society and, especially, the state is not sending them the correct signals.

One way to use the relatively swollen numbers of university and secondary students in countries with many illiterate adults would be to launch adult-literacy campaigns. However, only a few states of the region have ever tried to do this. In most cases, the explanation seems to be that the government fears the political impact of such campaigns: The students or the young people who will go to the slums and villages may hold more radical political views than the regime. Governments in Morocco, the Sudan, and Egypt may plausibly fear fostering contact between Marxist or, more likely, Muslim Revivalist students and the large numbers of illiterate adults, many of whom might be sympathetic to the political messages that usually are imparted along with literacy in such campaigns. Only if a regime feels politically secure and believes that it can control and shape the content of the materials used in literacy campaigns will such efforts occur.

It is no accident that the three countries that have tried to mount adult-literacy campaigns are Algeria, the PDRY, and Iraq: Each is ruled by a single political party, with a more or less well-defined ideology and with considerable experience in mass-mobilization techniques. However, only the Iraqi campaign seems to have succeeded in dramatically reducing adult illiteracy. The relatively difficult problems of the the other campaigns were mainly due to the lack of sufficient educated cadres to carry them out. In both Algeria and the PDRY, very few Arabs had been educated under the colonial regimes; still fewer were available for the arduous work of going into the countryside and slums to educate peasants and workers. However, the South Yemenis have continued to push for adult education, holding compulsory adult-literacy classes in all places of employment, and displaying considerable tenacity: Although the results of the campaigns of the mid-1970s were somewhat disappointing, the government proclaimed a second major campaign in 1983. This persistence is very likely to pay off in the near future.

The Iraqi campaign illustrates what can be done when an oil-rich state wants to diffuse adult literacy. The Ba'athists had long had an ideological commitment to the goal of universal literacy. They also had the resources that the oil boom of the 1970s provided. There had been literacy campaigns during the 1960s, but these had foundered through lack of information on the characteristics of illiterates, inadequate and insufficient textbooks, paucity of funds, and low motivation of the adult learners. From 1971 to 1978 the government conducted crash campaigns to train teachers. In November 1977 it conducted a census to determine the characteristics of the illiterate: 2.2 million illiterates, aged 15 to 45, of whom 70% were women. The government then passed laws requiring attendance at adult-literacy classes, made extensive use of trade unions and other "popular organizations," daily use of TV, and so forth. Different textbooks were prepared for peasants, workers, housewives, and soldiers.

As usual, these texts contained strong ideological messages: In Iraq, as in the PDRY, adult-education campaigns have been used to disseminate the regime's image of itself and of the society it hopes to build. To ensure female participation in classes, nurseries were provided. The impact seems to have been considerable: 84% of the target population attended classes, and many women left home for the first time to attend. The cost was high: Over $700 million was spent, a cost of approximately $350 per person reached by the campaign (Sousa 1982). But most development specialists would agree with the Baghdad regime that the investment was well worth it.

Increasing classroom size has not been a problem in Middle Eastern primary education. Indeed, available data indicate that the pupil-teacher ratio has declined in virtually all countries: Despite the increasing enrollments, the numbers of teachers has expanded more rapidly still. In any case, there is little evidence that learning or later performance is linked to class size (Colclough 1982). Of course, one may well question the *quality* of the teachers whose numbers have grown so rapidly: From 1970 to 1983 the number of primary teachers nearly doubled, the number of secondary teachers more than doubled, while the number of university teachers nearly tripled (UNESCO *Statistical Yearbook* 1975, 1980).

Probably more important than class size are pedagogical methods, teacher quality, and morale. All too often, primary schools mimic traditional *madrasa*s (Islamic schools, where boys memorize parts of the Koran), with their emphasis on rote learning, rather than stressing problem solving, writing skills, or creativity. Few teachers, especially in poorer areas, have access to any materials but simple textbooks and paper; even these may be in short supply. Teachers in the Middle East do not enjoy markedly high social status, and rural postings are too often assigned to those with the worst academic performance. The pay is typically quite low, in common with that of all civil servants.

Given such working conditions in the poorer countries, it is hardly surprising that many teachers seek employment in the oil states. Egyptian schoolteachers can make a minimum of *ten times* their domestic salaries in Saudi Arabia or Kuwait; small wonder that more than 50,000 of them are working abroad, while thousands more are seeking to leave. Indeed, one of the difficulties with maintaining, much less advancing, the educational systems of countries like Sudan and YAR is the departure of the small number of trained teachers to the Gulf States. More than 5,000 Sudanese teachers are *officially* out of the country, and the actual numbers are probably double that figure (Birks and Sinclair 1980a). It is clear that Sudanese teachers prefer working at high pay in the relative physical comfort of Saudi Arabia to enduring the low pay and extremely difficult living conditions of the rural Sudan.

Although a more extensive discussion of the consequences of international migration is offered in Chapter 14, a few points on the impact of migration on the educational systems of both sending and receiving countries are in order. First, given the extremely low levels of adult literacy in most of the major oil exporters, the rapid expansion of their primary enrollments required large-scale importation of teachers. Second, such teachers had to be fluent in Arabic; consequently, Egyptians as well as Jordanians and Palestinians were prominently represented. Third, such teachers usually dramatically improved their private welfare. Fourth, there is little evidence that such emigration outflows exceeded the recruitment and training of new teachers; as noted above, pupil-teacher ratios continued to fall during the 1970s in Egypt, Jordan, and other major suppliers of teachers. Fifth, although this implies that there were few negative consequences of the export of teachers in countries with high enrollment ratios, the same argument is much weaker in Egypt and the Sudan. After all, the favorable pupil-teacher ratios were achieved in part by slow growth of the numerator, by sluggish improvement in the (low) percentage of Egyptian and Sudanese children in school.

## SECONDARY AND VOCATIONAL EDUCATION

Prior to direct European control and the consolidation of large bureaucratic state systems, literacy in the Middle East was a skill limited to a relative few and, among Muslims, one valued more for providing access to the sacred text of the Koran than for its contribution to everyday life. As the range of government activities grew, so too did the need for literate, white-collar staff: clerks, accountants, and, although not many, managers.

After World War I, nationalist movements throughout the Middle East put mass education at the top of their list of demands. Their concerns were twofold. First, it seemed to nationalist leaders that Europe's strength in large measure stemmed from its educational systems and educated citizenries. As long as Middle Eastern societies were deprived of such systems and citizens, the societies would remain backward and subjugated.

Second, these same leaders decried the elitism inherent in the new school systems promoted by colonial powers in the Middle East. Secondary education was limited to a narrow stratum of the population, often the offspring of the indigenous well-to-do, whom the colonial authorities wished to keep on their side. The object of the systems was to produce the clerks necessary to staff the colonial administration itself as well as the banks and businesses that sustained the economic links between the colony and the metropole. Only a handful of Middle Easterners ever received a university education. With the exception of Cairo University, universities in Istanbul and Ankara set up by the independent Turkish republic, and the American University of Beirut, there were no universities in the region. The very fortunate could go to the United Kingdom (UK), France, Germany, or even the United States for advanced studies. In Algeria on the eve of the revolutionary war in 1954, out of a native population of 10 million, only 7,000 were in secondary school and only 600 had gone on to university-level studies. Although the elitism of the Algerian situation was more pronounced than elsewhere, it was a difference in degree, not in kind (for more on colonial Algeria see Chapter 15).

Thus the colonial authorities could and did use the educational system as an instrument to bestow favors on select groups and to produce the staff that would work in the trenches of the colonial administration. The nationalist leaders who criticized the elitism and manipulativeness of these policies knew whereof they spoke: Overwhelmingly they were among the elite and not infrequently cogs in the colonial administration's wheels.

In the interwar years a number of ideas became rooted in the popular mind, among them the belief that education and literacy are the rights of all citizens and not privileges. Once independence was achieved, nationalist leaders were held to this notion. In addition, the link between secondary education and stable, respectable white-collar employment was firmly established. All, from peasants and tradespeople to craftsmen and manual laborers, saw their children's education as the key to moving upward in society and also as a hedge against the day they would be too old or infirm to work.

The new states of the Middle East kept their promises in various ways. On the one hand, there was the temptation to yield to popular pressure and open the gates of secondary and university education nearly as wide as those of primary education. In most cases the financial costs of such a policy appeared prohibitive. Typically, per-student outlays in secondary school are two to three times higher than in primary school, and university outlays may be ten times higher. The demands for and costs of teacher training for secondary education are also commensurately higher. Alongside these concerns was the realization that the economy needed skilled craftspeople, technicians, and low-level supervisory personnel as much or more than it needed civil servants. The upshot is that in all Middle Eastern countries there is a marked selection process that takes place between primary (or preparatory) and secondary school. Some comparative figures are presented in Table 5.8.

Table 5.8   Percentage of Eligible Population Enrolled in Secondary School, 1976
            and 1984

|                    | 1976 | 1984 |
|--------------------|------|------|
| Algeria            | 19   | 47   |
| Egypt              | 42   | 58   |
| Iran               | 48   | 51   |
| Iraq               | 38   | 67   |
| Israel             | 39   | 74   |
| Kuwait             | 60   | 82   |
| Libya              | 65   | --   |
| Morocco            | 17   | 31   |
| Saudi Arabia       | 19   | 38   |
| Sudan              | 13   | 19   |
| Syria              | 50   | 59   |
| Tunisia            | 20   | 32   |
| Turkey             | 29   | 38   |
| YAR                | 4    | 10   |
| PDRY               | 19   | 19   |
|                    |      |      |
| France             | 85   | 90   |
| Japan              | 92   | 95   |
| Republic of Korea  | 63   | 91   |
| United States      | --   | 95   |

Source: World Bank, World Development Report, New York, Oxford University
Press, 1979, pp. 170-71; 1987, pp. 262-63.

The figures need to be taken with caution. Why the revolutionary PDRY has such low and unchanging secondary enrollments is inexplicable. Those with the lowest enrollment ratios in general are also the poorest economically, e.g., the Sudan and the YAR, but oil-rich Saudi Arabia's is surprisingly low (a reflection of low female enrollments?). The richest economies also have the highest enrollment ratios, e.g., Kuwait, Israel, and Iraq, while Algeria appears to have expanded its secondary system more rapidly than any of the other countries. But not even the highest MENA ratios approach those of upper-income countries. In 1984 the ratio in the United States was 95%; in Japan, 95%; in France, 90%; and in South Korea, 91% (a figure worth noting).

In an intermediate position in economic wealth and enrollments are states like Egypt, Iran, or Syria that have gone far to reduce the elitism of secondary education. The democratization process started in Egypt even before the military seized power in 1952. The main nationalist party, the Wafd, controlled the government and parliament in 1950 and, in what Kerr termed "a demagogic bid" (1965, 176), not only opened the secondary schools to anyone who successfully completed primary school, but also made instruction tuition free. After the abolition of the monarchy and the establishment of the Egyptian republic, the Free Officers continued these policies. In 1957 a usually tame Egyptian parliament rose up against an attempt to restrict admission of secondary school graduates to university and imposed a policy of tuition-free admission to universities for any Egyptian in possession of a secondary school diploma. A fatal sequence was thus established: All primary school graduates could go to secondary school, all secondary school graduates to university, and all university graduates were entitled to a government job.

Between 1952–1953 and 1976–1977 the number of secondary school students in Egypt rose from 181,789 to 796,411, or at a rate of 14% per annum. Primary school enrollment rose at exactly half that rate and university enrollments at more than double, or 32% per annum. None of this made educational or economic sense. Degrees were debased; they no longer certified known skill or educational levels and consequently lost their earning power. Tens of thousands of secondary school students were being turned out with inappropriate or poorly acquired knowledge. Universities, swamped by numbers, could do little to improve upon the job done at the secondary level. For most of the 75,000 graduates per year that the Egyptian universities were dumping upon the job market by the early 1980s, the government would have to create fictitious jobs. There was nothing fictitious, however, about the low salaries, relative to inflation, that they would receive and the promotion paths, clogged with the accumulated masses of their predecessors, that they would face. In these circumstances secondary school education could no longer be seen as the key to financial security, a good marriage, white-collar respectability, and support for parents in their old age.

This same bleak and politically ominous scenario can be run for a number of other states, especially those that followed programs of state-centered socialism (Egypt, Syria, Iraq, Tunisia, and Algeria, in particular). But due to fundamental similarities in demographic change, all Middle Eastern states suffer to some extent from this problem. We should add that as in the case of rapid population growth itself, the "problem" is one posed for the society and economy as a whole. For any *individual* some education is better than none at all, and the chance to be frustrated in one's career aspirations is better than to be denied those aspirations in the first place.

With that in mind, we may turn briefly to Morocco, a former French protectorate, a monarchy with no socialist pretensions, and, as shown in Table 5.9, a country where there is a severe weeding out of students between primary and secondary school. Yet here again we see an accelerated expansion of secondary and university enrollments while primary school enrollments increase slowly. In the latter years of this table, 1976–1977, educational outlays at all levels represented 15.5% of GDP. It is important to remember that as secondary and university enrollments grow more rapidly than primary, their share of total outlays grows even more rapidly. Per-student outlays in 1976 were 460 dirhams at the primary level, 1,913 dirhams at the secondary, and 6,262 dirhams at the university levels (in 1976, U.S. $1 = 4.4 dirhams).

In sum, the costly effort throughout the region to expand secondary and university education has to some extent backfired because it has proved impossible to maintain exacting standards of instruction at the same time.

Table 5.9   Enrollments in Morocco's Educational System, 1966/67-1976/77

|         | Primary | | Secondary | | University | |
|---------|---------------------|---------------------------|---------------------|---------------------------|---------------------|---------------------------|
|         | No. of Students | Rate of Annual Increase | No. of Students | Rate of Annual Increase | No. of Students | Rate of Annual Increase |
| 1966/67 | 1,072,721 |     | 241,730 |      | 6,799  |      |
| 1970/71 | 1,175,277 | 2.3 | 298,880 | 5.9  | 15,111 | 30.5 |
| 1976/77 | 1,667,773 | 6.9 | 524,555 | 12.6 | 45,085 | 33.0 |

Source: Mohammed Souali and Mekki Merrouni, "Question de l'Enseignement au Maroc," Bulletin Economique et Social du Maroc, Numéro quadruple 143-46, 1981, pp. 90-128.  Figures also include public and private primary and secondary schools.

Few young Americans can imagine what this system is like on a day-to-day basis. Schools, whether urban or rural, are primitive; drafty and cold in the winter, ovenlike in the spring. They are run-down due to inadequate budgets for maintenance: There may be no or very little artificial lighting, broken windows, missing blackboards, primitive and insalubrious plumbing, classrooms crowded with benches and desks looking like relics from a war zone. The din has to be heard to be believed. The students who suffer through this are often ill clothed and fed and must return to homes where there is no place to study and perhaps little understanding among the older generation of what modern education is all about.

It is moot under these circumstances whose morale is lower, that of the students or that of the teachers. For the latter, pay is low, teacher-student ratios extremely high, and support equipment nonexistent. That teachers resort to rote learning punctuated by long periods of chanting and calisthenics in what passes for the schoolyard is hardly surprising. Nor is their absenteeism. Young male teachers, thrust as bachelors into village schools, face long periods of sexual and social frustration. The teaching profession, like the diplomas it produces, has lost its prestige. Normal schools attract the least capable university students. It is a miracle that the system functions at all.

In this situation, privileged classes have reproduced themselves in part through their ability to put their children through an educational process that gives them career advantages and excludes most of their compatriots of a similar age. Thus, despite the professed ideal of the region's governments to make the educational system without cost and open to all, a number of practices have developed that have maintained its class bias.

One avenue is offered through private schools, although it is safe to say that nowhere in the Middle East is there a truly elite system of private secondary schools such as one finds in the United States, the UK, or even India. At one time Victoria College in Alexandria, Egypt, or Robert College in Istanbul played such a role, but that is no longer the case. Christian missionary schools in the past were occasionally sought out because of high-quality education and foreign-language training. But their day, in societies that are preponderantly Muslim, has passed. The Christian minority of Lebanon has always maintained good private educational institutions, and perhaps even the civil war has failed to disrupt them. It may be that today we are witnessing a resurgence of private Muslim education, although it appears to be confined largely to primary education. Its aim is, however, to safeguard Muslim values and practices rather than to promote the interests of a privileged class.

A second prop for the protection of privilege comes through the acquisition of foreign languages, especially English. Whether one points toward a career in industry, foreign trade, or banking and finance, mastering English, German, or French may be requisite to rising to the top. This brings us to the consequences, perhaps unintended, perhaps not, of Arabization, or Persianization, or Turkishization. Having all one's young citizens learn the national language is a logical and laudable policy, a blow for democratization and cultural revitalization. But those who learn *only* Arabic, Turkish, or Persian will be able to rise only so far in the civil service, in professions such as medicine or engineering, or in modern industry and finance. Some critics have seen in the efforts to Arabize a plot on the part of the privileged to keep control of the commanding heights, for their children can afford secondary schools with quality instruction in foreign languages and are likely to do their university studies abroad or in disciplines that require foreign-language competency.

This question is most relevant for ex-French North Africa. There indigenous civil service and professional elites were educated almost exclusively in French. Even after independence, French continued to be the official language of the government and the military. Such a situation was seen as absurd as the great bulk of the local populations were Arabic speaking and thus unable to share the discourse of those who governed them. The governments of Tunisia, Algeria, and Morocco began to Arabize school and then university curricula while slowly promoting Arabic as the main language of government. In theory, a North African today, monolingual in Arabic, has an equal chance with one who knows more than one language to achieve any position in society. In practice, it is probably still the case that access to technocratic and intellectual elites requires a mastery of French or English. The offspring of incumbent elites are the most likely to have that competency.

In many Middle Eastern societies the public school system may be the only one available to the well-off. Facilities and teaching quality are supposed to be uniform throughout the system. Everywhere it is the central government that finances school budgets, so the local tax base is not relevant to school quality. Still, it is the case that schools in urban areas are better equipped and staffed than in the rural world, and schools in wealthier districts tend to have lower student-teacher ratios and an atmosphere more conducive to learning. These kinds of variations in what are supposed to be systems of uniform quality are common throughout the world. One may add to them the fact that while the public system is free to all eligible children, the well-off can afford books, pens, and pencils, decent clothing, and decent food and housing for their offspring, giving them a range of material advantages over the poor.

Going well beyond these types of class bias is the phenomenon of tutorials. Most of our evidence is drawn from Egypt, but the logic of the phenomenon is so compelling that we feel that it must manifest itself elsewhere as well. In Egypt at the end of the secondary cycle students sit for a general exam. The scores obtained on the exam determine the university faculties to which the student will gain admission. Engineering and medicine require the highest scores and are, indeed, the most sought-after faculties. In short, high scores on the secondary school exam determine access to the faculties that will produce the next generation of elite members.

Enter the underpaid teacher and the anxious middle-class parent. The teacher wants to supplement his or her meager income, and the parent wants to give his or her child a leg up. The result is fee-based tutorials to prepare for the exams. Depending on the subject matter and the number of students in the tutorial, the fees can be very high, sometimes more than what a low-income Egyptian may earn in a year. In this manner a parallel educational system grows up, based on fees, a system that favors the rich and penalizes the poor. The parallel system helps ensure that the children of the well-to-do accede in disproportionate numbers to those professional disciplines that will be most highly regarded in terms of income and prestige. Akeel and Moore (1977) found that in the 1960s when the engineering profession was particularly attractive, given Egypt's big push in industry and construction, 43% percent of a sample of Egyptian engineering students came from bourgeois or "aristocratic" strata. Today, medicine, business, and computer sciences may be the hot fields, but the class bias has likely continued.

Having stressed educational strategies that reflect class bias, we must even more strongly emphasize that the mass educational systems set up in most Middle Eastern countries have been catalysts for real social mobility. The evidence for this assertion is fragmentary; systematic studies of the socioeconomic background of secondary and university-level students have not been carried out. We do not know how profound has been the democratization process in higher education.

All indications, however, point in the same direction, to wit, that the children of lower-middle-income strata, the petty bourgeoisie of crafts- and service people, the clerks, the teachers, and the agrarian smallholders, have seized the educational opportunities offered to them and moved well beyond their fathers in status and wealth. The phenomenon was first observed in the 1930s when in various countries admission to institutes of higher education, but most important, to officers' candidate schools, was determined by competitive examination. Hard-working, ambitious, intelligent young offspring of the lower-middle class outperformed all others and entered educational and professional domains that had been reserved to the upper classes. Gamal 'Abd al-Nasser, the son of a rural functionary, and a number of others who overthrew the Egyptian monarchy in 1952, entered the military academy between 1936 and 1938 and attained the rank of colonel in the postwar years. A similar process got under way in Syria a few years later and yielded Hafiz al-Assad and other officers of rural, lower-middle-class background.

With independence, the process accelerated. One of the most striking examples is that of Damascus University, where in 1968 half the student body was of rural origin, and only 65% of the students had fathers with university education (Hinnebusch 1979, 28–29). Rapidly expanding public bureaucracies, educational systems, state enterprises, and military establishments provided a growing job market for these young people. They also become functionaries in some of the more coherently organized political parties like the Republican People's party in Turkey, the Ba'ath party of Syria and Iraq, and the Neo- (now Socialist) Destour party of Tunisia. By contrast, it would appear that the offspring of peasants, salaried workers, and common laborers—that is, the majority of the low-income strata—have not gained access to secondary and university education in numbers that come near to being proportional to their weight in society. This simply reflects their lower representation in the primary school system (see above). Cutting across income levels is the continued bias against females throughout the educational system. Thus the democratization of education in the Middle East has been incomplete and promises to remain so in the future.

In recent years in many parts of the Middle East, there have been reassessments of mass-educational policies and sometimes timid, camouflaged attempts to slow the rate of increase in secondary school enrollments and to restrict admission to the universities. Such attempts are usually accompanied by efforts to orient primary school students and those who fail general secondary school exams toward vocational-training institutes. As in the United States, such institutes have been regarded as dead ends, and students and parents alike have gone to great lengths to avoid them. In Algeria in 1982, rumors circulated that the government intended to restrict university admission to only 5% of those completing secondary school. Furthermore, it was rumored that the government would not necessarily admit to university those passing the equivalent of a university entrance exam, the *baccalauréat*. In 1982, for instance, 100,000 Algerians passed that exam. The alternative to be offered was vocational, technical, and teacher training. On the strength of these rumors, widespread rioting among secondary school students broke out in Oran and other western Algerian cities.

All governments of the region have for years stressed the need for vocational and technical training for their youth. Egypt's goal in 1985 was to provide primary and preparatory education to all children and then orient 60% of all secondary students toward vocational and technical training. The remaining 40% would follow the traditional secondary school curriculum, with admission to university as the final target.

Egypt is a long way from achieving this distribution, as are all other states in the area. In the late 1970s about 18% of all Egyptian secondary-level students were in vocational and technical-training institutions. The Arab country with the highest proportion was Tunisia, with 22%, while Jordan had 13%. All the other states ranged between 2 and 6% (R. Paul Shaw 1983, 169). Again, if we take Egypt as representative, we find that most of the vocational students are being trained in commerce, probably simple accountancy, and relatively few in industry and skilled trades. As in many developing countries, there is still a marked preference for white-collar, desk-bound employment. The old respect for craftsmen does not appear to have survived into the twentieth century. Even when herded into vocational education, Middle Eastern students opt for potentially white-collar skills in accountancy rather than certifying themselves as electricians, mechanics, or plumbers.

These attitudes may be changing, however. The great construction boom of the 1970s in the Gulf States created a heavy demand for masons, carpenters, electricians, and the like. Wages for these trades rose rapidly not only in the oil-rich countries importing labor but in the sending countries as well. Within a few years, plumbers or mechanics in Egypt could earn far more than a university-educated civil servant. Moreover, in addition to the oil boom, a technological transformation of the region was taking place. Let us consider a few simple examples. In the cities, high-rise buildings entail elevators, which in turn require maintenance. The spread of air-conditioning in places of work and private homes also requires maintenance. Tractors and diesel pumps in the countryside likewise demand servicing. In short, there is a booming market for skilled repair persons. Substantial incomes can be earned in these fields, but that realization is slow in dawning on a populace obsessed with the respectability of university education and white-collar jobs.

It is not at all clear that a bigger public effort to promote vocational training would remove these bottlenecks. Too often, it appears, vocational training is mired in routine. There is little interaction with the markets for which the students are presumably being trained. The same skills are taught in the same way year after year without regard to changing needs and changing technologies. The result is students who may have to be retrained by their employers.

In fact it may make good sense for public authorities to help likely employers to design their own on-the-job training. For many trades this takes place anyway through the traditional system of master and apprentice. If one looks in any auto mechanic's workshop or notices who is carrying the plumber's tool bag, one is likely to see a boy learning the trade. Whether or not he also goes to school is irrelevant. He may be paid little more than subsistence, but working side by side with the master he will become familiar with a range of real-life situations—such as dismantling five different kinds of automobile engines—that the vocational trainee will not face.

On-the-job training in larger enterprises should be strengthened. The enterprise management knows its present and future needs far better than any government ministry, and it would have a strong incentive to do the training job well. State educational institutions have faced enough challenge in teaching functional literacy and numeracy that they might be content with performing those tasks better. Public efforts in vocational training could best be directed at helping design and finance on-the-job training programs that respond to real labor needs. There is also a major role for public authorities to play in retraining people rendered obsolete by changing technologies. The armed forces have, in general, been underutilized as an instrument for imparting technical skills to an important segment of the region's male youth.

The secondary and vocational school environment provides a special political chemistry. The main actors, students and teachers, have particular characteristics. The teachers are themselves young and most often male. They are of course educated but may well have aspired to a loftier or more remunerative career than teaching. As mentioned earlier, they may have too few resources and too many students to carry out their job effectively. Often they are politically aware, if not active, and there is some evidence that in recent years some of them have been ready recruits for Muslim fundamentalist movements. In the Arab countries, they may be monolingual in Arabic and resent the fact that this precludes their ascension to elite status. In sum, secondary school teachers are seldom content with their lot or with the system for which they work.

The same can be said for many secondary school students. Although they may have survived the screening process after primary school, access to university-level studies will be available to, at most, a quarter of them. And for those in vocational schools that possibility does not exist at all. We have then physically mature adolescents, often from low-income backgrounds, a cut above the mass of primary school students and with ambitions to match. They too are politically aware and at a point in their lives when high-risk political action may appeal to their sense of adventure or at least relieve their frustration. In their teachers they may find mentors, not much older than themselves, who can focus their actions.

Finally there is the school itself, a physical locale that brings the actors together on a day-to-day basis. As is the case for the mosque or the church, it is very difficult for the authorities to control political activities among people who congregate in a perfectly legal manner. When there are disturbances in schools, they are highly visible and noisy and spill out to disrupt life in entire city neighborhoods or small rural towns. The issues that trigger protests, the violence that may ensue, the reprisals, arrests, police beatings, immediately resonate through a much broader stratum of the population—parents, siblings, and other relatives, who all have a stake in the secondary student's education. A student protest over poor food in the canteen or increased fees may rapidly activate many people with a more extensive list of grievances (we shall return to some of these issues in Chapter 10).

These patterns are neither very new nor unique to the Middle East. Some of the region's better known political leaders came out of the teaching corps or received their political baptism as secondary school students. Probably the single most important Muslim political leader of the first half of the twentieth century was the Egyptian Hassan al-Banna, monolingual in Arabic and a primary school teacher, who founded the Muslim Brotherhood in 1929. Of a very different political persuasion were Michel Aflaq and Salah Bitar, Syrian secondary school teachers, who founded the Ba'ath party, which now rules in Syria and Iraq. Several of the nationalist movements in the Middle East, such as the Neo-Destour party of Tunisia, the Istiqlal of Morocco, the National Liberation Front (FLN) of Algeria, the Wafd of Egypt, and the Ba'ath, relied to some extent on schoolteachers and students to develop the local infrastructure of their organizations.

Whether we consider the adolescent Gamal 'Abd al-Nasser experimenting with the Young Egypt party (Misr al-Fatat) in the 1930s, or the lycée student Ait Ahmad Hocine, who was a militant in the Algerian People's party (PPA) and later one of the six historic chiefs of the Algerian revolution, we see a pattern of the political awakening and active political involvement of secondary school students from the 1930s on.

Leaders of the independent countries of the region are acutely aware of the strategic importance of both students and teachers at this level. Habib Bourguiba of Tunisia was able to harness them to his Neo-Destour party but lost some of them to his more militant rival in that party, Salah Ben Yussef. The shah of Iran, after 1963, tried to mobilize students and teachers in literacy campaigns in the countryside, while Houari Boumedienne, president of socialist Algeria, put them to work in 1972 on a survey of landholdings prior to an agrarian reform (Leca 1975). Kemal Atatürk and his successor, Ismet Inönü, saw secondary school teachers as the vehicles for promoting the secular values of the Turkish republic. Village institutes were created to train rural youth to be teachers and to carry the message of republicanism, secularism, and statism to the traditional rural populations. People's houses, functioning as local cultural centers, were set up to propagate the new credo to people outside the school system. In Egypt, during its most pronounced socialist phase in the mid-1960s, the single party, the Arab Socialist Union, relied on local schoolteachers, veterinarians, co-op officials, and other white-collar functionaries to break the influence of local landowning groups (Harik 1974, 81–100).

The foundations of regimes tremble when the regimes lose their grip on these actors. In November 1968, after an Israeli helicopter raid deep in Egypt had revealed the porousness of Egypt's air defense, secondary-level students triggered riots in Mansura, Alexandria, and Cairo that required military intervention to put down. In the course of the riots, the regime itself was denounced for its authoritarianism and corruption. It was probably President Nasser's most severe challenge in fourteen years of rule. A different kind of challenge was launched during widespread rioting in several Moroccan cities in January 1984. The spark had come from secondary school students protesting increases in school fees. The protests soon escalated into riots involving large segments of the population opposed to government-decreed increases in the prices of basic commodities. The police were unable to contain the disturbances, and the army, as in Egypt, had to be called in to put them down. Hundreds of people were killed (*MERIP Reports,* October 1984, pp. 3–10). King Hassan immediately rescinded the price increases. Turkey, in the late 1970s, was annually graduating half a million secondary students. Only a tenth of them could hope to enter the universities. One Turkish political party, the fascist National Action party, made a concerted and successful effort to recruit these youths. They became the shock troops of violent clashes with left-wing groups. The violence was so widespread that the Turkish armed forces seized power in September 1980 to restore order (Keyder 1979). Regimes that have to call upon the armed forces to deal with their own citizenry are under severe strain, but if the regimes hesitate to do so, as in Turkey in 1979, the military may take matters into its own hands.

## THE UNIVERSITIES

Prior to the twentieth century, the Middle East had no modern public universities. There were a few higher institutes of Islamic studies such as the Qarawiyin in Fez, Morocco, and the prestigious al-Azhar of Egypt. The first university on the Western model in the region was the American University of Beirut. It was private and established as part of the Protestant Mission in Lebanon. By 1925 Cairo University had been chartered as a fully public institution, and national universities were started in Turkey and Iran. The Hebrew University was founded in Jerusalem, in Mandate Palestine, in 1925. But these aside, there were no universities in the region until the 1950s and 1960s.

With full independence throughout the region, there was an explosion in the establishment of universities and in the number of students attending them. In Egypt between 1952 and 1985 the number of university students increased from 51,000 to over 500,000, while eight new universities were founded. Algeria, which had no universities in 1962, now has ten. In 1934 Tehran University was founded in Iran. By the middle 1970s another eight universities had been established in Iran, with total enrollments around 60,000. Turkey had an equivalent number enrolled at that time. Taking the Arab world as a whole, the proportion of the age group 18 to 23 years old attending institutes of higher learning grew from 4% in 1960 to 16% in 1980. In addition tens of thousands of Middle Easterners pursued university educations abroad. The distribution of Arab Middle Eastern students in the United States in 1978 is shown on Table 5.10.

The institutional expansion within the region necessarily sacrificed educational standards. For many years the growing economies and governments of the Middle East could absorb whomever the universities produced almost regardless of the quality of their preparation. By the

Table 5.10  Middle Eastern Students in the United States, 1978

| | |
|---|---|
| Algeria | 1,720 |
| Egypt | 1,590 |
| Iran | 45,340* |
| Iraq | 1,250 |
| Israel | 2,570 |
| Jordan | 2,850 |
| Lebanon | 4,380 |
| Libya | 2,290 |
| Saudi Arabia | 8,050 |
| Turkey | 2,020 |
| | |
| Total | 72,060 |

* Note that this was before the fall of the shah.

Source: Institute of International Education, 1980.

1970s, however, administrations were clogged with fairly young civil servants, expansion of public-sector enterprises had slowed, and, except in the Gulf, the construction booms of the 1960s were over. Clement Moore, for instance, found a marked slowing in the upward mobility of Egyptian engineers in the 1970s and foresaw a situation in which some 70,000 engineering graduates would be competing for 10,000 top-level positions (Moore 1980, 126). The far more numerous graduates of faculties of arts or commerce throughout the region are, by and large, unemployable. Only the strong demand in the Gulf economies for university-educated personnel has slowed the formation of substantial intellectual proletariats in several Middle Eastern countries.

Universities and institutes of higher learning exhibit a greater degree of class bias than secondary schools. There has undoubtedly been a certain measure of democratization, with members of the lower-middle class in particular bettering their position through access to a more open educational system. Still, findings from a survey of university applicants carried out in Turkey in the mid-1970s may be applicable throughout the region (Özgediz 1980, 507). Only 30% of all applicants were from rural areas, while 47% were from the three major cities, Istanbul, Ankara, and Izmir. The success rate in passing entrance exams was three times higher for applicants from upper-income strata than for those from lower-income groups.

We have already noted that certain disciplines and faculties within the university are seen as more desirable: Medicine, engineering, computer sciences are among them. In 1976 at the University of Ankara, the medical school received 17,858 applications, and 285 students were admitted. Students from high-quality secondary schools or those who have benefited from special tutoring are likely to be among the lucky few who enter the prestige faculties. The unlucky and unprivileged wind up in normal schools or train to be agricultural extension agents or social workers.

Access to higher education may reflect ethnic or sectarian origin. In Israel, while non-Jews constitute 17% of the population, they constituted only 3.3% of the university population in 1978–1979—up from 1.3% in 1964–1965. Whereas 20% of the Jewish population 14 years old or older had received postsecondary education, only 6.8% of the non-Jewish, e.g., Arab, population had received higher education. Israel is not alone in such implicit or explicit discrimination.

The first universities were all located in major cities. Cairo alone has three universities and well over 200,000 students. No regime likes to see that kind of concentration of potentially volatile young, educated people in one place. In recent years there has been a general move throughout the Middle East to establish provincial campuses. This policy serves several purposes. It demonstrates to more remote regions the government's concern to make higher education directly available to their populations. It helps satisfy the relentless demand from all sectors of the population for university education. And it eases the concentration of students in economic and political capitals, where their agitation is highly visible and disruptive. Unfortunately, many of the provincial universities dispense a thoroughly mediocre education. Even more than the older universities, provincial universities are understaffed, underfinanced, underequipped and overpopulated. In most instances they are monuments to political expediency.

Middle Eastern universities are preeminently and self-consciously political. Various elements within them claim to speak for the nation's intelligentsia as well as for the generation that will furnish the nation's leaders. By its very organization the university, in its research and instruction, touches upon all the issues that are of great moment to the nation as a whole. All the political currents of the nation will be manifested within the university. There is a constant battle within its walls for control over the institution, and particularly in the authoritarian systems that typify the region, the conduct of that battle is seen as a bellwether for the entire polity.

Student elections of one kind or another may be more hotly contested and less easily controlled than other elections in a given society. In the absence of other indicators of shifts in public opinion or in the relative weights of political forces, such elections are closely scrutinized. In 1959 and 1960 strong Communist showings in student federation and teachers' union elections in Iraq sent tremors all the way to Washington (Batatu 1978, 934). Every regime will have its tame student association or union to enter the fray. In single-party regimes, such as those of the Ba'ath in Syria and Iraq, the Socialist Destour in Tunisia, or the FLN in Algeria, the student union will be directly affiliated to the party. So too will associations of professors and administrators. In this way the university is supposed to remain a place of learning subordinate to the regime. But it seldom works out that way in practice. While student or faculty activists may be a minority of the university population, they are ubiquitous, visible, and highly motivated. Even within dominant associations there will be identifiable factions and leaders representing well-known trends or philosophies. The most visible and consistent over time in many countries have been leftist, if not Marxist, groups and factions sympathetic to the Muslim Brotherhood or other Islamic fundamentalist movements (see inter alia, Moore and Hochschild 1968; Abdalla 1985).

The Middle Eastern university is enveloped in contradictory symbols and practices. Its origins are Western, and most countries of the region at least honor the fiction of the physical and intellectual inviolability of the university. However, the sanctity of academic freedom as well as the campus itself are frequently violated. In many countries the university is called upon to "serve the revolution" or contribute to the development of the nation, slogans that mean in fact that it should remain subservient to regime goals, if not politically inert.[18] When university organizations or movements criticize the government precisely for betraying the revolution (e.g., Algeria in 1966 after Boumedienne seized power from Ben Bella), thwarting the development of country (Iran throughout the 1970s and Turkey in 1978–1979), or capitulating to its enemies (Egypt 1971–1972), then the spokespersons for those organizations are denounced as traitors. The Moroccan monarchy on occasion has simply drafted troublemakers into the armed forces.

The freedom of teaching and research is highly circumscribed. There may be subjects that cannot be researched and questions that cannot be asked. Classrooms will typically have their share of police informers. Some regimes have resorted to strong-arm tactics with party-affiliated toughs enforcing the proper line, breaking up unauthorized meetings, and intimidating students leaders. Israeli authorities have since 1967 engaged in a running battle with Palestinian students and faculty at Bir Zeit University on the West Bank. Still, the spirit of the university as an institution with a peculiar responsibility to the fate of the nation is kept alive, and university students are often prepared to take great risks in making their views known (Ashraf and Banuazizi 1985). The best among them will in all likelihood be the nation's future leaders. In fact student militancy has often been the stepping-stone to high official position, as incumbent leaders identify their challengers and set about co-opting them. It is for all these reasons that in national power struggles contenders may see capturing the university to be as strategically important as capturing the armed forces.

## CONCLUSION

Health and education are two policy domains in which nearly all Middle Eastern governments have promised their citizens rapid progress. They are domains in which until this century little progress had been made. It would be a rare Middle Easterner today who is not aware that he or she is saddled with the burdens of "ignorance" and disease. Progress in both domains has been rapid and real, but starting from such low bases has meant that many Middle Easterners—infants who die young or adults who remain illiterate—still suffer from the twin scourges. As we noted throughout this chapter, the progress registered is not commensurate, by international standards, with the average levels of income and per capita GDPs of these countries. Moreover, the rapid increase in population in the region will make the effort to catch up extremely costly. The effort, if it is made, will come at a time when many Middle Eastern governments are under severe pressure to *reduce* their spending and their costly welfare programs. Are healthier government accounts to be achieved at the expense of the health and education of the people in whose name they govern?

## NOTES

1. According to UNICEF, between 1975 and 1980, the average yearly number of infant deaths was 167,000 in Egypt, 195,000 in Turkey, 181,000 in Iran, 104,000 in Algeria, and 103,000 in Sudan. The number of such deaths, when summed over countries and over an eight-year period, greatly exceeds the death toll of even the most brutal military conflict in recent regional history, the Iran-Iraq war: Informed observers estimate the total number of casualties on both sides of that conflict at approximately 1 million during eight years of fighting.

2. His definition of class is based on educational levels, which, he argued, is closely correlated with other, more common measures like occupation and income. We will look at the relationship between literacy and health in more detail in this chapter.

3. That is, 45% of the variance of the dependent variable, LEB, may be attributed to variance in per capita incomes.

4. Diarrhea kills by dehydrating and by "starving" the victim, whose body cannot absorb the nutrients in his or her food. The disease caused some 45% of the deaths of children between birth and 5 years of age in Rabat in 1981, and 49% in Tunis in 1982. Such diseases are the leading cause of child death in Egypt and in other countries (UNICEF 1986).

5. The emergence of a chloroquine-resistant strain of malaria in Africa, a strain that is now spreading in the Sudan, is alarming. Unlike other diseases in the region, control and cure of malaria is neither simple nor cheap.

6. A comparable result can be obtained through multiple regression analysis of UNICEF data: Having a higher percentage of the population adhering to Islam *reduces* life expectancy at birth, when controlling for income per capita. However, the adverse impact of Islam is entirely explained by female illiteracy: When a variable for female illiteracy is introduced, the percentage of the population that is Muslim ceases to have any explanatory power (that is, its coefficient becomes statistically insignificant) (Richards 1987).

7. However, cross country regression analysis fails to support this (plausible) contention: As noted above, when controlling for female illiteracy, the percentage of the population that is Muslim has *no* effect on LEB or on infant mortality. Presumably it would, if "female autonomy" (which, under any reasonable definition, must be judged low in many Muslim countries) had an impact on health independently of female literacy.

8. Three high-income oil exporters—Bahrein, Kuwait, and Libya—plus Turkey and Tunisia.

9. Bahrein, Iraq, Israel, Jordan, Kuwait, and Turkey.

10. Segregation in Algerian schools formally ended in 1948, but the system remained strongly biased in favor of *colon* children until independence.

11. Since, in that case, the percentage change will be greater, the lower the original literacy number: e.g., an increase of literacy from 10% to 20% (100% change) seems more impressive than a change from 80% to 100% (a 25% change). For a full discussion, see Sen 1981b.

12. Note, however, that the basis of the calculation for Iraq is somewhat different than for the other countries and therefore overstates Iraqi achievement relative to other countries. As argued below, however, the Iraqi adult-literacy campaign seems to have been quite successful, and stands in marked contrast with the inaction on this front by most other countries.

13. It should be noted, however, that some observers believe that the data on enrollments give an excessively sanguine picture because they include over-age students and repeaters (Kavalsky 1980, 156).

14. Israel spent over 7% of GNP on education, while Turkey spent 3.4%. Numbers for Iran were not reported to UNESCO (United Nations Economic, Scientific, and Cultural Organization).

15. However, it is worth noting that Cuba spent 12% of its GDP to finance its ambitious educational reforms in the 1970s. It is also disturbing to note that spending per pupil in Turkey fell some 40% in real terms from 1980 to 1987 (*Economist,* June 18, 1988, p. 23).

16. The "social rate of return" on an investment is the internal rate of return, calculated using international (as opposed to distorted domestic) prices and taking into account externalities.

17. Gender bias is also apparent in the slow rate of improvement of primary school female enrollment.

18. In September 1961 Syria broke its political union with Egypt and brought about the demise of the United Arab Republic. Students at Cairo University and elsewhere demonstrated in favor of the union and against Syria. Egypt's President Nasser closed down the universities for having demonstrated at all.

# 6

# AGRICULTURE
# AND FOOD SECURITY

The Middle East cannot produce enough food to feed its population. Rapidly escalating demand and sluggish supply response have made the area the least food-self-sufficient region in the world. In this chapter we examine the political economy of this phenomenon. The emergence of this "food gap" does not mean (as some have implied) that agricultural supply has stagnated, although this has happened in some cases (Table 6.1). Rather, the more common experience has been that both public and private responses to the food deficit have failed to restore food self-sufficiency. The measures taken to reduce the disequilibrium between the rates of growth of demand and domestic supply are transforming agricultural production, rural class structures, and relations between both rural and urban citizens and their states throughout the region.

The agrarian sector provides many illustrations of our focus on the reciprocal determination of economic development, state policy, and class formation. The need to import food potentially threatens national independence, provoking state action. In many countries, state actors attacked powerful rural social classes by implementing land-reform programs. The "national projects" of national unification and economic development molded state policies toward agriculture. Although the "contributions of agriculture to development" are often presented as a "list" (Johnston and Mellor 1961), in fact there may be conflicts among goals, such as increasing the flow of investable resources out of agriculture, on the one hand, and the creation of a domestic market, on the other. Here different relations between farmers and the state have contributed to very different policy outcomes. And just as the varied actions of the state shape rural class structures, these structures, in turn, come to constrain policy options.

## THE FOOD GAP: AN OVERVIEW

The essence of the food-security situation in the Middle East is straightforward. Rapid population growth and per capita income expansion due

Table 6.1  Selected Agricultural Growth Rates, 1965-1985 (percent per year)

|  | Growth Rate of Agricultural Output | | Growth of Value-Added in Agriculture | Growth of Cereal Imports |
|---|---|---|---|---|
|  | 1965-80 | 1980-85 | 1970-85 | 1974-85 |
| Algeria | 5.8 | 2.1 | 5.7 | 10.4 |
| Egypt | 2.8 | 1.9 | 2.6 | 7.6 |
| Iran | 4.5 | -- | -- | 7.0 |
| Iraq | -- | -- | -- | 12.4 |
| Israel | -- | -- | -- | 3.4 |
| Jordan | -- | 6.4 | 3.7 | 13.1 |
| Libya | 10.7 | 7.3 | 9.7 | 4.7 |
| Morocco | 2.2 | 1.0 | 1.0 | 8.5 |
| Oman | -- | -- | -- | 12.4 |
| Saudi Arabia | 4.1 | 8.0 | 6.0 | 21.3 |
| Sudan | 2.9 | -5.5 | -1.0 | 19.6 |
| Syria | 4.8 | -1.4 | 6.0 | 10.5 |
| Tunisia | 5.5 | 4.2 | 5.4 | 7.9 |
| Turkey | 3.2 | 2.6 | 3.1 | -2.0 |
| UAE | -- | 13.3 | -- | 10.9 |
| YAR | 3.6* | 0.2 | 4.0 | 12.9 |
| PDRY | -- | -- | -- | 7.9 |

* 1970-82.

Source: World Bank, **World Development Report**, New York, Oxford University Press, 1987, p. 228.

to the oil boom of the 1970s increased the demand for food. At the same time, natural and social constraints (sometimes exacerbated by state policies) limited the domestic supply response. Let us first look at each side of the demand/domestic supply equation and then turn to the consequences of the resulting escalation of food imports. Then we shall examine the forms of state intervention in agriculture: land reform, price policies, and investment programs. The chapter concludes with a reprise on the role of the state in rural class formation.

There are three determinants of demand growth: population increase, per capita income advance, and the income elasticity of demand.[1] We have seen that MENA population growth rates are among the highest in the world, exceeded only by those in sub-Saharan Africa. Such population growth rates in themselves pose a challenge to food producers. But the very rapid growth of incomes during the 1970s compounded the task. For five countries, per capita GDP grew more than 5% per year, with incomes doubling in fifteen years.[2] With the major exception of Sudan, per capita incomes advanced swiftly in the region during the past fifteen years.

The impact of such income growth upon food demand depends, of course, on the specific foodstuff. Demand for cereals for direct food consumption (as opposed to use as livestock feed) grew at approximately 3.7% per year from 1966 to 1980; although this was mainly due to burgeoning population, increasing incomes accounted for roughly 25% of this growth.

Demand for cereals for livestock feed grew more rapidly, expanding at 4.8% per year. About one-fourth of all cereals consumed in the region is eaten by animals (Paulino 1986, 26). Regional meat consumption increased by more than 5% per year, far above the roughly 2.7% rate of regional population increase; in the most rapidly growing, oil-exporting countries, meat consumption soared: In Iran and Saudi Arabia, meat consumption increased by 19% and 12%, respectively, every year from 1966 to 1980 (Khaldi 1984, 19). Income growth was also the primary force pushing up the demand for products such as fruits and vegetables. In the Middle East, as in all other parts of the world, people who get richer eat more of everything, especially animal and horticultural products.

The demand for food in the region will continue to increase rapidly. Population growth is unlikely to fall dramatically, and even the recent collapse of oil prices has not reduced income sufficiently to have affected national food demand substantially. Food consumption is highly inelastic downward: Governments are likely to cut everything else (except defense) before they reduce the nation's (urban) food supply. It is reasonable to conclude that there will be little reduction in the food gap from the demand side.

Let us look now at the domestic supply response. Few countries could have met such a rate of growth of consumption from domestic supply alone. For example, for the entire century from 1860 to 1960, Japanese agricultural output never grew faster than 2.2% per year. During the twentieth century, U.S. agricultural growth has never exceeded 4% per year. Even the highly protected and subsidized agriculture of the Netherlands grew at "only" 4.3% per year from 1970 to 1982, while in the development textbook success story of Taiwan, agriculture grew at about 3.5% both before and after World War II. Such international comparisons help to put the "failure" of MENA agriculture in some perspective.[3]

In fact, by international standards, Middle Eastern agricultural output has grown quite respectably. According to the World Bank, the average annual rate of growth of agricultural output for low-income, middle-income, and developed countries was some 2.3%, 3.0%, and 1.8%, respectively, during the decade 1970–1980 (World Bank 1983b). As the data in Table 6.1 show, many Middle Eastern countries did better than this. Although regional growth has not been as rapid as in either Latin America or monsoon Asia, it has been considerably better than that in sub-Saharan Africa. MENA agriculture has lagged largely in relation to its own rates of growth of demand; the problem was *not* typically one of stagnation or retrogression, with the disastrous exception of the Sudan.

There are two ways to increase agricultural production: Bring new land into cultivation, and raise the productivity of existing farms. MENA countries must increasingly rely on the second option. Although about 45% of the growth of output from 1960 to 1980 came from area expansion, most of these gains were registered in the earlier decade; in the period of the oil boom, 1973–1980, some 88% of output growth was due to higher yields[4]

Table 6.2   Rates of Growth for Different Product Groups, Near East, 1975-1986
            (percent per year)

|                        | Growth of Production |
|------------------------|----------------------|
| Cereals                | 2.3                  |
| Fruit                  | 2.8                  |
| Vegetables and Melons  | 3.7                  |
| Meat                   | 4.5                  |
| Eggs                   | 8.0                  |

Note: "Near East" excludes Morocco, Algeria, and Tunisia.

Sources: Calculated from FAO Production Yearbook, Rome, FAO, various years.

(Mellor 1983; Khaldi 1984). Apart from the Sudan and perhaps some areas of Iraq, little cultivable yet still uncultivated land remains in the region. Output growth can only be accelerated by shifting from "extensive" to "intensive" growth. But this difficult and expensive process will require numerous state initiatives, and these will continue to transform Middle Eastern rural societies.

The aggregate data used so far conceal important differences among countries and among crops. The range of country performance has been wide indeed (Table 6.1). Agricultural performance was only weakly linked to overall economic growth during the 1970s; countries with rapid overall GDP rates have included agricultural success stories, like Syria in the 1970s, and relative failures, like Morocco. The two extremes may be Turkey, intermittently the sole cereal exporter of the region, and the Sudan, which experienced famine in 1983–1984 and again in 1987–1989.

The rate of growth of production of various crops has also varied widely. In general, in the Middle East as in Latin America, output of "luxury" foods like fruits, vegetables, poultry, and livestock products has increased more rapidly than that of cereals (Table 6.2). Much of this increase is simply the result of the working of Bennett's Law[5] and the higher income elasticity of demand for horticultural and livestock products. Price and credit policies may also contribute to these trends. Such developments do little to reduce the food gap; they may actually increase it, as, for example, increasing poultry production stimulates feed imports.

Those who try to meet the challenge of rapidly rising food demand from domestic production encounter various natural and socioeconomic constraints. The former are straightforward. The most important natural constraint is the unfavorable climate. Agriculture in the Middle East is truly "a gamble on the rains": Many countries face a high probability that production will fall at least 5% below trend in any year simply because of poor rainfall. For example, planners in the Maghreb must find supplementary foreign exchange to buy such "unusual" amounts of food four years out of ten.

The devastating droughts in the Maghreb and the Sudan underscore the climatic threat. In Morocco, production of wheat fell by nearly 40% from

1976 to 1977, while in the Sudan, millet and sorghum output fell by 38% and 58%, respectively, in 1982 and 1983, and continued to fall the next year. The social, economic, and political impacts were severe: Some 4–5 million northern Sudanese were forced from their homes, moving either into the Nile Valley or further south to less severely affected areas. In addition, multitudes of "drought refugees" fled to North African cities. Although these cases are extreme, all agricultural sectors in the region outside of Egypt[6] must contend with meager, variable rainfall.

Given such natural constraints, it is understandable that expanding irrigation looms large in agricultural plans. The experience and pitfalls of this response are examined below. Suffice it to note here that (1) irrigation has, of course, natural limits of its own, and (2) numerous social, economic, and political obstacles prevent the optimal use of existing and planned irrigation systems.

Social impediments to increasing agricultural production are no less severe than environmental ones. We may (loosely) divide such constraints into three groups: (1) skewed access to land and other "property rights" problems, (2) unfavorable terms of trade for rural producers due to overvalued exchange rates and specific taxation of agriculture, and (3) low levels of investment in agriculture and/or difficulties in fostering technological change that will improve the welfare of most rural inhabitants and also be environmentally sustainable over the long run. How did states respond to this mixture of rapidly growing demand and ecologically and socially constrained supply?

## THE POLITICAL ECONOMY OF FOOD IMPORTS

The states' first response was to import food. Food imports grew at an annual rate of about 12% from 1960 to 1980 (Khaldi 1984).[7] Such a response was attractive for both economic and political reasons. There were four economic reasons for the food import boom. First, as mentioned above, domestic production was (and is) highly unstable because of erratic rainfall. Second, the barter terms of trade moved sharply in favor of oil exporters/food importers. In 1970 a barrel of oil would buy roughly one bushel of wheat; by 1980, the same barrel would purchase six bushels, and even in May 1986 a barrel (of $14.00) oil would still buy over three bushels. Third, most MENA counties had ample supplies of foreign exchange; the balance of payments did not constrain food imports during the 1970s. (The 1980s are another matter.) Fourth, since most wheat importers in the region are small relative to the size of the international market, increased purchases have no impact on price; by contrast, domestic supplies were much less elastically supplied. Finally, in some countries urban-consumer tastes shifted away from local grains[8] toward bread wheat, a crop whose production was sometimes difficult locally.

Food imports also offered short-term political attractions. Given the demands of the urban population and the inelastic domestic supplies,

Table 6.3   Food Self-Sufficiency Ratios for Selected Foods and Countries, 1970
and 1981

|  | Cereals | | Vegetable Oil | | Meat | | Sugar | |
|---|---|---|---|---|---|---|---|---|
|  | 1970 | 1981 | 1970 | 1981 | 1970 | 1981 | 1970 | 1981 |
| Algeria | 73 | 40 | 26 | 11 | 97 | 87 | -- | -- |
| Egypt | 81 | 49 | 56 | 32 | 94 | 75 | 100 | 52 |
| Iran | 98 | 66 | 33 | 11 | 90 | 66 | 100 | 38 |
| Iraq | 91 | 47 | 15 | 4 | 98 | 44 | -- | -- |
| Libya | 25 | 20 | 42 | 28 | 60 | 30 | -- | -- |
| Morocco | 94 | 60 | 51 | 16 | 100 | 100 | 36 | 55 |
| Saudi Arabia | 22 | 7* | -- | -- | 38 | 27 | -- | -- |
| Syria | 73 | 84 | 100 | 90 | 100 | 75 | 17 | 24 |
| Tunisia | 61 | 54 | 100 | 99 | 98 | 84 | 10 | -- |

* Saudi Arabia was self-sufficient in wheat by 1984.

Source: U.S. Department of Agriculture, Middle East and North Africa: Situation
and Outlook Report, Washington, D.C., Economic Research Service, 1984, p. 17.


governments had to import if domestic consumption needs were to be
met. Food imports increase governments' control over strategic urban food
supplies. It is much easier for a government to monitor food that arrives
at one or a few ports than to collect grain from thousands of local markets.
Of course, governments could rely on private markets to do this, but state
actors fear ceding such a strategic domestic role to anyone else. Since
most states in the region subsidize urban consumption, and since urban
food supply is a national security issue, governments were and are reluctant
to rely primarily on private traders.

Money spent on imported food has, of course, an opportunity cost.
Stabilizing urban consumption implies that (inevitable) economic shocks
will have to be absorbed elsewhere in the economy (Scobie 1981). Reliance
on imported food also exposes a country to substantial risks should foreign-
exchange availability decline; the unhappy Sudanese experience noted
above was paralleled by events in Morocco and Tunisia in the early 1980s,
when drought and declining export revenues coincided. Yet during the
1970s the forces favoring increased imports were overwhelming.

The levels of food dependency shown in Table 6.3 prompted widespread
alarm. The risk of a politically motivated food embargo became something
of an obsession with many government planners. However, the effectiveness
of the "food weapon" has probably been overrated. First, the U.S. agricultural
lobby constitutes a powerful domestic force against restricting grain exports
to attain political goals. Even the zealously anti-Communist Reagan administration restored food exports to the Soviet Union to reduce economic
hardship for U.S. farmers. Second, the fungibility of grain and the multinational scope of the grain trade blunt the weapon's edge. Whether grown
in the Dakotas or Argentina, Number 2 Hard Red Wheat is the same
commodity. And in any case, relatively few countries depend heavily on
the United States (the only potential embargoer).

However, heavy reliance on food imports undeniably carries political risks. Three countries of the region purchase at least 20% of their total food supply from the United States: Egypt (25%), Israel (34%), and Morocco (20%). Furthermore, the percentage is higher in some cases for highly strategic *wheat* supplies: Egypt gets nearly 50% of all of its wheat and wheat flour from the United States. Since bread is the Egyptian staple, an interruption of supplies would be catastrophic. Moreover, the small size of the country relative to the world market suggests that the U.S. farm lobby would be less opposed to a politically motivated boycott against Egypt than to a similar action against the (much larger) Soviet market. Second, the effectiveness of the "food weapon" varies directly with the tightness of the market; although real grain prices have declined throughout the twentieth century, sudden periods of temporary shortages have occasionally driven prices up sharply, as in 1972. If wheat prices were relatively high, U.S. policymakers would face relatively little domestic opposition to a food boycott. Third, giving, rather than withholding, food aid is probably a more effective political instrument for the supplier. The United States has extended food aid as part of "policy packages" in which the recipient makes concessions to U.S. strategic instances; the Camp David Accords may be interpreted in this light. And of course, no country relies exclusively on comparative advantage and market forces in its food system.

Unsurprisingly, therefore, state reactions to the imbalance between domestic supply and domestic demand for food have not been limited to increasing imports. From the economic point of view, states could focus either on diversifying their exports (thereby increasing the stability of their foreign-exchange earnings) and/or launch programs to increase the share of domestic supplies to total consumption. For countries such as Egypt, there is really little choice but to pursue the first strategy. However, the problems of increasing exports are numerous. Not only must certain "macro prices," such as the exchange rate, reflect actual economic scarcities, but also marketing infrastructure and incentives must be well developed. Developments like these have important implications for the relationship between the public and private sectors, implications that are treated in more detail in Chapters 7–9.

Only a few states in the region have embarked on such an export-based food-security strategy, while nearly all have implemented at least some import-substituting agricultural policies. The effectiveness and the consequences of such policies depend upon the prior distribution of access to land, itself the product of past state actions. Although state policy toward agriculture throughout the region often operates in a "crisis mode," with difficulties of the balance of payments and food security driving decisions, in the recent past state actors have had somewhat wider scope for action. Their policies were accordingly shaped by "visions of development," by implicit analyses of why development was slow and of how to accelerate it. Whether states aimed primarily at extracting resources from agriculture or at developing a thriving domestic, largely rural, market for industrial products, how land was distributed and used was a major issue in policy decisions. But above all, and regardless of their development strategy, state actors sought to increase their own power over the countryside. The resulting legacy of land-tenure systems continues to affect the pattern of supply response to the food gap.

## LAND TENURE AND LAND REFORM

Both liberals (Johnston and Kilby 1975; Ranis 1984) and Marxists (de Janvry 1981) have argued that "bimodalism" (a few very large farms combined with many very small farms) perpetuates rural poverty *even if* agricultural output grows rapidly. The combination of such a land-tenure system with rapid population growth leads to increasing inequalities, environmental degradation, and other evils. Analysts in this tradition have often contrasted the pattern of development in Latin America, with its typically extremely skewed distribution of land, with that in East Asia, where much more equitable patterns of land tenure are the norm.

Although there are wide differences across the Middle East, we argue that (1) prereform land tenures more nearly resembled the bimodalism of Latin America than the small peasant systems of East Asia; (2) the state was, and remains, exceptionally active in shaping patterns of land tenure; (3) land reforms have reduced, but have not eliminated, the inequalities inherited from the past; (4) the state had mixed success substituting itself for the expropriated landlords as marketing agent, crop selector, and so forth; and (5) states have recently retreated from land reforms and especially from public-sector agriculture, a retreat that is part of a wider trend toward increased reliance on the private sector.

Let us first look at "prereform" experience. The phenomenon of large landholdings emerged in many areas of the Middle East and North Africa during the nineteenth and twentieth centuries. Although the process was dominated by relations between the state and local social groups, expanding markets for crops also provided opportunities for aggrandizement. When one considers the role of the state, one can make a few generalizations. First, throughout the region, indigenous states attempted to remove intermediaries between themselves and the tax-paying peasantry. The success or failure of such policies depended on local, regional, and international political forces. If the state could act without excessive external interference, and if the state's agents were sufficiently numerous and motivated, large landlordism was reduced or avoided. However, if the state had to rely on local intermediaries, the spread of private property rights in land and expanding market opportunities usually fostered the emergence of "bimodal" systems.

The critical variable was political: Could the central government dispense with local power holders and still provide security and collect taxes? In the areas of Anatolia and Thrace close to the Ottoman seat of power in Istanbul, small-scale farming prevailed (Aricanli 1986). In more remote areas, such as the Cukorova, Eastern Anatolia, or Syria, the Ottomans were less successful. Their need to rely on local intermediaries for tax collection and the maintenance of public order stimulated the conversion of various tax-collection rights into private property, engendering bimodalism. Remoteness from Istanbul was not a sufficient condition for such a development, however; other historical contingencies intervened. For example, to the extent that a local area had an exceptionally able or zealous governor, then local intermediaries were undermined, as in Iraq under Midhat Pasha and the Young Turks, who managed to reduce the power of the Arab tribal sheykhs and Kurdish *aghas* (Batatu 1978; Dann 1969).

The intrusion of European colonialism always fostered bimodalism. The pattern is most striking in the Maghreb, where agrarian changes resembled those of Latin America: Foreign conquerors seized the best agricultural land for themselves, relegating the indigenous inhabitants to marginal areas for subsistence farming, to wage labor on the European modern farms, or, commonly, to both. Between 1830 and 1880 *colons* and/or the French state seized nearly 900,000 hectares of land in Algeria; by 1962, 30% of the cultivated area was owned by *colons,* of which some 80% was held in large farms of over 100 hectares (Smith 1975). By 1914 nearly 20% of the arable land in Tunisia was in European hands, and over half of it belonged to only sixteen extremely wealthy absentee owners; by 1953 Europeans held nearly 1 million hectares in Morocco, concentrated in the fertile, well-watered plains of the west and north; the Italian Fascists seized some 500,000 hectares of land in Cyrenaica (Libya). The dispossessed indigenous population was forced onto more marginal lands, while the European farms enjoyed privileged access to government loans and other favors (Abun-Nasr 1971; Nouschi 1970). Population growth shortened fallows, extended cultivation into ever more marginal land, and reduced the amount of land available to each peasant family, even as large estates continued to expand (van der Kloet 1975). European occupation and settler colonialism in the Maghreb created land-tenure systems as bimodal as any found in Latin America.

"Indirect" colonial rule generated a similar result. The British in Iraq shored up the sheykhs and *aghas* because the British needed counterweights to (nationalist) urban groups and to the king (Batatu 1978, 78–100; Dann 1969, 4). By confirming the registration of formerly tribal land in the names of sheykhs, the British and later the independent Iraqi government placed vast amounts of cultivated land in a few hands: By 1953, 1.7% of landowners held 63% of the land, while nearly two-thirds of the population held less than 5% of the land; over three-fourths of the rural population was landless (Khafaji 1983, Ch. 7; King 1977). Introducing private property in an environment of relative land scarcity also created a bimodal land-tenure system in Egypt. Muhammad Ali had initially attempted to eliminate all intermediaries between the state and the peasants. When internal economic difficulties and British pressure forced him to decentralize, he granted land to court favorites, military officers, and the like. These actions laid the foundations for the class of large, typically absentee, landlords, known as pashas in modern Egyptian history. By 1900 large (over 50 *feddan* farms—1 *feddan* = 0.42 ha = 1.03 acres) covered 40% of the cultivated area of the country (Baer 1962; Owen 1986; Richards 1982).

Land reclamation and expansion also created large farms. As marshes and steppes were opened for cultivation, as rural security increased, and as markets expanded, richer farmers acquired much land. The British, to minimize their administrative costs, sold reclaimed Egyptian land in large lots, thereby ensuring that the wealthy would acquire the land. In Syria, the opening of the sparsely settled Jezirah during World War II enabled urban entrepreneurs to import agricultural machinery and to establish huge grain estates; land reclamation activities throughout the Maghreb largely benefited European settlers.

The prereform land-tenure systems may be summarized as follows:

> large estates, accounting for a quarter to four-fifths of privately owned land and in the main tilled by sharecroppers; a huge number of very small peasant proprietors, often with highly fragmented holding; short and precarious leases; high rents . . . large debts, rising land values; and a growing landless proletariat earning very low wages. (Issawi 1982, 138)

Both political and economic critiques were leveled at such systems. Landlords were alleged to be economic drones, mere rent collectors who took no interest in their lands and who failed to invest in industry. The historical record does not support the first allegation; large landowners in Syria, Egypt, and the Maghreb gave much evidence of being agrarian capitalists (Richards 1982; Owen 1986; Hannoyer 1980; Tignor 1984; Davis 1983). They also invested in urban activities, although in the Maghreb there is little doubt that often funds returned to the northern shore of the Mediterranean. Throughout the region the conjuncture of consolidating private property rights, weak or colonial states, and expanding economic opportunities increased the power of large landowners.[9]

The argument that such skewed landownership patterns were highly inequitable and contributed to the poverty of the land-poor or landless was more apposite. Rural inhabitants not only suffered from malnutrition, endemic diseases, and illiteracy but were also subjected to the arbitrary authority of local large landowners, who often regarded themselves as the only source of security and law on their estates. It is indicative that Iranian landlords measured their holdings not in hectares, but in "villages" (Keddie 1981; Hooglund 1982). Needless to say, such powers were commonly abused to keep their labor force poor and subordinate.

Attacking such political power lay at the core of land reforms throughout the region. Reformers expropriated enemies: Nasserists dispossessed the family and friends of Farouk; Syrian Ba'athists (often Alawi or Druze) took away the lands of urban (typically Sunni) merchant absentee landlords; the Algerian FLN seized the farms of fleeing *pied noir* colonists; Iraqi nationalists and Communists dispossessed the sheykhs who had often supported the deposed Hashemite monarchy. The extension of Iraqi reforms in 1976 to the Kurdish areas after the cessation of fighting there was aimed at undercutting the political base of secessionist Kurdish nationalist forces. Even the shah of Iran, shortly after he was reinstalled by the United States in 1953, agreed to launch a land reform mainly because he believed that this would weaken his opponents, such as friends of Mossadegh (himself a landowner) or the Shi'i *'ulema'* (Hooglund 1982, Katouzian 1981).

Various "developmentalist visions" also played a role in the theory and practice of land reforms. For example, the Kennedy administration, which viewed land reform as an alternative to revolution in Latin America after the Cuban revolution, urged the shah of Iran to implement a reform to improve his position. Arab reformers believed that a reformed agriculture would generate a larger economic surplus, which could be mobilized for industrialization, and that a peasantry freed from the shackles of "feudalism" would provide a wider market for domestic manufactures.[10] Some ruling parties (in PDRY, Iraq) accepted the Soviet view that only large-scale, collective agriculture could capture the agricultural surplus for industrial investment. But the fundamental goal was political, and in this respect most reforms were successful: Large landlords have ceased to exist as a political force in any country that has had a significant agrarian reform.

The contributions of land reform to equity and economic growth were more mixed. The Egyptian agrarian reform, which became the model for other Arab regimes, affected only 12% of the land area. Landless daily-wage workers were excluded from the reforms, since only tenants were believed to have the necessary agricultural experience. This pattern was repeated in Algeria, where the permanent workers seized the estates of the departed *colons.* When the land seizures were institutionalized under *autogestion* (self-management), temporary and seasonal laborers received nothing (Zghal 1977). Subsequent reforms of the 1970s affected some 30% of the rural population (Tuma 1978). In Iran only those who held *nasagh,* or cultivation rights (which implied ownership of oxen and thus relative prosperity), received land; the poorest rural residents, the agricultural laborers, or *khushneshin,*[11] were excluded from the reform. Nominal beneficiaries of land reform often received too little land to enable them to survive. In Iran, although estimates of the percentage of the population affected range from 22% (Katouzian 1981) to 92% (Hooglund 1982), some 75% of those receiving land got less than 7 hectares, which was insufficient to support a family (Hooglund 1982, 93). Hooglund summarizes the result of the Iranian land reform as the "creation of a small minority of profit-oriented farmers and a mass of poor peasants unable to support themselves from their holdings" (93).[12] (Table 6.4.)

The administration of land reforms often created serious production problems. In both Syria and Iraq, confiscating land proved far easier than redistributing it. Delays in redistribution, failures to provide credit and other complementary inputs, and above all the lack of trained rural cadres undermined agricultural production. By 1975 only about one-third of land

Table 6.4  Distribution of Landholdings, 1961-1982 (selected years) (percentages)

| | Year | Farms (Hectares) | | | | | Landholdings (Hectares) | | | | |
|---|---|---|---|---|---|---|---|---|---|---|---|
| | | 0-5 | 5-10 | 10-50 | 50-100 | >100 | 0-5 | 5-10 | 10-50 | 50-100 | >100 |
| Algeria | 1973 | 61.6 | 17.6 | 18.9 | 1.400 | 0.50 | 14.2 | 15.7 | 47.0 | 11.8 | 11.4 |
| Egypt* | 1975 | 92.5 | 5.2 | 2.3 | .004 | -- | 66.0 | 15.9 | 16.5 | 1.8 | -- |
| Iran | 1974 | 64.4 | 17.3 | 17.3 | 0.660 | 0.39 | 14.8 | 18.0 | 45.7 | 6.5 | 14.9 |
| Iraq** | 1979 | 39.7 | 25.4 | 32.6 | 1.200 | 1.20 | 6.9 | 12.4 | 39.7 | 6.3 | 34.8 |
| Jordan | 1975 | 63.5 | 17.0 | 17.4 | 1.400 | 0.70 | 13.6 | 14.6 | 41.9 | 11.6 | 18.3 |
| Lebanon | 1961 | 92.0 | 6.0 | 3.0 | <.500 | *** | 44.0 | 16.0 | 25.0 | 15.0 | *** |
| Libya | 1974 | 46.8 | 20.6 | 29.4 | 2.400 | 0.80 | 6.5 | 9.8 | 40.8 | 10.8 | 32.1 |
| Morocco | 1973 | 73.7 | 14.9 | 10.7 | 0.500 | 0.20 | 24.5 | 20.7 | 37.7 | 7.2 | 10.0 |
| Saudi Arabia** | 1979 | 75.4 | 11.1 | 12.1 | 1.000 | 0.80 | 14.3 | 10.4 | 31.5 | 8.7 | 35.0 |
| Syria** | 1970 | 56.4 | 17.4 | 23.5 | 1.800 | 0.90 | 10.7 | 11.3 | 45.7 | 11.1 | 21.1 |
| Tunisia | 1980 | 42.1 | 21.3 | 32.3 | 3.000 | 1.20 | 6.6 | 10.5 | 43.9 | 13.3 | 25.7 |
| Turkey | 1973 | 72.9 | 19.2 | 7.0 | 0.600 | 0.20 | 26.6 | 39.5 | 19.8 | 8.8 | 5.3 |
| YAR | 1982 | 88.5 | 7.4 | 4.0 | 0.000 | 0.10 | 43.5 | 22.5 | 29.4 | 1.2 | 3.3 |

\*    Figures for Egypt refer to feddans, not hectares.
\*\*   Some figures estimated by interpolation from other groupings.
\*\*\*  All holdings over 50 ha are reported together.

Sources:  AOAD, Yearbook, Arab Organization for Agricultural Development, 1984, and Dennis Tully, "Rainfed Farming Systems of the Near East Region," Aleppo, ICARDA, April 1986, mimeo, except: Turkey: official statistics cited in Ergun Özbudun and Aydin Ulusan, The Political Economy of Income Distribution in Turkey, New York, Holmes and Meier, 1980, p. 140; Iran: Afsaneh Najmabadi, Land Reform and Social Change in Iran, Salt Lake City, University of Utah Press, 1987, p. 117; Egypt: Ministry of Agriculture.

seized by the Iraqi state since 1958 had been given to farmers. Governments sometimes removed large landowners, who often had also supplied credit and seed to tenants, without replacing the landowners with anyone else. This was a function of continual political upheaval, as in both Iraq and Syria during the 1960s, and of the lack of sufficient cadres, a problem that was more serious in Iraq than in Syria, and that became less acute by the late 1970s (Springborg 1981).

In nearly all countries land reforms redistributed land as private property; even in the Communist PDRY, state farms occupy less than 25% of the cultivated land area (IFAD 1985). The Iraqis have also flirted with collectivized agriculture, once briefly in the early phases of land reform (1958) when the Communist party had considerable influence in decisionmaking, and again in the middle-to-late 1970s. Elsewhere, private ownership and family production have been the norm.

Most land-reform beneficiaries were obliged to join government-sponsored service cooperatives. Peasants farmed their own lands, but input supply, marketing, and often crop choice were regulated by the cooperatives. Restrictions on the sale or renting of land by land-reform beneficiaries are also common; some have argued that many countries now have a new "dual tenure" system composed of reformed lands hedged about with restrictions, on the one hand, and far less regulated, exclusively private lands, on the other (Tuma 1978). The cooperative system, pioneered in Egypt, also appears in Tunisia, Algeria, Syria, Iraq, and the PDRY. Initially designed as an (effective) mechanism to prevent loss of output while redistributing assets, such cooperatives became the principal instrument to channel resources out of agriculture toward industrial projects. Land reform was the handmaiden of state-led industrialization strategies.

Land reforms' limited coverage, the states' use of cooperatives to distribute and to subsidize inputs, and history's legacy often combined to generate a "new class" of rural rich, the more prosperous sections of the peasantry.[13] Such farmers had usually been the intermediaries between the state and the village. They often continued to play this role: Large landlords had been eliminated, while official cadres relied on the wealthy peasants for information and for social activities. Such farmers dominated their areas and ensured that government policies and cooperatives favored or at least did not threaten their own interests (Adams 1986). As shown on Table 6.4, in many countries of the region, substantial tracts of land are held by this intermediate stratum of peasants. Nevertheless, reforms throughout the region greatly reduced the gross inequities in land tenure that were inherited from the pre–World War II era.

Land reforms had widely varying consequences for efficiency and growth. As usual, the critical variables were political. In Egypt, where the ecological, political, and administrative conditions for reform were the most favorable, there is no evidence of any decline in output as a result of the reforms. The combination of retaining economies of scale of input supply and marketing through cooperatives with the advantages of family production on relatively small plots helped to produce this result. By contrast, the lack of adequate cadres and, above all, unsettled political conditions ensured that both the Iraqi and the Syrian reforms would have a high output cost. Despite the influence of poor weather, one can fairly blame much of the stagnation of grain production in those two countries during the 1960s on the politics of land reform.[14] However, some scholars have argued that even in such unlucky countries, peasants' responsiveness to price signals increased after the land reforms (Askari and Cummings 1978). We shall see that, unfortunately, these signals were often inappropriate.

Even if output declined, the total "take" of the state could increase, as happened in the Soviet Union during the 1930s (Nove 1969). The Egyptian system extracted over Egyptian pounds (£E) 700 million from agriculture in the "old lands" during the 1960s, mainly thanks to the profits made by selling heavily taxed cotton and sugarcane on the international market. However, much of these funds was squandered on relatively unproductive land reclamation, leaving little for industrial investment.

Few countries succeeded in "mobilizing the agricultural surplus for industrial investment" via land reforms and cooperatives. Land reforms, and the additional policy interventions discussed later in this chapter, also failed to eliminate rural poverty or to create a wide domestic market.

## TWO VIGNETTES:
## LAND REFORM IN EGYPT AND IRAQ

The two extreme cases of Egypt and Iraq illustrate the many issues raised by land-reform programs. This is especially instructive since the latter country attempted to follow the former so closely; yet politics and ecology combined to thwart ideology.

The Nasser regime gave land reform the highest priority. Politically, members of the government wished to deprive the friends and family of the deposed King Farouk of all influence. They also sought the passive support of the "second stratum" of the rural middle class and hoped to create political followers among small peasants. In addition, they wanted to substitute the state's power in the countryside for that of the deposed pashas. Economically, they wished to accelerate industrial growth by mobilizing an investable surplus from agriculture. They thought there was no trade-off between growth and equity, as their slogan, *al 'adl w'al-kiffayah* (justice and sufficiency), indicates.

The regime successively lowered the ceiling on landholding per family from 200 *feddans* in 1952, to 100 in 1961, to 50 in 1969; the latter remains the legal limit today. All of the reforms taken together affected only 12% of the cultivated area. Just under 342,000 families, amounting to perhaps 1.7 million people, or about 9% of the rural population, received land. However, much more land changed hands as an indirect result of the reforms: Large landlords were allowed to sell land privately rather than have it confiscated by the state. The main beneficiaries of these "distress sales" were the rich peasants (Radwan 1977; Abdel-Fadil 1975). By 1964, about one-third of the farm area was held in medium-sized farms (between 5 and 50 *feddans*); small farms (less than 5 *feddans*) covered about 55% of the area, with the rest in the (then still legal) 50 to 100 *feddan* range.

These land reforms, the fixed supply of land, rapid population growth, and Islamic inheritance law transformed the Egyptian land-tenure system. Very large private farms were entirely eliminated, and by 1975, small farms covered two-thirds of the cultivated area. Significant inequalities in the distribution of land persist, however. Rich peasants further consolidated their already strong position, and many landless peasants got nothing. Nevertheless, the equity gains were striking.

These achievements had a low output cost. There was no disorganization of production; agricultural growth rates were maintained as more land was brought into cultivation, and crop yields either remained the same or increased. The government achieved this result by successfully substituting itself for the pashas. The government created agricultural cooperatives, which at first covered only the reformed areas but were later (1961) extended throughout the country. These assumed the functions of marketing of cotton and of irrigation control formerly performed by the pashas' overseers; the cooperatives also dictated crop rotations and furnished inputs, especially fertilizer, whose consumption doubled in the decade after the coup. The Egyptian reforms eliminated bimodalism and also fostered further agricultural intensification.[15]

The Iraqi case presents something like a mirror image of the Egyptian experience. Prerevolutionary land tenure in Iraq was far more concentrated than in Egypt; consequently, land reform covered a much wider area. Furthermore, large areas of Iraq had only recently come under cultivation, and more important, many agriculturalists, especially in the south, had only recently settled. There was no cadastral survey, and boundaries were often vaguely defined. The costs of implementing any reform were higher than in Egypt because the population density was far lower and the transportation network was much worse. The agro-ecology was both more varied and less predictable than Egypt's, not only in the rain-fed areas of the west and north, but also on the irrigated lands of the Tigris-Euphrates rivers, whose irregular and formerly devastating floods had in the late 1950s only very recently been brought under a semblance of control. Finally, while virtually all cultivated land in Egypt was irrigated, large areas of Iraq were subject to highly variable rainfall.

Politics was as unhelpful as ecology to Iraqi reformers. Unlike Egypt, the country was sharply divided ethnically and religiously, between Shi'i and Sunni, Arab and Kurd. Again in contrast to Egypt, the political situation from the coup of 1958 until the early 1970s was highly uncertain, with four (typically violent) changes of government. Under such handicaps, it is little wonder that Iraqi land reforms failed to achieve their economic goals.

The reforms themselves may be divided into four phases: (1) the initial decrees of 1958, (2) a second law in 1970, (3) the extension of the reforms to Kurdish areas in 1975, and (4) a reversal of previous policy in 1981, when private enterprise in farming was encouraged for the first time. The reform of 1958 expropriated some 75% of privately owned land, an area about nine times as large as that taken over in Egypt; despite the agro-ecological diversity of the country, the state specified only two landholding ceilings, one of 250 hectares for irrigated land and the other of 500 hectares for nonirrigated land. Since there was no possibility of rapidly redistributing the land and creating cooperatives, the government expected landlords awaiting expropriation to manage the land and to supply inputs to their erstwhile tenants. Needless to say, most landlords quietly demurred. More-over, the limits of the land reforms were uncertain, as the Communist party's cadres tried to mobilize peasants to take direct action and to seize lands that had not been designated for expropriation by the central government.

It proved easy to seize land but difficult to redistribute it. Although the FAO had estimated that some 2,000 cooperative societies would be needed to replace the landlords, there were only 25 by 1963. Some 1.3 million hectares had been expropriated by then, but only 316,000 hectares had been redistributed. The remainder of the land was rented to peasants, typically on one-year leases. Such arrangements gave the peasants little interest in the long-run productivity of the land, and the government lacked the personnel to promote its interests. Although Iraqi agricultural statistics for the period are unreliable, production at best stagnated and probably declined in the first ten years of the reforms (Penrose and Penrose 1978).

When the Ba'ath returned to power in 1968, the party reduced the land ceiling further and confiscated an additional 1.5 million hectares of land. Although the redistribution of land accelerated after 1971, by the end of 1975, only one-third of the sequestered land had been distributed. The government seemed to place its hopes on increasing control over coop-eratives, on greatly expanding agricultural investment, and on establishing state farms. However, by 1975 less than 3% of the cultivated area was in state farms. The 1976–1980 Five-Year Plan called for the creation of over 300 collective farms and called for some 325,000 hectares to pass into the public sector. Increasing food-security fears as inefficient state farms re-sponded sluggishly to the explosion of demand and Saddam Hussein's attempts to weaken rivals in the Ba'ath party generated a "counterreform" of the early 1980s. The number of collective farms fell from 77 in 1979 to only 10 by 1983. Law 35 in 1983 permitted private entrepreneurs to rent land from the state on long leases (up to twenty years) with no land ceiling, while land-reform beneficiaries were permitted far more freedom to operate than ever before (Springborg 1986).

Increasing privatization of agriculture is not limited to Iraq. Throughout the region, the extensive experience with large-scale state farms has been disappointing. Whether in Tunisia in the 1960s, in Iraq and Syria in the 1970s, or in newly reclaimed lands in Egypt, wholly public-sector farms have been abandoned. In Algeria, 2,000 "self-managed" farms have been subdivided into 6,000 smaller and more specialized units, while "other land is being leased to state farm workers or coop members who want to farm privately" (USDA 1987, 23). Privately owned large farms fared little better: In Pahlavi Iran the large "farm corporations" set up by the shah not only disrupted rural society but also failed to out-produce medium-sized peasant holdings by any of several measures (Moghadem 1982). The large number of detailed local surveys conducted in Egypt over the past decade agree that very small farmers are at least as productive and efficient as larger ones. Small may not be beautiful, but big is surely sluggish. As the food-security problem loomed ever larger, governments from Algeria to Iraq turned toward the private sector to solve their domestic agricultural supply problems. For such a strategy to succeed, however, adequate incentives are necessary.

## PRICES, TAXES, AND SUBSIDIES

Government price policies have become the bête noire of orthodox development thinking. Many economists point to heavy taxation as a crucial impediment to more rapid growth of agricultural production (e.g., Schultz 1978). They commonly charge that the mechanisms chosen to transfer resources out of the farming sector distort farmers' incentives and spawn resource misallocations. Two types of price policies receive most attention: direct taxation, in which government-run marketing agencies enjoying monopsony or oligopsony power offer farmers prices well below those prevailing on world markets; and the indirect taxation implicit in an overvalued real foreign-exchange rate. The first mechanism is straightforward: Since farmers are offered lower prices, and since farmers are "price responsive," such policies weaken their incentives to produce. Because some crops are more heavily taxed than others, farmers reallocate land, labor, and purchased inputs toward less taxed, more profitable crops.

Overvalued exchange rates also weaken farmers' incentives. Such overvaluation creates excess demand for foreign exchange, which is then usually rationed by (often complex) government trade regulations. These policies lower the value of exports and raise the value of imports, while also increasing the prices of nontraded domestic goods relative to products that are traded internationally. The first effect hurts producers of export crops (e.g., cotton, rice, vegetables) and of the major import-competing crop, cereals. Furthermore, government rationing of scarce foreign exchange usually favors industrial and military users; farmers often stand last in line, finding that they must pay higher prices for inputs or consumer goods, if, indeed, they can get them at all. The increase in the relative price of nontraded to traded goods also hurts farmers, because a large portion of the sector's costs are nontraded inputs like land and labor,[16] while their outputs are, of course, traded. All of these effects reduce farmers' profit margins.

Such indirect taxation and trade-based distortions are in turn traced to import-substituting industrialization programs: The choice of such a development strategy thus implies biases against agriculture (Little, Scitovsky, and Scott 1970; Johnston and Kilby 1975; Timmer, Falcon, and Pearson 1983). The argument of the Dutch Disease follows similar lines: An overvalued real exchange rate creates incentives for labor and capital to move out of traded-good sectors such as agriculture into nontraded goods, like urban construction, real estate, and services. Both directly (price policies) and indirectly (exchange-rate policies), the strategy of import-substituting industrialization stands accused of undermining farmers' incentives throughout the region (e.g., Cleaver 1982; Ikram 1980). This position has not gone unchallenged; defenders of ISI have argued that governments must get revenue from somewhere, that international prices are highly unstable, that economists do not agree on how to measure the real exchange rate, and that deficient investment is much more important than price policies in explaining poor agricultural performance. Let us examine MENA experience with price policies.

First of all, we must divide the countries of the region into two groups: those that have substantial nonagricultural revenue sources (usually oil exporters) and those that have little choice but to rely on agriculture for the bulk of their tax revenues. Although foreign-exchange largesse is supposed to be detrimental to agriculture in models of the Dutch Disease, countries with surplus capital have often found ways to offset such problems. Their hefty oil rents eliminate the need to transfer resources from agriculture to other sectors, their demand for food has grown the most rapidly of all the countries in the region, and their food-security fears were (and are) acute. In response, major oil-exporting governments have lavishly subsidized their farmers. Thus Saudi Arabia paid farmers from five to six times the international price of wheat during the early 1980s, while simultaneously subsidizing inputs; the received wheat price has been roughly 225% above production cost (*Mideast Review 1985,* p. 212). Saudi government loans to farmers rose from under $5 million in 1971 to over $1 billion in 1983; from 1980 to 1985 the Saudi government spent some $20 billion on agriculture, mostly in the form of subsidies (*Economist,* April 6, 1985, pp. 80–83). The results have been spectacular for the key food-security crop: Wheat output rose by over 700% from 1971 to 1983, entirely replacing imports and actually creating a small export surplus. Libya, Kuwait, and the UAE also offer generous farm incentives. Both economic and ecological critiques have been leveled at these policies (e.g., Nowshirvani 1987), but food-security concerns swept them aside.

Countries enjoying less ample revenues have historically had little alternative to taxing agriculture (except borrowing) to finance industrialization and human-welfare programs. The allocational, equity, and political consequences of different types of taxation vary widely. We shall consider three types of government instruments: (1) direct taxation, i.e., taxing farmer's land or incomes, (2) using state-controlled marketing systems to tax certain crops, (3) overvalued exchange rates and other trade-policy instruments like tariffs and physical quotas.

Direct taxation of either income or agricultural land is not widely practiced in the region. Farmers are sometimes exempted from taxation because of hardship, as in Morocco after the devastating droughts of the early 1980s, or as part of an explicit policy of encouraging agriculture, as in Iraq in the early 1980s. In Egypt, the land tax remains extremely low, fixed at the level of land rents in 1952 until 1977 (Ikram 1980). Economists often advocate using a land tax, which has both equity and efficiency advantages (e.g., Hansen and Radwan 1982). However, such advice is rarely followed because rich farmers have repeatedly and successfully lobbied against it.

A much more common, and more distorting, means of taxing agriculture is to combine control of the marketing system with trade regulations. In the Sudanese Gezira Scheme, for example, the government enjoys a mar keting monopoly over cotton. By paying farmers less than the international price for the commodity that the government sells, the latter extracts resources from agriculture.[17] Egypt follows a similar system for cotton, sugar, and rice and implements as well as extensive quantity and area controls for other crops. Algeria, Morocco, and Tunisia do the same thing; the Algerian government's interventions are the most extensive, but even supposedly "liberal" Tunisia fixes the producers' prices for eight of the major farm outputs.[18] The Syrian government also interferes extensively in the food marketing system, although "parallel" private markets are also very active.[19]

The results of these policies for nominal protection coefficients (NPCs),[20] however, vary widely across countries and over time, even for wheat, the region's preferred food grain (Table 6.5). Differences over time are largely explained by changes in international prices, which were highly volatile during the 1970s; governments kept producer prices above import levels during 1971–1973, reduced their local prices relative to the soaring in ternational prices of 1973–1975, and increased relative local prices once again when international prices fell during 1977–1979. In short, governments stabilized prices during the 1970s.

NPCs are calculated using official exchange rates. If the currency is overvalued in real terms, NPCs understate the disincentive for farmers. An alternative calculation that corrects for exchange rate overvaluation is shown in Table 6.6. Many countries had overvalued exchange rates and offered farmers considerably less than the real international price for wheat during the 1970s. However, four countries, including two non–oil states, actually subsidized their wheat producers already in the 1970s. This has become increasingly the norm during the 1980s, as food-security fears have mounted. For example, the Syrian government paid wheat farmers about 30% more than the international price in the early and middle 1980s; maize farmers received over twice the international price, while sugar beet, sugarcane, and cotton farmers also received prices above international levels (World Bank 1986a). Some countries' farmers may enjoy prices above international levels because of "natural protection" due to transportation barriers: Thus

Table 6.5 Average Producer Price of Wheat as a Percentage of the Import Price (c.i.f.), 1971-1981

| | 1971 | 1972 | 1973 | 1974 | 1975 | 1976 | 1977 | 1978 | 1979 | 1980 | 1981 | Average |
|---|---|---|---|---|---|---|---|---|---|---|---|---|
| Algeria | 140 | 144 | 131 | 55 | 73 | 90 | 144 | 159 | 180 | 156 | -- | 127 |
| Egypt | 113 | 106 | 96 | 53 | 61 | 62 | 97 | 96 | 54 | 62 | 63 | 79 |
| Iran | 145 | 144 | 131 | 55 | 66 | 73 | 120 | 125 | 127 | -- | -- | 110 |
| Iraq | 142 | 113 | 126 | 49 | 52 | 56 | 89 | 79 | -- | -- | -- | 88 |
| Jordan | 121 | 118 | 116 | 54 | 66 | 73 | 133 | 119 | 115 | 109 | -- | 102 |
| Libya | 199 | 193 | 172 | 81 | 86 | 96 | 202 | 210 | 243 | -- | -- | 165 |
| Morocco | 130 | 137 | 149 | 85 | 99 | 96 | 175 | 162 | 184* | 189 | -- | 141 |
| Pakistan | 145 | 97 | 60 | 30 | 47 | 54 | 77 | 80 | 75* | 72* | -- | 74 |
| Saudi Arabia | 248 | 232 | 230 | 125 | 159 | 215 | 356 | 322 | -- | -- | -- | 235 |
| Syria | 107 | 103 | 126 | 53 | 64 | 68 | 110 | 106 | 99* | 94 | -- | 93 |
| Sudan | 146 | 149 | 179 | 82 | 85 | 109 | 149 | 140 | 168* | 158* | -- | 137 |
| Tunisia | 123 | 130 | 117 | 61 | 75 | 78 | 115 | 113 | 111* | 105* | -- | 103 |
| Turkey | 98 | 102 | 94 | 75 | 87 | 86 | 116 | 89 | 102 | 71 | 83 | 91 |
| Unit Value of Imported Wheat** US$/mt | 72 | 76 | 100 | 225 | 215 | 194 | 142 | 159 | 168 | 203 | 208 | -- |

* Producer support price.
** The average unit value of wheat imports for all countries in the region, calculated from the total volume of wheat imports and their dollar value, is used as an estimate of the c.i.f. import wheat price.

Source: FAO, Agricultural Price Policies in the Near East: Lessons and Experience, Rome, 1983, p. 7.

Table 6.6　Currency Overvaluation and Average Producer Prices for Wheat, 1971-
　　　　　1981

|  | Index of Currency Overvaluation* | Average Producer Official Exchange Rate | Price of Wheat Using Market Exchange Rate |
|---|---|---|---|
| Algeria | 178 | 127 | 71 |
| Egypt | 174 | 79 | 45 |
| Iran | 120 | 110 | 92 |
| Iraq | 118 | 88 | 74 |
| Jordan | 101 | 102 | 101 |
| Libya | 143 | 165 | 115 |
| Morocco | 104 | 141 | 136 |
| Saudi Arabia | 99 | 235 | 237 |
| Sudan | 181 | 137 | 76 |
| Syria | 107 | 93 | 87 |
| Tunisia | 115 | 103 | 90 |
| Turkey | 125 | 91 | 73 |

* Official dollar value of national currency as percentage of market value as
given in Pick's Currency Handbook.

Source (middle and last columns): FAO, "Agricultural Price Policies in the Near
East: Lessons and Experience," 1983, p. 8.

farmers in the YAR in 1982 received, on average, cereal prices that were
360% above those prevailing on international markets (World Bank 1986a,
Annex 1).

The actual tax burdens on agriculture that result from such systems is
a matter of dispute. The FAO study cited above found little correlation
across countries between low real NPCs and rates of growth of wheat
production (FAO 1984); this suggests that price policies are hardly the
sole explanation for sluggish agricultural growth. It does not, however,
prove that price policies are unimportant. In all countries only *some* crops
are taxed: In Egypt, for example, clover, vegetables, and fruits are unregulated, while in Tunisia, pulses, lamb, and most fruits and vegetables fetch
whatever price the market will bear. It is widely agreed that farmers are
highly responsive to price signals among crops. For example, Egyptian
farmers fled from cotton and rice into horticultural crops and from wheat
into clover, whereas Sudanese farmers in the Gezira switched their land
and labor away from heavily taxed cotton toward sorghum, peanuts, and
wheat. In Algeria, value-added in (taxed) cereals stagnated between 1974
and 1986; during this same period, value-added in vegetables grew at 7.4%
per year, that of fresh fruit at 4.3% (World Bank 1987; FAO Production
Yearbooks). In Egypt the value of the allocative distortions during the
1960s has been estimated at a sum equal to the size of the country's entire
balance-of-payments deficit (Hansen and Nashashibi 1975); a more recent
estimate (for 1980) places the losses at about 7.5% of agricultural output
or 1.5% of GDP (Alderman and von Braun 1984). In the Sudan, the incentive
bias against cotton reduced the average yield of that crop by roughly 50%
between 1974 and 1980–1981 (World Bank 1985); since cotton is that
country's largest export, such policies and the farmers' responses to them

exacerbated the country's severe balance-of-payments problem. There is little doubt that the resource reallocations brought about by distorted price signals have had important efficiency consequences.[21]

Price policies raise two major equity issues. First, since rural residents are usually poorer than urbanites, the transfer of resources out of agriculture is disequalizing. Second, wealthier farmers find it easier to evade government regulations and to shift resources out of controlled crops than do their poorer neighbors. Such arguments are highly plausible but should be treated with caution. First, the calculations upon which such conclusions are made require numerous assumptions; in particular, few studies are available that include an assessment of *all* input subsidies, including water subsidies and loan forgiveness, along with output taxes.[22] Second, in some cases, government policies may (perhaps unintentionally) favor the smaller farmers, as seems to be the case in Egypt (Alderman and von Braun 1984).[23] Such a case appears to be unusual; since most input subsidies accrue to richer farmers, the "inefficient and iniquitous" critique of output price policies has considerable force. Finally, most studies of Turkish farm subsidies agree that the lion's share of crop support benefits accrue to larger farmers, simply because subsidies are per unit of output and because, of course, larger farmers produce a larger total amount of crops.[24]

Although output price policies stimulate the reallocation of cropland, the responsiveness of agricultural output as a whole to price distortions is far less certain. Changing price policies is no panacea for the food gap. Several studies of Egyptian agriculture indicate that the responsiveness of the entire sector to shifts in its terms of trade is rather low (e.g., Alderman and von Braun 1984). Since this implies that price increases would have to be large if any substantial output response is to be expected, it is unsurprising that government officials, concerned with inflation and financing the cost of urban subsidies, fear such price increases. Presumably, the longer the time period, the greater the response: Price distortions may inhibit technological change and/or bias its direction in socially undesirable ways. However, it is worth noting that there are some surprises here: If Egyptian farmers received world prices for all crops, that country's production of wheat (the main food-security crop) would actually *decrease,* since Egypt lacks a comparative advantage in that crop.[25] Nevertheless, it is hard to believe that long periods of disincentives to agricultural production do not elicit farmer responses. It is probably not an accident that Turkey, which has offered price supports (i.e., subsidies) rather than crop taxes for over a generation, has had one of the strongest long-run performance of any country in the region.

The impact of overvalued exchange rates on agricultural performance also illustrates the complexity of the consequences of price policies. The Sudanese experience shows that overvaluation harms the production of important export crops. Again, however, the multiplicity of unfavorable factors in the decline of that country's cotton exports during the late 1970s counsels caution in placing excessive reliance on any one instrument to

solve agricultural problems. Acreage, yield, and therefore of course production of cotton fell sharply under the combined disadvantages of an
overvalued exchange rate (cotton exports were traded at the least favorable
of several different rates), special additional taxation of cotton production,
administrative failures (paying farmers late, delays in input deliveries),
deterioration of the Gezira-Managil irrigation system, and the acute shortage
of fuel for transport. A realignment of the exchange rate, along with reform
of the parastatals, abolition of some of the special taxes on cotton, and a
rehabilitation of the irrigation network led to a resurgence of production
of the cotton crop, from about 300,000 tons in 1980/81 to more than twice
that figure in 1984/85 (World Bank 1985; *Middle East,* May 1986).

The Turkish experience also suggests that exchange-rate reform will
not automatically lead to an agricultural boom. Despite the gross overvaluation of the Turkish lira from 1973 to 1977, that country's agriculture
performed quite well by international standards. The crisis of the balance
of payments, domestic inflation, rationing, and political violence contributed
to dramatic policy changes after 1979 (see Chapters 8 and 9). These
reforms followed orthodox lines: devaluation of the exchange rate, reduction
or elimination of input and consumer subsidies, granting of export subsidies.
There was a one-year boom in agricultural exports, due mainly to depressed
domestic demand. The (dollar) value of Turkish agricultural exports in
1985 was 22% below that of 1981 (Kopits 1987). Devaluations and reductions
in government subsidies have increased the price of agricultural inputs
more rapidly than those of outputs, catching farmers in a profit squeeze.
A few years ago the president of the Union of Chambers of Agriculture,
Osman Özbek, charged that farmers' purchasing power had declined by
over one-third during the previous six years (*Middle East,* March 1986, p.
44). Farmers, wholesale merchants, and processors dealing in import-
substitution crops could constitute an important lobby against the Özal
government's policies.

This leads us to the question of the political origins of such policies.
A prominent position holds that these lie in the "urban bias" of government
agencies and actors (Lipton 1977). Of course, ISI strategies are indeed
"biased" toward industry; their entire rationale is to increase the percentage
of national output coming from industry. Since such industries are usually
located in urban areas, there may be little difference between "urban bias"
and the imperatives of ISI. The latter requires a source of investable funds,
implies an overvalued exchange rate, and necessitates tariff protection.
Each of these implies some discrimination against agriculture. In this
sense, then, urban bias is the cause of pricing policies that distort agricultural
incentives.

Some distortions in incentives have been introduced because of the
government obsession with food security. To the extent that such a concern
derives from the power of urban political actors, then there is an additional
role for "urban bias" in the explanation of food-price policies. For example,
one of the reasons Sudanese farmers abandoned the cultivation of cotton

during the late 1970s was that the government tried to promote the production of wheat for domestic consumption—an ill-conceived food-security measure.

The role of food-security fears in policymaking indicates that state autonomy is alive and well in the agricultural sector. More often than not, governments respond to the outcome (e.g., accelerating balance-of-payments deficits) that farmers' responses to distorted incentives engender. In a balance-of-payments crisis, as in Sudan and Turkey, the state may have less autonomy vis-à-vis international actors, but there is little evidence that political lobbying by farmers has played a large role in recent policy shifts. To be sure, state actors are *constrained* by the threat of insufficient urban food supplies. Dramatic cuts in food subsidies *may* lead to urban unrest or even open riots; but, as we shall see, this is not always true. The political economy of food subsidies is complex; they are not merely Pavlovian responses to political bells.

Furthermore, an alternative source of investable funds lowers the taxation of agriculture. Countries that receive substantial foreign exchange can, and have, pursued policies more favorable to agriculture than the classical ISI model implies: Capital-surplus oil exporters heavily subsidize their agricultures, Turkish subsidization of agriculture dates from the 1950s and substantial U.S. aid inflows, and the burden of taxation of Egyptian agriculture declined during the 1970s when receipts from oil exports, workers' remittances, and foreign aid grew dramatically.

The link, then, between consumer food subsidies and low prices for farmers is indirect. Funds must be found to subsidize urban consumers, just as they must be obtained to undertake industrial investment. There is no *necessary* connection between food subsidies and low prices for farmers; it is, again, a question of the availability of alternative sources of government revenue. Saudi Arabia heavily subsidizes *both* producers and consumers because it can afford to do so; the cost of Egyptian food subsidies soared during the 1970s at the same time as the burden of taxation on agriculture declined—the financing of the subsidies was simply shifted to the general budget, which was bolstered by the additional revenues, described in the preceding paragraph. A country like Tunisia that both subsidizes food and lacks alternative revenue sources will no doubt be reluctant to modify adverse producer prices. But the issue is not so much one of urban bias as of external largesse and the mobilization of domestic resources by the tax system.[26]

## INVESTMENT AND TECHNOLOGICAL POLICIES

Although price policies are important determinants of agricultural development, they are hardly the whole story. Technological change is the core of development, and although relative prices influence such change, many other government interventions shape its speed and pattern. The development literature usually divides farm technological changes into two

Table 6.7   Share of Agricultural Investment in Total Public Investment, 1968-
            1985 (selected years)

| | Planning Period | % Agriculture in Planned Spending | Actual Spending |
|---|---|---|---|
| Algeria | 1970-77 | 12 | 15 (1970-73) |
| | 1980-84 | 12 | |
| Egypt | 1973-82 | 10 | 9 (1973-81) |
| | 1980-84 | 18 | |
| Iran | 1973-77 | 7 | |
| | 1977-81 | | 5 (1979-80) |
| Iraq | 1970-80 | 18 | 11 (1970-78) |
| | 1981-85 | 2 | |
| Jordan | 1973-80 | 6 | 7 |
| Libya | 1973-80 | 12 | 13 |
| Morocco | 1973-80 | 19 | 12 |
| | 1981-85 | 18 | |
| Saudi Arabia | 1970-74 | 2 | 5 |
| | 1975-80 | 2 | |
| | 1980-85 | 10 | |
| Sudan | 1970-80 | 26 | 24 |
| | 1980-83 | 24 | |
| Syria | 1971-80 | 25 | 7 |
| | 1981-85 | 17 | |
| Tunisia | 1973-81 | 13 | 13 |
| | 1982-84 | 14 | |
| Turkey | 1968-72 | | 11 |
| | 1973-77 | | 12 |
| | 1979-83 | 12 | |
| YAR | 1973-81 | 15 | 10 |
| | 1982-84 | 16 | |
| PDRY | 1971-79 | 33 | 34 |
| | 1981-85 | 17 | |

Source: FAO, "Strategies for Agricultural Investment in the Near East," 1984.

types: biological-chemical and mechanical (e.g., Johnston and Kilby 1975). Since the former type requires dependable water supplies, irrigation investment has long been a major form of state-sponsored technological change. We shall first discuss irrigation expansion, then turn to the "green revolution," or the diffusion of higher-yielding varieties (HYVs) of cereals, and conclude with an assessment of farm mechanization.

First, however, let us assess the share of agriculture in total investment. This share varies widely across countries (Table 6.7). Note, however, that the Sudan, a country with one of the highest shares, suffered from a serious famine in 1984.[27] Obviously, a large total share of investment in agriculture is not a sufficient condition for agricultural growth and development. However, it may be a necessary condition.

How much *should* countries invest in agriculture? Although it is often observed that agriculture's share of investment is well below its share of GDP, there is no reason why investment and output shares should necessarily be equal. The real issue is the productivity of investment, specifically the incremental capital-to-output ratio, or ICOR. Raj Krishna (1982) has argued that agricultural ICORs are likely to be considerably higher than had been

Table 6.8  Irrigated Area, Total (000 ha) and as Percentage of Total Cultivated
Area, 1970-1985 (selected years)

| | Irrigated Cultivation | | | | | | | |
|---|---|---|---|---|---|---|---|---|
| | 1970 | | 1975 | | 1980 | | 1985 | |
| | Area | % | Area | % | Area | % | Area | % |
| Algeria | 238 | 3.5 | 244 | 3.3 | 253 | 3.4 | 338 | 4.4 |
| Egypt | 2843 | 100.0 | 2825 | 100.0 | 2447 | 100.0 | 2486 | 100.0 |
| Iran | 5200 | 33.0 | 5900 | 36.0 | 4948 | 36.0 | 5740 | 39.0 |
| Iraq | 1480 | 30.0 | 1567 | 30.0 | 1750 | 32.0 | 1750 | 32.0 |
| Israel | 168 | 41.0 | 181 | 43.0 | 203 | 49.0 | 271 | 65.0 |
| Jordan | 34 | 9.0 | 36 | 9.0 | 37 | 9.0 | 43 | 10.0 |
| Lebanon | 68 | 21.0 | 86 | 26.0 | 86 | 28.0 | 86 | 29.0 |
| Libya | 175 | 8.6 | 200 | 9.7 | 225 | 10.8 | 234 | 11.0 |
| Morroco | 340 | 4.5 | 425 | 5.5 | 510 | 6.4 | 523 | 6.2 |
| Oman | 29 | 91.0 | 34 | 92.0 | 38 | 93.0 | 41 | 87.0 |
| Saudi Arabia | 365 | 42.0 | 375 | 34.0 | 390 | 35.0 | 415 | 35.0 |
| Sudan | 1750 | 15.0 | 1565 | 12.9 | 1600 | 12.9 | 1700 | 13.6 |
| Syria | 451 | 8.0 | 516 | 9.0 | 539 | 9.0 | 652 | 12.0 |
| Tunisia | 90 | 2.0 | 125 | 2.6 | 156 | 3.3 | 215 | 4.4 |
| Turkey | 1800 | 7.0 | 1980 | 7.0 | 2070 | 7.0 | 2150 | 8.0 |
| YAR | 210 | 16.0 | 230 | 17.0 | 245 | 18.0 | 247 | 18.0 |
| PDRY | 52 | 39.0 | 56 | 39.0 | 60 | 38.0 | 62 | 37.0 |

Source: **FAO Production Yearbook**, Rome, FAO, 1987.

formerly thought. Irrigation investment is often inherently expensive: The
High Dam at Aswan, for example, cost approximately $840 million. Fur-
thermore, since most "easy" investments have already been undertaken,
additional ones are likely to have higher ICORs, especially as the region's
agriculture increasingly shifts from extensive to intensive growth. Krishna
asserted that agriculture in most LDCs should receive at least 20% of total
public investment. By such a modified criterion, it appears that most
agricultural sectors in the region receive inadequate investment.[28] Actual
spending is usually less than planned (Table 6.7). With the exception of
embattled Iraq, all countries in the region show increases in nominal
spending on agriculture in the early 1980s compared with the late 1970s.
However, only Egypt, Sudan, and Saudi Arabia planned significant increases
in agriculture's share of total investment (FAO 1984). An agricultural
investment boom is not about to plug the region's food gap.

## Irrigation

Much, often most, public investment in agriculture in the region is in
irrigation: In recent planning periods irrigation received 60% of planned
expenditures on agriculture in Iraq, 60% in Jordan, 83% in Syria, 82% in
Saudi Arabia, 60% in YAR, and 61% in PDRY (FAO 1984). This is quite
understandable, given the ecology of the region and the fact that so far
all biological/chemical technical changes (such as HYVs) require dependable water supplies. The expansion of irrigation in the region by
country is detailed on Table 6.8. The rate of growth of the irrigated area

in the region during the past decade has been below that for many other developing regions.[29] For many countries the expansion has been disappointing.

The benefits of irrigation are evident: a larger cultivated area, (often dramatically) increased crop yields, and reduced risk to food supplies from fluctuating rainfall. The costs are equally apparent: negative ecological externalities, exacerbated by the neglect of maintenance, and poor management. In addition, state investment in irrigation often dispossesses some rural people, while bestowing large windfalls on others. Finally, concentrating on irrigation often implies neglecting rain-fed areas, where, apart from Egypt, most rural people in the area live. A brief glance at a few experiences in the region will help to highlight these issues.

Egypt, whose agriculture is entirely dependent on irrigation, has had as long an experience with sustained large-scale irrigation development as any other country in the world. Egypt's agriculture had been dependent on the Nile flood for millennia, but the country's irrigation system underwent a fundamental transformation in the nineteenth century with the transition to year-round irrigation, a transformation that only concluded in the 1960s with the completion of the Aswan High Dam. There are certain inescapable facts about Egyptian irrigation development: (1) summer irrigation made possible the production of cotton on a substantial scale and was thus an important part of that country's integration into the international economy during the nineteenth century; (2) year-round, dependable irrigation makes it possible for Egyptian yields to be among the highest in the world; for example, the High Dam enabled maize (until very recently the main rural foodstuff) yields to increase by over 70%; (3) The process of irrigation expansion not only redistributed land, especially in the nineteenth century, but also increased the role of the state in the countryside; (4) political forces have determined the pattern and timing of irrigation investment, with the result that the technological externalities that often accompany irrigation development were ignored and neglected (Waterbury 1979; Richards 1982).

The debate on the merits of the High Dam at Aswan has raged for at least thirty years. Although its problems were and are serious, the achievements of the dam are too often overlooked. First, there is no doubt that some form of "over year storage"[30] for Nile water was absolutely necessary to provide increased irrigation water to keep up with the country's expanding demand for food. Egypt's food-security problem would have been *much* worse much earlier without the dam. When the annual Nile flood was unusually low in 1972, the country's agriculture suffered relatively little— thanks to the dam. The devastating droughts that ravaged Ethiopia and Sudan in the early 1980s would have severely affected Egypt also—had it not been for the dam. Even with the dam, disaster has been narrowly averted: The level of Lake Nasser was only 147 meters in August 1988 (at 145 meters, the turbines of the dam would have had to be shut down). Second, there was really no alternative to the dam; all other technically feasible approaches faced insuperable political obstacles.[31] It is hardly surprising that given the need and given the alternatives, the High Dam at Aswan was constructed.

The technological externalities were severe, however. Some of these were unique to the High Dam: problems of shoreline erosion (because all silt was trapped behind the dam), decline in fish catches in lakes and in the Mediterranean, scouring of the Nile banks, and high evaporation losses of the water stored in Lake Nasser. However, the most serious problems were really not qualitatively different from problems that had repeatedly plagued the extension of year-round (i.e., summer) irrigation in Egypt for more than half a century: inadequate drainage and health problems. The problems of schistosomiasis and ancylostomiasis in Egypt are very ancient, but were certainly exacerbated by earlier (khedivial and British) irrigation works just as they were by the High Dam. From the point of view of agricultural production, however, the main problem with irrigation expansion both was and is the neglect of drainage. The ecological consequences of such neglect are straightforward: All water contains soluble salts and minerals, and even if farmers use water with maximum efficiency, inadequate drainage will permit these salts to accumulate, dramatically lowering soil fertility. By the late 1970s, this problem afflicted some two-thirds of Egypt's cropland.

The benefits of irrigation appear almost at once, while the costs of neglecting drainage only become apparent later. If governments face strong revenue pressures, and if they desperately want a success now, they usually succumb to myopia. This happened in Egypt both under the British (1890–1914) and under Nasser. In both cases, irrigation expanded while drainage lagged behind; in both cases, crop yields first soared, then stagnated. Politics and finance have conquered agronomy throughout the region: Salinity plagues Syrian, Moroccan, Sudanese, Tunisian, indeed, virtually every regional investment program in irrigation expansion.[32] Once the problem is recognized, large additional funds are required to remedy the problem, as in Egypt both in the 1920s and 1930s and in the 1970s and 1980s. The remedies are very expensive: The total outlay for field drains (still not completed) will exceed the cost of the High Dam itself. But the alternative to drainage installation is for substantial areas of land to go out of cultivation, as occurred in Syria until very recently (ICARDA 1979).

In Gulf countries and in Libya, irrigation projects often draw on groundwater. As in the southwestern United States, the temptation to remove more water than nature replenishes is severe. On the Tripolitanian coast of Libya, such activities have already led to the intrusion of seawater into the aquifer, endangering current water supplies. The current, massive "great man-made river," which will channel water from the south to the coast, relies entirely on fossil water (Allan 1981). Such projects offer no long-term solution to food-production problems, since they rely on a nonrenewable resource. But as with the Aswan High Dam, once the political commitment has been made, and especially once political enemies begin to denounce the project, any criticism of the scheme smacks of disloyalty. What Libyan would risk criticizing a project now officially referred to as "our national anthem"?

Irrigation's social and political effects are no less striking than its ecological difficulties. These investments confer differential benefits on rural social groups. The concentration of scarce funds on irrigation implies the neglect of the rural majority, farmers in the rain-fed areas. It is often argued that investments in such zones will not raise productivity dramatically and will create even more ecological problems than irrigation (Adams and Howell 1979). Although Sudanese agricultural investment concentrates on the more developed irrigated zones of the north and east, designing ecologically sound, productivity-enhancing development projects in the western Sahelian zones is a difficult task.[33] Even in more favorable rain-fed areas, the design of sustainable, productivity-enhancing investments faces significant obstacles. Countries like Libya have already probably pushed dry farming into areas where it can be sustained only with great difficulty and good luck (Allan 1981).

However, neglecting rain-fed areas in favor of irrigated zones is self-defeating: As population grows, the pressure on fragile, rain-fed environments rises, and deforestation accelerates, fostering soil erosion, greater flooding, and more rapid accumulation of silt in irrigation systems. While the irrigation systems are thus undermined, the surplus rural population migrates to the cities, compounding the economic, administrative, and political burdens on the state. In countries like Morocco and Sudan, the collapse of agriculture in some rain-fed zones due to drought and land mismanagement has created formidable social disasters.

Since we would expect the rate of return on investment in irrigation to decline over time, the continued emphasis on irrigation seems administratively and politically driven. In Morocco, for example, the World Bank has calculated that the IRRs (internal rate of return) on investments in rain-fed areas exceed those on irrigated lands by 50 to 100%, but the government continues to stress irrigation development (World Bank 1981). Rates of return on rain-fed agricultural projects also exceed those on irrigation in the Sudan (World Bank 1985). However, many regional governments have built up considerable expertise in hydraulic projects. Irrigation ministries are old and well established, and the technologies are well understood. Engineers and planners know how to build a dam; it is not surprising that they keep doing what they know best. Despite the disappointing experience with irrigation expansion, the relative ease of administration of irrigation systems is highly attractive to state actors. Last but not least, irrigation investment usually entails large and lucrative contracts to private-sector construction companies, which doubtless share some of the money with irrigation bureaucrats.

Administrative inertia provides only a partial explanation for the emphasis on irrigation, however. Food-security fears and the political clout of those favored by such investments also contribute to the outcome. States invest in irrigation hoping to reduce national food dependency. Irrigation works are complementary with the other subsidies that the Saudi government lavishes on its farmers. The problems of food security are at the moment pressing; the ecological difficulties of irrigation mismanagement and dryland neglect will appear only in the future. Once again, the lethal politics of the region produces the short time horizon of planners; this favors the short run over the future, but in this arid zone of the world, nature's revenge is often cruelly swift.

Irrigation also provides the state with an opportunity to extend its authority in the countryside and to pursue its "vision" of development. The Moroccan government has used irrigation development partly as a kind of substitute for land reform, and partly as a mechanism for bestowing benefits on the rural notables, who constitute such an important source of political support (Leveau 1985; Swearingen 1987). Although the World Bank recommended in the 1970s that farmers receiving the benefits of irrigation expansion be taxed, the advice has been ignored. Moroccan irrigation investment, like Mexican, has reinforced the position of the rural rich, exacerbating bimodalism. Farmers in the irrigated areas concentrate on high-value crops, leaving cereal production to the neglected rain-fed areas. Cereal output has stagnated; the final irony of the obsession with irrigation is that it fails to solve the food-security problem.

State actors often use irrigation to recast rather than to reinforce the social-class structure. For example, by developing new irrigated areas in the Ghab region, the Syrian Ba'athists could sponsor state cooperatives and bring in poor farmers from other areas as part of a land-reform effort. By carefully mixing different ethnic groups, the regime seeks to promote its vision of a "new society," no longer composed of Alawis, or Druze, or Sunnis, but of Syrian small farmers, dependent on the state. Many governments favor such developments because they offer tabulae rasae. The preference of the Egyptian government for (economically questionable) land reclamation over development of the existing villages of the Nile Valley may have this kind of explanation: Everything on reclaimed land can be planned from the top down, whereas in the Old Lands, development efforts must confront the complexities of existing social structures and power relationships (Métral 1980; Richards 1982).

Finally, the neglect of maintenance and recurring expenditures also bedevil irrigation systems. This is a widespread development problem, hardly limited either to irrigation or to the Middle East. It is especially serious there because, as most authorities agree, water is becoming increasingly scarce in the region, and as demand presses against inherently limited supplies, the imperative is for better management of already existing systems, for raising the returns to water, rather than for developing new systems. The efficiency of water use is low throughout the region. The combination of gravity-flow irrigation (which makes it cheap to apply water and difficult to monitor usage) and the absence of any pricing system engenders widespread overwatering, compounding salinity and drainage

Table 6.9   Distribution of High-Yielding Varieties of Wheat and Rice Throughout
            Developing Regions of the World, 1982-1983 (percentages)

| | HYWVs | All Wheat | HYRVs | All Rice | HYWVs and HYRVs | All Wheat and Rice |
|---|---|---|---|---|---|---|
| Asia* | 60.8 | 46.5 | 92.9 | 86.2 | 76.3 | 69.9 |
| Near East | 18.2 | 36.6 | 0.3 | 1.2 | 9.5 | 15.7 |
| Africa | 1.2 | 1.4 | 0.5 | 4.4 | 0.9 | 3.2 |
| Latin America | 19.9 | 15.5 | 6.3 | 8.2 | 13.3 | 11.2 |
| Total | 100.1** | 100.0 | 100.0 | 100.0 | 100.0 | 100.0 |

\* Excludes Communist Asia.
\** Total is greater than 100 due to rounding.

Source: Dana G. Dalrymple, **Development and Spread of High Yielding Wheat
Varieties in Developing Countries**, Washington, D.C., USAID, 1986, pp. 25-31.

problems. The result, in MENA as elsewhere, has been to try to increase,
rather than to ration, supplies. The absence of trained personnel and low
educational levels of farmers further impede the transition to a new water
regime that recognizes the inherent limitations of regional water supplies
and tries to devise systems to allocate water to its most productive use.
Once again, the neglect of the "ultimate resource" of human talent impedes
sustainable development strategies.

## High-Yielding Varieties: The Green Revolution

One of the benefits of improved water control is that it permits greater
use of fertilizer and the adoption of higher-yielding varieties of grain. Such
"packages" of improved inputs (often called the green revolution) raise
output per unit of land, in contrast with mechanical innovations, which
reduce production costs and make possible an extension of the cultivated
area, but which do little to raise crop yields (Binswanger 1986). Mechanization has spread more rapidly during the past fifteen years than have
yield-increasing technologies, with the notable and important exception of
fertilizer diffusion. But this must change soon: As we have seen, few
uncultivated but cultivable areas still exist in the region, so further output
gains will require higher yields. Yet as indicated on Table 6.9, MENA, the
cradle of wheat, has the lowest percentage of wheat area planted in HYVs
of any region of the developing world.

The obstacles facing diffusion of HYVs may be illustrated by comparing
the experiences of Turkey, Tunisia, and Egypt. Turkey has had the most
success. The government made a vigorous effort to diffuse the new varieties
by providing information on proper cultivation practices, by extending
credit for complementary inputs like fertilizer, and by continuing to support
wheat prices at levels well above costs of production for most farmers.
Nearly all farmers in the Aegean, Marmaran, and Mediterranean districts
had adopted the new seeds within five years of their introduction (Mann

1980, 212), while the "latifundista" areas still lag behind.[34] The introduction of the green revolution dramatically increased cereal production, but the gains were regionally concentrated. Even in the first season, some 70% of the farmers who adopted the new seeds were small farmers. In the relatively well-watered regions of Turkey, the green revolution was by no means confined to the rich. These unimodal areas have the best performance with HYVs anywhere in the region.

By contrast, in Central Anatolia the key to achieving higher wheat yields was adopting improved tillage to reduce weeds and to retain moisture; consequently, smaller farmers were at a disadvantage. Although rental markets for tractors exist, it is often difficult for small farmers to hire such services at the proper time, since the tractor owners naturally first plow their own land, renting out only the "excess capacity" of their machine. The complementarity of new seeds with lumpy inputs like tractors in Central Anatolia has, predictably, biased the benefits there in favor of better-off farmers.

Tunisian small farmers also faced constraints to adopting HYVs. Crop yields had fallen or stagnated since the early 1950s. The foreign owners of large farms began disinvesting in agriculture from the onset of independence talks in 1956 until the expropriation of their farms in 1964; responding to the abrupt departure of Europeans and to a vision of a socialist Tunisia, a sweeping land-reform program imposed cooperatization on a recalcitrant peasantry. The lack of incentives joined with peasant resistance to reduce yields further still. In a move reminiscent of later, parallel actions elsewhere (e.g., Iraq), the government retreated and returned much land to the private sector after 1969. At that point, the government joined with foreign donors to launch a program to spread the new wheat varieties. The rate of growth of agricultural output shot up from at only 2.0% per year during the 1960s to 5.1% during the 1970s.

It is essential to distinguish among the major types of cereals in Tunisia: The principal marketed cereal is bread, or soft, wheat, largely grown in the better-watered rainfed areas of the north.[35] Durum wheat, used for making pasta and couscous, is the subsistence crop in the north, giving place to barley in the drier south. Largely thanks to the diffusion of HYVs, yields of bread and durum wheat roughly doubled during the 1970s; barley yields showed more modest, but significant, increases. By 1982, two-thirds of land planted in bread wheat was in HYVs, and 36% of durum wheat was so planted (Dalrymple 1986, 52). Expansion was especially rapid after price reforms in 1977, when annual price increases were instituted. Although the area planted in cereals declined during the 1970s when farmers who could shifted to more profitable crops like fruits, vegetables, and animal fodder, cereal output increased thanks to the yield gains. The advances in supply have fallen well short of demand increases, but the situation would have been far worse without the diffusion of HYVs.

Given the markedly bimodal land-tenure system that Tunisia inherited from the colonial period, it is hardly surprising that the distribution of the producers' benefits from the diffusion of HYVs has been skewed. Bimodalism appears not only in the distribution of farms but also in crop choice and marketing. Although some 70% of bread wheat was marketed in 1981, only 36% of durum wheat was sold; the remainder is consumed on the farm. Over 80% of Tunisian farmers hold less than 20 hectares, but such farmers market only about 10% of their output. Such data indicate that larger farmers, who on average have about the same percentage of their land in cereals as do small farmers, plant largely bread wheat, leaving durum to their smaller neighbors. Large farms are also concentrated in the north, where better rainfall favors bread wheat cultivation.

Wealthier farmers were heavily favored by government allocations of credit and inputs; the main agricultural lending agency, Banque Nationale Tunisienne, made loans only to farmers holding more than 40 hectares; the bank's total loan portfolio in 1980 of Tunisian dinar (TD) 39.6 million may be compared with the TD 7.1 million lent by the two institutions that dealt with loans to small farmers.[36] Given the complementarity of HYVs and fertilizer and credit, it is remarkable how widely durum HYVs diffused in Tunisia. Although HYVs of bread wheat required many complementary inputs (e.g., tractor services, more careful water management), durum HYVs needed fewer resources and expertise; they also helped to meet the consumption needs of small farmers.[37] The Tunisian green revolution has really been two "revolutions": one for bread wheat (where the experience confirms the "reinforcement of inequalities" argument) and one for durum wheat (where the lot of subsistence farmers seems to have improved).

Egypt best illustrates the deleterious role of adverse pricing policies on the diffusion of yield-increasing innovations. It is worth remembering, however, that Egyptian crop yields and fertilizer use are already at exceptionally high levels; for example, among developing countries, only Korean rice yields exceed those attained in Egypt. However, most agronomists believe that the nearly ideal agronomic conditions of the country (excellent alluvial soil, adequate water supplies, sunshine nearly all year) create a potential for yields far above those currently attained for most crops grown in the country. It is instructive, however, that attempts to introduce HYV wheat in Egypt have failed. Although it might seem odd that a country with such a severe food-security problem and with such scarce land should have difficulty adopting a land-saving innovation like HYVs, the country's pricing policies have undermined their adoption. Short-stemmed HYVs yield less straw, and therefore less animal feed, than do traditional varieties; wheat also competes with *birsim* (clover), an unregulated, very lucrative animal fodder. When the government attempted to diffuse HYV wheat in the 1970s, farmers disdained the new seeds, because relative prices made the straw more valuable than the grain![38] Even today, despite price-policy modifications, there has been no green revolution in Egyptian wheat production, nor have most other crops come close to attaining their scientifically feasible maximum in the country. Although sufficient incentives are surely not a sufficient condition for technological change in agriculture, they are probably necessary.

## Mechanization

Agricultural mechanization has spread more widely and more rapidly than yield-increasing technological changes for the region as a whole. Indeed, farm mechanization has proceeded more rapidly in MENA than in any other region of the developing world (Binswanger 1986). Most of this mechanization has been "tractorization." Tractors are mainly used for primary tillage, transport, and power for irrigation pumps and portable threshers. Combine harvesters are utilized in some countries, but they are far less common than tractors. More sophisticated machines like seed drills, fertilizer applicators, and fruit and vegetable harvesters are much less prominent.

This pattern is consistent with the worldwide sequence of farm mechanization. Binswanger (1986) has suggested a very useful typology of farm mechanization by distinguishing between "power-intensive" and "control-intensive" operations. The former include tasks like water-lifting, primary tillage, and threshing, tedious tasks that require much physical energy. Farmers have had work animals to assist them with these jobs for many centuries. In contrast, control-intensive operations "require primarily the control functions of the human mind or judgement" (Binswanger 1986, 3); these include winnowing, pest control, and the harvesting of cotton, fruits, and vegetables. Grain harvesting is a hybrid, intermediate operation. Binswanger argued that power-intensive tasks are mechanized first, then intermediate jobs, and finally control-intensive operations. Although the first stage of mechanization may save some human labor, labor scarcity is not the key to the process; the critical economic consideration is the relative cost of machine and animal power. But as mechanization proceeds into the second and third phase, saving labor becomes an increasingly important motive. Mechanization of power-intensive operations has proceeded quite far in the region (Table 6.10). For example, in the Settat region of Morocco, over 80% of the land is tilled at least once a year by tractors (USAID 1986). On large commercial sorghum farms in the heavy-clay belt of central Sudan, all plowing is mechanized. In Turkey, the ratio of tractors to land area was 49 hectares per tractor in 1984/85, compared to 40 hectares per tractor in the United States (FAO 1986)!

The use of combine harvesters is spreading more slowly (Table 6.11). As we would expect, the diffusion of combines is furthest advanced in countries whose agricultural labor force has actually declined (Algeria, Jordan, and Iraq), or is relatively stable (Turkey, Syria). But combine harvesters are also adopted by large commercial farmers to avoid the problems of supervising large numbers of hand harvesters. Nevertheless, mechanization of harvesting is still far less advanced than tractorization in most countries. Finally, few countries in the region have proceeded very far with the mechanization of control-intensive operations.

Table 6.10   Ratio of Arable Land to Tractors, 1960-1985 (selected years)
             (ha/tractor)

|              | 1960  | 1965  | 1970  | 1975  | 1980  | 1985 |
|--------------|-------|-------|-------|-------|-------|------|
| Algeria      | 248   | 226   | 148   | 171   | 171   | 143  |
| Egypt        | 219   | --    | 156   | 124   | 63    | 54   |
| Iran         | 1,359 | 984   | 781   | 404   | 236   | 153  |
| Iraq         | 1,028 | 537   | 366   | 268   | 245   | 179  |
| Jordan       | 882   | 635   | 477   | 365   | 305   | 274  |
| Libya        | 885   | 776   | 694   | 155   | 148   | 76   |
| Morocco      | 648   | 633   | 611   | 376   | 327   | 278  |
| Saudi Arabia | 2,854 | 1,873 | 1,423 | 1,387 | 931   | 722  |
| Sudan        | 3,029 | 1,765 | 1,267 | 1,387 | 1,129 | 732  |
| Syria        | 1,064 | 803   | 647   | 367   | 206   | 149  |
| Tunisia      | 373   | 349   | 206   | 201   | 176   | 180  |
| Turkey       | 536   | 343   | 260   | 115   | 65    | 49   |
| YAR          | --    | --    | 2,980 | 1,334 | 675   | 628  |
| PDRY         | 272   | 171   | 142   | 150   | 124   | 152  |

Sources: Calculated from **FAO Production Yearbook**, Rome, FAO, 1961, 1966, 1971, 1976, 1981, 1986.


Table 6.11   Ratio of Arable Land to Harvesters, 1960-1985 (selected years)
             (ha/machine)

|              | 1960   | 1965   | 1970   | 1975   | 1980   | 1985   |
|--------------|--------|--------|--------|--------|--------|--------|
| Algeria      | 1,409  | 1,356  | 1,163  | 1,846  | 1,821  | 1,503  |
| Iran         | 15,358 | 11,907 | 9,547  | 7,454  | 5,713  | 5,113  |
| Iraq         | 3,757  | 1,908  | 1,287  | 1,088  | 1,434  | 1,981  |
| Jordan       | 22,634 | 13,684 | 9,460  | 7,184  | 5,750  | 4,660  |
| Morocco      | 1,710  | 2,213  | 3,001  | 2,843  | 2,501  | 2,636  |
| Saudi Arabia | 6,714  | 6,082  | 5,487  | 4,007  | 2,792  | 2,181  |
| Sudan        | 51,500 | 27,173 | 18,800 | 13,511 | 10,797 | 10,639 |
| Syria        | 4,744  | 4,403  | 4,190  | 3,011  | 2,410  | 2,014  |
| Tunisia      | 1,615  | 1,518  | 1,451  | 2,074  | 1,869  | 1,838  |
| Turkey       | 4,133  | 3,578  | 3,244  | 2,405  | 2,083  | 2,030  |
| PDRY         | 52,500 | 30,750 | 24,833 | 11,833 | 11,142 | 11,133 |

Note: Libya and YAR unavailable.

Source: Calculated from **FAO Production Yearbook**, Rome, FAO, 1961, 1966, 1971, 1976, 1981, 1986.


This pattern suggests that tractors are substituting as much for animal power as for human labor. A major reason for this is the very rapid rate of growth of demand for livestock products. The opportunity cost of using animals for work has increased (working animals produce less milk and meat than animals kept in stalls), providing incentives to mechanize power-intensive operations like land preparation.

Agronomic considerations also contribute to the mechanization of primary tillage in rain-fed areas. Rainfall is usually necessary to soften the ground before it can be plowed using animal traction. Given the highly erratic rainfall in many parts of the region, this can delay planting and reduce yields. In Tunisia, for example, a tractor can plow 1 hectare of dry upland in 2.5 hours; the same operation using two bullocks and a Mediterranean

Table 6.12    Estimates and Projections of the Agricultural Labor Force (x1000)
              in Selected Countries of the Near East Region, 1960-2000 (selected
              years)

|                       | 1960   | 1970   | 1980   | 1985   | 1990   | 2000   |
|-----------------------|--------|--------|--------|--------|--------|--------|
| **Main Oil-Exporting**   |        |        |        |        |        |        |
| Algeria               | 1,990  | 1,394  | 1,262  | 1,301  | 1,342  | 1,387  |
| Iran                  | 3,220  | 3,547  | 4,026  | 4,082  | 4,199  | 4,331  |
| Iraq                  | 972    | 1,125  | 1,081  | 1,043  | 1,049  | 1,073  |
| Libya                 | 200    | 150    | 137    | 131    | 127    | 118    |
| Oman                  | 97     | 102    | 140    | 163    | 163    | 165    |
| Saudi Arabia          | 871    | 1,019  | 1,333  | 1,490  | 1,599  | 1,729  |
| Subtotal              | 7,296  | 7,337  | 7,979  | 8,210  | 8,479  | 8,803  |
| **Main Non-Oil Exporting** |     |        |        |        |        |        |
| Egypt                 | 4,364  | 4,765  | 5,158  | 5,526  | 5,902  | 6,786  |
| Jordan                | 199    | 162    | 66     | 63     | 59     | 51     |
| Lebanon               | 199    | 130    | 106    | 90     | 86     | 69     |
| Morocco               | 2,195  | 2,333  | 2,594  | 2,746  | 2,860  | 2,950  |
| Sudan                 | 3,376  | 3,601  | 4,331  | 4,606  | 4,866  | 5,348  |
| Syria                 | 685    | 785    | 707    | 713    | 747    | 848    |
| Tunisia               | 663    | 559    | 668    | 648    | 630    | 549    |
| Turkey                | 10,991 | 11,361 | 11,146 | 11,385 | 11,418 | 11,335 |
| YAR                   | 973    | 1,024  | 1,013  | 1,103  | 1,226  | 1,561  |
| PDRY                  | 201    | 208    | 199    | 203    | 206    | 208    |
| Subtotal              | 23,846 | 24,928 | 25,988 | 27,083 | 28,000 | 29,705 |
| Total                 | 31,142 | 32,265 | 33,967 | 35,293 | 36,479 | 38,508 |

Source: FAO, "World-Wide Estimates and Projections of the Agricultural and Non-
Agricultural Population Segments, 1950-2025," Statistical Division, Economic
and Social Policy Department, Rome, December 1986.

plow takes 41 hours (USAID 1983). Only tractors can plow land in the
dry season, a practice that reduces weeds and improves moisture retention;
only tractors can provide the force needed to work the dense heavy clays
of central Sudan. Here, too, direct labor costs are a secondary consideration
in the mechanization of power-intensive operations.

   This does not mean that migration and the expansion of off-farm
employment play no role in mechanization. Because many operations require
much physical force, social custom has often allocated these tasks mainly
to adult men, a type of labor that is disproportionately affected by migration.
Although it is sometimes asserted that such migration has created "labor
shortages" in agriculture, these are usually temporally and spatially localized
(see Chapter 14 for a more extended discussion). For most countries, the
farm work force grew during the 1970s and is expected to keep expanding
into the 1990s and beyond (Table 6.12). Despite fifteen years of rapid
population growth and unprecedented migration, the absolute numbers of
farm workers rose in Turkey, Sudan, Iran, Saudi Arabia, PDRY, and YAR;
they declined in Jordan, Libya, Iraq, Lebanon, and Syria. Only in the latter
countries might we expect sectoral labor shortages. But we have seen that
tractorization has been very rapid in all countries.

State policy has often encouraged mechanization. Most countries of the region directly subsidize tractors, usually by offering cheap loans to purchase equipment and diesel fuel. Imported tractors are either directly subsidized, as in Saudi Arabia and Libya, or indirectly encouraged by overvalued real exchange rates. For example, in 1982 the Moroccan government began to promote farm mechanization by removing all duties and taxes on agricultural equipment and by expanding credit for such purchases. The real cost of a tractor fell by 30%, and not surprisingly, the number of tractors rose from 23,000 in 1978 to 40,000 in 1986 (USAID 1986). These policies, combined with growing incomes, accelerating demand for animal products, and, in some cases, shortages of young adult male labor have contributed to the rapid tractorization of the region.

The output gains from mechanization have not been impressive. This is consistent with the now-conventional wisdom, which denies the empirical existence "of a strong causal link between the availability of tractors and increases in crop yields, intensity levels or timeliness" (Binswanger 1986, 67). There are some exceptions: (1) dry-farming areas where mechanization appears to be complementary to the adoption of HYVs, as noted above for Tunisia and Turkey, and (2) instances when mechanization permits an expansion of the cultivated area, as in Turkey during the 1950s or in the Rahad irrigation project in the Sudan in the 1970s (Aricanli 1985). But the overall contribution of mechanization to augmenting food supplies has been modest. Tractors cannot plow under the food gap.

The distributional consequences of mechanization are also mixed. One might suppose that only large farmers could afford tractors and that mechanization, by replacing labor, should reduce the welfare of the poorest rural groups, the landless laborers. However, the evidence here is quite murky. In many countries in the region, rental markets for tractors are well developed; although there are some differences in the degree of mechanization by farm size, and although rental markets are hardly perfect, small farmers are by no means excluded from access to tractor services. For example, in many parts of the Egyptian Delta, land preparation is entirely mechanized, even for the one-quarter of the land area worked in farms smaller than one *feddan* (Richards and Martin 1983). In Tunisia, an estimated 80% of the cereal area (of which 79% is in small and medium farms) uses tractors for land preparation (USAID 1983). There is also little evidence that mechanization to date has generated unemployment, although the Turkish case may be an exception.

How ecologically sustainable are these new biological and mechanical technologies? All too often, future land productivity has been sacrificed to obtain short-term output gains. We have seen that such a problem plagues irrigation development in the region. The increasingly heavy use of agricultural chemicals, especially pesticides, may bode ill for the future as well. Egyptian farmers, in particular, use huge quantities of dangerous pesticides, including DDT. The expansion of mechanization and the extension of the cultivated areas into ever-drier areas pose similar environmental hazards. Some specialists believe that much of the outwardly impressive output gains in Syria have been obtained by pushing cultivation out into the steppe, into areas that should have been left as grazing lands (Jaubert 1983).

Sudanese experience highlights the dangers of ecologically destructive mechanization. For over a generation, various governments there have let out large (e.g., 1,000 hectare) tracts of land in "mechanized farm schemes" for the growing of sorghum and other crops (sesame, peanuts) under rain-fed conditions. Successive Sudanese governments underpriced land and ignored externalities: Although the government steadily increased the length of the leases (from one year from 1945 to 1954 to eight years until 1967 and to up to twenty-five years thereafter), the rental rates charged were very low. The government also offered subsidized loans to farmers for land clearance. Farmers were thus implicitly encouraged to clear-cut land, farm intensively for a few years, and then move on to repeat the process elsewhere. Although some regulations against ecologically abusive practices exist, poor transportation infrastructure and the weakness of local administrations render them nugatory. Many authorities believe that these practices have contributed to desertification and to the agricultural collapse of many dry-farming areas in the Sudan (Affan 1984; O'Brien 1985; ILO and Republic of Sudan 1985); others point out that most mechanized farm schemes are located well to the south of the most ecologically vulnerable zones of the Sudan (Simpson 1978). Such farms have also blocked nomadic livestock routes and have reduced potential farmland for small, traditional cultivators. However, they produce over 70% of the country's sorghum. In rain-fed as in irrigable areas, the tragedy of Middle Eastern agriculture has been the coincidence of ecological fragility with politically engendered economic myopia.

The experience of the Sudanese mechanized farm schemes is only one of a large number of cases in which government policies to subsidize rural credit have had unfortunate and unexpected consequences. Credit for input use is subsidized in nearly all countries; in nearly all countries richer farmers receive the lion's share of such credit, as we saw in detail in the Tunisian case. Similar stories can be told for virtually every country from Morocco to Iran. At the same time that the Sudanese government was subsidizing "soil mining" mechanized agriculture, only 3% of traditional farmers in the rain-fed sector had access to official credit; the rest had to rely on money lenders and small-scale crop merchants, who charged up to 250% per year for loans.[39] The causes and consequences of such subsidized credit schemes in the region are little different from experience elsewhere in the developing world: Transactions costs are lower for large loans, wealthy borrowers are better credit risks, and the political allocation mechanisms that substitute for price rationing typically favor bigger farmers. Subsidized credit has been one of the major mechanisms favoring rich farmers, encouraging farm mechanization and, too often, environmentally abusive farm practices (El Mesmoudi 1982; Adams and Graham 1981).

## CLASS FORMATION IN THE COUNTRYSIDE

State policy has shaped the pattern of supply response in every state in the region. Such policies have also been constrained by, and in some cases designed on behalf of, politically powerful social classes. But the relations of class, state, and development are reciprocal: State policies toward agriculture and the process of agricultural development have shaped, even created, rural social classes. In this section we shall briefly consider this process in more detail.

The vast literature from around the world on the "differentiation of the peasantry" has been generated by two schools: those who believe that the process of agricultural change polarizes rural society into a class of capitalist farmers and landless laborers, and those who argue that small peasant farmers are a much more tenacious feature of rural society. The first view, of course, is rooted in the Marxist classics of Lenin and Kautsky; the second perspective, while quite eclectic, may be traced back to the writings of Chayanov (1966). Such analysts argue that the difficulty of supervising agricultural labor implies that as in advanced capitalist countries, farm structures in the Third World are likely to evolve toward highly mechanized, family farm operations.

The evidence on this question from the Middle East varies widely by country and by region. We may distinguish a variety of paths of rural transformation and of the evolution of rural classes in the region. In some cases, former landlords have become capitalist farmers, investing in new agricultural technology and expanding their holdings at the expense of their smaller neighbors. This "Junker Road" may be seen in the Çukurova region of Turkey, in parts of Iran before the revolution, and in Morocco and Tunisia. Something similar occurred in Egypt and Syria before their land reforms. Indeed, one might argue that such a path would have been the dominant one had states not intervened with land reforms: Large farmers have long been profit oriented, and both new technologies and state policies have often favored them.

A second "path," which is especially prominent in countries that have had significant land reforms, is the steady strengthening of the economic and social power of the rural middle class. Such "kulak consolidation" has occurred in Egypt, Syria, Iraq, Algeria, and Iran. Some evidence from Iran suggests that the most efficient farm size is the intermediate one of the "middle" or "rich" peasant, rather than either tiny "microfundia" or large estates (Moghadem 1982). The technical advantages are usually strongly reinforced by the pattern of government intervention in rural areas. Not only did land reforms remove the large-estate holders as competitors to the social and political power of such rich peasants, but as we have seen, governments often could not really replace them, leaving rich peasants not only socially dominant but also in a position to take advantage of government input subsidies and, in some cases, to evade output controls.

Nevertheless, small peasants continue to farm substantial proportions of the cultivated area throughout the region (Table 6.4). Farms smaller than 10 hectares rarely account for less than one-fifth of the cultivated area. In countries like Morocco, such farmers work nearly half of the agricultural area, while in Egypt small farms cover roughly two-thirds of the cultivated area. Small farmers have been able to improve their situation during the past decade in three major ways: (1) by renting-in land and by cropping intensively, (2) by diversifying their income sources, not only by wage labor in agriculture but increasingly by nonfarm work in rural areas, and (3) by sending at least some household members to work either in major cities or abroad. The great potential that small farmers have for integrating crop and livestock production has also contributed to their survival in Egypt, Tunisia, and the wetter regions of Turkey. The ever-increasing demand for meat in the region may shore up peasant farmers for some time.

Diversifying income sources has been the second survival strategy of poor farmers. Many poorer rural people in the region now earn their living from a wide variety of jobs, including much nonfarm work. A recent nationwide survey in Egypt suggests that most small peasant households there now obtain a *majority* of their income from nonagricultural sources (Radwan and Lee 1986); a similar phenomenon has been observed in some Turkish villages (Uner 1986). Although as far as we know, the question has not been examined in the Middle East, there may be a symbiosis between "kulak consolidation" and this survival strategy, with the better-off rural middle class providing the sources of demand for simple handicrafts, luxury foods, and services, all of which tend to be labor intensive (cf. Mellor 1976). The third strategy, labor migration, may be the most important of all. It is very common for many young men in a family to leave the farm to work elsewhere, sending back remittances to their relatives in the villages.

There are reasons to doubt the long-run efficacy of these strategies in the face of population growth and a relatively fixed supply of cultivable land. Many poor farmers cannot adopt any of these strategies. A field study done in the late 1970s in Upper Egypt revealed a depressing downward spiral of increasing population pressure on a fixed supply of land, with little emigration and few changes in cropping patterns (Adams 1986). Even within a village, demographic variables (family size and the presence or absence of a young man who can emigrate) have become crucial in determining incomes. The rapid expansion of mechanization may have removed relatively few jobs in some countries (e.g., Egypt), but a continuation of official policy to push mechanization will, inevitably, reduce employment opportunities in farming. This has already happened in Turkey, the country with the most mechanized agriculture in the region (Uner 1986): Over 20% of the farm labor force is now unemployed. Government policies continue to favor large, capital-intensive livestock operations at the expense of promoting small-farmer production. Finally, and most important, the slackening of oil exporters' demand for unskilled labor will leave the remaining rural poor in a very difficult situation, as the supply

Table 6.13   Estimates of Rural Poverty in Selected MENA Countries, 1973-1982
              (selected years)

|  | Year | % of Rural Population in Absolute Poverty | Number of Persons (000s) |
|---|---|---|---|
| Egypt | 1978 | 25 | 5,518 |
| Jordan | 1979 | 17 | 236 |
| Morocco | 1979 | 45 | 5,309 |
| Sudan | 1982 | 70 | 9,987 |
| Tunisia | 1980 | 13 | 399 |
| Turkey | 1973 | 50* | -- |
|  |  | 78** |  |
| PDRY | 1978 | 20 | 227 |

\*   Farmers.
\*\* Farm laborers.

Sources: Turkey: Kemal Derviş and Sherman Robinson, "The Structure of Income
Inequality in Turkey, 1950-1973," in Ergun Özbudun and Aydin Ulusan, The
Political Economy of Income Distribution in Turkey, New York, Holmes and Meier,
1980, p. 111. All others: M. Riad Ghonemy, "Economic Growth, Income
Distribution and Rural Poverty in the Near East," FAO, 1984.

of workers in rural areas grows more rapidly than in the past decade, but
the demand for their labor grows more slowly, due to continued mechanization. Just as the emigration outlet for Turkish workers to West Germany
narrowed sharply in the 1970s, so too are openings for the emigration of
rural Egyptians to the Gulf contracting now. Regional and international
forces are eroding the viability of peasant survival strategies.

   Trends of rural poverty are as widely varied as the paths of agrarian
transformation in the region. We have already seen that health and literacy
standards in rural areas of the region are below what we might expect,
given official per capita income figures. The most common approach to
the study of poverty is to try to calculate an "absolute poverty line,"
usually the amount of income needed to avoid malnutrition, and then
determine what percentage of the population fails to receive such income.
This kind of methodology has its difficulties (see Chapter 10); nevertheless,
we present such calculations for the late 1970s in Table 6.13. The figures
vary widely, ranging from a high of 70% in the Sudan to a low of 13% in
Tunisia. Unsurprisingly, there are also regional differences: For example,
only about 6% of rural residents of northern Tunisia had incomes below
the poverty line, while nearly one-fifth suffered from absolute poverty in
the center and south of the country. It is instructive to note that Morocco,
whose per capita income exceeds both Egypt's and the PDRY's, has a
much higher proportion of rural residents in poverty than either of those
countries. Although countries like Turkey, Egypt, and Tunisia have made
some progress in alleviating rural poverty over the past generation, even
there large numbers of poor people persist, while countries like Morocco
have made little progress. And in the Sudan, absolute poverty for the
majority has turned into famine for millions. When combined with health,

nutrition, and educational statistics, the picture of "rural development" in the region is not a pretty one.


## CONCLUSION

The essence of the patterns of agrarian change in the region during the oil boom era may be summarized as follows. Population growth and rapidly rising incomes dramatically increased the demand for food. However, natural and social factors constrained domestic supply. Governments responded by importing food and by offering selective incentives for domestic producers. The ensuing "model" of agrarian change had the following elements: (1) abundant foreign exchange, directly or indirectly due to the oil-price revolutions of 1973 and 1979; (2) outflows of labor from the major agricultural producers; (3) accelerating imports to feed the cities; (4) input subsidies and specialty-crop promotion for larger farmers, accompanied by accelerating mechanization; (5) migration and (some) increased commercialization for small farmers, who, in certain countries, were able to adopt improved cultivation practices; (6) food subsidies for the urban population (See Chapter 10); (7) persistence of substantial pockets of absolute rural poverty; and (8) some attempts to improve farmers' incentives, a policy shift made possible by the increase in nonagricultural revenues from oil and aid.

This model came under considerable pressure during the 1980s. Since the engine of the process was foreign-exchange largesse, the decline in such revenues forced many governments to implement austerity programs. Morocco, Tunisia, Turkey, and Jordan have been forced to try to cut government spending and to promote exports. The North African countries faced particularly severe difficulties because the collapse of other export revenues coincided with increased debt burdens and a devastating drought. Although they seem to have gotten through the worst years, their room for maneuver remains very narrow. Even the wealthy Saudis have recently slashed price subsidies for wheat by over 50%.

The "political economy of austerity" that ensued has a number of implications for the food systems of the region. There is a renewed emphasis on export crops to increase foreign exchange; yet the largest nearby market, the EC, has become increasingly inaccessible since Greece, Spain, and Portugal were admitted to full membership. Government retrenchment has hit projects in rain-fed areas, where most peasants live, particularly hard. Understandably, planners mainly strive to maintain and if possible to augment urban food supplies. Consequently, they promote irrigation projects, subsidize richer farmers, and trade off future ecological viability for uncertain current production gains. The fears about food security goad them into a "wager on the strong," channeling the now-reduced resources toward larger, allegedly "more modern," farmers.

Such a strategy and such austerity threaten the food entitlements of both urban and rural poor people. The extent of austerity varies widely by country. The worst experience was in the Sudan, where famine affected thousands of people in 1984. It is unlikely that this ghastly experience will be repeated elsewhere in the region. Nor is it likely that urban entitlements (usually, food subsidies) will be withdrawn; resulting budgetary deficits may be covered by collecting "strategic rent" (although Egypt and Morocco are in a much stronger position here than, say, the Sudan). However, the process of social differentiation under the twin spurs of the food gap and state responses to this gap are likely to continue the process of social differentiation in the countryside. Unless MENA countries can adopt "equitable growth" strategies, the situation of those at the bottom of rural society is likely to remain grim. The reciprocal interaction of economic development, state policy, and class formation has failed to create a prosperous, just, and sustainable agricultural order. We now turn to the public sector, to see if it has done any better.

## NOTES

1. The formula is $D = n + y\ e$, where $D$ = the rate of growth of demand, $n$ = population growth, $y$ = the rate of growth of per capita incomes and $e$ = the income elasticity of demand, or the percentage change in quantity demanded for every 1% change in income.

2. Since the numbers used are for GDP, which excludes workers' remittances, income growth for countries like the YAR are underestimated.

3. It is true that the agricultures of some particularly favored *regions* of a country (e.g., the Indian Punjab or northwest Mexico) have grown at faster rates. Such success stories may have helped to persuade some MENA policymakers to seek such an area in the Middle East. The hope of turning Sudan into a regional "breadbasket" (or, with greater agronomic realism, a "feedbag" or "sugar bowl") elicited important initiatives from wealthy Gulf States. As we shall see, however, such initiatives have so far borne little fruit.

4. "Yields" = output per unit of land.

5. Bennett's Law holds that the percentage of calories derived from starches declines with income.

6. In Egypt 97% of the cultivated area is irrigated. Even Egypt must worry about rainfall in the Sudan and, especially, Ethiopia for the replenishment of the Nile waters.

7. For "basic staples," i.e., cereals and pulses. As usual, there is wide variance by country. Unsurprisingly, capital-surplus oil exporters' imports grew most rapidly.

8. Yemenis and Sudanese shifted away from sorghum and millet, Maghrebis away from couscous made from durum wheat, and rural Egyptians increasingly abandoned maize flour.

9. Something very similar happened in Latin America. See, among others, Grindle 1986, Ch. 3.

10. Few regimes seemed to realize that there might be a contradiction between extracting resources from peasant farmers and having them buy the products of local industry.

11. The term *khushneshin* actually means "those without cultivation rights," including fairly well-to-do village artisans and traders; however, the large majority of this category were landless agricultural workers (Hooglund 1982).

12. Others disagreed, arguing that the reforms transferred land to all tenant cultivators (e.g., Majd 1987). Majd did not discuss the issue of viable farm size, and he ignored issues of fragmentation after reform through Islamic inheritance law.

13. In Morocco, the main beneficiaries of the departure of *colons* were already wealthy: Over 300,000 hectares of *colon* land passed into the hands of private, invariably well-to-do, Moroccans after 1956 (Swearingen 1987).

14. See "Two Vignettes: Land Reform in Egypt and Iraq" for more detail on the Iraqi case.

15. The cooperatives also fixed prices for some outputs and for inputs, using these terms of trade to extract resources. The consequences of such "price policies" are taken up in the next section.

16. The appropriateness of this standard assumption in the Middle East is highly dubious; see Chapter 14 on labor migration.

17. The list of disincentives to Sudanese cotton production in the late 1970s was formidable: an overvalued exchange rate, explicit taxes on cotton, allocating the input costs of *all* crops in the Gezira Scheme from cotton, and long (sometimes up to two-year) delays in payments. As was common throughout the region, many of these problems were ameliorated in the early 1980s.

18. Price controls apply to cereals, olives, wine grapes, sugarbeets, milk, dates, beef, and poultry; prices for pulses, lamb, forage crops, fish, and most vegetables and fruits are uncontrolled (Cleaver 1982, 36).

19. The parallel market constitutes an important alternative for farmers to selling to the government. If the state's prices are too low, farmers simply sell privately: In years where the price gap between the two is very large (e.g., 1973), as much as 90% of Syrian grain is traded privately. Such a market acts as an important check and barrier to excessively low prices to farmers and probably contributes to Syria's exceptional agricultural performance (ICARDA 1979, 226).

20. "Nominal protection coefficient" is defined as the ratio of the domestic price divided by the international price, evaluated at the official exchange rate.

21. As we shall see below, such distortions may also contribute to socially questionable biases in the kinds of technologies that farmers adopt: The misallocations are not limited to the output side.

22. For Egypt, de Thier (1987) and Alderman and von Braun (1984) are exceptions.

23. In Egypt, while *crop*-price policies are still disequalizing, *livestock* products enjoyed substantial protection until mid-1986. Since small farmers have ample family labor resources, they have reallocated these to raise *birsim* and produce more animal products. Consequently, farmers holding less than 1 *feddan* actually receive about £E 6 per person per year as a *subsidy* from government output prices, while those holding between 1 and 5 *feddan*s lose about £E 6 per person per year, and those holding over 5 *feddan*s lose £E 80: By this account, Egyptian output price policies are progressive (Alderman and von Braun 1984).

24. The same distributional picture appears in OECD countries that support their domestic agricultural prices; dozens of studies have documented the skewed distribution of benefits of U.S. crop-price supports.

25. This does not imply that food security would actually be reduced by such a policy; Egypt can only achieve such security by maximizing the country's gains from trade: Self-sufficiency in basic grains could come only at an unacceptable cost there.

26. None of this means that Middle Eastern states do not discriminate in favor of urban areas in human-welfare expenditures, especially in health and education.

We merely suggest that a vaguely defined "urban bias" is not a very useful explanation for agricultural pricing policies.

27. The more recent famines in southern Sudan (1987–1989) are entirely politically generated, the result of the civil war.

28. However, as we shall see in more detail, countries like Libya may have invested *more* money than was wise, given that the subsequent projects have serious environmental consequences (Allan 1981).

29. The region's irrigated area grew at approximately 1.2% per year from 1970–1981, compared to 2.1% in South Asia, 3.2% in Latin America, and 2.3% for the world as a whole (World Resources Institute 1986, 48).

30. "Over year storage" was the phrase used to describe dams large enough to hold and impound enough water from the Nile flood (September) to have water available in the summer of the following year.

31. The so-called Century Scheme, which proposed combining use of the Equatorial lakes for water storage with a canal to bypass the Sudd swamp in Sudan would have required extensive investment in very remote and inaccessible areas with considerable dangers of local resistance: A modern-day version of this plan, the Jonglei Canal, remains unfinished because of the revival of the Sudanese civil war. Even more important, alternatives to the High Dam required the British colonial authorities to cooperate with the Nasser regime, which the former loathed; the British invaded Egypt militarily in 1956.

32. The massive irrigation projects in the U.S. Southwest, such as those along the Colorado River, face similar problems. Salinization is a constant danger in irrigated farming, and only very sophisticated technical and social arrangements can overcome it.

33. Significantly, however, some relatively simple, relatively neglected options (e.g., early-maturing/drought-resistant varieties of sorghum and millet) do exist, but problems of land tenure, and especially, of credit and marketing impede their diffusion.

34. Only 30% and 10% of the wheat area of the southeast and the east, respectively, is planted in HYVs (Dalrymple 1986, 54–55).

35. Some soft wheat is grown on irrigated land, but farmers with access to irrigation usually prefer to grow higher-value crops like sugarbeets, fruits, vegetables, or fodder.

36. The Caisse Locale de Crédit Mutuelle, whose loans decreased during the 1970s, and the Société de Caution Mutuelle. The total number of borrowers was less than 40,000, compared with just under 300,000 farmers holding under 20 hectares (USAID 1983).

37. Per capita consumption of couscous declined during this period by nearly 50% (Fikry 1983); as men left the countryside, women had to perform more field labor, encouraging them to substitute bread wheat for couscous, which requires more preparation time.

38. There were also technical difficulties, like shattering and disease, which inhibited the diffusion of HYV wheats in Egypt during the 1970s.

39. These are annualized rates; the actual loan period is usually no more than three to four months.

# 7

# THE EMERGENCE
# OF THE PUBLIC SECTOR

## THE LEGITIMACY OF
## THE INTERVENTIONIST STATES

Our concern in this chapter is to document and analyze the prodigious growth in the economic functions of the Middle Eastern state. Again, there is little that is unusual about the Middle East in this respect. What is striking, however, is the relative lack of variability in the size and scope of state intervention across countries that in other respects differ greatly.

Middle Eastern states are big: They employ large numbers of people as civil servants, laborers, and managers—sometimes, as in the case of Egypt, as much as one-half of the nonagricultural work force. These states monopolize resources: They control large investment budgets, strategic parts of the banking system, virtually all subsoil minerals, and the nation's basic infrastructure in roads, railroads, power, and ports. Whether size and resources translate into strength is a question to be examined on a case-by-case basis. Certainly the potential for strong states is there, especially when resources are coupled with control over, or control by, the military. There is, unsurprisingly, abundant contrary evidence that size spawns red tape and administrative paralysis, that resources are diverted into corruption and patronage, that authoritarian leaders cannot push administrative agencies at a speed and in the directions that the leaders would like.

There has been a widespread acceptance among the people of the Middle East of the legitimacy of an interventionist state. This is not to say that most Middle Easterners accept the legitimacy of the particular state under which they live—that frequently is not the case—but it is conceded in the abstract that the state and its leaders have a right and an obligation to set a course for society and to use public resources to pursue that course. Two principles flowing out of the Western liberal tradition are given short shrift. One is that state authorities, to the extent possible, should confine themselves to the maintenance of law and order, regulation (but not too much) of economic life, provision of basic social-welfare benefits (health and education), and defense of the borders. The Middle Eastern state has taken on functions vastly more complex than these, and its citizenry has endorsed the effort. Second, the emphasis is on the ends of state intervention, and checks and balances are not seen as preventing abuse of power but rather as impeding the state's course toward its goals. Therefore, to some extent, there has been an acceptance of a high concentration of power—economic, administrative, and military.

It can be argued that in Muslim society, political authority is legitimate only insofar as it promotes the interests of the community of believers, the *umma*. In so doing, the political authority safeguards Islam and serves God. All its administrative, fiscal, and military actions are undertaken in the name of the overriding objective of glorifying God and protecting his faithful. As in Latin America, this yields an organic image of society, a living community whose "health" the state must maintain.

There have been explicit formulations of this image of the ideal Muslim state. One of the most striking came out of Ottoman tradition as early as the eleventh century and is known as the "circle of justice." The circle is constructed around these maxims (as cited in Bianchi 1984, 84–85):

1. There can be no royal authority and kingdom (*mulk*) without the military.
2. There can be no military without wealth and treasure.
3. Wealth and treasure are produced by subjects (*reaya*).
4. The sultan maintains the subjects by making justice reign.
5. Justice requires harmony in the world.
6. The world is a garden, its walls are the state.
7. The state's support is the religious law (*shari'a*).
8. There is no support for the religious law without royal authority and kingdom.

Cultural antecedents notwithstanding, it is our conviction that it is more the politics of decolonization and development that account for the interventionist, organic state in the Middle East than it is history and culture. The caretaker states of the colonial era, concerned with law, order, and taxation, have logically evoked their opposites, states that impinge upon all aspects of life among their citizens. Moreover, the postcolonial state has seen as its duty the reparation of all the economic damage resulting from colonial policies. It must mobilize human and material resources on an unprecedented scale. The goal is to overcome "backwardness" and build a prosperous, educated citizenry, a diversified economy, and national power. These tasks and goals are culture blind. Hence we find basic similarities in the goal orientation and interventionism of states in societies with as widely varied cultural origins as Indonesia, India, Burma, Ghana, or Tanzania.

## THE STATE AS ARCHITECT OF
## STRUCTURAL TRANSFORMATION

It is not only outside observers but also the leaders of Middle Eastern states themselves that see their tasks in terms of "engineering," architecture, blueprints, and the like. They are designing new societies, and the state is that collection of agencies that will enable them to build what they have designed. Ideologies vary but not the perceived need for state intervention. And no state in the region has been able to pass up the exercise of elaborating a national plan.

The point of departure for the state is backwardness, a condition, it is alleged, imposed on the region by imperial powers. Its three major components are (1) the agrarian trap, whereby the economy is mired in the production of cheap agricultural commodities requiring an unskilled work force; (2) the system of production is perpetuated by denying education and the acquisition of modern skills to all but a privileged few; and (3) the trap is sprung through the international division of labor into which the backward agrarian economies are forcibly integrated. To break out of the trap requires a supreme effort, a kind of military campaign on three fronts. Only the state can coordinate the campaign and mobilize the inherently scarce resources needed to carry it out. So, along with the engineers and architects there are the inevitable Bonapartes, and as Tunisia's Habib Bourguiba has demonstrated, they need not all wear a marshal's uniform.

Resources were and are scarce: The area has an uneducated, poor population, an agricultural system characterized by small pockets of high productivity in a landscape of low yields, no or very little capital for investment. However ironic it may seem in retrospect, the leaders of the state saw the need for intervention in order to avoid wasting scarce resources. This would be achieved through comprehensive and rational planning. The effort would require an inventory of all available resources, a strategy for their development and utilization over time and in light of the profound structural changes that would take place in the economy and society as the plan unfolded, and the construction of the economic levers needed to implement the plan.

Throughout the region it was assumed that the private sector could not be relied upon to undertake this kind of resource mobilization and planning. The least critical saw the private sector as too weak financially, too close to a commercial and trading, rather than an industrial, past, and too concerned with short-term profit to be the agents of structural transformation. More severe critics emphasized the greed and exploitativeness of the private sector, its links to interests in the metropole, and its tendency to export capital rather than reinvest profit. Private sectors might be tolerated, but nowhere, save in Lebanon, did they enjoy legitimacy. Reliance on private entrepreneurs and on the law of supply and demand to allocate scarce resources would be wasteful, it was believed, and would not extricate the economy from its trap.

As important as efficiency for the state leaders was the question of equity. Gross inequalities in the distribution of assets in Middle Eastern societies, not to mention absolute poverty for large segments of the population, was associated with the colonial system of exploitation. A more equitable distribution of assets within society became a universal goal throughout the area, again regardless of ideology. Some states pursued redistribution with greater conviction than others but all espoused it as an ideal. The Great Depression, leading to absolute declines in the standard of living of rural populations, followed by the privations caused by World War II, sensitized Middle Eastern elites to these equity issues. It was again assumed that the private sector could do little to alleviate them and if left to its own devices, would probably aggravate them.

The Middle Eastern state took upon itself the challenge of moving the economy onto an industrial footing, shifting population to the urban areas, of educating and training its youth wherever they lived, raising agricultural productivity to feed the nonagricultural population, redistributing wealth, of building a credible military force, and doing battle with international trade and financial regimes that held them in thrall. These were goals widely held, if poorly understood, by the citizens at large. There were no impediments then to the expansion and affirmation of the interventionist state.

## ATATÜRK AND THE TURKISH PARADIGM

As we stress throughout this book, the Republic of Turkey has been an example if not a model for many of the other states in the Middle East. Because it achieved real independence in 1923 after successful military action against European forces (Italian, French, and Greek) that were bent on dismembering all that remained of the Ottoman Empire, Turkey showed what could be done to thwart imperialism. It possessed an inspiring leader, Mustapha Kemal "Atatürk," "father of the Turks," who built a secular, republican, nationalist system in Anatolia. His sweeping reforms, from the abolition of the caliphate to the introduction of the Latin alphabet, have been too well studied to require treatment here (inter alia, Lewis 1961). For our purposes it is important to note that by the late 1930s Turkey was endowed with a credible military structure, the beginnings of a diversified industrial sector, and a rapidly expanding educational system.

Atatürk's contemporaries looked on with varying degrees of admiration,[1] including Reza Khan of Iran, the man who was to found the Pahlavi dynasty. So too did Arab nationalist politicians, like Habib Bourguiba of Tunisia, who would lead their countries to independence. There were also students and young army officers in the turbulent 1930s who learned from the Turkish experience lessons they would come to apply in the 1940s, 1950s, and 1960s. An Iraqi officer who later participated in the Golden Square conspiracy to oust the British from Iraq attended Atatürk's funeral and wrote (Sahah al-Din Sabbagh, as cited in Hemphill 1979, 104): "I saw

signs of progress which amazed me . . . a social revolution in education
and economics, and in cultural and spiritual affairs. I saw the pride of the
Turks in their fatherland, pride in their nationalism, their self-reliance and
their independence."

In April 1931 Atatürk issued a manifesto that contained six principles
that were to be embodied in the 1937 Constitution of the Republic. He
declared that the society and the Republican People's party (RPP) that he
headed would be republican, nationalist, populist, secular, etatist, and
revolutionary. The principles of etatism (a term meaning "statism" and
taken directly from the French and having a strong Bonapartist flavor),
populism, and revolution will be our main concern here. The first provided
legitimation for a strongly interventionist state. Populism meant that the
masses were the object of political and economic policy and that distributive
issues were at the forefront of the policy agenda. The revolution lay in
Turkey's rejection of empire along with the sultanate and caliphate, Turkey's
militant republicanism, and its confrontation with the imperial powers of
Europe. Within a few years of the enunciation of these principles, Turkey
embarked upon an economic experiment that was to be emulated in several
countries following World War II (Hershlag 1968, 74): "Turkey became
first among the backward countries to conduct an experiment in planned
development, wth its first five year plan in 1934." It also built a large
public-enterprise sector and pursued a policy of import-substituting industrialization under the auspices of the state.

Turkey's trajectory toward this experiment was erratic, and there is no
question that the world depression forced Turkey to revise profoundly the
strategy that had prevailed in the 1920s. It is important to review these
antecedents. First, Turkey was in a shambles after World War I. The empire
itself had been destroyed and the Arab portions had fallen under French
or British control. The basically agricultural economy had been badly
damaged, especially in the fighting against the Italians, French, and Greeks.
Then, after the signing of the Treaty of Lausanne in 1923 between Turkey
and the major war victors, an enormous exchange of population took place.
Something like 1.3 million Greeks left Anatolia by 1926, taking with them
vital skills in commerce and trades. In their place came 400,000 Turks,
mainly peasants from Thrace, whom the rural world could absorb only
with difficulty.

Turkey inherited the Ottoman debts, which were finally settled at the
end of the decade. It was fortunate that no reparations were imposed upon
it as a successor to the empire that had fought on the side of Germany
in that war. The fact that Turkey signed a treaty of friendship with the
USSR in 1921 may have militated against vindictive policies on the part
of the allies. The Lausanne treaty did impose restrictions on Turkey's ability
to place tariffs on imports from Europe and hence to protect its own
nascent industries. Nonetheless, Atatürk from the outset was determined
to promote Turkey's industrialization and to liberate its economy from
dependence on the West. In February 1923, at the Economic Congress of

Izmir, these same goals were endorsed. Atatürk himself emphasized that national sovereignty had to be rooted in economic independence, and that an educated citizenry and an industrial base were both vital to such independence.

In contrast to what was to transpire after 1931, the republic's strategy was to rely on private-sector initiative and to avoid taxing the peasantry in order to finance industrial growth. The Organic Statute of 1924 declared private property and free enterprise to be the basic principles of the state. It reiterated the position of the Izmir congress that "the task of the state begins where the activity of private initiative ends." With the founding of the Iş (Business) Bank in 1924 to finance private enterprise, the state showed its willingness to foster the growth of an indigenous capitalist class (F. Ahmad 1981; Boratav 1981).

Again in contrast to what came later, the new republic implemented policies that were relatively favorable to the rural world. In 1924 the *'ushr* tax, or tithe, was abolished. This tax had generated as much as 29 percent of government revenue. Its abolition was of particular benefit to smallholders and poor peasants. In its place, the government introduced a land and unutilized-property tax that fell most heavily on wealthy landlords. Throughout the 1920s agricultural prices were allowed to rise. Although agricultural production was at an abnormally low ebb following the war, it grew by an impressive 58 percent between 1923 and 1932, while cereals alone increased by 100 percent. At the same time urban consumers had to pay high prices for commodities controlled by government monopolies: tobacco, salt, sugar, matches, alcohol, gasoline. In many ways this was the inverse of the "urban bias" that was to develop in the 1930s and 1940s when factory smokestacks were referred to derisively as "Atatürk's Minarets."

After 1929, with the onset of the world depression, agricultural prices collapsed. No nonagricultural private sector had yet emerged that could pick up the slack in the economy, even supposing that world economic conditions would have allowed such a development. As soon as the tariff restrictions of the Lausanne treaty had expired in 1929, and before the onset of the depression, Turkey introduced higher tariff barriers to protect local industry. As the world crisis affected the Turkish economy, there was not time enough to see if the private sector would respond to the protective measures.

When, on April 20, 1931, Atatürk launched the etatist experiment, he said (Hershlag 1968, 69), "We desire to have the Government take an active interest, especially in the economic field, and to operate as far as possible in matters that lend themselves to the safeguarding of vital and general interests, or, in short, that the Government ensure the welfare of the nation and the prosperity of the state." The RPP reaffirmed its support for private enterprise but went on to prescribe government intervention in agriculture, health, education, commerce, industry, and public works.

In May 1932 Turkey negotiated a historic interest-free twenty-year loan from the Soviet Union for the equivalent of $8 million. This may have been the first of its kind to a developing country, but it was the only one for twenty-five years. The loan was to be used to buy Soviet equipment for two sugar refineries and a textile mill at Kayseri. Repayament was to be made in Turkish exports to the USSR. The Soviets set up a special trade agency to implement the loan agreement, Turkstroj, which in 1935 negotiated with the Sümer Bank that Turkey had created especially to manage the project financing of the First Five-Year Plan. A pattern of economic assistance was thus established that was repeated in Egypt, Algeria, Syria, Iraq, Iran, and Morocco in the 1950s, 1960s, and 1970s.

In the year following the loan, Turkey drew up its First Five-Year Plan and began its implementation in 1934. Atatürk, like nearly every head of state we shall consider in these pages, headed a coalition of interests and ideological perspectives within his government and party. Left-of-center figures who had been offstage during the 1920s were given much more prominence during the etatist era. There was much more talk now of the "Kemalist Revolution," and the private-sector strategy of the earlier years was abandoned. Rather than the state's being the handmaiden to a growing private sector, it was now to seize "the commanding heights" of the economy and bend the private sector to its will. In this new atmosphere the state technocracy and party ideologues could denigrate the private sector and talk of the necessity of state intervention. The left-of-center voices found a forum in the journal *Kadro* (i.e., *cadre,* the French word used to designate a party organizer). The secretary-general of the RPP, Recep Peker, was known to be an advocate of forced-pace change "to tear away from a social structure the backward, the bad, the unjust and harmful, and replace them with the progressive, the good, the just, and the useful elements" (cited in Karpat 1959, 72). Finally, the prime minister, Ismet Inönü, a man who saw etatism primarily in terms of the political and administrative obligations of the state, was to some extent eclipsed by Celal Bayar, who saw the need for much more aggressive economic intervention on the part of the state. Bayar came out of the Iş Bank, became minister of economy in 1932 and then prime minister in 1937, when he replaced Inönü.[2]

In the view of its originators, the statist experiment was not socialist in nature or intent. Atatürk defined it by what it was not: liberal or socialist. Those in the Arab world who were to pursue similar strategies were more willing to call them socialist, but often qualified them as "Arab" socialist, and eschewed all notions of class conflict or rule through any one class.

The five-year plan itself was a blueprint for ISI, emphasizing local processing of Turkey's primary commodities and minerals. A major part of the program lay in developing the textile industry, utilizing Turkish cotton, and selling to a large domestic market. This kind of thrust is often associated with the so-called easy phase of ISI. Other industries of a similar nature are food processing, sugar refining, and simple assembly. But Turkey went somewhat further, launching projects in basic chemicals—super-phosphates, chlorine, caustic soda—as well as in cement, iron, paper and cellulose, artificial silk, and hemp.

Even prior to the five-year plan, the Turkish state owned several enterprises; there were processing plants associated with the tobacco monopoly, beet sugar refineries, a shoe factory, wool mills, and a cotton-weaving plant. It had taken over power generation and the railroads from foreign interests.

The First Five-Year Plan added some twenty new enterprises to the public patrimony. A State Office for Industry was set up in 1932 and by 1936 was empowered to inspect the accounts of private-sector industries and to enforce price and wage controls. The Central Bank had been established in 1930 as the bank of issue. In 1933 the Sümer Bank was created and absorbed the Bank for Industry and Mines. Sümer Bank provided financial management and supervision to state-owned enterprises, planned new projects, and invested in others coming under the plan. By 1939 Sümer Bank's holdings accounted for 100% of production in artificial silk, paper, cardboard, iron, and superphosphates; 90% of shoes, 80% of steel and lubricants; 70% of coke, 62% of leather, 60% of wool, and 55% of cement (Hershlag 1968, 92). The İş Bank went well beyond private-sector financing and invested in a number of joint ventures. The Eti Bank to finance mineral exploration, extraction, and marketing was set up in 1935. In this way the state in the 1930s had the financial leverage to orient all economic actors in accordance with plan priorities.

Work on drafting the Second Five-Year Plan was started in 1936 and the plan itself was formally adopted by the Grand National Assembly in September 1938, just before Atatürk's death. Over 100 new enterprises were planned. The first efforts at "industrial deepening" were projected. The Zonguldak-Karabuk region was slated to become a heavy-industrial-growth pole, built around coal, steel, and cement, and serviced by its own Black Sea port. A major effort was to be made in power generation, basic chemicals, engineering, and marine transport. Part of the plan was to disperse industry in order to benefit backward areas, especially Eastern Anatolia, as well as for strategic reasons.

Some of the seemingly inevitable side effects of this sort of "big push" strategy made themselves felt during the 1930s. The government ran a growing deficit, due in large part to an outsized bureaucracy. The civil service, not including the military or part-time personnel, reached 127,000 in 1938 and 184,000 in 1945 (Karpat 1959, 129). About 35% of the budget went into their salaries. The size of the civil service was due not so much to the overproduction of university graduates that characterized most of the Middle East by the 1960s as to the absorption of the personnel of the Ottoman bureaucracy set up to administer an empire. The deficit of the government stood at TL 13.8 million in 1930/31 and TL 125 million in 1939/40. Over the same decade Turkey was obliged to borrow abroad, from the Soviet Union, Germany, and the UK. Still, in contrast to the foreign indebtedness that developed throughout the region in the 1960s and 1970s, Turkey was able to finance most of its investment out of its own resources. The level of investment was modest by postwar standards:

The government was investing annually about 5% of national income, with another 5% coming from the private sector.

World War II interrupted the Second Five-Year Plan, and a period of severe privation ensued. Import substitution continued of necessity as Mediterranean shipping was disrupted during the hostilities. A major shift in the political domain after the war, leading to a two-party system and the victory of the Democrat party, which had come to oppose etatism, ushered in a liberal economic phase during the 1950s. Only after a military takeover in 1960 did Turkey return to etatism. By that time it had been joined by another half dozen states in the region.


## REPLICATING THE PARADIGM

It would be an exaggeration to suggest that other states in the Middle East slavishly imitated the Turkish experience. In fact, state-led ISI spread throughout the developing world in the years after 1945 and, as a strategy, had a logic independent of any single country's efforts. We shall see that among Middle Eastern states, the tremendous growth in publicly owned assets, and the development strategies associated with them, had varying sources of inspiration, some external and some internal.

We are distinguishing here between public-sector enterprise and other governmental agencies that employ the bulk of the civil servants. Generally, public-sector enterprises have their own statutes, personnel policies, and salary and wage scales. They are companies in the legal sense that make and sell products or deliver services for a fee. They enter the national marketplace directly and usually with great impact.

If we look at the developing world as a whole around 1980, we find impressive statistics on the weight of public sectors in their economies. On average the output of public-sector enterprise, exclusive of financial institutions (banks, social security and pension funds, insurance companies), accounted for 8.6% of GDP; these enterprises on average employed 47% of the manufacturing work force in the organized sector, utilized 27% of all manufacturing investment, and, on average, ran deficits equivalent to 5.5% of GDP (World Bank estimates). State-owned manufacturing enterprises frequently accounted for 25–50% of value-added in manufacturing. Some Middle Eastern states, especially Egypt, Algeria, and Syria, were well above these averages: Egyptian state-owned enterprises (SOEs) accounted for around 60% of value-added in manufacturing, and Syrian, 55%. The output of Algeria's and Egypt's SOEs reached 13% of GDP, while Syria's was close to 11%. Turkey's SOEs were, in 1980, producing about 8% of GDP and accounted for 25% of value-added in manufacturing.[3]

The question of publicly owned assets is important to this study in two ways. First, the assets are always the instruments of a given state's development strategy. In that sense, they shape production, absorb and allocate scarce resources, and orient patterns of consumption. This may help or hinder the development of private-sector activity. They are always instruments of political preemption and control, a proposition that will be explored below. Second, when we speak of publicly owned assets, we are obviously dealing with a fundamental aspect of property relations and hence of class. What the state owns, private individuals or firms do not. In theory, public ownership is ownership by the "people." The state acts as custodian, manager, and fiduciary on behalf of citizen-owners. The latter monitor the state through their representatives in parliament, or the party, or on the boards of directors of public enterprises. But this is almost everywhere a fiction. The state builds public enterprise to pursue ends that it alone defines.

The last statement, however, begs some crucial questions. The state cannot be taken as a homogeneous bloc. It always contains diverse interests and factions that prevail at different times and in different combinations. Furthermore, crude indicators of ownership and economic weight, such as those presented in the preceding paragraphs, tell us little of intent or direction. The states with the weightiest public sectors in the Middle East are to be found among the frequently conservative oil exporters. Moreover, in Turkey in the 1950s, despite the professed liberalism of the Democrat regime, the public-sector actually grew in size. More important, public enterprises may implicitly or explicitly be put, in part, at the service of the private sector (Turkey in the 1920s) or be designed to marginalize the private sector over time (Egypt after 1961). The weight of the public sector in either case may not vary much, but direction and intent are quite different.

The final begged question is whether or not the managers of public assets, those atop "the commanding heights," or those in control of "the major means of production," come to constitute a dominant class, which seeks to reproduce itself and to exclude others from the assets it controls. We shall try to advance some tentative answers to all these questions in the remainder of this chapter.

## Arab Socialism and State Enterprise

One set of Arab states adopted the Turkish paradigm and went well beyond it. These states' strategies were explicitly socialist, hostile to the indigenous private sector and to foreign capital, and aimed at far-reaching redistribution of wealth within their societies. The strategy has not always been sustained and on occasion has been officially abandoned (e.g., Egypt after 1974, Tunisia after 1969, Sudan after 1972). The principal experiences we have in mind are Algeria—1962 to the present; Egypt—1957 to 1974; Syria—1963 to the present; Iraq—1963 to the present; Tunisia—1962 to 1969; Sudan—1969 to 1972; PDRY (South Yemen)—1969 to the present (the only Marxist regime in the Middle East); Libya—1969 to the present (although the term *socialism* is avoided).

What all these have in common is a blueprint for the radical transformation of their societies and economies. In these states the campaign for growth, equity, and national economic sovereignty was no mere metaphor. Indeed,

Habib Bourguiba of Tunisia likened his country's quest for development to Islamic holy war, *jihad,* and said that Tunisians should be dispensed of the obligation to fast during the month of Ramadan just as if they were warriors.

A number of basic assumptions underlay these experiments: first, that profit and loss should not be the primary criteria by which to assess public-sector performance. Rather, the creation of jobs, the provision of cheap goods of first necessity, the introduction of new economic activity to remote or poor regions, and the achievement of self-sufficiency in goods of a strategic (in Turkey from the outset, sugar was considered a strategic good) or military nature would be more appropriate tests of success. Second, the market, that is, the forces of supply and demand, is inferior to planning and the application of administered prices. In market situations, goods of first necessity (food and clothing) are often the objects of speculation, and because demand for them is relatively inelastic, prices may rise precipitously. The state must set prices so that such goods are always within reach of the poorer strata. Similarly, the price of inputs and credits supplied to priority industries should not reflect their scarcity value.

The large-scale private sector was seen as untrustworthy. Most of the regimes under consideration nationalized it or sharply curtailed its activities. The private enterprise that remained was subjected to state licensing procedures and price and wage controls and had to compete with the public sector for scarce credit and foreign exchange.

Foreign investment was viewed with suspicion. Entire sectors of the economy, such as basic metals, chemicals, and minerals, were reserved exclusively for public-sector enterprise; neither foreign nor domestic private capital was to be allowed in them. The favored form of collaboration with foreign capital was through turnkey projects and management contracts in which foreign investors acquired no equity in the host country. Socialist Algeria, in the 1970s, was able to do billions of dollars of business with the United States, France, Japan, and other countries through such formulas.

The setting up of closed sectors for public-sector enterprise underscores another assumption: There is nothing inherently inefficient about monopolies. In many instances SOEs enjoyed monopolies in entire lines of production, or they were the sole purchasers (monopsonists) of certain inputs (raw cotton or sugar beets). Egypt, after 1961, took matters further, putting the entire banking, insurance, and foreign-trade sectors under public ownership. The supply of investable funds and the importation of vital production inputs thus became a state monopoly. For all this to work, to promote overall growth, industrialization, and a more equal distribution of income, required that the planners anticipate the interaction of all the economic variables that, today, computer models chew over, that the managers pursue efficiency even while protected by tariffs and monopoly status, and that the civil servants put in an honest day's work. By and large none of those requirements were met, but that is a story to be taken up in the next chapter.

*Egypt.* Egypt was the first Middle Eastern country in the postwar era to adopt a strategy of radical transformation. In many ways it was far more integrated into the world economy than Turkey. Egypt had been one of the leading exporters of raw cotton for nearly a century. The British occupation of Egypt after 1881, the economic dependency on Britain that ensued, and the role of the Suez Canal in world trade made Egypt's a classic colonial economy. As in Turkey, the world depression and World War II set Egypt on the path toward ISI. It was the Egyptian private sector, partly indigenous and partly foreign, that led this effort.

In 1952 the Egyptian monarchy was overthrown by a military coup, led by Col. Gamal 'Abd al-Nasser and a group of his colleagues known as the Free Officers. From 1952 to 1956 Egypt promoted public-sector growth but, as in Turkey in the 1920s, did so either to help the private sector or to undertake projects the private sector could not finance or manage. The old Aswan Dam was electrified to augment Egypt's power supply, and it was decided to promote a new, giant dam at Aswan to increase hydropower generation severalfold and to ensure a predictable supply of irrigation water to the agricultural sector. Work was begun on an iron and steel complex at Helwan and on a large fertilizer plant at Aswan.

It was not until the Suez War of November 1956 that the public sector grew at the expense of the private. Because of the participation of Britain and France, along with Israel, in a direct attack on Egypt, all assets owned by the former two in Egypt were taken over by the Egyptian government. The attack itself had been provoked by Egypt's nationalization in July 1956 of the Suez Canal Company.

With the wartime sequestrations of banks, trading companies, insurance companies, utilities, and some manufacturing enterprises, the Egyptian state found itself in possession of a very substantial patrimony. It was only then that the term *socialism* was adumbrated and that left-of-center voices in Nasser's coalition gained greater prominence. In 1957 Egypt contracted its first loan for economic assistance from the Soviet Union, followed in 1958 by a Soviet loan to help build the Aswan Dam. In 1957 Egypt began its first five-year industrial plan, with strong emphasis on state enterprise. By 1960 Egypt felt ready for a five-year plan for the entire economy.

After 1956 there was some evidence of private-sector disinvestment and profit taking and of growing suspicion between the private sector and the regime. The privately held Misr Group and Misr Bank were pretty much taken over by the state by 1960. The new Ministry of Industry was empowered to license and regulate all private industrial activity. The elaboration of the First Five-Year Plan was carried out without consulting the private sector, although the latter was called upon to mobilize about 55% of all investment over the five-year period.

The failure of the private sector to do so allegedly provoked a wave of nationalizations through the Socialist Decrees of July 1961. In one fell swoop, the Egyptian state took over most large-scale industry, all banking, insurance, and foreign trade, all utilities, marine transport, and airlines, and many hotels and department stores. The bulk of agricultural property remained in private hands, but new desert reclamation projects were owned by the state.

The First Five-Year Plan embodied a straightforward ISI strategy, combining aspects of the easy (textiles, sugar, automobile assembly, pharmaceuticals) and hard (heavy engineering, steel, chemicals, and fertilizers) phases. It generated 1 million new jobs and growth rates of 6% per annum. Yet in 1965 it ended in crisis.

The Achilles heel of ISI, whether under public or private auspices, is the economy's ability to earn foreign exchange. For the major oil exporters that at one time or another pursued an ISI strategy (Iran, Algeria, Iraq), this was not a major problem, but for Turkey, Egypt, and Syria, it certainly was. As Turkey learned in the 1930s, ISI often reduces imports of one kind—let us say, finished textiles or refined sugar—only to increase imports of another kind—e.g., raw materials such coking coal for new steel plants or capital goods such as turbines and power looms. Egypt's new industries were designed to market their products in Egypt. They did not have the economies of scale and basic operating efficiency that would have allowed them to export to other markets. Thus while they needed imports to function, they could not generate the foreign exchange to pay for those imports.

To finance its Second Five-Year Plan, Egypt had little choice but to try to borrow more heavily abroad. It was not very successful, and even the Soviet Union was reluctant to extend new lines of credit. At the same time the state's large outlays on construction and social services drove up domestic demand without commensurate increases in the supply of goods, so that inflation reared its head. Finally the fact that few SOEs were profitable and that many of them were being padded with redundant personnel in an effort to create jobs meant that the government had to resort to deficit financing to cover their losses. In short, although rates of growth in production and the delivery of services were quite respectable, the Egyptian state nonetheless faced an external and a domestic fiscal crisis.

The Second Five-Year Plan, which, like Turkey's, would have led to industrial "deepening" had to be abandoned for want of adequate financing. Then came Egypt's disastrous defeat in the June War of 1967 and Israel's occupation of the Sinai Peninsula. Egypt lost its oil fields there, the Suez Canal was closed to traffic, and tourism was badly disrupted. Egypt went into severe recession. Its strategy for radical structural transformation through public-sector enterprise had to be revised.

President Nasser died in September 1970, and his successor, Anwar al-Sadat, cautiously pursued a policy of economic liberalization aimed at reforming and streamlining the public sector, stimulating the Egyptian private sector, attracting foreign investment, and promoting exports. Public-sector enterprise was subjected to sharp criticism for its chronic inefficiency and huge operating deficits. While Egypt continued to produce five-year plans, they had clearly lost their mystique, and the notion of socialist transformation was downplayed. Egypt's initial blueprint, the crises that developed in its implementation, and the revision of the blueprint constitute a sequence that has been played out elsewhere in the region.

Even though heavily criticized, Egypt's public sector continued to grow throughout the 1970s. Entering the 1980s it included 391 companies employing about 1.2 million workers. The market value of its assets was about £E 38 billion. In 1983/84 its wage bill stood at £E 5.7 billion (over 20% of GDP) and over the period 1975 to 1982 had grown at 19% per annum. It accounted for 22% of total value-added in the economy. The return on its total investment was only 1.5% per annum.

If we add public authorities that run everything from the Suez Canal to the Aswan High Dam, and the civil service, to the core companies of the public sector, we then have a public and governmental sector with 3.2 million employees—i.e., a third of the total work force and over half of the nonagricultural work force—and over £E 90 billion in assets. Total public expenditures in 1980 represented 60% of GDP; total government revenues, 40% of GDP; and the public deficit, 20% of GDP. As one observer put it, "There are few, if any developing countries in the world with such high proportions" (Ahmad 1984, ix).

*Algeria.* Algeria is one of the few LDCs to rival Egypt in terms of the weight and extent of its public sector. To a greater degree than in Egypt, the overall size of the Algerian public sector was the result of ideology and long-term policy.

Independent Algeria emerged in 1962 out of seven years of revolutionary warfare against the French. Many of the leaders of the National Liberation Front (FLN) were committed socialists and occasionally Marxists. There were also many guerrilla fighters who were neither. The nature and intensity of their struggle made it inevitable that Algeria would confront France and the imperialist world in general. International business interests and the Algerian private sector itself were seen as likely enemies of Algeria's revolution (Leca 1975, 124). At no time did the state see its role as helpmate to the private sector, as Turkey did during the 1920s or Egypt up to 1957. The National Charter of 1976 reiterated a position that had been constant since 1962 (Benissad 1982, 29):

In Algeria, private property cannot be a source of social power. It cannot be the basis for exploitative relations between the owner and the workers. It can only function to the extent that it does not prejudice the interests of the laboring masses, nor constitute a brake or obstacle to the inexorable evolution of our society toward socialism. . . . In the industrial domain, the intervention of the national private sector is restricted to small-scale enterprise involved in the last stage of industrial transformation, downstream of the production or the imports of the public and socialist sectors.

Since 1966 the commanding heights of the economy have been reserved to the state. Collaboration with foreign firms was extensive but was carried out on a contract basis involving turnkey projects, technical assistance, and purchase of technology. Direct investment was carefully avoided. Like all states in the region, Algeria was the exclusive owner of all subsoil minerals. French companies that had developed the country's petroleum and natural gas deposits were nationalized between 1969 and 1971, so that the state had exclusive control over their production, refining, and marketing. The hydrocarbon sector, after the surge in world petroleum prices in 1973, came to represent over 30% of GDP.

In many ways Algeria could not have avoided heavy state intervention even if its official ideology had not been socialist. On the eve of independence, nearly all of the French settler community in the country, nearly 1 million strong, packed up and left. This was an exodus even more devastating than that of the Greeks from Turkey in 1922–1923. The French settlers had dominated modern farming, skilled trades, the small industrial sector, and government services. The new state inherited agricultural, industrial, and residential property. The first two were given over to "worker self-management" units. In the agricultural sector, over 2 million hectares were cultivated by about 130,000 permanent workers, on 2,000 farms. The state owned the farms, but, in theory, the workers had full control over their operations. The same formula was applied to industrial units. These consisted of about 400 small-scale enterprises, only 5% of which employed more than 100 persons, and having total employment of 15,000 workers.

In the early years, when Ahmad Ben Bella was president, the experiment in self-management was seen as putting power in the hands of the working people and constituting a barrier to the emergence of a dominating and domineering bureaucracy and technocracy. The period 1962–1965 was one of near-romantic populism and socialism, but already one could see government agencies arrogating basic decisionmaking power in all spheres of production. The FLN, which had seen many of its militants absorbed into the civil service, could do little to defend the populist experiment, and the workers themselves soon reverted to apathetic clock punching.

The romantic period came to an end in June 1965 when the minister of defense, Houari Boumedienne, overthrew Ben Bella and ushered in an era of "rational" top-down planned development that, implicitly, saw the masses as a source more of disruption than of revolutionary support. Worker self-management was paid lip service but was deprived of any effective autonomy.

Boumedienne met one significant challenge from Ben Bella's old coalition. In December 1967, Tahar Zbiri, the army chief of staff, and Abdelaziz Zerdani, the minister of labor, who was close to the General Confederation of Algerian Workers (UGTA), tried to engineer a coup against Boumedienne. Zerdani saw the Algerian development strategy moving toward authoritarian state capitalism in which the workers would be made to pay a heavy price while their unions would be muzzled. He appealed to his old friend Zbiri, like himself a Berber from the Aurès Mountains, and a former guerrilla fighter. The attempted coup failed, the conspirators fled, and Boumedienne, in close concert with his minister of industry, Abdesslam Belaid, pushed Algeria down the very path Zbiri and Zerdani tried to bar.

With the First Four-Year Plan, 1969–1973, Algeria launched a program built on heavy industry. Oil and natural gas were to serve two ends: First, they would be the feedstock for a modern petrochemical sector producing fertilizers and plastics; second, the earnings from their export would pay for the importation of plant and capital goods for planned steel manufacture and vehicle assembly. It was expected that the agricultural sector, especially the self-managed units, would be an expanding market for the new products (fertilizers, irrigation pipes, tractors). The local private sector was regarded as irrelevant to the effort and foreign firms were seen mainly as providers of technology. The slogan was "sow oil to reap industry."[4]

By the time Algeria initiated the Second Four-Year Plan, world petroleum prices had quadrupled. Unlike Egypt, Algeria faced no financing problems in the mid-1970s. In that sense, its experience emphasizes some of the inherent weaknesses of state-led ISI, for, by the late 1970s, major elements of the strategy had been called into question. Rather than the agricultural sector generating demand for new industrial products, there was a general decline in agricultural production, especially in the self-managed sector. Algeria became a major importer of food. Insufficient domestic demand coupled with tariff protection and monopoly position meant that public-sector industries operated below capacity and at high cost. They had little hope of exporting except to some of their East European creditors. Finally some of the imported technologies were so sophisticated, as in natural gas liquefaction, that costly units were frequently shut down for technical reasons.

Near the end of his life, President Boumedienne acknowledged the shortcomings. In his "state of the nation" address of March 1977, he warned (as cited in Nellis 1980b, 410): "Management is henceforth a battle to win, just as we have won that of investment. In truth, the problem of the management of the economy, and more particularly the production and service units will constitute our major concern for the coming years."

Boumedienne died on December 27, 1978. His successor, Chadli Benjadid, a former liberation army commander and a man who supported Boumedienne in 1965, was elected president in 1979. Since that time Algeria's public sector has been extensively overhauled (see Chapter 9). However, the public sector still dominates the Algerian economy. In the late 1980s there were some fifty public-sector companies and twenty authorities with assets valued at over $100 billion, employing 80% of the industrial work force and accounting for 77% of all industrial production. Add to this 260,000 civil servants and 140,000 teachers and other employees of the educational system, and one has 45% of the nonagricultural work force on the public payroll. Finally, the Algerian state in the late 1970s was able to invest the equivalent of 25–30% of GDP annually. This could not be achieved, however, without stimulating inflation and increasing the external debt, which stood at $14 billion in 1981. The collapse of international petroleum prices in 1984/85 forced Algeria to question the very premises of the strategies it had followed since the mid-1960s.

*Syria and Iraq.* We join the two countries together here mainly because since 1953 they have fallen under the domination of the same pan-Arab party, the Ba'ath, or Arab Renaissance party. Since its founding in Syria after World War II, this party has called for Arab unity and socialism and has tried to propagate its message throughout the Arab world. The major obstacle to its spread was perceived by its leaders to be Nasser's Egypt, especially when that country entered its socialist phase after 1961. Many of the policies of state intervention implemented by the Ba'ath in Syria and Iraq spring in part form its socialist ideology, but just as important, from the fears of Ba'athi leaders that Egypt's socialist transformation would dazzle the radical youth of the Arab countries.

Both Syria and Iraq, in contrast to Algeria, had substantial indigenous trading and landowning bourgeoisies and no foreign settler communities (inter alia, see Batatu 1978 and Khouri 1983b). Prior to the Ba'ath's coming to power, both countries pursued policies whereby the state helped the private sector through the development of infrastructure and banking credit. Neither country had made significant advances in industrial production, although Iraq enjoyed the revenues from a sizable oil sector.

In the 1950s, under the Iraqi monarchy, oil revenues gave the state tremendous leverage in the economy. The public Development Board annually absorbed 70% of those revenues and invested them mainly in infrastructural development. It was this policy that required deferred consumption and may have led to a situation in which elements of the Iraqi armed forces overthrew the monarchy in July 1958.

Almost immediately the new regime, led by 'Abd al-Karim Qassim, disbanded the Development Board and replaced it with a Planning Board and a Ministry of Planning. There was a major shift in investment away from infrastructure and agriculture and into industry. The Ministry of Industry was empowered to promote public-sector projects and to supervise and license private-sector activities (Penrose and Penrose 1978, 253).

The new regime, however, was not Ba'athist. Qassim was merely a nationalist army officer with leftist leanings. He tried, unsuccessfully, to balance Nasserist, Communist, and Ba'athist forces within his coalition, contend with Kurdish dissidence and apply a far-reaching agrarian reform. All the contenders battled for the hearts and minds of the officers corps, and it was in February 1963 that a group of Ba'athi officers overthrew and killed Qassim and set up a government presided over by Colonel 'Abd al-Salam 'Arif. This new regime moved in early 1964 to nationalize all banks, along with thirty-two large industrial and commercial firms. With these moves the state's share in large manufacturing concerns rose to 62% of gross output, 46% of employment, and 55% of wages. Once more the state had captured the commanding heights, and most observers concede that Iraq acted in order to steal the thunder from Egypt (Batatu 1978, 1,031; al-Khafaji 1983). One summit was not scaled. Oil production and export remained in the hands of an international consortium of oil companies, known as the Iraq Petroleum Company (IPC). Iraq did not have the skills to take over the fields or to undertake exploration on its own. Oil revenues were too vital to the economy to risk the interruption in the flow of oil that might occur through nationalization. Although Qassim in 1960 had revoked most of the IPC's concessions, no further actions were taken until 1972–1975, when full nationalization took place.

The nationalization coincided with the first big increase in world petroleum prices. With the oil sector under state ownership, the state's share in GDP rose to 75% in 1978, although if the petroleum sector is netted out, the state's share is a more modest 23%. By 1977 there were some 400 public-sector enterprises, employing 80,000 workers. They absorbed over 60% of all industrial and commercial investment (Stork 1982, 36; al-Khafaji 1983, 36). Total government employment in 1977 reached 410,000, or nearly half of Iraq's organized work force. As Batatu pointed out (1978, 1,123), if one adds to the civil servants and public-sector employees 130,000 members of the armed forces, 120,000 pensioners, and thousands of schoolteachers, "it becomes clear that . . . something like one fifth or perhaps one fourth of the inhabitants of Iraq would be depending directly upon the government for their livelihood and their life chances."

Between 1958 and 1961, Syria had been a member, along with Egypt and North Yemen, of the United Arab Republic (UAR). In those three years, under Egyptian pressure, land-reform measures were undertaken as well as some steps toward expanding public-sector enterprise. Egypt's Socialist Decrees of July 1961 alarmed the Syrian private sector, which feared they would be applied in Syria. In league with sympathetic army officers, these elements brought off a coup d'état that took Syria out of the UAR and installed a somewhat conservative, pro–private sector military regime in Damascus.

In March 1963, one month after the Ba'ath had come to power in Iraq, yet another military coup brought the Ba'ath to power in Syria. A year later, in May 1964, the regime took over the country's banks, and in the wake of private-sector protests in Hama, seven enterprises of "reactionary capitalists" were nationalized. Then in January 1965 the regime undertook far-reaching nationalizations. Assets worth $50 million were taken over, and the public-sector share in industrial production rose from 25% to 75%. Again part of the motive was to demonstrate to organized labor that Syria's socialist experiment was as radical and devoted to workers' welfare as Egypt's (in general, see Hannoyer and Seurat 1979; Chatelus 1982; Longuenesse 1985b). In fact, Syria structured its public sector exactly on the Egyptian model, using General Organizations to supervise production in specific sectors such as textiles, chemicals, metals.

A more radical wing of the Ba'ath seized power in 1966, but its militancy was manifested mainly in confronting Israel and sponsoring Palestinian guerrilla attacks. This faction's image was battered in the June War of 1967, and, in 1970, after an internal trial of strength, Hafiz al-Assad, minister of defense and commander of the air force, took power. The shift to some extent resembled that from Ben Bella to Boumedienne. Assad is an organization man, mistrustful of the masses and of revolutionary adventures. He relies on the large power structures of the country: the armed forces, the bureaucracy, the Ba'ath party, and the public sector—perhaps in that order. These instruments are used to control, preempt, and police, not to mobilize.

Between 1970 and 1982 employment in public-sector enterprises rose from 57,000 to 119,000, or, in the latter year, to half the entire industrial work force. In just two years the public-sector wage bill doubled, going from 3.5% to 6% of GDP. In 1979, Syria's total work force was about 2.1 million, of which about a third were engaged in agriculture. Combined public-sector and civil-service employment probably totaled 350,000. There may have been 230,000 Syrians in uniform and, although there is some overlap with the preceding categories, perhaps 200,000 members of the Ba'ath party (Drysdale 1982, 5–7). Some 220,000 workers, in both the public and private sectors, are unionized and under Ba'athi supervision. Again, as we have found in all the preceding experiments, not only does the state own "the major means of production," it controls through the payroll, the party, and the armed forces the most strategically situated elements of the work force.

This dominance in Syria and elsewhere has been achieved at the expense of economic efficiency. The strategic sectors became used to their privileges and to low levels of performance. The state hesitates to alienate them by asking more of them or paying them less. This holds true especially for the military: In 1981 Syrian defense outlays were 13% of GNP, placing it among ten nations worldwide to spend more than 10% of GNP on defense. Inflation and a growing external debt (it increased tenfold between 1970 and 1983 to $2.3 billion) plagued the economy, especially after the Syrian intervention in Lebanon in 1976.

Since 1978, Hafiz al-Assad and other leaders have talked cautiously of stimulating private-sector activity without jeopardizing the predominant role of the public sector (Picard 1981, 215). The same sorts of themes were sounded, with some emphasis on introducing market criteria in judging public-sector performance. Still the Syrian regime was not ready to concede that Syria is a "socialist society on the road to capitalism" (Sadowski 1985, 6).

*Tunisia.* Although since its independence in 1956, Tunisia has maintained uninterrupted civilian rule, it has built an interventionist-state system that resembles those of Egypt, Turkey, and Algeria. Habib Bourguiba founded the Neo-Destour party in the 1930s, rallied the small-scale trading and commercial groups, the professionals and intelligentsia, and the trade unions, and led the coalition to power (Moore 1965).

Although the size of the French settler community in Tunisia was smaller than that of Algeria, it nonetheless dominated the modern private sector.

Table 7.1   Evolution of Total and Industrial Gross Fixed Capital Formation in
Tunisia, 1962-1981 (percent)

|                          | 3-Year Plan 1962-64 | 4-Year Plan 1965-68 | 4-Year Plan 1969-72 | 4-Year Plan 1973-76 | 4-Year Plan 1977-81* |
|--------------------------|--------|--------|--------|--------|---------|
| **Total GFCF**           |        |        |        |        |         |
| Public sector            | 74.7   | 70.9   | 59.1   | 53.2   | 64.7    |
| Private sector           | 25.3   | 29.1   | 40.9   | 46.8   | 35.3    |
| Total GFCF               | 100.0  | 100.0  | 100.0  | 100.0  | 100.0   |
| **Industrial GFCF**      |        |        |        |        |         |
| Public sector            | 84.7   | 86.7   | 60.5   | 43.7   | 63.6    |
| Private sector           | 15.3   | 13.3   | 39.5   | 56.3   | 36.4    |
| Total Industrial GFCF    | 100.0  | 100.0  | 100.0  | 100.0  | 100.0   |

* Average for first three years of the plan.

Source: P. Signoles and M. Ben Romdane, "Les formes récentes de
l'industrialisation tunisiènne, 1979-1980," in GRESMO, L'industrialisation du
Bassin Méditerranéen, Grenoble, Presses Universitaires de Grenoble, 1983,
Table 4, p. 119.

There was no mass exodus of the settlers, as had occurred in Algeria, but the fact remained that there was no indigenous industrial bourgeoisie upon which the new state could rely to promote the country's structural transformation.

From the outset then, much as in Turkey in the 1920s, Bourguiba built a powerful state apparatus, to some extent gutting the Neo-Destour of its best *cadres,* subordinating the trade unions, and using the state to mobilize capital and raw materials to stimulate private activity. In 1962 Tunisia launched its first three-year plan, followed by a series of four-year plans. The state's role in resource mobilization was, until the 1970s, overwhelming (Table 7.1).

Tunisia in the 1960s was quite literally boxed in between the Arab world's two most ostentatious socialist experiments, Algeria's to the west and Egypt's to the east. By 1964 Bourguiba had decided that it was necessary to give a more radical cast to the Tunisian strategy. In October 1964, the Neo-Destour party became the Socialist Destour party and called for the "coexistence" of the public, private, and cooperative sectors. The first Four-Year Plan, 1965–1968, was to embody a socialist transformation of the economy: Cultivators were to be grouped into agricultural cooperatives and state enterprise would spearhead the industrialization drive. A young intellectual, Ahmed Ben Salah, active in the Neo-Destour and the unions prior to independence, was made secretary of state for planning and national economy, and was the driving force behind the experiment.

Both the extent and pace of state intervention had been dictated by Bourguiba's failing health. The Combatant Suprême, as he liked to be known, feared that the socialist experiment would be jeopardized if he were to die before it had been implemented. But Bourguiba's health was restored, and Ben Salah, by forcing the pace of cooperative formation, alienated much of the regime's petty capitalist and small landowning constituency. In 1969, Bourguiba turned on Ben Salah and put him on trial for treason. The statist experiment was overhauled, and Tunisia adopted a strategy of stimulating its private sector and promoting exports to the EEC. The shift in emphasis is shown clearly in Table 7.1 (see also Chapter 9). Still the Tunisian state is a dominant force in the economy and, through its modest oil exports, had substantial revenues at its disposal, especially in the late 1970s. Those rents explain the rising share of the state in gross fixed capital formation after a decline in the early 1970s. In 1982 the public-enterprise sector alone employed 180,000 persons, or over 11% of the work force.

*The Sudan.* The Sudanese economy is, among the major countries of the region, the most heavily dependent on its agrarian sector. Over 70% of the population is rural, and 55% of the work force is employed in farming, animal husbandry, or fishing. Prior to independence in 1956, Sudanese industry was based on agricultural processing: cotton ginning, seed crushing for edible oil and feed cake, soap manufacture. After a military coup d'état in 1958, the Sudanese state began an ISI strategy built around public enterprise. Once again the Egyptian example proved contagious. And as in Algeria, Egypt, Syria, and Iraq, the Soviet Union stepped in with technical assistance, planning advisers, and soft loans. The strategy was maintained during a turbulent return to civilian control between 1964 and 1969 and then was accelerated when Major Ga'afar al-Nimeiri seized power in May 1969. His coalition initially had a strong Marxist and Communist faction that engineered several nationalizations of foreign banks and indigenous private firms.

In the summer of 1970 al-Nimeiri purged his government of its Communist and Marxist members and within a year began to denationalize the assets he had just taken over. Since the early 1970s, the regime has acted to support private-sector growth, within the general ISI framework, but state enterprise is still the dominant economic force in the economy. Public companies dominate the sugar, textile, cement, food processing, and canning sectors and have a significant share of leather, edible oils, soap, and detergents. The 1 million–hectare Gezira Scheme is owned by the state. Cotton and groundnuts are grown on the scheme by 100,000 tenant farm families. It is one of the largest state-owned farms in the world and for years has been the backbone of Sudan's rural economy. The state also owns all mineral deposits, including some oil deposits in the south-center of the country, the Sudanese railroads, and all hydro- and thermal-power systems.

As has been the case for the other countries under consideration, the state in the Sudan is the country's principal employer. With over 400,000 people on the public payroll in 1977, exclusive of the armed forces, the state employed 8% of the entire work force and 21% of the nonagricultural work force (Table 7.2).

*The People's Democratic Republic of Yemen.* So little is known about the structure and functioning of the economy of the PDRY that our remarks

Table 7.2  Growth in Public Employment in the Sudan, 1955/56-1976/77

|                      | 1955/56 | 1976/77 |
|----------------------|---------|---------|
| Central government   | 31,283  | 119,115 |
| Local government     | 80,000  | 157,457 |
| Public corporations  | 65,125  | 132,144 |
| Total                | 176,408 | 408,716 |

Source:  Sudanow, December 1977, p. 11.

will be very brief. The PDRY is an oddity in nearly all respects. It emerged out of the old British protectorate of Aden in 1969. The modern economy was and is totally dependent on the activity of Aden port. The hinterland is a semiarid zone of traditional agriculture. It was the powerful port workers' union that propelled the country to independence. A National Liberation Front organized a dominant Marxist coalition built on the military and organized labor. Whereas the retail-trading sector and some agriculture have remained in private hands, the country's major assets—the port, storage, petroleum refining, manufacturing—are all in the public sector.

*Libya.* The Jamahiria, or "mass state," of Libya presents romantic rev-olutionary *and* Islamic programs combined, in an unacknowledged way, with a kind of cynical authoritarianism. As in all the major oil-exporting nations, the state dominates the economy by the simple fact of owning the petroleum and controlling the proceeds of its sale. That was the case under the Idrissid monarchy, and it has been the case since 1969 when the monarchy was overthrown by then-lieutenant, now colonel, Mu'ammar Qaddafi. He eventually elaborated a new theory of the state of the masses, the Jamahiria, which meant that all productive units and all workplaces were to be directly governed by popular congresses. Bureaucratic hierarchies, top-heavy party structures, elaborate command channels, were all depicted as antithetical to true popular democratic control. Libya's experiment, on paper, was one of worker self-management with a vengeance (see Fathaly and Palmer 1980).

Beginning in 1979 Qaddafi led an assault on private-sector interests unrivaled anywhere in the Middle East. He expropriated all private industry. In 1981 all bank deposits were seized without warning and a program to abolish retail trade by replacing it with state-owned supermarkets was begun (*South,* October 1985, 27–28). By this time three-quarters of the entire Libyan work force was on the public payroll (Anderson 1986). One doubts that the Libyan state and regime have really relinquished effective control of production and administration to popular committees. The oil and banking sectors appear to be under tight state control, as are the 60–70,000 men and women in the armed forces. Libya has multiyear development plans like other countries we have considered, and it is improbable that the leadership would allow the "people" to question, no less change, any of the plan's major parameters.

*Liberal Monarchs*

It may be that socialism entails a significant public sector, but the converse is not true. The monarchies of pre-1979 Iran, Jordan, and Morocco all profess liberal economic credos in which the private sector is to be the leading force. The role of the state is, once again, that of handmaiden to the private sector. Yet if we look at statistical indicators of state activity, we see that these three countries possess public sectors of a size and weight equal to those of the "socialist" countries. The monarchies highlight the general point that one should not confuse state ownership with socialism. Some "radical" regimes have waved the flag of public ownership to demonstrate their socialist bona fides, while "liberal" regimes have passed over in silence the substantial assets they control through state ownership.

*Iran.* Next door to Turkey in Iran a would-be Atatürk appeared on the scene following World War I. Colonel Reza Khan of the Persian Cossacks had de facto taken over the Iranian state by 1924, and it was his intention to proclaim a republic, have himself made president, and to build a power-state system as Atatürk was doing in Turkey. The Shi'ite clergy of Iran, however, vehemently resisted the plan for a republic and persuaded Reza Khan to proclaim himself shah (emperor) in 1925 and to found the Pahlavi "dynasty."

Aside from this nontrivial distinction, Reza Shah set about building a nation in the ethnically and geographically fragmented society he inherited from the Qajars. The state apparatus and the armed forces grew side by side, and, as in Turkey, the depression pushed the Iranian state into ISI. The private sector benefited from credit provided through the state Industrial Bank as well as from high tariff walls against imports. But the state did not wait to see how the private sector would respond to these incentives, and by 1941 there were public enterprises in textiles, sugar, cement, and iron and steel. Through consumption taxes and trade monopolies, the Iranian state, over the period 1926–1940, was able to invest some $400 million in industry and infrastructure, a very substantial sum for that era. Another $120 million was invested by the private sector. All this was done with very little foreign borrowing. The modest revenues from the sale of oil in those years were turned over to the military (Issawi 1978). Iran was neither populist nor revolutionary, but it was just as etatist as Turkey.

Reza Shah was sent into exile in 1941 by the Allies, who feared his collaboration with the Axis. His young son, Mohammed Reza Pahlavi, became the new shah. He did not consolidate his grip on power until his showdown in 1953 with the prime minister, Mohammed Mossadegh, a nationalist leader who brought under state ownership the British-controlled Anglo-Iranian Oil Company. After that time, Iran's economic strategy marched on three legs: petroleum exports, continued ISI, and a division of labor between the public and private sectors. State enterprise undertook the deepening process in iron and steel, copper, machine tools, aluminum, and petrochemicals, while a dynamic private sector, sometimes in joint ventures with foreign capital, moved into finished metals and special steels,

Table 7.3  Public and Private Shares in Gross Fixed Capital Formation in
           Iran, 1963-1977 (billions of rials)

| | Third Development Plan | Fourth Development Plan | Fifth Development Plan |
|---|---|---|---|
| | 1963-67 | 1968-72 | 1973-77 |
| Private | 77 | 141 | 319 |
| Public | 74 | 146 | 734 |

Source: H. Razavi and F. Vakil, The Political Environment of Economic Planning
in Iran, 1971-1983, Boulder, Colo., Westview Press, 1984, p. 76.

synthetic fibers, paper, automobile assembly, and sugar. Iran in 1944 established a Plan and Budget Organization and launched its first national plan. It was well ahead of all countries in the region in this respect, except Turkey.

The kind of division of labor was what one would have expected—it reconciled the regime's professed economic liberalism with a strong state presence in the economy. But in the 1970s a very significant shift in the division of labor occurred, one that contains lessons about the logic of public enterprise in the Middle East. With the first great surge in petroleum prices in 1973/74, the shah's state had at its disposal a tremendous volume of rents. Neither the shah, nor his advisers, nor the state technocracy proposed investing these rents in private-sector growth. Rather, the new funds allowed the state to expand and consolidate in an atmosphere in which public authorities either disregarded or were actively hostile toward the private sector (Razavi and Vakil 1984, 66; also Katouzian 1981, 237):

> The dream of the Great Civilization had established a subjective development goal in the Shah's mind. It was then necessary to refine the strategy of development. This was to be a Big Push type industrialization financed by oil revenues. Given that oil reserves were seen to have a twenty year horizon and that the Shah probably knew himself to be fatally ill, the speed with which the Big Push was to be implemented was to be of paramount importance in the shaping of expenditure patterns.[5]

Those expenditure patterns revealed a dramatic reorientation in the 1970s (Table 7.3). In 1973 the shah prophesied that by 1980 there would be no more than 2 million people, or 300,000 farmers, left in Iran's agricultural sector (Katouzian 1981, 304). In essence, the shah had resurrected his father's blueprint: a powerful state and a powerful military establishment. By the end of the 1970s, government investment and consumption represented 43% of GNP. Military expenditures, which neared $10 billion in 1978, were the equivalent of 10% of GNP. One-quarter of the nonagricultural work force, or 1.5 million people, were on the public payroll.

Let us extract a few general propositions from this example. First, regardless of the ideology of the regime, one of the major factors making for the expansion of the state's economic role is the *control* it offers the nation's leaders over resources and people. It denies those resources and people to other contenders for power. In this sense it is doubtful that the shah ever wanted a powerful and autonomous private sector to develop in Iran. A prosperous, subordinate, parasitic private sector, yes; a true national bourgeoisie, no. When given his monopoly over Iran's external rents in the 1970s, the shah showed the real content of his liberalism.

Has the Islamic Republic of Iran reversed this pattern since 1979? The question is of more than passing interest, for Iran's Muslim state could be something of a harbinger for the rest of the region. The constitution of the Islamic republic is explicit on the role of the public sector, which is to include "all major industries, foreign trade, major mines, banking, insurance, power, dams, major irrigation systems, air, sea, land and rail road transport." Shortly after Khomeini's return to Iran, a wave of nation-alizations took place in June and July 1979 involving 27 banks, insurance companies, and heavy industries, such as the Iran National Auto Works, with 12,000 workers, and the Behshahr Industrial Group, with 13,500. By the end of 1982, the National Industrial Organization controlled about 600 enterprises, with 150,000 employees. In addition, the Foundation for the Disinherited (Bonyad-e Mostaz'afin) was created to take over assets of the Pahlavi family, the Pahlavi Foundation, and the expropriated property of the shah's entourage including farms and apartment buildings (Bakhash 1984, 178–84; Ashraf 1984).

There has thus been no rollback of the state under the Islamic republic, yet it is clear that the new regime is deeply divided on the issue of state ownership and intervention in the economy. The Guardianship Council, whose duty it is to monitor the constitutionality of legislation, in 1982 declared unconstitutional land-reform measures passed by the parliament as well as the law giving the state a monopoly in foreign trade. Toward the end of 1985, the Assembly of Faqihs (Jurists) chose Ayatollah Hussein Ali Montazeri as the successor to Khomeini. Montazeri is known to have strong ties to the Iranian trading interests, the so-called *bazaaris*, and to be sympathetic to the private sector in general. There is nonetheless an important faction of radicals in the parliament, the Islamic Republican party, and in the Oil Ministry who seek to use the state to engineer far-reaching redistribution of wealth in Iranian society. In early 1988, Khomeini's pronouncements showed clearly that he was leaning in the direction of the more radical, statist elements. Since his death, and despite the emergence of the more pragmatic Hashemi Rafsanjani, the same tension continues unresolved.

*The Kingdom of Jordan.* The Jordanian economy is small, and since the Israeli occupation of the West Bank in 1967, badly truncated. It is a dynamic and growing economy but highly dependent on external assistance. In 1976/77, for example, when GNP stood at $1.7 billion, external assistance, exclusive of military aid, stood at $500 million.

The Jordanian state controls the economy in three ways. First, as the direct recipient of the external assistance, it is able to channel investment in the ways it sees fit. This has taken the form of large-scale joint ventures with state, foreign, and local private capital in fertilizers, cement, petroleum refining, and so forth. State pension and social security funds as well as the Housing Bank and the Industrial Development Bank are the conduits for substantial public finance. The state has a significant equity stake in private firms in mining (42%), manufacturing (23%), tourism (27%), transport (20%). It owns 90% of the shares of the Jordan Phosphate Mines Company, 100% of the Jordan Automatic Banking Company, and 99% of the Agricultural Products Manufacturing Company (Rivier 1980, 111, 206). The second lever in the hands of the state is the phosphate sector, which is the country's single largest export and foreign-exchange earner. The third lever is the defense budget, which stood at $246 million in 1978, or 15% of GNP.

The Jordanian private sector has been given the lead in promoting exports of fruits, vegetables, and manufactured goods to Arab and regional markets. If it were not at war with Israel and not so internally divided between Palestinians and non-Palestinians, Jordan would be a good candidate for an export-led-growth pattern à la Hong Kong or Singapore. Its relatively well-educated and hardworking population and its no-nonsense political leadership may still be sufficient to attract foreign investment and technology. There is no way, however, given its small population and narrow resource base, that Jordan could pursue an ISI strategy.

*The Kingdom of Morocco.* Morocco and Iran up to 1979 followed similar development strategies. Morocco, like Iran, had a substantial trading bourgeoisie that was never totally eclipsed by French economic interests during the protectorate, 1912–1956. The country's economic ideology has always been liberal and pro–private sector. Yet, like the shah, King Hassan II may be reluctant to see a national bourgeoisie with its own resource base gain an undisputed foothold in the economy. Finally, while Morocco is not an oil exporter, it has been the world's leading exporter of phosphates, and through the giant, public holding company, the Cherifian Phosphates Office (OCP), the state controls the single most important sector of the economy.

The state's control of the economy takes the form of direct ownership of assets (mines, railroads, dams, sugar refineries) and equity positions through public holding companies. The OCP and the Cherifian Foreign Trade Office (OCE) own assets themselves and have a controlling interest in a host of affiliated enterprises. The OCE, for example, between 1965 and 1975, helped launch twenty-five branch operations involved in citrus exports and wound up controlling about $5 billion in assets. In addition, the state controls a number of special investment agencies like the Caisse de Dépôt et de Gestion, which handles social security and pension funds, and the National Bank for Economic Development, which has been a favored channel for World Bank credits. As Claisse (1977, 878) has noted, the Moroccan public sector reflects basic contradictions in strategic objectives. As is the case in all public sectors, its managers seek its expansion

Table 7.4    Sources of Gross Fixed Capital Formation in Morocco, 1968-1977
             (selected years)

| Gross Fixed Capital Formation | 1968 | 1970 | 1972 | 1975 | 1977 |
|---|---|---|---|---|---|
| In millions of current dirhams | | | | | |
| Government* | 500 | 580 | 710 | 2,150 | 4,650 |
| Public enterprises | 950 | 1,050 | 950 | 3,400 | 4,530 |
| Of which: transfers | (390) | (500) | (400) | (1,190) | (1,940) |
| Other sectors | 740 | 1,360 | 1,520 | 3,310 | 6,170 |
| Of which: Housing | (250) | (440) | (580) | (1,130) | (2,180) |
| Total | 2,190 | 2,990 | 3,180 | 8,860 | 15,350 |
| | | | | | |
| In percentage of GDP | | | | | |
| Government* | 3.1 | 3.0 | 3.1 | 5.6 | 9.6 |
| Public enterprises | 5.8 | 5.4 | 4.2 | 8.9 | 9.4 |
| Of which: budget transfers | (4.2) | (2.6) | (1.7) | (3.1) | (4.0) |
| Other sectors | 4.5 | 7.0 | 6.6 | 8.7 | 12.8 |
| Of which: housing | (1.5) | (2.3) | (2.5) | (3.0) | (4.5) |
| Total | 13.4 | 15.4 | 13.9 | 23.2 | 31.8 |

* Includes civilian investments only.

Source:   World Bank, Morocco: Economic and Social Development Report,
Washington, D.C., World Bank Pub., October 1981, p. 25.

and dominance, even though the political system legitimizes the private sector and the public sector is called upon to protect the national economy against foreign capital, which is otherwise encouraged to enter.

The post-1973 surge in world petroleum prices was followed closely by a large jump in world phosphate prices. The Moroccan state found itself in control of windfall rents and, just as had occurred in Iran, used them not to invest directly in the private sector, but to expand the public sector. The 1973–1977 plan was revised in midcourse, with public investment targets rising from 11 billion to 29 billion dirhams (ca. $6 billion), destined mainly for the steel, sugar, cement, and chemical sectors. The number of public-sector firms increased from 137 in 1970 to 238 in 1976, and state equity in them from 700 million dirhams to 2.2 billion dirhams (el-Midaoui 1981, 234–38; el-Malki 1982, 175). The share of the government and the public sector in total gross fixed capital formation reached 19% in 1977 (Table 7.4). The Moroccan state employs well over 400,000 persons in the civil-service and public sector. There are at least another 150,000 in the armed forces and police. At least one-quarter of the nonagricultural work force is on the public payroll.

Since the big push in public-sector expansion in the mid-1970s, phosphate prices have tumbled, and Morocco's military involvement in the Saharan war has been costing the country $300 million per year. The government by 1983 had been driven into large public deficits and a cumulative external debt of around $10 billion. The government has been obliged to restrict its current expenditures and investment and to revert to its pre-1974 policy of stimulating the private sector and luring in foreign investment. While the number of enterprises in which it has a majority stake has increased, the share of the state in total equity of these companies has declined.

### Princes and Kings of Oil

The most conservative regimes in the Middle East, the princedoms of the Gulf and the Kingdom of Saudi Arabia, are also those with the largest state sectors. They are conservative in the sense that they share non-republican forms of government, a concern for the protection of Islamic values, a fierce anticommunism, and dominant classes with roots in older maritime and transdesert trading communities.

Their economies have been swamped by oil revenues. They combine small populations (Saudi Arabia is by far the biggest, with about 6 million inhabitants), little or no agriculture, no tradition of manufacturing, and a common resource, oil, which has generated tremendous rents. The share of the oil sector in the gross national products of these countries reached the following levels in 1980: Saudi Arabia—66%; Kuwait—51%; United Arab Emirates—65%; Oman—69%. Kuwait's lower figure merely signals that its rents have been diversified and that the country is drawing significant revenues from its foreign investments.

With this kind of financial clout at the disposal of the state, it was inevitable that all new investment programs would fall within the state sphere. For most of the princedoms, industrialization will never be a realistic option except in the petrochemical field, where public enterprises have formed joint ventures with foreign multinational corporations (Kubursi 1984). Private-sector activity is booming and occasionally crashing, as in the Kuwaiti stock market (known as Suq al-Manakh) scandal of August 1982 (Beblawi 1984, 232–34). But such activity is confined to trading and speculative investment, while the public sector dominates the productive sectors and, of course, the civil service.

The civil administration has grown prodigiously in all these countries. Kuwait's expanded from 22,000 in 1963 to 146,000, of whom 90,000 were foreigners, in 1980. Saudi Arabia's grew from 37,000 in 1962 to 232,000 in 1981, to whom we should add another 81,000 part-time or nonclassified employees (Ayoubi 1985; also Islami and Kavoussi 1984; Chatelus 1982, 23). The entire native Saudi work force in 1980 totaled 1.5 million, and there were 800,000 foreign workers in the country. Ayoubi saw this expansion as a function of increased educational output unaccompanied by significant industrialization. Public employment serves the purpose of political control of the educated. It also serves as window dressing: "a respectable and modern looking tool for distributing part of the oil 'loot' and for 'disbursing' largesse camouflaged in the language of 'meritocracy and national objectives'" (Ayoubi 1985).

Saudi Arabia has gone further and established a giant public-enterprise sector, with over forty corporations in housing, storage, agriculture and the Saudi Basic Industries Corporation (SABIC). In the plan period 1976–

1980 alone, Saudi Arabia disbursed $290 billion, which went into infrastructure, port development, and new industrial cities at Jubail and Yanbu. The 1980–1985 development plan, although less spectacularly funded, was designed to put Saudi Arabia on an industrial footing. Oil Minister Ahmad Zaki Yamani prophesied that Saudi Arabia would soon rank alongside Argentina, Brazil, and South Korea as a semi-industrialized country (*Middle East,* March 1984, pp. 25–27). Whereas the goal may be to shift some of the burden of industrialization onto the private sector, it is likely that even if significant industrialization takes place, it will involve mainly public-sector joint ventures with foreign capital.

## Israel and Post-Atatürk Turkey

*Israel.* Israel, for obvious political, social, and religious reasons, is a case apart, but in terms of the structure of its economy, the weight of the state, and some of its ideological predispositions, it shares many features with the socialist states of the Arab world and with Turkey. This sharing is all the more striking in that before there was any Israeli state at all, the Zionist community in Palestine had well-organized party and union structures and cohesive farmer-soldier communities in the kibbutzim. That a powerful and somewhat autonomous state grew out of such a highly structured civil society says much about the logic and attractiveness of the interventionist state.

It was David Ben Gurion, the first Israeli prime minister, who developed the doctrine of etatism (in Hebrew, *mamlachtiut*) and subordinated to the state his own socialist labor party, the Mapai, and its powerful trade union affiliate, the Histadrut. The Histadrut included in its membership about 70% of all Jewish wage earners in Palestine. In addition, the new Israeli state asserted its control over the Zionist defense force, the Haganah, which had fought successfully to achieve and then defend Israeli independence.

What Ben Gurion did in absorbing the labor movement into the state sector, gutting the kibbutzim of their most dynamic leaders, and putting the Mapai and the Israeli Defense Forces under state control is not unlike the process undertaken by another charismatic civilian, Habib Bourguiba, in Tunisia after 1956. As Ben-Dor pointed out (1983, 109), "there was an overwhelming paradox in a man trying to use his party as a base of power from which to destroy the party-state linkage."

There were, however, a number of factors that made Israel's experiment in state-building unique. First, there was the "acquisition" by the state of all the property previously owned by Arab Palestinians who had left their homes during the hostilities of 1948 (cf. Turkey 1923 and Algeria 1962). Second, the Jewish immigrant population of Israel doubled between 1948 and 1952, most of the newcomers were "Oriental," and the state had to undertake their economic, cultural, and social integration into what had been a predominantly Ashkenazi society. Third, Israel, like Jordan, has always been dependent on external assistance and financial flows, and it is the state that controls their disbursement. Between 1950 and 1974, for example, such assistance totaled $19.5 billion. Finally, the state runs Israel's military-industrial complex. Defense outlays were the equivalent of 17% of GNP in 1972 and 30% in 1979, probably the highest proportion in the world (in general, see Rosenfeld and Carmi 1976; Arian 1985; and Kimmerling 1983).

What had emerged in Israel by the late 1960s was a large, paternalistic welfare state with vaguely socialistic objectives and extensive public ownership. In this system, "the citizen would be perceived as an object available for the activities of the state and its bureaucracy, this latter serving as [a] paternalistic body deciding what was good for the citizens and for the collectivity as a whole. By definition, the reasoning of the authorities was better than and took precedence over the individuals and groups"(Kimmerling 1983, 99). The Israeli variant of statism was given practical effect by state-owned or state-controlled enterprise. Histadrut in the 1970s had 1.5 million members, or 80% of the employed work force. It in turn had controlling interests in several corporations: Solel Boneh in construction; the Koor holding company, with 250 industrial, financial, and commercial firms under its control (Koor is listed in the Fortune 500); Bank Hapoalim, and others. There are 200 corporations in Israel in which the government has at least 50% equity. In addition there are some 450,000 persons on public payroll, including the professional military, teachers, and municipal employees. Arian (1985, 36) estimated that in the late 1970s about 52% of the entire Israeli work force was employed by the state and Histadrut, with the remaining 48% in the private sector.

The Israel economy has paid a heavy and familiar price for *mamlachtiut*. Huge government deficits resulting from indexing wages to the cost of living, heavy defense expenditures, and various forms of subsidies produced triple-digit inflation in the mid-1980s. Despite flows of concessional aid and grants, Israel's external debt had risen to $12.5 billion in 1980, or 62% of GNP, the highest ratio in the Middle East. After the Labor Alliance lost power to the Likud in 1976, there were important modifications in the Ben Gurion formula, and some efforts at containing government expenditures and promoting exports through devaluation were undertaken. In 1986, Israel implemented a determined inflation-reduction program, cutting government expenditures, temporarily freezing prices and wages, and increasing tax receipts. Whether or not this program will lead to substantial erosion of the state sector is moot.

*Turkey Revisited.* Since Atatürk's death in 1938, Turkish development strategy has oscillated in intent, but the weight of the public sector has remained predominant. In the decade of the 1950s, i.e., the first ten years of two-party democracy, the Democrat party, led by Adnan Menderes and Bayar, rejected etatism in favor of a liberal economic policy to benefit commercial farmers and the industrial bourgeoisie. Nonetheless, during the 1950s eleven new SOEs were started, the initial objective of selling off some public enterprises was abandoned, and the share of public in

Table 7.5   Public and Private Shares in Investment in Turkey, by Plan Periods,
            1963-1987 (percentages)

|         | 1963-67 | 1968-72 | 1973-77 | 1979-83 | 1984-87 |
|---------|---------|---------|---------|---------|---------|
| Public  | 48.0    | 44.0    | 46.4    | 46.1    | 56.2    |
| Private | 52.0    | 56.0    | 53.6    | 53.9    | 43.8    |
| Total   | 100.0   | 100.0   | 100.0   | 100.0   | 100.0   |

Sources: Merih Celasun, Sources of Industrial Growth and Structural Change: The
Case of Turkey, World Bank Staff Working Paper No. 641, 1983, p. 103; and
TUSIAD, The Turkish Economy,'88, Istanbul, 1988, p. 9.

total investment rose from 38% in 1952 to 62% in 1959 (Roos and Roos
1971, 43).

The brief military takeover in 1960 ushered in another period of national
planning and state-led ISI. This thrust was modified in the Second Five-
Year Plan, 1968–1972, to put a greater burden of investment on private
industry. Subsequently, the RPP government under Bülent Ecevit, with the
Third Five-Year Plan, 1973–1977, resurrected the statist strategy, giving new
authority to the State Planning Organization and stressing intermediate
and capital goods industries (Walstedt 1980, 85–87; Hale 1981, 198–200).

At the end of the 1970s, the state sector remained the economy's center
of gravity. The public share in total investment had stayed fairly constant
for twenty years (Table 7.5), while public investment in the manufacturing
sector had risen from 34% in 1965 to 65% in 1980 (World Bank 1982,
218). Employment in SOEs had grown from 362,000 in 1970 to 646,000
in 1980, or the equivalent of 16% of the nonagricultural work force. In
the manufacturing sector alone, SOEs accounted for 32% of value-added,
36% of employment, and 43% of investment. Total investment in SOEs,
which stood at TL 7.2 billion in 1971, had risen to TL 282 billion in 1980.

## STATE CAPITALISM, THE STATE BOURGEOISIE,
## AND THE PROCESS OF ACCUMULATION

There is remarkable consensus among observers of widely differing
political viewpoints that the interventionist state in the Middle East (and
elsewhere) has given rise to a state bourgeoisie that controls but does not
own the major means of production and to a process of accumulation that
is called state capitalism.[6]

Let us first address the issue of accumulation. Following on the useful
distinction made by Fitzgerald for Latin America (1977, 70, 87), there are
two fundamental types of state intervention and capitalist accumulation.
Both aim at structural transformation of the economy. They are not mutually
exclusive and, as the Turkish case has shown, may oscillate over time.
The first is a process whereby the state helps nurture or strengthen a
private sector. It does so, as noted in the preceding pages, in several ways.
It provides roads, railroads, ports, and electrical power to stimulate economic

activity in general. Through its basic industries and mines, it provides raw materials (coal, oil) and semimanufactured goods (iron, aluminum, chemicals, synthetic fibers), which feed directly into private production. It provides cheap credit and protective legislation. It may take over failing private enterprises. In this process of accumulation, the state transfers surpluses on its own operations, profits if any, and external rents to the private sector. It tries to absorb all major risks for the private sector.

This has been the predominant process of accumulation in the Middle East, although it is important to remember that it is frequently interrupted and that within the state sector itself there are always powerful lobbies that decry the handmaiden role. It is worth repeating that the state, when it gains access to an increased volume of external rents, uses those rents to expand its own activities with little regard to the private sector: thus Iran and Morocco after 1973/74 and Tunisia after 1977 when its own oil revenues shot up. Structural crises may also provoke episodes in which the state sector mobilizes resources by and for itself: thus Egypt and Syria in the 1960s. By and large, however, we see the handmaiden process at work in Turkey since 1950, in Egypt since 1974, in Tunisia since 1969, in Morocco since 1956, in Iran since 1963, and in the Sudan since 1972. Israel also fits somewhat awkwardly into this schema. Leftist critics of the Ba'athi experiments in Syria and Iraq are wont to attribute the same role to state intervention in their economies (e.g., al-Khafaji 1983; Longuenesse 1979), but our view is that in both countries there are dominant coalitions committed to state power and, to some extent, to a socialist vision of society, such that the private sector is encouraged only insofar as it remains subordinate to the state, the party, and the plan.

The second process of accumulation is one in which the state undertakes all the resource mobilization and infrastructure development functions mentioned above, but captures the surplus of its own activities, of a substantial portion of private-sector profits and of external rents in order to finance its own expansion. The goal is for the state to dominate all aspects of resource allocation and to seize, once and for all, the commanding heights of the economy. When this process is under way, the slogans of "socialist transformation" or the "noncapitalist path" are generally used to describe it.

Turkey in the 1930s flirted with this strategy. Egypt explicitly adopted it with the Socialist Decrees of 1961 and then gradually dropped it after 1974. Algeria has described itself in those terms since 1962, although after Boumedienne's death in 1978 the regime has been more attentive to private-sector interests. Tunisia, between 1964 and 1969, adopted and then abandoned the strategy. Whatever the critics may say, Iraq and Syria have both adhered to it since 1963. Finally it may be that Libya, since 1975, has gone further than any country in the region outside the Marxist regime in South Yemen to strangle the private sector.

The term *state capitalism* calls attention to a basic dynamic in both processes: State enterprise, whether at the service of the private sector or of itself, may not involve any major revision of the relations of workers and managers to the means of production. The simple fact of public ownership does not mean the profit motive disappears or that the workers gain control of the surplus value of their own labor. "Exploitation," the counterpart of the drive for financial profit, does not disappear. Again critics on the left are especially inclined to see the state technocracy substituting itself for the private sector without any fundamental change in the relations of production. It is true that no regime has rejected financial efficiency and the generation of a surplus as legitimate criteria, *among others,* for measuring public-sector performance. There may be "exploitation" in the process in the form of surplus transfers from agricultural populations to the service and industrial sectors. The fact, however, that public-sector enterprises generally operate at a loss, reveal low levels of managerial performance, and carry more workers than they need must give us pause before applying the label "state capitalism" with much confidence.

We approach the concept of a state bourgeoisie with the same caution. There is a compelling logic to the *assumption* of a dominant state class (we discuss this class further in Chapter 15). After all, much of this chapter has inventoried the size and strategic importance of the assets owned by the state. They do constitute the "major means of production," with the exception of the agrarian sector, where the state nonetheless has the means to orient production. It stands to reason that the professional managers of public assets could develop the attributes of a class, standing as its members do in a similar position in relation to the means of production and sharing a common set of interests and goals, that is, class consciousness.

The existence of such a class is all the more plausible in that conventional class actors are weak or in decline. The old landowning classes have been destroyed by land reform, while an industrial bourgeoisie has yet to emerge. It thus seems plausible that the managers of public assets may fill this class vacuum, but the fact is that there is little evidence that they have ever done so.

This judgment is based upon an observable paradox in the identity of the state bourgeoisie. It cannot really ensure its own incumbency or its reproduction as a state class. A dominant capitalist bourgeoisie will, in the Marxist view, perpetuate its control of the means of production and pass that control on to its offspring through the juridical device of private property until the final showdown with the proletariat. But members of the state bourgeoisie have no legal title to their offices; they cannot transfer them, and the higher they are in the state hierarchy the less likely it is they will hold their own positions for very long. The fate of economic "czars" in the region is illustrative: Aziz Sidqi, the driving force behind Egypt's industrialization in the 1960s, disappeared from the scene in the 1970s; the same fate came to Algeria's minister of industry, Abdesslam Belaid, after 1980. Toward the end of his regime, the shah of Iran put under house arrest some of his longtime advisers like Prime Minister Amir Abbas Hoveida. Bourguiba tried his own acolyte, Ahmed Ben Salah, for treason.

The survival of the members of this class is dependent upon three factors: (1) their ability to move from position to position within the state hierarchy, (2) their technical competency, making them marketable in *any* milieu, and (3) their ability to build nest eggs (farms, businesses, investments, foreign bank accounts) outside the state sector. Seen in this light, the state bourgeoisie is a strange class indeed: Property is not the source of its power; it has no juridical claim to the positions that are the source of its power; and it cannot and may not even want to reproduce itself as a state class.

At any point we can "see" it as a class, merely by identifying those who are in formal positions of power and the resources they control. Thus Walstedt saw that in Turkey (1980, 187), "A self-perpetuating power group was born, linking bureaucrats, labor unions, and local politicians, that was far more powerful than any private capitalist power blocks operating in Turkey." Waterbury (1983, 260) saw 200–300,000 members of the state bourgeoisie in Egypt. But where are it and its offspring going? Perhaps into a private sector that it has helped foster? Or perhaps to other sectors within the state? Or perhaps out of the country altogether? Or finally perhaps back and forth across a public-private divide that for years has had little operational, and in states like Kuwait or Saudi Arabia very little juridical, meaning?

When social scientists do not know what is happening, they invoke "transitional phases." We can do no less. Powerful interventionist states with large public sectors, and the groups that dominate them, grew out of, on the one hand, the need to promote the structural transformation of their "backward" economies and, on the other, a kind of class vacuum in which a temporarily dominant class emerged on the strength of its education and competency rather than its property. The process of state intervention has contributed directly to the demise of some classes (large landowners, traditional trading bourgeoisies, craftsmen) and promoted others (capitalist farmers, bureaucratic middle classes, a small-scale manufacturing bourgeoisie). The process of intervention has also resulted in deep-seated crisis in the state sector itself and in the economy in general, calling into question the feasibility of continued intervention on the same scale as in the past. We are witnessing in several Middle Eastern societies a cautious retreat of the state and hence a gradual weakening of the state bourgeoisie. In some instances this is best seen as an effort to rationalize state intervention and to make it more efficient. Algeria is a case in point. In others, such as Turkey, an assertive private entrepreneurial sector may be ready to take over from the state the role of leading the development process. Falling in between are countries like Egypt and Tunisia where economic liberalization measures have been introduced in the absence of strong, self-assured private sectors (see Chapter 9). It is thus hard to know if we are at the dawning of a new era in which the state will confine itself to regulating market economies or merely in a period of stock taking and statist regrouping.

Whichever the answer, what has changed and changed dramatically over the past thirty years is the sense of confidence leaders and led placed in the efficacy of state intervention. That confidence is largely gone and the positive legitimacy granted state intervention has been replaced by a kind of resignation born of habit and the lack of alternative agents of change.

## NOTES

1. It is important to remember that for many Muslims, Atatürk is probably the most despised leader of the twentieth century, precisely because he abolished the caliphacy and tried to subjugate the Islamic establishment in Turkey.

2. Atatürk died in November 1938. Inönü became president, and Bayar resigned as prime minister. The latter returned to prominence after 1950 when Turkey's first open elections brought the Demokrat party, of which Bayar was a founder, to power.

3. A number of advanced industrial nations reveal similar proportions, especially Austria, Italy, France, and the UK.

4. The strategy owed a great deal to the French economist G. Destanne de Bernis. See his 1971 article.

5. The fear of time running out, as noted earlier, impelled Bourguiba to delegate broad powers to Ahmed Ben Salah in Tunisia's version of the Big Push.

6. On the state bourgeoisie, see, for example, Amin 1976, 8; Batatu 1979, 110; DERSA 1981, 263–83; Hannoyer and Seurat 1979, 127–33; Hussein 1971, 137–86; al-Khafaji 1983, 39–44; Longuenesse 1979, 9; el-Malki 1982, 163; Nellis 1980b, 417; Raffinot and Jacquemot 1977, 99; Trimberger 1978, 119; Walstedt 1980, 187; Waterbury 1983, 232–62. In addition to these authors, see, on state capitalism, Farsoun 1975; Gibb 1960; Lazreg 1976a, 1976b; Karpat 1959, 88.

# 8

## CONTRADICTIONS
## OF STATE-LED GROWTH

### THE NATURE OF THE PROBLEM

There is a growing but muted recognition that both the interventionism and the public enterprises have, by and large, malfunctioned financially and economically. Other than in the petroleum and banking sectors, the public enterprises have failed to generate profits and have constituted a net drain on state resources; to keep them afloat, they have required subsidized credit and inputs, foreign exchange at preferential rates, and constant flows of working capital and new investment. At the same time the public enterprises have not solved many of the social and economic problems they had been designed to address.

In many respects state-led growth achieved a great deal. Both absolute and per capita national output grew at respectable rates in most countries of the region, even before the massive infusion of oil rents during the 1970s and early 1980s. Structural transformation, whether measured by the share of industry in output or employment, also proceeded at rates that were not unfavorable in international comparative perspective (see Chapter 3). This performance was no mean achievement considering the speed of population growth, the heavy burden of defense expenditures, the limited natural resource base apart from oil, the initially low levels of literacy, and the perennial political instability of the region.

However, industry was often not internationally competitive; many "infant industries" never grew up, due to both price and technical inefficiencies. Overvalued exchange rates and domestic-price distortions led to serious misallocations, some of which we have documented earlier for both agriculture and industry. Too often, the wrong price signals led state managers and private economic actors to produce the wrong things with the wrong combination of inputs. Heavy industry grew rapidly, while agriculture and light industry were relatively neglected. International comparative advantage was often ignored. For example, in two of the leading industrial nations, Egypt and Turkey, much investment took place in industries where profitability was actually negative, if international prices are used for the calculation.

Furthermore, the multiple goals of state-owned enterprises (supplying cheap inputs to other industries, providing jobs for the rapidly expanding labor force) often gave the managers of these industries little incentive to minimize costs, even with a given technology. Capacity utilization was often poor (for example, the Algerian steel plant at El Hadjar operated at only 40% of capacity in the early 1980s; [Nelson 1985, 208]), leading to higher unit costs, which had to be either subsidized from the state budget or passed on in the form of higher costs to other industries. Usually the former approach was adopted.

Allocative efficiency and "X-efficiency"[1] were not the only problems with the state-led-growth strategy. The stress on heavy industry and import substitution failed to create sufficient jobs for the rapidly expanding work force, and, as we have seen in Chapter 6, the relative neglect of agriculture until the late 1970s contributed to the widening food gap. Finally, many countries continued to rely on external sources of investment capital and to accumulate large external debts. The goals of both social justice and national economic independence proved elusive.

Many countries of the region tried to invest more resources than were saved domestically. The "resource gap" (investment minus domestic savings) was large and in percentage terms considerably larger than that for other LDCs (Table 8.1). There was, and is, great variability in this indicator across countries and over time. Countries may be loosely assembled into several groups. Unsurprisingly, the oil-exporting countries typically save more than they invest: Indeed, this phenomenon has led to the creation of a new category of developing country by the World Bank, the so-called capital-surplus oil exporters, composed of Saudi Arabia, Libya, Kuwait, and the UAE. Other oil exporters, principally Iran, Iraq, and Algeria, have had adequate national savings to meet investment.[2] Another group of countries (Sudan, Morocco, Tunisia, Egypt, Syria, Turkey, Israel) had resource gaps in 1985 ranging from 2 to 11% of GDP. Two other countries (the YAR and Jordan) had massive gaps, 36% and 44% of GDP respectively. Mainly because of heavy debt repayments, domestic savings exceeded domestic investment in all middle-income countries from 1980 to 1985.[3] In comparison with this reference group, MENA countries have very large resource gaps (Table 8.1), filled for the most part with continued foreign borrowing and with aid from the United States, the EEC, and the capital-surplus oil exporters of the Gulf.

There were several reasons for this resource gap, but the inefficiencies of the state-owned enterprises certainly made an important contribution. For example, the "budgetary burden," or the net deficit, created by these enterprises was 4% of GDP in 1978–1981 in Tunisia and 3.5% in Turkey in 1978–1980 (Floyd 1984). These deficits contributed to high rates of inflation, which, in their turn, led to overvalued real exchange rates and therefore to uncompetitive exports and to domestic-price distortions. The

Table 8.1  MENA Resourcē Gaps, 1965 and 1985

|                          | GDI/GDP |      | GDS/GDP |      | Gap  |      |
|--------------------------|---------|------|---------|------|------|------|
|                          | 1965    | 1985 | 1965    | 1985 | 1965 | 1985 |
| Algeria                  | 22      | 36   | 19      | 38   | -3   | +2   |
| Egypt                    | 18      | 25   | 14      | 16   | -4   | -9   |
| Iran                     | 17      | --   | 24      | --   | 6    | --   |
| Iraq                     | 16      | --   | 31      | --   | 15   | --   |
| Israel                   | 29      | 16   | 15      | 9    | -13  | -8   |
| Jordan                   | --      | 31   | --      | -13  | --   | -44  |
| Kuwait                   | 16      | 21   | 60      | 30   | 45   | 9    |
| Morocco                  | 10      | 22   | 12      | 12   | 1    | -10  |
| Oman                     | --      | 30   | --      | 43   | --   | +13  |
| Saudi Arabia             | 14      | 31   | 48      | 21   | +34  | -9   |
| Sudan                    | 10      | 7    | 9       | -3   | -1   | -10  |
| Syria                    | 10      | 24   | 10      | 14   | --   | -11  |
| Tunisia                  | 28      | 27   | 14      | 20   | -14  | -6   |
| Turkey                   | 15      | 20   | 13      | 16   | -1   | -4   |
| UAE                      | --      | 31   | --      | 59   | --   | +28  |
| YAR                      | --      | 21   | --      | -15  | --   | -36  |
| **LDC Country-Group Averages** |   |      |         |      |      |      |
| Middle income            | 22      | 21   | 21      | 23   | -1   | +2   |
| Lower-middle-y           | 18      | 20   | 15      | 19   | -3   | -1   |
| Upper-middle-y           | 24      | 22   | 24      | 26   | 0    | +4   |
| Lower income, excl. China & India | 15 | 15 | 14   | 6    | -1   | -9   |

Note: PDRY unavailable.

Source: World Bank, World Development Report, New York, Oxford University Press, 1987, pp. 210-11.

failure to develop internationally competitive industrial (and agricultural) exports, combined with rapidly expanding domestic incomes and demand, exacerbated the deficit of the balance of trade. The public sector, originally created in part to generate foreign exchange, too often simply absorbed it.

State-led growth's failure to close the "twin gaps" between domestic savings and investment and between exports and imports contributed to the accumulation of large foreign debts. Some figures are given in Table 8.2. In most cases, there has been a marked increase in external indebtedness and a rise of the debt-service ratio (debt repayment as a percentage of export revenue). Although these debts are not nearly so large in absolute terms as those of Latin American debtors like Brazil (about $125 billion) or Mexico (about $100 billion), they have been large enough to narrow the options for policymakers and to increase the influence of international lending agencies in the policy process.

Finally, just as the goals of efficiency, growth, and national independence were only partially achieved, the ideal of increasing equality also proved equally elusive. More detail on patterns of income distribution is presented

Table 8.2   Estimated Amounts of External Debt, End of 1986

|              | External Debt (millions of U.S.$) |
|--------------|-----------------------------------|
| Algeria      | 24,020                            |
| Egypt        | 32,928*                           |
| Iraq         | 14,439                            |
| Jordan       | 5,530                             |
| Kuwait       | 8,357                             |
| Lebanon      | 1,694                             |
| Morocco      | 15,748                            |
| Oman         | 3,014                             |
| Qatar        | 620                               |
| Saudi Arabia | 14,290                            |
| Syria        | 4,008                             |
| Tunisia      | 6,454                             |
| Turkey       | 26,124**                          |
| UAE          | 9,084                             |
| PDRY         | 1,508                             |
| YAR          | 3,258                             |

\*   Excludes military debt.
\*\* 1985.

Sources: Middle East Economic Digest, December 12, 1987, p. 16, except Turkey: World Bank, World Development Report, New York, Oxford University Press, 1987, p. 45.

in Chapter 10. The employment problem has clearly not been solved, and the gap between rich and poor has often either widened or remained roughly constant. It appeared to many observers that those equity gains that were achieved had a high efficiency cost, as in expensive consumer-subsidy programs or in the swelling ranks of redundant public-sector employees. And as we have seen, the education and health systems seldom promoted a real equalization of human capital in the region.[4]

Despite high levels of redundant labor in SOEs, disguised and open unemployment remain serious problems in most Middle Eastern societies. Some redistribution of wealth has taken place through public-sector-employment drives and the location of SOEs in backward areas, but the distribution of income in most Middle Eastern countries remains highly skewed. The SOEs have not—again except for the petroleum sector—contributed to exports, while their import needs and hence claims on foreign exchange have remained high. Finally, although the prominence of agriculture in economic activity has diminished, it has been the service sector more than industry that has picked up the slack. It is not at all clear that centralized planning and state enterprise have accelerated the process of structural transformation.

Despite this generally acknowledged situation and the need for reform, little has been done in the past ten years. There have been efforts to stimulate the private sector, which we shall examine in the next chapter, and there has even been talk of "privatization," i.e., selling equity in SOEs to private investors. By and large, however, the economic weight of public enterprise in the Middle East has been little diminished in recent years.

There are a number of factors that explain this inertia; we shall explore them below.

## THE CONTINUED DOMINANCE
## OF PUBLIC-SECTOR ENTERPRISE

To recapitulate an argument made in the previous chapter, state enterprise has arisen within two broad developmental frameworks. The first is of an explicitly socialist and redistributive variety in which equity issues take precedence over profit-and-loss criteria in assessing state activities. When reform is first called for in such systems, it is in terms of making the public sector more efficient, reducing the deficits of specific enterprises, increasing monetary incentives for workers, allowing price increases, linking budgetary support and banking credit to performance, and perhaps even reducing the personnel list. The shift here is toward state capitalism. In Egypt that shift began in 1965 when Nasser first denounced the inefficient performance of the public sector, and in Algeria sometime between 1967 and 1969. Discipline, productivity, and profitability become the watchwords of the new era, but frequently they have remained slogans more than effective guides to improved performance.

The second framework includes countries that start out with state-capitalist experiments. Socialism was never at issue, and profitability, at least in theory, always took precedence over redistribution. Even by these criteria, however, the performance of SOEs in countries like Turkey, Iran, Morocco, and Saudi Arabia has been lackluster. When the issue of reform is raised in these countries, the main elements of the proposal are to use more public resources to stimulate private-sector activity directly and to privatize public-sector assets.

In neither framework have many steps been taken toward reform and privatization. After twenty or more years of strong state intervention in the economy, there are powerful bureaucratic, managerial, and political interests that stand in the way of any diminution of state economic activities.

It is not always possible to discern which groups, organizations, or class interests carry the most weight in promoting or defending the state's role in the economy. Organized labor is generally a staunch supporter because of relatively high wage levels and benefit packages and, above all, because of job stability and relatively light work loads. In many ways unions in the public sector constitute a labor aristocracy (see Chapter 15) and defend their privileges in the name of socialism and the toiling masses. When regimes begin to promote state capitalism, the unions find themselves in a difficult position. They sense that the public sector is under fire, and they seek to defend it against its critics. Yet they do not want to pay the price of greater efficiency, which entails higher productivity: more output per hour of work for the same pay. They may resist the introduction of incentive systems that reward individual or group performance and insist that pay and promotion be based on nondiscriminatory and "nonexploitative" seniority systems. In other words, they may try to sap the very logic of the state-capitalist thrust. Union leaders generally know that this is a dangerous game because if public-sector performance does not improve, its critics will inevitably call for disinvestment and privatization, an even worse outcome for the unions than state capitalism.

The managers of public assets are likely to resist efforts at reform. Frequently they have formed alliances of convenience with labor that have led to low productivity and high enterprise deficits. Managers may well prefer periodic bailouts from the state to the harder option of exacting higher levels of performance from the workers and from themselves.

The managers have generally been drawn to the public sector by its salaries and "perks," which are better than those found in the civil service and even in parts of the private sector. Although in the 1970s, when rates of inflation were high throughout the area, these salary advantages eroded, it is still the case that the work is less demanding and jobs and promotion are more secure than in the private sector. Individual managers may have good prospects for shifts into the private sector, but most public-sector managers will prefer the quasi-sinecures where they are. The opportunities for side payments and moonlighting compensate for deteriorating salary levels. Hence, we would expect resistance on the part of managers not only to efforts to make the public sector more efficient but also to efforts to privatize public assets.

Some segments of the civil service will also have a strong interest in the perpetuation of large public sectors. Whereas the autonomy of individual enterprises varies from country to country, in all instances government ministries directly oversee the activities of such enterprises. They draw up and supervise sectoral and enterprise budgets, review contracts, help design projects, and control personnel procedures. Thus, in the Ministries of Industry, Agriculture, and Defense, where the bulk of state enterprise is concentrated, extensive bureaucracies have developed to monitor them. The Ministry of Planning may plan public-sector activity, while the Ministry of Finance controls enterprise budgets, credit flows, and rates of corporate taxation (inter alia, see Roos and Roos 1971, 64). Auditing agencies check the books of hundreds of public-sector firms. Any reduction in the size of the public sector could lead to a reduction in the ranks of supervisory personnel. The civil servants may thus resist recommendations for greater operational autonomy of state enterprises in the context of state capitalism and recommendations to sell off parts of the public sector if privatization becomes a policy issue.

For some twenty years up to the early 1980s, the external donor community showed some predilection for public enterprise and direct state intervention in the economy. The degree of that predilection was not at all uniform. For example, the Agency for International Development (USAID) has never been a strong supporter of public enterprise, although there was a time when the U.S. government saw the Tennessee Valley Authority as a model for regional uplift that could be exported to the developing world. The attractiveness of public-sector enterprise to other donors lay in the possibility, so it seemed, to bypass cumbersome entrenched bureaucratic agencies in order to promote specific projects (e.g., fertilizer industries) or programs (e.g., diffusion of new varieties of wheat). For bilateral donors there was also the attraction that large public-sector enterprises could become important purchasers of equipment and technology from the donor's home economy. The point is that although the donors have in recent years become the major proponents of public-sector reform and privatization, there was a time not so long ago when they supported public-sector expansion.

Parts of the private sector frequently find it in their interest to have a large public sector alongside them. Large public enterprises in basic metals, plastics and petrochemicals, and other semimanufactures such as cotton yarn may support private-sector manufacturers with a regular and cheap supply of inputs—Turkey, Algeria, and Iraq are all notable in this respect. Likewise the public sector may prove a reliable and not very cost-conscious purchaser of private-sector goods, from automobile components to army uniforms. There are several observers who have concluded that the stirrings and growth of the private sector in several Middle Eastern countries, but most notably in Turkey and Egypt, are an assertion of class interests and that they are the principal force behind the gradual abandonment of state regulation of the economy. Private interests, sustained over decades by state contracts and protection, are alleged to be sufficiently powerful to force the state into retreat or at least to put it more directly at the service of the private sector (inter alia, Mursi 1976). Doubtless, some private interests will benefit from the process of liberalization that we summarize under the rubric *infitah* (economic opening), a term first used in Egypt in the early 1970s. We do not believe, however, that private class interests *caused* such policies. Moreover, it is not clear that private interests would have any stake in the reform of the public sector. They can have the best of two worlds through an inefficient public sector that continues to feed business to the private sector and that by comparison makes private enterprise performance look good. We take up these issues in much greater detail in Chapter 9.

The public sector and civil service together have been an important source of state revenues and savings that will not easily be abandoned or allowed to run down. All state employees represent a captive source of income tax and social security payments. Taxes and payments are simply deducted from salary and wage payments. Evasion is virtually impossible. Income tax and even social security payments outside the public sector are very difficult to collect and generally represent a tiny proportion of total government revenues. To take one example, in 1980, 60 percent of Egypt's total wage bill was paid out to civil servants and public-sector employees. Social security payments represented 10% of all government revenues, income tax on salaries of government personnel another 5%, profits tax on public-sector enterprise, returns on public assets and public-sector self-financing another 40%. Indirect taxes (sales tax, stamp duties) and tariffs and customs, a substantial proportion of which is levied on goods produced in or imported by the public sector and the government, accounted for another quarter of total revenues. External assistance represented 13% of total revenues. The remaining 7% came from corporate and income tax revenues from the nongovernmental sector and the proceeds on bond sales (Waterbury 1983, 202). The state sector in Egypt, taken in its broadest sense, was the source of most state revenues and the locus of a captive work force of 3 million employees.

It may well be that public sectors and big government tend to conserve their predominance in Middle Eastern economies, seemingly regardless of the ideologies of individual regimes, because of the extraordinary power they offer political leadership to preempt resources from actors outside the state system, to finance state activities, and to control strategic sectors of the work force. It does not surprise us to see leaders of self-proclaimed socialist regimes defending their public sectors, but at first blush, it seems surprising to see large and growing public sectors in nominally liberal or liberalizing economic systems such as those of Egypt, Jordan, or Tunisia. If one looks only at the sector of organized labor, the advantages of public-sector employment to *any* regime become clear. Writing on the situation in Turkey, Bianchi (1984, 231) pointed out:

> The conservative unions have focused on enlarging and asserting greater control over their core constituencies in state industry while leaving most of the newer organization in more difficult areas to others. Aided by the public sector's rapid adoption of automatic dues checkoffs and centralized collective bargaining, conservative unionists have come close to acquiring perfect representational monopolies over the state industrial workforce [which is 36% of the total industrial workforce]. Over 90% of the workers in state industry are now dues-paying union members, and about 80% of these belong to conservative unions.

Turkey's prime minister in the mid-1980s, Turgut Özal, may have disrupted this happy marriage of state power and union support through his privatization drive, but other leaders, from Egypt's Husni Mubarrak to Morocco's King Hassan, have proceeded far more cautiously. The economic risks of inefficient public enterprise may not outweigh the political risks of giving up the leverage over resources and people that public enterprise provides.

It is the political calculus of these two kinds of costs that determine the speed and manner with which political elites respond to the poor performance and fiscal burdens that characterize public-sector enterprise. To some extent equity (in the form of redundant labor, relatively high remuneration, and low productivity) and inefficiency have been combined and paid for through deficit financing and borrowing abroad. When foreign creditors refuse to advance new lines of credit until the fiscal mess is cleared up, a painful day of reckoning can no longer be avoided. One of Egypt's leading economists, Hazim al-Biblawi, wrote that the illusion had spread over the years that consumption could grow without sacrificing investment. Instead public and private consumption has grown at the expense of investment: "Nothing is accomplished in the economic realm without effort and sacrifice, or, as the American aphorism has it 'there's no free lunch'" (*Al-Ahram*, July 19, 1984).

The structural problems, if not crises, that have arisen in state-led-growth strategies have provoked essentially two kinds of response. One is that of structural adjustment and the other the deregulation and liberalization that we call *infitah*. The two are not separable in practice, but for analytic purposes we have separated them. Structural adjustment is the broader of the two concepts, and under it come efforts to improve state finances, control inflation, and in a general sense to allow market prices, reflecting real scarcities in the economy, to shift factors among sectors so as to achieve maximum efficiency in production and to favor real comparative advantage in external markets. We shall take up, in the remainder of this chapter, the implications of structural adjustment for Middle Eastern economies and, in the next chapter, the liberalization measures of *infitah*.

## THE POLITICAL ECONOMY
## OF STRUCTURAL ADJUSTMENTS

The failures arising from mismanaged ISI and public enterprise have been general across all the countries in the region that experimented with them. They were doubtless exacerbated in countries with no or very little petroleum reserves by the ratcheting up of world petroleum prices in the 1970s. Growing import bills coupled with stagnant exports led to burgeoning trade deficits that had to be financed by foreign borrowing, both commercial and multilateral. The reaction of most Middle Eastern countries to inflation in their import bill for petroleum and nonpetroleum products was to promote the expansion of their economies, perhaps with the long-range hope that such expansion would lead to increased exports.

Turkey, for example, found itself in one of the region's gravest economic crises in the late 1970s. It was governed by fragile and changing political coalitions, dominated by the Republican People's party (led by Bülent Ecevit) and the Justice party (led by Suleiman Demirel). Neither of these protagonists could afford to promote economic austerity for fear of alienating a significant part of the electorate. The result, in the words of Celasun (1983, 11), was that

despite the oil crisis and related external shocks, Turkey attempted to preserve its growth momentum under the Third Plan (1973–1977) through rapid reserve decumalation and massive external borrowing. Instead of relying upon internal adjustment to promote balance of payments improvement, the various coalition governments pursued expansionary policies, while allowing a decline in marginal savings ratios, and negative import substitution in the energy and manufacturing sectors.

Other countries replicated this scenario to some extent, although Turkey was unique in the nature of its party-competitive political system. What we see then is some degree of imported inflation, combined with high domestic-investment levels. The latter, unaccompanied by significant increases in domestic production, led to high domestic inflation. Governments responded to the inflation by resorting to ill-considered deficit financing in order to maintain salary levels and to cover the operating losses of public-sector enterprises. Foreign resources were used to pay for current consumption rather than to increase production. Eventually, as foreign debt snowballed, current borrowing was used to some extent to cover payments on past debt.

Without some fundamental restructuring of the basic parameters of the economy, the vicious circle described above would lead to debt default and economic collapse. It was to address the issues of restructuring the economy that the World Bank, in conjunction with the IMF and other multilateral lenders, developed strategies and multiyear loan programs for structural adjustment. These were no longer conjunctural, aimed at a particular balance-of-payments crisis or short-term disturbance in economic performance, but rather at the basic assumptions of development strategy. Ideally, structural adjustment could and should take place without sacrificing growth, but even then, the process necessarily entrains deflation and austerity for important segments of the population. Whether structural adjustment programs are leveraged by the World Bank and other donors or begun spontaneously out of domestic considerations (India has been notable in this latter respect), they go to the very heart of structural transformation: the balance between agricultural and nonagricultural sectors and the adjustment of policy and investment in favor of the former; the balance between public, private, and foreign enterprise; the amount of resources devoted to the public sector writ large; the balance between the ISI sector and sectors able to promote export-led growth.

The first steps toward austerity and restructuring have frequently been taken in the wake of balance-of-payments crises. Typically, the affected country turns to the IMF in order to borrow in excess of its quota in the fund. The IMF in turn disburses these funds in "slices" (tranches) as the country takes a sequence of steps to prevent a recurrence of the balance-of-payments shortfall. These first measures are part of a short-term stabilization program or standby agreement. Often the reform measures include reductions in government spending and increases in interest rates in order to dampen the rate of inflation and stimulate savings. Between 1956 and 1984 Egypt, Iran, Israel, Morocco, Syria, Tunisia, and Turkey entered into a total of fourteen such agreements.

Short-term remedies often proved inadequate to address deep-seated problems, and issues of structural adjustment, to be carried out over several years, became part of the agenda. In the early and mid-1980s, Turkey, Egypt, the Sudan, Tunisia, and Morocco were all wrestling with structural adjustment programs. Even countries that have experienced no severe balance-of-payments problems, such as Algeria and Iraq, have, because of problems of food security, unemployment, and poorly integrated domestic markets, spontaneously moved in the direction of structural adjustment. While countries that undertake structural adjustment programs at the behest of their major creditors frequently complain that economic reform is being rammed down their throats heedless of potential political upheaval, the converse may be equally true. The oil boom of the 1970s allowed the shah of Iran to finance large capital-intensive projects in the public sector, continue to neglect agriculture, and to generate high rates of inflation in an overheated economy. His failure to use Iran's petroleum rents for structural adjustment set the economic stage for his own downfall. As Bienen and Gersovitz (1985) have argued, stabilization and structural adjustment programs are as or more likely to contribute to political stability than to undermine it.

The simple fact is that the imbalances caused by years of unsuccessful state-led ISI are going to exact a high political price one way or another *unless* a particular country is able to borrow abroad indefinitely the resources it cannot generate at home. Otherwise some sort of "biting the bullet" will be unavoidable. Let us briefly review some of the typical measures that would have to be undertaken.

Generally, government deficits will have to be reduced to some target level—say, 4% of GDP. To do this governments may have to implement salary and hiring freezes and to slash investment budgets. Such measures go to the heart of the state's role of employer of last resort and may deny public-sector enterprise flows of investment to which it had become accustomed. Second, devaluation of the national currency may be called for. The object here is to promote exports, and it may be the agricultural sector that can most quickly meet the foreign demand induced by the new exchange rate. However, all imports will become more expansive. Industries reliant on imported raw materials and capital equipment will see their operating costs soar; urban consumers used to cheap food imports will likewise be hit; the military will find that its penchant for fancy imported armaments is costing much more. The short-term effects of devaluation can be devastating before its long-term benefits begin to be felt.

Structural adjustment programs will generally seek to stimulate national savings by raising interest rates. This in turn will tend to dampen consumption and inflation while making borrowing more expensive. The end of cheap or subsidized credit in the long run will encourage more careful project selection and a more efficient utilization of capital, but the short-term effect may be to put many firms out of business and many people out of work.

There will be measures to reduce administrative interference in pricing mechanisms and to allow supply and demand to determine price levels. Subsidies of consumer prices and inputs in the manufacturing sector may be reduced or phased out, increasing the cost of goods and the final price of manufactured goods. Subsidies on fuel, fertilizers, and agricultural-credit rates may be ended, raising the costs of agricultural production. Thus, despite a range of anti-inflation measures (reduced government spending and credit squeezes), the cost of living, especially for urban populations, may rise dramatically.

Structural adjustment generally entails a revision in the terms of trade prevailing between the agricultural and nonagricultural sectors. Policies that have held down the producer prices of agricultural commodities that feed into local industries (sugarcane, cotton, sugar beets) or of basic food crops (wheat, rice, oil seeds) may be raised to stimulate production. Presumably if production does increase, prices of such commodities will eventually fall, but the near-term effect may also be to raise the cost of living for urban populations.

Finally, there will be an effort to streamline the public sector and to stimulate the private. Public-sector enterprises will be called upon to increase productivity, reduce costs and idle capacity, generate a financial return on their investments, and, ideally, meet their investment needs out of their own earnings rather then relying on government financing of their deficits.

The effort to make the public sector more efficient will mean that redundant labor may be gradually let go, no new hiring may take place, and management will be called upon to concern itself with issues of inventory controls, waste reduction, market research, and quality control. At the same time, new sources of commercial credit to the private sector may be opened, and the public sector may find itself competing with local private or even foreign joint-venture enterprise in areas where it had previously enjoyed a monopoly position. It will be the private rather than the public sector that is targeted to lead an export drive to reduce the country's balance-of-payments problems.

To summarize: Successful structural adjustment will require at a minimum reduced government spending, a shift of investment resources from the urban to the rural sector and from the public to the private sector; a move away from a planned economy to one in which the market plays a major role in allocating resources; and, in the most general sense, a move to an economy in which equity concerns may be "temporarily" sacrificed to those of efficiency. The process is inevitably painful: Standards of living for people on fixed incomes and/or low- and middle-income urbanites may decline; privileged labor unions may find their wages and benefits eroding; educated and skilled youth may face an economy generating very little employment. Short-term economic contraction, it may be argued, is the price that must be paid to assure future sustained growth, but getting from the short to the longer term may prove politically impossible.

Two kinds of pitfalls must be avoided. The structural adjustment "medicine" must not be so powerful as to lock the economy in a downward spiral of contraction, business liquidation, unemployment, and slack demand. Judicious resort to government pump priming and foreign borrowing to keep the economy expanding will be called for. But the second pitfall is related directly to seeking that delicate balance between austerity and growth. The application of stabilization and structural adjustment programs may be so diluted that they achieve the worst of both worlds—a deterioration in standards of living for important segments of the population without the structural reforms that would set the stage for further growth.

Countries that enter into this process under pressure from the World Bank and other creditors may find that the pressure itself becomes a domestic political issue. No political leadership likes to appear to be bowing to outside forces, especially when what is at stake are *domestic*-policy issues. Indeed, some leaders may even try to raise their political capital at home by ostentatiously resisting the advice of their foreign creditors.

There are basically three kinds of response to such pressures that national leaders may adopt. The first is outright rejection, generally citing the deleterious consequences for equity and the likelihood of economic stagnation. In Turkey's turbulent party-competitive system in the 1970s, none of the major political leaders could afford to advocate belt tightening. A second gambit is to adopt a posture of rejection of some or all of the recommended reforms but to pursue their implementation in an unannounced way. Both Sadat and Mubarrak of Egypt from 1976 on followed that tactic to some extent. The risk of course is charges of hypocrisy and subterfuge when and if the game is revealed (Bienen and Gersovitz 1985, 749; Joan Nelson 1984, 986–91). Finally, leaders may accept the reforms but claim they are being adopted purely out of domestic concerns and because they make sense. One might view the reforms introduced in Turkey after the military takeover in September 1980 in this light.

The major risk, however, at least as it is perceived by political leadership, is that austerity will provoke violence, especially among urban populations. There have been several instances of cost-of-living riots in Middle Eastern cities, and we shall have more to say about them in Chapter 10. For the present, let us note that rioting severely tested the regimes of Morocco in 1965, 1982, and 1984, Tunisia in 1978 and 1984, Egypt in 1977, and the Sudan, where it may have been the catalyst to the overthrow of Nimeiri in March 1985. We have already noted the crisis into which Turkey's expansionary policies had driven the economy in the 1970s. High rates of inflation, flagging exports, escalating foreign debt, and huge government deficits were symptoms of a structural crisis that Celasun described as the exhaustion of the easy import-substitution possibilities in the early industries, and the need to move toward "trade improving investing programs" (1983, 12). Even before the military seized power in the midst of escalating civil violence, the civilian government, in January 1980, introduced sweeping policy changes that included sharp increases in the prices of public-sector goods, elimination of a wide range of price controls, a major currency devaluation, export incentives, favorable legislation for foreign investors, and curbs on government spending. It is moot whether or not this program

Table 8.3   Unemployment and Wages in Turkey, 1979-1983

|                        | 1979    | 1980    | 1981    | 1982    | 1983    |
|------------------------|---------|---------|---------|---------|---------|
| Unemployed             | 189,467 | 263,354 | 341,336 | 468,654 | 549,081 |
| Real gross wage TL/day | 75      | 56      | 52      | 50      | 51      |
| Real net wage TL/day*  | 41      | 29      | 33      | 31      | 32      |

* Net wages are net of insurance payments, income tax, stamp tax, and
"financial balance tax."

Source:   Annual Report of the Central Bank of the Republic of Turkey,
1983, Ankara, 1984, p. 110.

could have been implemented with the same force had the military not intervened to put an end to civil violence as well as to open democratic life. The trade unions and universities were muzzled, and the return to civilian government in November 1983 was under the strictures imposed by Turkey's senior officers. The figures in Table 8.3 give some indication of the impact of the austerity measures.

In Egypt, the challenge of structural adjustment was first posed un-equivocally in 1976. The country had fallen in arrears on payments on its commercial debt; the government deficit and domestic inflation were growing in lockstep, the public sector was riddled with idle capacity and large aggregate losses, and price disincentives prevented agriculture from taking up the slack. Egypt entered into a standby agreement with the IMF in the spring of 1976. Part of the reform package was to reduce the level of subsidies of several consumer goods in order to lower the deficit. In November 1976, President Sadat faced Egypt's first openly contested par-liamentary elections since 1952. He put off action on subsidy reductions until January 1977. When the price increases were announced, three days of severe rioting ensued in Alexandria, Cairo, and several other Egyptian cities. Sadat immediately revoked the price increases, and the stabilization program was shelved.

That Egypt's economy did not then founder was the result of great luck and some skillful political maneuvering. In the fall of 1977 Sadat made his historic trip to Jerusalem, in search of a peace that might, among other things, enhance Egypt's image as a home for foreign investment and that would lighten the burden of military expenditures on the economy. In fact, the Camp David Accords of March 1979, which established formal peace between Egypt and Israel, led to Egypt's ostracism from the Arab world and a drying up of Arab aid and private investment in the Egyptian economy. Sadat shared a Nobel Peace Prize with Prime Minister Menachem Begin, but the Egyptian economy did not directly benefit from their labors (nor did Israel's).

In the late 1970s, however, other processes, unplanned and unanticipated, were in train. The booming oil economies of the region needed manpower at all skill levels to implement their gargantuan development plans. By 1980 hundreds of thousands of Egyptian migrant workers were remitting to the home economy upwards of $3 billion per year. Recovery of oil fields

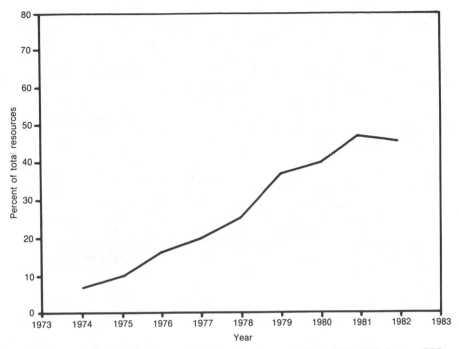

Figure 8.1 Share of exogenous resources in total resources in Egypt, 1974–1982. *Source:* IBRD, *Arab Republic of Egypt: Issues of Trade Strategy and Investment Planning,* Washington, D.C., January 1983, p. 5.

in the Sinai Peninsula, after years of Israeli occupation, coincided with a second surge in international petroleum prices. By 1980 Egyptian oil exports were earning the country $4.5 billion per annum. The surge in oil prices also was reflected in increased transit fees in the Suez Canal. These fees earned the economy nearly $1 billion in 1981/82. Finally, the peace between Israel and Egypt did stimulate tourism, which in 1980 generated $700 million in revenues.

Egypt was awash in unanticipated foreign exchange, and it became increasingly dependent on foreign rents (Figure 8.1). These external resources could have been used to cushion the impact of the structural adjustment process initiated in 1976 and aborted in 1977. Instead they were used to pay for increased consumption, mainly in the form of imports and increased consumer subsidies. They allowed Egypt to avoid structural adjustment rather than to make the process less painful. By the middle 1980s, a global oil glut was manifest and the bottom dropped out of international oil prices. Egypt's oil earnings plummeted, the demand for Egyptian labor in Arab oil-exporting economies slackened and the flow of remittances began to diminish, tanker traffic through the Suez Canal tapered off, and numerous terrorist incidents in 1985 and 1986 scared away tourists. Ten years after first nibbling at the bullet, Egypt was once again faced with the entire structural adjustment package. In the early 1980s, the World Bank and other donors became increasingly alarmed at Egypt's economic prospects in light of softening petroleum prices and the lack of domestic economic reform. More than one report noted that Egypt's only option for the future was to increase the export of manufactures in the near and middle term, but because of the inefficiencies of public-sector enterprises and the misallocation of investment resources that resulted from the heavy demands of the public sector on public finances, Egypt was losing its competitive edge in international markets. A 1983 World Bank report put the matter succinctly and starkly:

> Egypt's public finances are extraordinary in several respects compared to those of other countries at similar income levels. The public sector's dominance in its economy requires the mobilization and expenditure of a vast amount of resources. Total public expenditures are 60% of GDP, total revenues are 40% of GDP and the public-sector deficit is 20% of GDP. There are very few, if any, developing countries in the world with such high proportions. These heighten the normal fiscal issues of the efficiency, equity and development impact of public-sector economic operations.

The reforms envisaged by the bank and others involved the following areas:

- Reduction of consumer subsidies, which were running at about £E 4 billion per annum in the early 1980s or circa 7% of GDP.
- Energy pricing and conservation: Petroleum products in Egypt were priced at about 16% of the world prices prevailing in the early 1980s; this indirect subsidy to the rest of the Egyptian economy was worth $2.5 billion per annum.
- Exchange-rate management and trade policy; i.e., devaluation and export promotion.
- Tax reform to introduce a unified, global income tax-rate structure.
- Agricultural production policies to improve the terms of trade between the agricultural and nonagricultural sectors and to promote agricultural exports.
- Public-sector reform; under this rubric the bank envisaged only reforms that would improve efficiency, that is, resort to what we called above the state-capitalist route. Specifically, SOEs should be given greater financial and managerial autonomy; they should sell their products/ services at their real market value; they should pay market wages to attract skilled labor but should also shed redundant unskilled labor; the role of the state sector as employer of last resort should be ended. The bank did not recommend privatization or divestiture.

These reforms were advocated at a time when bank forecasters sketched out oil-price scenarios that they thought were fairly pessimistic. They saw a decline in world prices to about $25 per barrel but thought that price would hold, at least in nominal terms, throughout the 1980s. In fact, by 1986, the price had dropped to around $15 per barrel. Egypt's day of reckoning seemingly could no longer be postponed.

In the mid-1980s Egypt had become one of the world's major debtor nations, with over $38 billion in foreign obligations (not including Soviet military debt) and annual debt service charges running in excess of $4 billion (i.e., as much or more than earnings from the export of oil). Since the late 1970s, Egypt's military debt to the United States had grown to $4.5 billion and interest on that debt ran at 13% per annum. "Peace," as anyone would have predicted, did nothing to lessen the economic burden of Egypt's military preparedness. In 1986 Egypt had fallen $1 billion in arrears in some of its foreign payments.

The Egyptian government's internal debt in the middle 1980s had reached nearly £E 30 billion or about $20 billion at the market exchange rate prevailing at that time. The budgetary deficit of the government, already at 16% of GDP in 1981/82, was forecast to reach 23% of GDP in 1986. An acceptable level from the point of view of the World Bank and the IMF is around 4%. The annual financing requirements of SOEs alone at that time were well in excess of £E 1 billion and were met largely by overdrafts on public-sector banks and the printing of money.

President Mubarrak came to power in 1981 after the assassination of President Sadat by Muslim extremists. The new president was only too aware of the depth of alienation of large segments of Egypt's youth, faced with soaring costs of living and a shrinking domestic job market. To take on structural adjustment reforms at the very moment that external markets for Egyptian labor were beginning to contract must have seemed as politically suicidal as it was economically inevitable.

Several other Middle Eastern states have to varying degrees shared in Egypt's distress. The *Economist* (July 20, 1985) surveyed one of these states and noted the following symptoms: inflation running at 180–200% per annum; the highest per capita foreign debt in the world ($6,200 per person); unemployment running at 10% of the work force; an absolute decline in the standard of living; and an annual growth rate of GNP of about 1%. The causes of the disease were seen as lying in a defense establishment that annually absorbed 20% of GNP; a "massive welfare state"; subsidies of basic consumer goods; indexing wage increases to the cost of living; a "huge socialist bureaucracy—encompassing not only trade unions but also banking, transport, farming, insurance, education"; the dampening of private initiative through public quasi-monopolies, and "irresponsibly disbursed American aid." Public-sector expenditures were at a level equivalent to 30% of GNP and the deficit, in 1984, at about 16% of GNP. The trade deficit had reached $2.5 billion in 1984. The country surveyed by the *Economist* was Israel.

Prime Minister Shimon Peres promoted austerity measures that went much further than any attempted in Egypt. He slashed the government budget from $12 to $10 billion, including outlays on housing, education, welfare, and civil service salaries. Some $800 million in subsidy reductions were being planned. Simultaneously, the government set its sights on promoting high-tech exports as well as military hardware, the latter of which earned the country over $1 billion in 1984.

Once again we find the issues of increased efficiency and productivity linked to a reduction in public expenditure, a cutback in social-welfare programs, the containment if not privatization of public enterprise, and an export drive. As in Turkey and Egypt, Israeli politicians must calculate the political costs of the adjustment process—will lower-income Oriental Jews suffer more than the Ashkenazim? What will be the impact on Israeli and non-Israeli Arabs? Will Israelis respond to austerity by increased emigration or demonstrations or both? In none of the three countries we have looked at is anyone arguing that the sacrosanct financial requirements of the military should be reduced.

It would appear that we are at the end of a major developmental phase in Middle Eastern societies and perhaps in LDCs as a whole. State-led growth has brought about a certain amount of structural transformation, but rapid population growth has overwhelmed the income-raising effects such transformation was presumed to yield. The state has overextended its capacities to manage and guide increasingly diversified economies. It was able to give a big push to industrialization but unable to deal with the complexities of industrial deepening, the efficient use of labor and capital, and the need to export in highly competitive world markets. Part of the complexity and diversity that state intervention brought about lay in the creation of new class actors and interests that benefited from state policies (land-reform beneficiaries or the recipients of subsidized credit) or from state business (the whole range of subcontracting). Over time, these groups have become entrenched in their economic niches, absorbing resources, saving and investing in such a manner that they developed some economic autonomy and the means to lobby effectively vis-à-vis the state. Indeed, many state functionaries joined their ranks.

It is too early to predict that the state technocracy and political leadership, increasingly aware of the limited reach of the state and under pressure from the donors, will pass the baton to private actors. What is sure is that the next thirty years of structural transformation in the Middle East will be far more difficult than the first thirty. Neither the aid flows nor the buoyant international markets of the 1960s and 1970s are likely to prevail in the coming few decades. Population growth rates have declined only marginally, and absolute numbers of the rural population and the urban poor have continued to grow. There are no obvious ways to reconcile the political and economic demands of these young and increasingly educated populations with the need for a reduction in state investment, welfare budgets, and public-sector payrolls. The easy phase of import-substituting industrialization may also have been politically easy compared to the challenges that structural adjustment will generate in the coming years.

## NOTES

1. "X-efficiency" arises when an enterprise's total costs are not minimized because the actual output from given inputs is less than the maximum technologically possible level.

2. Iran and Iraq joined their poorer brethren in facing a resource gap once they embarked on their mutual slaughter, but there are no international data on this issue for these two countries after 1980. Unofficial estimates place Iraq's debt at as much as $90 billion, while Iran has entirely depleted its accumulated reserves (*Middle East,* July 1988).

3. For lower-middle-income countries, the difference between domestic savings and domestic investment was +2% for all middle-income countries, −1% for lower-middle-income countries, and +4% for upper-middle-income countries.

4. It should be added that liberalization and *infitah* policies, to be discussed in Chapter 9, have done little better on the equity front; indeed, for some countries, such as Turkey, they have worsened inequalities.

# 9

# THE EMERGENCE
# OF *INFITAH*

*Infitah* (economic opening) is a generic term for shifts in state economic policy toward increased emphasis on the private-sector, reform of public-sector decisionmaking, opening to international markets, and greater reliance on market forces. The specifics vary across nations, but many states of the region have moved in this direction. These changes are best understood as the product of three forces: the difficulties and contradictions of state-led growth, class actors either spawned or strengthened by such growth, and influence from abroad. This chapter will outline the basic logic of these policy shifts, illustrated by sketches of five countries' experiences (Egypt, Tunisia, Turkey, Algeria, and Iraq). The stress will be on the interaction of economic growth and structural change and policy; although the chapter concludes with a glance at the question of the role of class actors in these policy changes, a full discussion of this issue is postponed until Chapter 15.

Throughout the region, and despite national differences, the disappointments and problems of state-led growth engendered responses that shared common themes. Virtually all of the countries of the region have moved away from the earlier vision of complete (or nearly so) public-sector dominance of the economy. States with markedly different official ideologies share this tendency. Just as the state sector expanded as much in the conservative oil states of the Arabian Peninsula as it did in self-proclaimed socialist ones, so also has the *infitah* phenomenon occurred not merely in conservative Turkey and pro-Western Egypt but also in "socialist" countries like Algeria and Iraq. The timing and degree differ, but strengthening the private sector and shifting the performance criteria for public-sector enterprises are found throughout the region.

These changes may be interpreted as the response of one of our independent variables, "state policy," to the imperatives of another, "economic growth and structural transformation." However, explaining these changes also requires understanding current class forces, themselves the outcome of past policies, growth, and structural changes. Moreover, the extent to which social classes as opposed to the state apparatus and leadership itself have "determined" policy varies widely from one country to the next; despite *infitah,* state autonomy persists. The international dimension partly explains this phenomenon: Insofar as a country "opens up" to the rest of the world, the state will have a central role in mediating between the domestic society and international actors. In the next section we will offer a brief outline of some major countries' experiences with the *infitah* phenomenon. We conclude with a brief discussion of class and state actors, national and international.

## A SURVEY OF COUNTRY EXPERIENCES

We must distinguish between the capital-surplus oil exporters like Saudi Arabia and the other relatively industrialized countries. In the former, the state has rapidly expanded its activities in the past decade, although it has often done so by delegating and subcontracting tasks to private entrepreneurs. In these most conservative of political economies, the industrialization process has to a significant extent recapitulated the public-private division of labor of the earlier industrializing countries like Turkey and Egypt: The public sector has led the way, and the private sector has played the role of subcontractor and poor relation. The reasons for the dominance of the public sector were, as usual, practical rather than ideological. Indeed, ideologically these governments are firmly committed to private property and enterprise. However, only the state could plausibly mediate successfully between sophisticated multinational contractors and the local society. Only the state had the resources to undertake projects as massive and capital intensive as, for example, the Saudi petrochemical complex.

But even in these states, there are signs of policy shifts designed to strengthen the private sector. Indeed, one journal labeled these initiatives "the biggest programme of privatisation ever undertaken in the Middle East" (*Middle East,* April 1985, p. 12). Although this may be hyperbole, the Saudi Fourth Development Plan (for 1985–1990) explicitly aims at strengthening the private sector. Interestingly, such a move is justified on essentially nationalist grounds: to reduce dependence on foreign labor and goods. The government orchestrated the sale of shares in the Saudi Basic Industries Corporation (SABIC) by offering $10 billion worth of stock (20% of the total value) for sale to Saudis and citizens of Gulf Cooperation Council states. The issue was oversubscribed, the government sold additional shares, and there were numerous discussions of privatizing other major state enterprises (*Middle East,* April 1985, pp. 12–14).

The Saudi government has taken this path not merely from ideological preference (although officially the government has always favored a "leading role" for the private sector), but also from necessity born of economic austerity. With the softening and then collapse of world oil prices, public-sector spending could remain at previous levels only if the regime was willing to continue to draw-down its (enormous) financial reserves and ultimately, to begin borrowing abroad. Although the Saudi government did indeed draw-down its investment portfolio, the regime's legendary caution would not permit it simply to continue spending and to borrow. Instead, it hoped that the private sector could provide the engine of growth to the economy. In particular, the private sector was to lead the way in industry, which, with the completion of most of the vast construction projects of the oil boom era, was now planned to provide the principal stimulus to national growth.

The Saudi experience illustrates a common problem with this strategy: Private entrepreneurs are being asked to perform unaccustomed roles in a time of economic recession and uncertainty. Their response has been understandably cautious. Saudi entrepreneurs have proved reluctant to move out of more traditional investment areas like real property and commerce into industry. And as elsewhere, the private sector not only profits from government spending and subsidies but also clamors for more of the same. The so-called Peace Shield defense program, under which foreign companies (e.g., Boeing) holding contracts to modernize the kingdom's air defense system must simultaneously invest in high-technology manufacturing ventures in the kingdom, is a clear example of state-fostered private-sector growth. The extensive Saudi agricultural-subsidy package is another. The lesson here, as elsewhere, is that the "public" and the "private" sectors are not necessarily rivals or, in some cases, even easily distinguishable.

Our main concern is with the more advanced countries. We shall illustrate our argument by a brief consideration of the experiences of five countries: Egypt, Tunisia, Turkey, Algeria, and Iraq. There were several reasons for choosing these countries. First, all except Tunisia are relatively large economies. Second, Tunisia was the pioneer of *infitah*, while Egypt has given us the name of the phenomenon. Third, we have a kind of continuum of relative "state/private-sector" strengths within *infitah*. Turkey, where the bourgeoisie is strong and where the attempt at a "free market" export-led strategy has gone the furthest, lies at one end; Iraq and Algeria, whose private sectors, despite recent changes, remain clearly subordinate to the state, stand at the other end. Egypt and Tunisia fall somewhere in between.

## Egypt

The Egyptian *infitah* was a response both to internal problems with state-led growth and to shifts in the international economic and political environment. By the early 1970s, the Egyptian economy suffered from several maladies: stagnant productivity in the (overwhelmingly public) industrial sector, lagging agricultural growth and growing food imports, a serious imbalance of trade, and a large resource gap. How could the country maintain the "social compact" in the face of rapid population growth without accelerating the growth of productivity? And where were the investable resources for such change to come from if not from abroad, given that the Egyptian state under Sadat had no more intention of "sweating" the population than had Nasser?

The international conjuncture presented a chance to address these problems. The oil boom of the 1970s offerred Egypt the prospect of enhanced capital inflows from the major oil-exporting countries of the Gulf, from workers' remittances, and ultimately, from direct oil sales. But such opportunities required changes in the economic institutional environment. How were conservative Saudi (or U.S. and West European) investors to be persuaded to put money into such a tightly state-controlled economy? How could Egyptian workers abroad be enticed to repatriate their savings if the grossly overvalued exchange rate, so typical of ISI regimes, was maintained? Furthermore, the country had to buy food from the only available suppliers: the advanced industrial countries of the West.

As Abdel-Khaleq has pointed out, the term "economic opening" is a bit of a misnomer, because it implies that the Egyptian economy under Nasser was closed to trade, which, of course, it was not. In fact, what happened may be better described as a "turning West" (Abdel Khaleq 1981). Under Nasser the Egyptians had engaged in barter trade with Eastern European countries, mainly exchanging agricultural products and other raw materials for industrial goods. Of course, such trade did not generate any convertible currency, which Egypt needed to buy Western equipment and foodstuffs. A geographical restructuring of trade was certainly a central component of the *infitah* strategy. The percentage of Egyptian mechandise exports going to the OECD countries rose from 28% in 1965 to 53% in 1985, while the respective percentages for the Eastern Bloc fell from 38% to 7% (World Bank 1987, 226).

However, geographical reorientation of trade hardly exhausts the policy changes of *infitah*. Other goals were to attract capital from the oil states of the Gulf, to lure Western investment and technology through joint ventures with Egyptian public or private enterprises, to promote exports and the private sector, and to improve the productivity and competitiveness of the public sector. The legislative centerpieces of this effort were two laws on joint ventures, Law 43 of 1974 and its amendment by Law 32 of 1977, and legislation that extended the benefits of these laws to purely Egyptian companies, Law 159 of 1981. Also critical were the liberalization and partial privatization of foreign trade, the "own exchange" system to finance private-sector imports, repeated exchange-rate devaluations leading ultimately (in 1987) to the unification of the exchange rate, reorganization of the public sector in 1975 and again in 1983–1984, restructuring of the banking system, and a host of changes in publicly administered prices (e.g., raising of electricity rates and other fuel prices).

The results of these policy shifts, combined with the changing international conjuncture, have been quite mixed. There is no question that the first ten years of *infitah* witnessed a dramatic escalation of economic growth in Egypt: Per capita GDP growth rates rose to 8–9% per year. Although these rates have slowed during the oil bust of the mid- to late 1980s, Egyptian growth rates have remained well above those of the 1960s.

Unfortunately, this improved growth performance was as much the result of windfalls as of domestic policy shifts. It is true that the ratio of domestic savings to GDP rose sharply from 8.5% in 1974 to 16% in 1985. The improvement looks less impressive when juxtaposed with the Nasserist heyday: In 1965, some 14% of domestic output was saved. However, the most striking change came in the investment ratio, which soared from 18% to 25% in the same period. This was made possible by oil exports, workers' remittances, Suez Canal revenues, tourism, and, after 1979 and the Camp David Accords, an increased flow of U.S. bilateral aid. As many observers pointed out at the time, all of these sources of savings were highly dependent on the state of the regional and world economy in general and on oil prices in particular. They had little to do with improvements in labor (or capital) productivity in the Egyptian economy. Such foreign largesse did provide a "window of opportunity" for reform, and although some important changes were implemented, much remained the same.

*Infitah* did not solve Egypt's balance-of-trade problem. Indeed, the liberalization of imports exacerbated it: The balance of trade, in the red some $1.2 billion in 1974, remained in deficit, $5.3 billion, ten years later (IMF 1987). The balance of agricultural trade, negative since the early 1970s, continued to deteriorate. By 1985, 25% of Egypt's imports were foodstuffs. Industrial exports also failed to take off, and commodity exports were increasingly dominated by petroleum products. Workers' remittances rose rapidly enough to prevent a severe balance-of-payments crisis, but they never were as large as the trade imbalance. As a result, the foreign-exchange gap continued to grow and, with it, foreign indebtedness. External debt rose from approximately $3 billion in 1974 to $24 billion in 1985 and $50 billion in 1988. Already in 1985, debt service (payments of interest and principle) consumed one-third of the value of Egyptian exports (World Bank 1987).

However, we believe that it would be an error to attribute these problems exclusively to the policies of *infitah*. First, as an oil exporter, Egypt suffered from the Dutch Disease. Unless the exchange rate is very carefully managed, sudden foreign-exchange inflows create serious problems for the traded-goods sectors of agriculture and industry. Second, much investment in nontraded goods, such as in housing and infrastructure, was essential, given their seriously dilapidated state after over a decade of neglect. Third, some important changes in industry have occurred: The role of the private sector in the economy has increased, and important reforms in the public sector have been implemented.

Let us first look at the private sector. Foreign investment failed to provide all that its advocates had hoped. It is true that by 1980, about 17% of total investment was in (private) joint ventures of Egyptians and foreigners. However, most of this money has gone into financial services, tourism, or, to the extent that it has been invested in production, into the production of goods for upper- and middle-income consumers. Ironically but predictably, foreign investors in Egyptian industry favored the import-substituting sectors that offered substantial protection from foreign competition.

The domestic private sector has been at least as active as the joint ventures. Private investment has been especially notable in tourism, construction (which is now almost entirely privatized), and land reclamation. The share of the private sector in industrial production rose from 23% in 1974 to 32% in 1982 to 40% in 1985 (*al-Ahram al-Iqtisadi,* May 18, 1987). Finally, one should not overlook the "underground economy," estimated in 1980 to generate some £E 2.1 billion worth of transactions (Abdel-Fadil 1983). The Egyptian private sector has certainly grown markedly, just as the policymakers of *infitah* intended.

It would be a grave mistake, however, to believe that the private sector has grown at the expense of the public sector. This was not part of the intention of policymakers, and it has not happened. In the first place, the Egyptian public sector remains very large; recall that in the mid-1980s public-sector value-added was some 22% of the nation's total, and the sector employed one of five Egyptian workers. Second, the Egyptian government affects every decision of private-sector entrepreneurs, especially those in industry, through its pricing policies of public-sector output. The Egyptian government wants the private entrepreneurs to *complement,* not to *compete with,* public-sector activity. Such "assigning a role to the private sector" is very much in the Nasserist tradition. And such continuity makes many private entrepreneurs nervous: They remember that when the private enterprises failed to carry out such a role, Nasser nationalized them. Their lives are not simplified by the often contradictory signals coming from the state. For example, during a foreign-exchange crisis in January 1985 the government suddenly placed severe restrictions on private entrepreneurs' access to imports and just as suddenly removed these barriers. Such policy lurches not only make private investment planning difficult, they also remind private business who is really in charge.

The Egyptian public sector has also undergone considerable restructuring. Many public-sector industries experienced rapid rates of growth of output (often above 10% per year) during the 1970s. More significantly, these growth rates were unaccompanied by employment growth; consequently, labor productivity also grew rapidly. Public companies were no longer required to hire new university graduates, leaving that task to the government bureaucracy itself. This certainly helped to reduce the overemployment in these industries that plagued them during the 1960s. Although some of this improvement in labor productivity took the form of capital deepening (increasing the amount of capital per worker), a World Bank study found that for some fifteen major industries, this process was much less pronounced in Egypt than in countries with comparable growth rates like the Republic of Korea (ROK), Yugoslavia, or Turkey. Much of the growth in the Egyptian public sector was increasing productivity of *all* inputs, or, in economists' language, growth in total factor productivity. This indicates that Egyptian public-sector industry has been catching up with the standards of productivity elsewhere in the world, surely an encouraging sign (World Bank 1983a).

Yet despite these achievements, the Egyptian economy is in serious trouble. The central problems of food dependency, external indebtedness, employment creation, pervasive price distortions, and government deficits remain. The equity consequences of *infitah* are as hotly debated as they are unclear; unquestionably there have been losers as well as winners in the process. Perhaps what is most important is the widespread perception that the economic reforms have benefited a well-placed minority of the population but have left very large segments of the population behind. *Infitah* responded to the problems of state-led growth, was first aided and then hampered by the international conjuncture, and implemented important changes. But the state retains a dominant role in the economy, and the basic problems of providing food, jobs, and basic consumer goods for the mass of the population continue to cast a shadow over the Valley of the Nile.

## Tunisia

If Egypt provides the prototype of *infitah*, Tunisia was the pioneer. The Tunisian economy saw a sharp shift toward state-led growth in the 1960s, followed by an equally dramatic reversal of the trend in the 1970s. These policies aimed to increase the role of the private sector, to stimulate foreign investment, and to diversify exports. Tunisian experience also illustrates our argument that successful realization of the goals of these policy shifts is highly dependent on external economic and political circumstances. This is especially critical in Tunisia, given the country's small population and limited natural resource base. Tunisian development strategy since the demise of Ben Saleh has continued to stress the development of human capital and of agriculture. During the 1970s and 1980s, the strategy has also (1) increasingly relied on the private sector, (2) stimulated foreign investment, (3) sought to diversify Tunisian manufacturing and exports, and (4) tried to improve the performance of the public sector. As we shall see, some notable successes may be attributed to this strategy. However, the problems of mounting international indebtedness and inadequate employment creation remain unsolved.

The critical original institutional changes were (1) the 1972 investment code, which offered concessions such as ten-year tax exemptions to firms that produced for export markets, and (2) the 1974 extension of this code to foreign investment, which was intended to supply the Tunisian market. Tunisia was the first country to sign an agreement with the World Bank that guaranteed in advance the terms of compensation for any future nationalization (World Bank International Arbitration Agreement). The trend toward liberalization, which did not solve serious balance-of-payments and employment problems in the 1980s, was nevertheless extended further in the sixth plan: In 1986–1988 the government removed virtually all state controls on investment in industries deemed to sell in competitive markets (about 60% of industrial production according to the World Bank) and implemented an extensive reform of industrial prices (essentially decontrolling them).

The result of the early reforms was a modest increase in foreign investment and a larger role for the private sector. Most foreign investment went into tourism and textiles, two of the country's largest earners of foreign exchange. Other investments have occurred in industries like automobiles (e.g., an Opel joint venture). However, foreign investment remains quite small in Tunisia and declined when the economy needed it the most in the early 1980s: from $339 million in 1982 to only $62 million in 1986 (IMF 1987). Presumably, the political instability of the last years of Bourguiba's rule contributed to this weakness. The Tunisian case still stands as a warning against any belief that foreign investment constitutes a panacea for development problems.

As in Egypt, the Tunisian reforms have hardly led to the demise of the public sector. It is true that in the late 1960s about 86% of investment in manufacturing came from the public sector, and by 1976 only 40% was located there. However, the IMF estimates that the output of SOEs as a percentage of total GDP remained roughly constant at about 25% from 1969 to 1979 (Short 1984). In 1981 SOEs still accounted for just under 60% of the value of manufacturing output. And until the reforms of the mid-1980s, the budgetary burden of SOEs (i.e., their losses that had to be covered from the public treasury) actually increased—from 1.7% of GDP in 1968/69 to 4.0% in 1978/81 (Floyd 1984).

There has emerged a sort of "division of labor" between the (growing) private sector and the public sector. As a rough generalization, we may say that the state retains control of intermediate-goods production while ceding most of the production of consumer goods to the private sector. State-owned enterprises continue to dominate industries that either were deemed "strategic" or were characterized by marked economies of scale: steel, fertilizer, and phosphoric acid production, oil refining, flour and sugar milling (the last two being central to the government food-security program). In some of these areas (phosphoric acid, pesticides, pharmaceuticals), the state has entered joint ventures with foreign investors. One can see here the streamlining, rather than the dismantling, of the basic premise of state-led growth: The public sector should dominate the commanding heights of the economy, supplying the intermediate goods that private industry needs. Another example of this structure is in leather goods: The state owns the largest tannery in the country, but all final consumer leather goods are produced by the private sector.

An important exception to this generalization is the textile industry, where the large government SOE coexists with Tunisian domestic and foreign firms. This sector has been modernized through state action. The industry attracted considerable foreign private investment during the 1970s and is the prototype of what the government would like to accomplish through joint ventures: to follow the country's comparative advantage by building on the long commitment to human-capital investment (see Chapter

5), creating employment and generating exports at the same time. By 1985 the industry contributed nearly one-fifth of the country's exports (compared with 2% twenty years earlier).

The performance of the Tunisian economy under this *infitah* policy was quite respectable during the 1970s: GDP per capita grew at the rate of 5% per year from 1970 to 1980, the savings ratio increased from 13.5% in 1970 to 20% in 1985, while the investment ratio remained fairly steady at around 27–28%. Manufacturing value-added grew at the commendable rate of 9.7% per year from 1970 to 1984. As in Egypt, however, much of this growth was fueled by oil exports, workers' remittances (from France and then Libya), and tourism—all vulnerable to events beyond the Tunisian government's control, and all of which declined markedly (if only temporarily in the case of tourism) in the 1980s. Nevertheless, Tunisia did make progress in diversifying its exports. Manufactured goods accounted for 13% of exports in 1965 but 37% in 1985. The share of textiles, in particular, grew rapidly from 2% of exports in 1965 to 18% in 1985.

But this performance was not sufficient to offset the effects of the international conjuncture of the 1980s on the Tunisian balance of payments. International recession, drought, rising European protectionism, and falling oil prices, combined with government reluctance to slow the growth of the economy (and therefore imports), fueled the accumulation of external debt (over 75% long-term), which rose from $106 million in 1970 to $2.2 billion in 1985. The Muhammed Mzali government instituted some halfhearted reforms, including the change of consumer-subsidy programs that provoked the riots of January 1984. The government then retreated, but the problems became even more severe: By the summer of 1985 the country had only a few days of import cover left. At this point, the government had little choice but to turn to the IMF and accept the standby agreement that it had proudly avoided for so long. Tunisia adopted the usual recipe: Cut the budget, cut investment, reduce subsidies, devalue the currency. The trade deficit did fall by about 10%; this was entirely due to the compression of imports, as exports continued the decline that began in 1982. Such policies also exacerbate the already serious unemployment problem; the government claims that unemployment is running at about 10%; unofficial estimates run much higher. The entire program was overwhelmed by the collapse of oil prices in 1986; Tunisia in the late 1980s continues to face severe problems of external debt and employment creation. But the government of Zine al-Abdine Ben Ali strongly believes that an *infitah* strategy offers the only egress from these difficulties.

### Turkey

Turkey offers perhaps the most thoroughgoing attempt to open up a strongly "inwardly oriented" economy. Recall that Turkey was the pioneer in the region (and indeed, anywhere in the Third World) in ISI; its experience illustrates the policies and problems of such a strategy. After first concentrating on consumer products, the government promoted the production of intermediate and capital goods during and especially after World War II. The usual instruments were chosen: tariffs and quantitative restrictions on imports; an overvalued exchange rate to facilitate the importation of machinery and raw materials; state-owned enterprises, concentrated in eight large holding companies in sugar, textiles, pulp and paper, petrochemicals, nitrogen fertilizer, cement, iron and steel, other chemicals, and machinery. The aims were also the usual ones: the promotion of growth and national independence. There was only a weak ideological bias against the private sector. Instead, a kind of division of labor, similar to the Tunisian case, can be seen: The public sector, concentrated in capital-intensive industries with large economies of scale, was to provide the inputs necessary for private industry and agriculture. Indeed, by 1980, the private sector, typically operating smaller plants producing consumer goods, accounted for about 70% of manufacturing value-added.

The results of such state-led growth also resembled the experience elsewhere in the region. Growth was respectable and steady, but not spectacular: GDP grew at 6.3% in the 1950s, 6.0% in the 1960s, and 5.9% in the 1970s. The economy was very strongly oriented to the domestic market: The export/GDP ratio was low (only 5% of GDP in 1980), and nearly all manufactured output (some 95% in 1980) was produced for home consumption. The country suffered from the usual "dual gap" (between investment and domestic savings, and between imports and exports), from serious unemployment problems (despite massive emigration to the EC), from persistent government deficits due in large part to financial losses of state-owned enterprises, and, increasingly in the 1970s, from accelerating inflation, which, in turn, exacerbated the other problems.

These difficulties are best understood as the outcome of the interaction of Turkish policy and the external environment. Exchange-rate and tariff policies favored imports and discouraged exports. By 1979 the effective rate of protection on Turkish manufactures had reached 68% (Kopits 1987), but quantitative restrictions were even more important: About 80% of all imported goods were subjected to some kind of restriction. Manufacturers and farmers had strong incentives to produce for the domestic market; exports accordingly grew very slowly (5.5% per year, 1965–1980: less than the rate of growth of GDP, which means that exports were a declining share of output). The resulting imbalance could be sustained because of workers' remittances and foreign aid. These sources dwindled in the 1970s when the recession in Europe and conflict with the U.S. Congress over Cyprus coincided with the oil-price increase and a soaring import bill. But rather than deflating, successive Turkish governments opted to keep growing, in a policy very similar to that adopted by the Third World's largest NIC, Brazil. Like that country, Turkey financed such a "growth first" policy by accumulating foreign debt, which had reached $16 billion by 1980.

The policies of inward-oriented state-led growth did not solve the country's employment problems. Despite the long history of industrial development, even in the late 1980s over half of the labor force is employed in agriculture. Job creation lagged well behind the growth of the labor force; by 1979 there were 1.5 million unemployed workers out of a labor force of 16 million, and another 800,000 agricultural workers were underemployed. By the crisis years of the late 1970s, employment creation had slowed from its usual 3–4% per year rate to under 2% annually (Kopits 1987; Reynolds 1985). Rural-urban migration continued nevertheless, and the *gecekondu,* neighborhoods inhabited by the unemployed, newly urbanized rural migrants, became fertile recruiting grounds for violent political groups, whose activities further destabilized the political economy. Finally, the state-owned enterprises, asked to perform multiple functions and lacking significant competition, generated losses, which were covered from the general budget; the "budgetary burden" of SOEs grew steadily, from under 1% of GDP in the 1960s to 1.8% in 1970–1973, 2.3% in 1974–1977, and 3.5% in 1978–1980. Inflation accelerated, reaching triple digits in the first three quarters of 1980 (Kopits 1987). The country was unable to withstand the second oil shock of 1979, and governmental ineffectiveness in halting the deterioration of the economy, along with escalating political violence, led to the military coup of 1980, which inaugurated the Turkish version of *infitah.*

The policies implemented were those of a classic IMF stabilization package, reminiscent in many ways of the policies adopted in the Southern Cone of Latin America in the 1970s. The Turkish lira was sharply devalued, and a "crawling peg" (i.e., continually downward adjusting) nominal exchange-rate regime was implemented; between 1979 and 1986 the lira fell 2,000% against the U.S. dollar in nominal terms. Tariffs were reduced and quantitative restrictions on imports lifted; many prices (e.g., gasoline, cement, steel, textiles, electricity, fertilizer, paper) were increased in an effort to eliminate SOE losses, encourage efficiency, and reduce the government deficit. Turkish planners tried to dampen inflation by restraining the rate of growth of the money supply and credit. State-owned enterprises were reformed; managers were paid on the basis of performance as measured by commercial criteria, and employees were hired on a contract basis. Trade unions were weakened or destroyed with the usual violence; real wages plumetted, lowering costs and reducing domestic demand. For four years (1981–1985) exporters enjoyed tax rebates and subsidized credit while nonexporting firms faced sharp increases in the real cost of borrowing. Finally, the government asserted repeatedly its intention to increase the role of the private sector, not only through stimulating the growth of existing firms, but also by privatizing some SOEs and by attracting direct foreign investment (Kopits 1987).

What have been the results of this most serious and consistent attempt at *infitah* in the region? Although it is still too early to pass a final judgment, we can say that the policy shift has certain notable successes to its credit, especially in the promotion of exports. At the same time, it has clearly failed, at least to date, to solve certain other fundamental problems.

Easily the most notable success has been the increase in exports, especially the export of manufactured goods. The rate of growth of exports rose to over 25% per year between 1980 and 1985; exports grew rapidly during the next two years as well. Whereas the ratio of exports to GDP was only 5% in 1980, it had risen to 15% in 1985. Manufactured exports grew even more rapidly, at a rate of 35% per year, 1980–1985, rising from just over one-third of exports in 1980 to over three-fourths in 1985. These industrial exports were quite diversified, ranging from textiles to iron and steel to machinery to chemicals. Trade was also reoriented toward the Middle East. Whereas the percentage of exports going to MENA countries was about 22% in 1980, five years later other countries of the region were taking over two-fifths of Turkish exports. If Egypt's *infitah* was a "turning West," Turkey's was initially a "turning South (and east—to Iran)."[1] The trade gap has been cut (but not eliminated), and Turkish products are now competing vigorously in international markets. This export performance is all the more remarkable given the unfavorable external environment. The early 1980s saw the softening, and then the collapse, of oil prices, weakening demand in the oil-exporting states, at the same time as the European Community and the United States became increasingly protectionist. Moreover, Turkey's terms of trade deteriorated during the period. It is true that Turkish exporters fared well by exporting to their war-torn neighbors, Iran and Iraq, which received one-quarter of Turkey's exports in 1985. However, Turkish exports to the EC grew at 18% per year in the first half of the 1980s, despite recessions and protectionism. This was a real achievement.

Turkish performance in the 1980s also offers plenty of ammunition for those who would argue that *infitah,* "export-led growth" strategies leave many problems unsolved. First, although the government has succeeded in reducing the rate of inflation from its triple-digit peak of 1980, inflation remains stubbornly high by regional standards; after an initial fall in the rate, it has showed signs of accelerating: from about 30% in 1986, to 55% in 1987, to 75% in 1988 (*Economist,* June 18, 1988). Budgetary reforms have reduced, but have failed to eliminate, government deficits. The overall government deficit fell from over 5% of GDP in 1980 to a low of 2.1% in 1982, rose to 4.9% in 1984, fell again until 1986, only to rise by nearly one-half in 1987 (Kopits 1987; *Middle East Economic Digest* [*MEED*], December 19, 1987, p. 60). The culprit was *not* the SOEs, whose losses were sharply cut.[2] Rather, the problem seems to have been caused by high and rising interest payments, export subsidies and transfers to localities on the expenditure side, and poor tax performance on the revenue side (tax receipts as a percentage of GDP fell to 18% by 1985, below the average for lower-middle-income countries—World Bank 1987). Although about one-third of the deficit was financed with foreign borrowing, the rest was monetized, fueling inflation.[3]

A second, related problem has been the slowing down of GDP growth and the charge that much of the increase in exports has simply been a transfer of output from domestic to foreign markets without any real increase in production. Of course, because the percentage of exports in GDP has roughly tripled since 1980, the charge is true, and, indeed, the transfer was a goal of policy. But critics imply that the strategy of outward orientation is failing to generate the kind of linkages and growth that the architects of this orientation promised. It is true that the rate of growth of GDP in the early 1980s was well below historical norms (4.5% compared to about 6.0%). During 1986 and 1987, however, growth improved to 5.5–6.0%. Two further points are apposite. First, the initial years of the decade witnessed a stabilization program, during which growth was *supposed* to fall as the price of regaining macroeconomic equilibrium. Second, the rate of growth of *manufacturing* during 1980–1985 *exceeded* that of 1965–1980 (7.9% vs. 7.6%, respectively).

Nevertheless, the critics may have a point, although it is still too early to be sure. The investment ratio (gross domestic investment/gross domestic product—GDI/GDP) has fallen to historic lows; at the same time, there has been an even larger decline in the domestic-savings ratio. The "savings gap," only 1% of GDP in 1965, stood at 4% in 1985. Since government investment has remained quite stable during the 1980s, these developments imply that private-sector investment has declined. So far, at least, the expanded role for the private sector that the Özal *infitah* strategy envisaged has failed to materialize. High credit costs and the orientation of much private-sector activity to the (depressed) domestic market may explain part of this relatively poor performance.

The promised privatization of various public-sector firms has also moved quite slowly, blocked by legislative hurdles, bureaucratic obstacles, and political calculations. Change here was especially slow during military rule, perhaps because Kemalist generals did not want to relinquish state control of strategic industries. Despite journalistic fanfare, Özal's government has also done relatively little. It has begun selling off state minority interests in private-sector companies (*MEED,* December 19, 1987, p. 61) and has drawn up a master plan for privatization, which remains only a document. Direct foreign private investment has also grown sluggishly, amounting to only $400 million between 1980 and 1985 (Kopits 1987). It is possible that such investment may develop more rapidly in the near future; the business press is certainly full of reports of joint ventures in a wide variety of manufacturing operations. It is probably too early to pass judgment on the shifting roles of the public and private sectors in Turkey, but at least to date, any change in the relative weights of the private and public sectors has been in favor of the latter (see Table 7.5), because the high real interest rates of the stabilization program have strangled private investment. Finally, the "open door" to foreign capital has been largely ignored by the invitees.

Despite the rapid growth of exports, Turkish foreign debt remains large, in excess of $26 billion. There has been a substantial increase in short-term debt (now over 25% of total debt), and the debt service now consumes roughly one-third of exports. This debt trap may help to explain why the very rapid growth of exports has not stimulated more rapid overall economic growth in Turkey.

Finally, of course, there are losers in this strategy. Domestically oriented industrialists have faced very high borrowing costs, increased input prices, and depressed markets. Workers have also lost. There is dispute over the extent of the decline in wages, but even the IMF admits that real pretax wages fell over 3.0% per year for five years. The Turkish trade union federation claims that Turkish workers' real wages have fallen 20% since 1980, while others would place the decline at around 40% over five years. These are serious losses; the highest estimate would have Turkish wages falling as much as in many Latin American countries where military dictatorships implemented similar policies.[4] The government and the IMF assert that the new economic strategy also created over 800,000 jobs from 1981 to 1985. Nevertheless, the employment problem is far from solved; unemployment increased from 12.1% of the labor force in 1977 to 14.8% in 1980 to over 16% in 1986 (IMF, *Financial Times,* November 5, 1986, p. 19). The situation in the rural areas is even worse: Over 100,000 agricultural jobs have been lost since 1980, but the agricultural-labor force has continued to grow. More than one of five agricultural workers is now unemployed. The government argues that it is not responsible for the slowing down in the traditional employment safety-valve of emigration or for the decline in agricultural employment. The first point is plausible, but the second one is not.

Indeed, the final problem with Turkish *infitah* has been its impact on the agricultural sector. After an initial jump of 50% from 1980 to 1981, agricultural exports declined for the next four years. Production growth has been sluggish, and employment and farmers' incomes have stagnated. Bad weather explains some of this poor performance: There was a serious drought in 1985. However, the *infitah* policies also contributed to the outcome. Recall that Turkish agriculture has been subsidized since the 1950s; many Turkish scholars (e.g., Somel 1986) have argued that a central part of the political economy of such subsidies was the desire of state planners to create a domestic market for Turkish manufacturers. It follows that an *infitah* policy would remove these subsidies; advocates of this policy would be unconcerned with the decline in purchasing power of farmers. Indeed, they might even welcome such a development, since the policy would assist the shift of production toward international markets. Farm subsidies were cut, both by lowering subsidized output prices and by raising the prices of subsidized inputs. Increases in government farm price supports were usually held below the rate of inflation, while the price of fertilizer increased nearly *tenfold* between 1979 and 1982. In view of past Turkish agricultural success, and given the regional food-security problem, one of the most serious long-term costs of the Turkish *infitah* may be the stagnation of the region's most successful agricultural sector.

*Algeria*

The Algerian state has always played *the* major role in that country's industrialization process. Algeria offers perhaps the most extreme example of the strategy of using revenues from hydrocarbon (oil and, increasingly, natural gas) exports to create a strong heavy-industrial base. All foreign trade, utilities, transportation, and banking are run by the central government. More than three-quarters of manufacturing output comes from the public sector, and much of wholesale and retail trade is nationalized. Such state dominance of the economy had roots in both the conditions of independence and the ideology of the ruling FLN. The appearance of *infitah*-like phenomena there is all the more remarkable given this past history, ideology, and institutional structure.

The state-led growth strategy has several notable accomplishments to its credit. Algeria's GDP has grown very rapidly, over 6% per year in the quarter-century since independence. From a colony whose economy was monopolized by foreigners and devastated by a bloody independence war, Algeria has become an upper-middle-income country, ranking approximately thirtieth in the world in per capita GNP (World Bank 1987). This high rate of growth was not achieved merely by the grace of geology (hydrocarbon reserves) but by a draconian policy of investing over one-third of national income for more than twenty years, one of the highest investment ratios in modern economic history. Algeria has constructed one of the best road systems in the region, a very sophisticated petroleum and gas industry, and a large basic metals and machinery industry. In 1980, 27% of the work force was employed in industry, the same percentage as in the Republic of Korea and Brazil. All of this was achieved within one generation of a bloody independence war that claimed perhaps 1 million lives.

Despite these achievements, serious difficulties emerged during the late 1970s. Excess capacity, low productivity, overcentralization, unemployment, massive urbanization, and one of the most seriously neglected agricultural sectors of any country of the region were among the bitter fruits of the development strategy of the Boumedienne regime. Labor productivity had actually *fallen* in both the hydrocarbon and the nonoil public-industrial sector.[5] The rate of worker absenteeism ranged between 10 and 20%, about one-fifth of all workers left their jobs each year, and "factory discipline became extremely unsatisfactory" (Bennoune 1988, 141). The iron and steel complex at El Hadjar was operating at only 40% of capacity in the early 1980s, thereby forfeiting economies of scale and raising costs to all final users of its output. Two-thirds of Algerian basic food was imported, and unemployment was estimated at 16% in the cities and 18% in the countryside.

These problems can be traced to the strategy of concentration on heavy industry and to management problems of SOEs. The economic argument for developing heavy industry was based on linkage effects: These industries were to provide the basic materials for others, which would supply the population with their needs. It is true that basic metals and energy industries have high forward linkages.[6] However, they are also very capital intensive and create relatively few jobs. Worse, in Algeria they were run as monopolies, giving enterprise managers little reason to be efficient. These industries were also located in and around the major cities of Algiers, Constantine, and Oran. Such industrial location further stimulated rural-to-urban migration, already massive because of rapid population growth and the neglect of agriculture. This exacerbated the severe problems of the cities.

The Benjadid regime has attempted to redress these problems without abandoning state control of the economy. This is *"infitah* with a socialist face," which began in 1982. First, there has been a clear shift in the allocation of investment. Metals and hydrocarbon received a smaller share, while lighter manufacturing, agriculture, and social services got more emphasis. Second, the public sector is being reorganized. Some 66 huge SOEs were broken up into 474 smaller companies by 1985 (Bennoune 1988, 264). For example, both the giant National Corporation for Transport and Marketing of Hydrocarbons (SONATRACH), and the National Steel Corporation (SNS), the iron and steel monopoly, have each been divided into thirteen separate companies. Now eleven separate firms make the various cars, trucks, and agricultural machines formerly produced by the National Corporation for Mechanical Construction (SONACOME). The autonomy of management has been strengthened, and it is hoped that these companies will operate more efficiently. It is encouraging that capacity utilization rose from an average of 30–40% in the late 1970s to 75% in 1984.

The government instituted a program to raise labor productivity by improving incentives. Industrial workers now receive not only the basic wage and a supplement (based on working conditions) but also, for the first time, a bonus linked to productivity. If a worker or work group meets its quota, he or it receives an additional 20%; the workers get 30% if they exceed the quota. These reforms were introduced in 1982; some assert that since then, productivity has increased by over 10%: an improvement, but not exactly a revolution.

The regime has also sought to encourage the private sector both by giving support to Algerian entrepreneurs and by attracting foreign private investment. The private sector accounted for about one-fourth of manufacturing output in 1985; its activities continued to be concentrated in light-industrial products. As elsewhere in the region, private entrepreneurs existed in a symbiotic relationship with the public sector, obtaining inputs from the public sector and/or selling their output to the giant companies; some observers have pointed out that their greater profitability is partly the result of subsidized inputs (e.g., Bennoune 1988). The 1982 investment code reduced the tax rate on profits and expanded credit for industries likely to generate foreign exchange (e.g., tourism). The amount of foreign currency that such firms could import legally was doubled, and the establishment of some 660 new private firms was approved. Foreign private direct investment rose from virtually zero to $280 million in 1984. Whereas

previously nearly all contracts with foreign companies were turnkey arrangements, for the first time foreign firms are being allowed to operate
facilities (in joint ventures) in the country. The two most visible are in
telecommunications (Sweden's Ericsson Co.) and in automobiles (Italy's
Fiat Corp.).

Part of the reason for pushing liberalization and an increased role for
the private sector is the old goal of independence. The Algerian government
wants to reduce its dependence on foreign suppliers and contractors, not
only for political reasons, but also to reduce the burden on the balance
of payments created by the repatriation of profits. Ironically, an important
motive of the current economic liberalization in Algeria is import substitution. For example, the government has tried to favor private Algerian
bidders on contracts for the GK-2 gas pipeline, on dam projects, and for
the largest planned project in the country, the Bellara steel works (*MEED,*
December 19, 1987, p. 37).

A critical force driving all of these policy changes has been the country's
mounting indebtedness. There are major discrepancies in estimates of the
size of the country's debt; in 1985 the World Bank reported Algerian debt
at $15 billion, while for the same year the OECD's figure for Algeria was
about $24 billion. Despite austerity programs of reducing investment
spending, pruning government recurrent expenditures, and slashing imports
by over 10% in one year, the government was forced to return to international
capital markets in 1987. There is little evidence that the restructuring of
the economy under Benjadid has alleviated the problem of international
debt.

Algeria continues to face serious problems of external indebtedness,
unemployment, bureaucratic inefficiency, and agricultural neglect. The regime has tried to tackle all of these concerns through limited liberalization,
encouragement of the private sector, and decentralization, but it has had
decidedly mixed success. For example, in 1986 about 116,000 new jobs
were created, while about 173,000 new job-seekers entered the labor market
(Bennoune 1988, 295). However, as elsewhere in the region, this certainly
does not imply that a continuation of the old policies would have been
more successful. It is hard to see how any actual Algerian regime could
have avoided something like the reform program that has been implemented.
As in Tunisia, the response to difficulties has been to press ahead with
the reform program; the riots of October 1988 seem, if anything, to have
deepened the regime's resolve to pursue an *infitah* strategy.

However, the limits of the process should also be stressed. The Algerian
state under Benjadid has no more intention of relinquishing control over
long-term resource allocation than does the Soviet government under
Gorbachev. The private sector is still being *assigned* a role *by* the state:
"the encouragement of private companies through a revived Chamber of
Commerce is directed by the government, which employs Chamber officials"
(*MEED,* November 7, 1987, p. 5). And decentralization may actually increase
the centralization of power: The center now confronts, instead of a few

powerful ministries, a myriad of much smaller enterprises. In the absence of a thoroughgoing market system, the presidency may actually have a *larger* coordination role than previously.

## Iraq

Like Algeria, Iraq in the 1980s offers a record of policy shifts that seems more of a *perestroika* (restructuring) than an *infitah*. As in Algeria, the Iraqi state has long played the central, independent role of turning oil money into factories and infrastructure. As in Algeria, the state-led policy encountered some constraints, and as in Algeria, the Iraqi state has tried to encourage the growth of the private sector and to reform SOEs without ceding any real economic (much less political!) control to the private sector. Of course, unlike the case in Algeria, in Iraq some of these developments are really best understood as a response to military exigencies (a kind of "war capitalism"). Iraq presents an example of a very limited, highly tentative, easily revokable *infitah*.

Like most of the "Arab socialist" countries, successive Iraqi regimes have nationalized the basic industries in the country. Actually, given the low level of industrial development before 1958, it would perhaps be more accurate to say that the government "created" public industries by channeling oil revenues into state-owned industrial projects. Before 1963, the regime's main economic intervention was in agriculture, launching the agrarian reform discussed earlier. In that year, over 75% of industrial output in "large" firms was in the private (largely Iraqi) sector. Sweeping nationalizations in that year and subsequently led to public-sector dominance of industry: Over 60% of output and half of employment in large enterprises was in the public sector (Fattah 1979). By 1972 just under three-fourths of output in such enterprises was in the public sector; this figure showed almost no change during the next decade: The rates of growth of output of public and private large industry were almost exactly the same (18.7% and 18.6%, respectively) between 1972 and 1982 (calculated from data in Sluglett and Sluglett 1987, 233). However, during those same years, output from industrial establishments employing fewer than ten people grew at a rate of 25%. Iraq shows the same "division of labor" between public and private sectors as other countries of the region: The state controls the bulk of industries with substantial economies of scale and/or producing intermediate goods and leaves smaller industry producing for domestic consumers to the private sector.

The stability of public and private shares during the 1970s suggests that *infitah* was limited in Iraq during that decade. This is not surprising: There were two strong centralizing forces at work in Iraq. First, the oil boom greatly increased the revenues of the central government. With exports of between 2.5 and 3 million barrels per day (b/d), oil revenues were some $26 billion, and foreign-exchange reserves stood at about $35 billion. Second, the Ba'ath party increased its political dominance over every aspect of social life. Non-Ba'athists were purged from the civil service, the Ministry of Interior employed more than 150,000 people (some 25% of public employees), and the death penalty was prescribed for non-Ba'athist political activity by any former member of the armed forces (in a country with universal male conscription). Human rights abuses were widespread as the dictatorship of the Ba'ath party, and the personality cult of Saddam Hussein, were consolidated (Sluglett and Sluglett 1987). It is not surprising that evidence of an economic "opening up" is very weak in such a political atmosphere.

The Ba'ath regime also used its swelling oil revenues to create supporters and to build infrastructure and factories. This tendency seems especially pronounced in the construction industry. The great majority of this activity, which is about 80% as large as all of manufacturing, is in the private sector, mainly working on contract for the state. This case rather dramatically illustrates an important point about the data base underlying all discussions of *infitah:* The problematic nature of the categories of "public" and "private" in many states of the region. Iraqi construction firms are privately owned; that is, their profits accrue to certain specific individuals. But they get their money by working for the government; they are hardly "in opposition" to the state in any way.

There is also little evidence of a dramatic restructuring of Iraq's geographical and political trading pattern during the 1970s. Iraq had already "turned West" during the first phase of the oil boom. Despite its friendly relations with the Soviet Union, Iraq had always sold most of its oil to the West, Japan, and Third World nations. Like most oil exporters, the Iraqis sought to obtain the highest-quality technology with their oil money, no matter where the technology came from. Consequently, they gave out huge, lucrative contracts to firms from all over the world, especially Western, Turkish, Japanese, and Korean firms. Imports from the Eastern Bloc, already only 11% in the mid-1970s, were a mere 6% by 1979 (Sluglett and Sluglett 1987, 240).

The usual problems of the state-led growth strategy appeared in Iraq as elsewhere: inefficiencies, noncompetitive industries, overstaffing. For example, outside observers commented on the sluggishness with which decisions were made in the public sector; they attributed this to fear: No manager or public servant wanted to be wrong lest he and his family suffer unpleasant consequences (Townsend 1982; Sluglett and Sluglett 1987). However, given the extent of oil revenues and the political attractiveness to the Ba'athists of retaining control, there were few pressures to change this pattern during the 1970s. Oil constituted over 90% of the value of Iraqi exports; as long as its price remained high, there would be no balance-of-payments pressure severe enough to engender dramatic internal change. Whereas balance-of-payments pressures ultimately may have forced change in countries like Turkey and Tunisia, nothing like this was visible in Iraq before 1980.

Of course, what did prompt change in Iraq was the war with Iran. The cost of the war, increasingly difficult to pay for with falling oil revenues, led Iraq into deep indebtedness to the Saudis and other peninsular Arab states. Such costs, along with manpower shortages, increased the need to reduce inefficiencies. The 1982 Ba'ath Party Conference upbraided public-sector industrial managers for "low levels of production and low technical standards, especially in middle management" (Crusoe 1986, 43). The private sector was encouraged to become more active in providing the consumer goods that the government needed to maintain morale. Law 115 of 1982 and Company Law 36 of 1983 increased the ceiling on private-sector investment by over 1,000% and offered various tax benefits to private firms. The latter were also guaranteed subsidized raw materials and duty-free import of machinery. As discussed earlier, *infitah* has been more extensive in the agricultural sector, as dwindling oil revenues and escalating war costs made a narrowing of the food gap imperative.

The limitations of the Iraqi *infitah* must be emphasized, however. The government has no intention of relinquishing political or economic control to anyone. Rather, it hopes to streamline the existing system. In a manner reminiscent of the early 1960s in Egypt, the Ba'ath wants the private sector to participate actively in achieving the *government's* goals. For example, if the state believes that urban markets lack eggs, it simply "instructs" private poultry farmers to switch to egg production (Crusoe 1986). It is unlikely that these instructions are ignored, but it is equally unlikely that such an *infitah* will effect many deep changes in the Iraqi political economy.

## ECONOMIC GROWTH, CLASS, AND THE RISE OF *INFITAH*

We believe that the *infitah* phenomenon must be understood as, at least in part, arising from the exigencies of the development process itself, as well as from the international economic conjuncture. State-led growth in the countries of the region succeeded in raising living standards but encountered certain difficulties. First, the program of import-substituting industrialization failed to save foreign exchange. Not only did imports of intermediate goods and machinery increase as part of the inward-oriented industrialization effort, but also exports of manufactured goods or agricultural products failed to grow sufficiently quickly to offset these increased imports. Second, the domestic-supply response to the accelerating growth of demand for food compounded this problem of the external balance. State-led growth policies reorganized agriculture and reduced inequalities through land reforms (Algeria, Iraq, Egypt), but the implementation of these reforms (Iraq), the taxation of agriculture (Egypt), and/or the neglect of crucial investments in the sector (Algeria, Iraq, Egypt, Tunisia) contributed to the sluggish supply response. Large sums accordingly had to be spent on food imports. Only the oil exporters were spared the resulting pressure for change that came from the persistent balance-of-payments deficit.

A third problem was the failure of the non–oil exporters to bridge the gap between investment and domestic savings. This gap was exacerbated by policy. State-owned enterprises failed to generate savings; indeed, they incurred losses that had to be covered from the general budget. Given the deficiencies of revenue collection, such losses contributed to the government deficit, which in turn was monetized, fueling inflation. Such inflation then further undermined the external balance by revaluing the real exchange rate, which discouraged exports and stimulated imports.

Fourth, the state-led growth strategy failed to eliminate inequalities. Rural-urban disparities remained wide, fostering migration, which strained housing and other urban infrastructure. Job creation lagged behind the growth of the labor force. This problem, too, was exacerbated by policy. Excessive capital intensity and high incremental capital-to-output ratios reduced the number of jobs created with limited investment funds. A variety of labor-market imbalances were also observable; this was especially true in SOEs, where job guarantees often reduced labor effort and exacerbated wage gaps between the formal and informal sectors. Governments like Egypt's that adopted ad hoc "solutions" to the problem, like guaranteeing to all university graduates a job in the public sector, only compounded the problem.

The evident national differences in responding to these problems are the fruit of past history, especially with respect to the ideological commitment of governments to state-led growth (e.g., high in Iraq and Algeria, lower in Egypt) and to the strength of domestic private-sector actors (weak in Algeria and Iraq, stronger in Egypt, strongest in Turkey). Consequently, a variety of responses is to be expected. Nevertheless, almost any conceivable response would have involved increasing reliance on markets, the private sector, and some decentralization of decisionmaking in the public sector. We have noted that in each of the cases considered above, none of the policy reforms have succeeded in eliminating the basic problems of indebtedness, the "twin gaps," and employment creation. This hardly means that the reforms were therefore either failures or unnecessary. One only has to look at recent developments in the PRC and the Soviet Union to see that even governments that are the most ideologically committed to state control are forced to follow such a path.

Such shifts are easier to understand when we consider the ideological dimension. Recall our argument that the key "image of the future" was not a Socialist Commonwealth, but a strong, prosperous, independent Nation. Nationalism, not socialism, was (with few exceptions) the driving force behind policy selection. Socialism was not an end in itself, but rather was seen as a means to a (nationalist) end. To the extent that experience with state-led growth was disappointing, state managers, top bureaucrats, and political leaders may have been (and may be) willing to try to limit state economic activity.

Of course, alternative explanations of the *infitah* phenomenon are readily available (e.g., Mursi 1976; Bennoune 1988; al-Khafaji 1983). Some believe that *infitah* arises as a result of the power of international capital, usually employing the agencies of the World Bank and, especially, the IMF (Hussein

1982). Others believe that the changes were brought about as a result of a "class project" of the domestic bourgeoisie, be it state, *grande,* or *petite.* Although we postpone a full discussion of the issue of the shifting balance between class power and state autonomy until Chapter 15, here we would reiterate our basic position that state policy is the outcome of *both* class forces *and* the logic of economic growth and structural change. Policies must be conceived and implemented by real actors, but those same actors need opportunities if they are to pursue their goals.

Take the issue of the role of international forces in creating *infitah.* The international conjuncture certainly contributed both to the extent of the economic difficulties and to the leverage of external and internal actors. For non–oil exporters (and even for Egypt), balance-of-payments pressures both exacerbated internal conflicts (e.g., Turkey) and necessitated either more exports, fewer imports, or increased capital inflows from abroad. Any and all required policy change. For some countries these problems were made especially severe by declining terms of trade (particularly true for oil importers in the 1970s and oil exporters in the 1980s). Oil exporters at first did not face such problems, but public-sector waste, mounting food gaps, and persistent unemployment pushed countries like Algeria to embark on reforms also. The fall in oil prices obviously increased the urgency of such change. And for the Iraqis, the exigencies of war produced *infitah.*

The most important components of the external economic conjuncture that contributed to *infitah* were declining terms of trade, increased international interest rates, rising indebtedness, and the recession of the early 1980s. Of course, the importance of these forces varied from country to country. Major oil exporters were relatively immune from such pressures until the early and middle 1980s. Major oil importers, such as Sudan and Turkey, were very vulnerable much earlier. The point is not whether "internal" or "external" forces were more important; it is simply that the interaction of these forces with domestic difficulties not only created a sense of urgency (and often, a very palpable crisis) but also increased the leverage of external agents.

These external agents were (and are) the major international agencies (especially the IMF), bilateral donors, and foreign multinational corporations, especially multinational banks. The IMF has been a critical "player" in policy outcomes in Morocco, Tunisia, Egypt, Sudan, and Turkey. Arab donors have played important roles in Iraq (after the war began), Syria, Jordan, and Sudan, while multinational banks have played an important role in Turkey.

What do these actors want? For bilateral donors like the United States and Arab Gulf States, political stability is the first goal. Syria can avoid significant internal reform despite a very large deficit on the balance of trade because the Saudis and others give them aid to buy them off. These donors also, however, typically share the IMF's economic perspective. The IMF clearly prefers private enterprise to public and has a standard "policy mix" for correcting balance-of-payments problems: Devalue (and, if possible, float) the currency, cut government spending, and eliminate price distortions to reduce inflation, improve efficiency, and shift resources from nontraded goods to tradables and from imports to exports.

Despite all of these considerations, it must be emphasized that the IMF (or other international actors) cannot simply dictate policy. Even a country so deeply in difficulty as the Sudan has resisted the fund's pressures; bankrupt Sudan, faced with famine and civil war, nevertheless simply refused to pay its debt and was suspended from the fund in 1985. Sometimes governments can play one international actor off against another. For example, the IMF has repeatedly demanded reform of the Egyptian food-subsidy system; with the exception of 1977, the Egyptian government just as steadfastly refused to make more than cosmetic changes in that program. The government found aid from an unlikely source: the Reagan administration, which clearly placed Egyptian political stability above free-market principles. Furthermore, these international actors require the cooperation of domestic actors: the Özals, Sadats, and Mubarraks. Without such assistance, the foreigners fail. And of course, the presence, pressure, and resources of these external actors are useful allies for those domestic actors who want to push an *infitah* privatization agenda even if the balance-of-payments problems are manageable (e.g., Egypt in the early 1980s).

This leads us to the second set of alternative explanations for *infitah:* those that stress the role of domestic class actors. We have seen that part of the original logic of the state-led growth strategy was the absence of a strong, domestic bourgeoisie. We have also seen that the typical pattern was, not complete state control of all economic activity, but rather a division of labor between the public and private sectors. As growth, for all its deficiencies, proceeded, the private sector was strengthened: Contractors, suppliers, users of state-produced and -subsidized inputs, sellers to protected national markets—all were able to accumulate privately as a result of the expansion of the state sector.

The relative strengths of this "state-nurtured" bourgeoisie vary considerably from one country to the next. As a generalization, such a bourgeoisie is strongest in Turkey and Tunisia, less so in Egypt, and weakest in Algeria and Iraq. For the latter three countries, we must add another "class actor," the technocrats or "state bourgeoisie." It is very likely that Bennoune (1988) was correct in characterizing the upper echelons of the Algerian state as being divided between those committed to state-led growth and those in favor of some form of *infitah.*[7]

The real issue here is one of political interpretation. Two questions must be asked: What did the private capitalists and/or state managers want? And just how were they able to influence policy? We saw in Chapter 8 that many domestic capitalists have little reason to clamor for the wholesale dismantling of the public sector; surely this is one reason why the state sector remains so strong, despite *infitah.* But even had they wanted full privatization of industry and decontrol of prices, how would they have implemented these policies in the face of considerable opposition? What gave them the opportunity to carry out their "project" (whose existence we question), if not the contradictions of state-led growth itself? Here we only pose these questions, postponing our answers until Chapter 15.


## CONCLUSION

*Infitah* should be seen as the outcome of three interacting sets of forces: class actors, often fostered by earlier state-led growth policies; serious economic difficulties, generated both by state-led growth policies and by the international conjuncture; and pressure from international actors. Although it is much too early to say much about the specifics of the process, it is likely that *infitah* policies will have consequences for class formation. And as earlier, the international conjuncture will continue to be critical. For example, can the Turkish export drive be sustained if there is sluggish growth in both Western Europe and the oil exporters of MENA?

Finally, it is important to note what *infitah* does *not* mean. It does not mean that the public sector is about to be dismantled, even in Turkey. It does not mean that the state is ceding to "civil society": This may happen, to some extent, in Turkey and Egypt; it is much less likely in Iraq or Algeria. Rather than a *retreat* of the state, *infitah* is better conceived as a *restructuring* of state activity, always mediating between society and international actors, still responsible for the basic welfare of the population, and continuing to formulate the goals and strategy of economic development and structural change.


## NOTES

1. This trade pattern has been reversed again during the past three years, with the oil bust in the Middle East.

2. Government transfers to SOEs as a percentage of GDP changed as follows: 1980, 4.8%, 1981, 3.3%; 1982, 3.2%; 1983, 2.5%; 1984, 1.3%; 1985, 0.7%. (Kopits 1987, 38). State enterprises, however, contributed to inflation from 1985 to 1987 by borrowing heavily: Their borrowing was over 4% of GDP in 1987 (*Economist,* June 18, 1988). They dealt with their deficits by raising their prices, also contributing to inflation.

3. Because of the government's difficulty in controlling inflation, the real exchange rate has remained stubbornly high. Although the nominal Turkish lira has depreciated over 2,000% against the dollar since 1980, the real lira has only depreciated by 25% (Kopits 1987, 40).

4. From 1964 (the date of the military takeover) until the early 1970s, Brazilian real wages fell over 40%.

5. In hydrocarbons, output per worker had fallen from 2.4 million Algerian dinars (AD) in 1967 to AD 306,000 in 1978; in non–oil industry, the decline was from AD 36,800 in 1967 to AD 31,500 in 1978 (calculated from data in Bennoune 1988, 142–143).

6. Yotopoulos and Nugent (1973) found that basic metals and nonmetallic minerals ranked first and second, respectively, in forward linkages among eighteen industries in LDCs.

7. We do not, however, share his assumption that the latter were somehow necessarily "pro-French" or opposed to Algerian industrialization.

# 10

# URBAN POLITICAL ECONOMY

The Middle East has long been dominated by its cities. Even in 1800, after several centuries of decline, perhaps 25% of the population of Greater Syria and 10% of Egyptians lived in cities of over 10,000 (Issawi 1969, 102–03). Cities dominated their rural hinterlands and were focal points of the extensive international trade system linking Europe to Asia. Landlords and rulers alike lived in the cities, not in the countryside as did their European feudal counterparts. The *medina* was the center of gravity of economics, politics, religion, and intellectual life. This historical legacy continues today. The cities of the region hold most of the industry, a large and growing percentage of the labor force, and the bulk of government officials. They contain most of the modern health facilities and universities; they are the centers of drama, film, television, publishing, and intellectual life generally. Their residents generally enjoy higher incomes, and better standards of health and education than do their rural cousins. Cities also display severe economic and political problems, many of which are caused by the rapidity of urbanization: acute housing shortages; insecure and unremunerative employment; water, power, and sewage failures; and political riots.

The overall picture of urbanization is shown in Table 10.1.[1] The region is more urbanized than China, India, Southeast Asia, or sub-Saharan Africa, less so than Latin American (where about 70% of the population lives in cities). For the larger countries of the region (Morocco, Algeria, Egypt, Turkey, Iran), from two-fifths to over one-half of the population live in cities. In many cases, the urban population is concentrated in one or two very large cities. Over 40% of urban Moroccans live in Casablanca and neighboring Rabat; Baghdad contains more than half of all urban Iraqis and nearly 20% of the total population. In 1970 Beirut was home to over 60% of the urban population of Lebanon. The region's (and Africa's) largest city, Cairo, holds over 12 million inhabitants, making it roughly as large as New York City.

*263*

Table 10.1  Growth of Urban Population in the Middle East, 1965-1985

|  | % Urban | | Urban Growth Rates | |
|---|---|---|---|---|
|  | 1965 | 1985 | 1965-80 | 1980-85 |
| Algeria | 38 | 43 | 3.8 | 3.7 |
| Egypt | 41 | 46 | 2.9 | 3.4 |
| Iran | 37 | 54 | 5.5 | 4.6 |
| Iraq | 51 | 70 | 5.3 | 6.3 |
| Israel | 81 | 90 | 3.5 | 2.4 |
| Jordan | 47 | 69 | 5.3 | 4.0 |
| Kuwait | 78 | 92 | 8.2 | 5.1 |
| Lebanon | 49 | -- | 4.6 | -- |
| Libya | 29 | 60 | 9.7 | 6.7 |
| Morocco | 32 | 44 | 4.2 | 4.2 |
| Oman | 4 | 9 | 8.1 | 7.3 |
| Saudi Arabia | 39 | 72 | 8.5 | 6.1 |
| Sudan | 13 | 21 | 5.1 | 4.8 |
| Syria | 40 | 49 | 4.5 | 5.5 |
| Tunisia | 40 | 56 | 4.2 | 3.7 |
| Turkey | 32 | 46 | 4.3 | 4.4 |
| UAE | 56 | 79 | 18.9 | 5.5 |
| YAR | 5 | 19 | 10.7 | 7.3 |
| PDRY | 30 | 37 | 3.2 | 4.9 |
| Lower-y LDCs | 17 | 22 | 3.6 | 4.0 |
| Lower-middle-y LDCs | 27 | 36 | 4.5 | 3.7 |
| Upper-middle-y LDCs | 49 | 65 | 3.8 | 3.2 |
| High-y oil-exporters | 40 | 73 | 9.5 | 6.0 |

Source: World Bank, World Development Report, New York, Oxford University
Press, 1987, pp. 266-67.

   As is true throughout the Third World, MENA cities have grown swiftly.
We will explore the causes and consequences of this growth in the next
section of this chapter. We anticipate by pointing out that although urban
population growth is very important, rural-to-urban migration is probably
the critical component of the process (but, as usual, the data are uncertain
and there is much variation across countries). We then turn to a more
detailed analysis of urban labor markets. As is well known, these markets
are complex but can be usefully divided into three segments: a public
sector, a private "formal" sector, and a private, "informal" sector. The
informal sector consists of all those working in small-scale workshops, as
street sellers, hawkers, itinerant artisans, jobbers. How large is it? Who
works in it? What role can this sector, especially small-scale industry, play
in meeting structural adjustment problems and employment and growth
difficulties? How is it linked to other sectors? How flexible are urban labor
markets? We offer some tentative answers to these questions in the third
section.

   We turn next to a brief discussion of the problems of housing and
infrastructure. This is but one of a number of aspects of the larger question
of urban poverty and of income distribution. We review the empirical
evidence both for equity and for the extent of poverty and then summarize
the consequences of the oil boom and bust, and of *infitah* and austerity,

for the urban poor. The costs of structural adjustment programs are primarily borne in the cities: Not only does the demand for urban labor typically fall, but consumer subsidies are usually a prime target of austerity measures. We briefly consider the origin and the fiscal and equity consequences of these subsidy programs.

Cutting these subsidies has sometimes stimulated significant political protest. When does this happen, when not, and why are among the questions asked in the concluding part of this chapter, where we consider the politics of Middle Eastern cities.

## THE PROCESS OF URBANIZATION

In this section we focus on two questions. First, what explains the differences in the percentage of the population that is urban within the region? Second, what are the sources of the growth of urban populations?

The diverse weight of cities in populations within the region, ranging from a low of around 20% in Sudan and YAR to about 90% in Kuwait and Israel, is broadly consistent with a simple expectation: The higher the per capita income, the higher the percentage of the population that is urban. Of course, this is not a causal statement; indeed, it is much more plausible that increased urbanization and rising per capita incomes are both the result of the economic growth process and, especially, of industrialization.

One of the most important aspects of urbanization in the region is its speed. MENA cities have grown very rapidly during the past generation (Table 10.1). This rapid growth has had three sources: reclassification,[2] natural growth of the urban population, and rural-to-urban migration. Although it is not possible to give precise estimates of the relative weight of each of these factors, we shall present evidence that suggests that rural-to-urban migration usually accounts for at least half of the growth of cities.

A very crude calculation would be to assume that rates of natural increase (fertility minus mortality rates) are the same in urban and rural areas. Then the rate of rural-to-urban migration (plus reclassification) could be approximated as the difference between the rate of growth of cities and the overall rate of population growth. (We will argue below that such a procedure seriously underestimates the role of rural-to-urban migration in the urbanization process; this more than compensates for the overestimation that results from including reclassification with migration.) These calculations are shown in Table 10.2.

Several generalizations may be made, keeping in mind the very crude quality of the data and assumptions. Rural-to-urban migration accounts for about one-third to one-half of the growth of cities in Morocco, Turkey, Iran, Saudi Arabia, and Iraq. This is roughly the same ratio as is common elsewhere in the developing world (Todaro 1984; Sethuramen 1981). In several other countries, the role of migration in urbanization was rather larger: In the period 1965–1980, more than half of urbanization in seven countries (Sudan, YAR, Tunisia, Jordan, Lebanon, Oman, and Libya) can

Table 10.2   Rural-Urban Migration as Percentage of Urban Growth, 1965-1985

|                       | 1965-1980 | 1980-1985 |
|-----------------------|-----------|-----------|
| Algeria               | 21        | 11.0      |
| Egypt                 | 17        | 18.0      |
| Iran                  | 42        | 33.0      |
| Iraq                  | 36        | 43.0      |
| Israel                | 20        | 23.0      |
| Jordan                | 51        | 7.5       |
| Kuwait                | 15        | 14.0      |
| Lebanon               | 65        | --        |
| Libya                 | 54        | 42.0      |
| Morocco               | 40        | 40.0      |
| Oman                  | 56        | 34.0      |
| Saudi Arabia          | 41        | 30.0      |
| Syria                 | 24        | 35.0      |
| Tunisia               | 50        | 38.0      |
| Turkey                | 44        | 43.0      |
| UAE                   | 16        | --        |
| YAR                   | 74        | 66.0      |
| PDRY                  | 38        | 47.0      |
|                       |           |           |
| Lower-y LDCs          | 25        | 33.0      |
| Lower-middle-y LDCs   | 44        | 32.0      |
| Upper-middle-y LDCs   | 42        | 38.0      |
| High-y-oil exporters  | 45        | 28.0      |

Note: Assumes rural and urban population growth rates are the same.

Source: Calculated from World Bank, World Development Report, New York, Oxford University Press, 1987, pp. 266-67, 254-55.

be explained by migration. By contrast, Egypt shows quite a low rate of rural-to-urban migration (so measured).

   This methodology seriously underestimates the importance of rural-to-urban migration in urban growth. First of all, the assumption that the rate of population growth is the same in rural and urban areas is dubious. A priori, we would certainly expect both fertility and mortality rates to be lower in urban areas. Recall that much of the variance in fertility rates can be explained by income differences. Since, as we shall see in more detail below, average urban incomes are typically 1.5 to 3 times higher than rural incomes, we would expect urban fertility rates to be lower. Female literacy is higher in the cities, and infant mortality is usually lower: Both suggest that urban fertility should be lower than rural. However, since mortality is also very probably lower in urban areas, it is uncertain whether overall rates of natural increase are lower in the cities than in the villages.

   For some countries, we have direct evidence that suggests that urban rates of fertility and mortality are considerably lower than rates in rural areas. For example, the Turkish rural population is growing roughly 40% faster than the urban population (Kuran 1980). When differential population growth is included in the analysis, about 60% of urbanization in Turkey is attributable to migration (Todaro 1984). Similarly, Egyptian rural fertility exceeds urban: In 1975–1976 the total fertility rate was 3.9 in Cairo and Alexandria, 5.0 in urban Lower Egypt, 6.0 in rural Lower Egypt, and 6.8 in rural Upper Egypt (National Academy of Sciences 1982a, 3). However, mortality rates are also higher in rural areas, so the rates of population growth in urban and rural areas may not be significantly different.

What is more, the high rates of natural increase in the cities are not independent of rural-to-urban migration. There is much evidence that this form of migration is often undertaken by whole families and is especially prevalent among the young. The transfer of population of childbearing age to the cities obviously raises the rate of urban natural increase (Todaro 1984). A substantial portion of children born in the cities have parents who have recently arrived from the countryside. When this factor is taken into consideration, it seems clear that for most countries of the region, rural-to-urban migration is the single most important explanation for the rapid growth of urban areas.

In any case the absolute numbers of rural migrants to cities has been very large during the past generation. For example, In the mid-1970s in Turkey, up to 650,000 rural residents arrived in the cities every year; by the 1980s, 800,000 arrived every year (Danielson and Keleş 1980). From 1968 to 1977 just under 1 million rural Iraqis moved to the cities, especially to Baghdad and Basra (Sluglett and Sluglett 1987). Between 1967 and 1979, 1.3 million Algerians moved from the countryside to the cities (Bennoune 1988). The phenomenon of rural-to-urban migration is a crucial process in the political economy of the region.

It is no secret why rural people come to the city. Throughout the world, economic motives predominate in the decision to migrate. The most widely accepted model of the process (Todaro 1969) posits that the decision to migrate is based upon the difference between the incomes that rural migrants expect to earn in the city and those that they can earn in the countryside. This framework combines the rural "push" with urban "pull" factors. Some more recent arguments have held that migration may be part of a family strategy of income maintenance; one brother goes to town to seek work, while others remain behind (Stark 1984). However, the evidence in the region suggests that most rural-to-urban migration is of entire families; this seems to be the case for Iraq (Sluglett and Sluglett 1987), Iran (Kazemi 1980a), Turkey (Danielson and Keleš 1980), Egypt (Hopkins 1983), and Morocco (World Bank 1981). Still more complicated models have been formulated, trying to link together all of the different markets that might influence the migration decision (so-called computable general equilibrium models) (Kelley and Williamson 1984b). Such models stress the role of terms of trade between agriculture and manufacturing and faster productivity growth in (usually urban-based) manufacturing.

Although differences in rural versus urban wages and incomes in MENA are not excessive by Third World standards, they are substantial, usually on the order of 1.5 to 3.0.[3] Of course, a potential migrant has to consider the risk of failing to find a job in the cities, a risk usually measured by

urban-unemployment rates. Measuring unemployment in developing countries is difficult. Official, measured unemployment rates are often quite
high in the region: 16% (Turkey, 1985); 25% (Tunisia, 1983); 20% (Iran,
1982); 16% (Algeria, 1983); 8% (Jordan, 1983) (Kopits 1987; Nelson 1979;
Johnson 1988; Nelson 1985a; World Bank 1986a). Although Egypt's measured
unemployment rate was about 5% in 1980 (Hansen 1985), by the end of
the decade it had approximately doubled (Assaad 1989). Even if we take
the higher numbers at face value, and even if we assume that rural workers
have no difficulty finding jobs in the countryside, migrating to the city is
still a good investment.[4]

In fact, of course, the incentives to migrate to cities are even stronger
than the simplest version of the Todaro model implies. First, since none
of these countries have unemployment-insurance schemes, it is likely that
many of those listed as unemployed are actually working in low-paying,
irregular jobs in the informal sector. We will look at this sector in more
detail in the next section. Here we simply point out that in some countries
(e.g., Turkey, Iran), rural migrants are often first employed in this sector.
Second, there is direct evidence that migrants obtain urban jobs fairly
quickly: A World Bank study in Morocco found that more than 70% of
migrants found work in less than three months, and that the urban
unemployment rate in 1976 for urban residents born in the countryside
was less than one-half that for those born in the city (World Bank 1981,
247). Third, recall that in some countries there is substantial unemployment
in rural areas.[5]

It may be objected that the cost of living in rural areas is lower than
in the cities. Two points should be considered here. First, such cost
differentials are rarely as large as the differences in nominal wages. Although
housing may be more expensive in the cities, extensive food-subsidy systems
(see "Income Distribution and Poverty"), usually confined to the cities,
reduce food costs to urban dwellers to the same or even lower levels than
those in rural areas. Since food usually constitutes over half of the total
expenditure of poor persons in MENA countries,[6] food subsidies significantly
reduce the rural/urban cost-of-living differences.[7] Second, other benefits
of urban life, like better educational and health facilities, further widen
the gap betwen real incomes in urban and rural areas.

Finally, in some cases people have left rural areas because they could
not survive there. Much of the recent growth of North African and Sudanese
cities is due to the influx of "drought refugees," people whose crops or
rural employment prospects were wiped out by bad weather. Government
neglect of rural areas (Algeria) or misguided policies (Iraq, Iran) have
also played a major role in creating incentives for rural people to move
to town.

Two other tributaries of rural-to-urban migration flows are spreading
rural education and the Dutch Disease. Young men who receive some
education pour out of the countryside in large numbers, often taking their
families with them. One study of rural migrants to Tehran found that over

two-thirds were literate, compared with overall rural literacy rates of about 20%. Over two-fifths of farmers with a primary education wanted to move to the cities (Kazemi 1980a). This is, of course, a universal phenomenon: Educated people everywhere leave the farm for the cities. One of the ironies of development is that successful educational programs in rural areas swell urban populations.

The Dutch Disease likewise fostered rural-to-urban migration. The shifting of the terms of trade against agriculture, the disproportionate concentration of spending in the cities, and, especially, the construction boom of the 1970s widened the gap between rural and urban incomes, increased the probability of finding jobs in the cities, and thereby stimulated migration. In some countries this process interacted with the phenomenon of international labor migration. In Egypt, for example, nearly one-half of the urban construction labor force left the country to work in the Oil States. Since the demand for domestic construction labor shot up at the same time, the incentives for unskilled rural residents to move to the city became overwhelming.

## EMPLOYMENT AND LABOR MARKETS: "FORMAL" AND "INFORMAL" SECTORS

Where do all of these urbanites find jobs? For many countries of the region we may divide urban labor markets into three major sectors, each with its own characteristics and pay levels: public, private "formal," and private "informal." The public sector is in turn divisible into bureaucracies and state-owned enterprises. Employment in it is typically very stable: It is almost impossible in many cases for a worker to lose his job. However, this greater security is often purchased at the price of lower wages. Until recently, the public sector has often provided the first jobs for the growing masses of educated and semieducated young men.

The private formal sector varies greatly in size but is often the smallest of the three sectors. There are several definitions, but usually a minimum of ten to fifty workers is required to classify an enterprise as belonging to this sector. Additionally, workers in it are assumed to have some job security, although less than in the public sector. Under these assumptions, the distinction between "formal" and "informal" sectors becomes roughly similar to the "dual labor market" hypothesis for developed-country labor markets.[8] Private formal-sector workers often receive higher wages than their counterparts in the public sector. In some countries (e.g., Turkey, Tunisia) many may belong to trade union organizations. Some analysts (e.g., Harberger 1971) treat this and the public sector as "protected" sectors, offering wages above market-clearing levels, a situation that then naturally creates queues of workers seeking to get these jobs.

Finally, there is the urban informal sector. The definitions of this sector vary considerably in the literature. Sometimes the term is used as a euphemism for "slum dwellers" or "poor people." Some analysts (e.g.,

Charmes 1986) treat it as a residual catergory, embracing all jobs and activities that do not fall into either the public or the private formal sector. Some define it as comprising all self-employed persons, plus those employed in firms employing fewer than ten workers, plus the unskilled, casual labor employed by larger firms. One careful study for Egypt argued that the informal sector there consisted of (1) small-scale manufacturing and handicraft work, (2) itinerant and jobbing artisans (masons, carpenters, tailors), (3) personal services (servants, porters, watchmen), and (4) petty services and retailing activities (car washers, street hawkers and vendors, garbage collectors) (Abdel-Fadil 1983).

Despite the diversity of definitions, all agree on certain characteristics. There are few, or no, barriers to entry in the informal sector. Capital per worker is very low, and incomes fluctuate considerably both seasonally and annually. The sector usually employs a higher proportion of women, children, and young adults than other sectors. Some analysts argue that both the output markets and the labor markets are highly competitive (Kuran 1980). Others see competition as restrained by the limited area of search of both employers and employees: Information on this labor market is thought to be highly imperfect (Hansen 1985). We do not have enough detailed, rigorous studies to be able to assess these arguments yet.

How large is the informal sector? Given the diversity of definitions, it is not surprising that we find considerable difference of opinion. In Egypt, for example, one analyst (Abdel-Fadil 1983) argued that it is about 16% of the urban labor force, whereas two others believe that it is closer to 41–43% (Hansen 1985; Charmes 1986). Numbers also vary across countries: YAR, 70%; Morocco, 57%; Algeria, 18%, Tunisia, 36%; Turkey, 36%; Iran, 35% (World Bank 1979; Charmes 1986; Kuran 1980; Johnson 1988). Given the differences in definitions and the often rather poor data quality (many of the members of the urban informal sector escape enumeration by labor-force surveys or censuses), we may conclude that the informal urban sector employs at least one-third to one-half of the labor force. This is roughly comparable to what has been found in studies of other parts of the Third World (Sethuramen 1981, 214).

Many assume that rural migrants usually find their first jobs in this sector and that wages are well below those elsewhere. Although evidence exists to support both contentions, there is considerable diversity across countries. Consider the equation of "migrant" with "informal-sector worker." Students of Turkey, Iran, and Sudan seem to agree that rural workers have mainly found jobs in the informal sector (Kuran 1980; Scoville 1985; Ghosh 1984). In Egypt, in contrast, many rural migrants can and do find jobs in the public sector, even if they are illiterate: Throughout the 1970s and 1980s, government employment grew more rapidly than that of any other sector (Hansen and Radwan 1982; Handoussa 1988).

Part of the original conceptualization of the informal sector was that its participants were accepting lower income in that sector while they waited to get the better-paying jobs in the public and private formal sectors.

This, of course, implies that wages and incomes are in fact lower in the informal sector and that individuals do move from one sector to another. The evidence on this point is scarce and mixed. One study of Turkey found that average incomes in the formal sector in 1963 were about twice those of the informal sector; by 1973 the ratio had declined to 1.8 (Kuran 1980).[9] The same study asserted that mobility is limited between the informal sector and formal sector: More than half of those whose first job was in the informal sector were still employed there ten years later. Moreover, earnings in the informal sector in Sudan seem to be *greater* than those for unskilled workers in the formal sectors, even though most rural migrants found work in the informal sector (Ghosh 1984). At this stage of our knowledge, we cannot draw any firm conclusions here. It is very likely that informal employment is more. remunerative than rural employment; the relation between informal and formal private-sector remuneration is less clear. Much of the informal sector remains *"terra incognita,* recently discovered but with an unknown interior"(Hansen 1985, 7).

We now turn to the questions of how these sectors interact, and of how their relative roles have changed over time. Although, as usual, there are numerous exceptions and qualifications, the following generalizations may be made. The formal sectors are relatively more rigid than the informal; public-sector wages influence pay in the other sectors; the increasing budgetary crisis has (often) reduced the role of the public sector, while the importance of the informal sector has grown. Wages and employment in the informal sector are largely market determined. Because of the ease of entry and exit, these are probably (imperfectly) competitive markets, with differences in information, product differentiation generating some (unknown) divergences from a purely competitive model.[10] By contrast, both the private and the public formal sectors have certain rigidities, which are greatest in the public sector.

Public-sector wages and employment are "administered" or politically determined: They are very insensitive to supply and demand forces. Pay is largely determined by civil service grades, which are almost entirely a function of (formal) educational levels and years of experience (e.g., Sudan, Egypt, Turkey). Public-sector employment often acts as an "employer of last (or first) resort." The extent to which this is true varies from country to country, and, in nearly all cases, the austerity of the 1980s has diminished this function of the public sector. Young Jordanians usually find their first job in the public sector and move to the (more remunerative) private sector after acquiring experience. In countries with an "Arab socialist" institutional legacy (e.g., Egypt, Sudan, and Iraq) the government hires any university graduate, regardless of training, who cannot find another job.[11]

Such policies have several consequences. First, they have bloated government bureaucracies and have promoted the pursuit of academic training of any sort, regardless of its utility to the development process. At the same time, the higher incomes available in the private sector and especially in the Oil States have contributed to serious shortages of highly skilled manpower in the public sector. Second, public-sector pay scales create a kind of floor under private-sector wages, even for unskilled labor. Minimum-wage legislation has a similar, related impact in some countries (Egypt, Turkey). Private-sector wages usually exceed those in the public sector for comparable skills in Egypt, Sudan, Iraq, and Jordan. For example, in Khartoum the average unskilled manufacturing wage seems to be determined by the public-sector wage plus a markup of about 12% (Ghosh 1984), whereas Jordanian accountants can make 75% more money in the private sector (World Bank 1986a). However, public-sector employees usually enjoy various fringe benefits (such as pensions) that may as much as double the effective wage. The public sector in the region usually combines shortages of highly skilled personnel with surpluses of poorly paid, but secure, unskilled employees.

Because public-sector employment is a realistic option for nearly all job-seekers, they have an incentive to wait for it or to combine it with private informal employment. The phenomenon of "moonlighting," or multiple jobs, is very widespread in MENA cities; most Egyptian public employees also work in the private sector.[12] This suggests that there is considerable mobility between sectors, but as far as we know, there are few detailed studies of this.

Such mobility does not seem to have removed all wage differentials. Not only are private-sector wages usually higher than those in the public sector, but also the gap increased during the 1970s. For example, wages in the Iraqi private sector rose five times as much as those in the state sector during the oil boom (Sluglett and Sluglett 1987, 249). Something similar, although less extreme, happened in Egypt, Sudan, Jordan, and Syria. Since the presence of moonlighters plus those waiting for public-sector jobs swells the supply of labor to the informal sector, the explanation for the existence and increase in this wage differential must lie on the demand side of the labor market. In particular, that phenomenon was one of the consequences of the oil boom, with its increased demand for services of all kinds, the massive construction boom (publicly funded but usually privately executed), and the large-scale emigration of labor and influx of remittances in some countries.[13]

In some countries analysis of labor markets is further complicated by the presence of trade unions. Although many countries have official unions, independent unions are really limited to Israel, Turkey, Tunisia, and the Sudan and existed in Iran under the shah. Although the ability of unions to act independently varies greatly across countries and over time, a few generalizations are possible. First, they are confined to the public and private formal sector and are strongest in the public sector. There is contradictory evidence concerning the percentage of the labor force that is unionized: For example, in Turkey, estimates range from 15% to 56%.[14] Around 1980, the membership of the Union General de Travailleurs Tunisiens was about 175,000; the total manufacturing work force (including mining) was a little over 400,000.[15] During the 1970s, Turkish unions attempted to keep wages increasing at least as fast as inflation, contributing to the inflationary spiral there. In Turkey, as elsewhere in the world, union activity was largely defensive, trying to prevent its membership's welfare from declining. Although these unions have been able to achieve some greater stability of employment and modest improvements in working conditions for their members, they have probably also increased the degree of segmentation between the formal and informal sectors. Unions were greatly weakened by the military coup in 1980, when many union leaders, especially those of the Confederation of Progressive Trade Unions (DISK), were arrested.

What are the implications of this labor market structure for unemployment? A prominent argument holds that much of the "disguised" and open unemployment in the cities is the result of the job guarantee and other formal-sector rigidities, which create a queue of (usually young) job-seekers waiting for a government post. Open unemployment is concentrated among young men, especially those with some education. For example, in Jordan in 1979 some 55% of the total unemployed were between the ages of 15 and 24; perhaps 17% of job-seekers in this age group were unemployed; and about 70% of these unemployed young men had at least a primary education (World Bank 1986a). In Morocco the share of 15-to-25-year-olds in total unemployment rose from 50% in 1971 to 70% in 1976 (World Bank 1981). Iranian unemployment in the 1970s was also concentrated among such people (Halliday 1979); and in 1980, Egyptians "without work experience" were six to eight times as likely to be unemployed as those "with work experience" (Hansen 1985, 18). All of this is at least consistent with the "waiting for the *mugama'a*" hypothesis.

Demand forces, however, obviously also contribute to unemployment. In Morocco, for example, both the public and private formal sectors are quite small relative to the total size of the labor market. Unions are weak, and the World Bank noted approvingly the country's "flexible labor market." Yet not only is youth unemployment widespread, but underemployment is also common: In 1981 nearly one-sixth of the urban "employed" were working less than forty hours per week (*Annuaire Statistique du Maroc* 1984, 49), and the pool of the unemployed is growing at 18% per year (USAID 1986). The World Bank also noted that most temporary workers worked much less than full time, earning low incomes despite finding jobs with relatively good wage rates per day. The bank's speculation that such unemployment is "voluntary" is redolent with the current "blaming the victim" fashion: It is much more likely that the underlying cause of such developments are the continued influx of rural migrants, the high and rising incremental capital output ratios,[16] and the sluggish growth of the economy as a whole.

Turkey and Egypt furnish further confirmation of the importance of the demand side in generating unemployment. Recall that Turkish unemployment rates soared during the early 1980s, when labor unions were weakened or crushed (presumably increasing "labor market flexibility") and demand declined. In Egypt, the growth rate of the labor force rose from 2.1% per year, 1960–1976 to 2.9% from 1977–1980. Hansen showed that these changes cannot be plausibly explained by changes in population growth rates or the age structure of the population. He concluded that labor-force participation increased during the "*infitah* boom," as formerly "discouraged workers" or the "disguised unemployed" emerged to seek work (Hansen 1985, 16–17).

We have seen that most countries of the region face austerity and are trying to reduce the size or at least the rate of growth of employment in the public sector. This suggests that the importance of the informal sector will continue to increase. Because of the diversity of the informal sector, the crucial question is not just whether *jobs* will increase but whether jobs with potential for increasing productivity and incomes will be created. Here the key seems to be small-scale manufacturing enterprises, with potential for upgrading, rather than the myriad personal services so often (erroneously) identified with the "informal sector."[17] One study of Egypt found that such "minifactories" were not only more labor intensive but also used capital as least as efficiently as did larger enterprises (Davies et al. 1984). However, their evidence also suggests that hours are long (around fifty hours per week) and wages low in such activities.

Governments have done relatively little toward creation of such jobs, except through overall macropolicies. On the one hand, measures to foster the private sector might help the informal sector, especially if they allow small-scale entrepreneurs to compete for scarce inputs. On the other hand, austerity-induced recessions and tighter credit clearly do little to help such small-scale enterprises. Whether these small firms, with their typically personalized marketing arrangements, can create the many jobs that the burgeoning labor force will require seems moot. But it is safe to predict the continued importance and expansion of the informal sector in the immediate future.

## HOUSING AND INFRASTRUCTURE

Probably the most visible and pressing problem facing both the increasing numbers of urban residents and their governments is the provision of adequate housing. The rapid growth of urban populations has ensured that demand for housing would outstrip supply, spawning shortages, overcrowding, and/or soaring rents. Governments have been forced to allocate substantial sums to housing construction. Since these funds have been perceived as diversions from growth-enhancing industrial investment, they have often been severely constrained. Although some countries (Algeria, Turkey) have recognized the need to increase urban spending, many others have cut urban budgets as part of austerity measures.[18] Such changes have induced some policy changes and, in particular, a (further) shift toward the private sector as a provider of housing.

A few examples may illustrate the magnitude of the problem. Moroccan cities have been growing by 1,000 people *every day*. Although the supply of housing units roughly doubled between 1973 and 1977, the shortfall (demand minus supply) increased from 390,000 units in 1973 to 800,000 units in 1977 (World Bank 1981). In the early 1980s, an average of 7 Algerians were living in a three-room apartment; the estimated shortfall of public housing units was about 1 million (Nelson 1985a, 152–54; Bennoune 1988), and in 1982, the FLN estimated that "over two million families were in urgent need of accommodation" (Bennoune 1988, 243). Turkey needs to add 350,000 new homes every year to keep up with urban growth; in 1986, construction was approximately half of this figure (*Economist,* June 18, 1988).

Perhaps the worst situation is to be found in urban Egypt. Although the situation has been improved by a decade-long housing and infrastructural construction boom, the deterioration in urban Egypt due to a combination of rapid urban growth and niggardly investment from 1956 to 1973 has still not been fully rectified. By 1975 the housing shortage in Egyptian cities was estimated at over 1.4 million units (Mohie el-Din 1982), with over three persons *per room* the Cairo norm. Much of the existing housing stock was decidedly substandard: 23% of urban households had no electricity, over one-sixth had no access to potable water, and nearly two-thirds lacked sewage hookups (Mohie el-Din 1982). Much of modern Cairo, where vast districts (Masr al-Qadima, Sayyida Zeinab, Darb al-Ahmar, Gamalia, Bulaq) are almost uniformly run-down and substandard,[19] deserves the term *slum.* More than a half million Cairenes live on rooftops, and unknown thousands[20] live in the tombs of the Mamluks.

As usual, there are sharp differences in access to housing by social class. At the upper end of the social scale, every city in the region has neighborhoods of well-maintained, comfortable, often elegant housing inhabited by the well-to-do. In the Maghreb, upper- and middle-class Moroccans, Tunisians, and Algerians often occupied the dwellings of the (often hastily) departed French. Moroccan cities boast new residential developments, with comfortably low densities; even densely populated Cairo has its favored districts, like Zamalek, Doqqi, and Maadi. The problem of urban housing in the MENA countries is, as everywhere, primarily a problem of the relatively poor.

The "class bias" of the housing problem partly reflects two facts: (1) in all countries, most housing construction is in the private sector, which, of course, responds to ability to pay, and (2) public-sector housing, or indeed any subsidy schemes for low-income housing, has been inadequately funded, or misconceived, or both. In some cases, class bias has been an official element of policy: In the Moroccan plan of 1973–1977, the first goal of housing policy and spending was to meet the needs of those with the ability to pay (World Bank 1981). In Tunisia, although the large majority of units built under the 1977–1981 plan was designed to satisfy the needs of the poor, the average cost of new units was out of reach for the poorer half of the population (Nelson 1979, 101).

Some policies intended to benefit the poor have been misguided. Two of these seem especially prominent: rent control legislation and attempts to "clean up" shantytowns. Official rent control in Cairo has had the usual effects: (1) it depressed private investment in housing; (2) it led to the substitution of "key money" for rent and other ways to circumvent the rules; (3) it discouraged people from moving, presumably either reducing the flexibility of the labor market, increasing the demand for (grossly inadequate) urban transportation, or both. In short, it engendered inefficiencies, with little compensatory increase in equity (Mohie el-Din 1982).

Most of the cities of the region are surrounded by squatter settlements: neighborhoods of relatively poor urbanites, with nonexistent or insecure title to the land they occupy, living in dwellings made of very crude materials. The various national names illustrate their nature: *bidonvilles* (tin-can cities: Morocco, Algeria), *gourbivilles* (peasant-style mud-hut towns: Tunisia), or *gecekondu* (housing built overnight: Turkey). In 1981 about one-quarter of urban Moroccans and Turks lived in such settlements; in some cities, the proportion was much higher: Nearly two-thirds of the population of Ankara live in *gecekondu,* with over two people per room. Southern Tehran, Northern Cairo, Omdurman, and Casablanca have similar conditions. Most of these people are recent rural migrants: One study for Turkey estimated that 85% of *gecekondu* residents came from the countryside (Danielson and Keleş 1980).

Until fairly recently, states were hostile toward these urban formations. Not only were they unsightly, but their presence often forced urban administrations to extend already overstretched electric, water, and sewage facilities. Governments tried to prohibit such construction and even attempted to tear down existing structures.[21] Two factors undermined these policies. First, residents themselves have resisted such actions (Iran, Turkey). Second, *infitah* strategies implied greater fiscal austerity and increased reliance on the private sector; both suggested that the government should leave shantytowns alone. Many governments have now revised their anti-shantytown policies, embracing at least some of the arguments of John Turner, who observed twenty years ago that shantytown residents, like anyone else, would try hard to improve their own housing if they felt secure (Turner 1969). Self-help rehabilitation of the *bidonvilles* is now government policy in Morocco; the Turkish government tries to offer low-cost loans to cooperative housing projects in the *gecekondu.* The available evidence vindicates Turner and the new policy approach. Turkey's *gecekondu* are considerably more substantial than equivalent shantytowns in Latin America, more solidly built and usually connected to electricity (*Economist,* June 18, 1988). The *gourbiville* residents of Tunisia replace the orignal mud walls first with brick, then with cement blocks.

For all the urban problems of the region, one remains relatively minor in comparative terms: street crime. In sharp constrast to many Latin American, sub-Saharan African, or North American cities, there are very few areas of major Middle Eastern cities that are unsafe for men to walk at any hour. People complain, as everywhere, about crime, but there is nothing even remotely resembling the anomie and random violence of Lagos, Bogota, or Los Angeles in Cairo, Istanbul, or Casablanca. It is a tribute to the social cohesiveness of Muslim societies that this nearly universal plague of the modern world has been relatively mild in the region.

## INCOME DISTRIBUTION AND POVERTY

How has income been distributed among the urban population? How well have governments met their stated goal of achieving a more equitable distribution of the national product? And how satisfactory has government performance been in reducing the incidence of poverty? What policy mix plausibly accounts for the observed pattern? In this section we will examine the (scanty) evidence on income distribution and poverty and then briefly consider the impact of state policy on both. Since many policies have been examined in more detail in earlier chapters (health, education, agriculture, public/private sector), we shall conclude the section by focusing on consumer-subsidy policies.

The study of income distribution presents both conceptual problems and data difficulties. Conceptually, we may distinguish three broad types of income distributions in political economy: the "functional," the "extended functional," and the "size." The first refers to the distribution of income between the factors of production of labor, capital, and (sometimes) land. This form of distribution boasts the most highly developed theoretical framework; it has been a major focus of political economy since Smith, Ricardo, and Marx. However, it suffers from the deficiency of its origin: The classical political economists believed (with some justification for nineteenth-century England) that the major social categories that were relevant for social and political analysis were landlords (rent of land), capitalists (return on capital), and workers (wages of labor). As we have repeatedly argued in this book, the concept of social class may be indispensable in analyzing the political economy of the region; however, the division of society into the three classes of classical political economy will not help much. We need a much more refined sociology: one that takes into account, for example, the differences between government bureaucrats and wage earners in the private sector. For such purposes, we need an "extended functional distribution." Unfortunately, as far as we know, estimates of this distribution exist only for Turkey in 1973 (Derviş and Robinson 1980). They stratify the Turkish population into eleven different groups and then estimate the income shares of each.

Our main focus will be on the "size" distribution. Here, too, there are conceptual issues. First, what is the unit of analysis? Are we interested in the distribution of income among *persons* or among *households*? To a large extent, this will depend on the purpose of analysis. Since the overwhelming majority of Middle Easterners live in families, the data are almost invariably for households. Distribution within the household and differences in household sizes are therefore typically ignored. For some purposes (e.g., child nutrition) these considerations might be very important, but we will ignore them due to the lack of data.

A second conceptual issue with the "size" distribution concerns its interpretation. We usually consider the whole distribution, ranking the population according to income only, and assuming that an additional unit of income has the same welfare consequences for every household, no matter how poor or how rich. This amounts to espousing a particular version of the utilitarian theory of justice.[22] However, if we focus on the incomes of the very poorest people only, we are implicitly (or often explicitly) appealing to a Rawlsian theory.[23] An Islamic theory would be concerned not merely with the actual distribution-as-outcome but also with the process by which income had been acquired, and with the problem of (illegitimate) absolute poverty among members of the *umma*. We will adopt a somewhat eclectic approach, presenting the "utilitarian" evidence as well as "absolute poverty" data, which would interest utilitarians, Rawlsians, Muslims, Marxists, and, indeed, anyone holding a universalist perspective.

The study of income distribution of any sort in the region is also plagued by very serious data deficiencies. The World Bank's *World Development Report* (1983b) lists income distribution data for only three MENA countries, Egypt, Turkey, and Israel. Furthermore, the information reported for these countries is fifteen years old. Other data can be gleaned from a wide variety of sources, and we will present these data. The coverage, however, is quite poor and is restricted to certain countries: Egypt, Turkey, Morocco, Iran in the 1970s, and Israel being the principal countries for which we have information.

Such data deficiencies are not surprising. First, no country in the region except Israel has the kind of thorough and effective income tax collection system that generates the kind of data that scholars of OECD countries have at their disposal. Accordingly, most information about income distribution comes from sample surveys. These face a formidable problem: Respondents may not tell the truth about their incomes, fearing that the tax collector is peering over the shoulder of the survey researcher. In some cases it is easier to get information on "expenditures" than on income, and we will utilize such data. By definition such numbers omit savings; since these are usually greater among the rich than among the poor, the data underestimate the degree of inequality of the distribution of income. They also notoriously undercount both the very poor and very rich. They are, at best, only a very rough approximation of income distribution.

Similar conceptual and data difficulties surround discussions of poverty. Since the days of Adam Smith or even before, political economists have recognized that poverty is a relative social concept. Even attempts to construct "absolute poverty" lines (below which people are malnourished), contain social analysis, since the amount of calories someone needs depends upon that person's size, occupation, and geographical location. Furthermore, we can only translate a minimum caloric consumption level into a minimum income by making assumptions on what people eat and how they obtain it (e.g., at what prices). These are obviously social categories. And of course, few of us would say that a person who *only* had enough to eat was "not poor": The concept of poverty inevitably has a notion of "minimally adequate" clothing, housing, and so on.[24] Since the concept of poverty is socially determined, it is unsurprising that even within the same society, we can find quite different estimates.

A final issue concerns the question of "relative performance." If we assume (as we certainly do) that inequality is excessive in the region, we are compelled to ask, Relative to what? We will ask (as we have so often done in this book) how the MENA countries compare with other developing countries. A kind of consensus about how the distribution of income changes with development has emerged: Inequality increases in the early stages of economic development, but for middle-income countries (a category that includes all MENA nations except Sudan), policy choices can lead to dramatically different distributional outcomes. We will therefore try to summarize the consequences of state policies for equity and poverty alleviation.

Some summary data (Gini coefficients) on the size distribution of expenditure or income are given in Table 10.3. We also list there the attempt by Adelman to calculate average Ginis for several broad categories of LDCs in 1960 and 1980. These data suggest that in global comparative perspective, there is nothing particularly remarkable about the distribution of income in the region.[25] But the low data quality should make us *very* cautious about any generalizations here.

It is often more intuitively appealing to present the disaggregated data from which the Gini coefficient is calculated.[26] To answer questions like: "How much do the poor (or rich) get?" we need to present something other than Gini ratios. Unfortunately, we have very sparse and spotty data coverage. For example, the World Bank reported early 1970s data on the top and bottom of the distribution of expenditure in Morocco and Tunisia. It also reported the Moroccan data for 1960; these data show a clear deterioration in the distribution of income there, a deterioration that does not seem to have been reversed in the subsequent decade and a half. We also report the figures given by the World Bank (1981) for an overall "average" distribution for the entire region[27] (Table 10.4). It should be remembered that these are data on expenditures, which are almost always more equitably distributed than income.

Data on the size distribution of income are available for Turkey, Egypt, and Israel (Table 10.5). To put these numbers in comparative perspective, note that the richest 20% in Brazil, Mexico, Venezuela, and Peru receive, respectively, 67%, 58%, 54%, and 61% of income, while the poorest 40% in those countries get 7%, 9.9%, 10.3%, and 7%, respectively. It is instructive to note that the poor (bottom 40%) in Egypt (with about 16.5% of income)

Table 10.3  Gini Coefficients for Income Distribution, 1955-1983 (selected
          years)

|  | Gini (Year) |
|---|---|
| Egypt | .429 (1958)[a] |
|  | .37  (Rural-1958/59)[b] |
|  | .40  (Urban-1958/59)[b] |
|  | .40  (Urban-1964/65)[b] |
|  | .37  (Urban-1974/75)[b] |
| Iran | .47  (1969)[a] |
| Iraq | .568 (1956)[a] |
| Israel | .316 (1957)[a] |
| Morocco | .486 (1955)[a] |
|  | .500 (1965)[a] |
| Tunisia | .516 (1965)[a] |
|  | .530 (1971)[a] |
| Turkey | .51  (1973)[c] |
|  | .50  (1978)[d] |
|  | .52  (1983)[d] |
| Sudan | .393 (1969)[a] |
|  |  |
| Low-income countries | .407 (1960)[e] |
|  | .450 (1980)[e] |
| Middle-income, non-oil | .603 (1960)[e] |
|   exporting | .569 (1980)[e] |
| Oil-exporting | .575 (1960)[e] |
|  | .612 (1980)[e] |

Sources: [a]"Towards Alleviation of Poverty in Sudan," FAO Rural Poverty Study,
1978 (unpublished);  [b]John Waterbury, "Patterns of Urban Growth and Income
Distribution in Egypt," in G. Abdel-Khalek and R. Tignor, eds., The Political
Economy of Income Distribution in Egypt, New York, Holmes and Meier, 1982;
[c]Kemal Derviş and Sherman Robinson, "The Structure of Income Inequality in
Turkey, 1950-1973," in Ergun Özbudun and Aydin Ulusan, The Political Economy of
Income Distribution in Turkey, New York, Holmes and Meier, 1980;  [d]Merih
Celasun, "Comment: Income Distribution and Domestic Terms of Trade in Turkey,"
METU Studies in Development 13, 1 and 2 (1986);  [e]Irma Adelman, and Sherman
Robinson, "Income Distribution and Development: A Survey," in H. B. Chenery and
T. N. Srinivasan, eds., Handbook of Development Economics, Amsterdam, North
Holland, 1988.

Table 10.4  Distribution of Household Expenditure, 1959/60 and 1970/71
           (percentages)

|  | Morocco | | Tunisia | MENA Average |
|---|---|---|---|---|
| Household Income Group | 1959/60 | 1970/71 | 1970/71 | 1970/71 |
| Top 5 | 18.0 | 20 | 17 | 21.4 |
| Top 20 | 43.4 | 49 | 42 | 48.6 |
| Bottom 40 | 18.0 | 12 | 15 | 15.0 |
| Bottom 20 | 7.0 | 4 | 6 | 5.3 |

Source: World Bank: Morocco: Economic and Social Development Report,
Washington, D.C., World Bank Pub., October 1981, p. 222.

Table 10.5 Size Distribution of Income in Turkey (1973), Egypt (1974), Israel (1979/80), by Households (percentages)

| Household Income Group | Percent of Income Received in | | |
|---|---|---|---|
| | Turkey (1973) | Egypt (1974) | Israel (1979/80) |
| Bottom 20 | 3.5 | 5.8 | 6.0 |
| Second 20 | 8.0 | 10.7 | 12.0 |
| Third 20 | 12.5 | 14.7 | 17.7 |
| Fourth 20 | 19.5 | 20.8 | 24.4 |
| Top 20 | 56.5 | 48.0 | 39.9 |
| Top 10 | 40.7 | 33.2 | 22.6 |

Source: World Bank, World Development Report, New York, Oxford University Press, 1987, pp. 252-53.

receive a higher share than the poor in Sri Lanka (15.9%)—a country justly famous for its "pro-poor" policies—or than any lower-middle-income country for which the World Bank reports data. For upper-middle-income nations reporting data, only in socialist Hungary (20.5%) and Yugoslavia (18.7%), Israel (18%), and the Republic of Korea (16.9%) do the poor receive a larger share than in Egypt. However, the Turkish poor, receiving 11.5% of national income in 1973, fared worse than the poor in any other reported middle-income countries outside of Latin America except the Ivory Coast and Malaysia.[28] (All figures from World Bank 1987, pp. 252–53.) This share deteriorated further to 9.6% in 1983 (Celasun 1986), which was slightly lower than the share of the Mexican poor in 1977 (9.9%).

But before we conclude by congratulating the Egyptians on their achievements, let us look at the diversity of estimates of income distribution there. This can be taken as illustrative of the extent of our ignorance of the subject in the whole region. For example, a 1976 study argued that the bottom 60% of Egyptians received 30% of income, the middle 30% got 32%, while the richest 10% got 38% (Eckaus, McCarthy, Mohie el-Din 1978). Although this is quite close to the World Bank's estimate for the poor, it is much higher for the share of the very rich (bank's estimate: 33%). And a still later study (Mohie El-Din 1982), finds that the bottom 75% of Egyptians got 25% of the income, the next 20% received 21%, while the richest 5% took a modest 54% of income![29]

Although Mohie el-Din's estimate may exaggerate the skewness of Egyptian income distribution, there is (some) evidence that the distribution of income in urban areas deteriorated during the 1970s (Table 10.6). The share of the wealthy increased; the share of the very richest increased proportionately the most. The stability of the share of the very poorest is probably explained by the generous food-subsidy system (see below). At the same time, the share of the bottom 50% in rural areas improved, as did that of the richest in those areas. These numbers are consistent with what we might expect in Egypt during the *infitah* period: Emigration pulled up rural wage rates, improving the lot of the rural poor, while the boom in financial services, real estate, and other skill-intensive services

Table 10.6  Egyptian Income Distribution, 1974/75-1981/82 (percentages)

|  | 1974/75 | 1981/82 |
|---|---|---|
| **Urban household income group** | | |
| Bottom 10 | 2.3 | 2.3 |
| Bottom 50 | 24.0 | 23.1 |
| Middle 30 | 28.9 | 26.6 |
| Top 20 | 47.1 | 50.3 |
| Top 10 | 32.1 | 37.2 |
| Top 5 | 21.7 | 28.7 |
| **Rural household income group** | | |
| Bottom 10 | 2.2 | 3.3 |
| Bottom 50 | 24.6 | 25.0 |
| Middle 30 | 29.4 | 28.1 |
| Top 20 | 46.0 | 46.9 |
| Top 10 | 31.4 | 33.6 |
| Top 5 | 21.8 | 24.9 |

Source: Al-Ahram al-Iqtisadi, #871, September 23, 1985, pp. 34-35.

disproportionately favored the urban rich. However, this information must be treated cautiously: There is evidence of increasing *equality* among wage earners during the 1970s (Hansen and Radwan 1982, 28-29), and no one knows much about the impact of workers' remittances on family incomes.

Some information is available on the functional distribution for Egypt over time. The share of wages in national income rose from 45% of GDP in the late 1950s, to 50% in the early 1970s, only to fall to 44% in 1975, 40% in 1978, and 36% in 1979 (Ministry of Economy, in Waterbury 1983, 212). These numbers, however, can be easily misinterpreted: First, as we have seen above, "wage earners" are themselves quite diverse—a simple model of class based on classical political economy will not do. Second, the category "nonwage income" includes government receipts from oil sales, the Suez Canal, and so forth. It is unclear which social groups have benefited most from these revenues. Third, remittances are undercounted in these calculations. Nevertheless, these numbers are at least consistent with the data in Table 10.6 that show a deterioration in the distribution of income in favor of the upper, property-owning classes in the largest Arab country.

We now turn to consider the question of absolute poverty in the region. Here, too, the "data" represent informed guesses. Some of these are presented in Table 10.7. These numbers are of the crude "head count" variety: After a "poverty line" has been selected, the number of people who fall below this line are enumerated. As noted earlier (note 24), such a measure omits any discussion of how far below the poverty line poor peoples' incomes fall. Despite these difficulties, several points deserve emphasis. Overall, about 20% to 25% of the population of the region (excluding Sudan), or about 40 to 50 million people, were poor in 1977 (Kavalsky 1980). Second, it is often argued (e.g., Adelman and Robinson 1988) that absolute poverty is concentrated in the rural areas; the World

Table 10.7 Estimates of Absolute Poverty in MENA Countries, 1977

|  | Number of Poor (millions) | As % of Population |
|---|---|---|
| Algeria | 3.0[a] | 17[a] |
| Egypt | 10.0[a] | 26[a] |
|  |  | 35[b] |
|  |  | 48[c] |
| Iran | 8.7[a] | 25[a] |
| Iraq | 1.5[a] | 13[a] |
| Jordan | 0.2[a] | 7[a] |
| Morocco | 7.0[a] | 38[a] |
| Lebanon | 0.6[a] | 21[a] |
| Syria | 1.2[a] | 15[a] |
| Tunisia | 1.0[a] | 17[a] |
| Turkey | 8.0[a] (1973) | 19[a] |
|  | 12.5[d] (1973) | 30[d] |
|  | 12.0[e] (1978) | 25[e] |
|  | 16.0[e] (1983) | 30[e] |
| YAR | 0.7[a] | 14[a] |
| PDRY | 0.4[a] | 24[a] |

Sources: [a]Basil Kavalsky, "Poverty and Human Development in the Middle East and North Africa," in Poverty and the Development of Human Resources: Regional Perspectives, World Bank Staff Working Paper No. 406, 1980, p. 145; [b]Saad Eddin Ibrahim, "Social Mobility and Income Distribution in Egypt, 1952-57," in G. Abdel-Khaleq and R. Tignor, eds., The Political Economy of Income Distribution in Egypt, New York, Holmes and Meier, 1982 (urban); [c]John Waterbury, The Egypt of Nasser and Sadat: The Political Economy of Two Regimes, Princeton, N.J., Princeton University Press, 1983 (urban); [d]Kemal Derviş and Sherman Robinson, "The Structure of Income Inequality in Turkey, 1950-1973," in Ergun Özbudun and Aydin Ulusan, The Political Economy of Income Distribution in Turkey, New York, Holmes and Meier, 1980; [e]Merih Celasun, "Comment: Income Distribution and Domestic Terms of Trade in Turkey," METU Studies in Development 13, 1 and 2 (1986).

Bank guessed that about 80% of total MENA poverty was in the countryside (Kavalsky 1980). This latter estimate may be too high, however: In Morocco two-thirds of the very poor live in the countryside, while more than two-thirds of the Turkish poor are farmers and farm laborers (USAID 1986; Derviş and Robinson 1980). But in Egypt about 35% of rural households are poor (Radwan and Lee 1986, 87), compared with 35% (Ibrahim 1982b) to 48% (Waterbury 1982) in urban areas; since the population is about evenly divided between city and countryside, these figures imply that at least half and perhaps a majority of the Egyptian poor live in the cities. Similarly, a nutritional study for Iran in 1973 found much greater malnutrition in Iranian urban areas than in the countryside (Katouzian 1981).[30]

Who are the urban poor? In Turkey, about 40% are unskilled laborers, with artisans in the informal sector constituting another one-third. Interestingly, nearly one-fifth of government employees are poor; over half of all unskilled laborers and one-third of all artisans are poor (Derviş and Robinson 1980, 110–11). These numbers should remind us that the categories of "the poor" and "the informal sector" are not the same. A study of Egypt likewise argued that the number of the poor employed in the formal sector exceeds the number in the informal sector (Abdel-Fadil 1983). Not only are about 50% of workers earning the minimum wage employed in the private formal sector, but low-grade clerks and messengers working for the government are also poor. For both Egypt and Turkey, available evidence suggests a deterioration in the relative-income position of all government employees and, probably, an increasing incidence of poverty among their lower ranks. Finally, poverty is partly a function of demography. If an entire family of six depends on one male unskilled laborer for its consumption, that family will almost certainly be poor in any country in the region.

There is relatively little evidence on changes over time in either the percentages or the total numbers of poor people in the region. However, although the growth process in some countries (Morocco, Turkey, perhaps Egypt) may have increased inequalities during the past decade, this deterioration may not have been sufficient to offset the increase in national incomes. One observer guessed that the percentage of absolutely poor people has declined over time in YAR, Jordan, Tunisia, Syria, Algeria, Iraq, and perhaps Iran (Kavalsky 1980, 145). The Tunisian government claimed that the proportion of the poor declined from 27% of the population in 1967 to 16% in 1977 (H. Nelson 1979, 120). In 1980, some 11.8% of the urban population and 14.1% of the rural population were officially enumerated as "poor" (Tunisian Republic 1982; cited in Ghonemy 1984, 34). There seems to have been a decline in both the percentages and the absolute numbers of the rural poor in Egypt (Radwan and Lee 1986); unfortunately, comparable estimates for the urban population are unavailable. Recent direct evidence on Morocco is not available; however, the nominal minimum wage remained unchanged from 1977 to 1982, while inflation was at least 10% per year. For Turkey, in contrast, the percentage of the total poor fell from 1973 (about 30%) to 1978 (about 25%) and then rose until 1983 (30%) (Celasun 1986). This means that there were about 3.5 million more poor Turks in 1983 than ten years earlier.

Although direct evidence is scarce, we can use indirect evidence and theory to complement the picture drawn above. The relationship between social structures, government policies, and economic growth patterns on the one hand and poverty reduction and changes in distribution on the other have been intensively studied during the past generation (for a useful review, see Adelman and Robinson 1988). Several major points of consensus have emerged. Policies that reduce poverty and inequality include: asset redistribution (especially of land), mass education, and price systems that encourage the growth of demand for unskilled labor. We have looked at all of these in previous chapters: land reform (Chapter 6), education (Chapter 4), and price policies (Chapters 6–9). International comparative research has demonstrated that the most successful examples of growth, equity, and poverty alleviation (Republic of Korea, Taiwan) have combined all three of these policies in a vigorous and coordinated manner.

MENA countries' performances on redistribution of physical and human capital and on employment generation have varied widely. It is therefore unsurprising that we find considerable diversity in improving equity and removing poverty. The better performers seem to be Egypt, Tunisia, Syria, and Iraq, all of which redistributed land and promoted education. The first three countries' labor markets have also benefited greatly from emigration, while Iraq has used its petroleum resources to generate a high demand for labor. The answer to why such countries have not done as well as the "baby tigers" of East Asia may be sought in previous chapters: land-reform difficulties and failures, biases against agriculture, educational shortcomings, and industrialization and trade policies that reduced the labor intensity of production and the rate of growth of production of labor-using manufactured goods.

The argument that the best guarantee of growth with equity is to "redistribute first, grow later" (Adelman and Robinson 1988) finds negative illustration in Morocco's and Turkey's poor performance on equity enhancement and poverty reduction. Neither country has undertaken any significant redistribution of assets; both countries for long periods pursued import-substituting industrialization policies, which were unable to absorb unskilled labor into productive employment sufficiently rapidly. The poor in both countries benefited from labor emigration to Western Europe but then faced the closing of that "safety valve" by the 1980s. And both countries have been confronted with serious budgetary and trade problems, in turn leading to austerity programs.

The stabilization policies outlined in the previous two chapters pose a considerable threat to equity and poverty reduction. Proponents of these policies argue that although their implementation may worsen poverty in the short run, they set the stage for dramatic gains later on. Such policies should eliminate biases against labor-intensive production and against the rural sector. But, of course, the logic of these policies is to *reduce* domestic demand; unless there is a boom in exports, there will be a decline in employment, as the Turkish experience in the 1980s shows. In addition, a fall in real wages is part of the strategy of shifting resources toward exports and reducing inflation. Such a fall increases poverty, since wages are the major component of income for unskilled workers; the number of poor Turks increased by about 4 million (from about 12 million in 1978 to about 16 million in 1983) (calculated from Celasun 1986). Although Keynes reminded us that "in the long run, we are all dead," for the poor in the Third World, the long run is very short indeed. If reforms reduce the bias against agriculture, they may help the rural poor; however, in Turkey, as we have seen, the reverse occurred.[31] Stabilization measures have had similar consequences in Tunisia and Morocco, while Egypt has been able to use its international political position to stave off the kind of reforms that might increase growth tomorrow but that will surely also increase poverty today.

Stabilization packages always call for a reduction in government spending. In particular, creditors usually demand a reduction in consumer subsidies. This, of course, is a highly charged issue in the region's political economy: Proposed subsidy cuts have provoked riots in Algeria, Egypt, Morocco,

Tunisia, Jordan, and the Sudan. Most countries in the region try to subsidize at least bread consumption; many extend these subsidies to other goods, with Egypt having the most extensive (and costly!) system, which covers thirteen different commodities.

The methods used to implement these subsidies vary from country to country, but all share certain features. Prices of bread and flour are kept low by state subsidies paid to millers. Governments usually control the import of subsidized commodities, often through state monopolies. If there is private-sector involvement in marketing (e.g., in Tunisia), the system of subsidies becomes more complex.

The critical feature that all of these systems share is that they are "untargeted": Bread is not rationed but is available for purchase by anyone in unlimited quantities at a low price. Even when other subsidized commodities are rationed, virtually every household, regardless of income, is entitled to a ration book: In Egypt, over 90% of households are eligible (FAO 1984, 17; Alderman 1986, 184). Such broad coverage both increases budgetary costs and reduces the subsidies' contribution to equity.

The budgetary burdens can be exaggerated, however. By far the most costly system is the Egyptian one: Total subsidies, which were nearly 20% of government expenditure in 1979, fell to roughly 9% in 1986/87. Food subsidies made up over half of all subsidies (de Thier 1987). For most other countries, the budgetary burden of food subsidies has been still lower: Morocco, 3.2% of government expenditure (1979), Sudan 1.3% (1980), Syria, 7.2% (1977), Saudi Arabia, 0.6% (1980) (FAO 1984, 20). There are also other, implicit burdens. The stabilization of food consumption in an economic world of continuous shocks implies that something else must become still more unstable: In Egypt, this seems to have been industrial investment and imports of capital goods and intermediate inputs (Scobie 1981). If the subsidies are not paid for by taxation, they contribute to the budgetary deficit and, therefore, to inflation. This has made them a prime target of stabilization policy mongers. Although low prices to consumers are often blamed for low farm-gate prices, there is no necessary connection: Subsidies have to be paid for by taxation, but there is no law that says that agricultural taxation must carry the weight alone, or even in large part. This is a fiscal question: What can the government tax? In Egypt, research has shown that the fiscal burden of consumer subsidies was gradually shifted from farmers to the general population in the period from the end of the 1960s to the early 1980s, a shift made possible by the influx of external resources (Alderman and von Braun 1984). Moreover, the dramatic expansion of the Egyptian subsidy system during the 1970s occurred in a context of rapid economic growth: Only one-seventh of the growth of resources available to the economy between 1971 and 1980 was devoted to food subsidies (Alderman 1986, 189).

Food subsidies are vitally important for the urban poor.[32] Of course, the poor always spend a high percentage of their income on food. For example, the average percentage of income spent on food in Morocco was 58%, but the poorest two quartile of the population spent four-fifths of their income on food, one of the highest ratios in the world (USAID 1986, 18).[33] The poorest quartile of Khartoum residents spend about two-thirds of their income on food (Youngblood et al. 1983). Poor Tunisians spend around 60% of their incomes on food; for them, the subsidy cuts of January 1984 constituted a 20–25% cut in real income (J. Nelson 1985, 29). Poor Egyptians receive about 15% of their total incomes in the form of food subsidies (Alderman and von Braun 1984).

There can be little doubt, then, that the system of food subsidies helps the poor, preventing the kind of widespread hunger that is the fate of the poor in so many other countries (including the United States). It is equally indisputable that the current system is a highly inefficient means of meeting this worthy goal. Most benefits accrue to the nonpoor; even the well-to-do consume subsidized food. The upper 75% of Khartoum residents consume five loaves of subsidized bread for every one consumed by the poorest 25% (Youngblood et al. 1983, 55). The poorest 40% of Moroccans receive only about 20% of that country's subsidies (J. Nelson 1985). Every rich Egyptian received about £E 24 of food subsidies in 1981/82, compared with about £E 19 for each poor Egyptian (Alderman and von Braun 1984).[34]

Such resources obviously have alternative uses; most countries of the region have been trying to improve the "targeting" of these subsidies. Egypt has begun to issue ration cards differentiated by income level (de Thier 1987); Tunisia and Morocco have been raising food prices and trying to restrict access to subsidized food. However, this is difficult for both political and administrative reasons. The political angle stems from the fact that many of the "nonpoor" are not exactly prosperous. Although many Tunisians employed in the informal sector received incomes above the poverty line, they spent over half of their money on food. The price hikes of 1984 reduced their real incomes by approximately 14% (J. Nelson 1985, 30–31). Governments do not wish to antagonize these "near poor"; they are much more numerous than the "absolutely poor" and include many (politically volatile) students.

Administratively, any food-subsidy system has "leakage"; the most effective targeting mechanism is a food-stamp system (Reutlinger and Selowsky 1976), but such a system requires literacy. Unless the food stamps are indexed, their purchasing power will decline in an inflationary economy, jeopardizing the welfare of the poor.[35] Another targeting idea is to limit subsidies to an "inferior" food grain. However, partly as a result of food subsidies, the staple cereal of the urban poor is now the same as for the rich: wheat bread. But subsidies for "luxury foods" (e.g., meat in Egypt) could clearly be reduced. The budgetary savings, however, would be quite small.[36] Because of the pressure of debt and stabilization policies on the one side and of popular protest on the other, governments are likely to move slowly in modifying food-subsidy systems.

## SUMMARY:
## WHAT SORT OF URBAN WORKING CLASS?

What sort of working class do we find in the region? For all the geographical diversity, we can point to a few commonalities. The working class is growing in size. It is a composite of the urban-born and recent arrivals from the countryside. In many countries (e.g., Algeria, Tunisia, Egypt, Sudan, Turkey, Syria, Iraq) the class is segmented by sector of employment (government/private, formal/informal) and degrees of job security. Many of these people are self-employed, and a large fraction of wage earners work in small establishments, where industrial relations are quite personalized, often even a family affair. The working class is also united by relatively low incomes; the constant problem of finding a job; if not for fathers, then for sons; and overcrowded living conditions. Most members receive at least some consumption subsidy from the state, which both makes it possible to survive and politicizes consumption. These people have many grievances. In the next section, we turn to how they and other urbanites express their frustrations politically.

## URBAN POLITICS AND POLITICAL VIOLENCE

Large and medium-sized cities in the Middle East and in other LDCs may be a stage for disruption and violence. The theatrical potential of cities evokes a level of concern on the part of governing elites that the countryside, no matter how important economically, can seldom match.[37] Relatively small groups of determined people—from spontaneous rioters to urban guerrillas—can disrupt and paralyze urban centers that sit astride national communications grids (railroads, ports, telephone systems, the international airport) and that contain heavy concentrations of industry, the chief bureaucratic installations of the government, the foreign diplomatic and press corps, the major universities, and so forth.

In the 1940s and 1950s there had been widespread expectations that throughout the developing world, the shantytowns would provide an endless stream of young, poor, unskilled, uprooted males ready to answer any appeal to violence. The image that was developed was one of people stripped of their village, family, and kin associations, thrust into a money economy where jobs were scarce and exploitation of the unskilled common, and where anomie, or normlessness, predisposed the "uprooted" to seek a new identity in radical movements through targeted and random violence.

The picture, while not wholly inaccurate, as we shall see below, has major flaws. Shantytown populations, by and large, have turned out to be fairly responsible urban dwellers (J. Nelson 1979, presented the new picture). Often they have reconstituted kin, ethnic, and religious associations in their new abodes. We have seen that generally they have been able to find work. When city authorities have legalized access to the land on which they had been squatters, they have invested their labor and earnings in home improvement. They are upwardly mobile, and however grim the shanty slums may appear to the outsider, their inhabitants vastly prefer life there to life back in the village (see, inter alia, Danielson and Keleş 1985). For the most part, shantytowns have not been hotbeds of political agitation and violence.

The second source of slum dwellers is located in the inner city, in old, decaying, substandard housing, much of which may be condemned and is certainly unsafe to inhabit. A third or more of a given city's population may live in such quarters, and the residents may be second- or third-generation migrants or trading and craftspeople of long standing in the city. Second-generation migrants may have forgotten why their parents left the village and see only the poor services offered them by the municipality; the broken sewers, crowded schools, collapsing buildings, and mounds of refuse that often make these quarters more forbidding than the shantytowns (see Wikan 1980). The solidly urban service and craftspeople may recall a bygone era when they enjoyed status and a higher level of income, before modern industrial production, department stores, and the like invaded their world. In short, residents of these quarters may be more violence-prone than those of the shantytowns.

Another source of potential actors is to be found in the ranks of organized labor. The reasons are obvious. Trade unions present a command structure for, and sometimes a tradition of, confrontation and militancy. They can respond rapidly, coherently, and on a sustained basis to unfair labor practices (i.e., plant or industry-specific), cost-of-living issues (city or national in scope), or to ideological and political causes. Strikes among dockers or bus and train drivers can shut down cities and ports, and worker demonstrations of whatever nature may act as a catalyst to the involvement of other, less organized groups. But because organized labor is usually a small fraction of the entire work force, governments are willing to make large financial settlements to buy the goodwill of union leaders. Conversely, in most Middle Eastern countries, strikes are illegal, and the threat of arrest and imprisonment is not idle (as the secretary-general of Tunisia's General Confederation of Tunisian Workers [UGTT], Habib Achour, learned in 1978). As we shall see in Chapter 12, corporatist arrangements through which the state co-opts union leadership have been the preferred strategy to deal with labor.

High school and university students are viewed by municipal and national authorities with particular alarm. They have relatively little to lose—few are married or hold jobs and are thus willing to take big risks. Terminating their education is a real threat, often acted upon, but committed university militants may discount that threat, and many high school students may feel their education is of little worth anyway. It is, moreover, part of student culture everywhere to take political stands, to be the nation's or the "movement's" conscience, to confront, be bloodied, go to jail (on Egypt, see Abdalla 1985). No Middle Eastern society has been spared student agitation and violence, and in some (Morocco, 1965, 1984; Sudan, 1964,

1985; Turkey throughout the 1970s; Egypt 1968, 1977; Iran, 1978–1979) regimes have been shaken or fallen. When students go into the streets, they draw not only other students but perhaps organized labor and the slum dwellers as well.

Although they tend not to be the initiators, segments of the urban trading and merchant strata may be important actors in urban-based challenges to the authorities. The mass clanging down of iron shop-shutters in congested urban commercial districts is a time-honored and dramatic signal that even the better-off have had enough. Shopkeepers have closed down to support the war against the French in Algiers in 1958; against Israeli occupation of the West Bank, sporadically since 1967 and on a regular basis since 1987; against the awarding of a monopoly in tobacco trade to foreigners in Tehran in 1896; against the ending of Islam as the religion of state in Syria in 1966; against the shah in his final months in Iran in 1978.

Finally we should pay attention to what Marxists would call "lumpen" elements. All cities are full of people who in fact are rootless or, if organized, are so in ways that enjoy no respect or legitimacy: beggars, prostitutes, dope pushers, scavengers, drifters, and derelicts. Time and again, political protest draws in the lumpen elements, and organized confrontation may degenerate into random looting. Few observers in the last decade or so have failed to note the striking presence of the very young in all forms of urban violence. These are preadolescent or early adolescent street urchins, kids playing hooky, runaways, orphans, and beggars. They take physical risks that even older students avoid, and they suffer casualties that the authorities generally try to cover up.

By looking at specific instances of urban violence we may better appreciate how these various elements combine. One of the most frequent forms of violence has been the cost-of-living riot or demonstration. The issue, as noted, has become acute as various countries try to reduce their deficits through cuts in consumer subsidies, but there were instances of this form even in the 1960s. A sharp rise in the price of sugar in Morocco in 1965 triggered massive rioting in Casablanca, with scores of dead, and led to the suspension of parliament and a state of emergency that lasted for the rest of the decade. In June 1981 there was a repeat of this scenario in Casablanca, with 66 "officially" killed (600 by other accounts).

In August 1983, the Moroccan authorities reduced consumer subsidies on average by 20% and raised public-sector salaries by an equal amount. No violence occurred immediately. But then in January 1984, riots broke out all over northern Morocco, as well as at Oujda and Marrakech. Casablanca this time was not a major locus of the violence. What had happened? Poor political management allowed several grievances to come together simultaneously. Secondary school students were already on strike because of an increase in the fees required to sit for the baccalaureat exams. In northern Morocco, where contraband trade with the two Spanish enclaves of Ceuta and Melilla helps prop up economic life, very high exit fees were imposed on Moroccan traders. Rumors, probably well founded, were rife that new subsidy cuts were in the offing. Finally, in preparation for an Islamic summit at Casablanca, a number of Moroccan cities had been stripped of their police so that they could protect the conferees at the summit. Student strikes and demonstrations turned into cost-of-living riots, and the local forces of order in several cities were unable to contain them. Twenty-nine people "officially" lost their lives, while some estimate the real number to be around 400 (Clément 1986).

Similar cost-of-living riots occurred in Tunis and other Tunisian cities in 1978 and 1984 (in the latter, 89 were "officially" killed), in Egypt in 1977 (about 90 dead), and in Khartoum in 1982 and 1985 (number of dead unknown). Surely the most quixotic of these outbreaks was the one in Beirut in the summer of 1987 when Lebanese interrupted their civil war to demonstrate against the precipitous fall in the international value of the Lebanese pound. Algeria, which for nearly twenty-five years had experienced little urban violence, was rocked by cost-of-living riots in the fall of 1988, and the Kingdom of Jordan followed suit in the spring of 1989.

National leaders are loath to admit that these riots reflect real grievances, for that would be to admit that the government cannot feed its own people. Generally, the head of state blames the riots on outside agitators—Zionism, Khomeini, Marxists, or Qaddhafi have always been ready at hand. Nevertheless, the same heads of state typically give away the game by rescinding the measures that gave rise to the protest: Sadat, Bourguiba, and King Hassan all responded in that manner. Needless to say, with such precedents it becomes all the more difficult to reintroduce the measures, just as these precedents make it more likely that people will resort to violence in the future because it worked so well in the past.

We should be cautious, however, in accepting the counterclaims of pure spontaneity behind cost-of-living riots. Organized political groups, from Muslim militants to Marxist radicals, are generally forewarned of impending shifts in government pricing policies and are ready to incite allied groups to go into the streets. It is unlikely that their actions are decisive, but there may be more orchestration to some riots than meets the eye. In the winter of 1986, thousands of Egypt's security police, made up of young, rural, terribly underpaid, but armed, conscripts, rioted against an alleged plan of the government to extend their tour of duty by one year. A number of those arrested were found to have amounts of money on them equivalent to several months' pay. The conclusion, not ever proven, was that Muslim groups had paid many of them to protest.

There have been outbreaks of violence or demonstrations driven by political issues. Perhaps the most important single instance came on January 26, 1952, in Cairo. In a day of rioting and arson, downtown, "European" Cairo was set ablaze as denizens of the Old City (low income, substandard housing) and of the tombs in the city of the dead went on a rampage. The Black Saturday riots had been triggered by an assault on an Egyptian police post in the Suez Canal Zone by British troops who suspected the police of harboring terrorists. The riots introduced such a sense of interregnum and *fin de régime* that Nasser and his coconspirators accelerated their plans to seize power and did so the following July.

Hanna Batatu recounted that in March 1959 the Iraqi Communist party (ICP) tried to pressure Gen. 'Abd al-Karim Qassim, the Iraqi head of state, into giving the party four seats in the cabinet. At that time the party probably had no more than 2,000 members, but it was able to put *half a million* people in the streets of Baghdad. Who were they? Surely very few of them were committed Marxists. Many of them may have come out of the "somber wretchedness" (Batatu 1978, 49) of the largely Shi'ite slums, and there were surely students and members of the white-collar intelligentsia.

Perhaps those half million Iraqis responding to the marching orders of the ICP were in composition similar to the millions of Iranians who demonstrated against the shah exactly twenty years later. In Iran a broad coalition of urban interests sustained direct confrontations with the Iranian police and military for most of a year. Although Ayatollah Khomeini's recorded instructions and urgings, sent from his exile in Paris, may have been the real force behind the movements, other groups, including students, bazaar merchants, organized labor, radical political organizations, all contributed to what became an urban-based revolution.

In Chapter 15 we shall look at this revolution in greater detail. For the moment let us note that it involved constant street demonstrations and confrontations throughout 1978, strikes by labor and civil servants in the last quarter of the year, strikes by bazaar merchants, and after the shah left Iran in the hands of a caretaker government (Prime Minister Shapur Bakhtiar), arms finally found their way from disaffected elements of the armed forces to the civilian groups in the streets.

The most systematic account of the revolutionary process during 1978 is provided us by Ashraf and Banuazizi (1985), and they saw the three major components of the movement as the "young intelligentsia," both left secular and radical Muslim, the *bazaaris*, and the clergy, or mullahs. They saw the *bazaaris* as including shopkeepers, merchants, and artisans (1985, 29):

> Several factors contributed to the importance of the bazaar in the revolution. First, the closing of the bazaar as an act of protest was a time-honored tradition, which had a far more direct impact on the daily lives of the people than strikes at schools or other institutions. Second, the bazaar, a highly congested and closely-knit community, was an ideal site for collective actions of protest. And, third, the merchants, shopkeepers and other members of the bazaar provided important financial backing for the revolution.

The two authors noted the absence of participation of slum dwellers in the violence and, like Kazemi (1980b), stressed the involvement of second-generation migrants and the urban unemployed. Ashraf and Banuazizi estimated the scope of the violence during the twelve months of 1978, a period of cyclical urban riots and mass demonstrations, as follows (1985, 22):

| | |
|---|---:|
| Number of demonstrations | 2,483 |
| Number of participants | 1,600,000 |
| Number of strikes | 1,207 |
| Number killed | 3,008 |
| Number wounded | 12,184 |

In the last two months of 1978, demonstrators were joined by an estimated 5 million workers and employees involved in strikes, and in the first two months of 1979, according to Ashraf and Banuazizi, virtually the entire adult population demonstrated in one fashion or another against the shah.

The final two examples we shall look at are (so far) atypical for the region as a whole. One is that of Turkey's urban violence during the 1970s. The patterns that developed were more akin to those in Argentina, Italy, and West Germany of the same period than to anything in the Middle East. The Turkish political arena underwent a kind of centrifugal process by which radical leftist, fascist, and occasionally Muslim militant groups took up arms and warred among themselves. There appears to be little doubt that fascist groups, such as the Grey Wolves, were the primary instigators of the troubles. They fought for control of university campuses, assassinated both one another and "marked" political leaders, and used the shantytowns to hide out. By 1980, 20 to 30 Turks were being killed every day, and the total number of political deaths reached 5,000.

The beginning and the end of the decade were marked by military takeover, in each instance partially justified by the need to restore law and order. It was organized labor that provided the occasion for the first intervention (Bianchi 1984, 202):

> In June 1970 industrial workers in the Istanbul-Izmit area joined in a massive march to protest a new law regulating union organization and collective bargaining. The march soon erupted into a workers' riot involving over one hundred thousand demonstrators in the largest and most violent worker protest in Turkish history. Tanks and paratroopers were mobilized to quell the rioting, which had caused large-scale damage at over one hundred work sites. The organizers of the demonstration were accused both by the government and rival labor leaders of fomenting class warfare and staging a rehearsal for a proletarian revolution. Nine months later, after the government's economic austerity policies had led to an unprecedented wave of political protest that included virtually every organized sector of Turkish society and urban guerrillas had launched a Tupamaro-type campaign of bank robberies and kidnappings, the General Staff deposed the beleaguered Justice Party government in what many feared was a rehearsal for a Turkish "Eighteenth Brumaire."

During the 1970s, labor continued to disrupt the economy, if not urban life per se. The following figures show the growth in strike activity (Margulies and Yildizoğlu 1984, 18):

| Year | Strikes | Strikers | Days lost |
|------|---------|----------|-----------|
| 1963 | 8       | 1,514    | 19,739    |
| 1970 | 72      | 21,150   | 220,189   |
| 1977 | 59      | 15,628   | 1,397,124 |
| 1980 | 220     | 84,832   | 7,708,750 |

In 1977, the 80,000 members of the Metal Workers Union (Maden-İş) went on strike for eight months.

The combination of political organizations settling accounts with arms and growing labor agitation as the two-party system polarized between the secular and increasingly left-leaning Republican People's party of Bülent Ecevit and the center-right, probusiness Justice party of Suleiman Demirel finds no equivalent anywhere in the Middle East.

Lebanon and Beirut offer the other unique case. When civil war broke out in 1976 many assumed that it would go on only so long as it did not disrupt commerce and banking. That point was reached and passed years ago. Anyone who stayed in Beirut, Tripoli, Sidon, or their immediate hinterlands had to be either armed or in a position to hire protection. As the fighting increased, many businesspeople and much of the intelligentsia left the country. The streets were given over to armed militias, some affiliated to older political parties, such as the Phalanges (Kata'ib), or to the Palestinian resistance, or to the various Shi'ite factions. It is clear that in Lebanon the young men of the slums, the squatter settlements, and the refugee camps have taken over the cities and staked out highly fortified enclaves. The small-scale merchants, traders, craftsmen, and service people who stay on must pay off the local powers, but as money comes in from outside to finance the war, and as it finds its way into the pockets of the militias and their dependents, business can be good.

After twelve years of carnage and fifty or sixty thousand dead, it is hard to discern any more what causes and issues drive the violence. Religion and confessional balances, greater economic equality among religious confessions, the survival or liquidation of the Palestinian refugees, the never-ending need to avenge an avalanche of deaths are all at stake. Power hunger and, by now, habit have transformed Beirut into a city where no central authority holds sway and where violence is the norm and its absence a curiosity. Khalaf believes that pervasive violence has finally produced the reality of Durkheim's anomie (1987, Chap. 11). Years ago a Beirut newspaper published a cartoon of a man on his apartment balcony during a short-lived cease-fire, blasting a submachine gun round into the night sky. His neighbor shouts at him, "What's wrong?" to which he replies, "Oh, nothing much. I just can't seem to get to sleep."

The cities of Iran and Lebanon may point toward the future. Every outbreak of urban violence in the Middle East since the Iranian revolution has had an Islamic component, and in some instances that was the only component. In late 1979 the Great Mosque at Mecca was seized by a heterogeneous group of Saudi fundamentalists and allied pilgrims from all over the Muslim world. It took weeks for Saudi security forces to flush them out. In the summer of 1987, Iranian pilgrims, under instructions from Ayatollah Khomeini, staged demonstrations at Mecca that Saudi security forces confronted with force. Over two hundred demonstrators and policemen were killed.

In January 1980, armed bands, apparently having infiltrated from Libya, briefly seized the Tunisian mining town of Gafsa and proclaimed a set of Islamic revolutionary goals. Since then the Tunisian regime has periodically met militant Islamic groups with force. Neighboring Algeria has dealt ruthlessly with similar challenges, and its cities have been relatively free from Islamic agitation. The riots of the fall of 1988, however, were to some extent led by prominent Muslim spokesmen.

After President Sadat's assassination in October 1981 by Muslim extremists, hundreds of those associated with the plot made their stand in large provincial cities, especially Mansura in the Delta and Assiut in Upper Egypt. In the latter, pitched battles were fought and several hundred were killed. The violence there pales in comparison to the confrontation between Syria's Muslim Brotherhood and its archenemy, the "Alawite" regime of Hafiz al-Assad. The brotherhood, accused of an assassination campaign against Alawite army officers, holed up in the old Sunni city of Hama. President al-Assad ringed the city with artillery and leveled parts of it in order to flush out the brethren. The death toll may have been in the thousands.

We seem to be seeing developments that neither the older vision of violence going hand in hand with massive migration and unemployment nor the more recent vision of the docile shantytowns and perhaps violence-prone second-generation migrants would have predicted. Urban violence now is taking a predominantly religious form. Its organizers, and to some extent its shock troops, are drawn from a particular stratum of the urban population. They tend to be young men, and some women, from provincial cities, who come to large metropolises to pursue higher education. They tend to come from solid families, rather than broken homes, and they have been raised within an Islamic value system. In confronting the big city, they are shocked by the luxury, debauchery, cosmopolitanism, and materialism that these conurbations typically display. The university campuses themselves appear to be venues of uncontrolled mixing of the sexes and centers for the propagation of debased Western mores. These young people are thus a segment of the rural-lower-middle class with professional aspirations (see Chapter 15, in which the "provincials" are discussed more fully) and high religious ideals. They are willing and able to organize small, disciplined groups of followers that infiltrate state agencies, the junior officers corps, and the security forces. Or if they feel that the corrupt state monster cannot be taken from within, they withdraw in small cellular communities, and like the Prophet at Medina, prepare to take society from without (see Ibrahim 1980; Sivan 1985; al-Ansari 1986).

Such leaders and groups do draw on other sectors of the urban society, and, indeed, in Lebanon the slum dwellers appear to have been the shock troops for all the contending factions, be they religious, partisan, or mercenary. These groups will also often enlist the support of militant members of the *'ulema',* who lend the lay militants some doctrinal legitimacy, and they may count on support from a broad spectrum of actors, from well-to-do officers in the armed forces to schoolteachers, clerks, and petty traders.

All the actors that previous theories of urban unrest would have suggested as likely participants are currently present in large numbers on the Middle Eastern urban scene. We believe, however, that the catalysts to their activation will come primarily from the young Muslim activists who have become prominent since the late 1970s. They may capitalize on economic grievances: unemployment, poor living conditions, neglect by the authorities. We also expect that cost-of-living riots, more or less independent of religious instigation, will likely occur in the future as regimes implement austerity programs. Still, these young, provincial, educated migrants to the city, with no sure place in the political and economic systems created by the large, secularizing states of the region, are no epiphenomenon and are here to stay.

By the turn of the century the Middle East will be overwhelmingly urban, and it is likely that in most countries there will be one or more cities with several million inhabitants. These growing urban markets may well drive up the prices of rural produce and thus stimulate agricultural production. That is the good news. The urban populations, however, will bear the brunt of the austerity measures introduced as part of structural adjustment programs. Except for the very rich, all urban dwellers will suffer, but the ones that will feel the pain most acutely will be those on fixed incomes and those with the educational qualifications for middle-class status but for whom appropriate employment will be in increasingly short supply. To some extent managing the national economy and managing the cities will become coterminous.

## NOTES

1. Because these numbers are based on different national definitions of "urban," they are only suggestive of rough orders of magnitude.

2. "Reclassification" means a change of a given village from the "rural" to the "urban" category simply because of the increase in its population.

3. Some examples are Syria, 1.7 (Ghonemy 1984, 26); YAR, 2–4 (World Bank 1979; Commander and Burgess 1988); Egypt 1.7 (Ghonemy 1984); Iran 3.2 (Nattagh 1986); Turkey, 1.5–3.0 (Danielson and Keleş 1980); Tunisia, 2.1 (Ghonemy 1984); Morocco, 2.2 (Ghonemy 1984), Jordan 2.5 (Ghonemy 1984); Sudan, 2.8 (Ghonemy 1984). It is common for the ratio between low-income urban and low-income rural to be at least 2.5 (e.g., Turkey, 2.7 [Derviş and Robinson 1980, 112]).

4. The expected value of moving to the city is given by the formula: $E(v) = PU*YURBAN - PR*YRURAL$, where PU is the probability of finding an urban job, YURBAN is urban income, PR the probability of finding a rural job, and YRURAL is rural income. As long as $E(v)$ is positive, it pays to migrate. Assuming that PR $= 1.0$, we may rewrite the formula as $E(v) = PU*(YURBAN/YRURAL) - 1$. If

the probability of finding a job is 1 − unemployment rate, using the *highest* measured employment rate cited in the text, 75%, implies that as long as urban incomes are even one-third higher than rural incomes, migration would pay.

5. For example, Iran, 14% (Kazemi 1980a, 42); Algeria, 40% (H. Nelson 1985a). Elsewhere, however, the rates seem to be very low: e.g., Egypt, 2% (Hansen 1985).

6. One study estimated that the poorer 44% of Moroccan households spend over 80% of their income on food (USAID 1986, 18); poor Egyptians spend about 60% of their incomes on food (Radwan and Lee 1986, 96).

7. Because food subsidies are also effective in rural areas, this is less true for Egypt than for other countries of the region. See below, and Alderman and von Braun 1984, 37–51. However, during the 1970s the rural price index increased more rapidly than did the urban (Mohie el-Din 1982, 24), a further indication that differences in cost of living did little to offset incentives for cityward migration.

8. This hypothesis divides the labor market into the "primary" market, where the pay and conditions are attractive, job security a function of seniority, and the possibilities of promotion good, and the "secondary" market, with low-paying, dead-end jobs with little or no security or possibilities for advancement (Doeringer and Piore 1970).

9. By contrast, the gap between average rural and urban informal-sector incomes increased slightly during the same period.

10. These are conjectures. We do not have any thorough, in-depth studies of the extent of competition or other aspects of the wage, output price, and employment formation in this sector.

11. This guarantee was gradually suspended in Sudan between 1973 and 1980 (Ghosh 1984).

12. Such employment usually does not show up in official statistics, which means that actual participation in the informal sector is even larger than the estimates given above.

13. For example, the rapid growth of informal-sector trade in the YAR has been plausibly explained as the consequence of the massive volume of remittances there (Meyer 1986).

14. Mumcuoğlu (1980) gave a figure of 15% in 1977. Yet the same article contains data that suggests that about 3 million out of about 5.7 million nonagricultural workers (about 56%) were unionized! Since Turkish workers could belong to more than one union, this figure contains considerable double-counting. Hale gave numbers that suggest that about 35% of the nonfarm labor force was unionized (Hale 1981, 218).

15. It is notable that the number of trade union members (135,700) exceeded the UN estimate of the total number of manufacturing employees in establishments of more than 10 workers.

16. USAID estimated that Moroccan ICOR rose from 3:1 in the early 1970s to 8:1 in the early 1980s. The agency attributed this phenomenon to protectionist, ISI policies and to "poor programming of public investment" (USAID 1986, 20).

17. Such services are only a subset of the informal sector, which also includes small workshops and minifactories.

18. Tunisian public spending on housing fell from TD 137 million in 1986 to TD 91 million in 1987, while Algerian national plans have increased housing investment from DA (Algerian dinars) 60 billion in 1980–1984 to DA 96 billion in 1985–1989 (Economist Intelligent Unit 1987, p. 18; Nelson 1986, 153).

19. For an extensive discussion, see Waterbury 1978.

20. A former governor of Cairo estimated the number at 1 million ten years ago (Waterbury 1978).

21. "At dawn . . . it is not uncommon to see the fog that regularly covers Algiers thickened by the smoke of fires destroying these illegal slum dwellings" (Entellis 1986, 104).

22. The utilitarian theory of justice holds that society should maximize the welfare (utility) of all members of society, weighting all individuals equally. Using income as a proxy for welfare implicitly assumes that there is a constant marginal utility of income. Many social thinkers believe that a declining marginal utility of income is a more reasonable assumption.

23. In a nutshell, this theory holds that society should maximize the welfare of its worst-off member. Rawls (1971) argued that this would be the rational choice of societies' members if they were to choose a distribution rule for society while "behind the veil of ignorance," that is, without knowing where *they* would wind up in the distribution. He argued that since each of us might have the bad luck to be on the bottom, a rational strategy would be to "maximize the minimum," or choose his rule. One might discern similarities with the religious dictum: "There but for the Grace of God go I."

24. For a thorough and rigorous discussion, see Sen (1981a), Chapter 2. All concepts of poverty presented here are the "headcount" measures, which Sen rightly criticized because they do not contain information about "how far below" the poverty line poor peoples' incomes lie. To our knowledge, the only attempt to construct a "Sen Index" (which remedies this problem) for the region is for rural Egypt, by Radwan and Lee (1986).

25. Needless to say, this does *not* imply that current levels of inequality are morally acceptable or "fair" in *any* way!

26. Because the reference standard of the Gini coefficient is so extreme (perfect equality), the number is quite insensitive to changes in distribution, especially in changes in incomes of the poor. For a good textbook discussion of this point, see Gillis et al. 1987.

27. The source does not say how they arrived at these numbers; they should be treated with considerable caution.

28. Countries whose poor fare better than those in Turkey include several that are not noted for their egalitarianism: Indonesia (where the poor get 14.5%), the Philippines (14.1%), Portugal (15.2%), Thailand (15.2%), and El Salvador (15.5%).

29. This estimate, however, is based on figures for electricity consumption, which requires assumptions on the income elasticity of demand for electricity.

30. The figures were 64%, urban; 29%, rural. However, it is very difficult to believe these urban numbers, in view of the presence of a food-subsidy system.

31. The percentage of the agricultural population that was poor rose from 42% in 1978 to 51% in 1983 (Celasun 1986).

32. Egypt is the only country with effective food subsidies in the rural areas.

33. Indeed, such a figure is difficult to believe. But it is likely that the poorest Moroccans spend about two-thirds of their income on food.

34. It is often asserted that the price of bread is so low that it is wasted, being fed to chickens or other animals. However, Alderman and von Braun's careful study of Egypt found that only about 5% of bread distributed is fed to animals (1984).

35. Recent research has shown that this happened in Sri Lanka. The austerity-induced shift to a food-stamp program in 1978 led to a reduction in food consumption by the poorest 25% of Sri Lankans (Edirisinghe 1987).

36. In fact, subsidies for energy place a far greater burden on the Egyptian economy than do food subsidies (de Thier 1987).

37. If rural dissidents happen to be in a position to control a strategic resource, as is the case for Iraq's Kurds in that country's oil-bearing region and for the southern Sudanese, who could control both the head of the White Nile and the country's major oil deposits, then the countryside can match the cities in arousing the concern of the government.

# 11

# POLITICAL REGIMES: AS THEY ARE AND AS THEY VIEW THEMSELVES

We are on treacherous ground, but in good company, when we try to label the political regimes of the Middle East (inter alia, Binder 1957; Hudson 1977). *Regime* refers not only to a type of government but also to ideology, rules of the game, and the structuring of the polity in a given nation. *Regime change* is no mere changing of the guard or cleaning out city hall; it is, rather, profound structural change in all forms of political activity. Regime change may be revolutionary, as in the violent shift from a monarchical to a republican regime in France in 1789 or from Pahlavi dynastic rule to the Islamic republic (some would say "theocracy") in Iran in 1979. Regime change may, however, be relatively peaceful and incremental. Turkey moved between 1946 and 1950 from a single-party, authoritarian regime to a two-party system with openly contested elections. Egypt has been creeping hesitantly since 1971 from Nasser's single-party, authoritarian, and socialist regime toward a more liberal, multiparty system in which private economic interests have come to play a legitimate role. Hinnebusch (1985) has characterized the Nasserist regime as "authoritarian-populist" and Sadat's as "post-populist authoritarian-conservative."

There is no dearth of cumbersome labels for Middle Eastern regimes, and both their number and terminological complexity testify to the difficulties observers encounter in making coherent generalizations about the nature of regimes. There are a number of pitfalls into which one easily stumbles. The first one is that in the Middle East, not without reason, we tend to personalize regimes, equating or confusing them with their founders. We talk of the Nasserist, Kemalist (Atatürk), or Bourguibist systems as if to say, "le régime c'est moi!" Doubtless for these giant figures there is a good deal of truth in equating their systems to their personae. Waterbury (1983) argued that the death of Nasser in 1970 in itself signaled the end of a regime and necessarily set the stage for a new one. But it is an abuse of the term *regime* and of empirical reality to succumb to the temptation to see all leadership changes as constituting regime changes. Constant and violent power struggles within the Ba'ath hierarchy in Syria and Iraq since the mid-1960s have not constituted regime changes. The triumph of the more managerial Hafiz al-Assad over the more populist Salah Jadid in Syria in 1970, or the eclipse of Ahmad Hassan al-Bakr in the face of Saddam Hussein in Iraq were only in-house power shifts, which did not significantly alter the nature of the Ba'athi-military regimes of those two countries.

A second pitfall is taxonomic; we tend to classify regimes merely by describing what they appear to be doing at a given point in time. Rather than capture the essence of the process of regime formation, consolidation, and decay—that is, classifying by understanding the *dynamics* of regimes— we say regime X is "authoritarian-socialist," or "radical Islamic," or "patriarchal-conservative." Now that public-sector enterprises are everywhere being compared unfavorably to those of the private sector, and now that there is considerable talk of putting the former on the auction block, at least one scholar is using the term "authoritarian-privatizing regimes." In this way there is a tendency for each regime to become its own type, and if the regime changes, a new type must be invented to describe it. All one needs to do is summarize what the new regime does in a new hyphenated label. The reader can play the game to her or his heart's content.

One must be on the lookout for a third pitfall. One way to avoid superficial and descriptive labeling is to focus on the dynamics of social and economic change within societies and how they are or are not reflected in the nature of the regime. We then may be able to see the extent to which regime change is the product of social and economic change. For instance, in 1962 there was an abrupt regime change in North Yemen. The quasi-medieval theocracy known as the Imamate was overthrown through a military coup d'état and a socialist republic proclaimed. Legally, a profound change had occurred, but Yemeni society had scarcely changed at all. Even to the present time, the republican regime has not restructured the Yemeni polity or the political rules of the game. By contrast, one could argue that the downfall of the shah of Iran in 1979 and the proclamation of the Islamic republic came as the result of rapid and profound social change in Iran in the 1960s and 1970s. The large cohorts of literate, urban, upwardly mobile Iranians that the shah's own educational system had spewed forth could no longer be contained within the paternalistic, authoritarian, and repressive regime the shah had inherited from his father. While an Islamic republic was surely not the only possible regime alternative to the shah, and while the shah's downfall itself was not inevitable, Iranian society was clearly ready for some profound restructuring of the polity.

We have, in our discussion of public sectors in Chapters 7 and 8, classified regimes in part according to how they manage publicly owned assets. The three major categories are (1) regimes that use these assets to generate surplus for further state expansion at the expense of the private sector, (2) those that use assets to act as a handmaiden to private entrepreneurs, and (3) those that seek to transfer public assets to private hands. We tried to delimit the major factors leading given regimes into one or another of these modes as well as the likely consequences of their adoption. In what follows, we extend the analysis to the major policy domains of the region's regimes in order to move beyond descriptive understandings of their dynamics.

## SOCIALIST REPUBLICS

Of all the regime types that have characterized the Middle East since World War II, the most prevalent have been the socialist republics. As was the case for economic growth strategies and state intervention in the economy, the Turkish republic of the 1920s and 1930s, although never espousing socialism, was the forerunner and the model for several regional neighbors. Egypt, Syria, Iraq, North Yemen, the Sudan, Tunisia, and Algeria have all replicated to some extent the Turkish model. One should also include Qaddhafi's "mass state" in Libya and the Marxist regime in South Yemen. Not only are these regimes numerically dominant, but they have also demonstrated considerable longevity:

Egypt: 1952–present (with a significant regime transformation beginning in 1971)
Syria: 1963–present
Iraq: 1963–present
Algeria: 1962–present
Sudan: 1958–1964 and 1969–1985
North Yemen: 1962–present
Tunisia: 1956–present
Libya: 1969–present
South Yemen: 1968–present

The interwar experience of Atatürk's Turkey set the main themes and gave them real meaning in the construction of the Turkish polity. The quest for independence and national sovereignty, the ability to stand up to the great powers, was seen as rooted in a strong industrial economy and a cohesive citizenry. Former Ottoman *subjects* had to become proud Turkish *citizens,* educated, enlightened, unburdened of the fetters of religious obscurantism, hardworking, and patriotic. Atatürk was a practitioner of nation-building, a term that was to come into vogue in Western modernization literature (e.g., Deutsch and Foltz 1966; Emerson 1960) long after Atatürk's death.

Nationalism, etatism, republicanism, revolutionism, populism, and secularism were the watchwords of the Turkish experiment. The 600-year-old Ottoman Empire and the Islamic caliphacy were ended in 1923. Atatürk and his lieutenants, inspired by the writings of Ziya Gökalp, himself inspired by Emile Durkheim's *The Human Division of Labor,* sought a society in which all class conflict and parochial loyalties were suborned to citizens' functional or occupational roles. "Solidarism," i.e., the building of an integrated, conflict-free society, characterized an outlook that spread throughout the Middle East. Religion was to be the affair of individuals, not of the state, which would remain resolutely secular and rationalist, especially in the education it dispensed through the public school system. The political guarantor of the nation's integration was to be a single party, to mobilize the citizenry rather than to compete for power against other parties, which, in any case, were only sporadically tolerated. The Republican People's party, while the creation of the regime, became an important organization in its own right.

As we have already pointed out, the Turkish experiment put the state center-stage. This was to be an activist, interventionist state, rather than a set of agencies and bureaucracies over which political factions fought for control. Together with the military, the Turkish state rose above society and sought to reshape it in the image that Atatürk and his lieutenants thought desirable (see Trimberger 1978). This was a state with a purpose and with goals—to build a modern nation and modern Turkish citizens. The hurly-burly of electoral politics, the unfettered expression of political differences, or, worse yet, the outbreak of class conflict could, it was believed, only deflect the state from its lofty purpose.

This understanding of the proper role of the state and of the uses of public power spread throughout the Middle East in the post–World War II era and was at the heart of the socialist republican experiments. The late Malcolm Kerr, in a powerful essay on Arab radical notions of democracy (1963, 10–11), wrote that this radicalism was

> characterized by a moral preference—not just a tactical preference—for maintaining the maximum degree of unity of purpose and action at all political and social levels, by an emphasis upon the virtues of group solidarity and the evils of individual self-absorption and self-seeking, by a mistrust of competition, bargaining and the promotion of special interests; and by a vision of strong government as a liberator rather than a danger to liberty.

Much the same argument, under the rubric of "organic statism," has been advanced by Stepan (1978) for Latin American states. Stepan saw organic statism as arising out of the heritage of Roman law and the history of the Catholic church. He thought it unlikely that organic statism would find many echoes in the Middle East, but Kerr, writing twenty years before Stepan, noted that the Islamic reformists of the early twentieth century (principally Egypt's Muhammed 'Abduh) had originated from the first attempts to organize the Muslim community as a "morally purposeful society," under one leader (the caliph), sharing a common interest in service to God, under a single law (the *shari'a*), which assured the moral and political solidarity of all members. In this conceptualization "power is good or bad according to the righteousness of its possessor" (Kerr 1963, 10).

Atatürk tried to redefine the purpose and to strip it of its religious underpinnings, but the morally purposeful state was still the linchpin of his nation-building. Many other Middle Easterners, while seeing much to admire in republican Turkey, were disturbed, indeed often shocked, by Atatürk's vehement secularism. Tunisia's Habib Bourguiba, among the Arabs, came closest to emulating Atatürk's ideas and practices, but few other Arab leaders dared try to separate national from religious identity, or to separate "church" from state.

We may note now, in anticipation of discussion yet to come, that the strengthening of Islamic challenges to many of the existing Middle Eastern states can be seen in large measure as stemming from the conviction that these states have failed in their mission. Some Muslim activists believe that the republican socialist mission was misconceived, if not blasphemous. Atatürk, for many pious Muslims, is the century's greatest villain, the man who ended the caliphacy and separated the Turkish state from serving the community of Muslim believers (the *umma*). What Islamic radicals seek is to put the state, once again, to its God-given purposes of promoting the unity and strength of the *umma*. There is, thus, conflict over state purposes, but no conflict over the belief that power used for the right purposes should be unchecked and unbalanced.

## Nasserist and Bourguibist Variants

In July 1952 a group of Egyptian officers of the rank of colonel or below seized power and ended the monarchical rule of the descendants of the old Ottoman governor in Egypt, Muhammed Ali (1804–1841). A republic was soon proclaimed, and a respected senior officer, Gen. Muhammed Naguib, was made its president. All existing political parties were abolished in 1953, and in 1954, the Muslim Brotherhood (al-Ikhwan al-Muslimun), while not legally a party, was abolished after one of its members attempted to assassinate Col. Gamal 'Abd al-Nasser. Having swept the political arena clean, the new regime sought to build its own monopoly political organization from the top down. It was called the Liberation Rally, and a good deal of its founders' programmatic priorities are embodied in its slogan, Unity, Discipline, and Work. With the parties and politicians who had lived on factionalism and debilitating partisan conflict out of the way, the new leaders hoped the populace would close ranks, put its shoulder to the wheel, and, led by the armed forces, the embodiment of the nation's will to survive, stand up to the imperialist powers.

In these early years the talk was much more of revolution than of socialism. It was only after 1956 and the acquisition of extensive economic assets taken over from the British and the French (see Chapter 7) that a socialist ideology gradually took shape. But whatever Nasser's understanding of socialism, he was always clear about the need for unity and solidarity. Egypt's second monopoly party, founded in 1957, was called the National

Union. As he was to say frequently thereafter, Nasser stated that it was not a party because parties mean partisanship and partisanship means dividing the body politic and that would not be tolerated. The National Union, rather, was an assembly of all the nation, the organizational manifestation of its unity of purpose.

After the abrupt nationalizations of 1961, the regime committed itself to socialism and the building of yet another monopoly party, the Arab Socialist Union (ASU). Nasser's goal was to use this party to extend Egyptian influence throughout the Arab world. Within Egypt it tried to organize the citizenry along functional lines. There were five broad categories—the peasants, the workers, the intellectuals and professionals, the national capitalists, and the troops—bound up in what was called the Alliance of Working Forces. One of the objectives of the socialist revolution and the Arab Socialist Union was to achieve "the melting away of class differences." As in Atatürk's Turkey, the rhetorical emphasis was on unity, cohesion, devotion to the national cause as defined by the state, and the peaceful resolution of class differences by the redistribution of national wealth through state policies. A unified Egypt would carry the socialist revolution to the rest of the Arab world, and greater Arab and socialist solidarity would protect the region from the forces of neo-imperialism and from Zionism. Reality and rhetoric did not mesh very often in Egypt or elsewhere, but we are concerned here with trying to capture the spirit of the experiment.

The origins of the Bourguibist and Destourian regime in Tunisia were far different from those of Nasserist Egypt. Habib Bourguiba, a young lawyer from Monastir in Tunisia, captured the nationalist movement of that country from an older generation of leaders and in 1934 founded a mass-based party, the Neo-Destour (the New Constitution party). The party came to mobilize organized labor, white-collar professionals, the intelligentsia, and provincial merchants and commercial farmers into a powerful coalition. The Neo-Destour helped win independence from the French in 1956, and Habib Bourguiba served as president for thirty-one years until he was deposed in the fall of 1987.

Bourguiba had all Atatürk's instincts; his project for Tunisia was republican (he ended the old quasi-monarchical institution of the dey), secular, populist, and, more than Atatürk, imbued with a kind of French rationalist vision of the state that was Napoleonic in spirit. Socialism was not initially part of the project, but redistributive policies certainly were. In 1964, however, Tunisia entered a short-lived socialist era. The Neo-Destour party became the Socialist Destour, and the new minister of planning, Ahmed Ben Salah, formulated a state-led plan for the formation of agricultural cooperatives and public-sector industrialization. Egypt to the east and Algeria on Tunisia's western border were ostentatiously promoting similar socialist experiments, and Bourguiba may have felt compelled to join the bandwagon.

The experiment, having been implemented too rapidly, raised considerable opposition within Bourguiba's old coalition, especially among provincial merchants and capitalist farmers. In 1970, Ben Salah was dismissed and eventually jailed. The socialist experiment was ended, but all other aspects of the Bourguibist state were continued. It must be stressed that Bourguibism, while similar to Atatürkism, differed in one major respect—it was resolutely nonmilitarist. Bourguiba always argued that Tunisia could never be a credible military power and that he would not condone the building of a large military establishment that would only consume unwarranted amounts of scarce investment and perhaps thrust Tunisia into the cycles of military intervention in politics that have plagued the rest of the Middle East.[1] Tunisia would have to use diplomatic skill rather than military power to defend its independence.

Twenty years after independence most observers saw Tunisia as one of the best organized polities in the Arab world. Hudson compared Arab regimes in terms of three levels of political legitimacy. The first, personal legitimacy, refers to leaders who enjoy the support and respect of their populations but who may not be able to transfer their own legitimacy to the programs and institutions they have sought to develop. The second type of legitimacy is ideological, whereby citizens respect a regime's professed ideology and principles but not necessarily its leaders, who may fail to honor those same principles. Finally, there is structural legitimacy, whereby citizens respect and accept the rules of the political game, the programs of the government, and the way in which goods are distributed in society. In Hudson's view, Bourguiba and the Tunisian regime enjoyed legitimacy along all three dimensions and in that sense were probably unique in the Arab world. In 1977 Hudson wrote: "Tunisia may be considered as perhaps the most politically modern of the revolutionary Arab states, in terms of secularism, rationality, and institutionalized participation. Certainly it has been one of the most stable" (1977, 378).

Yet even as Hudson wrote, he noted that in 1975 the National Assembly proclaimed Bourguiba President for Life. The proclamation foretold a breakdown in the rationality of the regime, the reenforcement of the cult of the indispensable leader, a violation of the ideal of meritocracy and political accountability. Like Atatürk before him, the leader (the *za'im,* as such power figures are known in the Arab world) apparently did not trust the citizens (that the new rationalized political system was to create) to choose or change their leaders. For all their emphasis on national unity and purpose, the leaders of the socialist republics never leave office voluntarily. Atatürk and Nasser died in harness and Bourguiba, in his 80s and increasingly senile, was ushered into retirement by General Zine al-Abdine, the man he had appointed minister of defense. None of these leaders could accept the full political logic of the systems they sought to build.

With age and physical decline, Bourguiba became more and more manipulable by figures in his entourage. There were, in the 1980s, occasional flashes of his old political skills, but the modernizing presidency became increasingly the focal point of intrigue and personal vendettas, as if Tunisia had tired of the French model of the state and had resurrected the Ottoman seraglio. In June 1986, at the congress of the Socialist Destour, Bourguiba simply appointed a new central committee, a body supposedly elected by party members, and dismissed the careful and unflamboyant Prime Minister Muhammed Mzali, a man who had been seen as Bourguiba's successor. Mzali, it is said, had differed with the president over the conversion of the educational system to the use of Arabic, and many felt that he had mishandled the internal-security situation, but as important in his downfall were purely personalistic factors. It was well known that Bourguiba's niece Saida Sassi (herself 60 years old) was settling a personal score against all the protégés of the president's estranged wife, Wassila Bourguiba, who had been a power broker in her own right. Mzali was one such protégé and, with Wassila in the United States, had lost his protector. Most Tunisians clearly hope that the country's new leadership will be able to restore some of the political coherence of the first decade of independence.

The Sudan and North Yemen have witnessed regimes in the past twenty-five years that were to some extent Nasserist in their structures and programs. But the societies onto which these regimes were imposed were and are very much different from that of Egypt or Tunisia, let alone Turkey. North Yemen is a still-tribal society, with backward agriculture and very little industry. The society is, as well, divided between the mainly Shi'ite tribesmen, from whom the former Imams were drawn, and urban Sunni Muslims, from whom many members of the modern Yemeni officers corps have been drawn. Sunni officers seized power from the Imam in 1962, proclaimed a republic, and reached out to Nasser's Egypt for support. Shi'ite tribes did not accept the new regime and looked to Saudi Arabia to help restore the Imamate (note that the Saudi monarchy is organically linked to Wahhabite Sunni Islam but, in the face of socialist republicanism, willing to support a Shi'ite royalist cause). Five years of civil war ensued, in which a large Egyptian expeditionary force found itself incapable of subduing the tribes in their mountainous home territories.

The Egyptian expeditionary force was withdrawn at the time of the June War of 1967, and the contending Yemeni factions reached a fragile modus vivendi that preserved the republic but reintegrated royalist leaders into positions of power. A succession of Yemeni army officers have governed the country ever since, and their comings and goings have often been bloody. What we now see in North Yemen is a peculiar hybrid regime—a military presidential structure, authoritarian and vaguely socialist in intent, living uneasily with a still largely rural society, peopled with colorful tribal leaders and warriors festooned with cartridge belts, traditional Yemeni daggers, and submachine guns galavanting about the countryside on Suzuki motorcycles. The economy depends on workers' remittances and international assistance. The most lucrative agricultural product of the country is a mildly narcotic shrub whose leaves (*qat*) are chewed assiduously by most Yemenis. Rapid urbanization and spreading education may provide a more fertile ground for "modernizing" military leaders, but they could just as easily yield a generation of Muslim radicals. Then the questions would be whether the radicals were predominantly Sunni or Shi'i and whether or not that cleavage would paralyze them. In any event, trying to invent an apt label for the North Yemeni regime is a futile endeavor.

The Sudan, the largest country in Africa in surface area (Algeria is second) is also one of the continent's poorest. Like North Yemen, the Sudan is still overwhelmingly rural and agricultural, with its 25 million inhabitants scattered over a territory the size of the United States east of the Mississippi. One-third of the population, living in the southern region of the Sudan, consists of black Nilotics who for the most part are neither Muslim nor Arabic-speakers, while the other two-thirds are of mixed Arab stock, Sunni Muslims, and speak Arabic.

In 1958, only two years after independence, a military regime was established under the leadership of Gen. Muhammed Abboud. Bearing some resemblance to the Nasserist regime in neighboring Egypt, it put an end to a multiparty system that had ineffectively governed the country between 1956 and 1958. The regime emphasized themes of national unity and solidarity and tried to deal militarily with dissidence among the southern populations. It drew up a national economic plan and promoted state industries.

The growing war in the south was the principal cause of the downfall of the Abboud regime in 1964. For five years civilian parties and politicians, organized around the country's two major Muslim brotherhoods (the Ansar and the Khatmiya), sought to construct a liberal political system and to bring an end to the fighting in the south. Failing on the second count, they crippled their liberal experiment.

In May 1969 Col. Ga'afar al-Nimeiri seized power and established a regime that was explicitly Nasserist. A few months later Mu'ammar Qaddhafi established a similar regime in Libya. Both Nimeiri and Qaddhafi looked to Nasser as a revered leader, as a source of inspiration for their own experiments, and ultimately, as a protector who could come to their rescue if need be. Nasser died only a year after the two young officers had come to power.

Al-Nimeiri, in his first two years, dealt with the religious power centers in the Sudan, taking on the Ansar militarily, dispersing their adherents, driving their leaders into exile, and seizing their rural properties. He then turned on Marxist supporters in his government and, in a bloody sequence of coup and countercoup in July 1970, physically eliminated several prominent Marxists and Communists. Like Nasser in 1953, Nimeiri had cleared the political arena and into it he cast the Sudanese Socialist Union, yet another "alliance of working forces," derived directly from Egypt's Arab Socialist Union. Central planning was resurrected, and there was a great surge in the funding of public-sector industries. Most important, al-Nimeiri negotiated an end to the fighting in the south and granted local autonomy to the three southern provinces.

But Sudanese society neither was ready for republican socialism nor easily tolerated the authoritarian politics of young army officers. As in

Yemen, traditional loyalties to brotherhoods and religious leaders and to regions and tribes were very much alive, and al-Nimeiri eventually was absorbed in elaborate games of patronage, payoffs, and balancing rivals, games that sapped the regime of much of its socialist energy. These games were interspersed with a half dozen attempted coups, the frequency of which may have driven al-Nimeiri deeper into drink, the only habit he shared with Atatürk, and into corruption. Although only half Bourguiba's age, al-Nimeiri lost the logic of his political project and succumbed to the intrigue of his own seraglio. He probably never enjoyed much legitimacy of any sort; he was personally uncharismatic, his ideology was muddled and unconvincing, a blind imitation of Egypt's, and his political and economic structures were flimsy, never taking root in the society. His one achievement, ending the civil war in the south, was undone by his penchant for divide and rule, which eventually alienated his own supporters among the southern populations.

In the early 1980s al-Nimeiri became a kind of "born-again" Muslim. He threatened to apply *shari'a* law throughout the country, including the non-Muslim south. By 1983 the south was again in full revolt, led by John Garang. In the north, al-Nimeiri combined a ferocious Muslim piety with a vast spoils system by which his civilian and military cronies pilfered the public purse. The Sudanese intelligentsia and uncorrupted elements of the armed forces overthrew al-Nimeiri in March 1985. A fragile civilian regime has been reestablished, while the civil war in the south continues to rage on. Al-Nimeiri ruled sixteen years, exactly as long as Nasser, but at the end of the period he had left virtually nothing of his experiment behind.

### Radical Socialist Variants

Turkey, Egypt, and Tunisia developed their socialism hesitantly, if at all, and their socialist experiments were short-lived. Egypt for a brief period in the early 1960s espoused "scientific socialism," with a fairly explicit Marxist content, but more conservative forces in Egyptian society advocated "Arab socialism," which presumably eschewed class conflict and anything smacking of atheism (see Mahfouz 1972). In 1971 Bourguiba enunciated an understanding of socialism that probably was and is shared by a number of other regimes (as cited in Entelis 1980, 156):

> In our eyes socialism is neither a philosophical belief nor an uncompromising social doctrine. It is not an end in itself. It is a means of achieving a precise objective, namely development. . . . By definition our socialism is distinguished from other socialisms by three fundamental aspects: (1) it rejects the class struggle, (2) Government seeks to control and direct rather than eliminate private or collective property; finally, (3) we do not believe it necessary to sacrifice the present generation to guarantee the well-being of future ones.

Socialism thus meant attention to equity and distributive issues, public ownership of some means of production, the acceptance of private property, and the drive for development, i.e., the mission of the purposeful state. It did not mean indoctrination, the moral and spiritual reshaping of humans, or the assumption that social action necessarily be organized along class lines. It certainly did not mean the dictatorship of the proletariat or even the direct control of publicly owned enterprises by the workers themselves.

By and large, all Middle Eastern socialist regimes, except the People's Democratic Republic of Yemen, adopted similar outlooks. What makes some regimes more radical than others has generally hinged on their conduct of foreign policy rather than their domestic politics. Thus the regimes of Algeria, Syria, and Iraq in the 1970s and 1980s had come, de facto, to positions similar to Bourguiba's, but all three were aggressively anti-imperialist, too friendly with the USSR to suit the United States, and, significantly, bogged down in foreign adventures: Algeria in the Saharan war with Morocco; Iraq in the large-scale hostilities with Iran; and Syria in the Lebanese cockpit.

That Algeria is not more revolutionary and radical than it is, is something of a surprise. Algerian socialism and its organizational underpinning, the National Liberation Front, were shaped in eight years of brutal warfare with France between 1954 and 1962. The FLN at the time of independence was not a top-down party like the Arab Socialist or the Sudanese Socialist unions. Like the Neo-Destour, it had come out of the crucible of nationalist struggle, but in Algeria that struggle had been violent and prolonged. Some believed that once independence had been won, the FLN would lead Algeria down a Marxist-Leninist path similar to Cuba's.

Organizationally and in terms of its leadership, the FLN was a heterodox coalition of all the major participants in the war for liberation. Its secular, socialist, and even Marxist image was owed to the young intellectuals who had constituted its "external team" and who had made the Algerian cause known throughout the world. Their radical views were embodied in the two fundamental documents of the revolution, the Tripoli Program of 1962 and the Charter of Algiers of 1964. Algeria's first president, Ahmad Ben Bella, was not unsympathetic to their views. In the early years of independence the radicals were able to promote worker self-management (with Yugoslav advice) on agricultural land taken over from departing Europeans and in abandoned or nationalized factories. Algeria also became a major voice in the Non-Aligned Movement and identified strongly with Palestinians, the African National Congress of South Africa, and liberation fronts in Vietnam, Angola, and Mozambique.

But alongside the articulate and cosmopolitan radical intelligentsia were other major forces, far less committed to radical transformation of Algerian society. The guerrilla fighters were mainly mountain and steppe Berbers, fervent nationalists and pious Muslims, eager for their share of the spoils of victory, but by no means doctrinaire socialists. Indeed they had always been suspicious of and hostile toward the citified and seemingly atheist intellectuals.

The guerrillas (*mujahidin*) did not have a monopoly of arms in independent Algeria. The major armed forces were large professional armies that had been trained and billeted in Tunisia and Morocco in the final years of the war, although they saw little action. Their principal spokesman was Houari Boumedienne, the first minister of defense and the man who would seize power from Ahmad Ben Bella in June 1965. Boumedienne was a graduate of Egypt's major center of Islamic learning, al-Azhar. He had little sympathy for Ben Bella's secular socialist allies or for the ragtag bands of guerrillas that had born the brunt of the fighting.

Boumedienne's seizure of power ushered in an era that was in many ways Nasserist. The new president, like Atatürk, Nasser, and Bourguiba, was obsessed with rational and orderly national development. He liked good organization and good management, and as we saw in Chapter 7, he launched Algeria onto the path of state-led heavy industrialization. The era of romantic socialism and strident internationalism ended; the era of the planner and the technocrat began.

The FLN, while enjoying a legal monopoly within the political arena, was increasingly marginalized under Boumedienne (Leca 1975; Roberts 1984). It was no longer to be an instrument of mass mobilization but rather, like the ASU in Egypt, an instrument to control Algerians while the state marshaled the nation's resources for the development effort.

Real power passed to the armed forces and the bureaucracy. In the absence of a national parliament and a permanent constitution, the supreme authority in the country was the National Council of the Algerian Revolution (CNRA). Typical of the secretiveness of Boumedienne, the full membership of the CNRA was not made public. Several of the members came from the so-called Oujda Group, that is, military associates who had been with Boumedienne in Oujda, Morocco, during the revolution and when the first units of the Army of National Liberation were being trained.

Few, if any, Middle Eastern regimes had ever so divorced themselves from their mass base, or so discouraged popular participation, as Algeria's. Boumedienne himself was a private, dour man who never sought popular acclaim. Yet ironically, toward the last years of his regime, it could be said that Boumedienne, his statist, technocratic socialism, and his efforts to remake the Algerian economy all enjoyed considerable legitimacy.

That legitimacy was not unmitigated. In 1976 the regime organized debates in all sectors of society to formulate a new National Charter. Sharp criticism of corrupt officials and heavy bureaucratic procedures poured forth. After this letting off of steam, the National Charter was approved. Notably, it talked of Algerian socialism consisting in a transclass alliance. The idea of internal class struggle was downplayed, while that of Algeria as a "proletarian" state struggling against the forces of imperialism was emphasized (Nellis 1983, 372). With that the regime went back to business as usual until the death of Boumedienne in 1978. He was succeeded by another member of the Oujda Group, Chadli Benjadid, who has encouraged some economic liberalization but has not made the regime any more accountable to the Algerian citizenry.

Since 1963 Iraq and Syria have been ruled by national branches of the same party, the Ba'ath or Arab Renaissance party. There are many ironies

in the history of the Ba'ath. It was founded after World War II by two
French-educated schoolteachers from Syria: Michel Aflaq (Greek Orthodox)
and Salah Bitar (Sunni Muslim). Its mission was to capture power somewhere
in the Arab world and then to work for Arab and socialist unity among
all Arab states. The ironies are that in the 1960s the Ba'ath contested
Nasser's Arab Socialist Union for preeminence among the region's youth.
Between them, Nasserists and Ba'athists divided the Arab world. The enmity
between Nasserists and Ba'athists took a violent turn in Iraq in 1959, but
it was eclipsed by the rivalry that developed between Ba'athist Syria and
Iraq after 1968. It is hard for the outsider to discern any profound doctrinal
differences between the two regimes, and one suspects that older geopolitical rivalries between two states sharing the Euphrates Basin may have
as much to do with the enmity as anything else.

The structure of both regimes is rather similar. While civilians built
the party in both countries (Aflaq and Bitar in Syria, and the Shi'ite civil
servant Fu'ad Rikabi in Iraq), they were tempted to recruit supporters
among the officers corps in both countries and seek power by means of
coup d'état rather than the ballot. Unlike the Neo-Destour, which fought
openly for Tunisian independence, the Ba'ath won power through stealth.
Its popular base of support in both Syria and Iraq has always been narrow.
In Iraq around 1980 the Ba'ath had only 25,000 full members although
there were 1.5 million "supporters" (Helms 1984, 87). Hinnebusch (1979,
21) put party membership in Syria at 100,000 in the mid-1970s. The Ba'ath
has always followed a Leninist predilection for a vanguard rather than a
mass-based party.

The military allies of the Ba'ath have tended to take it over and marginalize
it much as Boumedienne did to the FLN in Algeria after 1965. In Iraq
there is the Revolutionary Command Council (RCC), which groups the
major military figures of the regime and, like Algeria's CNRA, is the real
locus of decisionmaking. Alongside it is the Ba'ath Regional Command
(the Iraqi branch of the Ba'ath), whose membership is quite similar to
that of the RCC. Finally there is the National Command, supposedly the
heart of the pan-Arab organization and of which Michel Aflaq (d. 1989),
at odds with his native Syria, was the titular head. The National Command
has no power at all.

The structures of the Syrian Ba'ath are not greatly different. The military
retain effective power but use the Ba'ath party to legitimize their preeminence. In February 1971, President Hafiz al-Assad, an air force officer, was
reappointed to his position by a body called the People's Council. The
council had itself been appointed by the Ba'ath Regional Command and
included 173 Ba'athis, 40 Nasserists, and 8 Communists. Assad clearly
wanted to portray himself as president of *all* Syrians, not just Ba'athi
Syrians.

Both the Iraqi and Syrian politico-miliary elites tend to be drawn from
regional and sectarian minorities. In Syria, Assad, many of his closest
associates, and a number of those upon whom he trampled before and

since seizing power in 1970 have been drawn from the Alawite religious sect, an offshoot of Shi'ism, and from the poor hinterland of the Latakia region. As Hinnebusch noted (1979, 17), "The Ba'ath recruited from all those who were outside the system of connections, patronage or kin on which the old regime was built: the educated sons of peasants, the minorities, the rural lower middle class, the 'black sheep' from lesser branches of great families." The wearing of the Ba'athi label and the espousal of Ba'athi socialism has not been enough to persuade many (mostly Sunni) Syrians that Assad's regime is other than a clan of power-hungry Shi'ites masquerading as socialists. Still Assad has reached out to Sunnis, and their presence in the Ba'ath has been growing. The party is well organized and pervasive; it is not a paper organization like the Sudanese Socialist Union. Sadowski probably had it right in this assessment (1985, 3): "Twenty-two years in power have changed the Ba'ath from a revolutionary movement into a virtual appendage of the state. But this transformation did not destroy the party's influence. Along with the army and the bureaucracy, it remains one of the foundations of the Assad regime."

The Ba'ath came briefly to power in Iraq in the winter of 1963, on the shoulders of the military, and was moved out by a "palace" coup led by Abd al-Salam 'Arif, a Nasserist of sorts, who sought close relations with Egypt. An agreement with Egypt of May 1964 provided for a loose form of union between the two countries and for the setting up in Iraq of the "Arab Socialist Union–Iraqi Region." Egypt had temporarily won Iraq from the Ba'ath. In terms of domestic policy, however, there was little to choose between Nasserists and Ba'athists. 'Arif's nationalization of over thirty industrial firms in May 1964 would have fit easily into a Ba'athi program, as would all other aspects of his state-led growth (see Gotheil 1981; Penrose and Penrose 1978; Springborg 1981).

The June War of 1967, in which the Iraqi armed forces played no significant role, may have undermined whatever legitimacy the 'Arif regime still enjoyed. In July 1968 the Ba'ath came to power once again through a military coup. Iraq's new president was Gen. Ahmad Hassan al-Bakr, but the real power of the regime lay with the prime minister, Saddam Hussein, a Ba'athi militant since his student days and a hardened veteran of the nation's internal police. Few Middle Eastern leaders have ever had as much experience with "dirty tricks" as Saddam Hussein.

Both Hussein and al-Bakr, along with several other stalwarts of the new regime, were from central Iraq, especially the provincial town of Takrit. Iraq's new masters were bound by shared blood, their home region, and the fact that they were Arab Sunni Muslims. The Takriti clan in Iraq has become the functional equivalent of the Alawite clan in Syria. There has been bloodletting among Takritis but not rivaling the violence wreaked on Shi'ite fundamentalists, Kurdish dissidents, and any others foolish enough to challenge Saddam Hussein. When al-Bakr died in 1982, Hussein, in the midst of the war he had launched against Iran, became president. He has nurtured a cult of his own personality that is unparalleled in the Middle East.

His state, like Assad's, rests on the pillars of the armed forces, the internal police, the bureaucracy, the party, and his clan. Iraq's ideology has no more teeth to it than Tunisia's. Batatu has dismissed the 1968 Ba'ath party constitution as formulating "a mild form of middle-class socialism." It tries to combine acknowledgment of Islam and pan-Arabism with the ideals of social justice, the end of exploitation, the right to use private property subject to state regulation, and "a guided national economy based on the cooperation of the public and private sectors" (Batatu 1978, 1,084).

Both Ba'athist regimes have redistributed income, promoted growth, spread literacy, and in general have improved the economic lot of their citizens. The two leaders, in spite of, or because of, their foreign adventures, appear to enjoy some popular support. Neither regime has opened any avenues for political participation or accountability. It may be true that the full members of the Ba'ath have considerable influence at the local level, but they are but a tiny fraction of the adult population (see Helms 1984, 91).

It is difficult to know if Ba'athi ideology enjoys much legitimacy, but, as Batatu suggested, it may be so amorphous as to threaten no one. Those who do not accept the legitimacy of these regimes and their leaders are Sunni Muslim fundamentalists in Syria and Shi'ite fundamentalists in Iraq, the Kurdish dissidents in Iraq, and remnants of the commercial bourgeoisie in both countries. Corruption and the crushing costs of war may take their toll of regime legitimacy. Let us not forget that both regimes were born and have survived through conspiracy supplemented by police repression (see Mullen 1984). The word *trust* seems totally absent from the Syrian and Iraqi political lexicons. The utopian vision of Arab socialist unity that Aflaq and Bitar cherished has long been forgotten.

When we approach South Yemen, the old Aden Protectorate, we find Marxism-Leninism in an unlikely place. South Yemen is socially and ecologically an extension of the North Yemeni highlands. It receives less rainfall and thus has only limited agricultural potential. Traditionally it had survived on maritime trade. Its remote, arid valleys were populated by highly stratified tribal lineages dominated by a religious notability, the *sayyid*s, putatively descended from the Prophet (Bujra 1971). The *sayyid*s dominated trade and helped carry Islam to the Far East (e.g., Malaysia, Indonesia). In this peculiar society the British established one of the world's major ports, Aden, servicing the British fleet and shipping in transit to India and beyond. With the opening of the Suez Canal in the last third of the nineteenth century, the port of Aden became a vital link for handling Red Sea maritime traffic. It was made a crown colony and its hinterland was put under a British protectorate.

In the port a modern work force developed, consisting of dockers, maintenance personnel, clerks, customs officials, suppliers, traders, bureaucrats, schoolteachers, and the like. Many were drawn from the tribal interior and, like many other Middle Eastern peoples, as individuals struck an indeterminate balance between their status in the modern world and their deeply rooted identity in blood-tribal and religious networks.

Throughout the 1960s, while the rest of the Arab world consolidated its independence, and while the civil war wore on in neighboring North Yemen, nationalist agitation in the port of Aden grew in strength. Abdullah al-Asnag, a labor leader, founded the People's Socialist party, which in turn was part of the National Liberation Front (NLF), to spearhead the movement. The NLF in 1968 took over the government of South Yemen from the departing British. Earlier in the decade it had been inspired by the Arab National Movement (ANM), originally a Nasserist organization founded in Beirut. The NLF and the ANM moved steadily leftward in the 1960s, rejecting both Ba'athism and Nasserism as their espousal of scientific socialism deepened.

With independence, the NLF adjusted its internal alliance. The organized labor wing and especially its moderate leader, Abdullah al-Asnag, lost out to a group of intellectuals and a rural constituency of poor tribal peasants who had long chafed under the dominance of the *sayyid* class. Something of a Maoist scenario was enacted: Revolutionary intellectuals allied with oppressed peasants surrounded and captured the city.

Since 1968 the People's Democratic Republic of Yemen (PDRY) has been the country in the Middle East most closed to outsiders and has been virtually ignored by the foreign press. In 1986 when factions within the NLF fought each other for control of the state, the world briefly focused on this country of only 2 million people, but once the fight ceased, so did the attention. Soviet advisers may have a good idea of how the PDRY conducts its politics, as might migrant Indian workers and merchants, but neither tend to write down their impressions. Thus we are left in the dark. Part of the PDRY's drift into obscurity was a function of the fact that the Suez Canal was closed to shipping between 1967 and 1976, which had devastating consequences for Aden's economy.

One of the NLF's principal ideologues, Abd al-Fattah Ismail, early on expressed his movement's scorn for the moderate socialist experiments we have already examined. He dismissed the structures of Algeria, Egypt, Syria, and Iraq as "self-styled socialist parties that are petty bourgeois in ideology and class makeup. . . . The conciliatory politics of the petty bourgeoisie is even more dangerous for the popular national democratic revolution than the overtly hostile politics of the feudal-bourgeoisie alliance. On the class question the worst thing is the politics of the 'golden mean'" (as cited in Hudson 1977, 356).

Nonetheless the NLF's Marxist-Leninists did make some concessions to Yemeni society; the constitution of the PDRY declares Islam to be the state religion. Indeed no Arab state has dared disestablish Islam, although Bourguiba may have toyed with the idea and radical Ba'athists in Syria actually struck the state religion clause from the Syrian constitution in 1966, only to have it restored by Hafiz al-Assad.

The NLF is an explicitly mobilizational party seeking to activate the working class, which includes women, students, and soldiers. It is also the supreme authority in the land, eclipsing the government and the Supreme People's Council as the locus of decisionmaking. The NLF can be conceived of as a vanguard party, penetrating all sectors of society through mass organizations set up along familiar functional lines: peasants, workers, soldiers, students, women. On paper there would be little to distinguish the NLF from the Ba'ath, but it would seem that its effective role in running the state and the level of indoctrination of its cadres clearly set it apart from all other Arab revolutionary parties.

From the mid-1970s on, predictable cleavages between moderate and radical wings of the NLF were exacerbated by the country's economic crisis. In the early years of the decade, the regime had backed a liberation front in Dhofar Province, part of the Sultanate of Oman, in the hope of spreading and consolidating the revolution. The front was eventually subdued, however, through a combination of Jordanian, Iranian, and Pakistani military support to the Omani sultan and the largesse of Saudi Arabia awash in foreign exchange after the surge in international oil prices in 1973.

The PDRY was in desperate economic shape in the mid-1970s. It had lost business through the closing of the Suez Canal and also had to pay much higher prices for its petroleum imports. Saudi Arabia was willing to bankroll the PDRY out of its difficulties in exchange for the abandonment of the Dhofar Liberation Front and some move away from the regime's espousal of Marxism-Leninism. The chairman of the Presidential Council, Salim Robaya Ali, was sympathetic to the Saudi overtures, while Abd al-Fattah Ismail, secretary-general of the NLF, was opposed.

Robaya Ali prevailed for a time; the regime became regionally well mannered, although it hosted a large Soviet military presence and maintained close relations with the revolutionary regime in Ethiopia and the most radical factions of the Palestine Liberation Organization. But the conflict between socialist radicals and moderates had not been definitively resolved. Moreover, when once again it burst forth, it was clear that older forms of tribal loyalties contributed to what appeared to be purely ideological or strategic disputes.

For a time, when Abd al-Fattah Ismail replaced Robaya Ali as president, the radicals appeared dominant, but in 1980 he in turn was replaced by the moderate Ali Nasr Muhammed, who became both president and secretary-general of the NLF. Ismail went into exile in Moscow, but his supporters put increasing pressure upon the regime for his return. Curiously, the Soviet Union was not eager to have Ismail back in the PDRY, devoted Marxist though he was. The USSR cautioned Ali Nasr against allowing him to return, but in February 1985, yielding to internal pressure, Ali Nasr did so anyway. Over the next year Ismail mobilized his supporters to take over key positions in the party's politburo. It was simply a question of time before that politburo would calmly depose and dispose of Ali Nasr. Against this creeping coup d'état, Ali Nasr launched a preemptive coup in January 1986. He seemed to lack the heart to fight his opponents to the end, and as armed conflict engulfed the city of Aden, he fled to his tribal homeland at Abyan and then into exile. Ismail and the hard-liners were back in power even as the PDRY faded once again from the headlines.

In all this discussion we have not mentioned Palestine for the simple reason that there is no Palestinian state or even a government-in-exile (although in 1989 steps toward such a government were being taken). We can talk of Palestinian ideology or ideologies, the organization of the Palestine Liberation Organization (PLO) and its component parts, such as al-Fatah, and its strategies in confronting Israel. However, we cannot say how it would run a state, what would be the role of the liberation fronts, the guerrilla fighters, the structuring of the economy, the place of public and private enterprise, the place of religion and of ethnic and religious subgroups. The Palestinians as a would-be nation deserve far more attention than we give them, and we suspect that were they ever to win sovereignty in some part of their homeland, some variant of the socialist republic model would be erected. Beyond that we do not care to speculate.

## THE LIBERAL MONARCHS

The kings, princes, and sheykhs of the Middle East have fostered very different polities from those of the socialist republics. The purposeful state, bent on development and military might, its citizenry tightly organized, mobilized, and, above all, unified, has not characterized the monarchical systems of the region. Of course, it has not even characterized the socialist republics themselves, which, more often than not, have failed to achieve unity or development.

The distinction we wish to make is subtle and not always apparent from the written record. The shahs of Iran, father and son, were modernizers and little tolerant of ethnic and sectarian cleavages in their society. Like Atatürk they dealt with these cleavages by force. King Muhammed V and Crown Prince Hassan of Morocco likewise dealt ruthlessly with Berber dissidence in 1959. Monarchs seem as concerned by integration as republican presidents. The monarchs have also espoused the cause of economic development and have marshaled state resources and large technocracies to pursue them. All have paid lip service to an even distribution of national wealth. Most, in function of their own national resources, have sought military credibility; the last shah was obsessed by that goal.

So what makes the monarchs different? In our view there are two main factors. First, all claim some degree of the divine right to rule. Even King Hussein of Jordan, a descendant of the Prophet, can invoke his blood as a qualification to rule. The shah claimed that he spoke to God and that the Pahlavi dynasty had a divine mission to rule Iran. The king of Morocco uses the Koranic title: Commander of the Faithful. King Fu'ad, father of Egypt's last monarch, Farouk, tried in the 1930s to lay claim to the caliphacy, which had fallen victim to Atatürk's militant secularism. The point is that the monarchs do not rest their legitimacy on the expression of popular will or sovereignty. They are responsible, not before the people, but before God. The distinction may be somewhat artificial in that few Middle Eastern leaders, republican or monarchical, have ever enjoyed much legitimacy, but the rival sets of symbols evoke powerful emotions in Middle Easterners.

Three times a year on great state occasions the king of Morocco would ride forth on a white stallion, led by a descendant of the old palace slave guard, with the king protected by the embroidered parasol, symbol of royal authority. Before him were the ranks of the Moroccan meritocracy who served at his pleasure: Ministers, generals, governors, *'ulema',* all knelt before the king, foreheads to the ground, in an ultimate gesture of fealty and self-effacement. The general populace was admitted to the palace grounds to witness this display of divine power.

It is true that Middle Eastern presidents, e.g., Bourguiba, tend to rule as if they were monarchs, but none could ever get away with such symbolic identification with God and concomitant distancing from the populace. The only president to make much of his working relationship with the Almighty was Ga'afar al-Nimieri of the Sudan, and he lasted only two years after having told his people of his new status.

The second factor has to do with the handling of diversity and pluralism. Here the monarchical game is subtle and close to hypocritical. On the one hand, monarchs speak in terms of the nation and decry all the fractious elements in society that impede national unity. But while decrying these elements, monarchs do not deny them legitimacy so long as they behave according to the rules of the game as defined by the monarchy. What the monarchs want is a plethora of interests, tribal, ethnic, professional, class based, and partisan, whose competition for public patronage they can arbitrate. None of these elements can be allowed to become too powerful or wealthy, and the monarch will police and repress, or entice and divide factions that are becoming too entrenched. The monarch's rule is to divide, chastise, and regulate, but not to humiliate or alienate important factions. The shah in the 1970s, fat with oil revenues, thought he could violate this rule.

The rhetoric of this game is paternalistic; kings talk of themselves as fathers to their societies or, as King Hassan has described himself, as a shepherd to a flock of occasionally errant sheep. They suggest that if all behaved selflessly and for the national good, all would be better off, but, alas, children will be children, and the king must settle their petty squabbles. He is thus *above* all factions and party to none, especially in that he answers to God alone.

But he must have the factions and the squabbles. It is the role of arbiter and supervisor of the distribution of patronage and state resources that makes him relevant to the political game. He must propagate the belief that were he ever to disappear, the system would disintegrate into a chaotic war among all the petty contenders for spoils. "Après-moi le déluge" is very much the motto of Middle Eastern monarchs. Their populations have not always believed in their indispensability, and monarchies have been overthrown with some regularity: King Farouk of Egypt in 1952, King Faisal of Iraq in 1958, the Imam of Yemen in 1962, King Idris of Libya in 1969, and the shah of Iran in 1979. The first four all fell to military coups that may or may not have expressed popular sentiment. Only the shah was the victim of direct popular action.

If Atatürk was the model leader of the socialist republics, King Faisal I of Iraq may be seen as the model of the modern Middle Eastern monarch. His task was formidable. In return for his services to the British during World War I, he was plucked out of his native Hijaz in the Arabian Peninsula and plunked down in Iraq, which had become a British protectorate. He was made king of an unlikely realm that included Shi'ites and Sunnis, the latter divided between ethnic Kurds and Arabs. Faisal had to rely on his descent from the Prophet (e.g., His being a *sharif*) and his prestige as the former protector of the Holy Places of Mecca and Medina.

Like all monarchs, Faisal had to assure himself of direct control of the armed forces, though in the Iraqi case these were no more than an internal police force. Here he relied on Arab officers from the Ottoman armies who had been loyal to him prior to 1921. These stalwarts were mainly Sunni Arabs from Iraq. Faisal, after suppressing a large tribal revolt in 1920, sought to associate traditional Shi'ite leaders with the new state, and Kurds were given quotas in public appointments. As an outsider, Faisal had little choice but to portray himself as above the fray of Iraqi politics (Batatu 1978, 26). His probity and evenhandedness made him an enlightened leader, and his death in 1933 ushered in an era of lesser figures, who eventually led the monarchy to its doom.

The monarchy of independent Morocco also emerged out of a protectorate, in this instance that of the French (1912–1956). The nationalist Istiqlal party had used King Muhammed V as the symbol of the nationalist struggle, but with independence the king took his distance from the party, abetted its scission in 1959, from which the National Union of Popular Forces emerged, and encouraged the formation of rival parties. In other words he deliberately increased the number of factions and political clans in the system, the better to assert his role as arbiter.

Shortly after independence Berber dissident movements in the Middle Atlas and Rif mountains elicited a sharp military response, but at the same time Mohammed V encouraged the formation of a Berber party, the Popular Movement. Mohammed V's wife, the mother of King Hassan, is a Middle Atlas Berber.

Mohammed V died in 1961 and was succeeded by his son, Hassan II, whom his father had put in direct control of the Royal Armed Forces. Hassan never relinquished his control over the military, although he was nearly overthrown twice by the military, in 1971 and in 1972. He assiduously followed the divide-and-rule tactics of his father, weakening parties, trade unions, and regional interests, but never destroying them or pushing them out of the political arena. Even the Moroccan Communist party, after having been being dissolved a few years after independence, was allowed to reestablish itself legally in the mid-1970s. King Hassan puts himself forward as the final protector of all interests; the parties against military intervention; the military against civilian bungling; the Berbers against the Arabs, and the Jews against the Muslims. Hassan II may not be loved, but most Moroccans now do believe that the monarchy is vital to the country's stability.

Reza Khan, the founder of the Pahlavi dynasty, was, it will be recalled, inclined to follow Atatürk's path and model his state after Turkey's republic. Although he was persuaded to adopt a monarchical form of rule, much of his reign was characterized by the crushing of all regional, tribal, and ethnic dissidence and the building of a centralized state and powerful military. Although Reza Khan built a powerful state, he left a place in its political arena for the weakened tribal leaders, for regional interests, and for the clergy. As in Morocco, as long as these groups played by the rules laid down by the shah, they could represent their interests legitimately.

The shah's son, Mohammed Reza Pahlavi, even after surviving his confrontation with the nationalist prime minister, Mohammed Mossadegh, in 1953, never managed the political game with the same forcefulness and assurance as his father. His efforts to fabricate political parties (see Chapter 12) and to exclude others parties of the Mossadegh era or before, such as the Tudeh and the National Front, merely produced a kind of vacuum that could be filled only by clandestine political groupings, either radical Islamic or radical secularist, and the notorious internal police, the Iranian Security and Intelligence Organization (SAVAK). Rather than dealing with formally constituted parties and interest groups, as the king did in Morocco, the shah tried to manipulate large categories of the population—the secular intelligentsia; the clergy; the bazaar, or traditional retailing, bourgeoisie; a new state-dependent private entrepreneurial bourgeoisie; organized labor; and civil servants. Heady with the massive oil earnings accruing to the state treasury in the 1970s, the shah neglected many of these constituencies; he found himself in the late 1970s with only two sources of support, the armed forces and the United States, and a large source of indifference, the peasantry. All other constituencies had turned against him. He had lost his role as the accepted, indeed indispensable, arbiter of the political game.

Other monarchs also profit from cleavage and enhance their relevance to the functioning of state power by perpetuating it. King Hussein strides the cleavage between a majoritarian, highly educated Palestinian population and a largely Bedouin minority that dominates the Jordanian armed forces. The Bedouin look to King Hussein to protect their privileged position in the armed forces and to "contain" the Palestinian intelligentsia and entrepreneurial bourgeoisie. Jordan is eloquent testimony to the fact that the cleavages that allow monarchs to survive are precisely those that can and do bring them down.

Similarly, the Sabah ruling family of Kuwait and the Saudi monarchy find themselves astride major cleavages. In Kuwait, which, strictly speaking, is a princedom (emirate), the fault line is unidimensional. Over 40% of the entire population is non-Kuwaiti, as is a majority of the work force (see Chapter 14). The economy and the administration is thus dependent upon these more or less long-term worker-migrants. At the same time the Kuwaiti royal family has established a National Assembly, whose members are chosen by an electorate that numbers no more than 60,000 and from which all foreigners are excluded. The Sabah family cannot claim to speak for or represent the foreign workers, but it can and does manage the two communities. It must also worry about the Shi'ite minority within the native Kuwaiti population.

The Saudi monarchy manipulates a host of internal fissures. There are the regional divisions between the Nejd, from which the royal house of Saud is drawn, and the more urban, trade-oriented Hijaz. There are the inevitable fraternal divisions within the sprawling royal family, with its several thousand princes. It was a young prince who assassinated King Faisal in 1975. Indeed if power is a resource and the House of Saud shares it among its sons, there is a Malthusian crisis in store. Rival princely lineages maneuver for official positions in the government and armed forces (the officers corps is dominated by Saudis of royal blood), government contracts and business licenses, and the myriad of financial and trading privileges the Saudi state is able to dispense. The kingdom is still in the hands of the direct offspring of 'Abd al-'Aziz, the founder, but once the current generation passes from the scene, there will be an enormous pool of princes available from which to choose the king, but no clear rule to guide the selection.

In writing of European monarchies, Max Weber classified this kind of regime as "patrimonial," and many observers, including Hudson (1977) and Islami and Kavoussi (1984) have applied it to the monarchies of the Middle East. Trusted officials, of royal or common blood, are granted sinecures that generate income for their holders and that resemble the prebends that were granted royal vassals in medieval Europe. If the trust is broken, the prebend or sinecure is taken back by the royal authority and distributed to another. The downfall in 1986 of the "commoner" Sheykh Zaki Yamani, for nearly fifteen years the minister of petroleum and chief architect of Saudi oil policy, illustrates both the longevity of tenure and the abruptness of termination that inhere in the use of royal prerogative. Yamani was relieved of his position in the midst of intense negotiations within OPEC over new production and pricing arrangements.

The Saudi monarchy, like the Kuwaiti emirate, faces a large foreign work force, over 43% of the entire working population. Alongside it is a growing Saudi professional middle class (Rugh 1973), whose claims to status are based on training and competency. While certain individuals from this class, like Yamani and Hisham Nazir, have risen to positions of great power, there is nonetheless an inherent incompatibility between the power achieved through the accident of royal birth and that resulting from professional training. In many ways the regional environment holds much greater danger for the Saudi monarchy than does the domestic political arena. Saudi Arabia is territorially huge, sparsely inhabited, poorly defended and enormously rich. Saudi Arabia's neighbors, especially Egypt, Iraq, and Iran, have often looked covetously toward this exposed wealth. The Saudi regime must thus pursue a delicate regional balancing game that may in fact help it manage the dynamic equilibrium of factions and interests within the kingdom. The major and perhaps most destabilizing link between the regional and the domestic arena is the foreign work force, and containing and sanitizing it is the regime's single greatest political challenge.

## PLURALISM WITHOUT MONARCHS

There are only three countries in the Middle East that have indulged in liberal electoral politics for sustained periods of time: Israel, Lebanon, and Turkey. The Sudan had one chance between 1964 and 1969, while Egypt has pursued a highly controlled liberal experiment since 1976. Turkey has oscillated between freewheeling electoral politics in the 1950s and 1970s and military rule in the 1960s and early 1980s. Since 1983 another attempt has been made to revive civilian electoral politics. Only Israel since its creation in 1948 has maintained a democratic regime, but that distinction must be qualified by its strict policing of the Arab populations it inherited in 1948. The Israelis have never allowed an autonomous Arab party to function in its political arena.

Turkey has failed to achieve a stable party system, and in the 1970s it suffered from a series of coalition governments whose component interests were so diverse that no coherent economic policy could be implemented. Sound economic management fell victim to the political expediency of the Justice party, the lineal descendant of the Democrat party of the 1950s and of the Republican People's party—now "radicalized" and more overtly socialist under the leadership of Bülent Ecevit than at any time under Atatürk. The military, as already noted, put an end to this situation, tried to put Turkey's economic affairs in order, and then, under carefully controlled circumstances, including the banning of most parties functioning before the 1980 coup, allowed new elections to be held in 1983. Turgut Özal's Motherland party won a narrow majority, and he became prime minister. General Kenan Evren, who had led the coup in 1980, became president. He and the top brass will watch closely Özal's economic management and handling of issues of law and order and may not hesitate to intervene once again to correct a deteriorating situation. Turkey is subject to a kind of democratizing pressure, however, that no other country in the region faces. There is a national consensus of sorts that Turkey should join the European Common Market. To do so will require not only far-reaching restructuring of the Turkish economy but, as well, adhering to European legal standards of liberal democracy. Rule by generals, repression of labor, suppression of Kurdish or religious political organizations cannot be made compatible with entry into the EEC.

Lebanese democracy after 1946 fascinated Western political scientists. Here was a society that the French protectorate authorities had organized along sectarian or confessional lines. Seats in parliament were distributed in a ratio of 6:5 between Christians and Muslims, and subdivided among the several sects in both religious communities. The 1946 National Pact, elaborated by the principal leaders of the Maronite and Sunni sects, consecrated the French arrangement. Henceforth a Maronite Christian was to be president; a Sunni, prime minister; and a Shi'ite, president of the Chamber of Deputies. Positions in the civil service and the armed forces were likewise distributed along confessional lines.

In a manner most theorists of modernization would find reprehensible, Lebanon had quite literally enshrined religion in politics. People ran for office or voted, won jobs or lost them, and occasionally came to blows as members of specific sects. There was no separation of "church" and state, but somehow the system seemed to work. The press was free, debate open and vigorous, elections held on a regular basis, although not without tampering, and Lebanon served as a small island of political refuge and free enterprise for the rest of the region.

Yet the fragility of the confessional balance was apparent to some early on (see especially Hudson 1968). Most obvious was the fact that confessions became more rather than less rigid as office and spoils were distributed along confessional lines. Except at the elite level there were few cross-cutting alliances, and candidates seldom had to seek votes outside their own confessional constituencies. Second, while population growth and migration gradually transformed the Christians into a minority (see Chapter 4), they continued to control the presidency and a majority of the deputies. Camille Chamoun, who was president up to 1958, altered the constitution so that he could succeed himself, thereby triggering a brief civil war that presaged what was to happen in 1975. Chamoun was forced from the presidency and was replaced by Gen. Fu'ad Chehab (a Maronite), who restored law and order and talked about deconfessionalizing Lebanon. He was unable to make much headway, as his talk of position through merit seemed to non-Christians to favor Christians, who enjoyed generally higher levels of education and training.

The fruits of Lebanon's booming merchant economy were not equally shared among the populace. The oligarchs of the economy came from all sects but were dominated by the Maronite banking elite. Yet the sharing of economic interests among the very wealthy cut across confessional lines, and, some have suggested, the oligarchs saw it to their advantage to promote confessional conflict so that class-based politics might be avoided.

Finally, after the June War of 1967 and the conflict between King Hussein and the PLO in 1970, nearly 200,000 Palestinians, many of them armed, sought refuge in Lebanon. They are not citizens and cannot vote, but as they were mainly Muslim, Lebanese Christians feared their gradual absorption into the local arena. Were that to happen, all semblance of balance among confessions would be lost. It was the Maronite Christian Phalange

(Kata'ib) party that precipitated the civil war in 1975 in an attempt to disarm or expel the Palestinians. In the ensuing years the Lebanese state collapsed and at least four statelets (Maronite, Druze, Shi'ite, and Palestinian) emerged, the Lebanese armed forces became only one among several militias, and confessionalism became a question not merely of voter identification but of life and death.

A system that had inspired some of the highest hopes for Western-style democracy in the Middle East now inspires little more than despair and incomprehension. The Lebanese may have lost 50–60,000 people out of their tiny population in the first decade of fighting. When one looks at the ex-country's embedded confessional mosaic, it would seem that here if anywhere is a society in need of a king who would be above all parties and backed by a loyal palace guard to regulate the political game. Lebanon desperately needs the functional equivalent of King Faisal I of Iraq.

Israel's democratic system is old and vigorous but should not be taken for granted. As in Turkey, old political coalitions such as the center-left Israel Labor party (MAPAI), which dominated Israeli politics in the first two decades, have broken down and reassembled. Now the major cleavage in Israeli Jewish society is between secularists with some commitment to socialism and a strong welfare state, and a conservative coalition increasingly characterized by an aggressive religious nationalism. Menachem Begin's Likud alliance, which dominated Israel politics from the mid-1970s to the mid-1980s, has been home for Israelis favorable to private-sector growth, religious claims to the occupied territories, and repressive policies toward Israel's Arab minority. The bulk of Likud's following has come from Oriental and Sephardic Jews, who tend to be somewhat less educated than the dominant Ashkenazi elites and somewhat lower in the hierarchy of incomes. Moreover, their commitment to the democratic process is suspect. The growing fascination of young Israelis, both Oriental and Ashkenazi, with the religious nationalists of the Gush Emunim movement and the proto-fascist Rabbi Meir Kahane, could strain to the breaking point the system's ability to maintain democratic practices. The question is, as in Lebanon, whether or not the system can absorb a large, possibly majoritarian, non-Jewish population and still preserve the logic of one citizen, one vote. For many Israelis the answer has come, over time, to be no. That leaves those Israelis two options—expulsion of the Arabs from Israeli territory, whatever its final boundaries, or second-class citizenship for Arabs. Neither option can fail to weaken Israel's commitment to democracy.

## CURIOSITIES OR MODELS FOR THE FUTURE?

In 1977 Col. Mu'ammar Qaddhafi proclaimed a regime that is unique in the Middle East and in the world. After initially modeling his regime after the Nasserist state, Qaddhafi introduced what he called the Jamahiria, or mass state. Qaddhafi invented the term and the regime. Its intent is to abolish all intermediaries between the people, or masses, and their leaders. There are to be no political parties and no mass organizations, which would only produce new oligarchs. All agencies, enterprises, and places of work are to be run by the employees themselves, through Revolutionary People's Councils. Formal administrative hierarchies are to be undone or at least closely supervised by the people's councils. Simultaneously, the mass state tried to terminate wage payment for work, nationalize retail trade, and end all rents—all this in the name of the eradication of exploitation.

The blueprint is breathtaking, but its implementation is not visible. Key bureaucracies built around the oil and banking sectors seem little affected by massism, and there is no evidence that the armed forces have been taken over by the revolutionary committees. In June 1986, after the U.S. air strike against Libya, Qaddhafi in typical fashion unilaterally resurrected the Revolutionary Command Council, including four officers who had participated in the 1969 coup d'état against King Idris. Qaddhafi did this without consulting the Revolutionary Committee Movement, in whose name he spoke.

The idea of the mass state seems vacuous when it is recalled that, like Saudi Arabia's and Kuwait's, 40% of Libya's work force is foreign, as is 50% of its managerial and professional personnel. Foreigners cannot be members of revolutionary committees, and it is inconceivable that they are not paid wages. Libya in the final analysis is simply another rentier state with an idiosyncratic and autocratic leader, who confuses theatrics with institution building. His staging is for the benefit of the Libyans, but without oil rents and worker migrants, the show would end. We suspect the Libyan "model" will have little appeal elsewhere.

By contrast, the Islamic Republic of Iran may be attractive to wide segments of Middle Eastern society, whether Shi'ite or Sunni. Even ten years after the downfall of the shah, it is too early to say that a new regime has fully taken shape. We suspect that it will take a definitive end to the Iran-Iraq war (a distinct possibility at the time of writing) and the stabilization of the new leadership after the death of Ayatollah Khomeini in June 1989 before the regime will show its true colors. Still some features of the Islamic republic are clear. First, the direct role of the Shi'ite clergy in politics has been firmly established despite the serious reservations of a number of respected ayatollahs (Teleqani, Shariat Madari, inter alia). Thus we now hear of the "mullacracy" of Iran or the reign of the ayatollahs (Bakhash 1984). The mullahs control the major institutions of the state, the parliament, the Foundation for the Disinherited, the Revolutionary Guard, and before it was dissolved in 1987, they controlled the Islamic Republican party. It is doubtful that we shall soon see a retreat of the clergy from politics.

Second, like the socialist republics, the Islamic republic stresses unity, combining the overriding element of being Muslim with the secondary element of being Iranian. In the months following the departure of the shah, various ethnic and linguistic groups forcefully put forward claims for greater recognition in the new polity than had ever been accorded them under the shah. As Ayatollah Khomeini and the clergy consolidated their grip on the new state, mainly through the elimination of leftists and liberal moderates such as Bani Sadr and the venerable Mehdi Bazargan, these claims were denied. Revolutionary Guards were dispatched to crush Kurdish, Turkomen, and other groups agitating for a new place in the republic. When war broke out with Iraq in September 1980, this kind of subnational agitation became at once blasphemy and high treason.

While pluralism is officially condemned, the new regime does share one characteristic with the monarchies we have examined, and that is the denial of the principle of popular sovereignty. Sovereignty is God's alone, and although in the Islamic republic the people elect their representatives, those who rule are ultimately responsible before God and not before the people. Rulership cannot be inherited; rather it is the duty of the council of the foremost clerics to judge and select the best qualified leaders in view of protecting the believers, applying God's law, and protecting the republic. Moreover, a Constitutional Council reviews all parliamentary legislation to assure that it conforms to the *shari'a* and to the Iranian constitution. The principle in operation here is the "trusteeship of the jurisprudents" (*vilayet al-faqih*), whereby the elite of the clergy, on the strength of their learning, assure that the people, in practicing Islamic democracy, do not stray from "the straight path."

Finally, as in the socialist republics, there are two major tendencies in domestic and foreign affairs that are loosely referred to as moderate and extreme, or conservative and radical. In the domain of foreign policy, the radicals advocate unyielding opposition to the United States and the West, the source of materialism and debased morality, and confrontation with all regional states that have "deviated" from Islamic practices. The moderates, in contrast, may be willing to accept an Islamic revolution in one country, seeking normalcy in regional relations, accommodation with Ba'athi Iraq, and a modus vivendi with the West, whose technology Iran so badly needs. Ayatollah Rafsanjani, the principal force behind the cease-fire negotiated with Iraq in August 1988, represents the "moderates."

These two tendencies in foreign affairs do not mesh very well with similar groupings in domestic policy; that is, foreign policy radicals may be domestic moderates and vice versa. One part of the coalition that Khomeini led was directly linked to the Iranian private sector, especially the commercial groups often labeled the *bazaaris*. This wing advocates respect for private property and free enterprise and a minimal amount of state intervention in economic affairs. It is bolstered in its position by several jurisprudents who argue with reason that the *shari'a* in no way interferes with private-property rights so long as the better-off pay the *zakat,* or religious tax destined for the poor. This tendency has support in the Constitutional Council, which declared illegal a fairly radical land-reform act passed by the parliament. In 1985, moreover, 181 expropriated industries were returned to their former owners.

Arrayed against this tendency are the radicals, identified primarily with Prime Minister Hossein Mousavi and Ayatollah Montazeri, the latter of whom having been designated for a time to succeed Khomeini. The radicals emphasize the egalitarian and redistributional duties of the Islamic revolution and advocate state intervention to overcome disparities in income and the distribution of assets. Their position was strengthened by the need of the state to mobilize resources for the war with Iraq, entailing deep intervention in all economic affairs.

For nearly seven years, Ayatollah Khomeini skillfully mediated between these two groups and made sure that neither became dominant. In the mid-1980s, there were some indications that the conservative, pro-private-sector wing had enhanced its strength. Then, in the winter of 1988, Khomeini issued an authoritative opinion that no judicial body had the right to overrule the legislative acts of the *majlis*. With this he signaled a major shift in favor of those with a radical domestic agenda, including land reform and the nationalization of foreign trade. The subsequent elections to the *majlis* in the spring of 1988 returned a substantial majority to those identified with the radical wing of the political elite. Only after a forced peace with Iraq has been negotiated in terms that inevitably will be seen as unfavorable to Iran, and after a long process of factional sorting out following Khomeini's death, will we be able to gauge the grip of the radicals on the levers of power within Iran.

## FUTURE REGIMES: SOME SPECULATIONS

Certain features of the Islamic Republic of Iran have had undeniable appeal throughout the Middle East. That country has combined three elements that have been notably lacking or have eroded in other Middle Eastern regimes. There has been, first, the adherence to the basic tenets of Islam in a nearly puritanical fashion. The regime is moral and authentic—no imported ideologies here. Second, the regime has successfully projected an image of equally distributing the burdens of development and war; the legitimacy crises faced by other Middle Eastern elites that are seen as corrupt and compromised have not yet afflicted the Iranian regime, although a humiliating peace with Iraq could alter that judgment. Third, Iran has militantly and successfully confronted the West and the United States. It has gone its own uncompromising way and demonstrated to some perhaps that God will help those who help themselves.

The Islamic republic is far from being universally admired. Minorities within Iran, secularist elites, many woman, and leftists have paid a high price in post-Pahlavi Iran. Similar groups throughout the Middle East will not welcome the spread of the revolution. Although Saddam Hussein of Iraq is anything but universally admired, these same groups can only rejoice that his nominally socialist and secular regime has been able to withstand the relentless onslaught of the Iranian war machine. Certainly, Shi'ite groups inside Iraq, such as al-Dawa, which may have looked forward to an Iranian-backed Islamic republic, have had the rug pulled from under them. Other Arab countries have radical Islamic factions that in combination with support from key military units, might be able to initiate an Islamic revolution but almost surely not make it stick—the Sudan, Morocco, and perhaps Tunisia are candidates.

If Islam triumphs politically, it is far more likely to be in the form of what we call Islamic praetorianism. The model here comes from the regime of Pakistan under Gen. Mohammed Zia al-Haqq, itself in jeopardy since his death in a plane crash in August 1988. It is an authoritarian military regime in which a large public sector works closely with a private banking and industrial bourgeoisie. Zia al-Haqq invoked Islam to justify a highly skewed distribution of income and the absence of democratic politics. Islam in this situation is used to legitimate economic and political hierarchy and military rule. It is conceivable that Ga'afar al-Nimeiri might have built such a regime in the Sudan, and it is possible that Iran might evolve in that direction. Morocco, were King Hassan to die or be overthrown, and Egypt could also see similar regimes. Note, however, that we are talking of possibilities and not probabilities.

Lebanon has provided a model of political disintegration and chaos. For a time, as Iran pressed its advantage in southern Iraq, there was a possibility that Iraq might be dismembered among Shi'ites and Sunnis, Arabs, and Kurds. That kind of turmoil in Iraq could drive Turkey to intervene militarily at least to secure its southeastern borders. Just as Syria and Israel have carved out spheres of influence in Lebanon, Iran and Turkey could find themselves in the same position vis-à-vis Iraq. The other country in the region that is already in the process of disintegration is the Sudan. Financial collapse and the continued insurrection in the southern provinces have reduced the capacity of the government to control its own territories. With nine African nations along its borders, including Egypt, Libya, and Ethiopia, there will be inevitable temptations for the Sudan's neighbors to exert control over various parts of the country.

Israel may have to deal with the ironic threat of lapsing into some variant of European fascism. Religious chauvinists could build a superiority complex among a significant portion of the Jewish population and try to render the state free of Arabs. One assumes that the basic values of the original Zionist settlers will yet prevail, but the frustrations of forty years of war, tension, and more recent economic crisis on the lower-middle strata of Jewish society could produce a violent form of nationalism and intolerance.

Abrupt departures from existing patterns, such as we have seen in Libya since 1969 or in Iran since 1979, are not likely to be the norm. Rather we would expect to see the evolution of most regimes in certain predictable directions. One likely evolutionary path is toward what we shall call party-dominant spoils systems. For instance, in Egypt, Tunisia, and Algeria, a single party is already dominant, e.g., the National Democratic party of Egypt and the Socialist Destour of Tunisia, while the FLN of Algeria is uncontested. At the same time these parties have tended to become large bureaucratic appendages of the state and have lost whatever ideological and mobilizational zeal they may have once had. Concomitantly, these regimes show significant movement toward more economic liberalism, with a growing role for private-sector activity. As socialism diminishes as a guide to values and economic organization, the party may come to be a monopolist distributor of, or broker for, state patronage and spoils. If there are major political struggles, they will take place within the party and the upper echelons of the state. These regimes may well become civilian, and of course in Tunisia the regime always has been so. But they will remain authoritarian, staging carefully controlled elections, and trying to assure that strategic interests always have sufficient access to patronage so as not to turn against the regime. Mexico's regime and the Institutional Revolutionary party (PRI) provides the model, and Tunisia may come to approximate it more readily than Egypt or Algeria. But note that such regimes could as easily move toward the Islamic praetorian model, whose leaders judge the need to invoke Islamic values as crucial to their survival.

Turkey has some likelihood of sustaining a controlled multiparty regime within a liberalizing, private sector–oriented economy. But all this will be contingent on the ability of the economy to continue to export and grow. A renewal of the economic crisis of the late 1970s could lead to a reentry of the military into direct control, with a possibility of the establishment of an Islamic praetorian regime.

It must be kept in mind that all the above are informed speculations about the future, not predictions. What we do predict is that change will be evolutionary, not revolutionary, and that a common element in the evolutionary process will be a critical reassessment of, and diminished role for, the state. We do not believe that the prevalence of military dictatorships in the region will lead, as in Latin America, to a process of redemocratization. There do not appear to be Alfonsíns or Sarnays waiting in the Iraqi, Syrian, Algerian, or Yemeni wings. Civil society and especially the middle classes of the region have not yet taken on the political weight they have acquired in Latin America. Yet we feel intuitively that we are at the end of an era in the process of regime formation. A generation has gone by since most Middle Eastern nations won independence, and many hopes for democracy, economic growth, and national strength have been dashed. Disillusionment, cynicism, and anger have infused the political atmosphere among leaders and led. There is a sense that the existing regimes have "exhausted" themselves (Khoury 1983a) and that something new has to be tried. Whatever *is* tried, regimes will have to deal with a high level of skepticism, on the one hand, and heightened political awareness, on the other, among the citizenry they helped shape.

## NOTES

1. It was, therefore, ironic that it was a general and the minister of defense, Zine el-Abdine Ben Ali, who deposed Bourguiba in the fall of 1987 as mentally unfit to govern—a "medical" coup d'état.

# 12

# SOLIDARISM
# AND ITS ENEMIES

The integrated, cohesive citizenry, about which Middle Eastern leaders have spilled oceans of ink and over which waves of rhetoric have crashed, remains a distant goal. The erosion of optimism and elite will that accompanied the long and dangerous wielding of power has been matched by the disillusionment and cynicism of citizens. Sensing that alienation, leaders have been driven to divide and rule rather than to unite, to contain rather than to mobilize, to repress rather than to inspire. The rhetoric of solidarism still prevails, but political practice has deviated sharply from the older goals. Some of the obstacles to the new society have lain in older forms of social and political insurance: clans, ethnic groups, tribes, and religious sects; units that, among other things, protect their members from the vagaries of powerful states and markets (see Migdal 1987). To see these forms as atavistic is to lose sight of their redefined roles in the new state systems of the contemporary Middle East.

Permeating them, but separate from them, is the bedrock of Islam, which provides a set of standards by which political leadership may be and is judged. When leaders who profess some obeisance to Islam fail in their statist enterprises, they are seen as exposing the *umma* to mortal danger. If they are not aware of their error, they must be removed and replaced by rightly guided leaders. But if they err knowingly, it is possible that they are the agents of satanic power. For many Muslims, Atatürk, Nasser, and Mohammed Reza Shah were all such agents.

There are, by contrast, obstacles to solidarism of quite a different order. Leaders nearly obsessed with control have emasculated the very political organizations they created to mobilize and integrate the masses. At the same time, in organizing strategic sectors of the working population, they have created real occupational associations that have gained organizational and political skills and substantial bargaining power. Concomitantly the disbursement of large state-investment budgets and the very real economic growth that has occurred in some Middle Eastern societies have transferred resources to white-collar workers, skilled trade unionists, capitalist farmers, and a few entrepreneurial groups that are now in a position to contest, cautiously, certain state policies.

Finally had Middle Eastern leaders been able to nurture some sort of broad ideological and programmatic consensus, it might have been possible to keep all these old and new actors within the political game. But ideologies fabricated by house ideologues or, worse yet, by bureaucrats in Ministries of Culture, Information, and National Guidance, have failed to penetrate strategically placed elites, no less the people as a whole. There is, we argue, a kind of organizational and ideological vacuum in the Middle East that several sorts of actors are trying to fill. Incumbent elites with the economic and coercive might of the state at their disposal still have the upper hand, but they may lack the conviction or confidence to use it.

## SMALL GROUPS AND CLIENTELIST POLITICS

One trap we must avoid is to see older forms of political organization and action as direct reenactments of their forbears. A tribe and tribal loyalty in the twentieth-century Middle East are qualitatively different phenomena than their seventeenth- or eighteenth-century antecedents. So too are sects, ethnic groups, families, and coteries. What has changed momentously is the degree of state and market penetration into all sectors of Middle Eastern society. Just as economic subsistence is a thing of the past, so too is political isolation. Central authorities are now able to place effective claims on ever-growing proportions of societies' wealth, but they tend to do so in arbitrary and sometimes punitive ways. Markets, having captured large producing populations, do not behave predictably. And for those who play the national political game, the stakes are high, with death, imprisonment, exile, or at best, forced retirement as probable outcomes. Parties and formal associations have not yet provided effective means to protect members from the new order. People retreat into or invent "security groups" as much to protect themselves as to promote their own interests. One may find in a small band of friends, members of one's tribe, ethnic group, home region, or religious sect a framework for mutual support, accountability, shared obligations, or plain psychological reassurance that no formal organization can offer. The more people adhere to these nonrecognized, loosely organized forms of political and social action, the more the formal associations and political parties lose their cohesion and viability. Leaders may react in one of two ways or both simultaneously: Beat the political fragments into submission or, abandoning solidarism, try to manipulate them through state patronage.

What Bill and Leiden (1984, 74–131) have called the genes of Middle East politics are a congeries of small and nonexclusive units that are of varying degrees of cohesion and durability. Throughout the area, we find political and economic actors associating with small clusters of cronies of similar status. The members of these groups help each other along in their careers, for it is likely that at any particular time some will be doing better than others and can promote the interests of the less fortunate in the group. People who are from the same village or region or perhaps from the same university class, or who share common blood descent or are related through marriage, may come together in such groups. Whether it is a question of Iran's *dawreh*s (circles) or Egypt's *shillas*, cronyism is an important form of political and economic insurance (Bill 1972b; Springborg 1982; Moore 1977).

One often hears of clans in Middle Eastern politics. Sometimes we find fairly persistent coteries at the elite level, such as the Oujda group or clan in Algeria, an alliance of perhaps a dozen men brought together in the building of the Army of National Liberation in Oujda, Morocco, in the late 1950s. Note, however, that like so many of these groupings, they are fragile, and power struggles within them can be brutal. Despite the fact that a member of the Oujda group, Chadli Benjadid, succeeded Boumedienne to the presidency, most of its other stalwarts have disappeared from the scene. So too the members of Egypt's Revolutionary Command Council (RCC), which seized power in 1952. Several members were classmates in the staff college in the late 1930s and served together in various postings and in the 1948 war with Israel. Over the years after 1952, members dropped away in disgrace, exile, or early retirement. Anwar Sadat had been a marginal member of the RCC, but with his assassination in 1981 none of the original twelve officers was still in a position of power, although a number remained alive.

We hear also of the Takriti clan in Iraq and the Alawi clan in Syria. Unlike the two examples mentioned above, these clans combine cronyism with common regional and sectarian loyalties. Moreover, both Hafiz al-Assad and Saddam Hussein have to some extent surrounded themselves with confidants from their own blood lineages. Again, as the parables of Cain and Abel or the Hatfields and the McCoys would warn us, consanguinity and feuding go together. Clans of the Takriti or Alawi sort do not preclude internecine struggle unless there is an outside threat posed to the clan as a whole. One should not doubt for a minute that were there to be a violent change in governing elites in Iraq or Syria, the new incumbents would ferret out all real or *suspected* members of the Takriti and Alawi clans; that realization makes elite clans cling to power all the more tenaciously and frequently at the expense of their rationalist and egalitarian ideals.

Interrelated families may act as units in the political sphere. Hanna Batatu, who wrestled through more than 1,000 pages in sorting out the issues of class, ethnicity, and other "primordial sentiments" in Iraqi society, noted that (1978, 28) "it must not be forgotten that the real unit of class is not the individual but the family, and that members of one middle class family pursue different professions." Waterbury (1970) traced family alliances used for political ends among the Moroccan elite and bourgeoisie. As suggested by Batatu, bourgeois families, through marriage and education, place offspring in several professional domains—business, the officers corps, law, the clergy—so that familial flanks are protected against all eventualities. Khoury (1983b, 94) found similar patterns in interwar Damascus and concluded, "The political field in Damascus was restricted to the interaction of powerful family units."

Springborg (1982) drew up a detailed portrait of a sprawling Egyptian political family, the Mareis, tracing the family's role in Egyptian politics over a number of generations. The persistence of these family "genes" in Egyptian politics was given no acknowledgment, no less legitimacy, in the socialist rhetoric of the 1960s in Nasser's Egypt, but it is significant that President Sadat evoked the image of the family as the backbone of Egyptian society, a unit that implied hierarchy and the peaceful resolution of internal disputes. Sadat constantly cast himself in the role of the patriarch of the Egyptian family, the head of an entire social hierarchy.

Yet another manifestation of small-group genes lies in pervasive patron-client networks. Unlike clusters of cronies, clientelistic groupings bring together people of very different status and power. The patron is the power wielder, and his clients need his protection. In turn they render him a number of services that enhance his power and hence his ability to continue to act as their protector. The classic example in the Middle East and elsewhere is the large landowner. He monopolizes in a given locale the most precious fixed asset, land. He controls access to it, and his clients are his tenants, laborers, and sharecroppers. He protects them physically, he supplies them agricultural inputs and monetary credit, he helps them out if they fall ill and helps pay for extraordinary events such as marriages and funerals. The clients in turn produce for him, supply him free labor for a host of menial tasks, vote for him if elections are an issue, fight for him if he is attacked by outsiders. In this classic example the patron controls what are called "first-order resources"—land and money. As long as he maintains his local monopoly, his clients will have little choice but to seek his protection. Migration might be an option, but in some countries, such as Iraq in the interwar years, peasants with outstanding debts could not legally migrate. Peasants are chronically in debt. Agrarian reform has everywhere eroded the power of the classic rural patron.

Today with the growth of large bureaucratic states that invade and regulate all aspects of one's life, the patron is more likely to be a broker. While he may continue to control first-order resources (see Adams 1986), his real services to his clients will come through his ability to deliver public goods or to protect his clients against various forms of state action. In this sense he brokers access to state resources. He may help procure a birth certificate, a work permit, a commercial license, a passport, or any of the other vital pieces of paper that the modern state routinely requires but does not routinely deliver. He may help place a son in secondary school or the university, find a migrant a job in a public agency or factory, get the courts to drop charges for a misdemeanor, swing a loan through the agricultural credit bank, and so forth. What the patron receives in return is somewhat amorphous. In the few systems in which votes count, he will surely receive votes, but his relative weight in the political system may well hinge on his ability to demonstrate the size and cohesion of his group of clients. If he is perceived as being able to "deliver" his clients, even in elections where official candidates receive 99.9% of the votes, or to keep them out of mischief, such as street demonstrations, union strikes, or land seizures, the higher authorities will make sure that public resources sufficient to maintain his clientele are put at his disposal.

It has been the case that as the socialist and solidarist élan of several of the radical republics began to wane, the large, all-encompassing parties that they set up became simple conduits for the distribution of state patronage. Party cadres, rather than educating, indoctrinating, and mobilizing the populations with which they dealt, fell into the role of broker, establishing their reputation on their ability to deliver state resources to their clients. From their intended role as members of the vanguard, they became ward heelers. The party thus became an instrument in the slow drift of the leadership into divide-and-rule politics; the cadres were there, not to encourage the masses to do something, but to reward them for doing nothing. Putting as kind a light on this as possible, some observers have referred to this deal as a "social pact or contract."

In several other political systems, such as monarchical Iran and Morocco, Lebanon up to 1975, Israel, and Turkey during its liberal phases, party patronage was an open and accepted aspect of the political system. The Lebanese system took these practices to a perhaps fatal extreme: Patronage networks were organized within confessional groups. The kingpins of the system, the *za'im*s, or *zu'ama* (plural), thus used private and public resources to reenforce the confessional boundaries of the country. The channels through which money, jobs, and protection used to flow now move arms and ammunition. The *zu'ama* have by and large given way to a generation of street fighters, who may be incapable of bringing an end to the fighting.

## THE FAILURE OF PARTIES

In the early literature on political development and nation-building, great attention was given and hopes attached to the independent role of political parties in the process (see La Palombara and Weiner 1966). Western polities had been built around parties that organized citizens, helped them formulate their demands and transmit them through elections or through the corridors of power to makers of public policy. For the Middle East, political scientists attached great hopes to the two-party competition that emerged in Turkey in the 1950s, to the luxuriant party pluralism of Lebanon, and to the rational, efficacious single-party regime of Tunisia.

By and large these hopes and expectations have been deceived in the Middle East. There has indeed been an abundance of political parties, but with rare exceptions they have never contested elections. Seldom have they sought to represent constituents or, as organizations, challenged their own regimes. Those enjoying legal monopolies of "representing" citizens, like Egypt's ASU or Algeria's FLN, rejected the label party—having no rivals, they needed no partisans. Through some mysterious chemistry in which freedom of speech, open debate, and freedom of choice were notably absent, the front or union would distill the essence of the popular will and transmit it, for policy action, to the regime's leaders. It did not take long for the citizens to recognize this hokum for what it was.

More liberal experiments fell into their own kinds of sham. Iran, Morocco, and Jordan, monarchical regimes with carefully policed multiparty systems, and Sadat's Egypt all boasted party-competitive systems. But like several of their socialist counterparts and, in Egypt's case, predecessor, the parties that were to compete for power were created from above and the outcome of elections was more or less known in advance (Hamied al-Ansari 1986, 203).

The shah of Iran habitually dabbled in the fabrication of parties. He established in the 1950s a loyal opposition party, Mardom, and a loyalist party, the Melliyun; eventually they came to be known as the Yes party and Yes Sir! party. Leading up to the elections of summer 1960, Cottam recounted (1964, 297):

> the Shah seemed determined to play seriously with his two parties. Since neither party had been permitted the independence to develop a distinctive personality, however, the fascination of this game was limited to the Shah and the candidates. Rumor in Teheran had it that Melliyun had been allotted two seats for each seat given Mardom, and as the returns began coming in this appeared indeed to be the pattern. The Shah was so confident of his ability to control the election and still maintain a democratic motif that he permitted an influx of correspondents from the world's press.

After 1963, the shah had tired of his two creations and replaced them with the Modern Iran party, run by the young technocrats who engineered the White Revolution of 1963. Then in 1975 he founded the Rastakhiz (Renaissance) party and made Iran a one-party state.

Similarly, the Moroccan monarchy tried to displace existing and in most ways "real" parties, not by abolition, as Nasser did in Egypt, but by siring its own party and controlling election results. Hassan II attempted this in 1963 through the Front for the Defense of Constitutional Institutions (FDIC), but it won only a narrow majority in parliament, which the king then dissolved in 1965. Not until 1976 was another round of legislative elections held, and this time the palace discreetly backed a "nonparty," the so-called Independents, mostly rural and urban Yuppies with no party affiliation. The Independents won a large majority in the new parliament. In the next round of elections in 1984 the palace backed a new party, the Constitutional Union, which swept aside all contenders except the venerable old nationalist party, the Istiqlal.

The Middle East has seen some real parties that seek to organize constituents, win votes, and influence policy. It has also seen some contested elections. Turkey in the 1950s and again in the 1970s was the scene of electoral struggles between the Republican People's party and the Democrat party, and their lineal descendants that would look familiar to most Americans and Europeans. In Israel, older parties, like Mapai, have broken apart and regrouped, but elections are real, partisan loyalties deep, and power is at stake. Much the same could be said of Lebanon's confessional parties up to the outbreak of the civil war in 1975. In the Sudan the Khatmia and Ansar religious brotherhoods, through their party fronts, have waged battle on three different occasions: 1956–1958, 1964–1969, and again with the first civilian elections in 1986 after the downfall of Nimeiri. Sadiq al-Mahdi, leader of the Ansar and head of the Umma party, won a parliamentary majority and became prime minister (Lesch 1986). His inept economic management and his inability to find any solution to the civil war in the south led to yet another military takeover in July 1989.

We should not overlook the ground-up parties, organized in nationalist struggle or in defense of specific interests and classes. We have already discussed the Neo-Destour of Tunisia, but the Wafd party of Egypt, standard-bearer of Egyptian nationalism, is back in action again thirty years after its dissolution by Gamal 'Abd al-Nasser. Morocco's nationalist party, the Istiqlal (Independence) hangs on in the king's carefully controlled political arena. In some countries Communist and Socialist parties, often born in illegality and the objects of constant repression, have developed strong organizations and toughened cadres that compensate for their small membership. We should mention here the Tudeh (Toilers) party of Iran, and the Communist parties of Syria, Iraq, Sudan, Egypt, Tunisia, and Morocco. Morocco also boasts the National Union of Socialists Forces, a non-Marxist party that broke away from the Istiqlal and has become a resilient organization. The Communist party of Israel has always enjoyed legal existence and has competed for votes in Israel's elections. Its major vote bank, perhaps ironically, lies in Israel's Arab population. In Lebanon, where the term *legality* no longer has any meaning, parties have become private armies, or perhaps it is vice versa.

These examples of party success do little to disperse the general gloom enveloping partisan activity in the Middle East. There are four main causes of party atrophy in the region. The first, outlined above, is that parties have been created from the top down and seldom strike roots in the population in whose name they claim to speak. With a stroke of a pen Anwar Sadat dissolved Egypt's Arab Socialist Union in 1975, and there was not the slightest murmur from the "masses" or the party's cadres. The same fate fell to the Sudanese Socialist Union in 1985, and there the "masses" were positively jubilant.

The second cause resides in the hesitancy of leaders to use the parties they have created to mobilize the people, to make them participate in national politics and to share responsibility. Time and again, parties have been used to control and *de*mobilize the populace. Laced through with police informers, parties have become associated with the repressive apparatus of the state—in Iraq, Saddam Hussein, a "policeman," runs both the party and the government. Party cadres, all too often, are bureaucrats who have been seconded to the party from the civil service and whose careers will ultimately be determined in their ministries, not in the party.

Third, the economic strategies of many Middle Eastern states has brought forth a technocratic elite of planners, financial experts, managers, and engineers whose quest for orderly and disciplined change reenforces the party's mission as an instrument of control, especially in the workplace. Boumedienne's Algeria best represents this concept of party organization and technocratic supremacy.

Finally, for those parties that were alive and well prior to independence, there was a marked tendency afterwards to gut them of their best cadres to staff government agencies in an ever-expanding state apparatus. Party militants became government bureaucrats, and the parties were left without any lofty mission and very few experienced organizers. The Neo-Destour, the Ba'ath in Syria and Iraq, and Algeria's FLN have all been victimized by this phenomenon.

## THE TENETS OF SOLIDARISM

A vast body of literature now exists dealing with "corporatism" in European and Latin American society (e.g., Schmitter 1974). Only Bianchi (1984) has tried to apply corporatist analysis to a Middle Eastern (Turkey's) political system. The word *corporatism,* to the best of the authors' knowledge, does not even exist in any of the languages spoken in the region. But although the term itself may be foreign to the Middle East, its logic certainly is not. To oversimplify, corporatist ideologies conceive of societies as organic entities, much like the human body. Societies have functioning parts that perform specific kinds of tasks. The brain (the government) and the nervous system (the party) control these parts and make sure they work harmoniously together to achieve a desired end (once again the teleological mission of the state and society). They *must* work harmoniously together; just as one's arms and legs cannot be at odds with one another if one is to walk, so too the functioning parts of the society must be coordinated for the body to live healthily. Occasionally diseases set in; foreign bodies (the Jews in Nazi Germany) must be purged; conflict may produce paralysis; a specific functioning part may atrophy.

The corporatist imagery comes out of European fascism. It condemns two kinds of conflict models of politics: the Marxist and the liberal. In an organic society neither can there be any place for class conflict nor is any organization along class lines permitted. Likewise the liberal model that posits open competition among a myriad of opposed interests and parties cannot be accepted. In the corporatist model, conflict is pathological; it can never be seen as healthy.

Thus corporatist systems structure organization and representation around the major functional groups in society—agricultural producers, industrial producers, entrepreneurs, white-collar workers, the armed forces. We have already seen how this sort of categorization has manifested itself in Egypt, Algeria, and elsewhere in the Middle East. Such functional categories cut vertically through horizontal strata of wealth and poverty. Agricultural producers may range from a landless tenant to a capitalist farmer, entrepreneurs from a street vendor to a factory owner, and so forth. Corporatism prescribes representation by function and wedges people of disparate power and resources into the same functional box. In contrast to European experience, what has been missing in Middle Eastern corporatism (and in Latin America as Cardoso 1979 pointed out) is a strong party organization as in Hitler's Germany or Franco's Spain. We may be thankful perhaps that Middle Eastern corporatism has been aimed at domestic stability and order and not at external conquest. Again, demobilization and containment of potentially conflicting groups in society have been the objective of corporatist formulas.

It is tempting to adduce historical and cultural antecedents for Middle Eastern corporatism, much as Stepan has done for organic statism in Latin America (Stepan 1978). Medieval and premodern Islamic political theory is replete with treatments of the state as analogous to the human body. Ottoman theoreticians employed what Norman Itzkowitz has called the pharmacology of Islam, comparing the four basic classes of society: men of the sword, the pen, negotiation, and husbandry to the four humors of the body: phlegm, blood, yellow bile, and black bile (see Bianchi 1984, 84–85). And as we have noted earlier, the concept of the *umma,* the community of Muslims, is inherently hostile to conflict and emphasizes the harmony of brotherhood through submission (Islam) to God's will.

Whatever historical and cultural predispositions there may be for the twentieth-century manifestations of corporatism, we argue that those manifestations must be seen as new and culturally neutral. They emerge as a function of state-building and market penetration in an age when no government can afford to condone wide disparities in the distribution of wealth. Significantly, Ziya Gökalp, the ideological muse to the Young Turks and to Atatürk, in elaborating his ideas on "solidarism," relied more on Emile Durkheim than upon theoreticians of the Islamic state.

Corporatism becomes an arm in the struggle to contain large segments of the population that are officially entitled to a fair share of the national pie but that in fact are denied that share as the development process channels resources away from consumption (what the "toiling masses" want) and toward investment and, concomitantly, speculation (what the state elites and private entrepreneurs want as long as their own consumption is not curtailed). It is rare that the relatively disenfranchised masses— peasants, workers, low-income white-collar workers—feel that they are adequately represented through corporatist structures, and they are quite literally bought off by consumer subsidies, guaranteed employment schemes, and a blind eye to moonlighting, peculation, and low productivity.

There is perhaps a predisposition to corporatism that emerges in the contemporary period from the nature of military organization. No modern organization more resembles the corporatist ideal than the military. Here is a relatively large, complex organization divided into functionally specific services, in turn subdivided into functionally specific corps (e.g., engineers, logistics, supply, communications) and task-defined field units (artillery, infantry, armor). The activity of all functioning parts is minutely planned and supervised by the chiefs of staff and chiefs of operations. While the lines of hierarchy, of subordination and command, of officers and recruits, are sharply drawn, military ethos calls for harmony among all units and all levels of command. Insubordination entails court martial, dishonorable discharge, and in times of hostilities, death. The military is a quintessentially purposeful organization, and all of its functioning parts must be subordinated and directed to the pursuit of specific goals and targets. Although it is hard to advance concrete evidence, we can plausibly speculate that the prevalence of government by the military in the Middle East over the past thirty years may have brought to power men who, by their training and the evolution of their military careers, were disposed to organize civil society along corporatist lines.

With this possibility in mind, let us turn once again to the great innovator Atatürk, who in May 1935 set forth his conception of society in terms that were to be echoed throughout the Middle East after 1950 (as cited in Özbudun 1981, 88):

> The source of will and sovereignty is the nation. The Party considers it an important principle that this will and sovereignty be used to regulate the proper fulfillment of the mutual duties of the citizen to the State and of the State to the citizen. We consider the individuals who accept an absolute equality before the law, and who recognise no privileges for any individual, family, class, or community to be . . . populist. It is one of our main principles to consider the people of the Turkish Republic, not as composed of different classes, but as a community divided into various professions according to the requirements of the division of labour for the individual and social life of the Turkish people. The farmers, handicraftsmen, labourers and workmen, people exercising free professions, industrialists, merchants, and public servants are the main groups of work constituting the Turkish community. The aims of our Party . . . are to secure social order and solidarity instead of class conflict, and to establish harmony of interests. The benefits are to be proportionate to the aptitude, to the amount of work.

There is very little that one can add to that vision; its terms were taken up by Nasser, Bourguiba, Boumedienne, various Ba'athists, Ga'afar al-Nimeiri and at least certain subthemes by Mu'ammar Qaddhafi, David Ben Gurion, and the shah of Iran. Perhaps only Lebanon has failed to experience attempts at corporatist organization, although Gen. Fu'ad Chehab (1958–1964) may have had leanings in that direction.

## Corporatism and Parties

There are four major sociopolitical issues with which corporatist organization and ideology have done battle. The first is the role of political parties. We have noted elsewhere that many Middle Eastern leaders have been hostile to partisan competition. They have seen it as divisive, destructive, and a potential conduit for direct foreign intervention in domestic affairs. The common pattern has been the dissolution and legal abolition of all political parties and the establishment of monopoly fronts to represent "all the people." Egypt from 1953 on, Algeria since independence in 1962, and the Sudan between 1969 and 1985 established corporatist monopolies in the Arab Socialist Union, the National Liberation Front, and the Sudanese Socialist Union. The Ba'ath regimes of Iraq and Syria, and the Socialist Destour of Tunisia, have allowed for coalitions of the dominant party with small marginal groupings such as Communists, Nasserists, and liberals, but there has never been any question of these groupings being allowed to organize freely or to play anything but a subordinate role.

## Corporatism and Class

The second issue is that of containing class antagonisms. Corporatist regimes sometimes deny their existence, as in Atatürk's 1935 speech, or acknowledge their existence but refuse to allow any organization along class lines. This notion was at the heart of Nasser's socialism, which sought the "melting away of class differences" through a peaceful and harmonious redistribution of national wealth. There is no question that everywhere corporatism has been aimed at Marxists and any attempts to incite class conflict. But while European corporatism was aimed directly at containing the radicalization of the industrial proletariat, that class has yet to acquire much weight in the Middle East.

Corporatism need not be a mechanism for the defense of the interests of the upper bourgeoisie; in fact it is more likely to appeal to middle- and lower-income groups. But almost never does it seek to give proportionate and effective weight to the poor majority of the adult populations of the Middle East. Nasser's unilateral bestowal of 50% or more of all elected seats throughout all the branches of the ASU and the National Assembly to peasants and workers was window dressing.

## Corporatism and Labor

This leads us to our third issue, organized labor, which refers mainly to workers in industry, mining, municipal services, and transportation, but might also include organized agricultural labor. Corporate regimes pursue dual strategies vis-à-vis labor. One is to encourage organization and unionization. Strategically placed labor, mainly in public-sector enterprises and the transportation sector, may receive favorable wage and social-benefit packages. Such workers are co-opted by the the corporatist state; their leaders are given significant roles in the "party" organization, in legislative assemblies, and sometimes in the government itself. In exchange for favorable unionwide wage and benefit packages, union leadership is expected to keep the rank and file in line. The second strategy is to segment the labor force, relying on the organized-labor elite to keep the economic wheels turning while looking over its shoulder at the majority of unorganized labor in the urban informal sector, in the private sector, and in the countryside, people who would clearly love the jobs of the labor elite.

In Algeria Boumedienne purged the unions (the peak organization, the General Confederation of Algerian Workers, or UGTA) of militant leadership in 1967 and subordinated the unions to his statist industrialization drive. The 1971 Charter of Socialist Management of Enterprise installed an ineffective system of worker participation in management. Every major workplace would have an elected Assembly of Workers, but the latter included management as well as labor. The clear goal of Socialist Management was and is to increase production, not proletarian democracy (DERSA 1981, 132; Nellis 1977, 549). We have already expressed some skepticism with respect to the much more radical Libyan experiment of people's bureaus, or councils (see Glavanis 1984, 139; Vandewalle 1986).

Labor leaders co-opted into the corporatist power structure must walk a fine line between serving the state leaders and maintaining some semblance of credibility among the rank and file. Sometimes the balancing act is impossible to maintain. In 1966 the dominant Türk-İş labor confederation in Turkey condemned a strike in a glass works. This led to the hiving-off of a faction of Türk-İş and the founding of the radical Confederation of Progressive Trade Unions (DISK). By 1970 DISK had 40,000 members, and Türk-İş 700,000, but DISK became an active element in the agitation of the 1970s. When the military took over in 1980, DISK was disbanded and many of its leaders arrested.

A similar process unfolded in Tunisia. The General Confederation of Tunisian Workers (UGTT) had been a pillar of the Destourian coalition before and after independence. Anytime labor leaders appeared ready to use the organizational strength of the UGTT in any way that conflicted with regime goals, Bourguiba had them removed. Throughout the 1970s and the readjustment of the Tunisian economy after the Ben Salah statist experiment, the UGTT was led by Habib Achour. In 1978 cost-of-living riots broke out in several Tunisian cities. The rank and file of the UGTT were hit hard, yet the regime wanted Achour to condemn the violence. In order not to lose support among his following, Achour had to take his distance from the regime. He was jailed, but the relative autonomy of the UGTT had been asserted.

Cost-of-living riots occurred once again in January 1984 when the regime sought to reduce consumer subsidies. It could no longer rely on the relatively pampered members of the UGTT to remain aloof from the agitation. During the sixth plan, 1982–1986, the regime called for a "social dialogue" and announced that the consultative Economic and Social Council would be transformed into the National Council for Social Dialogue and that in each ministry Social Peace Commissions would be created (Baduel 1983). But corporatist discipline appeared to have broken down. After Habib Achour was once again jailed, the UGTT called, in May 1984, for a boycott of local elections and even threatened to run its own list of candidates in the 1986 legislative elections.

Corporatist discipline is always hard to maintain. Sometimes the regime will tolerate strikes and labor agitation in the private sector but forbid them in the public, as public enterprise is the motor of national development and, in any case, already is owned by "the people." The Algerian Charter of Socialist Management of Enterprise states (DERSA 1981, 125): "If private enterprise is characterized by a permanent contradiction between the interest of the owner and those of the workers . . . in the socialist enterprise the interests of the producers and those of the state are indissociable." Such double standards have seldom spared public enterprise strikes, no matter how illegal. In 1977, only one year after the adoption of a new national charter, there were 129 strikes, involving 31,000 workers, in the Algerian public sector (DERSA 1981). Egypt experienced major strikes twice in 1968, as workers demanded that military officers responsible for the debacle of the June War of 1967 be given severe sentences by the military tribunals. In 1977 dockers at Alexandria kicked off three days of cost-of-living riots that spread through most Egyptian cities. We should note also that certain unions, because of their long history and/or strategic position in the production process, have often asserted their organizational autonomy: One thinks of the phosphate miners of Khouribga in Morocco, the port workers of Basra in Iraq and Aden in the PDRY, and the railway workers in the Sudan.

One of the unexpected results of corporatist experiments is to inculcate organizational skills and eventually some sort of autonomy from the state in the very functional groups the experiment was designed to control. The evolution of the Confederation of Egyptian Labor is instructive. Its autonomy was limited in the Nasserist-socialist era, when rhetoric in favor of the working man was at a high pitch. During the Sadatist era of economic liberalization, the confederation's leadership was co-opted into prominent official positions and its leader, Sa'ad Muhammed Ahmad, was made the minister of human resources, a post he held for nearly a decade. By the time of Sadat's death in 1981, "the Confederation had become the largest, wealthiest and most representative association in Egyptian society" (Bianchi 1986, 438). Under Mubarrak, the confederation became an effective veto group, notably in precluding any further joint ventures between public-sector companies and foreign investors. Corporatism had thus "provided union leaders with new means for defending workers' interests and, ironically, for limiting the decisional autonomy of the authoritarian regime in critical issues" (Bianchi 1986, 434).

Increased autonomy need not entail greater radicalism. The trend in Turkey and Egypt, and perhaps elsewhere, is for unions and professional associations to become important economic enterprises in their own right.

With dues, special funds, and pension funds at their disposal, unions and associations have invested in businesses, run cooperative-housing schemes and hospitals, launched banks to mobilize their members' savings, and even participated in joint ventures with foreign capital. In this way the organizations develop a stake in the overall smooth functioning of the economic system; their members' interests are better served through the general ability of the economy to generate profits, an ability not enhanced by strikes and agitation. Political co-optation through corporatism has to a limited degree been replaced by co-optation into the economic establishment.[1] There is a potential marriage, already familiar in the West, of big capital, whether public or private, and big labor (see Chapter 10).

The gradual distancing from close corporatist control that several Middle Eastern labor organizations have undergone has been replicated to some extent in business and professional associations (especially those of lawyers, journalists, and engineers). Corporatist organizations, like public-sector enterprise, have tended to fall into the hands of bureaucrats, clock punchers with little motivation. Just as production and profits have suffered in the parastatals, ideological commitment and indeed unity itself have suffered in corporatist fronts. The decay of corporatist structures has paralleled the erosion of elite confidence in its ability to change society. In the process (Bianchi 1984, 130), "the network of public professional associations operates, not as a centralized system for harmonizing and balancing similarly organized functional units, but as a series of channels for selectively distributing unequal privileges and rewards within and among differentially organized, competing social and economic sectors."

Rather than displacing patronage, corporatist structures have simply absorbed it. Social harmony then becomes a function of patronage carrots and the formidable stick of highly trained internal police forces.

## Corporatism, Sectarianism, and Ethnicity

The fourth issue with which corporatist frameworks must grapple is that of ethnic and sectarian identity and conflict. This is a vast question and one that has vexed Middle Eastern leaders as much as it has fascinated outside observers (see, for example, Coon 1958; Bates and Rassam 1983; and Eickelman 1981). Although we shall deal all too cursorily with this topic under the rubric of corporatist containment and solidarism, the reader should be warned that the topic warrants much fuller treatment.

It may be that most of us implicitly adopt a Marxist supposition that the really intractable conflicts in society revolve around issues of class and the maldistribution of wealth. Communalism and sectarianism by contrast have been seen in the modernization literature as anachronisms that would slowly erode in the face of economic development, literacy, and nation-building (inter alia, see Lerner 1959). But as any observer of the persistence of racial discrimination in the United States knows, issues of blood, skin color, and creed may not be susceptible to treatment through public policy.

It may in fact be easier to redistribute wealth through public policy than to wash away these parochial loyalties, prejudices, and conflicts.

The major corporatist experiments in the Middle East have to some extent foundered on the rocks of ethnic and sectarian loyalties. As early as 1926 Atatürk confronted a Kurdish rebellion with Islamic overtones in Eastern Anatolia. It represented the first major challenge to the new secular, republican regime. Nasser was challenged by the Muslim Brotherhood in 1954 and 1965. Coptic Christian and Muslim confrontations became commonplace in Egypt during the Sadat era, and eventually Muslim extremists assassinated him. Habib Bourguiba early on had to back away from his own secularizing proclivities, and today Tunisia has one of the strongest Muslim fundamentalist movements in the Arab world. Finally, Lebanon has been destroyed as a nation by sectarian strife, not just Muslims versus Christians, but Shi'is versus Sunnis, versus Druze, versus Maronites, etc.

The issues become murky when sect or ethnic groups overlap with relative wealth or deprivation. Lebanese Shi'is have for long been the underclass in Lebanon's economy, whereas the Maronites have formed the core of the business elite (Nasr 1985). Oriental Jews in Israel have been in a situation similar to that of the Shi'is in Lebanon. In North Yemen, Shi'i tribesmen fought Sunni townsmen in what might be seen as a confrontation between two modes of production.

In certain instances we have a multidimensional overlap of ethnic origins, distinctive language, shared sect, geographic location, and a common economic way of life. When all these factors come together, the ethnic-sectarian issue becomes particularly intractable. The two most outstanding examples in the Middle East are the Kurds, perhaps 20 million strong, whose mountain homeland sprawls across the borders of Turkey, Iran, and Iraq. Turkey has ruthlessly suppressed all attempts at Kurdish self-determination. The shah, and later Khomeini, dealt successfully but not definitively with sporadic Kurdish insurrections. In Iraq, however, Kurdish dissidence has been chronic and has seriously hindered Arab-dominated elites in Baghdad from consolidating their rule. As noted, Iraq's cease-fire with Iran in the summer of 1988 allowed the former to turn its military energies against its own Kurdish populations, using chemical weapons in the process.

The second example is that of the black, mainly Nilotic, populations of the southern Sudan, roughly one-third of the country's total population and land area. These people are non-Arab, speak tribal languages other than Arabic, are for the most part non-Muslim, and live as cattle raisers, fisher folk, or subsistence farmers in the vast swamps and savannas of the south. Since 1955 there has been a chronic state of civil war in the southern Sudan, interrupted for about a decade, 1974–1983, during the Nimeiri regime. The fighting has periodically led to the toppling of regimes (1964 and 1985) and crippled the economy.

More often the issues are less clear cut in the Middle East. Ethnic and sectarian groups may not be geographically fixed, may have considerable degrees of inequality among members, and may share important characteristics with majority populations, such as language (e.g., Shi'a Arabs in Iraq) or religion (e.g., Muslim Berbers in North Africa). The result is a multidimensional set of actors. It is hard to know at any point what factor is driving the actors—ethnicity, region, religion, or class status. Batatu beautifully captured all the richness of the confusion (1978, 868) in describing a revolt in the city of Mosul in northern Iraq in March 1959:

> The events of March at Mosul illumined with a flaming glare the complexity of the conflicts that agitated Iraq and disclosed its various social forces in their essential nature and in the genuine line-up of their life interests. For four days and four nights Kurds and Yezidis stood against Arabs; Assyrian and Aramean Christians against Arab Moslems; the Arab tribe of Albu Mutaiwit against the Arab tribe of Shammar; the Kurdish tribe of al-Gargariyyah against Arab Albu Mutaiwit; the peasants of the Mosul country against their landlords; the soldiers of the Fifth Brigade against their officers; the periphery of the city of Mosul against its center; the plebeians of the Arab quarters of al-Makkawi and Wadi Hajar against the aristocrats of the Arab quarter of ad-Dawwasah; and within the quarter of Bab al-Baid, the family of al-Rajabu against its traditional rivals, the Aghawat. It seemed as if all social cement dissolved and all political authority vanished. Individualism, breaking out, waxed into anarchy. The struggle between nationalists and Communists had released age-old antagonisms, investing them with an explosive force carrying them to the point of civil war.

What we should bear in mind is that ethnicity and sectarianism should be seen as resources that can be drawn upon when they best suit the needs of an individual or a group. They need not be a badge that is worn constantly and with unalterable intensity (see Kasfir 1979). There are times, when communal tensions run high, when clans are settling scores, when sectarian or ethnic witch-hunts are under way, that an individual cannot shed the ethnic or sectarian label with which he or she was born. In calmer circumstances, however, an individual may act as easily in terms of his or her occupation or class position.

The examples of the Kurds and of the black populations of the southern Sudan are those of peoples seeking at a minimum regional autonomy and, in the case of the Kurds, national independence. These populations at various times sought to opt out of existing systems. That desire was not shared by all Kurds or by all southern Sudanese. Today the leaders of the rebellion in the southern Sudan claim they seek a socialist transformation *within* the nation. Still, these two movements have seen little to be gained from the regimes with which they have done battle.

In contrast, most ethnic dissidence has had as its aim to opt in to existing political systems, to use violence or its threat to extract more resources from the central authorities: roads, schools, clinics, industrial projects, and so forth. Even though the Turkish authorities give no recognition to their Kurdish minority, they have nonetheless invested heavily in large dams, hydropower projects, and agricultural schemes in the Kurdish heartland of Eastern Anatolia. The Kurds of the Islamic Republic of Iran also tried to fight for a more favored position in the newly established republic. Whether Khomeini's violent response forced the Iranian Kurds toward opting out remains to be seen. Similarly, the Berbers of Algeria and Morocco have confronted the central authorities to augment the Berbers' position in the political establishment and to draw more resources to their home regions. Their status is highly complex. Their regions of origin are generally mountains or steppes, and generally poor. For this very reason out-migration has been heavy. Several North African cities are majority Berber in population, and hundreds of thousands of Berbers have worked in France and other European countries. Berbers are a crucial part of the North African urban proletariat. Finally, in both Algeria and Morocco many Berbers enjoy elite status, with prominent roles in the state technocracy, party leadership, and the officers corps. The interests of North African Berbers are not homogeneous, and for that very reason there has never been a unified Berber front, no less a movement, to opt out of existing political systems (see Gellner and Micaud 1972; Roberts 1982, 1983).

When religious identity is invoked, it tends to take two forms. First, religious minorities generally adopt a defensive posture, trying to guarantee some degree of legitimacy and freedom of practice within the majority society. Some minorities have not fared well; but none worse than the Baha'is in Iran. Historically in the Middle East, the most violent repression of a religious minority was that of the Armenians in Turkey at the beginning of this century, and since 1948, the year in which the state of Israel was founded, Jewish minorities in the Arab countries have experienced varying degrees of repression, although the right to practice their religion has never been questioned.

The second form is that taken by religious movements within the dominant Islamic majority. Here the objective is to transform existing political systems, to force them from without or to change them from within to adhere to the *shari'a* and to Islamic principles. There is no question of opting out here, only of exerting the force of the putative majority in whose name Muslim militants claim to speak.

In summary, it is the case that no sectarian or ethnic groups can be analyzed or understood within their own terms of reference. In every instance there will be at stake elements of the distribution of scarce resources, of making concessions that might jeopardize national unity, of reacting to minority demands in such a way as to call the regime's legitimacy into question. Just as sectarian or ethnic groups are the enemies of corporatist solidarity, so too are they often the enemies of class formation and consciousness. Sectarianism and ethnicity, more often than not, cut across class lines. No corporatist or class-based organization has succeeded in fully co-opting or defanging ethnic and sectarian groups. Until national political systems can provide institutions and rules of political conduct that are reliable and respected, such groups will continue to act as buffers against the arbitrary use of state power.

Let us note finally that minorities have the pesky habit of living on strategic real estate: Iraq's Kurds live in the oil-bearing region of their country, and their dissidence is a loaded gun pointed at the head of the Iraqi regime. So too, the southern Sudanese sit on that country's recently discovered oil reserves but, more important, control the headwaters of the White Nile. Central authorities almost always suspect strategically located minorities of colluding with hostile foreign powers to destroy the nation, and sometimes those authorities are right.

## THE FAILURE OF IDEOLOGY

For over three decades the official ideologies spawned in the Middle East shared several common themes, all similar to if not derived from Atatürk's and the Turkish republic's six principles. National strength, meaning freedom from imperial control coupled with a strong economy and strong armed forces, was both a goal and a promise. Building a new citizen and a new sense of citizenship was a second ideological tenet, something that would be achieved once foreign control had been ended and domestic oppressor classes, such as large landowners, and comprador businesspersons eliminated. Mass literacy, public health, and a booming planned economy would take care of the physical and work needs of the population, giving each adult a new sense of dignity and self-worth. The psychic needs of the populace would be satisfied through the mass party, which would educate new generations in nationalist and civic duties. Every regime espoused the equitable distribution of the benefits of economic growth. Some called this concern socialism and some not.

Curiously, all of these themes can be found in Western modernization literature of the 1950s and 1960s: the inculcation of new civic values and future-oriented behavior among the citizens through mass education and the mass media. The literature of nation-building could, in spirit, have been written by Atatürk or Nasser. The shah of Iran, King Hassan of Morocco, King Hussein of Jordan, and, indeed, the Saudi monarchy have been as concerned with modernization and national strength as the more obvious socialist republican leaders. If one goes over the rhetoric of the White Revolution launched by the shah in 1963, one finds familiar themes of destroying the feudal landowners through agrarian reform, of redistributing national wealth through selling shares to workers in private and public industry, of bringing literacy to all the people, and of liberating women. Ten years later the shah added the national-military dimension, proclaiming that within a decade or so Iran would become a world military power.

Had the planned, state-dominated economies worked up to expectations, had the expansion and quality of education and social services kept pace with unchecked population growth, and had Middle Eastern nations built measurably powerful military establishments (only Turkey, the Middle East's sole member of NATO, and Israel can be said to have done so), then perhaps the accompanying ideologies might have had some impact upon broad strata of Middle Eastern society. But all the performance failures, from unprofitable public enterprise to repeated military setbacks for some Arab armies, rendered the rhetoric hollow and ultimately a target for derision and anger. Khoury (1983a) has rightly written of regime "exhaustion," the collective playing out of a set of policy and ideological options by an entire generation of Middle Eastern leadership. The statist, socialist, and implicitly secularizing experiments of the past thirty years have resolved few of the problems they promised to tackle, and there is a general sense that their proponents have few cards left to play. Other than in Iran and perhaps Saudi Arabia, the one option that has not been tried is Islamic government and, by default, its hour may yet come.

It is tricky business to analyse any religion as a social phenomenon, that is, as something produced and held to by various people because of social change and stress. For true believers, God's word and faith in the Almighty need no explanation that puny mortals can adduce. Thus to treat Islam as an ideology, or Islamic resurgence as a political movement, is to speak a language different from that of its practitioners. We cannot resolve this kind of tension and, cognizant of the judgmentalism involved, proceed to treat militant Islam in its political and ideological, rather than theological, aspects.

Many Muslims claim that there has been no resurgence; Islam has always been the dominant motif for Middle East populations, but that fact was obscured to outside observers by the rhetoric of secularizing leaders who controlled the institutions of power and the media. Moreover, they argue, Western observers have a visceral interest in seeing Islam, Western Christendom's old nemesis, disappear. There is no gainsaying that Islam has permeated Middle Eastern society profoundly over the centuries, and because it is a religion that pays great attention to law and political rule, it has direct implications for rulership in Muslim societies.

Moreover, because the nineteenth- and twentieth-century confrontation of the Middle East with the West was seen by many Middle Easterners as another enactment of an ancient struggle between Christianity and Islam, and European colonialism as an effort to snuff out Islam once and for all, nationalist resistance and Islamic reaffirmation became inextricably intertwined. For the Berber mountaineers who made up the fighting forces of Algeria's liberation movement, it would have been impossible to separate their sense of "Muslimness" from their Algerian national pride. For many Muslims there is not and should not be any separation of nation and religion nor any separation of "church" and state.

Many Muslim theologians and laypeople believed that the dominant statist experiments after World War II were totally misguided in their attempts to define a separate and diminished religious sphere, to separate Islam from politics, to reduce the *'ulema'* to mere bureaucrats, to bury the *shari'a* in an avalanche of Western-inspired civil-law codes. Nearly all political leaders could feel the repressed heat of Muslim militants; Nasser,

Atatürk, and the shah, among others, broke up their organizations and put the leaders in jail. Significantly however, nearly all republican constitutions in the Middle East state that the president must be a Muslim, and several declare that Islam is the religion of state and that all law must conform to the *shari'a*. Leaders from Nasser to Saddam Hussein have frequently invoked Muslim themes to try to legitimize their rule, and few have failed to make the pilgrimage, ostentatiously, to Mecca. And we should not forget that several "secularizing" leaders, including Nasser and Boumedienne, were in fact pious Muslims who performed their religious duties regularly.

The current rise of Islamic militancy is partially a function of the hesitancy of incumbent elites to continue to repress and harass militant groups. It is not that these groups are so powerful, but rather that the population as a whole varies between indifference and hostility toward the incumbent elites. While relatively few might welcome Islamic government, a far broader swath of the population shares the moral indignation of the militants. Incumbent elites are aware of this popular state of mind and hesitate to confront the militants for fear of isolating themselves further.

Another explanation of the phenomenon is largely sociological and directly drawn from theories of social strain. The general line of argument is that the most active militants tend to be young males with a high school or university education. They usually come from provincial cities and from solid and religiously observant families. The argument is that these young, educated Middle Easterners gravitate toward large, cosmopolitan cities in search of further education or work. There they are confronted with upper-class behavior that they see as decadent, if not perverted. On university campuses women mix freely with men; they expose their arms, legs, and faces; even the working masses may be corrupted through drugs and alcohol. The result, it is alleged, is that these highly motivated people are led to assert their Islamic values and to reject the existing political and social system. Some believe that society as a whole is corrupt and unredeemable. Like the Prophet himself, who left Mecca and built the new religion at Medina, these groups believe that one must leave the corrupt society, rally the few true believers, and conquer the corrupt from without (thus, the Repentance and Holy Flight group of Egypt). Others feel that incumbent elites and dominant classes must be directly assaulted from within and that the masses will follow the Islamic puritans. This was the path followed successfully by the supporters of the Imam Khomeini in Iran and the path the assassins of Anwar al-Sadat hoped to follow (see Ibrahim 1980; Sivan 1985; Kepel 1986; Ansari 1986, 211–30). There is also the more moderate line followed by the Muslim Brotherhood in Egypt and elsewhere of challenging the regime but doing so within the rules of the game as laid down by the regime itself.

There is clearly a large grain of truth in the sociological theory, but militants in Iran, Egypt, and elsewhere are just as clearly drawn from social sectors other than the provincial intelligentsia. Young male migrants in unskilled and semiskilled positions in Iran's urban centers were the shock troops of the revolution. Traditional merchants groups and petty entrepreneurs throughout the area, but notably in Turkey, Iran, Tunisia, and Syria, have been consistently attracted to militant Islamic causes (inter alia, see Fischer 1982; Sunar and Toprak 1983). In all too brief summary, we suggest that the three factors: the failure of elite confidence, the exhaustion of the regimes themselves and popular support for them, and the strains of rapid change, which have impinged upon some social groups more than others, must all be weighed in any explanation of contemporary militant Islam.

We also argue that the intertwining of Islam and nationalism should not be undone artificially. Several authors have suggested that while nationalism was the dominant ideology of the 1950s and 1960s, Islam has become the dominant ideology of the 1970s and 1980s (see, inter alia, Arjomand 1984; Ibrahim 1982a). It may be, however, that what we are witnessing is the same bedrock of religio-nationalism (which sustained the Algerian revolution), with a greater emphasis today on the religious symbols and values. Nationalists like Michel Aflaq recognized the religious content of Arab nationalism and built Islam into the otherwise secular Ba'athi conceptualization of the unified Arab nation. One wonders how Iran's tenacity in its war with Iraq could be explained in religious terms alone. Surely the fierce strain of Iranian nationalism that Mossadegh personified in 1953 was recast in the Islamic drive of Imam Khomeini. Similarly, Saddam Hussein must invoke religious symbols, along with the Arab nationalist ones, to rally Iraqis to the flag. He repeatedly compared the current conflict to the battle of Qadassia, through which the Arabs first brought Islam to what is today Iran. Ajami (1978/79, 78) has argued that Arabism is dead, but nationalism, we argue, is alive, well, and wedded to Islam.

There is one last sociological phenomenon that should be mentioned. Both individually and collectively, there is frequently an espousal of militancy for militancy's sake, virtually without regard for its ideological content. Individual leaders have often oscillated between political extremes; Marxists or leftist radicals in their youth and Islamic fundamentalists in their autumn years (Akram Hawrani of Syria and Ahmed Ben Bella of Algeria are examples). What may best explain these gyrations is the simple quest for activism, the need that many politically aware Middle Easterners feel to do something to move their societies and to challenge the corruption and complacency of incumbent elites. In May 1959, according to Batatu (1979, 900), the Iraqi Communist party pressured the government of 'Abd al-Karim Qassim for greater representation in the cabinet. Although the party had no more than 20,000 members, it was able to put 300,000 demonstrators into the streets of Baghdad. What did these people understand by their demonstration? How much Marxism could they possibly have mastered? Can we see as their counterparts twenty years later the hundreds of thousands of Iranians who repeatedly filled the streets of Iranian cities in support of Ayatollah Khomeni? Did the latter know anything more about the doctrine of trusteeship of the jurisprudents than the former had known

about the class dialectic? Probably not. What we may presume the masses
saw in both movements was a tool with a cutting edge and leaders prepared
to help them shape their own destinies.

## SOLIDARISM AND
## ECONOMIC LIBERALIZATION

Perhaps the most profound challenge to solidarism and corporatism will
emerge in the general process of streamlining, if not reducing, the degree
of state intervention in the economy. The political controls that corporatism
affords various regimes will be difficult to maintain if the state begins to
cede control of important economic resources to the private sector.

Whether out of conviction or convenience, Nasser always argued that
there would be no real democracy in the midst of poverty, no matter what
the constitutional guarantees. A poor man cannot truly exercise his sovereign
right to choose. Hence the state must manage the economy so that poverty
is overcome and socialist democracy may prevail. But as the goal of socialist
prosperity receded, so too did that of socialist democracy. Now in "liberalizing" Turkey, Prime Minister Turgut Özal has voiced a new orthodoxy
that Nasser would have found abhorrent: "We believe that the free market
and democracy must go hand in hand" (Speech at Council on Foreign
Relations, New York, March 1985).

Özal's prescription for democracy may not be compatible with corporatist
structures. It raises the important question whether economic liberalization
necessitates some form of political liberalization. We have argued consistently that political elites of varying ideological persuasions have been
reluctant to see national resources transferred from the state domain and
into hands beyond the direct control of the state. Increasingly dynamic
private sectors, increasingly autonomous trade unions and professional
groups, private banks and organizational pension funds, all suggest that
the state is losing its grip on major economic levers and that wealth and
employment may be accumulating more rapidly outside than within the
state sector. From strong material bases outside the state, new class actors
may be able to challenge incumbent elites. Thus, the stakes are high: On
the one hand, incumbent elites realize that the state has overreached its
capacity to manage economic growth and must retreat, while, on the other,
they fear that retreat in the economic sphere may lead to the erosion of
political controls.

This need not be the outcome, but it is certainly a strong possibility.
There are many examples among developing countries in which dynamic
private sectors, relatively autonomous interest groups, and increasing resort
to market mechanisms to distribute resources have been combined with
strong authoritarian and corporatist political controls. Indonesia, South
Korea, Pakistan, and Mexico are all important examples. But the process
of redemocratization that has taken place in Brazil, Peru, Argentina, and
South Korea may indicate the outer limits to which corporatist authoritarianism combined with economic liberalization can be pushed.

In the Middle East, regional conflicts (Arab-Israeli, Iran-Iraq) may give incumbent leaders a justification for imposing strict political controls on their citizenries, but these controls are likely to become more and more artificial and more and more resented. If Islamic regimes proliferate in the region, a new rationale for corporatist authoritarianism may be found, but Iran, like Pakistan, will find itself faced with the same dilemma of allowing strategic resources in society to be privatized while trying to exert political control over groups with the economic wherewithal to resist.

Redemocratization is not an issue in the Middle East; there has been precious little democracy in the region in the past. Democratization is, however, a distinct possibility as economies diversify and middle-income groups grow in size. That possibility is strongly conditioned by external conflict and the alleged need to close ranks domestically, by world economic trends that may choke off economic liberalization, and by cultural predispositions to political systems that emphasize organic unity and eschew all forms of open conflict. But if this array of formidable obstacles remains within manageable proportions, tensions within the enfeebled statist experiments of the Middle East may give rise to more pluralist political and economic systems.

## NOTES

1. Several Middle Eastern regimes have experimented with selling shares of public enterprises to the workers, in the hope that those shares would encourage workers to work harder in order to boost profits and thus returns on their holdings. The unplanned growth of union and professional-association capitalism has probably been more effective in achieving those ends.

# 13

# THE MILITARY
# AND THE STATE

Throughout recorded history the geographic Middle East has been the arena for sweeping military encounters. Enduring geopolitical struggles between the two great river systems—the Nile and the Tigris-Euphrates— date back to the pharaonic and Babylonian dynasties. As perhaps the world's most important crossroads, the area has been fought over by Greeks, Romans, Assyrians, Persians, Turks, Mongols, Crusaders, and, latterly, the imperial powers of nineteenth-century Europe. As Islam spread across this area, it was carried, so to speak, in the saddlebags of Muslim generals. Kemal Atatürk, the Gazi, or warrior, is but the most recent in a long line of military heroes of epic proportions.

There are those who see the area, its peoples, religion, and culture, as deeply impregnated with a fascination for military strength and valor, inspired perhaps by the early Islamic conquests and the martial traditions of largely tribal societies. We raise the issue of some sort of cultural predisposition merely to signal its currency, if not its prevalence, in much of the literature loosely referred to as "orientalism." Such cultural characterizations must always be treated with care and skepticism, although, like many stereotypes, they may contain a kernel of truth.

## THE SALIENCE OF THE MILITARY
## IN MIDDLE EAST POLITICS

What is undeniable is the prevalence of military conflict in the Middle East since World War II, carried out on a scale and with an intensity that has been rivaled only in theaters such as the Indo-Pakistani or the Indo-Chinese since the 1930s. The area has witnessed one major war for national liberation and independence in Algeria (1954–1962). Among independent states, the most salient example is that of the Arab-Israeli conflict, which has resulted in four major wars and several thousand deaths. Accompanying this intractable confrontation have been extraordinarily bloody civil wars in Lebanon (1976–), the Sudan (1959–1971 and 1983–), North Yemen (1962–1968), and Oman (early 1970s), while the Iraqi government has sporadically fought its Kurdish minority. King Hussein of Jordan engaged armed elements of the Palestinian Liberation Organization in savage battle in September 1970, and Algeria and Morocco have fought each other since 1976 in the ex-Spanish Sahara, which Morocco has claimed as its own territory, but which the Polisario Liberation Front, with Algerian backing, has tried to win for itself.

The most spectacular and grisly of these conflicts has been the Iran-Iraq war, which raged from 1981 until a cease-fire in the summer of 1988. In most ways it was a conventional war, with large regular and irregular armed focus confronting each other with very high levels of fire power and means of destruction, including poison gas. Perhaps as many as a million died in what became a conflict to rival those of Korea in the 1950s and Vietnam in the 1960s.

Alongside these major military confrontations, there has been a constant stream of smaller incidents: brief border skirmishes (Egypt-Libya, Morocco-Algeria); shows of force (Jordan-Syria, Syria-Iraq, Israel versus all its neighbors); invasions of longer or shorter duration (Turkey in Cyprus, Libya in Chad, Israel and Syria in Lebanon, Iraq in Iran, and then Iran in Iraq).

This simple listing of military conflicts says nothing about causes and motives; they are complex and specific to each particular theater or conflict. All that the listing tells us is that the Middle East has had more than its share of military violence and, predictably, has devoted more of its human and material resources to defense and war-making than have many other regions of the developing world.

It is also undeniable that Middle Eastern societies have experienced prolonged periods of rule by the military. Military or quasi-military government has been the rule rather than the exception in the region. Even when, de jure, regimes are headed by civilians, it may be the case that the power wielders are military officers who have left their uniforms in the closet. Atatürk himself was the first general to follow this path and to insist that those of his officer colleagues who wished to pursue political careers do likewise. Ismet Inönü, his vice president and successor, led the way in resigning from the armed forces. Still it is hard to see Atatürk's regime as other than quasi-military. Next door to Turkey, Reza Shah, commander of the Iranian cossacks, founded a monarchy, but throughout his rule his regime was reliant upon the military. His son Mohammed Reza Pahlavi continued to rely on his military establishment and in fact owed his throne in 1953 to the initiative of General Fazlollah Zahedi, who, in coordination with the Central Intelligence Agency (CIA), arrested the civilian prime minister and opponent of the shah, Mohammed Mossadegh.

As the Arab countries gained their independence, several fell under nearly uninterrupted military rule. Since 1949 Syria has known only brief periods of civilian rule. Today Hafiz al-Assad may wear a suit to work, but he and his fellow Alawi officers constitute the power elite of the government and of the Ba'ath party. Iraq, since the toppling of the monarchy in July 1958, has had constant military rule, although one should note that Saddam Hussein comes out of the internal police rather than the military. Several of his closest associates from his home area of Takrit are strategically placed in the military and in the Iraqi Ba'ath party (although Helms 1984, 131, noted the increasing civilianization of the regime). Similarly the Yemen Arab Republic since 1962, the People's Democratic Republic of Yemen since 1969, the Sudan between 1969 and 1985, Algeria between 1965 and 1978, and Libya since 1969 have been ruled by the military.

One should not belittle, however, the possible significance of the "civilianization" of military regimes. Over time the moves that initially may be largely symbolic, such as dropping military titles and substituting mufti for uniforms, may lead to a real transfer of power and control to civilian hands. That transfer took place in dramatic fashion in Turkey in 1950, although the military has intervened in politics in 1960, 1971, and 1980. In Egypt and Algeria in the past decade there has been a process of creeping civilianization, with nonmilitary technocrats playing increasingly prominent roles in economic and social policymaking. But the two presidents, Husni Mubarrak and Chadli Benjadid, were professional military officers and maintain close links to their senior officers corps. Key positions in internal security and administration, national defense, and foreign affairs are still reserved for senior officers.

Some regimes, like Iran from the 1920s until 1979, have had no formal military cast to them. One thinks of the other major monarchies: Jordan, Morocco, and Saudi Arabia. In all three countries, the king is intimately linked to the military. Members of the royal family, if not the king himself, direct the Ministry of Defense, command key units in the armed forces, and review all promotions in the officers corps. Before becoming king, Prince Hassan of Morocco was put in command of the Royal Armed Forces by his father, and King Hussein, whose throne is dependent upon the support of the largely Bedouin Jordan Legion, has always been a king in uniform.

There are a handful of regimes that have had a reputation for civilian predominance. Tunisia has enjoyed uninterrupted civilian government since 1956, the size of the military has been contained, few military men have played any role in the civilian administration, and there have been no serious attempts at military intervention. President Bourguiba, with single-minded purpose, built his coalitions among civilian forces and insulated his regime from military influence. However, as we shall see below, in recent years the size and cost of Tunisia's military have been growing substantially. Moreover, it was the minister of defense and now head of state, Gen. Zine al Abdine Ben Ali, who deposed President Bourguiba in 1988.

We have already discussed, in Chapters 11 and 12, Turkey's peculiar oscillation between civilian and military rule since 1950. The president of the republic is still a general. Indeed Kenan Evren led the coup in September 1980 that ended nearly a decade of turbulent civilian government. But if Turkey is one day to enter the European Common Market, it will have to convince its future partners that its civilian institutions are firmly and irrevocably anchored.

There was a time when Lebanon appeared to be a solid civilian republic, but looks were deceiving. Civil war broke out in Lebanon in the summer of 1958, at the time of the overthrow of the Iraqi monarchy. The violence provoked U.S. military intervention. President Camille Chamoun, a civilian, was judged to have mishandled the situation, and was replaced by Gen. Fu'ad Chehab, like Chamoun a Christian. For six years under Chehab, Lebanon was under lightly veiled military rule. Between 1964 and 1976, Lebanese presidents were civilian, but their presence did not head off the civil war that, since 1976, has devoured civilian institutions, the Lebanese armed forces, and the country itself in vicious fighting.

Israel has escaped military rule, but here too looks may be deceiving. Indeed, soon after independence, Prime Minister David Ben Gurion feared a coup d'état engineered by the leaders of the outlawed Jewish terrorist organizations (principally, the Irgun, led by Menachem Begin). It is an irony of sorts that Begin went on to become prime minister himself some thirty years later through the ballot box. More important, however, is the thorough intermingling of the civilian and military spheres in Israeli politics and in the economy. Israel is a nation in arms. It has fought four major wars. It has faced terrorist threats of various kinds. It maintains a large defense industrial base, and many public activities are regulated by concerns of national security. The military does not have to seize power in Israel to get its own way because on most issues it is already positioned to get what it wants. Moreover, many of Israel's most visible politicians have come out of the military: Moshe Dayan, Itzhak Rabin, Haim Bar-Lev, Ezer Weizmann, Rafael Aytan, and Ariel Sharon, to name but the most illustrious (for a contrasting view, see Gutmann and Landau 1985, 191). We do well to remember, however, that it is an abuse of reality to draw hard and fast distinctions between civilian and military spheres, just as it is between public and private sectors (see Bienen 1983).

So far, with the possible exception of Turkey (Sunar and Sayari 1986), there has been little pressure for civilianization and democratization in the Middle East such as we have seen in Argentina, Brazil, the Philippines, and South Korea. Whether or not such a process requires a large and assertive middle class and a powerful private sector is moot, but several Middle Eastern societies appear to have both (one thinks mainly of Egypt, Turkey, Morocco, Israel, and until 1979, Iran). Only two countries, however, have witnessed the ending of military or quasi-military rule as a result of civilian pressure: the Sudan and Iran. The two are, needless to say, remarkably different in their socioeconomic configurations. Still, in Iran, the shah's enormous repressive apparatus, built on the armed forces and the secret police (SAVAK), was neutralized by persistent street demonstrations and strikes orchestrated by both the Iranian Muslim organizations and the radical leftist groups. It would be hard to describe the new Islamic Republic of Iran as civilian but equally hard to describe it as a military dictatorship. The regular military have been contained by a dominant coalition of the clergy (the mullahs) and the irregular Revolutionary Guards (Pasdaran). It is this coalition that, with Khomeini's fervent blessing, prosecuted the war with Iraq. The Islamic republic is thus a strange, if not unique, mutant of Samuel Huntington's praetorian state, led by "priests" and armed religious militants (see below).

In the Sudan, a military regime under Gen. Ga'afar al-Nimeiri had led the country to economic disaster; the regime was paralyzed in the spring of 1985 by massive demonstrations in Khartoum, spearheaded by middle-class professionals. The pattern is reminiscent of South Korea and the Philippines, but the overwhelmingly agrarian and impoverished nature of the economy and society places the Sudan at the antipodes of the other two societies. The Sudan's third experiment in democratic government came to an ignominious end in the summer of 1989. The elected coalition government of Sadiq al-Mahdi proved totally incapable of taking measures to deal with the economic crisis or to find a compromise to end the civil war in the south. The Sudanese military stepped in once again to end civilian rule. Still, before yielding to pessimism, one must never lose sight of India's remarkable experiment in democracy and civilian rule, now in its fifth decade. Dominant rural populations and low standards of living can sustain democratic politics.

## GOOD GUYS OR BAD GUYS?

In the 1950s and 1960s, in the literature generated under the rubric of "political development," there was a tendency to look upon military regimes in LDCs with some favor. Military officers were seen as modernizers, men with a nationalist vision, a strong sense of discipline and organization, and a commitment to the values of a meritocracy. For many observers, the military could build nations, just as they had built their armed forces, out of the heterogeneous religious, ethnic, or linguistic particles of their societies. They would transform the economy, develop the infrastructure, expand the educational system, and see to it that hard work and competence were rewarded with official recognition and advancement. In short, their vision was national, whereas that of their compatriots was seen as parochial; they were organized and disciplined, while their citizens were still mired in the supposed fatalism and petty jealousies of traditional societies; they believed in performance, though their countrymen trusted in fate or luck. If freewheeling democracy had to be sacrificed, temporarily, to the exigencies of building a nation and transforming an economy, that appeared an acceptable price to pay.

The Middle East provided the prototypical military modernizer, Mustafa Kemal Atatürk,[1] who was emulated by a few others—Reza Khan, Gamal

'Abd al-Nasser, and Houari Boumedienne. In a more optimistic era, Halpern saw the military as embodying the hopes and objectives of the new, professional middle class, that propertyless class that achieved its status through training, competency, and performance, and that, more than peasants or workers, would act as a revolutionary force in Middle East society. The military was its vanguard (Halpern 1963, 274): "The army in politics cannot become an institution above the battle. It intervenes as a partisan, representing a new class with whom the majority in the country does not yet share a common consciousness."

A decade or more later neither the military nor their presumptive class allies were viewed with the same enthusiasm. Huntington, in his influential book, *Political Order in Changing Societies* (1968), wrote with faint distaste about praetorian regimes that might be necessary evils to restrain the demands of segments of the population for a range of social and economic benefits that hard-pressed governments could not meet. The praetorians provided the "order" necessary to allow the economic development process to proceed without unmanageable unrest. An equally unromanticized vision of the capabilities and limitations of military autocracies, but this time from a neo-Marxist perspective, was presented in Trimberger's (1978) *Revolution from Above,* which examines Turkey, Egypt, Peru, and Japan.

While in the last twenty-five years the Republic of Korea has best exemplified the kinds of praetorian functions Huntington attributed to Third World militaries, the counterparts in the Middle East that come closest to his model are Iran under both shahs, Turkey under Atatürk, and Algeria under Boumedienne. The experiments of Nasser in Egypt and the Ba'athi military in Syria and Iraq do not fit well because they have neither really suppressed popular demands for *economic* benefits nor driven forward the development process to the degree they had hoped.

In the analysis of Latin American politics in the last two decades, O'Donnell has advanced a variant on the praetorian model that he called "bureaucratic authoritarianism" (1978). He argued that in those LDCs that have pursued strategies of import-substituting industrialization, there comes a moment when the "easy" substitution phase ends and when a process of "deepening" must be initiated. This entails moving from the manufacture of consumer goods to the manufacture of intermediate and capital goods, i.e., sophisticated machinery, heavy engineering goods, the full range of basic metals. It may entail cutting costs so that industries that had grown fat on captive domestic markets can compete in international markets. O'Donnell predicted that as deepening got under way, it might require a military authoritarian regime to discipline the work force and hold down wages. The military would ally with elements of the civilian technocracy responsible for designing and planning the deepening strategy and with foreign multinational corporations that would provide the technology and expertise.

This model, developed largely with Brazil and Argentina in mind, has been judged deficient even for Latin America (Collier 1979), and in the

Middle East the only regime that has approximated it has been Turkey since the military coup of September 1980. That coup was provoked by years of growing political violence and a profound economic crisis that called into question Turkey's long-standing strategy of ISI. The generals, allied to civilian technocrats like the current (1989) prime minister, Turgut Özal, muzzled the labor unions and the universities, cut social outlays, and pushed through an export-led growth strategy that required Turkish industry to become competitive in international markets. Although after elections in 1983 the armed forces nominally returned to the barracks, President Evren is a general, and it is implicitly clear that the officers corps stands behind Özal's economic policies. One should note that, not deepening, but rather export promotion, is really the issue for the new strategy. In addition, while the Özal government would like to attract foreign investment and technology, not too much has been forthcoming. Nonetheless O'Donnell's propositions do alert us to some of the dynamics of the growth strategy instituted in Turkey after 1980.

It is difficult in the 1980s to unearth anyone who finds merits in military or quasi-military rule. The downfall of the shah, Ferdinand Marcos, Ga'afar al-Nimeiri, and the military regimes in Argentina, Brazil, and Guatemala were greeted, at least initially, as unmitigated blessings. There is a sense that whatever degree of order and discipline the military have been able to provide, it has been outweighed by the choking off of the free flow of information and ideas, and the blocking of the assumption of responsibility on the part of ordinary citizens for their economic and political affairs. With a few exceptions, notably South Korea, the military has not promoted real economic growth, no less deepening. In fact, Latin American scholars have begun to talk of de-industrialization under the (former) praetorian regime in Argentina and the incumbent praetorians in Chile.

While the military clings stubbornly to power in the Middle East, its role as a transforming and dynamic institution has been discredited just about everywhere. In the Arab countries, it has not even been able to achieve any military successes, and the 1967 debacle stands as a watershed in the "exhaustion" of the military regimes. President Sadat once uncharitably remarked that his illustrious predecessor, Gamal 'Abd al-Nasser, had for all intents and purposes died in June 1967. Also military regimes have been unable to deliver on many of their economic promises. Instead they have built up inefficient public sectors that contribute mightily to the public deficit and costly military establishments that exacerbate both the deficit and the external debt.

There is, among the middle classes of the region, a general sense that the military must be pushed out of politics and out of economic management. In some countries, notably Egypt, Turkey, and the Sudan, that process has begun, but even there it is reversible, and in most of the others, the military still reigns supreme. What is interesting to note is the total transformation in the way scholars interpret military rule. In thirty years we have moved from an image of them as revolutionary modernizers ushering in a new age to one of Mamluks; heavy-handed, power-hungry bunglers, who act as impediments to economic growth and who rule by the use or threat of coercion.


## THE ECONOMIC WEIGHT OF THE MILITARY

Conventional wisdom has long posited that heavy outlays on defense and war-making divert scarce resources away from directly productive investment (the old guns and butter trade-off) and human-capital formation (education, health). For once, conventional wisdom may be right. There is a counterargument with respect to the LDCs that suggests that large defense expenditures may act as an economic stimulus. They finance heavy industry (armaments); the acquisition of advanced technologies; the formation of skilled personnel, from truck drivers to radar operators; and the provision of employment. Defense expenditures or a large military establishment may attract foreign aid and investment and thus enhance the country's foreign-exchange position. The most widely noted presentation of this position comes in Benoit (1973).

The argument has provoked a great deal of debate, and many cross-national surveys tend to refute Benoit's findings (for a summary, see Ball 1983). Fredriksen and Looney (1983), for example, found that defense outlays bear a high opportunity cost, shifting resources from "high growth development projects" that entail a reduction not only in public outlays but in dependent private outlays as well. Only countries flush with foreign exchange (e.g., Saudi Arabia) show any positive correlation between defense outlays and economic growth; otherwise, the two compete against each other.

What can the Middle East tell us about this debate? Unfortunately, nothing very conclusive. When defense expenditures in all regional groupings in the developing world are compared, those in the Middle East certainly come out the highest. When oil prices were at their peak, Middle Eastern countries were spending $40 billion a year on defense, with Iran and Saudi Arabia leading the way. Petroleum revenues of course allowed some countries to indulge in this luxury, but Egyptian outlays were about $3 billion per annum, while Syria and Morocco spent about $2 billion. Of the fourteen countries worldwide that in the late 1970s spent more than 10% of their GNP on defense each year, eight were in the Middle East. Chatelus (1983, 19) calculated that Syria was spending 93 times as much on defense as on health, while Saudi Arabia was spending 8 times as much. By some estimates (*Middle East,* July 1988, 19), in eight years of fighting, Iraq had incurred debts of $85 billion.

One would suppose that such defense burdens would cripple most economies, at least those without significant petroleum earnings. But there is no correlation in the Middle East between defense expenditure as a proportion of GDP and rates of growth (Figure 13.1). Moreover, large outlays and relatively high rates come together in a few instances. One

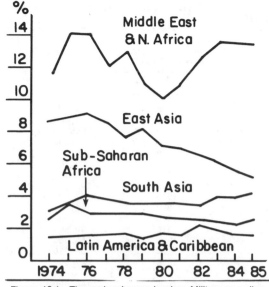

Figure 13.1  The regional arms burden: Military spending as a percentage of GNP, 1974–1985. *Source:* Adapted from U.S. government sources and published in *South* (London), September 1988, p. 6.

cannot conclude from this that defense expenditures contribute more than direct public or private investment to economic growth, nor can we assume a causal relation between high defense outlays and growth. We may estimate, counterfactually, the returns on alternative uses of the moneys devoted to defense, but practically nowhere in the world is there any assurance that reduced defense budgets would result in increased outlays on, say, social welfare or infrastructure. Defense outlays are laden with the symbols and sentiments of national pride and survival. People seem prepared to accept disproportionate public investment in defense. They and their leaders may find less justification in using equivalent resources to reduce adult illiteracy or line irrigation ditches.

Similarly, as Benoit pointed out, big defense establishments attract foreign-resource flows; first, because they represent big markets for arms exporters and, second, because they are located in geopolitically strategic regions. Great and lesser powers can buy political and strategic leverage through the supply of arms and military expertise that no other sphere of economic activity can offer. In the same vein, there is often a large concessional component in the pricing and the financing of the arms deliveries; indeed in the Middle East, billions of dollars worth of arms have been given away annually. As is the case with domestic military

Table 13.1   Socioeconomic Weight of Middle Eastern Military Establishments,
             1973-1985

|  | Annual GDP Growth Rate: (%) | | Defense Expenditure/GDP (%) | Size of Armed Forces | Armed Forces Personnel/Total Population (%) |
|---|---|---|---|---|---|
|  | 1973/84 | | | 1984/85 | |
| Algeria | 6.4 | | 2.0 | 169,000 | 0.80 |
| Egypt | 8.5 | | 11.0 | 445,000 | 1.00 |
| Iran | 0.5 | (1980-85) | 8.0 | 704,500 | 1.60 |
| Iraq | 5.3 | (1960-80) | 51.0 | 845,000 | 5.50 |
| Israel | 3.1 | | 17.0 | 149,000 | 3.50 |
| Jordan | 9.6 | | 11.4 | 70,200 | 2.10* |
| Libya | 3.0 | | 3.0 | 71,500 | 2.00 |
| Morocco | 4.5 | | 4.3 | 205,000 | 1.00 |
| Saudi Arabia | 6.0 | | 19.0 | 67,500 | 0.70 |
| Sudan | 5.5 | | 3.0 | 40,300 | 0.20 |
| Syria | 7.0 | | 18.0 | 392,500 | 3.90 |
| Tunisia | 5.5 | | 5.0 | 40,500 | 0.50 |
| Turkey | 4.1 | | 4.4 | 654,000 | 1.60 |
| YAR | 8.1 | | 18.0 | 36,550 | 0.50 |
| PDRY | -- | | 15.0 | 27,500 | 1.30 |
| United States | 2.3 | | 6.5 | 2,144,000 | 0.80 |
| Japan | 4.3 | | 1.0 | 243,000 | 0.15 |

* Population figure includes West Bank.

Sources: GDP growth rates from World Bank, World Development Report, 1986, New
York, Oxford University Press, July 1986; expenditures and size of armed forces
from Institute of Strategic Studies, The Military Balance, 1986-1987, London,
Garden City Press, 1986, pp. 78-79, 92-112.

expenditures, it is unlikely these grants would have ever materialized for
nonmilitary development purposes, at least not on the same scale.

The figures in Table 13.1 need to be treated with great caution because
they do not always measure the same things. For example, under the
column heading Armed Forces Personnel, the Iraqi figure must include
reserves and paramilitary personnel, whereas the Israeli does not include
reserves. Also defense expenditures do not, in most cases, include arms
and equipment supplied by foreign governments on a concessional basis.
Thus, except in the case of Iraq, the figures understate the real share of
military outlays in gross domestic product. For example, over a period of
several years Israel has received upwards of $2 billion in arms annually
on a grant basis from the United States. Likewise, between 1982 and 1986,
Egypt received about $2.4 billion in U.S. grants of military supplies. Saudi
Arabia has supplied arms concessionally to various clients or countries
whose goodwill it seeks (Morocco, Iraq, Syria, inter alia), and Turkey's
military budget is partially financed through its membership in NATO.
Official arms *sales* to the region, while down from the high levels of the
late 1970s, still totaled $16 billion ($4.9 billion to Iraq and $3.1 billion
to Saudi Arabia) in 1983. These sales are probably not included in the
expenditure figures in Table 13.1.

There are still at least eight Middle Eastern countries that spend in excess of 10% of GDP on defense, yet those outlays do not appear to have slowed economic growth except in the cases of Iran and Iraq. Reliable figures on Iraqi GNP for the early 1980s are not available, and presumably the high rate of growth registered over the period 1960–1980 has been reduced as a result of armed conflict and falling petroleum prices. We have better information for Iran (Amirahmadi 1986; Alnasrawi 1986) that shows a sharp decline in Iranian GNP growth from 1977 to 1980 (i.e., in the last years of the shah) and a hesitant recovery from 1980–1985. Iran, however, had not achieved in real terms the GNP level of 1977.

Given the number of unresolved conflicts in the region and actual or potential civil wars, it is unlikely that defense outlays will be reduced significantly in the coming years. It is an ominous sign that Tunisia, the least militarized of any Middle Eastern society, is now spending 5% of GDP on defense.

The weight of the military can be measured in other ways. In several of the large Middle Eastern states there has emerged what President Dwight Eisenhower once termed a "military-industrial complex." Israel, Egypt, Turkey, and Iran, most notably, have developed extensive armaments industries that occupy a particularly important niche in their nations' economies. The importance lies in three elements. First, the military-industrial sector includes some, if not the most, advanced technological undertakings of these economies. We find research into and direct use or manufacture of strategic technologies, including supercomputers, nuclear fission, lasers, advanced telecommunications and remote sensing, telemetry, missiles, and so forth. Second, these undertakings are almost exclusively within the public sector, although in Israel and Turkey some component manufacture is contracted out to the private sector. But the fact remains that the transfer and adaptation of high technology with obvious civilian applications is monopolized by the military establishment, and anyone, civilian or otherwise, who has the expertise and desire to work with such technologies becomes a servant of that monopoly. The military-industrial complex tends to invade the civilian sector of the economy, competing directly with private producers and providers of services. Third, these growing economic domains have become important sources of foreign exchange through sales of arms. Arms exports have been crucial to Israel's balance of payments for many years, but Egypt too, partially as a result of Iraq's needs for arms, has seen the value of its military exports rise from some $1 billion in 1986 (see Springborg 1987) to an estimated $4 billion in 1988/89.

Let us look at some concrete examples of the range of undertakings of these complexes. Turkey's military industries employ over 40,000 people, and in 1985 Turkey exported some $400 million in arms. These factories and facilities are involved in overhauling M-48 tanks, manufacture of optical equipment, assembly and manufacture of Huey helicopters and F-16 jet fighters, submarines, patrol boats, tank guns, and missiles. Significantly, some of Turkey's large private industrial conglomerates, especially, Koç

MANAŞ and ENKA, are licensed to manufacture ground-to-air missiles, Black Hawk helicopters, heavy trucks, and armored vehicles (see Karaspan 1987; *MEED,* September 7, 1985).

Egypt's defense industry is several decades old; under Nasser it expanded from manufacture of munitions and light arms into aeronautics and even took an ill-fated leap into ballistic missiles. But real expansion occurred under President Sadat, especially after 1975 when Saudi Arabia and some other Gulf States agreed to finance the Arab Military Industrialization Organization (AMIO) to act as a manufacturer of a range of advanced weapons for all Arab countries. Egypt became the home for the AMIO, and when, as a result of the Camp David peace accords with Israel, the Arab financiers pulled out of the project, it became an entirely Egyptian undertaking. Between the AMIO and the original defense industries, the complex comprises some twenty-four factories, with a work force of 70,000 to 100,000 and production worth about $350 million per year (Stork 1987). It assembles French Alpha jets, manufactures components for MIGs, assembles helicopters, and, at Benha Electronics, assembles radars.

During the 1970s the shah of Iran sought to make the Iranian military the dominant force in the Gulf and a rival to India in the Indian Ocean. The purchase of arms and military technology ran at more than $4 billion per annum and led to contracts and licensing arrangements with a host of multinational suppliers: Northrop, Lockheed, Bell Helicopter, Leyland, Daimler-Benz, and others. The Islamic republic inherited this complex but has had to look to other sources of supply: the PRC, the USSR, Sweden, Turkey, and the international arms market. Likewise, Saudi Arabia, on the strength of its petroleum revenues in the 1970s, has bought entire military technologies and industries. For instance, Saudi Arabia's Peace Shield air-defense system is bringing in billions of dollars in radar equipment and computers. There will be local assembly and manufacture of electrical equipment (Westinghouse), helicopters (Boeing), and the setting up of training centers. Contracting and supervision are carried out by the Saudi Basic Industries Corp. and the Ministry of Defense (*MEED,* September 7, 1985).

It is Israel, however, that has gone the furthest in the development and sophistication of its military industries. Israel's technical expertise is without equal in the region. Its research and development facilities put it on an equal footing with the most advanced nations of the world. It is one of the world's major arms suppliers. The Uzi submachine gun is a standard weapon in many national armies. Its scientists have provided Israel with all the requisites to assemble and deliver nuclear bombs and warheads. The country had the necessary expertise to design and manufacture a jet fighter, the Lavi, possessing all the capabilities of the U.S. F-16c. The real question for Israel was whether or not it could afford the Lavi. Both Israel's Treasury Department and the U.S. government opposed it as an unnecessary burden on the economy. It would have cost $200 million a year to develop the aircraft. Ultimately Israel had to abandon the project. The Lavi dilemma is symptomatic of a larger problem of Israel's defense establishment. It is a case of the tail wagging the dog. Israel wants to be self-sufficient militarily and in *all* technological domains. But its own armed forces could never generate sufficient demand to sustain, economically, the range of military industries that national security would require. Thus Israel must seek markets abroad, mortgage its balance of payments to military exports, and suffer the opprobrium of being a "merchant of destruction."

Perhaps the most important aspect of the Middle East's military-industrial complexes is that they have tended to become powerful economic enclaves and, because of their strategic nature, not fully accountable to parliaments or auditors. They are in a position to harness important private-sector clients and, indeed, to invade civilian markets. They own property, productive assets, financial institutions, and they can negotiate foreign and domestic loans and put out contracts. Frequently it is alleged that these assets and points of leverage are used by the officers corps to line their own pockets and those of their clients.

Turkey may have pioneered in the building of a military-economic enclave. After the military coup of 1961, the Armed Forces Mutual Assistance Fund (OYAK) was set up. Its financial resources come from a 10% levy on the salaries of all commissioned and noncommissioned officers, and the purpose of the fund is to pay these officers pensions upon their retirement. By the middle 1970s some 80,000 officers were paying into this fund. Its assets were estimated at $300 million by 1973, and Bianchi (1984, 70) described it as "the country's largest and most diversified industrial conglomerate."

OYAK has grown substantially since then and has controlling interests in the Turkish Automotive Corporation, MAT corporation for truck and tractor manufacture, the OYAK Insurance Co., TUKAS Food Canning, and a cement plant. It owns 20% of Petkim (petrochemicals), 8% of Turkish Petroleum, 42% of OYAK-Renault, for automobile assembly and manufacture, and 7% of a Goodyear subsidiary (Ayres 1983).

Both Bianchi and Ayres have pointed out that OYAK's empire was encouraged by the Turkish government and was to serve as a model for other professional associations and pension funds that could mobilize resources for development purposes more easily than the government itself could through direct and indirect taxation. OYAK's activities have been replicated by special funds such as the Foundations for the Air Force, the Navy, and the Ground Forces. Prime Minister Özal has tried to bring these funds under a single direction, the Defense Industry Development and Support Administration. What should be kept in mind, however, is that OYAK and the other funds have bridged a gap between the military establishment and the private economic sector. Since Ottoman times and even under Atatürk, the military has seen itself as an independent entity, a guardian of the nation's interests, and to some extent a watchdog against private greed. The military depended upon state budgetary appropriations for its needs. Now OYAK and the special funds are dependent on direct investments in the national economy and in joint ventures with foreign and domestic corporations. The economic interests of the officers corps have become firmly wedded to the performance of the Turkish economy and to that of its private sector.

Other actors in the Turkish military enclave operate directly in the civilian domestic market. The Military Electronics Industry, Inc. (70% owned by the Ground Forces Foundation), manufactures telecommunications and telephone equipment under license; the Military Battery Industry, Petlas Tire Co., the Sivas Textile Industry, and the Electronics Industry (ISBIR) are all controlled by the foundation and sell products in civilian markets. Likewise the Machinery and Chemical Industries Establishment runs twenty factories, with 20,000 employees. Six of these factories produce textiles, steel, chemicals, and machine tools (Karaspan 1987).

Egypt, especially since the advent of Field Marshal Abu Ghazala in 1981, has followed a similar path. Military industries had already claimed a portion of civilian markets for products including truck motors, telephone equipment, optical lenses, fans, air conditioners. Annual production for civilian consumption reached circa $300 million in the early 1980s.

In 1978 the National Service Projects Organization was established, and once Abu Ghazala got hold of it, its range of activities was greatly expanded. The army corps of engineers assisted civilian contractors in bridge and road construction. Armed forces communications experts implemented the refurbishing and expansion of the telephone systems of Cairo and Alexandria. Most spectacular was the armed forces' direct entry into food production, allegedly so that in time of hostilities they could assure their own supply of food. But what has transpired has been a capital-intensive plunge into desert reclamation, hot-house cultivation of vegetables, and commercial production of eggs and poultry. Springborg estimated the value of food produced by the military at £E 488 million (or roughly $200 million) in 1986. Private producers have cautiously complained, particularly after military production drove down the price of eggs, that by using conscripts as free labor the military had an unfair advantage over the private sector. These protests may be outweighed by the ability of the military to let lucrative contracts to private firms, assure supply of produce to designated wholesalers, and, through a network of retired officers relocated in private and joint-venture firms, maintain a far-flung system of clients and cronies.

Nearly all Middle Eastern military establishments have exhibited similar characteristics. Some have "cleaner" reputations than others: The Algerian armed forces have undertaken a wide range of public-welfare projects, such as construction of the trans-Saharan highway, the University of Constantine, and 1,000 "socialist villages." They have also been engaged in emergency relief operations to aid victims of floods or earthquakes (Roberts 1984). Doubtless through the wide range of goods, services, and arms that the military purchases, there is ample opportunity for officers to pocket their 5%, do favors for friends, evade import regulations, and so forth. Still, to date the Algerian armed forces have not earned the same reputation for corruption as some of their neighbors.

The Sudanese military, under the long tenure of Gen. Ga'afar al-Nimeiri (1969–1985), became mired in corruption, cronyism, and abuse of power. In the trials of various officers following Nimeiri's downfall, many of the details of a story that was already well known became available. In the Sudanese case, the presidency was enmeshed in the military. In fact, after a coup attempt in 1976, Nimeiri normally resided in the military command compound in Khartoum. Close colleagues among the senior officers (including in the waning years Vice President Omar al-Tayyib), the cabinet, and the top officials of the Sudanese Socialist Union amounted to an alliance of patrons who used civilian and military budgets indiscriminately to let contracts to private-sector clients and to large multinationals like Lonrho, Tenneco, Tri-Ad (Adnan Khoshoggi), and Daewoo (South Korea). This same clique made percentages off oil purchased at high cost from international traders and, it is alleged, was paid handsomely to orchestrate the evacuation of Ethiopian Falasha Jews across Sudanese territory.

The lynchpin of the military enclave was the Military Economic Board (MEB) (see Bienen and Moore 1987), which was heavily involved in the foreign-trade sector and was a major participant in the local foreign-exchange market. For instance, the MEB became the exclusive importer of a certain brand of cigarettes and tried to take markets away from the country's only local manufacturer and distributor. The board's frequent entries into the unofficial but tolerated local foreign-exchange market were of such magnitude that they could drive down the traded value of the Sudanese pound. For military insiders the possibility of profiting from these currency gyrations could not be passed up.

How far the rot had spread is not known (see, for example, Khalid 1985). It was, after all, Gen. Sawar al-Dahab, left in command when al-Nimeiri departed for Washington (never to return), who deposed the president and proclaimed a transitional period of one year to civilian rule. He was responding in part to the vociferous protests of the Sudanese middle classes but also in part to the anger of younger officers who felt that al-Nimeiri had dragged the image of the Sudanese armed forces in the mud.

Similar but not quite so dramatic accounts have been made about the Syrian military. The Syrian armed forces were drawn into the Lebanese civil war in 1976 and wound up in effective control of east and northeast Lebanon as well as of access to Beirut. Mildly austere, socialist Syria thus met anarchic Lebanon, where freewheeling entrepreneurs still managed to thrive in the midst of the fighting. Lebanon imported a range of consumer goods that Syrians craved, and the armed forces found themselves in a position to control the movement of such goods. The result was inevitable: a sprawling black market in everything from tape decks to automobiles, operated by Syrian officers, with astronomic profits distributed through several subnetworks.

In some ways the chief racketeer was the president's own brother, Rifaat al-Assad, in command until 1984 of an elite praetorian guard known as the Defense Detachments. Sadowski gave a vivid portrait (1985, 7):

He had been the "kingfish" of Syrian patronage. His power derived not only from the military units he commands, but also from his vast array of civilian clients. He sponsored cliques of *nouveau riche* businessmen in Damascus and Aleppo. He bankrolled al-Rabita, a highly-subsidized fraternity for students and intellectuals. He controlled extensive business interests in Lebanon (everything from East Beirut cement plants to hashish trade in the Beqa' Valley) which he guarded with his personal militia, the Fursan al-Arab. And he was not above using his troops and clients to secure even petty favors, from "week-end wives" to nightclub seats.

Even without the profiteering spawned in the Lebanese cockpit, the Syrian military control an important economic enclave. They have been involved in public works, construction, basic industry, farm production, and the manufacture of batteries, bottled mineral water, and furniture. The largest military corporation is the Military Housing Organization (Longuenesse 1985b, 18).

## THE MILITARY AND NATION-BUILDING

Recent studies of the process of state formation in Western Europe have emphasized the crucial role of military rivalry and war (for example, Tilly 1975). It is argued that the perceived need to build powerful military forces obliged central authorities to extend their administrative grip on their societies, reduce the autonomy of the feudal estate, and extract through taxes the resources needed to pay for the military effort. Over time this process gave rise to strong, centralized states and, as war was an inherent part of the scheme, to proto-nationalism.

We may legitimately ask whether in the Middle East a similar process is under way. The answer is an equivocal "no," or perhaps, "not yet." Certainly war, or its threat, has been a constant in regional affairs since World War II, but, with a few exceptions, that fact has not notably promoted national integration and a common national identity. Perhaps our time horizon is simply too short. Moreover, because arms and what we might call geopolitical rents have been so readily available, and on soft terms, to Middle Eastern belligerents, the region's states have not had to develop an extractive capacity commensurate with their military burdens.

Nonetheless, there are very important exceptions to these generalizations. There is little doubt that war has been a determinant factor in shaping Israel's national identity. There, the nation in arms is an everyday reality. The Israeli Defense Forces, moreover, have been used since 1948 as a primary instrument for integrating the culturally diverse Jews of the diaspora, teaching them Hebrew, socializing them to the values of the state, and erasing differences among them through a common uniform and shared drudgery. Note that the only non-Jews who participate in this experience are the Druze. It is still the case that Israel, more than any other state in the region, has used its armed forces as a school for the inculcation of a new culture.

Turkey and Algeria have approximated that model as well. Like Israel, the Turkish republic was born and consolidated as the result of military victory, a commodity that hardly any other Middle Eastern societies have enjoyed in recent centuries. Likewise, Algeria's guerrilla armies forced the French to negotiate for Algeria's independence. It may be stating the obvious to say that military success can be claimed by all elements of a nation and serve as a symbol of national accomplishment, while defeat or perceived inferiority provokes a divisive search for culprits and traitors. Thus in 1931, Atatürk could *credibly* claim a role for the Turkish Armed Forces that could be matched only by the leaders of Israel and Algeria (Tachau and Heper 1983, 20): "the Turkish nation has . . . always looked to the military . . . as the leader of movements to achieve lofty national ideals . . . when speaking of the army, I am speaking of the intelligentsia of the Turkish nation who are the true owners of this country. . . . The Turkish nation . . . considers its army the guardian of its ideals."

We can hardly address this issue without considering Iran and Iraq. In 1988, after these two countries had slugged it out for over eight years, they reached a tenuous cease-fire. They are both societies with profound religious, linguistic, and ethnic cleavages. They contain colossal obstacles to national integration. Yet one of the astonishing elements of the combat was that each nation has more or less kept unity in the ranks. Iraq's Arab Shi'a did not defect and act as a fifth column for Khomeini, nor did Iran's Arab Shi'a rally to the Arab nationalism of Iraq's Ba'ath. Both countries, it is true, have dealt with sporadic outbursts of Kurdish dissidence.

It is hard to imagine that these years of mobilization and supreme sacrifice have not built some powerful sense of nationhood in both countries. That sense may not be able to survive a humiliating defeat (we know what defeat in 1967 did to the Arab psyche), but neither side has scored a major triumph. Both governments may have developed organic links to their peoples that could survive a formal peace. There are other ways to build a nation, and any of them are preferable to war. We cannot, however, overlook war's impact on the formation of national identity and the building of strong links between regimes and citizens. The cost must be emphasized: the annihilation, as in Europe during World War I, of a substantial part of an entire generation of the two nation's youth, but it may be out of this inexcusable carnage that the stuff of unifying national myths is taken.[2]

## THE REGULAR MILITARY AND
## CIVILIANS IN ARMS

The several self-proclaimed revolutionary regimes of the Middle East have all had to confront in one way or another the issue of arming the people. In Algeria, Iran, Israel, and the PDRY, where the people were to some extent already armed when new regimes were founded, the issue was particularly sensitive. In other countries, such as Morocco and the Sudan, irregular guerrilla forces had to be absorbed into the regular military.

We can state as a general rule that the regular military view with alarm the arming of civilian militias and party paramilitary groups, not to mention the poking about in military affairs of political commissars. Regimes have come unstuck over this issue. In 1965 Ahmad Ben Bella, the president of Algeria, contemplated arming civilian groups under the auspices of the National Liberation Front. His minister of defense, Houari Boumedienne, saw this as an implicit statement that the Army of National Liberation was not capable of defending the revolution and that Ben Bella wanted a paramilitary force loyal to him to hold Boumedienne's power in check. In June 1965 Boumedienne toppled Ben Bella and there was no further talk of party militias.

A similar drama unfolded in Syria in the late 1960s. Salah Jadid, a senior Alawi officer and leader of the military command in the Ba'ath, sought to organize a Ba'athi militia to engage Israel in guerrilla warfare. This was clearly a major issue in driving him apart from his erstwhile ally, Hafiz al-Assad, who was minister of defense. In September 1970, in the wake of King Hussein's crushing of the PLO in Jordan, Hafiz al-Assad had Jadid arrested and took over the presidency of the republic.

Nasser tried to use the Arab Socialist Union as a counterweight to the Egyptian armed forces in the 1960s, firmly under the control of Field Marshal Hakim Amr. Left-wing officers out of the intelligence branch were given the green light to organize people's militias to form "popular resistance" units in the event that Israel tried to occupy Egypt. After the 1967 defeat and the suicide of the field marshal, neither the Arab Socialist Union nor the people's militia appeared quite so important in checking the regular military and were disbanded.

In Iraq, following the overthrow of the monarchy in 1958, General Qassim for a time relied on the People's Resistance Force of the Communist party to assist him in any confrontation with his own armed forces, with Ba'athis, or with Nasserites. By June 1959, however, he was led to strip them of their weapons and to limit their patrols (Batatu 1978, 907). Once the Ba'ath was in power it organized its own militias. They were consolidated in 1970 into the Popular Army, commanded by Taha Yasin Ramadhan, first-deputy prime minister. The army guarded Iraq's frontiers, acted as a security force in rural areas, and was intended to be a watchdog on the regular military. Its size may have doubled from 200,000 to 400,000 members after the outbreak of hostilities with Iran (Helms 1984, 100).

In Morocco, Algeria, and the Sudan, the regular military had to disarm and absorb into its ranks the remnants of guerrilla forces. In Morocco these came from liberation armies operating, in the two years prior to independence, in the northern mountains, the southern deserts, and in some big cities, while in Algeria they came from the guerrilla armies in the interior *wilayas*, or military zones, of the FLN. In the Sudan, after the granting of autonomy to the southern provinces in 1971, the Sudanese army absorbed large numbers of freedom fighters into its ranks. One of them, Col. John Garang, deserted in 1983 and has led a major insurrectionary movement in the south ever since.

Iran offers an example, not yet played out, of irregular forces absorbing the regular military. The key actors are the Revolutionary Guards, or Pasdaran, who became a nationwide militia at the service of the Islamic Republican party (until that party was disbanded in late 1987). Many of their leaders came out of the radical secular leftist Mujahidin al-Khalq before 1979. They were introduced to radical Shi'ite Islam through the teachings of Ali Shariati and were drawn to Ayatollah Khomeini because of his fiercely anti-imperialist and antidespotic stance. After Khomeini came to power, these militants turned on their erstwhile leftist allies, hounding them out of the country or physically eliminating them. They organized the revolutionary tribunals that meted out arbitrary justice to a host of presumed enemies of the republic. They waged war against the Kurds and were instrumental in the seizure of the U.S. Embassy in Tehran. With time they took on the role of a security-force-cum-vigilante group in the countryside.

The regular armed forces were relatively powerless to oppose the ascendancy of the Pasdaran, as the senior officers corps had been so badly compromised in its loyalty to the shah. The armed forces were given an opportunity to refurbish their image in the war with Iraq, and to some extent they have done so. But the Pasdaran, along with the ill-trained volunteers, or *basij,* enhanced their image in Iran through human-wave assaults on Iraqi positions and other suicidal exploits. Their heroic self-sacrifice and battle experience probably led some of the leaders of the Pasdaran to envisage slowly absorbing the regular Iranian armed forces into their own ranks and command structure.

The Pasdaran have become a very powerful force in Iranian politics. They may number a couple of hundred thousand, they are armed, control substantial financial resources through institutions such as the Foundation for the Disinherited, and they espouse a common militant brand of Shi'ism. They have had powerful allies among the mullahs, such as former prime minister Mousavi, and in the elections of spring 1988 to the *majlis,* a majority sympathetic to their outlook was returned.

Some observers believe that Khomeini and other religious leaders were fearful of the Pasdaran and used the regular military to hold them in check. In the aftermath of Khomeini's death, they are still a force to be reckoned with. If they maintain unity in their ranks, they can become king makers, but, perhaps fortunately for more moderate elements in Iran (such as those who dealt with the United States in the Iran-Contra imbroglio), unity among leaders has so far eluded the Pasdaran. Moreover, the reverses inflicted on them and the regular Iranian military by the Iraqis in the spring of 1988 are unlikely to close their ranks.

It is in Israel that one finds the most "comfortable" equilibrium between the professional military and armed civilians. The Israeli Defense Forces were born in the kibbutz movement and the irregular Haganah before independence in 1948. Although the Haganah was rapidly professionalized after 1948, it has never forgotten its civilian origins. More important, Israel's ability to mobilize its adult population quickly, and its system of reserve training for all males until an advanced age, have blurred most boundaries between soldiers and civilians. Israelis board buses and sit on park benches with their sidearms with the same nonchalance as a New York yuppie totes his or her attaché case. Because the military is so closely integrated into Israeli society, the nation's leaders do not fear an armed citizenry.

## CONCLUSION

On the whole, the prominent and long-lasting role played by the military in Middle East politics has not been positive, although we cannot know, of course, whether civilian elites would have performed better. By and large, military regimes did not achieve the kind of structural transformation of their economies or the industrial deepening that they invariably announced as their goals. However, the heavy outlays on the military and on war preparedness that their incumbency has entailed appear to have done little to impede fairly rapid rates of economic growth. The real question is whether these rates could have been more rapid still in the absence of such heavy outlays.

It has certainly been the case that direct rule by the military has not enhanced the military performance of the region's armed forces, at least in the Arab-Israeli theater. Turkey boasts a formidable fighting force, but one that has not really been tested since the Korean War (the Cyprus invasion was not a real test). Israel has been militarily successful under uninterrupted civilian government. The ultimate price of the battle testing of the Iranian and Iraqi armed forces may be the quasi-destruction of their civilian economies and the annihilation of the flower of their youth.

The military has been the catalyst, or at least the conduit, for the introduction of advanced technologies into the region. Military industries and research and development facilities are often the most advanced of their nations and have a wide range of civilian applications. However it is less clear the extent to which these technologies are merely imported as opposed to being absorbed into the scientific community. At a more mundane level, and with the major exception of Israel, the armed forces of the Middle East have not been extensively used to impart literacy and vocational training to their recruits. Most countries maintain some form of universal conscription, and most of the recruits may come from rural backgrounds, so there is a real opportunity to build the nation's human resources during the years its youth is in the ranks, but that opportunity has not been widely seized.

Perhaps where the military have had the most far-reaching impact has been in the area of state-building—the "creation of order," in Samuel Huntington's terms. Frequently, military officers have come from outside the dominant classes (Lebanon was a notable exception) to the extent there were or are dominant classes. The officers believed in the use of state power and agencies to remake the social profile of their societies.

In that sense the military were the quintessential architects of state autonomy (see Trimberger 1978). Over time their interests may come to be identified with some of the class actors whose very existence depended on state initiatives. The Turkish military have now developed shared economic interests with the national bourgeoisie, and a similar process has begun in Egypt and Algeria. In Israel the intermingling of the economic interests of the military (retired or active), government officials, the Histadrut, and the private sector form a seamless web.

The military has done more to build state apparatuses than to create strong economies. We noted in Chapter 12 that the very nature of military training and the functional division of the armed forces may have predisposed officers to a corporatist vision of society as a whole. Thus, together with the strengthening of the state apparatus and of the public sector, we find military rulers structuring the political arena along corporatist lines. Order has taken precedence over mobilization, organic unity over pluralism, discipline over spontaneity. Corporatism is hard to impose for long periods of time and hard to swallow, especially for the middle classes. When it is combined with failed state enterprise, botched provision of services, and corruption, the middle classes grow restive. In the Sudan they undid the regime of Ga'afar al-Nimeiri. Elsewhere they are exerting an embryonic but unmistakable pressure for civilianization, if not democratization. Still the military have the ultimate answer to this pressure in their arsenals. The question is whether they still have the will to use it.

## NOTES

1. For two positive views of Turkey's "modernization," see Lerner 1959 and McClelland 1963.

2. It bodes ill for national unity that within days of its cease-fire with Iran, Iraq launched an offensive against its own Kurdish population, using chemical weapons in its assault.

# 14

# LABOR MIGRATION, REGIONALISM, AND THE FUTURE OF THE OIL ECONOMIES

Middle Eastern intellectuals have long harbored dreams of unity. Before the rise of secular nationalism, Muslims cherished a vision of one polity under one ruler: the Dar ul-Islam under the caliph, the Prophet's successor. Although the Iranian revolution may have revived such aspirations for some, for most Arabs they were replaced by hopes of secular unity. There have been several attempts to actualize these visions politically. The most famous was the formation of the United Arab Republic under Nasser, when Egypt and Syria merged for three years (1958–1961). However, Nasser's reforming military regime coexisted uneasily with a Syrian polity still dominated by wealthy merchants and landlords, and the system collapsed when Syria unilaterally withdrew in September 1961. Recalling Marx's dictum on how history repeats itself,[1] Qaddhafi's Libya has attempted to merge with Egypt, Sudan, Tunisia, Syria, and most recently, Morocco. These ventures have puzzled political pundits and yielded very little in the way of concrete political unification.

Although there were many reasons for these failures, the limited economic intercourse among modern Middle Eastern nations contributed. Like most areas of the developing world, they sold their goods, purchased their imports, and admitted capital from the developed countries of the West, not from each other. But the increasing integration of economic life that characterizes the entire world has certainly not bypassed the Middle East. During the past fifteen years, economic integration of the region has accelerated dramatically in some ways, while remaining stubbornly limited in others (Kerr and Yassin 1982).[2]

A simple classification of integration would be for the movement of goods and of factors of production across national boundaries in the region.

Table 14.1  Percent of Total Merchandise Exports of MENA Countries Going to
OECD, Eastern Bloc, Oil Exporters, and Other LDCs, High y 1965 and
1985

| | OECD | | Eastern Bloc | | Oil Exporters | | LDCs | |
|---|---|---|---|---|---|---|---|---|
| | 1965 | 1985 | 1965 | 1985 | 1965 | 1985 | 1965 | 1985 |
| Algeria | 90 | 92 | 2 | 1 | -- | -- | 8 | 8 |
| Egypt | 28 | 53 | 38 | 7 | 1 | 2 | 33 | 38 |
| Iran | 67 | 74 | 2 | 0 | 1 | 0 | 30 | 26 |
| Iraq | 83 | 33 | 1 | 0 | 0 | 0 | 16 | 67 |
| Israel | 72 | 74 | 1 | 0 | 0 | 0 | 27 | 26 |
| Kuwait | 56 | 49 | 0 | 0 | 1 | 4 | 44 | 47 |
| Lebanon | 43 | 14 | 3 | -- | 35 | 66 | 19 | 20 |
| Libya | 97 | 43 | 0 | 0 | 0 | 0 | 3 | 57 |
| Morocco | 80 | 65 | 6 | 5 | 0 | 3 | 14 | 27 |
| Saudi Arabia | 71 | 60 | 0 | 0 | 8 | 0 | 21 | 40 |
| Sudan | 56 | 29 | 9 | 0 | 4 | 36 | 31 | 34 |
| Syria | 26 | 40 | 14 | 15 | 8 | 4 | 53 | 42 |
| Tunisia | 61 | 81 | 3 | 1 | 3 | 4 | 32 | 15 |
| Turkey | 71 | 51 | 10 | 3 | 0 | 9 | 19 | 37 |
| UAE | 69 | 75 | 0 | 0 | 2 | 1 | 30 | 24 |
| YAR | -- | 23 | -- | 0 | -- | 13 | -- | 64 |

Source: World Bank, World Development Report, New York, Oxford University
Press, 1987, pp. 226-27.

Table 14.1 shows the pattern of interregional exports. There does not seem
to be any general pattern here; among non–oil exporters, four countries
have increasingly sold their goods to other LDCs (Sudan, Morocco, Turkey,
and Lebanon), two (Egypt and Tunisia) sell a higher proportion of their
output to developed countries now compared to twenty years ago, while
the geographical orientation of Israeli exports has remained essentially
stable. Of oil exporters, both Algeria and Iran have seen an increase in
the share of exports (overwhelmingly oil) going to OECD countries; the
rest now sell a higher percentage to other LDCs. Despite this variety, it
is fair to conclude that the old "dependency" syndrome of "all trade with
the First World" has weakened in many countries. Nevertheless (and
unsurprisingly from an economic point of view) ten of the sixteen countries
of the region listed in Table 14.1 depend on sales to OECD countries for
about half or more of their export revenues. The pattern for imports is
even more striking. Only the PDRY get as much as a quarter of its imports
from other Middle Eastern countries; most get less than one-sixth. Even
oil importers, buying their fuel from their brethren, buy far more from the
West. Integration through intraregional trade has eluded the Middle East.

Integration of factor markets has gone much further. As we have seen
above, national states have taken a central role in the investment process
within most countries, whatever the official ideology. The major oil-exporting
countries spent most of their increased incomes between 1974 and 1984
on their own internal-investment projects, Most of the surplus was held
in short-term liquid assets in the OECD countries, but some money was
channeled toward their poorer neighbors as economic aid. Such assistance

took the form of both direct, bilateral aid and contributions to "development funds" and other multilateral agencies.

A wide variety of private, public, and mixed banks engaged in international lending exists in the region. The lending to LDCs by surplus-capital MENA nations gave preference to other countries of the region and countries in the wider Islamic world. Lending policies have typically been conservative, concentrating on areas where managers already have some expertise, e.g., petroleum refining, tourism, real estate.

Perhaps the most notable attempts to use capital as an instrument of economic integration have been the various development funds of the region. The earliest of these (the Kuwait Fund for Arab Economic Development) was founded in 1961, to be followed by the Arab Fund for Economic and Social Development (established by the Arab League in 1968), and the Abu Dhabi Fund for Arab Economic Development (founded in 1971). These funds are run along World Bank lines, extending loans for development projects ranging from railroads and fertilizer plants, to sewage and water-supply systems, to livestock and crop-production schemes. Like the "pre-McNamara" World Bank, loans are typically for infrastructural construction and output-increasing projects, rather than for rural development. The latter, however, does receive some limited Arab oil money through the UN's International Fund for Agricultural Development, which began lending in 1977, combining OPEC and OECD money and specializing in lending to small farmers in poorer countries throughout the Third World.

The Arab Fund has had the most self-conscious political agenda. In addition to development loans to specific countries, it has consciously sought to promote the regional economy in at least three ways. First, it has invested in the Pan-Arab Communications Network, including development of an Arab Communications Satellite. Second, it has promoted the development of the Arab Military Industrialization Organization to manufacture weapons for Arab armies. The international aspects of this project were terminated by the Camp David Accords, leaving Egypt to go it alone, as discussed in Chapter 13. Given its relatively large and well-developed industrial sector, much investment had concentrated on Egypt. But when Egypt was expelled from the Arab League, this evaporated. Third, the Arab Fund established the Arab Authority for Agricultural Investment and Development (AAAID), allocating investments toward Sudan in an attempt to reduce regional dependence on imported grain and sugar.

These activities have not been exceptionally successful. At the same time, they have had some impact, and the political commitment to their long-range goals appears to be unshaken by various setbacks. For example, AAAID mounted five projects in the Sudan in an attempt to lessen the Gulf States' food imports from the OECD. Projects included mechanized farming, poultry production, sorghum and oil seeds production, vegetable farming, and dairy production. By their own account, these projects have suffered from serious management problems and remain unprofitable. Public-sector managers and university experts initially oversaw operations, an unfortunate choice, since neither group had much experience in running enterprises needing to show a profit. This is now changing; the financial losses are dismissed as a necessary cost of promoting "regional food security," and new projects are in the pipeline. Perhaps "learning by doing" will, in time, reduce the costs of these projects. Despite these problems, the political commitment to economic cooperation remains unshaken: Plans for huge new mechanized sorghum and livestock-production schemes in western Sudan are under way.

In summary, deliberate attempts to integrate the political economies of the region at the level of the state, of trade flows, and of capital and investment have been relatively unsuccessful. Far more important has been the unplanned, more or less spontaneous, integration of labor markets. Indeed, labor migration on a historically unprecedented scale has been a fundamental force in transforming national political economies even as it integrated the most remote areas of the most backward countries into the regional economy. The rest of this chapter is devoted to a discussion of this phenomenon.

## LABOR MIGRATION: AN OVERVIEW

Economics has driven most labor migration in the region. With the politically crucial exception of the Palestinian refugees, most Middle Easterners have left their homes to seek higher incomes rather than to flee political persecution.[3] The proximate cause of the migration is the enormous gap in wages between the sending and the receiving countries. For example, an unskilled rural Egyptian could earn *thirty times* more money when working at a Saudi construction site than he could on an Egyptian farm. Jordanian engineers could double or triple their incomes by going to Kuwait. This dramatic difference has, of course, two components: very low wages in the poor countries and dramatic increases in wages in the oil states.

The low wages in the sending countries were the result of low productivity in agriculture and the failure of previous industrialization to absorb surplus labor. The cause of the upward spiral of wages in the oil countries is similarly straightforward: The demand for labor shot up, while domestic-supply response was limited by economic, social, and political factors. On the demand side, the explosion of oil prices in the 1970s flooded the treasuries of the oil-exporting states, which then launched ambitious development plans and investment projects. These implied huge increases in the demand for labor of all types, from construction laborers to computer programmers, from doctors to doormen.

However, domestic labor supply was constrained by demographic and sociopolitical factors. The Gulf States and Libya have relatively small populations. As we saw earlier, they also have young populations. Usually at least 40% of the indigenous population is less than 15 years old and a majority is younger than 20. It follows that the size of the economically active population and of the domestic labor supply is smaller than that found in countries with a similar population but an older age profile. Limited female participation in the labor force further exacerbated the shortage of domestic workers in the oil-exporting states. Too often, males of working age were illiterate and unskilled. Those few who were skilled were often attracted to public-sector employment, especially in the armed forces. Finally, government subsidies of food, housing, medical care, transportation, reduced incentives of local people to take unpleasant or difficult jobs. Meeting from domestic sources the huge demand for labor that the oil boom stimulated was simply impossible. Foreigners were needed, and they came in unprecedented numbers.

This is not to say that migration in the region began with the oil boom. The modern history of migration in the region may be roughly divided into four phases. During the first phase, prior to 1974, more than 80% of immigrating workers were Arabs, mainly Egyptians, Syrians, Yemenis, and Palestinians. The major characteristics of the Gulf labor market during this period were the relatively narrow wage differentials between sending and receiving countries and the high skill level of many migrant workers. Further, Iraq and Oman, which became major labor importers during the 1980s, were net exporters of manpower. The second phase began with the oil-price increase of 1974. During this period the absolute numbers of Arab immigrant workers rose dramatically, with immigration from poorer countries like Egypt and the Yemens being especially prominent. Some estimates of the size of these flows are shown in Tables 14.2 and 14.3. It must be emphasized that such figures are and can be only approximations; the problems of data quality and comparability are severe. Accordingly, estimates of the numbers of migrant workers vary greatly: For example, Egyptian government sources claimed up to 3 million workers abroad in the early 1980s; although one study placed the total number of migrant workers in Iraq at 15,200, an alternative source offered estimates of 65,700. The estimate of perhaps 1.3 million migrants in the whole region in 1975 should probably be treated as a lower boundary.

The third phase covers the latter part of the 1970s and the early 1980s. Further oil-price increases in 1979 approximately doubled government revenues in a single year. This stimulated still more ambitious development plans, yet more lavish projects, and even more generous social-welfare programs. By 1980, an additional 700,000 men were at work in Saudi Arabia and the other Gulf States alone, while the number of migrant workers in Iraq had increased more than ten times, to about 750,000 (Table 14.3). The number of expatriate workers in Libya had risen from just under 50,000 in 1973 to over 400,000 in 1980, by which time they constituted about one-third of that country's labor force (Sherbiny 1984a). As usual, there are sharply contrasting estimates of the total number of workers: The ILO estimates the total number of workers in Saudi Arabia in 1980 at 1 million, only two-thirds of the figure presented in Table 14.3.

In addition to the increase in the total number of workers, two other trends stand out during this period. First, the share of Arab migrant workers in the total expatriate work force declined from about 43% in 1975 to about 37% in 1980 as Indians, Pakistanis, Sri Lankans, and other Asian workers flocked to the region. Not only was the wage gap even greater for these countries than for some of the poorer Arab countries, but state policy in the Gulf favored these workers. As non-Arabs they were believed to be less likely to stay in the Gulf and were perceived to be politically safer than potentially recalcitrant Egyptians, Yemenis, Lebanese, and Palestinians. Second, the growth of demand for unskilled labor slowed as major infrastructural projects were completed, while that for skilled workers to operate the completed projects accelerated.

The fourth phase began with the decline in oil prices in late 1982. The fall in oil revenues curtailed some development projects in the region. In turn, the growth of demand for foreign workers slowed down in some countries, while the trend toward a shift in the composition of demand toward more skilled workers and away from the unskilled continued. This trend has very recently accelerated: The value of construction contracts in the region fell by 25% from 1986 to 1987 (*South,* September 1987, p. 65).

However, as of 1985, only Iraq, fighting a major war, actually had reduced its labor imports.[4] An estimate of the numbers of migrants in 1985 is shown in Table 14.4. There is little sign of decreased immigration into Saudi Arabia, the largest importer of labor. Indeed, the stock of workers in the kingdom rose by about 1 million from 1980 to 1985. This is not surprising; the kingdom's Third Development Plan of this period allocated even larger funds for development projects than did the second plan. As usual, one can easily find contrasting estimates. Some (e.g., ILO) argue that the stock of workers in Saudi Arabia rose by less than 200,000 from 1980 to 1985. Whatever the figures, despite the softening and then decline of oil prices, Saudi Arabia increased its labor imports during the first half of the 1980s. The number of workers in Kuwait increased, but only very slightly, from about 380,000 in 1980 to perhaps 430,000 in 1985; the number of new work permits in Kuwait fell over 59% from 1983 to 1985 (*Economist,* September 6, 1986, p. 67). Countries such as Qatar and the UAE also show only very modest increases in immigrant workers. The consequences of this deceleration in the growth of demand for immigrant workers and its shifting distribution are taken up below.

It should be emphasized that the above data refer to the stock of workers in a country at any one time. The total number of workers who have *ever* participated in work abroad is of course much larger than the stock in any specific year. Data on the "turnover" of workers do not exist. However, if the average length of stay abroad is two to three years, the total number of workers who had ever emigrated for employment between 1974 and 1988 would have been four to seven times larger than the stock of workers in 1974, even assuming that the stock remained constant from 1974 to 1986. But using even our conservative estimates, the stock roughly tripled during this period. Of course, workers did "repeat," go, return home, and go again. Nevertheless, we would guess that between 12 and 21 *million*

Table 14.2  Arab Migrant Workers in the Near East Region, 1975

| Country of employment | Country of Origin | | | | | | | | | | | |
|---|---|---|---|---|---|---|---|---|---|---|---|---|
| | Egypt | | YAR | | Jordan/Palestine | | PDRY | | Syria | | Lebanon | |
| | No. | % | No. | % | No. | % | No. | % | No. | % | No. | % |
| Bahrain | 1,237 | 0.3 | 1,121 | 0.4 | 614 | 0.2 | 1,122 | 1.6 | 68 | 0.1 | 129 | 0.3 |
| Iraq | 7,000 | 1.8 | -- | -- | 5,000 | 1.9 | -- | -- | -- | -- | 3,000 | 6.0 |
| Jordan | 5,300 | 1.3 | -- | -- | -- | -- | -- | -- | 20,000 | 28.4 | 7,500 | 15.1 |
| Kuwait | 37,558 | 9.4 | 2,757 | 1.0 | 47,653 | 18.0 | 8,658 | 12.2 | 16,547 | 23.4 | 7,232 | 14.6 |
| Libya | 229,500 | 57.8 | -- | -- | 14,150 | 5.3 | -- | -- | 13,000 | 18.5 | 5,700 | 11.5 |
| Saudi Arabia | 95,000 | 23.9 | 280,400 | 96.6 | 175,000 | 66.1 | 55,000 | 77.9 | 15,000 | 21.3 | 20,000 | 40.3 |
| Oman | 4,600 | 1.2 | 100 | 0.0 | 1,600 | 0.6 | 100 | 0.1 | 400 | 0.6 | 1,100 | 2.2 |
| Qatar | 2,850 | 0.7 | 1,250 | 0.4 | 6,000 | 2.3 | 1,250 | 1.8 | 750 | 1.1 | 500 | 1.0 |
| UAE | 12,500 | 3.1 | 4,500 | 1.6 | 14,500 | 5.5 | 4,500 | 6.4 | 4,500 | 6.4 | 4,500 | 9.0 |
| YAR | 2,000 | 0.5 | -- | -- | 200 | 0.1 | -- | -- | 150 | 0.2 | -- | -- |
| Total | 397,545 | 100.0 | 290,128 | 100.0 | 264,717 | 100.0 | 70,630 | 100.0 | 70,415 | 100.0 | 49,661 | 100.0 |
| All employing countries | | 30.7 | | 22.4 | | 20.4 | | 5.5 | | 5.4 | | 3.8 |

Country of Origin

| Country of employment | Sudan No. | Sudan % | Tunisia No. | Tunisia % | Oman No. | Oman % | Iraq No. | Iraq % | Somalia No. | Somalia % | Morocco No. | Morocco % |
|---|---|---|---|---|---|---|---|---|---|---|---|---|
| Bahrain | 400 | 0.9 | -- | -- | 1,383 | 3.6 | 126 | 0.6 | -- | -- | -- | -- |
| Iraq | 200 | 0.4 | -- | -- | -- | -- | -- | -- | -- | -- | -- | -- |
| Jordan | -- | -- | -- | -- | -- | -- | -- | -- | -- | -- | -- | -- |
| Kuwait | 873 | 1.9 | 49 | 0.1 | 3,660 | 9.5 | 17,999 | 87.3 | 247 | 3.8 | 47 | 1.8 |
| Libya | 7,000 | 15.3 | 38,500 | 99.6 | -- | -- | -- | -- | -- | -- | 2,500 | 98.2 |
| Oman | 500 | 1.1 | 100 | 0.3 | -- | -- | -- | -- | 300 | 4.6 | -- | -- |
| Qatar | 400 | 0.9 | -- | -- | 1,870 | 4.9 | -- | -- | -- | -- | -- | -- |
| Saudi Arabia | 35,000 | 76.3 | -- | -- | 17,500 | 45.6 | 2,000 | 9.7 | 5,000 | 76.4 | -- | -- |
| UAE | 1,500 | 3.2 | -- | -- | 14,000 | 36.4 | 500 | 2.4 | 1,000 | 15.2 | -- | -- |
| YAR | -- | -- | -- | -- | -- | -- | -- | -- | -- | -- | -- | -- |
| Total | 45,545 | 100.0 | 38,649 | 100.0 | 38,413 | 100.0 | 20,625 | 100.0 | 6,547 | 100.0 | 2,547 | 100.0 |
| All employing countries | | 3.5 | | 3.0 | | 3.0 | | 1.6 | | 0.5 | | 0.2 |

Source: J. S. Birks and C. A. Sinclair, "International Migration and Development in the Arab Region," ILO, Geneva, 1980. (The authors used a wide variety of official sources for their estimates.)

Table 14.3   Estimates of the Numbers of Arab Migrant Workers in Saudi Arabia
             and the GCC States, Early 1980s

| Country of Origin | In Saudi Arabia | In GCC States |
|---|---|---|
| Egypt | 800,000 | 1,150,000 |
| Iraq* | 3,250 | 44,760 |
| Jordan/Palestine | 140,000 | 227,850 |
| Lebanon | 33,200 | 54,850 |
| Oman | 10,000 | 33,450 |
| Somalia | 8,300 | 12,200 |
| Sudan | 55,600 | 65,470 |
| Syria | 24,600 | 67,150 |
| Tunisia/Morocco | 500 | 920 |
| YAR | 325,000 | 336,145 |
| PDRY | 65,000 | 83,845 |
| Total | 1,465,250 | 2,076,640 |

* In 1980 there were approximately 750,000 foreign workers in Iraq.   ("Labour
Immigration in the Gulf States: Patterns, Trends and Prospects," Quarterly
Review of the Intergovernmental Committee for Migration, January 1986).

Note: GCC = Gulf Cooperation Council, which includes Saudi Arabia, Kuwait, UAE,
Qatar, Oman, and Bahrain.

Source: R. Owen, Migrant Workers in the Gulf, Minority Rights Group Report,
London, No. 68, September 1985.

Middle Eastern workers have worked abroad in the oil states during the past fourteen years. Most of the male population of some countries, like the YAR, have worked in Saudi Arabia at least once. A recent survey of over 1,000 rural Egyptian families found that one-third of all males had worked abroad, mainly in Iraq (Richard Adams, personal communication, November 1987). One direct estimate places the number of Egyptians who migrated at any time during 1973–1985 at 3.5 million, roughly one-third of the labor force (Fergany 1988). The socioeconomic consequences of migration are *much* larger, and the benefits probably much more widely shared, than the numbers in the tables would suggest.

Who are these migrants? Although the composition of the migrant work force varies from one sending country to another, in all countries the vast majority are young adult males. For example, one study of Sudanese migrants found that over 90% were men, and over 60% were between 18 and 30 years old (Berar-Awad 1984). A survey in Egypt found that the average age was 32 (Fergany 1988). Similar patterns have been observed in the YAR and Jordan. By contrast, the educational and occupational composition of migrants varies markedly across countries. Emigrants from Sudan and Jordan are largely skilled. The ILO survey cited above found that only 11% of Sudanese migrants were illiterate, compared to a national illiteracy figure of over 75%. About 63% of the migrants in the ILO sample possessed some skills (Berar-Awad 1984). Relatively skilled workers tend to predominate among non-Arab Asian labor, although there are many low-skilled service workers (cleaners, maids). However, emigrants from YAR are over-

Table 14.4  Numbers of Foreign Workers in Gulf States, by Country of Origin, 1985 (000s)

| | Total | | Egypt | | Jordan | | Yemen AR | | Yemen PDR | | Others | |
|---|---|---|---|---|---|---|---|---|---|---|---|---|
| | No. | % | No. | % | No. | % | No. | % | No. | % | No. | % |
| Bahrain | 85 | 2.3 | 4 | 0.5 | 4 | 1.5 | 5 | 0.6 | 2 | 2.0 | 70 | 3.9 |
| Kuwait | 430 | 11.5 | 137 | 18.4 | 70 | 26.2 | 24 | 3.0 | 11 | 11.0 | 188 | 10.3 |
| Oman | 145 | 3.9 | 7 | 0.9 | 7 | 2.6 | 3 | 0.4 | 1 | 1.0 | 127 | 7.0 |
| Qatar | 108 | 2.9 | 16 | 2.2 | 8 | 3.0 | 8 | 1.0 | 3 | 3.0 | 73 | 4.0 |
| Saudi Arabia | 2,500 | 67.0 | 500 | 66.9 | 158 | 59.2 | 720 | 90.0 | 75 | 75.0 | 1,047 | 57.7 |
| UAE | 462 | 12.4 | 83 | 11.1 | 20 | 7.5 | 40 | 5.0 | 8 | 8.0 | 311 | 17.1 |
| Total | 3,730 | 100.0 | 747 | 100.0 | 267 | 100.0 | 800 | 100.0 | 100 | 100.0 | 1,816 | 100.0 |
| % of Total | 100.0 | | 20.0 | | 7.2 | | 21.4 | | 2.7 | | 48.7 | |

Source: Economic and Social Commission for Western Asia (ESCWA), "Study on Impacts of Returning Migration in Selected Countries of the ESCWA Region," DPD/86/14, United Nations, March 1986 (in Arabic).

whelmingly unskilled and rural. The World Bank estimated that between two-thirds and three-fourths of the half-million Yemenis abroad in 1982 were from rural areas (World Bank 1986c). Still other countries occupy an intermediate position: Although many skilled Egyptians have emigrated, it is likely that a majority of emigrants from that country have had relatively low skill levels: Fergany's survey found that a majority of migrants came from rural areas and that only about 10% of emigrants had a university education (Fergany 1988, 17).

## THE IMPACT OF LABOR MIGRATION
## ON SENDING COUNTRIES

### Emigration, or "People Out"

There is much debate on the impact of labor migration on sending countries. Unfortunately, although the controversy is heated, it is often unenlightening. Different analysts often have different values: What is "collapse of the national culture" to one may be seen as "integration into the modern world" by another. Prejudices abound, as when from the comfort of their lavishly furnished living rooms rich officials decry peasant migrants' spending money on television sets and tape decks. These prejudices and value conflicts are difficult to confront or to clarify because the existing data are so poor. We do not really know how many people have been affected directly by migration. Still less is known about the indirect effects on localities. The debate on the impact of labor migration is too often a clash of ignorant armies in the night.

Few dispute the private benefits of emigration: If the benefits were not extensive, people would not leave their homes to work abroad. The fundamental force driving the private decision to migrate is the huge gap between local and foreign wages. This gap is especially large for unskilled, rural workers who obtain construction jobs, as in the Egyptian example given above. The gap is also large for skilled and technical workers. For example, the average weekly pay in Jordan for professionals in 1979 was only 37% of weekly pay in Saudi Arabia, while Jordanian managers and administrators, when working in Jordan, earned only 20% of Saudi wages (World Bank 1986a). Although immigrant workers often have to finance travel abroad, these costs are reduced by labor contractors and by various private information systems ("when you get to Riyadh, contact Uncle Ahmed"), which typically involve whole villages and urban neighborhoods.

Recently some analysts of labor migration have stressed that the appropriate unit of analysis is not the individual but the household: One or two members may be selected to seek work abroad, while others remain behind to tend the store or the farm, to retain government jobs and so forth (Stark 1984). Such a context implies that immigrant workers can afford a longer job search than can an unsupported individual migrant. This reduces the riskiness of unemployment and increases the incentive to migrate. Such "household strategies" have been employed by millions of Middle Eastern families, and there is every reason to suppose that in most cases, the strategy has contributed to the welfare of the emigrant's family.

Few deny these private benefits. The debate over the impact of labor migration focuses on the social costs and benefits. This debate may be decomposed into a dispute about the net social benefits of three aspects of the migration process: "people out" (emigration), "money back" (remittances), and "people back" (return migration). Let us consider these in turn.

Perhaps the central question in debate over emigration is its impact on employment and its role in creating labor shortages. Those who applaud the migration phenomenon argue that emigration acted as a safety valve for sending countries' labor markets by providing jobs for the unemployed. The critics counter that most migrants were already employed, and maintain that emigration has fostered labor shortages that have impeded development.

We must distinguish among different types of labor in assessing these arguments. We would hazard the generalization that emigration has been very beneficial for constrained labor markets for relatively unskilled workers, thereby reducing levels of unemployment and increasing wages for the underprivileged. Although some seasonal, short-term labor bottlenecks may have been created, there is little evidence that such phenomena have reduced output. However, although emigration may have also helped to alleviate the chronic unemployment of university graduates, the "brain drain" has made it very difficult for poorer countries' public sectors to find qualified skilled personnel. These shortages and the continual turnover of highly trained people contribute to the woes of the public sector.

Although it is often true that those who migrate were already employed, the departure of such workers creates new openings for those who remain behind. For example, the initial exit of perhaps 40% of the urban construction work force from Egypt during the middle and late 1970s, combined with increased construction demand, pushed up construction wages. The effects did not stop there: The domestic construction boom stimulated migration of agricultural labor to the cities, which in turn contributed to the most dramatic growth of agricultural real wages in that country's modern history. Similar ripple effects have been noted in the YAR and Jordan.

The focus of the labor-shortage debate for unskilled labor is on the agricultural sector. Some believe that labor migration has created pervasive labor shortages that constrain agricultural development. However, the evidence suggests that such "shortages" are primarily temporally and spatially localized. They are mainly a problem of shortages of adult male hired labor in seasons of peak demand for certain crops: They usually occur on larger, commercial farms and in certain geographical regions. By contrast, family labor is typically not in short supply. Furthermore, these shortages are likely to be "temporary disequilibria" rather than "long-run structural" problems.

The continued growth of the rural labor force and the deceleration of the demand for unskilled immigrant labor in the oil-exporting countries suggests that the experience of the 1970s was historically anomalous: The shortages of that decade may be replaced by surpluses in the late 1980s and the 1990s. Table 6.13 shows the actual and the projected trends in the absolute size of the agricultural labor force in selected countries of the region. For most countries, the farm work force grew during the 1970s and is expected to continue to grow into the 1990s and beyond. Of course, the growth of the nonagricultural labor force is still more rapid. Nationwide labor shortages are a myth. The case for sectorwide shortages in agriculture in most countries is also weak. Despite the scale of both internal and foreign migration, the absolute numbers of the agricultural labor force increased in YAR, PDRY, Turkey, Sudan, and Egypt between 1970 and 1985. In the YAR, the agricultural labor force declined between 1970 and 1980 but then resumed its earlier increase. There has been a decline in the agricultural labor force in Jordan, Syria, Iraq, and Lebanon. Other indicators, such as trends in the amount of cultivated land per rural worker or in real farm wages tell a similar story: For some countries there is evidence of a tightening of rural labor markets (e.g., increasing real farm wages in Egypt, increases in land per worker in Jordan and Syria). However, for most countries of the region, the safety valve of migration has relieved, but has not eliminated, the pressure of population and labor-force growth upon job opportunities.

In addition, the labor force will very probably grow faster than the demand for immigrant labor in the oil-exporting countries or in the industrialized countries. Before the sharp decline in oil prices, the World Bank (Sherbiny 1984b) estimated that the annual demand for immigrant labor of all types in Saudi Arabia would expand at 2.9% between 1985 and 1990. The UN estimated that during the same period the annual growth rates of the labor force in Jordan would be 4.3%, Egypt 2.9%, and the YAR 3.1% (FAO 1986). The growth of demand for labor in the oil-exporting countries will not absorb as large a proportion of the region's labor force in the 1990s as it did during the past fifteen years.

If emigration created sectorwide shortages in any country, it should have done so in the YAR. Of all the sending countries, YAR has the largest percentage of its rural labor force out: In 1982 about 500,000 rural Yemeni men were working abroad, compared to an agricultural labor force of just over 1 million. Yet a World Bank study of the YAR's agricultural sector found that the average direct agricultural-labor requirements were less than one-fourth of available supply: The bank argued that there was no agricultural-*sector* shortage of labor even in a country where one-third of the total agricultural labor force was abroad (World Bank 1986c).

This hardly means that large-scale emigration has created no economic problems in agriculture or elsewhere in the economy. First, the growth of cereal production may have been slowed by the departure of labor. Cereals face strong competition from imports and sometimes significant taxation:

It is difficult for local cereal farmers to pass on the increased cost of labor in the form of higher prices. This problem is probably most severe in marginal ecological areas where some farms have simply been abandoned, as in YAR and Jordan.

Second, because rural labor markets in the region are often poorly integrated and because labor migration tends to be "selective," with some villages supplying many workers and others sending far fewer, local labor bottlenecks do emerge. Some observers have generalized this argument to the national level. Birks and Sinclair (1979) maintained that for Egypt the segmentation of labor markets and the problems of mobility of labor from one part of the economy to another have magnified the effects of labor emigration. So, when construction workers leave, they can be replaced only slowly and with difficulty. Although labor markets are indeed not the perfectly functioning ones of neoclassical economic textbooks, such problems proved to be much less severe than Birks and Sinclair argued. Egyptian agricultural wages have followed unskilled construction wages fairly closely, and despite massive emigration, the absolute numbers of construction workers has increased. The "segmentation" argument seems more applicable to the local, rather than the national, level.

Third, there has been a change in the demographic composition of the labor force: The farm work force is aging (in Tunisia, it is claimed that a majority of farmers are now over 55 years old), and the percentage of the labor force that is female appears to be increasing.[5] Here again there are reasons to question how serious a constraint on production this has been. The aging of the farm work force has been observed in every country in the process of development. This has not constrained output, partly because of the increased mechanization of agriculture. We saw earlier that such mechanization is spreading rapidly in the region.

The economic significance of the "feminization" of the farm work force depends on the extent to which women's labor can substitute for men's. This substitutability varies widely by country and by task. Even if women can perform all farm tasks, the result is likely to be that women are even more overworked than they were previously. This may be detrimental to their health and possibly to the health of their children. It is possible that high female illiteracy, combined with various forms of gender discrimination (e.g., by male-run cooperative societies), impedes technological progress on female-run farms. However, we are not aware of any data or studies that can document the allegation that the increasing percentage of farm work done by women has constrained agricultural production.

Finally, because labor shortages are peak-season shortages of adult male hired labor, they often affect wealthier commercial farmers more than small family farmers.[6] This phenomenon has been observed in Egypt, YAR, and Tunisia (Taylor-Awny 1984; World Bank 1986c; USAID 1983). Although it is common in many countries for even small farmers to hire some peak-season labor, a much higher percentage of farm work is conducted by hired workers on large commercial enterprises than on small subsistence farms. What is more, small farmers often respond to emigration-induced shortages of hired labor by using family labor more intensively, by reallocating family labor (e.g., having women do jobs formerly carried out by men), and by entering into a variety of complex labor-sharing arrangements in which households swap labor with each other. None of these options is usually open to larger farmers, who in some areas of Egypt are increasingly resorting to sharecropping or more extensive mechanization as a response.

In summary, although emigration of adult males from rural areas of the region has created certain short- to medium-term adjustment problems, the available evidence does not support allegations that migration has created labor shortages, which in themselves have constrained the growth of agricultural production. The same point holds for the exit of unskilled urban workers as well: There is simply no evidence that unskilled-labor shortages have retarded industrial growth or the building of infrastructure in the region. We believe that the emigration of unskilled labor has created far more benefits than costs for the sending countries.

The balance of social costs and benefits for the emigration of skilled manpower is somewhat more complicated. By definition, skills cannot be reproduced overnight. Accordingly, the supply of skilled workers is relatively inelastic. As a general rule one could argue that the greater the skill, the longer the period of necessary training, and therefore the greater the interval of shortages induced by emigration. However, as conventional economic theory would predict, these shortages seem to have been fairly brief, as the ever-increasing number of new labor-force entrants replaced the departed migrants.

Many teachers, engineers, computer programmers, and high-level managers went to work in the Gulf. We would suggest that the domestic private sector has been able to compete with Gulf State employment much more successfully than the public sector. Contrast, for example, the experience of engineers and programmers in the booming construction and financial sectors with the fate of the educational system in Egypt. There is little evidence that private construction activity has been unable to attract and retain highly qualified professionals such as engineers and architects. By contrast, the public educational system of that country has seen a massive outflow of teachers. Since their departure impedes the eradication of illiteracy, the social cost of such emigration may be very high indeed. Labor migration may also adversely affect higher education: Some university faculties at Cairo University (e.g., economics, statistics, commerce) had up to one-third of their regular faculty abroad during the late 1970s.

The reason for this differential performance is simple enough: Public-sector wages in the sending countries for comparable skills are much lower than in the private sector. It is especially difficult for the poorest countries like Sudan and the YAR to retain the (essential, but very scarce) skilled manpower necessary for high- and middle-level management of even a scaled-down public sector. Why should a Sudanese engineer work on roads in his own country when he can make at least three times as much money doing the same work in Saudi Arabia? For countries like Egypt, the problem may be less severe, since the public sector has been so grossly overstaffed that the exit of many such workers might even have a positive effect on productivity! But in Egypt too, however, the problem is that it is the "best and brightest" who tend to go abroad.

But even assuming that the demand for expatriate labor in the Gulf remains fairly constant, the growth of the labor force, the large expansion of secondary and higher education of the past two decades, and the more modest economic growth prospects of the post–oil boom era suggest that surpluses, not shortages, of many types of skilled workers will characterize the next decade. For example, despite having had some 40% of its work force abroad, Jordan has suffered from *surpluses* of engineers, teachers, and managers (World Bank 1986a). To some extent, however, these surpluses are deceptive: There are surpluses of *new* engineers and managers, of young professionals beginning their careers, combined with *shortages* of older, more experienced professionals. But the scarcity of such workers can be as easily attributed to earlier underdevelopment as to migration.

In summary, the impact of the first aspect of labor migration, "people out," has on balance helped the economies of sending countries. Millions of unskilled workers and their families have improved their living standards; there is little reason to suppose that economic growth would have been more rapid in these countries had these workers remained at home; the so-called labor shortages have been largely seasonal, short-run disequilibria, with the exception of the emigration of the most skilled professionals, especially from the poorest countries like Sudan.

### Remittances, or "Money Back"

Workers go abroad to save money, which they hope to bring back home. They usually succeed. Some official estimates of the magnitude of remittances in selected countries of the region are shown in Table 14.5. These remittances are a crucial source of foreign exchange for many countries. Indeed, for YAR and Egypt, the value of remittances exceeds that of any commodity exports. Remittances often pay for a substantial fraction of imports, especially in YAR, PDRY, Egypt, Jordan, and Morocco (Table 14.6).

These official figures for remittances represent only the tip of the iceberg. Much money enters labor-exporting countries via unofficial channels (Choucri 1986). For example, an ILO survey observed that only about 13% of remittances to Sudan from Saudi Arabia and Kuwait come through national banks. Between one-half and three-fourths of the total value of remittances were simply carried by hand (Berar-Awad 1984). Applying this ratio to national figures would mean that total Sudanese remittances in 1985 were over $1.9 billion, rather than the offical $249 million. Although the extreme weakness of the Sudanese banking system and the gross overvaluation of the Sudanese pound in 1985 may make that country's experience special,

Table 14.5  Official Remittances of Migrant Labor in Selected Countries of Origin, 1973-1986 (millions of U.S.$)

| | 1973 | 1974 | 1975 | 1976 | 1977 | 1978 | 1979 |
|---|---|---|---|---|---|---|---|
| Egypt | 123.0 | 310.0 | 455.0 | 842.0 | 988.0 | 1,824.0 | 2,269.0 |
| Jordan | 55.4 | 82.0 | 172.0 | 401.8 | 420.8 | 468.0 | 509.0 |
| Morocco | 211.0 | 299.0 | 482.0 | 499.0 | 546.0 | 702.0 | 891.0 |
| Sudan | 6.3 | 4.9 | 1.5 | 36.8 | 37.0 | 66.1 | 115.7 |
| Turkey | 1,234.0 | 1,466.0 | 1,398.0 | 1,104.0 | 1,068.0 | 1,086.0 | 1,799.0 |
| Tunisia | 91.0 | 106.0 | 131.0 | 128.0 | 152.0 | 204.0 | 271.0 |
| YAR | -- | 135.5 | 270.2 | 675.9 | 987.1 | 910.1 | 936.7 |
| PDRY | 32.9 | 42.8 | 58.8 | 119.3 | 187.3 | 254.8 | 297.9 |

| | 1980 | 1981 | 1982 | 1983 | 1984 | 1985 | 1986 |
|---|---|---|---|---|---|---|---|
| Egypt | 2,791.0 | 2,230.0 | 2,481.0 | 3,688.0 | 3,981.0 | -- | -- |
| Jordan | 666.5 | 921.9 | 932.9 | 923.9 | 1,027.8 | 846.2 | 984.4 |
| Sudan | 209.0 | 322.0 | 107.1 | 245.8 | 276.8 | 248.6 | 89.3 |
| Tunisia | 301.0 | 331.0 | 361.0 | 346.0 | 304.0 | 259.0 | 354.0 |
| Turkey | 2,153.0 | 2,559.0 | 2,189.0 | 1,549.0 | 1,855.0 | 1,762.0 | 1,703.0 |
| Morocco | 1,004.0 | 988.0 | 840.0 | 888.0 | 847.0 | 965.0 | 1,394.0 |
| YAR | 1,069.5 | 777.4 | 911.4 | 1,084.4 | 995.5 | 763.2 | 527.4 |
| PDRY | 322.5 | 378.7 | 429.7 | 439.5 | 479.5 | -- | -- |

Sources: IMF, International Financial Statistics Yearbook 1986, Washington, D.C., and July 1987 Country Tables (line 77 afd: Private Unrequited Transfers).

Table 14.6 Official Remittances as a Percentage of Imports and Exports in Selected Countries in the Near East Region, 1973-1986

|  | 1973 | | 1974 | | 1975 | | 1976 | | 1977 | | 1978 | | 1979 | |
|---|---|---|---|---|---|---|---|---|---|---|---|---|---|---|
|  | Imports | Exports | Imports | Exports | Imports | Exports | Imports | Exports | Imports | Exports | Imports | Exports | Imports | Exports |
| Egypt | 13.4 | 11.0 | 13.2 | 20.5 | 11.6 | 29.9 | 22.1 | 55.3 | 20.5 | 57.9 | 27.1 | 105.0 | 59.1 | 123.3 |
| Morocco | 18.4 | 23.2 | 15.7 | 17.5 | 18.8 | 31.2 | 19.1 | 39.2 | 17.1 | 41.9 | 23.6 | 46.6 | 24.2 | 45.5 |
| Jordan | 16.8 | 75.9 | 16.8 | 52.9 | 23.5 | 112.4 | 39.9 | 194.1 | 30.5 | 169.0 | 31.2 | 157.0 | 25.9 | 126.3 |
| Sudan | 1.4 | 1.5 | 0.7 | 1.4 | 0.2 | 0.3 | 3.8 | 6.6 | 3.4 | 5.6 | 5.5 | 12.8 | 10.4 | 21.6 |
| Tunisia | 13.3 | 21.6 | 9.4 | 11.5 | 9.2 | 15.3 | 8.4 | 16.2 | 8.3 | 16.4 | 9.5 | 18.1 | 9.5 | 15.1 |
| Turkey | 59.2 | 93.7 | 38.8 | 95.7 | 29.5 | 99.8 | 21.5 | 56.3 | 18.4 | 60.9 | 23.6 | 47.5 | 35.5 | 79.6 |
| YAR | -- | -- | 71.3 | 0 | 91.9 | -- | 163.7 | -- | 94.9 | -- | 70.9 | -- | 62.8 | -- |
| PDRY | 19.2 | 32.9 | 10.2 | 18.8 | 18.2 | 34.2 | 29.0 | 67.4 | 34.4 | 103.5 | 44.3 | 132.7 | 32.2 | 63.9 |

|  | 1980 | | 1981 | | 1982 | | 1983 | | 1984 | | 1985 | | 1986 | |
|---|---|---|---|---|---|---|---|---|---|---|---|---|---|---|
|  | Imports | Exports | Imports | Exports | Imports | Exports | Imports | Exports | Imports | Exports | Imports | Exports | Imports | Exports |
| Egypt | 57.4 | 91.6 | 25.4 | 69.0 | 27.3 | 79.5 | 35.9 | 114.8 | 37.0 | 126.8 | -- | -- | -- | -- |
| Jordan | 27.8 | 116.1 | 29.1 | 125.8 | 28.8 | 124.1 | 30.4 | 159.3 | 36.9 | 136.7 | 31.0 | 107.3 | 115.8 | 384.5 |
| Morocco | 23.6 | 41.1 | 22.5 | 41.4 | 19.5 | 40.7 | 24.7 | 44.3 | 21.7 | 39.0 | 25.1 | 44.2 | -- | -- |
| Sudan | 13.3 | 38.5 | 21.4 | 49.1 | 8.4 | 21.5 | 18.2 | 39.4 | 24.1 | 44.0 | 16.3 | 33.5 | 10.7 | 3.7 |
| Tunisia | 8.5 | 13.5 | 8.7 | 13.2 | 10.6 | 18.2 | 11.1 | 18.7 | 9.6 | 17.0 | 9.4 | 14.9 | 15.5 | 25.2 |
| Turkey | 27.2 | 74.0 | 28.7 | 54.4 | 24.8 | 38.1 | 16.8 | 27.0 | 17.5 | 26.4 | 16.0 | 22.1 | 15.4 | 22.8 |
| YAR | 57.7 | -- | 44.2 | -- | 59.9 | -- | 68.1 | -- | -- | -- | 29.3 | -- | -- | -- |
| PDRY | 21.1 | 41.5 | 26.7 | 62.4 | 26.9 | 54.1 | 29.4 | 65.2 | 31.1 | 74.3 | -- | -- | -- | -- |

Sources: Calculated from IMF, International Financial Statistics Yearbook 1986, Washington, D.C., and July 1987 Country Tables; remittances from Country Tables (line 77 afd: Private Unrequited Transfers); exports and imports from World Tables (70d and 71d).

a qualitatively similar phenomenon has been observed in other countries (e.g., YAR, Jordan, Syria, and Egypt).

Critics of remittances' effects at the macro level focus on two alleged phenomena: the tendency for remittances to be spent on imports rather than domestic production and their contribution to inflation. These two effects are mutually exclusive: If money is being spent on foreign goods, it should have no impact on domestic inflation. To the extent that domestic supply can respond to the increased demand, the result should be economic growth, rather than simply inflation. Of course, there are numerous constraints to expanding the output of domestic goods and services in the economies of the region, as we have seen. But workers' remittances are hardly responsible for these constraints, which were often induced by inappropriate government policies. The way in which money enters the system may contribute to inflation: To the extent that remittances move outside of the banking system, the government may lose control of the money supply, as Egypt did until the spring of 1988.

The principal area of debate on the microeconomic effect of remittances concerns the division of the funds between consumption and investment, and the types of investments that are selected. A substantial proportion of remittances is devoted to direct consumption. Such spending improves the welfare of the migrants' families, because a majority of migrants from most countries are from rural areas. Rural per capita incomes are only one-half to one-third of urban incomes in most countries of the region. Although migrants are typically not the most impoverished rural people, their ranks include many poor persons, such as landless laborers. Given the level of incomes of many migrants, it is hardly surprising that a large proportion of remittances are spent on consumption.

However, the total amount of remittance money that is invested is substantial. In Egypt, for example, one estimate for 1980/81 calculated that some 25% of gross investment and fully 80% of private-sector investment were financed by remittances (Lesch 1985); others would question such high figures. Some criticize the form that such investment takes. Critics fault migrants for placing their savings in housing, consumer durables, dowries, and land. They assert that too little of these funds moves into productivity-enhancing investments, like machinery, small workshops, and improved agricultural techniques.

The critics are correct about the distribution of investments. Remittances are often spent on housing. One survey in Egypt found that over one-fifth of remittances were so used; a similar proportion was reported in a study of Sudanese migrants' spending (Berar-Awad 1984). Parallel patterns have been found in Turkey, Tunisia, and Morocco. Other priority items of expenditure include furniture and simple household articles (some 58% in one Egyptian case study) (El-Dib, Ismail, and Gad 1984). Few who have been inside the homes of Egyptian, Yemeni, or Moroccan manual workers would criticize this use of remittances, especially in the rural areas. Better housing improves the quality of life of rural people and contributes directly to meeting basic human needs. To the extent that poorly ventilated, poorly heated or excessively hot, vermin-ridden housing is a threat to human health, the spending of remittances on better housing may be viewed as an investment in human capital. Although building on irreplaceable agricultural land constitutes an Egyptian national disaster, faulty incentives may be more reasonably blamed than migration.

Remittances are frequently invested in land. Even poorer emigrants from Cairo sometimes buy plots on the edge of the city, intending to build houses there. Since the supply of land is inelastic, the increased demand has pushed land prices sharply upward. Of course, not all of the rise in land prices can be attributed to remittances. Land-price increases occurred primarily in the highly inflationary environment during the decade of the oil boom. From California to Kuwait, investors move into real estate in inflationary periods. More recently, in most countries of the region, these prices have softened considerably. For example, the average purchase price of irrigated land in Jordan fell by about 40% between 1983 and 1986 (FAO, unpublished data). Land prices in Egypt have also declined.[7]

Some remittances have found their way into productive investments, such as irrigation equipment, small workshops and factories, or transportation equipment (trucks and cars). But these investments probably constitute a relatively small proportion of the total spending of remittances. This is hardly the fault of the migrants or of the phenomenon of emigration. Instead, it is more plausible to attribute the lack of investment of remittances in productivity-enhancing technologies to national policies that reduce the profitability of such investments. For example, the ambiguous attitude of many governments of the region toward private-sector manufacturing, combined with overvalued real exchange rates and other macromanagement problems, discourages the kind of industrial investments that critics of the current pattern of remittance spending would prefer.

The fact that so many remittances do not move through the banking system further reduces their use for productivity-enhancing investment. Weak and unstable financial systems have discouraged people from using banks. Returned migrants often keep their savings literally under the mattress; although they save, they cannot be expected to create their own investment opportunities. Banks have performed their function of financial intermediation between savers and investors rather poorly. Overvalued foreign-exchange rates further dissuade migrants from forwarding their savings through official channels. Recent exchange-rate reforms in Egypt provide an example of what policy shifts can accomplish: The realignment of exchange rates in the summer of 1987 led to an increase in bank deposits of perhaps $750 million. Many of these funds were remittances of Egyptian workers abroad. Sound banking systems and realistic foreign-exchange rates could improve the use of remittances.

Although some charge that spending remittances on automobiles contributes to the monstrous urban congestion of cities like Cairo, subsidized motor fuel and the failure of urban management are more likely culprits.

The diffusion of motor vehicles in the countryside is a healthy development. One of the causes of local labor shortages is the lack of information and the difficulties of substituting workers from one village for (departed) workers in another. Improved communication and transportation contribute to increased market integration. In some countries, e.g., Sudan, the transportation bottleneck is especially severe. In such a case, it is desirable that a certain proportion of remittances be spent on transportation.

The problem is that complementary public investment in roads and other infrastructure often lags, especially in Sudan, where now virtually all new roads are being built by foreign-aid donors. One challenge for policymakers is to determine how to channel remittances into needed public and semipublic goods and services, especially in rural areas. It is difficult to entice private funds into irrigation works, roads, public-health facilities, schools. One promising attempt to solve this problem is the Rural Development Associations of YAR, in which *zakat* (the Islamic tithe), levied on all income, is allocated to wells, schools, and roads (Cohen 1981).

The combination of labor migration and remittances does undermine the potential for an export-led growth strategy. To the extent that wages in the oil countries contain an element of oil rent, and to the extent that these rents have "seeped" into the wage structure of sending countries, the latter will find it difficult to compete in exporting labor-intensive commodities. Some critics of emigration have argued that labor exports were an alternative to the export of labor-intensive manufactured goods (Katanani 1981).

However, this was not really a choice for most countries: The political policies, institutions, and entrepreneurial skills needed for successful export of manufactured goods were nowhere in sight in the region in 1973, and these things take time to create. Imagine how many changes the Egyptian government of the early Sadat years would have had to undertake to begin to compete in the fiercely competitive international market for textiles! The exchange-rate regime, the tariff structure, the domestic-communications infrastructure would all have had to be altered radically. Furthermore, the manufacturers of these products in Egypt were SOEs, hardly famous for their flexibility and attention to consumer tastes. By contrast, all the government of Egypt had to do to facilitate labor exports was simply to cease to prohibit them. In the short run, there was really no choice. In the longer run, however, the instability of labor exports and the absence of the numerous dynamic linkages that characterize the growth of manufactured exports suggest that, once again, history has not been kind to the political economies of the poorer, more crowded nations of the region.

## Return Migration, or "People Back"

The vast majority of migrants want to return to their homes. Neither they nor the receiving countries view labor immigration as permanent resettlement. Most migrants do return home; the large majority come back at least temporarily, for major holidays or for important family events such as weddings. The more important question concerns the behavior of migrants who return home for good: what kind of economic contribution do these men make? How will national labor markets absorb the likely increased return flow of workers in the wake of the oil-price decline?

Many, perhaps most, migrants return to their village or urban neighborhood of origin (Amin and Taylor-Awny 1985). It is also likely that formerly landless agricultural workers will not return to agricultural work, even if they come back to their villages. Some village studies find that returnees often set up small businesses, such as taxi services, shops, and, occasionally, small factories. Returnees may have acquired new skills (e.g., a farm laborer turned construction worker), although there is little direct evidence on this issue.

Return migration on a substantial scale has already become a major issue for many sending countries. The fall in oil prices, the completion of major construction projects, and the increased competition of non-Arab Asian labor in the smaller Gulf States have all contributed to the gradual reversal of labor flows. This, of course, poses very serious problems for the sending countries. The declining importance of remittances as a source of foreign exchange is already evident in some countries. In the YAR, remittances fell about 20% from 1983 to 1985. In just two years (1984 to 1986), Egyptian remittances plummeted 50%, from $4 to $2 billion.

At the same time that the economic stimulus of remittances falls, the labor market must absorb not only the returnees but also the young people who seek their first jobs. These youths, not the returnees themselves, are the people who are most seriously affected by return migration. The returning migrants have often accumulated savings and acquired or sharpened skills abroad. They are relatively well placed to compete effectively in a tightening job market or to become successfully self-employed. But this is much less true for the semieducated youths who pour onto the job market in ever-greater numbers.

Returning migrants who cannot find jobs and who are deprived of migration outlets may cause political problems for the sending countries. For example, it is widely believed that the large-scale forced return of southern Tunisian migrants from Libya contributed to the riots in towns like Gafsa in 1984. Probably the greater danger, however, is simply the continued deterioration of employment opportunities: the shutting or narrowing of the safety valve.

## THE IMPACT OF MIGRATION
## ON SOCIAL CLASS AND EQUITY

It is difficult to make generalizations about the class consequences of migration, not only because so little reliable data is available, but also because the spotty available evidence suggests that the windfall gains of emigration have been fairly randomly distributed across social classes. Engineers and farm workers, doctors and drivers, teachers and mechanics, have all participated. Migration does offer a clear avenue of upward mobility for those able to emigrate. It may well help to reinforce the survival of small family farms and strengthen some elements of the small urban entrepreneurial class. It leaves behind many white-collar workers, especially those employed by the state. Access to migration opportunities has become an important variable in class differentiation, alongside of more conventional factors like ownership of land, workshops, and equipment, and access to education. As such, it probably has the result of making the class structure more complicated, and almost certainly, more fluid.[8]

The impact on poverty is clearer than its effect on income distribution or on the class structure. Emigration and remittances have reduced rural poverty, the worst poverty in the region. In Egypt, for example, emigration dramatically reduced the ranks of landless laborers, historically the poorest of the poor in that poor country. An ILO survey found that although 23% of all Egyptian villagers received remittances, 75% of the poorest 30% of villagers received them. For the absolutely poorest people, who are often disabled single persons, remittances constituted more than 75% of their (extremely meager) incomes. For the third poorest income decile, 40% of their income came from remittances. The poorest fourth and fifth deciles obtained more than 30% of their incomes from agricultural wage labor; the real wages of farm workers more than doubled in the last decade, largely thanks to emigration (Radwan and Lee 1986; Richards and Martin 1983).

Similarly, emigration and remittances have ameliorated the grinding rural poverty in the YAR. Researchers report improved food and nutrition and better housing. The fact that sharecropping contracts now commonly allocate a higher percentage of the crop to the tenant is also evidence that poorer groups have benefited relatively as well as absolutely. In the Middle East, as everywhere, migrants often come from very poor and disadvantaged regions: from western Sudan, from Upper Egypt, and from southern Tunisia.

However, it seems clear that migrants are usually not the very poorest rural inhabitants, simply because migration requires some money to finance the journey abroad. However, labor contractors and family networks can often bring these costs down within reach of quite poor Middle Easterners. Furthermore, the very poorest Egyptians do seem to benefit from migration via remittances. Nevertheless, migration is unfortunately neither large enough nor stable enough to alter radically the serious problems of rural and urban poverty in the region.

## THE IMPACT OF MIGRATION
## ON RECEIVING COUNTRIES

The economic benefits of migration to the receiving countries are clearly very large. The major oil exporters simply could not have undertaken their large-scale development projects without foreign workers, who made possible the rapid physical capital formation and infrastructure construction of the oil-boom period. Saudi nonoil GDP grew at 10.5%, 13%, and 8.9% for 1970–1975, 1975–1980, and 1980–1983, respectively; in the UAE nonoil GDP expanded at 14.1% per year from 1975 to 1980. Immigration of teachers also enabled the oil countries to embark on the rapid expansion of their educational systems.

Such rapid economic growth and construction of physical and social infrastructure would have been impossible without the dramatic inflow of foreign labor. As explained above, the enormous increase in the demand for labor that such expansion implied could not be met from domestic supply alone. By 1980, 53% of the Saudi labor force was foreign, while 78% of Kuwait's workers and 89% of the UAE's work force came from abroad. Even in Iraq, with a much larger indigenous work force than the other states, 14% of the labor force was foreign in 1980 (Sherbiny 1984b). The dependence of the Gulf States on foreigners for labor has no parallels in modern economic history.

The combination of such rapid economic growth with these massive influxes of foreign workers of all types has had some unusual social and political consequences. To some extent, labor immigration has severed the "normal" link between economic growth and structural change on the one hand and class formation on the other. Locals can and have avoided manual labor; they can continue to be merchants, soldiers, and bureaucrats. Some fear the long-run impact of the identification of hard work with foreigners—by implication, something that is less than perfect. To be sure, immigrants from poorer countries do the hard, dirty, and dangerous work in all rich countries. But only in the Gulf do the foreign menials outnumber the local leisured.

In the Gulf, as everywhere, large-scale immigration has created political problems. Although these have proved manageable so far, as we argued earlier, immigration is the greatest political challenge facing the Saudi and Kuwaiti regimes. There is first a problem of the legitimacy of denying citizenship rights and benefits to fellow Arabs and Muslims. States that base their legitimacy on Arab nationalism (as in Iraq) or on Islam (as in Saudi Arabia) face contradictions when they deny other Arabs or Muslims the same treatment as nationals. However, ideological pronouncements notwithstanding, even the Iraqis (who require no visas from Arab migrants on the grounds that they are "citizens of the Arab Nation") treat their citizens differently from other Arab workers.

This problem may be more acute the longer migration continues and as the children of migrants are born in the host country. However, the Kuwaitis have refused to extend citizenship to the children of Palestinians, many of whom have been born in Kuwait; a "Kuwaiti" is still defined as someone who had relatives on both sides of the family living in Kuwait in 1920! Such considerations underlay the tolerance, and even preference, shown by the smaller Gulf States toward non-Arab Asian immigrants: It was believed that they would not *want* to stay. And in any case, conflict between stated principles and actual practices are hardly uncommon in the Gulf, as elsewhere.

Large-scale influxes of foreigners make national security agencies nervous. The disquiet in the Gulf was compounded by the volume of immigration, the political volatility of the region, and the relatively underdeveloped national-security apparatus in many Gulf States at the beginning of the 1970s when immigration soared. States handled these threats by implementing laws that insisted that all but a handful of immigrants be on short-term contracts, by forbidding job changes unless the original employer agreed, and by requiring all workers to leave the country for a specified period once their contracts had expired. They refused to allow the families of any but the most skilled professionals into the country. They mounted particular vigilance against special security threats such as Iranians after the Islamic revolution in Iran. The Saudis tightened security beginning in 1978 and with even more vigor after the Great Mosque incident of 1980. In particular, they sought to guarantee that *hajjis* (pilgrims) would return to their own countries and not use the pilgramage as a means to slip into the country in search of work. Finally, the Gulf States resorted extensively to particular devices, such as the use of turnkey construction contracts, in which the general contractor supplied the workers, whose departure was guaranteed by the company itself.

Although the Gulf States tried to beef up enforcement by importing foreign police experts (and, in some cases, foreign soldiers and policemen, like Pakistanis in Oman and Saudi Arabia) and by investing in expanded police equipment (e.g., computers), they continued to rely primarily on more traditional, personalized enforcement mechanisms. Effectively, the employer's right to hire and fire became a political prerogative to retain or expel a worker from the country. Not only could employers report a worker to the Ministry of the Interior, but also by simply dismissing him or her, the employer ensured that the worker would have a legally irregular status. Employers usually took the worker's passport upon arrival and would not return it until the contract expired.

In summary, the wealthy labor-importing states are a bit schizophrenic about labor immigration. On the one hand, they need these workers for their economies and have become accustomed to the benefits of greater money incomes and wider personal services that such migrants make possible. On the other hand, they fear being overwhelmed by the influx; they worry about losing their cultural values in a sea of foreigners, they dread the possibility of political activism by the immigrants, who, however much they may have improved their status relative to their conditions at home, are clearly underprivileged in the context of the Gulf States themselves. There is little indication that this contradiction will be resolved soon. It is likely that the Gulf States will remain dependent on immigrant labor for some time and that they will continue to dislike this dependence.

## CONCLUSION:
## THE RETURN OF SURPLUS LABOR?

Labor migration has transformed the political economy of the region. Huge numbers of urban and rural citizens of the poorer countries of the region left their homes, often for the first time, for extended stays abroad. Their departure, their remittances, and their return have all had important consequences for their families, villages, neighborhoods, and national economies. Although the dreams of unity remain far from realized, the economic interdependency engendered by labor migration is historically unprecedented (Ibrahim 1982a). It is no longer possible to talk sensibly about "the Egyptian" or "the Jordanian" labor market, without simultaneously discussing Saudi, Kuwaiti, and Iraqi employment opportunities. Labor markets, if nothing else, have become thoroughly integrated across national boundaries. The workers of the Middle East have mingled together on a historically unprecedented scale during the past fifteen years.

Since this integration was fundamentally driven by the spending of oil revenues, it may prove to be fragile. Whatever the future trend of oil prices, it is unlikely that the experience of the 1970s will be repeated. It is clear that the construction boom of that decade has ended; the demand for unskilled labor should slacken, by most accounts (e.g., World Bank). But predictions of massive returns of labor have so far not been borne out by events; this does not mean that it will not happen, perhaps even as this is written. It does seem that the citizens and governments of the oil states have acquired a taste for imported servants, and it will be some time before there are enough locals to staff the technical positions that the newly constructed petrochemical industries and infrastructure require. It is likely that foreigners will comprise a substantial proportion of the labor force of the Gulf States for many years to come.

However, the dynamism of labor migration as a force for raising wages and living standards in the poorer rural areas of the region is unlikely to be repeated. The rapid growth of population and of the labor force in these areas will very probably exceed any future demand from abroad: The old problem of surplus labor may make a comeback. However, experience elsewhere suggests that some of the social effects of rural emigration are irreversible: The young will continue to try to leave, even if the conditions are less favorable than those that faced their elder brothers. Finding these people jobs will remain an essential task of all governments of the region. Critics who charge that the emigration phenomenon simply provided windfall gains, which were squandered while the labor force continued its inexorable growth, may yet have the last word.

## NOTES

1. "First as tragedy, then as farce" (*Eighteenth Brumaire of Louis Bonaparte*).

2. Cultural integration among the Arabs has been proceeding apace for several generations. We do not attempt to analyze this complex, and vitally important, phenomenon here.

3. However, the Lebanese and Sudanese civil wars have also created large numbers of political refugees from those countries, while the authoritarianism of most countries of the region has guaranteed that nearly all of them have spawned at least some political exiles.

4. Official Iraqi data on labor imports do not exist, making all statements about that country even more speculative than for others. Some observers believe that there has been no decline in the numbers of foreigners (especially Egyptians) in Iraq.

5. UN data show an increase from the mid-1970s to the mid-1980s in the percentage of the farm work force that is female (FAO 1986). This may be due to the emigration of males, or it could simply be the result of improved data collection. Women's work in agriculture has long been undercounted. Women residing on family farms may perform various farm tasks along with domestic chores. These women are often listed as "housewives" rather than as "agricultural workers" (see Dixon 1980).

6. This fact may explain the popularity of "labor shortage" arguments with Agricultural Ministry officials, who, plausibly, are more subject to lobbying by large commercial farmers than to complaints by small peasants.

7. This is partly because of new, more stringent government regulations against building on agricultural land.

8. There are very few studies of the impact of emigration on income distribution. Fergany (1988) compared the Gini coefficients of income distribution of migrants and nonmigrants before (1973) and after (1984) migration. He found that the Gini coefficient *fell* for nonmigrants but rose for migrants. He then asserted that this shows that "labor migration during the period (1974–1984) militated in the direction of increasing income inequality in Egypt" (p. 13). However, since he also found that the large majority of migrants were uneducated rural men, this conclusion is dubious.

# 15

## CLASS INTERESTS
## AND THE STATE

Our purpose here is to sketch out how state policies have contributed to class formation and the ways in which class interests have manifested themselves. We shall take the occasion to rehearse earlier discussions of state initiatives in agrarian reform and nationalizations, economic liberalization (*infitah*), and higher and professional education. We shall pay particular attention to the petite bourgeoisie, which for many observers has been the driving political and economic force behind the state systems of the region. We shall also try to assess the role of class in the two violent social revolutions that have occurred in the Middle East in this century: the Algerian and the Iranian.[1]

### THE COLLAPSE OF TRADITIONAL CLASSES

One cannot but be surprised at the ease with which the independent states of the Middle East contained or broke the power of significant economic interests in their societies. Batatu summarized the conventional wisdom when he wrote (1978, 221), "All this is but another confirmation of the elementary truth that no class will for long accept a change adverse to its interests without opposition or violence." However elementary that truth, the history of the Middle East in the twentieth century does not bear it out. The only entrenched indigenous class in the region has been the landowners, and their roots are fairly shallow, no deeper than the middle of the nineteenth century, when private title to land was extended to the rural notability by revenue-hungry governments. Still, in Egypt, Iraq, and Syria, landowners were seen as the dominant class between the two world wars, and their power was reputedly great in Iran and to a lesser extent in Turkey during the same period.

The fact is, however, that when faced with determined governments promoting aggressive agrarian-reform projects, the landed classes have given up without a fight. That was the case in Egypt after 1952, although one

Upper Egyptian landlord did, briefly, defy the military government. Successive land-reform measures were pushed through in Syria and Iraq after 1958 without any reported resistance by the landlords. Algeria carried out an agrarian reform in 1972 against a far less entrenched landowning class that had grown up only since independence in 1962. The shah, between 1963 and 1966, stripped Iran's latifundists of much of their land. In all these instances, the major challenges faced by the architects of agrarian reform were bureaucratic inefficiency, lack of extension agents and agricultural credit institutions, but not opposition from landlords.

We should not belittle the fact that Turkey has been unable to implement a far-reaching agrarian reform, that in Eastern Anatolia there remain traditional latifundists, and that commercial farmers have carved a niche for themselves in Turkey's party system, where delivering the rural vote is important. No Turkish government has yet had the will to take these interests on. In Tunisia, Planning Minister Ben Salah's efforts in 1968/69 to bring the entire agricultural sector within a system of cooperatives was read as the first step on the road to collectivization and successfully resisted by the commercial farmers of the Sahel region. It may be that the Turkish and Tunisian examples tell us that commercial farmers who perform vital functions in agricultural production, who live in the countryside, and who often help organize the countryside politically for the regime, can better defend their interests than the older landlord class. Finally, in no instance were landlords utterly stripped of their land. All received compensation of some kind and were allowed to retain some portion of their holdings. That they were not literally liquidated may have made nonresistance more palatable to them.

The Middle East has not known until recent decades an indigenous entrepreneurial class except in Lebanon. Morocco's trading and manufacturing bourgeoisie from the city of Fez is also a partial exception. Nowhere did an indigenous private-capitalist class control the means of production. If such a class is to emerge anywhere in the region, we would expect that it will be in Turkey.

Frequently, entrepreneurial functions were carried out by combinations of large foreign interests, nonnational intermediaries such as the Armenians, Jews, and Syro-Lebanese in Egypt, or by outright foreigners like the Greeks in Egypt. There were also members of various indigenous minorities, legal citizens in their countries of origin, but vulnerable to repression on the part of dominant majorities. The Shi'ite Chalabis of Iraq; Turkey's Armenians; Egypt's, Morocco's, or Iraq's Jews; Iran's Baha'is, Jews, and Armenians are cases in point.

None of these entrepreneurial interests, no matter how economically powerful, were fully integrated into the political system. They never enjoyed full legitimacy and were seen as "foreign" and suspected of being at the service of imperialist interests. There were of course exceptions, like the above-mentioned entrepreneurs from Fez who launched Morocco's nationalist movement in the 1930s, and like Talaat Harb of Egypt, who founded

Bank Misr and what became the Middle East's largest textile complex at Mehallah al-Kubra. Nonetheless, polyglot entrepreneurial classes were fairly easy targets for nationalizations or simple harassment and shakedown.

There was one notable exception to these generalizations. Conservative business interests in Syria, allied with like-minded members of the armed forces officers corps, engineered a coup d'état in September 1961 that ended Syria's union with Egypt and interrupted Nasser's efforts to extend his nationalizations of July 1961 to Syrian enterprises. The conservative government that ruled in Syria until the Ba'ath seized power in March 1963 did not undo many of the nationalizations that had taken place, although it did raise the ceilings on landholdings first imposed in 1958. In early 1965, a little more than a year after seizing power, the Ba'ath regime swung leftward and nationalized 106 private enterprises. This time the entrepreneurial class was powerless to resist (see, inter alia, al-Ahsan 1984, 306).

## RURAL CLASS ACTORS

The great landowning classes of the Middle East have nearly everywhere been stripped of much of their land assets. This does not mean that the old landowning class has been physically liquidated, jailed, or put on the breadlines. Its members have often been able to make successful transitions to commercial or industrial enterprise. Others have become, on reduced holdings, prosperous capitalist farmers. Land ceilings, tenancy and rent reforms, and large public-credit schemes shifted the balance of economic and political forces in the countryside so that smallholders could find alternatives to the landlord's control over access to land and capital.

What we find in the wake of agrarian reform is the emergence of three important sets of actors. The new "capitalist" farmers, whom we referred to in Chapter 6 as on the "Junker Road," are an important force not only in societies that have experienced superficial land reform but also in those that have engineered profound changes in rural-property relations. In Turkey commercial farming in cotton, tobacco, sugar beets, wheat, hazelnuts, orchards, and vegetables has been important to the economy since World War II (Mann 1980), and commercial farming interests have been close to the Democrat and then the Justice parties (now called the True Path), which opposed the Republican People's party of Atatürk and Inönü. More than any others, these interests were able to block significant land-reform legislation (Hale 1981, 185). By contrast, powerful farming interests in Morocco's citrus sector were the beneficiaries of land sales on the part of departing French settlers. Many of these sales required the authorization of the king and his key ministers and thus should be seen as part of the royal patronage system (Waterbury 1970). In Algeria, former revolutionaries, bureaucrats, and army officers were able to acquire, surreptitiously, if not illegally, 400,000 hectares that had been owned by French settlers. Kaid Ahmed, one of the "historic" chiefs of the FLN, managed to acquire 3,000 hectares near Tiaret, and he exemplifies the gradual transformation of revolutionary sacrifice into personal aggrandizement. He was fired by Boumedienne in 1972 (Raffinot and Jacquemot 1977, 292, 366). Alongside officials like Kaid Ahmed were traditional Algerian landowners, in the less-favored agricultural zones, who began to modernize their holdings. In Egypt we find a middle-range landowning class drawn from former large landowning families (see Ansari 1986), urban interests that have moved into commercial agriculture, and an entrenched group of some 200,000 medium-size landowners whose position in the countryside is now several generations old (Binder 1978). A final example is that of the Sudan, where urban-based merchants and businessmen have, with easy public credit, launched themselves into extensive, tractor-based cultivation of sorghum, both for export and domestic consumption. In short the dominant rural interests now consist of commercial farmers, sometimes absentee, and often owning urban assets or exercising urban careers.

The next rural interest or stratum to be considered is that of the medium-size landholders. They differ from the capitalist farmers in degree, not in kind. They will tend to have smaller holdings that may be farmed by the labor available to an extended family. Hence, they do not often hire labor, except during peak seasons (although in Egypt, hiring-in may take place in any season). They may still produce for family subsistence and thus tend to be somewhat less integrated into regional and national markets. Concomitantly, their economic interests are less diversified, being almost wholly bound up in agriculture or animal husbandry. Almost surely they will have come, not from fallen gentry, but rather out of the ranks of the smallholders, perhaps as beneficiaries of land reform. They may enjoy considerable political power at the local level.

The final rural group to take into account is the large mass of smallholders. These hover near or above the subsistence level. They may have to lease-in land or hire out family labor in order to make ends meet. They will be only partially integrated into markets, although in Egypt that integration is likely to be fairly complete. Curiously, their interests and activities may be, of necessity, more diversified than those of the medium landowners. For instance they may be tenants as well as landowners; they may hire out as laborers, engage in petty trade or factory work in the slack season or migrate abroad.

Their economic existence is precarious, subject to adverse prices, natural disasters, fragmentation of holdings through inheritance, inadequate sources of credit, seizure of assets for debt, and so forth. In this respect they are not different from landless tenant farmers and rural labor. But in contrast to tenants and laborers, they own land, no matter how little, and for that reason they tend to enjoy a higher social status. Keeping in mind that Table 15.1 refers to only one country, Iraq, and that all others in the region may present different profiles, one can say that its figures indicate some reasonable orders of magnitude.

How has public policy influenced the emergence of these rural class actors? We have already stressed the key role of land reform, but some

Table 15.1  Socioeconomic Stratification of Iraq's Rural Population, Mid-1970s

|                                          | Number  | %     |
|------------------------------------------|---------|-------|
| Agriculture wage laborers                | 34,601  | 3.9   |
| Quasi-proletarian landless               | 91,680  | 10.3  |
| Poor smallholders                        | 138,520 | 15.6  |
| Smallholders above subsistence           | 366,721 | 41.5  |
| Medium landowners                        | 183,361 | 20.7  |
| Capitalist farmers and feudal remnants   | 71,539  | 8.0   |
| Total                                    | 885,422 | 100.0 |

Source: 'Issam al-Khafaji, The State and the Evolution of Capitalism in Iraq: 1968-1978, Cairo, Dar al-Mustaqbal al-Arabi, 1983 (in Arabic), p. 125.

additional comments are necessary. In a number of Middle East societies, redistributing land from the very rich to the very poor and middling was intended to broaden the base of property ownership in the countryside. That in turn was seen as politically stabilizing—creating for the regime a new contingent of rural clients among the beneficiaries of reform[2]—and economically desirable, in that there is brought into production for market a whole stratum of newly entitled, hardworking petty capitalists. To varying degrees the reforms in Iran between 1963 and 1972, the 1952 Egyptian reform, and the distribution of settler land in Morocco in the 1960s and 1970s all had such objectives in mind.

In the more radical reform programs, especially in Egypt (1961–1966), Algeria, Iraq, and Syria, the formulators were often self-proclaimed socialists and occasionally Marxists, and they advocated a gradual transition to collective forms of property and the abolition of rural private property. Nowhere did the ideologues have their way, and everywhere we have seen the wings of radical reformers clipped. Ben Salah's mildly radical project was wound up in Tunisia in the 1970s (Alan Findlay 1984). In Algeria, the self-managed farm experiment in 1987 was reorganized into cooperatives in which the former workers were granted private-property rights.

As the returns to *some* forms of rural production grew, urban-middle-class investors saw a way of protecting their salaried income against inflation. Bureaucrats, merchants, lawyers, professors, party leaders, and military officers bought land, herds, machinery, and orchards to run as commercial investments. They came to represent not only a hedge against inflation but also a potential source of support after retirement, or, simply, a good investment. Rural and urban interests thus came together in a myriad of joint ventures. In Egypt, for example, there were 300 "modern" poultry farms in 1975. By 1984 their number had grown to 18,623! Public institutions had advanced more than £E 750 million (ca $400 million) in credits to set up poultry and egg farms. Interest rates were subsidized, as was the sale of chicken feed. The result was that the government's target of 7.5 billion eggs per year by the year 2000 was reached in 1985. Owners were actually destroying chicks and eggs to keep prices up (*al-Ahram al-Iqtisadi*, No. 858, June 24, 1985).

Government investment projects enhanced the value of rural real estate. This is especially true of large irrigation projects that bring new land into cultivation or increase the productivity of land already cultivated. Under the shah, Khuzistan was singled out for irrigated development, Morocco has followed its multi-dam project, Turkey, and Egypt and the Sudan have already extended irrigation through several giant hydroelectric and water-storage projects. As a general rule we may say that large irrigation schemes will give rise to new class actors and powerful new rural interests (for one case study, see Barnett 1977). If the schemes do not, it will be because they have failed technologically or economically.

A last consideration in explaining the resurgence of rural capitalism is the recent official recognition of the need to generate exports. Morocco, Tunisia, Turkey, Egypt, and the Sudan, most notably, all stagger under large external debts and potential payments crises. All have announced their intention to stimulate agricultural exports to help relieve foreign-exchange pressures. It is believed that agriculture may be able to respond more quickly to the export challenge than can the industrial sector. It is also believed that private producers with as little state control as possible should be given the chance to respond to the challenge.

None of these groups has attained the political weight enjoyed by the former landowning elites in countries like Egypt, Iraq, and Syria. However, their economic importance has been growing precisely as the older strategy of urban-biased, import-substituting industrialization has been found wanting. That policy did succeed in creating expanding urban and industrial markets for rural products, and the capitalist farming groups have been well positioned to supply them.

Over the past twenty years, these groups have begun to lobby successfully for a certain number of policies that enhance the profitability of their undertakings. Primary among them are price increases for what they produce, in effect, ending the old system of state-administered pricing that underpaid farmers in order to supply cities and factories with cheap agricultural produce. Governments have not responded to demands for incentive pricing quickly or uniformly, but they have responded. They have done so as much in recognition of poor agricultural performance as in deference to the wishes of farm lobbies.

Rural capitalists are predictably demanding less government interference in *some* respects—pricing, marketing—but not in all. They also want their governments to maintain policies of subsidized credit, so that they can purchase inputs, like fertilizer and machinery, cheaply. They call for cheap electricity rates and the delivery of irrigation water at no or nominal charge. They oppose efforts to tax proportionately the growing value of their production or of their land.

The means they have employed to achieve these ends are various. We usually conceive of lobbying in the democracies of the advanced industrial states taking place before legislation or authoritative governmental decrees are enacted. Pressure is brought to bear on elected representatives and key actors in the administration in order to bring about desired legislation or to head off undesirable laws. Failing this, interest groups threaten to shift votes, strike, withhold produce until they get their way.

It is often argued that in developing countries the lobbying process is fundamentally different. Interest groups, perhaps assuming that it is difficult, if not impossible, to influence unaccountable governments and rubber-stamp parliaments before legislation is made, devote their efforts to sabotaging or neutralizing legislation *after* it is made. Evasion of land-reform ceilings is a widespread case in point.

Among rural interest groups in the Middle East, we find examples of both kinds of lobbying. In Egypt the rural middle class since the early 1970s has been able to block taxes on orchards, raise the base rate on which rents are calculated, reintroduce legal sharecropping contracts, and exempt privately reclaimed land from the land ceilings. Like Egypt's business and banking associations, rural capitalist interests are beginning to behave like conventional lobbies.

Similarly in Turkey, agrarian capitalists have had a political voice for decades. And in Turkey there has been, over fairly long periods of democratic rule, the real question of who gets the rural vote. Prosperous farmers who, to some extent, can deliver that vote, have effective leverage over agrarian policy. Turkey has turned away from import-substituting industrialization only in the last decade, but its agricultural sector had begun to perform well prior to that because in the 1960s and 1970s politicians had an incentive to deliver favors to the rural electorate. Improved roads, large hydroelectric projects, and incentive pricing have led to the buildup of rural wealth. In Iran in the early 1980s, commercial farming interests were able to block legislation introduced in the *majlis* that would have deepened the shah's land reform. Although some land seizures were eventually approved, the Council of Guardians in 1983 ruled the proposed land ceilings unconstitutional (Bakhash 1984, 196; Ashraf 1984).

In other instances, however, we find evidence of postlegislative lobbying and maneuvering. The Ben Salah reforms of the late 1960s in Tunisia, as mentioned above, provoked an organized response on the part of capitalist farmers, especially among the olive growers of the Sfax region, that threatened to weaken the rural organization of the Socialist Destour party. In the face of that threat, President Bourguiba withdrew his support of the reforms and abandoned Ben Salah.

Smallholders do not have the political leverage to lobby in either manner. Their tactics are much more indirect. They may default on public loans (but so do the medium-size owners), and ignore the government's cropping recommendations or deliberately neglect the crops the government has promoted. They may allocate more of their time to nonagricultural pursuits, or leave the countryside altogether for work in the cities or abroad. In systems where votes count, even symbolically, their interests cannot be ignored. Their ability to protest is not rooted in organized interest associations but rather in what Scott has called "everyday forms of peasant resistance" (1985).

In sum, the more privileged producers in the Middle Eastern countryside have gradually come to place important constraints on the ability of governments to formulate and implement agrarian policies. Because of their growing wealth and increasing awareness of shared interests, because of their important economic allies in government, the professions, and in urban business, and because of their potential to boost exports, they have been able to reduce state autonomy vis-à-vis the still-dominant rural sector. Their current preeminence, moreover, is in no small measure the result of previous government policies of land reform, agricultural credit, and differential pricing.

## THE STATE, THE PETITE BOURGEOISIE, AND THE NEW MIDDLE CLASS

Let us recall that heavy state intervention in the industrialization process was premised on the absence of, and sometimes hostility toward, private entrepreneurial initiative. But even in states such as Egypt, Algeria, Syria, and Iraq that set about limiting the scale and range of private industrial activities, large state-investment programs, the letting of contracts, and the supply of basic industrial inputs from public-sector enterprises, all served over time to build significant private-sector interests, dependent on the state but also thoroughly familiar with state agencies and their top administrators.

In different countries, private sectors have exhibited varying degrees of strength and influence on policy. Until 1976 Lebanon's business elite, dominated by Christians but containing representatives of all confessions, in effect controlled the state apparatus. It was in pre-1976 Lebanon that Marx's famous dictum that the state is the executive board of the dominant class came closest to realization in the Middle East. In Turkey, a new private sector was born in the shadow of a powerful, autonomous state, consolidated itself in the 1950s, and now is in a position to veto state-economic policy if not determine its content. At the present time the interests of the state and the large capitalist enterprises *coincide* in the pursuit of export-led growth. This does not mean, however, that private interests have come to dominate the Turkish state. Rather, both sets of interests control major human and material resources and can constrain each other's autonomy. In Iran in the 1970s, under the shah, the private sector may have been moving toward such an equilibrium with state interests, but since the founding of the Islamic republic, that trend has been arrested. The merchant class, or *bazaaris*, rural capitalists, and small-scale manufacturers may have come through the revolutionary process in good shape, but the large industrialists, whose fortunes could not have been made without the shah's assistance, are the objects of opprobrium and sometimes judicial pursuit. Egypt's and Tunisia's private-industrial sectors, by contrast, appear to be growing in wealth and experience along the same lines as Turkey's, and it would not be surprising to find that in fifteen years they may be able to affect state-economic policy in a major way.

In Algeria, Syria, and Iraq, while small doses of liberalization have been applied, the faint stirrings of private-sector industrial activity are still dominated by state controls, and state autonomy from class interests is still very real. These countries, along with Libya and the PDRY, stand at one end of a scale of state autonomy, while Morocco, Turkey, Kuwait, and the Sudan stand at the other.

## The Petite Bourgeoisie

Because it has been so difficult in the Middle East to discern a dominant class in the conventional sense—i.e., a landlord class or an entrepreneurial bourgeoisie—many analysts have cast the petite bourgeoisie in that role. To bring this off requires considerable legerdemain. If this class is "small" in its undertakings, how has it become dominant? If it is highly diversified internally, and seldom aware of itself as a class, why have other classes, particularly landowners or foreign economic interests, collapsed in its face? If it has been strong enough to take political power, why has it needed an interventionist state to help organize its economic interests?

Analysts, generally on the left, have saddled the petty, or petite, bourgeoisie with a host of sins. Its members lack vision, and their "class project" is murky. It is their nationalism and anti-imperialism that renders them in a limited sense progressive, but it also predisposes them to a kind of fascism and chauvinism that they try to mask by socialist slogans. When they sponsor state-socialist experiments, their own greed and lack of ideological commitment aborts the experiment. Ultimately they sell out to big capital, whether domestic or foreign, or use state socialism to build the private fortunes that will allow them to constitute an economically dominant class in their own right. So goes the critique.

This kind of analysis has been variously applied to the regimes in Egypt, Algeria, Iraq, and Syria. It has been inspired, in part, by postwar Marxist thinkers, like Kalecki, who wrote of the "intermediate regimes" of the Third World. He saw the weakness or absence of "big business" in these countries giving rise to a "ruling class" made up of, the rich peasantry and the lower-middle class. State capitalism was then adopted as a strategy to build the productive forces of society and to create "executive and technical openings for ambitious young men of the numerous ruling class" (Kalecki 1972, 164). Kalecki looked on India and Egypt as prime examples of what he had in mind.

These themes have been independently advanced by a number of authors to help explain the evolution of state capitalism and socialism in the Middle East. Writing of the entire Arab world, Amin stated (1976, 8), "Far from committing suicide as a class, the petite bourgeoisie engenders within itself a 'state bourgeoisie' each time that it undertakes the leadership of the anti-imperialist movement."

Mahmoud Hussein applied exactly the same kind of analysis to Nasser's Egypt. Hussein argued that an "elite" of the petite bourgeoisie roots itself in the state apparatus, disengages itself from its own class, and becomes a dominant state bourgeoisie. For a time it needs the support of the workers and for tactical purposes pursues redistributive policies and mouths socialist slogans. But sooner or later it yields to the quest for personal enrichment, breaks its alliance with the working class, and enters into an "objective" situation whereby state capitalists exploit the working class (Hussein 1971, 188, 281).

We may recall Fu'ad Mursi's proposition that a parasitic private sector, fat with the profits of doing business with and for the state, pushed Egypt's state capitalist regime toward economic liberalization and the open-door policy. Hussein stood Mursi's position on its head and argued that the state capitalists have to nurture this private sector in order to carry out their individual strategies of aggrandizement. Whichever line of causality one follows, the result is the same: The petite bourgeoisie engenders a new dominant class that exploits the masses through state capitalism and pilfers state resources for its own private ends.

The situation in Algeria has been depicted by Raffinot and Jacquemot (1977, 99; see also Lazreg 1976a) in similar terms. After 1967 (i.e., Boumedienne's squelching of Tahar Zbiri's brief coup attempt) one has seen "the emergence of a real state bourgeoisie, issued from the petty and middle bourgeoisie, but which succeeds in becoming autonomous by assuring itself the appropriation of the means of production—but not their juridical title—and by forging a specific class consciousness based on its common interests."

None of these authors foresaw a situation in which the state bourgeoisie turns on the state itself, begins to liquidate its economic assets and to transfer them to sections of the petite bourgeoisie, strengthened economically after two or three decades of state capitalism. Instead, these authors implied a situation in which state capitalism perpetuates itself until its inherent tendency to exploit the working masses brings about some sort of revolutionary upheaval. Perhaps the Iranian revolution of 1978–1979 can be partially explained in such terms (see below). But the Iranian example points instead to another failing of the authors cited above, who did not foresee that the petite bourgeoisie would take over the leadership of the Islamic fundamentalist movement, with its proclaimed enmity to state socialism (see Fischer 1982).

To come to grips with the petite bourgeoisie necessitates an exercise in disaggregation that Amin, Hussein, Raffinot and Jacquemot failed to carry out. The petite bourgeoisie strictly speaking should refer only to property-owning, mainly self-employed entrepreneurs in trades, services, petty manufacturing, and farming, who seldom hire labor. This "class" may find itself in conflict with big capital, whether foreign or domestic, which invades the markets of the petite bourgeoisie through mass production and which crowds it out of credit markets. Its members, however, probably aspire to the ranks of big capital. If, as in Egypt, a socialist regime takes over large private enterprises and confers on the petty capitalist sector a legitimate place in the corporatist structure as "nonexploitative" capitalists, then it will support such a regime. We should not forget that a coincidence of interests between a state and a set of class interests need not mean that those class interests dominate the state.

The petite bourgeoisie, in this fairly strict sense, is numerically very significant in the Middle East. Traders and retailers may alone constitute 5% of the total work force and in absolute terms represent considerable numbers: In the mid-1970s there were about 500,000 retailers in Iran and in Egypt 670,000, or in 1976, 18 retailers for every 1,000 Egyptians. In Iraq in 1977 traders made up 8.5% of the total work force (al-Khafaji 1983).

The service sector, which includes white-collar employees, also represents hundreds of thousands of self-employed barbers, repairmen, tailors, shoemakers, and so forth. It would be safe to conclude that the petite bourgeoisie constitutes 10–15% of the total work force in most Middle Eastern countries. In some countries they have been a recognized political force for some time. The *bazaaris* of Iran have been important actors on the political scene at least since the Tobacco Strike of 1895. When allied with the clergy, they have made regimes tremble. The shah in 1975 made the mistake of blaming them for Iran's high rate of inflation and allowing elements of the Rastakhiz party to harass and arrest merchants. In so doing the shah drove the *bazaaris* into the arms of the mullahs. In Turkey, small-scale provincial capital is seen as an increasingly significant political force, wedded to Islamic resurgence as in Iran and wooed by the Motherland party of Turgut Özal, the True Path party of Suleiman Demirel, and the Refah (Prosperity) party of Necmittin Ebarkan.

Frequently the petite bourgeoisie is lumped together with the lower-income members of what we have called the new middle class: white-collar professionals whose status is not dependent on the ownership of property, of which they typically have little. Longuenesse (1978, 1979) has rightly emphasized that in Syria, who rules is not so much the petite bourgeoisie but rather what she called the intermediate stratum, educated white-collar professionals. They "are largely the product of capitalist development, the extension of the market, the multiplication of banks, the development of schooling, and the intensified involvement of the government in social and economic life" (1979, 3). Longuenesse showed the relative importance of both the petite bourgeoisie and the intermediate stratum in the Syrian work force over the period of the 1960s (Table 15.2).

In Syria and perhaps in Iraq as well, the Ba'ath party, the military, and, to some extent, the state enterprises have been the vehicles for the ascension of provincial lower-middle-class professionals. We shall have more to say about these "provincials" below, but it is important that we not overstate the differences between them and the "traditional" petite bourgeoisie. We speculate that the intermediate strata to which Longuenesse referred may be the offspring of the traditional petite bourgeoisie. For example, Ashraf

Table 15.2    Class Structure of Syrian Society and Percentage of Active
              Population, 1960 and 1970

|  | 1960 | % | 1970 | % |
|---|---|---|---|---|
| Industrial and | | | | |
| commercial bourgeoisie | 19,750 | 2.2 | 10,890 | 0.7 |
| Rural bourgeoisie | 39,640 | 4.5 | 8,360 | 0.6 |
| Working class | 159,720 | 17.9 | 257,380 | 17.6 |
| Agricultural proletariat | 182,720 | 20.5 | 130,400 | 8.9 |
| Petite bourgeoisie: | | | | |
| Productive | 51,300 | 5.8 | 103,350 | 7.0 |
| Nonproductive | 59,600 | 6.7 | 112,740 | 7.7 |
| Intermediate strata | 132,530 | 15.0 | 234,930 | 16.0 |
| Small peasantry | 243,460 | 27.4 | 608,540 | 41.5 |
| Total | 888,720 | 100.0 | 1,466,590 | 100.0 |

Source:  Elizabeth Longuenesse, "The Class Nature of the State in Syria," MERIP
Reports 9, 4 (May 1979), p. 4.   Reprinted with permission from MERIP Middle
East Report, 1500 Massachusetts Ave., N.W., #119, Washington, D.C. 20005.

(1984) noted the dramatic shift in the composition of the Iranian *majlis*
before and after the 1979 revolution. In the last of the shah's parliaments,
the new middle class—bureaucrats and professionals—held about 47% of
the seats, while landowners, mullahs, and *bazaaris* controlled the rest.
The *majlis* elected in 1980, however, was composed of 30% schoolteachers
and professors, 50% mullahs, and a smattering of merchants, shopkeepers,
professionals, and bureaucrats. What is particularly interesting is that 30%
of the deputies came from peasant families, 26% from shopkeepers' families,
and 29% were the offspring of mullahs. Prime Minister Özal is an engineer
by training, and his ascendency in Turkey has been described as representing
that of the professionally trained sons of the provincial petite bourgeoisie
(inter alia, see Arat 1987). The Middle East may be living through a kind
of Jacksonian era in which the frontier comes to the city and ascends to
power. The landlords have been pushed aside, the urban notability suppressed or exiled, and foreign capital eliminated or circumscribed. It does
not appear that the urban petite bourgeoisie filled this vacuum. Rather,
aggressive, upwardly mobile "provincials" have successfully contested this
space.

The military has been the prime avenue for their ascent. Again we
should keep in mind that it is not the provincial bourgeoisie per se that
is in question but rather its professionalized offspring. Several members
of the Revolutionary Command Council that seized power in Egypt in 1952
came from families of the provincial petite bourgeoisie. Nasser, the son
of a rural civil servant, is a prime example. Binder (1978), emphasizing
the fact that several Free Officers came from the stratum of middle-range
landowners, suggested that Egypt's revolution embodied the aspirations of
"the rural middle class." We do not entirely agree with that assessment,
but it is a fact that the post-1952 regimes have given a prominent place
to political leaders of rural origins. We suspect that post-1952 Egypt

resembles Turkey, where from 1920 on, the Kemalist movement and state was partly based on an alliance "between the military-bureaucratic elite at the national level and small-town and rural notables at the local level" (Özbudun 1981, 84).

Likewise in Iraq, the advent of Gen. 'Abd al-Karim Qassim in 1958 ushered in Iraq's Jacksonian era. Qassim was the son of a carpenter and small landowner from al-Suwairah in southeast Iraq. He was succeeded by the Arif brothers from Dulaim in the northwest, in a violent transition of power, and they by the Takritis from the "Sunni triangle" of the Central Euphrates (Batatu 1979, 112–13). In the period 1958–1963, 36% of all cabinet seats went to Iraqis from localities of less than 200,000 inhabitants. Between 1963 and 1968 that proportion rose to 63%, and then under the Takritis to 75%. Twelve of fifteen members of the Iraqi Revolutionary Command Council after 1968 were from the Sunni triangle. Eight of fifteen were from peasant families, two from families of tradesmen, three from families of policemen, and there was one son of a teacher and one worker's son (al-Khafaji 1983, 177).

The same phenomenon has been analyzed in Syria by Hinnebusch (1979) and Van Dam (1981), among others. The Syrian Ba'ath, before coming to power, recruited heavily among rural schoolteachers and young professionals of rural origin, particularly among the Alawi and Druze minorities. Let us not forget that the founders of the Ba'ath, Michel Aflaq and Salah Bitar, were schoolteachers.

In 1969 both the Sudan and Libya witnessed coups engineered by provincial officers in the armed forces: Mu'ammar Qaddhafi, from a Bedouin family, seized power in Libya, while Ga'afar al-Nimeiri, from the northern Nile province of Dongola, deposed a civilian government in the Sudan. The leadership of Algeria's FLN during its armed phase was drawn from the rural petite bourgeoisie (see Quandt 1969; Zartman 1975), and two of the best known civilian nationalists, Ferhat Abbas and Yussef Ben Khedda, were rural pharmacists.

In sum, we should keep in mind three major components of the petite bourgeoisie: the small-scale trading and manufacturing segment, the lower echelons of the new middle class, and those drawn from both segments but of specifically rural origin. But even if one can specify where they are coming from, it is more difficult to see where they are going. Nellis (1980a, 506) has referred to the petite bourgeoisie as a "chameleon category, an intermediary group able to shift its policy position quickly from proletarian to bourgeois." Likewise, Longuenesse has noted that because the segment she called the intermediate stratum sells its labor, it bears affinity to the proletariat, but its ideology relates it to the bourgeoisie (1979, 3). Writing of lower-middle-class activists of rural origins on Iranian campuses in the 1970s, Arjomand (1984, 44) stressed their Janus-like qualities, their ability to espouse democratic and liberal goals or a kind of neofascism and intolerance.

The petite bourgeoisie is in every sense volatile. If it is a class, it does not wish to remain as it is but aspires to some other status, indeed to some other social order. It does not seek to reproduce itself as a class. Its role in the Middle East, and just about everywhere else, has been to push its children on to higher education and the professions. Its members drive themselves and drive their offspring. They are highly competitive and, in David McClelland's terms, high-need achievers.

The petite bourgeoisie not only tries constantly to cast off its skin, but it is ideologically changeable as well. Its constant is a penchant for activism. In Syria it has carried on the traditions of Akram Hawrani, the scourge of the landowning class around Hama in the 1950s. From its ranks have come the cadres and leaders of the secularist Ba'ath party. In Iran it has filled the ranks of the Pasdaran (Revolutionary Guards) and of the Islamic Republican party. No one better captured the radicalism and ideological inconsistencies of the petite bourgeoisie than Ali Shariati, who attracted to his eclectic polemics both radical leftists and militant Muslims. Hoogland (1980, 6) has paid particular attention to rural migrants to the cities, young men who live in the villages but work in the cities. These "rurbanites," he said, generally have a primary school education and in the 1970s were drawn into political activism: "The literal fusion of a nationalist ideology with a religious ideology was crucial in mobilizing these young men into political activity."

Along with their activism, another common trait of the members of the petite bourgeoisie, especially of its rural members, is a concern for religion.[3] Hassan al-Banna, the founder of the Muslim Brotherhood, was able to tap into both this activism and this religious concern. The wedding of the two has carried forward to the contemporary period. Bianchi, reporting survey results from Turkey in the early 1970s, concluded (1984, 291, 311), "There is a clear curvilinear relationship between religiosity and urbanization: those who were raised in provincial capitals or small towns score significantly higher on our index of religiosity than those who were raised either in villages or in Istanbul, Ankara, and Izmir"(291). In the succeeding fifteen to twenty years, other observers, both of Turkey and of other Middle Eastern societies, have called our attention to the fact that religiosity and activism have attracted the better educated and younger members of the petite bourgeoisie, but the provincial city and small rural towns retain their peculiar importance as venues for the politicization of the provincials.

Undeniably, then, these three segments, cobbled together under the label "petit bourgeois," have been particularly dynamic actors in the political field of the Middle East. By default they have become candidates for the role of "dominant class," or, more modestly, as the seedbed for a new dominant class. We suspect that this view attributes too much importance to them and implies that as a class, they share an identifiable set of interests and a strategy to promote them.

Our uneasiness is rooted both in abstract logic and in empirical anomalies. It is hard to imagine a class that is capable of overcoming landowners, domestic big capital, and foreign interests and of seizing the state but that is simultaneously incapable of organizing its own economic interests without resorting to state socialism and public-sector enterprise. If the class project of the petite bourgeoisie is to build itself into a respectable *grande bourgeoisie,* one would expect that it would make sure to transfer nationalized assets to private ownership and to use public financial institutions to mobilize the funds necessary to build large, private enterprises.

One answer to this is that, as Kalecki (1976) suggested, the petite bourgeoisie does not have the skills and experience to build a big capitalist sector, and it must gain those skills in the protective shadow of state enterprise. But how can we accept this answer and at the same time accept that this same class has the capacity to run complex state agencies and to manage state enterprises—because, we are told, it is the scions of the petite bourgeoisie that staff the state sector?

The empirical basis of our uneasiness also provides an alternative explanation. The leaders of these alleged petit bourgeois regimes have often displayed considerable hostility toward the commercial and trading sectors of their society. In Tunisia and Egypt in the 1960s, and in Algeria and Libya in the 1970s, the regimes tried to nationalize various segments of private retail and wholesale trade and to take over trucking and other privately owned commercial transport. Ahmed Ben Salah, the architect in the late 1960s of Tunisia's ill-fated experiment in state socialism, reminisced about his attempts to regulate domestic trade (Nerfin 1974, 63):

> The Tunisian is not given to investment. He has remained since the time of the Phoenicians, a trader. He trades without system, moved only by the desire to get rich quickly. . . . Where has all the money gone won by Tunisia's importers, all its exporters, all those who enjoyed more or less real monopolies . . . ? Who among them built anything, created an enterprise? No one. No industry, no factories, nothing. We realize that it was trade, the plethora of traders, not only the plethora, but the very structure of internal trade, that was at fault, that made national savings disappear into thin air.

Ben Salah's contempt for the class that he and many others are alleged to represent was shared by Nasser, Boumedienne, Qaddhafi, and others. They reached accommodations with the petite bourgeoisie only because the state was incapable of nationalizing their activities with any reasonable degree of efficiency. Moreover, unlike big local or foreign capital, the petite bourgeoisie did not appear to present any political threat to the state socialist regimes. Beginning in 1967 and throughout the 1970s, as the petite bourgeoisie became increasingly involved in Muslim militant movements, a political threat did become manifest and may be partially due to the hostility its members had encountered in various socialist experiments.

What can we conclude? First, that many regimes in the Middle East in the 1960s were indeed of petit bourgeois origin, but, second, that their leaders had, by and large, an antibourgeois (whether petit or grand) mentality. They were not the creatures of their class. However, the petite bourgeoisie, internally divided into its provincial professional and trading segments, was practically the only possible pool of recruits for staffing the rapidly expanding state system. These systems were inherently cumbersome and inefficient, but not because the petite bourgeoisie as a class plotted to sabotage them. Rent-seeking behavior, corruption, and sweetheart deals with the private sector were and are part of the decay of bureaucratically managed development strategies. Elements of the petite bourgeoisie that had indeed profited from state business over the decades stood ready to benefit from economic liberalization and the partial retreat of the state in the 1980s. Our error would be to assume that they planned it this way.

## The New Middle Class and the State Bourgeoisie

The other major urban class actors are the professionals, or new middle class, and the state bourgeoisie. As we have seen, the initial plunge of state agencies into social and economic engineering led to the formation of new professional interests in unprecedented numbers: schoolteachers, university professors, accountants, military officers, medical doctors, engineers, and even lawyers saw their ranks greatly expanded. They were the new meritocracy, and their status was based on training and performance, not wealth. Again, we may turn to Iraq for an example of the distribution and growth of the professional, new middle class (Table 15.3).

Let us review briefly the state policies that reenforced private industrial and commercial activities as well as expanded the ranks of the professionals. First, tariff walls designed mainly to protect public enterprise also protected private enterprise from foreign competition. Second, in most of the region's economies an implicit public-private division of labor developed. The public sector concentrated on lumpy, big capital projects in infrastructure (e.g., hydropower schemes, railroads) and intermediate goods (steel, fertilizers, plastics, paper). The private sector was allowed to capture major consumer markets in textiles, appliances, processed foods and beverages, and the provision of services. In some countries there might be direct competition, perhaps in cement or sugar production, but as a general rule state enterprise took upon itself the production of intermediate goods that the private sector could then acquire at low cost and feed into its own production process (on Iraq, see al-Khafaji 1983; on Algeria, Leca and Grimaud 1986).

The state has also disbursed significant portions of its investment through supply and construction contracts to the private sector. Particularly in the early years of state-led industrialization drives, much of the effort came in the form of building plants and infrastructure. Many private fortunes have been made through subcontracting. Cronyism and patronage are almost invariably involved in this process. Ahmad Osman, head of Egypt's giant Arab Contractors, has won contracts on everything from construction of the Aswan High Dam to bridges across the Nile, but he also built private homes for military officers at nominal cost and supplied government officials with foreign exchange when they traveled abroad. Similarly in Iraq, al-Khafaji found that of the country's thirty-one major private contracting firms, seven were run by Takritis with close ties to the ruling clique.

Table 15.3   Major Categories of the Urban Middle Classes and Their Growth in Iraq, 1958 and 1968

| | Number | |
|---|---|---|
| | 1958 | 1968 |
| Professionals, main components | | |
| Government and private elementary-<br>and secondary-school teachers | 20,154 | 56,436 |
| University teachers | 600* | 2,068 |
| Army officers | 4,000* | 10,000* |
| Registered engineers** | 1,270 (1959) | 6,534 |
| Registered lawyers** | 1,361 | 1,948 |
| State physicians** | 1,192 | 1,574 |
| Others | 2,000* | 3,000* |
| State pensioners and officials,<br>and employees of middling income | | |
| Officials and employees (other than state<br>physicians, teachers, and engineers) | 27,000* | 85,000 |
| Civil and military pensioners | 15,000* | 37,000* |
| Trading, industrial, and service components | | |
| Retailers | 36,062 (1956) | 76,000* |
| Self-employed industrial enterprisers and owners<br>of small-scale industrial establishments<br>employing one to nine workers | 21,733 (1954) | 26,690 |
| Owners of small or middling service<br>establishments | 10,546* | 20,000* |
| Employees of private commercial and industrial<br>firms | 7,000* | 9,000* |
| Subtotal | 147,918 | 335,250 |
| Dependents (subtotal x 4) | 591,672 | 1,341,000 |
| Total | 739,590 | 1,676,250 |
| Urban population of Iraq (in millions) | 2.6 | 4.9 |
| Middle classes as percentage of urban population | 28.0 | 34.0 |

*   Estimated or partly estimated.
**  A small segment of these professionals belonged to the upper classes.

Source: Hanna Batatu, The Old Social Classes and the Revolutionary Movements of Iraq, Princeton, N.J., Princeton University Press, 1978, p. 1126.  Reprinted by permission.

In the same vein, the state purchases goods and services from the private sector. Private truckers may haul public produce, private textile manufacturers supply the armed forces or the public hospitals with uniforms, private components manufacturers supply public-sector automotive plants, or private accountants audit public enterprises.

Finally, the state increasingly has helped bankroll the private sector through cheap industrial credit. This has been an uneven process. Public-sector enterprise has often competed directly with the private sector to obtain credit from the public banking system. Second, many private-sector firms have been unwilling to open their books to public bankers as a prerequisite for loans. Nonetheless in the past decade or more, lending institutions that specialize in loans to the private sector have become more and more common. Some, like Morocco's National Economic Development Bank (BNDE), date back to independence, while others, like Egypt's Industrial Development Bank, are far more recent. Very often the World Bank and/or USAID have encouraged the founding of such institutions and have provided much of their initial capital with the goal of stimulating private enterprise. In addition to such institutions, liberalization has often led to a resurgence of private banking (not yet in Algeria, Iraq, or Syria) and allowed the private sector to compete for domestic savings and the foreign-exchange earnings of workers abroad. We should add to these the network of Islamic banks and savings institutions, the most prominent of which is the Faysal Islamic Bank, domiciled in Saudi Arabia.

As the private sector has grown in economic strength and, less obviously, in ideological legitimacy, the public-sector corps of managers, or "state bourgeoisie," has found itself on the defensive. When state enterprises were first being launched, these men were depicted as the implementers of development. It was, as noted, a time of optimism, unbridled ambition, and faith in the state. University graduates were sucked up into growing state sectors and enjoyed rapid promotion. Alongside the generals and the politicians, technocrats were in the public eye: ministers of industry like Egypt's Aziz Sidqi or Algeria's Abdesslam Belaid, architects of whole plans like Tunisia's Ahmed Ben Salah, or technical collaborators like the shah's Abbas Hoveida, or finally, managers of vital sectors, such as Saudi Arabia's petroleum minister, Zaki Yamani.

With time the initial élan petered out. Public enterprise performed poorly for all of the reasons we have alluded to in previous chapters, but the managerial corps itself was debased. Political leaders could not resist using managerial positions for patronage, putting retired military officers out of harm's way, or paying off party faithful, as in Turkey, after successful elections. The political ideology of managers in Egypt, Algeria, and the Ba'athi regimes has been a criterion for promotion or firing, and religious purity must surely be a prerequisite for managerial positions in the Islamic Republic of Iran. Because the top-level managerial career was unstable and subject to arbitrary and unpredictable political whims and infighting, managers increasingly seized the moment to line their pockets and to build an economic hedge against an uncertain future. As the years went by, there was a growing and dynamic private sector willing and able to cut deals. Closed bidding, kickbacks, dummy companies, silent partnerships, embezzlement, and theft of inventory became commonplace. The public-sector manager could look forward to early retirement, a lateral move into a private-sector firm, sometimes foreign owned, where he could capitalize on his knowledge of how the public sector works.

So the state bourgeoisie has much to be defensive about. It is hard to defend enterprises that operate at chronic loss and are shot through with corruption. As we shall see below, many managers want to reform the system, but many others are willing to take what they can and then bail out.

The situation is quite different for many of the professions. Their members' skills are not specific to public or private activity but can serve both. Medical doctors now spend more time in private practice than in public hospitals or health clinics; lawyers have growing private-sector clienteles; the cautious decontrol of the press in a number of countries (Turkey, Egypt, Tunisia, Morocco, Sudan) has opened up a new range of possibilities for journalists; accountants still serve the government but can look to a growing private sector for new opportunities; the same story holds for engineers, computer experts, stenographers, nurses, and, to a lesser degree, schoolteachers. The public sector still maintains some employment monopolies: radio and television, the national airlines, the railroads, defense industries, and university education (although Turkey has two private universities). The private sector has yet to make inroads into these domains. It is the case, however, that the new middle class is no longer a creature of the state. Rather it is astride the state and the private sectors and can move between the two.

The policy agenda of these urban class actors varies widely. The state technocracy approaches the future with at least three strategies in mind. There are some ideologues who want to run public-sector enterprise as it has always been run, with an emphasis on social welfare, with suspicion of any profit-and-loss calculus, and with certain economic activities reserved for public enterprise. Others want to move toward state capitalism, that is, to run public enterprises essentially as one would private enterprise. Financial profitability would become the basic criterion for judging performance, firm managers would be autonomous and free from political interference, ownership (by the state) would be separate from management, and public enterprise would have to compete with private and foreign enterprise. The third position is that of partial liquidation of the public sector. Some managers advocate liquidating losing enterprises, selling others to the private sector, and retaining for state ownership only vital services and some strategic industries (perhaps mining, basic metals, and armaments). The important point is that the state technocracy does not confront liberalization united in a common set of objectives.

The private sector is likewise divided. Large industrial enterprises, like Koç in Turkey, have the financial resources, managerial talent, and technology to take risks and to compete internationally. Smaller-scale enterprise, long used to protection and perhaps undemanding public-sector customers, are not eager for the market to reign supreme. Like the rural capitalists, the urban private sector wants simultaneously more and less state intervention. By and large, the private sector would like less regulation and lighter taxes. For example, the private sector prefers to see an end to complicated licensing procedures, changes in labor laws that would allow easier hiring and firing and differential pay scales, greater flexibility in disposal of foreign exchange, and a simplification of import and export procedures.

However, many private-sector actors do not want the state to get out of the provision of subsidized credit, to cease supplying intermediate goods

|  | Personal Deals | Collective Action |
|---|---|---|
| Before policy is made | 1. Payoffs, bribes, threats, promises, trades | 2. Lobbying, advocacy, agenda-setting, voting |
| After policy is made | 3. Payoffs, bribes, threats, promises, trades | 4. Noncompliance, sabotage, protests |

Figure 15.1  The influence matrix

at low cost, to curtail the letting of large contracts to the private sector, or to lower protective tariff walls. All this is to say, once again, that the public and private sectors share a symbiotic, not an adversarial, relationship and that the retreat of the state will not be uniformly welcomed, or encouraged, by the private sector.

Our last task is to examine the instruments that state, professional, and private interests have used in promoting their goals. The same prelegislation lobbying versus postlegislation maneuvering and sabotage applies here and is depicted schematically on Figure 15.1.

Resort to political parties and vote getting (Figure 15.1, box 2) has been rare for Middle East private sectors. There has not been a "business" party anywhere in the region. However, there are now parties in whose constituent parts business figures prominently. Turgut Özal's Motherland party and Suleiman Demirel's True Path party both seek to represent private business interests in Turkey. Mustapha Kemal Murad's Liberal party in Egypt claims to speak for business interests but has no more basis for that claim than the Wafd or the dominant National Democratic party. In Morocco, the grand old party, the Istiqlal, was built in the 1930s around a core of important entrepreneurs from the city of Fez.

Business interests are generally wary of partisan identification. It can be dangerous to be on the losing side, and the wiser strategy is to keep open communications to all political contenders. Public authorities have responded by allowing business its profits while trying to deny it the political kingdom. Nowhere does the business community enjoy real solid prestige and legitimacy, so its low political profile suits all concerned. One suspects that the first businessmen to build political careers will be those explicitly defining themselves as "Islamic," claiming to serve the *umma* rather than individual acquisitiveness.

Private interests prefer to act through their associations that speak for general concerns (Chambers of Commerce and Industry) or specific interests (such as Associations of Importers, Bankers, Textile Manufacturers). These can lobby legitimately for specific policies and, if they fail, try to influence the implementation of policy after the fact (see Bianchi 1985).

One of the most spectacular and devastating weapons in the private sector's postpolicy arsenal is capital flight. If government policies on interest rates or exchange rates do not correspond to private interests, the response may be a hemorrhage of privately held foreign exchange abroad, further weakening the national currency and fueling inflation. In recent years Turkey and Israel have met and dealt with this kind of postpolicy response by their private sectors.

If capital flight is not the issue, capital "strikes" may be. Egypt's five-year plan announced in the spring of 1987 calls for the private sector to mobilize half of all planned investment, or circa £E 20 billion ($10 billion), over the five-year period. The appeal is unrealistic, and some private-sector spokesmen have said so. Many businessmen can remember the First Five-Year Plan of 1959, in which an equally ambitious private investment target was announced. When the private sector failed to meet the target, Nasser used the issue to justify the nationalizations of July 1961. Once again the Egyptian private sector faces a unilateral policy decision for which it may have to bear responsibility. Private capital may be even less willing to come forth than would have been the case had the state not invited the private sector to share the investment burden fifty-fifty.

When we examine the dilemma of the state managers faced with liberalization, we may be seeing the state turned against itself. State interests can fit into the influence matrix (Figure 15.1) as easily as private. The state, we reiterate, is not monolithic, and various interests within it can lobby for policies (for greater investment in a given sector, for special pricing arrangements, for foreign-exchange allocations) or try to deal with the consequences of policies already made. The set of policies embedded in liberalization provide excellent examples of the range of possibilities. One sees clearly that the objectives of political leadership may diverge widely from those of important managerial and bureaucratic interests. Even ministries may be divided against themselves. For instance, the Ministry of Finance may advocate privatization of public enterprises in order to reduce budgetary deficits and to generate a new source of public revenues through the sale of shares. At the same time, the ministry may lose revenue through forgone excise taxes, and it may lose administrative leverage through its ability to oversee, monitor, and control all fiscal operations of public enterprises.

So far the experience of liberalization in Turkey, Egypt, Tunisia, and, to a lesser degree, in Algeria has not been openly opposed by state agencies and interest groups. Having neither solid economic performance nor the achievement of sustainable social welfare goals to claim as accomplishments, state managers and bureaucrats in the civil service have had to concede the ideological game. Their power comes to bear in implementation. Bureaucratic red tape, a form of collective action, or the bargaining for special deals on an enterprise-by-enterprise basis are the most common forms of resistance. And there is always the very real possibility that the private sector will bungle its new economic tasks and that through short-term speculation and capital flight, it will once again become the villain. Moreover, protectionism abroad may defeat export-led growth strategies, and bring import substitution back into favor. Conceding rhetorical points and biding one's time may be the best strategy for vested interests in the public sector.

The growth of professional associations has been parallel to and partially linked to the growth of the private sector. Initially, professional associations were part of the corporatist framework put in place by the political authorities, who wanted to keep the educated and the highly trained under close scrutiny. The associations, such as trade unions, then began to develop leadership skills, organizational experience, and economic assets. As a result of economic liberalization, they have begun to invest their pension funds in private enterprise, to run their own banks, and to own housing and hospitals for their members. The new middle class is thus in the process of becoming collectively propertied. Turkey's military pension fund, OYAK (see Chapter 13), is the most striking example of this, but Egypt's Engineering Syndicate with special residential areas, housing co-ops, medical facilities, and a bank is also a model. Professional associations may be more important in the future than individual capitalists and enterprise in determining the nature of private-sector activity and in shaping the contours of state autonomy.


## CLASS AND REVOLUTION
## IN THE MIDDLE EAST

The Middle East has known two "social revolutions" (Skocpol 1983) since World War II, that is, far-reaching social and economic change, sometimes violent, initiated by forces outside constituted governments. The two cases are Algeria and Iran, and they are to be contrasted with the "revolutions from above" (Trimberger 1978) carried out in Kemalist Turkey, Egypt after 1952, and Syria and Iraq after 1958.

It is well known that one cannot read from situations of objective exploitation or oppression the likelihood of uprisings and revolts, no less revolutions, led by the oppressed. There have to be a number of mediating variables present before situations of "objective" exploitation and oppression give rise to revolutionary movements. A crucial variable is the cohesion and determination of the groups and classes in control of the state apparatus as they face mass unrest. Skocpol has suggested that when the state tries to extract more revenues from society, often in order to meet an external, military challenge, the extractive policies themselves provoke cleavages within dominant elites and paralyze the state as it confronts challenges from the oppressed, most often from the peasantry. That, all too cursorily, is how Skocpol approached the revolutions in France (1789), Russia (1917), and China (1949).

The two cases under consideration here—Algeria and Iran—do not fit any revolutionary paradigm very well, although bits and pieces of various theories help us understand bits and pieces of each revolutionary experience. Let us begin with Algeria's revolution, which took the form of a colonial war. This revolution has received surprisingly little attention in terms of the major social components contributing to the fighting and their presumed motivations.[4] What we know is largely circumstantial, to wit, that most of the fighting took place in the countryside (with the brief and disastrous exception of the Battle of Algiers in 1958) and mainly in the Berber-speaking areas of the Aurès and Kabyle mountains. Do we conclude that the fighting was then carried out by Berber peasants? The answer is more complex and inconclusive.

To a large extent, the bulk of the fighting had to take place in the Aurès and Kabylia because the terrain was suitable for guerrilla operations and not too remote from major urban centers that were home for most of the European population and that were the ultimate targets of the FLN. We know from Quandt and others that many of the guerrilla leaders were Berber or Berber-Arab, that they had had at most a secondary school education, and that they came overwhelmingly from smaller towns of eastern Algeria, specifically the Constantine region, Kabylia, and the Aurès (Quandt 1969, 151). None were peasants per se but, like the provincials discussed above, were drawn from the ranks of petty traders, schoolteachers, low-level civil servants, and skilled craftsman.

It is in the nature of guerrilla warfare that the numbers under arms are few: As elsewhere, even as in China, the Algerian revolution did not involve a mass insurrection, either rural or urban. At the outbreak of fighting in November 1954 there may have been no more than 800 *maquisards,* and as the war neared its end in 1962, there may have been 10,000 fighters in the six interior military districts of the National Liberation Front/Army of National Liberation (FLN/ALN) and 40,000 men in Tunisia and Morocco who did not see combat.

What is more important is the attitude of the unarmed civilian population. A simplistic reading of Algeria's pattern of stratification on the eve of the revolution would yield a two-class society. On the one hand, there were 1 million Europeans, 80% of whom lived in the main cities, monopolized government, modern farming and manufacturing, the professions and skilled trades, banking and commerce. Their children enjoyed universal primary education, made up about 90% of the secondary school population and about 98% of all those from Algeria who went to France for higher education.

Alongside this dominant European settler class were 9 million native, Muslim Algerians occupying all the subaltern positions in Algerian society: workers in European-owned factories, enterprises, and farms; low-level civil servants, interpreters, court clerks, telephone operators, unskilled labor for the public-works department, and the like. A minority of Algerian children received a primary school education, a tiny elite, mainly of Kabyle extraction, went on to secondary school, and in 1954 only 70 living native Algerians had had, after 124 years of colonial rule, a university education. The Europeans had seized the best agricultural lands on the coastal plains and had pushed the original populations back into the steppes, where soils were poorer and rainfall undependable. The major outlet for nonagricultural employment became, over time, the French metropolitan labor market, in which some 200,000 Algerians had found employment by the mid-1950s.

There were of course many Algerians who benefited from the system of European domination or at least found ways to promote their own interests within it. There was a body of local administrators, civil servants, schoolteachers, and representatives elected to local councils who enjoyed some prestige within the colonial hierarchy. There was a "traditional" landowning stratum engaged in extensive agricultural production and animal husbandry in the steppes. They were the backbone of a rural notability upon which the French administration relied to some extent to maintain order in Algeria's vast hinterland (let us not forget that Algeria, although predominantly desert, is over five times the size of France). There was also a stratum of smaller Algerian landowners precariously poised between commercial and subsistence agriculture (Launay 1963). Finally, there was the Algerian service sector, ranging from pharmicists, to grocers and barbers in the shantytowns of the big cities, who dealt largely with poor Algerian clients.

One fact is pretty clear: The large agricultural work force employed in European vineyards and farms was not an active participant in the armed revolution. If there were any rural actors of significance from the areas of European settlement, they were the commercial smallholders, especially in the west of Algeria (Oranais), who, Wolf (1968, 211–50) speculated, saw their ascendancy toward a more secure place in domestic markets blocked by the European settlers. The "middle peasants" fit that classification in the sense that they were midway between commercial and subsistence agriculture as well as between parochial and national political identities. As Wolf put it (1968, 234), "Reformist Islam provides the cultural form for the construction of a new network of social relations between clusters of middle peasants in the countryside and the sons of the urban elite of the hinterland towns."

Curiously, perhaps, the most consistent source of FLN recruits came from areas of the least European penetration: the Aurès and Kabylia. One might speculate that they were moved by the neglect their poor regions (Algeria's Appalachia) had experienced from the central authorities. Overgrazing and overcultivating these mountainous areas had been major factors in pushing out Berber migrants, who found their way in tens of thousands to Algiers, Marseilles, Paris, and just about everywhere in France. So while these areas were to some extent geographically remote and peripheral to the Algerian economy, they were, through labor migration, intimately bound to the metropolitan industrial economy. The Federation of Algerian Workers in France was a crucial source of funds for the FLN throughout the war and became known as the seventh *wilaya*. Many of the guerrilla leaders were "bridge" figures, Berbers who knew the peasants and *maquis* of the Aurès and Kabylia through having been raised in the small towns of the two regions, but who also knew France through having served in its army or worked in its factories.

It is doubtful that the FLN could have won its war against France militarily. The president of France, Charles de Gaulle, decided to cut France's losses in Algeria by granting independence and to rebuild good relations with other Third World nations as quickly as possible.

We might see in this decision the kind of cleavage in the ruling groups to which Skocpol alluded. Throughout the period of the Fourth Republic in France, the settler community in Algeria demanded higher levels of investment and a larger military effort from metropolitan politicians increasingly reluctant to provide those things. Four years after the collapse of the Fourth Republic, in the summer of 1962, Algeria's dominant European class packed up its bags and left. It was not literally driven out but must have believed that it would be simply a matter of time before it would be.

In its essence this exodus constituted a far-reaching social revolution, although one that did not flow ineluctably from the violence and bloodshed of the eight years that had preceded it. The FLN seized an abandoned colonial superstructure and proceeded to fill it with state socialism.

Iran's revolution differs from Algeria's in several respects. It was not, of course, the result of a colonial liberation struggle but, rather, of the mobilization of large segments of the Iranian populace against its own regime (although many would argue that the shah was a U.S. puppet and hence the revolution did represent a liberation struggle against an outside power). The Iranian upheaval did not last as long as Algeria's; there was really no more than a year of massive civil unrest. Finally, although the changes in Iran's political superstructure have been dramatic—an emperor replaced by an Islamic republic—the changes in the socioeconomic structures of the country have not been so far reaching as those in Algeria. By contrast, the fact that tens of thousands and, on occasion, hundreds of thousands of unarmed Iranians confronted the shah's police and troops over a period of a year reveals a level of mass mobilization unequaled in Algeria between 1954 and 1962.

Who made up these Iranian masses? Not the peasants, although they had plenty of reason to complain (see Kazemi and Abrahamian 1978). Hooglund (1982, 138–52) argued that rural opposition to the regime came mainly from landless petty traders and, as Wolf had argued for Algeria, from middle peasants owning between 7 and 10 hectares. The latter resented the fact that the state, even after the White Revolution of 1963, failed to make available to them the credit and inputs that would have allowed them to make a successful transition to capitalist farming. Hooglund also called our attention to "shuttle peasants," rural youth residing close to urban centers in which they found nonfarm work. Shuttle peasants linked the unrest in the cities to close-by villages.

The activists in the Iranian revolution were mainly urban. One standard explanation is that the shah, in his megalomaniacal quest for regional economic hegemony, allowed the Iranian economy to overheat in the mid-1970s, thereby causing high rates of inflation (Razavi and Vakil 1984). Abruptly in 1976, he agreed to various deflationary, contractionary policies, cutting back sharply on public investment. Projects came to a halt in midstream, and tens of thousands of workers, many of them recent migrants in the construction sector, were laid off. Scoville (1985, 153) completed the picture: "Several million unemployed and grossly underemployed, many of whom were recent migrants, were roaming the streets of Iran's cities. In such a context, the world recession and changing development policy had disastrous effects . . . the economic stage was set for the Iranian revolution."

The stage was set, but the actors had not yet taken their places. To understand how they did requires an examination of factors that can only be described as conjunctural. First, the United States, Iran's superpower ally since 1953, took its distance from the shah under President Jimmy Carter. Elected in 1976, he urged the shah to rein in SAVAK, respect human rights, and allow greater political liberties. The shah, in mid-1977, complied to some extent, and various sectors of civil society were emboldened to press their demands more forcefully. The shah's tentative liberalization divided the regime, for there were hard-liners in the military and in the shah's immediate family who wanted to meet all challenges with brute force. The second conjunctural element was the shah's health. He, and probably some close to him, knew that he had terminal cancer. He was on heavy medication. It appears that his own vacillation and hesitancy regarding the proper course to follow were a function of his poor health.

It is legitimate to ask whether there would have been a revolution in Iran if Carter had not been president and the shah not seriously ill. We must guard against the trap of assuming the presence of ineluctable social forces and keep in mind that whatever the level of objective grievances, it may require a breakdown in the cohesion of dominant groups or the ruling coalitions (including external backers) to open a space for the expression of those grievances.

The form taken by the revolutionary movements was Shi'ite. The first demonstrations in Qom were provoked by newspaper attacks, in the controlled press, on Ayatollah Khomeini in January 1978. In the ensuing months, demonstrations, clashes, and deaths led to memorial marches, more clashes, and more deaths. Cassettes recorded by Khomeini in exile in Paris were smuggled into and distributed throughout Iran and helped orchestrate the movement (see Ashraf and Banuazizi 1985). The shock troops appeared to be the urban un- and semiemployed. The leaders were a combination of leftist revolutionaries, Islamic radicals, and the mullahs, or clerics. Important supporters were found in the trading and bazaar communities, alienated by the shah in 1975 (see Bakhash 1984).

For some, however, the decisive period came in the fall of 1978 when a combination of the "new middle class" and organized labor threw its weight behind the people in the streets. The crucial petroleum workers' union struck all of Iran's oil fields and refineries. Civil servants in the Central Bank, the Planning Board, the post office, and the customs department all went out on strike. Several newspapers were struck by their employees. The Tehran bazaar closed its shutters for more than a month. Two members of the Planning Board and thus, objectively, members of the new middle class, summed up white-collar power thus (Razavi and Vakil 1984, 97): "The bureaucracy, ostracized by the Imperial Commission and blamed publicly for being unable to do the impossible [i.e. manage the deflationary economic policies], was to pull down the regime by going on strike in late 1978, thereby adding its substantial weight to the long list of discontented." In the midst of all this, the shah revealed the disarray and dissensus within his own party by arresting 132 of his closest followers on charges of corruption and abuse of human rights. He put under house arrest the head of SAVAK, Gen. Ne'motallah Nasiri, and the long-time prime minister, Amir Abbas Hoveida. As the number of protests, as well as killings, mounted, the armed forces began to lose heart. Once the shah left the country, on February 11, 1979, discipline in the armed forces began to break down. Only then did arms find their way into civilian hands.

Skocpol's frame of analysis is not of much use in understanding this situation, as she herself admitted (1982; cf. Arjomand 1986). In 1978 Iran faced no major external threat; its extractive policies did not split the ruling block asunder; and the peasantry was not drawn into the violence of the past year. It is not at all improbable, moreover, that a healthy shah and a resolute U.S. ally could have ridden out the storm, much as has Pinochet in Chile since 1973. We certainly do not mean to suggest that this would have been *desirable,* merely that it was possible, and that there was nothing *inevitable* about the Iranian revolution. The Algerian uprising against the French did have the air of inevitability to it.

Once the Islamic republic was established, the kinds of changes introduced through public policies did not aim at overturning the existing socioeconomic structures. By and large, private property has been protected, the wealthy farming class has avoided any far-reaching agrarian reform, and the merchant class has been restricted only by normal wartime measures against speculation and price gouging. The public sector has grown through the takeover of all the assets of the royal family and of convicted collaborators of the old regime. The secular intelligentsia and some business interests have fled the country or gone underground. As important as these disruptions may be, they were not the goals of public policy. These were aimed more at the religio-cultural realm, cleansing the Iranian soul of all its Western accretions, enforcing Islamic morality, ensuring that women covered their faces and bodies, that Iranians observe their religious obligations, and that commitment to Islam be a requisite for all public positions and even admission to institutes of higher learning. The Iranian revolution has so far been a bourgeois revolution that dismantled a regime founded on a big state sector allied with large-scale domestic and multinational capital and replaced it with a big state sector allied to the merchant and petit bourgeois strata of the cities and small towns.

## CONCLUSION

State autonomy has been reduced in the Middle East by the very process of state intervention in the economy. The expansion of the state apparatus led to the formation of a large public-managerial stratum, if not a state class. The same expansion created a tremendous demand for trained personnel of all kinds. As much as the military officers, the engineers were at the vanguard of these new cadres (see Moore 1980). Similarly, the concentration of investment capital in the hands of the state led, through the implementation of state development plans, to the dispersion of investable capital among a great number of dependent, private-sector businesses. For some Marxists, it was the concentration of wealth in the hands of these dependent capitalists that led to the aborting of various socialist experiments and the pressure to deregulate and liberalize the economy so that the new private wealth could be invested profitably—and legally (inter alia, see Mursi 1976).

There is another explanation, not necessarily in conflict with the Marxist one, that posits that liberalization is best seen as an attempt by the state to reassert itself and to regain control over the economy. This view holds that state leadership has come to realize that its elaborate system of controls, regulations, licenses, administered prices, and inflexible exchange rates drove much economic activity underground, where it could not be monitored, oriented, or taxed. The gray and black economies came to rival the legal economy. Vast fortunes made from evasion and rent-seeking behavior had totally undermined the statist project (Lal 1987). Paradoxically, liberalization can thus be seen as the only means by which the state can regain control over the direction of the economy. It is unlikely, however, that the state in most Middle Eastern societies will ever again enjoy the same degree of autonomy as it did in the past from the major interests and classes that constitute civil society. We have seen in the past few decades, in the larger economies, a prodigious growth in urban, educated professionals. Alongside them and competing with the state for their skills are rapidly expanding private sectors in manufacturing, commercial agriculture, the services, and trade. Both professional and entrepreneurial interest groups have begun to organize and to press their causes in the corridors of state power. This process of greater definition and assertiveness of parts of civil society cannot easily be reversed. The parts themselves, the new rural and urban entrepreneurs and the large new middle class, have in great measure been created as a result of state policies. They are already strong enough to constrain state initiatives in several domains, and the day may not be far off when they may be in a position to capture the state itself.

## NOTES

1. The violence that led to the founding of the People's Democratic Republic of Yemen might marginally qualify as a social revolution, but the extent of that

violence appears no greater than that preceding Moroccan and Tunisian independence. The country's small size, the peculiar dualism of the developed Aden port and a nearly premarket rural hinterland, and the PDRY's geographic remoteness reduce the lessons we can draw from its experience.

2. Huntington (1968) referred to this as Stolypinism, after the czar's minister who pushed through a conservative land reform in Russia at the beginning of this century.

3. We do not know if the Ba'athis of Syria and Iraq or the cadres of Algeria's FLN offer serious exceptions to this proposition. In Syria provincials from minority backgrounds may seek protection against the Sunni majority in espousing secularism. Secularism among the rank and file in Iraq's Ba'ath or Algeria's FLN may be only skin deep.

4. There has been an enormous amount written about the revolution in a general sense. The best journalistic account is contained in the four-volume study by Courière (1968, 1969, 1970, 1971); the fullest historical account in Horne (1978). An attempt to understand the revolution's leadership may be found in Quandt (1969) and its social bases in Launay (1963) and Wolf (1968).

# 16

## CONCLUSION

We have documented and tried to explain the vast political and economic change that the Middle East has undergone in the last forty years. The extent of that change, and in many respects its very nature, do not clearly distinguish Middle Eastern nations from the rest of what is loosely called the Third World. The two major variables that do seem to characterize the Middle East are an unusually high incidence of regional conflict and violence, with attendant diversion of human and material resources to the pursuit of those conflicts, and the general spread of Muslim fundamentalism and militancy. It should go without saying that neither armed conflict nor religious fervor are exclusive to the Middle East, but their juxtaposition and indeed interrelatedness do produce a peculiarly Middle Eastern phenomenon.

What is astonishing is that despite the investment of colossal resources and energies in the pursuit of destroying enemies, the region as a whole is more prosperous, its citizens better educated, its wealth more evenly distributed, and its nations more firmly rooted than forty years ago. As was suggested in Chapter 13, conflict may in fact have promoted the processes of development (an argument about which we are quite skeptical) and of nation-building (a claim that seems more plausible).

Unquestionably for *most* of its inhabitants, the Middle East is a better place in which to live than it was even a couple of decades ago. The middle classes, largely urban and earning their living in the service sector and as professionals with advanced training, are both the cause and the major beneficiary of the general rise in standards of living. But we should not forget that in the countryside extensive road networks have been built, irrigation systems introduced to formerly arid areas, electricity brought to villages and schools, dispensaries, veterinary services, agriculture extension services, and rural credit provided to much if not all of the rural population. Some countries pursued rural uplift and state welfare in general, with a strong egalitarian, populist, and occasionally socialist commitment. Others may have done so defensively so as not to look less caring than their populist neighbors. But whether one speaks of Jordan, Pahlavi Iran, and

Morocco, or Algeria, Syria, and Egypt, the overall distributional results are not very different.

Still, it should be abundantly clear from what has preceded that we believe that this new relative well-being is not built on firm foundations. There are several failings that are shared by many regimes in the region. No country has built an industrial base that can withstand international competition, although Turkey and Israel have made important strides in that direction. A great deal of industrialization has taken place, but it has been highly protected, often allowed to become technologically obsolete, and is not sustained by much indigenous research and development capacity. Moreover, to pay for this imperfect industrialization, several states have heavily taxed their agricultural sectors, thereby inhibiting more rapid agricultural growth, and have borrowed heavily abroad. The new industries have rarely been able to earn foreign exchange to help service the external debt (Turkey again is the major exception), and only the oil exporters have kept themselves out of payments crises.

Middle Eastern states in the past decades have tried by and large to achieve high rates of growth and high levels of consumption. This is a very hard equation to solve over any extended period of time. Again, the oil exporters could afford to strive for both, but countries without petroleum increasingly paid for investment by deficit financing and borrowing abroad. Countries like Egypt were able in part to fill this resource gap—the difference between national savings and investment—through external rents: worker remittances, Suez Canal fees, and tourism receipts. But in Egypt and elsewhere in the 1970s the big questions of raising the productivity of capital and labor, of restructuring industrial production to compete abroad, and of adjusting domestic prices to reflect real scarcities were simply avoided. Some countries hoped that their strategic significance would earn them financial support from the big powers, and for Morocco, Egypt, and Jordan, among others, that gamble paid off. For the Sudan it did not, and that country's economy has suffered profoundly. Even for the others, however, there are limits beyond which great powers or regional powers will not extend new lines of soft credit unless the borrowers do something to make their economies efficient.

Economic and societal development in the Middle East has too often consisted in educating and training new kinds of economic actors, but not in increasing the productive capacity of the economies. Engineers, accountants, schoolteachers, agronomists, stenographers, communications technicians, airline pilots, pharmacists, and computer experts are there in their tens and hundreds of thousands. In many instances they could have been better trained, but they are more than adequate for many of the challenges at hand. Yet they have been consistently mis- and underemployed, assigned to positions more often than not where their talents and initiative are stifled and unrewarded, and where seniority is the principal criterion by which one advances. The growth of the professional middle class, as Moore (1980) argued a decade ago, has become the surrogate for real economic development.

The middle classes in all their forms are better defined by their modes of consumption and styles of life than by their place in the mode of production. Amin (1975) made this point in the early 1970s, and it is no less valid today. Because style of consumption is so crucial to the maintenance of one's middle-class status, regimes that rely on the middle classes for support are hard put to curb their consumption and reduce their standard of living. But this is precisely what must be done now, in the late 1980s, and it clearly poses the most momentous political challenge to incumbent regimes.

It is not helpful to note that had Egypt and other countries begun the adjustment and austerity programs fifteen years ago when external resources were more abundant and external debts much smaller, they might now be on a relatively healthy economic course. They did not, however, do that, and it is only fair to add that the international banking system in the mid- and late 1970s encouraged them to borrow through real negative interest rates, rather than cut back on imports and overall consumption. Now the fifteen years have gone by, Egypt has added about 15 million new Egyptians to its population, and all the structural problems are still there to be addressed. Other countries in the region have begun to take on the challenge. Turkey in 1980, Israel in 1985, Algeria in 1986 are the most prominent examples. In Turkey there is no question that income distribution has worsened considerably and that organized labor and the lower and middle classes have suffered major real reductions in income. Turkish democracy will be put to a severe test in the coming years.

Yet the picture is by no means all gloomy. The period in which state-led ISI prevailed, and still prevails, witnessed the building of national infrastructure in railroads, ports, and power generation. Many of the industries started may not have been appropriate, but production and managerial skills were built and a certain mastery of technology achieved. Several Middle Eastern societies are relatively well equipped to undertake new economic tasks, and the early phase, while creating many of the problems that must be addressed, also has provided the solutions. That Iran was able to conduct a war and manage an economy in a period of declining petroleum prices is a tribute not so much to Khomeini as to the cumulative impact of twenty-five years of rapid social and economic change.

Politically, it would have to be said, Middle Eastern countries have not been at all successful. If we judge several of the regimes by their own criteria, we see that they failed to develop any coherent mass base to sustain their claims to populist support. Corporatist formulas, grouping citizens according to their functions and professions within single-party, single-ideology systems, turned out to be little more than bureaucratic attempts to control the active population. The base became increasingly divorced from the leadership, and as ideological commitment failed to take hold, the police became more prominent agents in the control process. Egypt under Nasser, Algeria, Syria, Iraq, and even Iran in the 1970s exemplified regimes that would not concede any real voice and responsibilities to the very people in whose name they spoke. Nor were they able to meet their own economic development goals or to build effective military forces; hence, they failed on all fronts. We have spoken frequently of regime exhaustion and the failure of secular ideologies, and both are perfectly apt terms.

Many Middle Eastern regimes, judged by other criteria, could be said to have achieved remarkable stability, a factor that has eluded many states in Latin America, sub-Saharan Africa and parts of Asia. Egypt since 1952 has witnessed two peaceful transfers of presidential power. King Hassan has been on the Moroccan throne since 1961, and King Hussein on Jordan's since 1952, although both monarchs have been targets of violence. The shah of Iran ruled uninterruptedly from 1953 to 1979. Assad of Syria and Hussein of Iraq have each been in power for nearly twenty years, while Mu'ammar Qaddafi is the doyen of Middle Eastern republican heads of state. From one perspective, this is comforting, for stability and predictability can only be good for economic development. But from another, it is highly disquieting because it implies the subjugation and alienation of increasingly educated populations that for decades have been given little say in their own governance.

When one looks at countries that have not had that kind of stability the message is very hard to read. Turkey has experienced three military coups since 1960, and during periods of civilian rule, changes in government have been frequent. Yet outside of Israel, Turkey is the most economically advanced country in the region, and its press, parties, and parliament are testimony to a high level of democratic practice. Israel, likewise, has achieved high standards of living and a kind of oligarchical democracy (Arian 1985) that is vibrant and exciting—if you are a Jew. If you are a Palestinian Israeli you are both economically and politically inferior. Until Arab Israelis are fully integrated, economically and politically, into Israeli society, the country's claims to full democracy will ring hollow.

Then there is Lebanon and the Sudan. We said earlier that most Middle Eastern societies form more solid nations today than they did a few decades ago. We would have to say the reverse for Lebanon and the Sudan. The sad irony is that both countries have enjoyed fairly long periods of civilian democratic government. Lebanon, like Israel, knew a kind of oligarchical democracy and a laissez faire economy that brought extraordinary prosperity to the country in the 1960s. Whether one seizes on internal factors of sectarian selfishness and maldistribution of wealth or on external meddling and provocations, the result is that Lebanon has ceased to exist. The Sudan, by contrast, never rose so high nor sunk so low. Still, as a state in effective control of its territory and in a position to stimulate the economy nationwide, it ceased to exist some time after 1983. The restoration of civilian rule in 1986 has produced governments incapable of dealing with the southern insurgency and equally incapable of managing what remains of the national economy. Once discredited, the civilian leaders were again brushed aside by the military. There is no light at the end of the Sudanese and Lebanese tunnels.

Perhaps the most striking political difference between the 1950s and the 1980s is the crisis in confidence that nearly all regimes have experienced. The 1950s, it must be stressed, was a period of considerable optimism in the developing world. On the one hand, development economists and bilateral and multilateral sources of foreign assistance gave encouragement to activist states that set about the mobilization of national resources for the development effort. These external mentors, having themselves participated in state-guided efforts to pull Western economies out of the world depression and out of the wreckage of World War II, felt that Third World states could act with similar effectiveness. Moreover, a certain amount of central planning and price administration seemed perfectly appropriate. On the other hand, new regimes were confident that they could bring off the development task without relying on weak private sectors, market forces driven by monopoly and speculation, or foreign private investment, which appeared likely to compromise newly won independence. Leaders of these countries felt sustained by a reserve of nationalist goodwill and a willingness (though it was illusory) to sacrifice for and comply with the leaders' grand designs.

In this kind of atmosphere all good things were seen to go together. Resource utilization would be planned rationally, administrators would conscientiously carry out their duties, the citizens would actively support the development programs, both growth and rising incomes would result, all so that new resources would become available for new rounds of planned development. A virtuous circle indeed. But as we have seen, it became reality only during very brief moments, and usually with attendant costs in foreign indebtedness or domestic price distortions that swamped the plans in subsequent phases. These were only a few of the unintended consequences we mentioned in Chapter 2.

Many things—sometimes all things—went wrong, and the combination of factors varied from country to country. The problem that no one addressed with much vigor was that of rapid population growth and the enormous demand that young populations created for the delivery of services and the expansion of job opportunities whether or not the jobs were truly needed. In addition, protection of import-substituting industries created gross inefficiencies at the same time that the industries themselves developed little capacity to earn foreign exchange in highly competitive external markets. Rather than leading to self-sustaining industrial growth, they became a net drain on public resources—another broken link in the virtuous circle.

Bureaucrats behaved rationally, not altruistically. Regulations meant to rationalize economic activity created barriers, or gates, among public agencies and between them and client groups in the society. Those officials who guarded the gates began to collect fees to open them, especially because their salaries, while predictable, and their jobs, while stable, were also low and dull. Nationalism was no antidote to officials trying to reach or sustain a middle-class way of life.

Concomitantly the citizenry, operating in centralized, top-down political structures, were given no effective means to call their officials and leaders to account. There was taxation but little true representation. The strategically placed, the professional middle class, was usually co-opted through material rewards and some real power. The rest could choose apathy, rioting, or the political equivalent to the parallel economy—local, informal politics in which vital resources were distributed in ways over which the state had little control. The Muslim political counterculture became the most positive and overt manifestation of the parallel political system, but in general the upshot was that the state found itself in less and less control of both economic and political life.

There were also the external shocks. It was an exceptional Middle Eastern state that did not find itself engaged in war—sometimes (Iraq, the Sudan) against parts of its own population. We will never know these conflicts' true cost in development forgone. So too there were the fears, sometimes fulfilled, of foreign intervention. The 1956 Suez War, the 1958 landing of U.S. Marines in Lebanon, and the 1979 Soviet invasion of Afghanistan are the most dramatic of such interventions, but subversion, destabilization, saber rattling, and the like have been commonplace in great-power dealings with the Middle East. In fairness one should note that Middle Eastern states employ the same means among themselves.

The external economic environment has not been unkind to the Middle East, but for most states the possible advantages of greater involvement in international trade were, with the exception of the oil exporters, not explored. This avenue toward driving the circle in a virtuous direction was not taken. The result by the mid-1970s was indeed regime exhaustion, with leaders assailed by doubt, pressured by external friends and enemies, and confronted by the indifferent or hostile gaze of a generation of young citizens they had educated and tried to win over.

Sadat, at a moment when Egypt was ostracized by other Arab leaders, dismissed them all as dwarfs. Only in relative terms was his stature any greater. The true giants have all passed from the scene. Atatürk inspired an entire generation of political leaders in the Middle East. Reza Khan dragged Persia into statehood. Nasser inspired such fear and admiration throughout the Arab world that even those who hated him had to copy him in some respects; King Faisal of Saudi Arabia was a notable exception and in his own right considerably more than a dwarf. Within the narrow confines of Tunisia, Habib Bourguiba was a giant for decades but in the end diminished beyond recognition. Ben Gurion was to Israel what Atatürk was to Turkey. Curiously, the extraordinary Algerian revolution yielded no Fidel or Che, but rather the quixotic Ben Bella and the dour Boumedienne. The last remaining colossus, the Ayatollah Khomeini, died in June 1989. No one since Nasser has so marked the contemporary Middle East, setting the themes, defining good and evil, friends and enemies, with a moral force that obliges all other leaders to react. And like Nasser, those that feared him the most have still had to buy part of his militant Islamic package, to debate him, as it were, on his own turf and in his own terms.

It is hard to know what constitutes institutional or leadership legitimacy in the Middle East, although Hudson's *Arab Politics* (1977) remains the most systematic effort to try to do so. Populations of roughly similar economic standing, occupational distribution, and educational attainment appear to attribute *some* legitimacy to leaders and institutions as dissimilar as the monarchies of Jordan and Morocco, the "mullahcracy" of Iran, or the republics of Husni Mubarrak and Chadli Benjadid. How much legitimacy is moot. We see Khomeini and Qaddhafi as more popular, and yet more feared and hated, while Saddam Hussein and Hafiz al-Assad appear to rule by big sticks, small carrots, and fiercely loyal clans. How many Middle Easterners would be truly sorry to see any of them go? How many Middle Easterners would breathe a sigh of relief, like most Tunisians when Bourguiba was "retired," or dance in the streets like most Sudanese when Nimeiri was overthrown? Perhaps they would pour into the streets to call back a disgraced leader. The Egyptian people did this in June 1967 when Nasser resigned, and their message as much as anything was, "don't walk out on us, now that you've gotten us into this mess."

Political logjams, however, may be breaking up, particularly where the weakest or the least flamboyant leaders are concerned. The signs and the causes are many. One cause is relative failure. Granted, the states and their leaders cannot do it all, but having designed systems in such a way that they must accept the blame for all their failings, then sharing responsibility with the citizenry may not be such a bad thing. The people have to be implicated in the failures, made to bear part of the responsibility, and hence more likely to accept the costs of solutions. The state *cannot* do it all: drive production, create jobs, redistribute income, educate, clothe, and house. But it has the principal levers in hand that affect these goals, and the citizenry unavoidably awaits solutions from the masters of the state. It may not be such a bad thing, in the eyes of the leaders, for the private sector to take over some of these levers, to absorb some of the responsibility for growth, wage levels, and general welfare. Moreover, as we have pointed out elsewhere, economic liberalization may be a way to let the parallel economy become visible, to measure its level of activity, and having legalized and measured it, tax it.

The change in the economic role of the state, from direct producer and orchestrator to one of regulator and referee, allows resources to accumulate in private hands. It seems naturally to tend toward political liberalization in the sense that new economic and professional interests will want to organize to protect and extend their advantages. This by no means need entail institutionalized democracy but rather a space in which interests and groups can legally contend. It has happened in Turkey, a few years after military rule, where eight parties are active, but where Communists on the one hand and Kurdish activists on the other cannot legally organize.

It is happening in Egypt, which is still an essentially one-party presidential system. It is happening in Morocco, where some politicians would like to see King Hassan or his son become the equivalent, not of Queen Elizabeth II, but rather of Juan Carlos of Spain.

The growth of the middle classes probably means that business cannot go on as usual. However fragile or temporary democratization and re-democratization may be in countries as diverse as South Korea, the Philippines, and Argentina, it appears to have been the project of the middle classes. We suspect that these classes in the Middle East want to be recognized as responsible and mature; they want direct responsibility for governance, not merely co-optation by praetorians and authoritarians. Many may seek empowerment through militant Islam with greater or lesser degrees of sincerity or hypocrisy. There is, in any case, no reason to expect them to be committed liberals. Authoritarianism of various kinds may find favor with them as long as they have a meaningful role in it. External conflict and martial law have kept the middle classes in an iron cage in countries like Iraq and Syria. Civil war or Revolutionary Guards have driven them to migration or to dissimulation as in Lebanon and Iran. Curiously, however, in much of the Third World in the latter part of the twentieth century, the force for change is proving to be not the peasantry or the proletariat, champions of the 1950s and 1960s, but the white-collar middle classes. Halpern (1963) said as much twenty-five years ago, but he was at least that many years premature.

We also must stress once again the internal differentiation of the middle classes. Some of the most intense competition and conflict occurs *within* their ranks. The petite bourgeosie in trade and small-scale manufacturing fears the big industrialist, whether private or public, as well as the big industrialists' allies in international business. The lower ranks of the white-collar clerical and professional groups see their way to higher status blocked by relatively young high-ranking administrators who rose to the top during the expansionary periods of the 1960s and 1970s. When one can identify groups that seem to be losing their rank, prestige, and functional importance in society—let us say the mullahs in Iran after 1963—or groups whose ambitions for upward mobility are being thwarted, there we will find middle-class and would-be-middle-class recruits for radical movements. Today those movements seem all to be defined in religious terms, with the exception of Turkey's neofascist National Action party. Whatever form they may take, the goals will be social promotion and political empowerment.

If one juxtaposes the various middle-class agendas to the programs of belt tightening and structural adjustment that many Middle Eastern countries are contemplating, one creates a potentially explosive situation. Again, implicating strategic middle-class interests in the austerity measures through cautious democratization may be the wisest political course, and Egypt, Tunisia, Morocco, and Turkey seem to be following it. Another element that serves to diffuse group interests and to head off the crystallization of broad-based grievances is the changed nature of economic life itself.

As the states renege on various parts of their social contracts, as inflation becomes a fixed aspect of everyday existence, as individuals and families are increasingly left to their own devices, people tend to respond by individualistic scrambling and by narrowly focused survival strategies with short time horizons. These constraints apply not only to the middle classes but also to virtually anyone seeking a livelihood in the urban environment or through migration. This serves the purposes of power wielders who are not unhappy to see potential adversaries caught up in the rat race. Some, if not most, people are able to stay even in this race, but only through taking on extra jobs and engaging in the informal, local-level politics of procuring the vital goods (licenses, credit, jobs) that are traded locally even if their ultimate source is the state itself. But not everyone makes it in the race, and even those that do are under enormous strain. A small elite visibly prospers in such times, living in a sense off the desperate scramble of the others, and that situation breeds anger, envy, and indignation. It literally exploded in Iran in 1978–1979 and nearly has in Egypt, Morocco, and Tunisia at various times since 1977. None of the structural causes of this situation have been removed, nor will they be in the near future. The stakes of political management would thus appear higher than ever in the Middle East.

The burdens of austerity weigh even more heavily on the region's poor, be they urban or rural. A continuation of slow or negative growth has grim implications for their lives, as wages fall and entitlements erode. Lowered spending on health, education, and rural-development programs threaten to reverse the tentative gains that were achieved on these fronts during the era of the oil boom. Populations keep growing, translating into ever-larger numbers of young people who must be fed, housed, educated, and employed. The food gap continues to mount, ecological depradations proliferate, and the burden of debt rises inexorably. Both in simple humanitarian and in long-run development terms, the region cannot afford to neglect human welfare. There is evidence that political leaders realize that a "Mexican scenario" of drastic falls in growth rates, living standards, and employment offers no long-run solution to the crisis of state-led growth and poses unacceptable political risks. But the easy exit of a vast natural-resource boom, which characterized the 1970s in much of the region, is unlikely to open again.

It is a much more difficult time than thirty years ago, not merely because resources are so severely stretched against growing populations, but also because so many experiments undertaken with confidence and enthusiasm have failed and an entire political generation is weighted with fatigue and self-doubt. Although the Islamic idiom seems to prevail, the countries in which it has been applied—principally, Iran and Saudi Arabia—do not offer appealing models for the rest of the region. As a decade has transpired since the shah left Iran, we see a country that has fed its people on war, religious repression, and bigotry. It gives pause to the most committed of Muslims, and it has given backbone to secularists in a number of Middle

Eastern countries. Thus, without tested models and without long-term strategies, the Middle East enters a long period of austerity and restructuring. In part, some of the successes of the most recent decades, especially the establishment of a diverse middle class, are what will make this restructuring particularly painful. The talent upon which the effort will succeed or fail is embodied in these classes, and it seems inevitable that they will become directly responsible for its design and implementation.

# REFERENCES

[Please note that *MEJ* is the *Middle East Journal* and *IJMES* is the *International Journal of Middle East Studies*.]

Abdalla, Ahmed (1985), *The Student Movement and National Politics in Egypt,* London, Zed Books.

Abdel-Fadil, Mahmoud (1975), *Development, Income Distribution and Social Change in Rural Egypt (1952–1970): A Study in the Political Economy of Agrarian Transition,* Cambridge, Cambridge University Press.

———— (1980), *The Political Economy of Nasserism,* Cambridge, Cambridge University Press.

———— (1983), "Informal Sector Employment in Egypt" in R. Lobbon, ed., *Urban Research Strategies for Egypt,* Cairo Papers in Social Science, American University in Cairo, 6, 2 (June), 16–40.

Abdel-Khaleq, Gouda (1981), "Looking Outside or Turning NW? On the Meaning and External Dimension of Egypt's *Infitah,* 1971–1980," *Social Problems* 28, 4 (April), 394–409.

Abdel-Khaleq, Gouda, and Tignor, Robert, eds. (1982), *The Political Economy of Income Distribution in Egypt,* New York, Holmes and Meier.

Abdel-Malek, Anouar (1968), *Egypt: Military Society,* New York, Vintage Books.

Abun-Nasr, Jamil M. (1971), *A History of the Magrib,* Cambridge, Cambridge University Press.

Adams, Dale W., and Graham, Douglas H. (1981), "A Critique of Traditional Agricultural Credit Projects and Policies," *Journal of Development Economics* 8, 347-66.

Adams, Martin E., and Howell, John (1979), "Developing the Traditional Sector in the Sudan," *Economic Development and Cultural Change* 27, 3 (April), 505–18.

Adams, Richard H., Jr. (1986), *Development and Social Change in Rural Egypt,* Syracuse, Syracuse University Press.

Adelman, Irma (1984), "Beyond Export-Led Growth," *World Development* 12, 9 (Sept.), 937–50.

Adelman, Irma, and Robinson, Sherman (1988), "Income Distribution and Development: A Survey," in H. B. Chenery and T. N. Srinivasan, eds., *Handbook of Development Economics,* Amsterdam, North Holland.

Affan, Khalid (1984), *Towards an Appraisal of Tractorisation Experience in Rainlands of Sudan,* Development Studies and Research Centre, Faculty of Economic and Social Studies, University of Khartoum.

Ahmad, Feroz (1977), *The Turkish Experiment in Democracy, 1950–1975,* London, Royal Institute of International Affairs (RIIA), Hurst and Co.

———— (1981), "The Political Economy of Kemalism," in Kazancigil and Özbudun (1981).

Ahmad, Iftikhar (1981), "Pakistan: Class and State Formation," *Race and Class* 22, 3, 239–56.

Ahmad, Sadiq (1984), *Public Finance in Egypt, Its Structure and Trends,* World Bank Staff Working Papers, No. 639.

Ahsan, Syed Aziz al- (1984), "Economic Policy and Class Structure in Syria: 1958–1980," *IJMES* 16, 301-23.

Ajami, Fouad (1978/79), "The End of Pan-Arabism," *Foreign Affairs* 57, 2, 355–73.

———— (1981), *The Arab Predicament,* New York, Cambridge University Press.

Akeel, H. A., and Moore, C. H. (1977), "The Class Origins of Egyptian-Engineer Technocrats," in C.A.O. van Nieuwenjuijze, ed., *Commoners, Climbers, and Notables,* Leiden, Brill, 279–92.

Akgüç, Öztin (1979), "The Development of the Public Sector in Turkey's Mixed Economy," in Mükerrem Hiç, ed., *Turkey's and Other Countries' Experience with the Mixed Economy,* Istanbul, Istanbul University Press, 433–57.

Alderman, Harold (1986), "Food Subsidies and State Policies in Egypt" in Richards (1986b), 183–200.

Alderman, Harold, and Braun, J. von (1984), *The Effects of the Egyptian Food Ration and Subsidy System on Income Distribution and Consumption,* Washington, D.C., IFPRI, Research Report No. 45.

Allan, J. A. (1981), *Libya: The Experience of Oil,* Boulder, Colo., and London, Westview Press and Croom Helm.

Alnasrawi, Abbas (1986), "Economic Consequences of the Iran-Iraq War," *Third World Quarterly* 8, 3 (July), 880–83.

Amin, Galal (1975), *The Modernization of Poverty: A Study of the Political Economy of Growth in Nine Arab Countries, 1945–70,* Leiden, Brill.

Amin, Galal, and Taylor-Awny, Elizabeth (1985), *International Migration of Egyptian Labour: A Review of the State of the Art,* Ottawa, International Development Research Center (IDRC), May.

Amin, Samir (1970), *L'accumulation à l'échelle mondiale,* Paris, Anthropos.

———— (1976), *La Nation arabe,* Paris, Editions de Minuit.

———— (1982), *The Arab Economy Today,* Zed Press, London.

Amirahmadi, Hooshang (1986), "Economic Operations in Post-Revolutionary Iran," paper presented at the Middle East Studies Association (MESA) annual meeting, Boston, Nov. 20–23.

Amouzegar, Jahangir (1983), *Oil Exporters' Economic Development in an Interdependent World,* IMF Occasional Paper No. 18.

Anabtawi, Samir (1983), "Arab Institutions of Higher Learning and Their Own Manpower Development," in Ibrahim (1983), 125–38.

Anderson, Lisa (1985), "The State in the Middle East and North Africa," paper presented at APSA meeting, New Orleans, Aug. 29–Sept. 2.

———— (1986), *The State and Social Transformation in Tunisia and Libya, 1930–1980,* Princeton, N.J., Princeton University Press.

Anderson, Perry (1980), *Lineages of the Absolutist State,* 2nd printing, London, Verse Editions.

*Annuaire Statistique du Maroc* (1984), Rabat, Kingdom of Morocco.

Ansari, Hamied al- (1986), *Egypt: The Stalled Society,* Albany, N.Y., SUNY Press.

Aoufi, N. el- (1980), "La Marocanization et le développement de la bourgeoisie," *Revue juridique, politique et économique du Maroc,* No. 7.

Arat, Yeşim (1987), "Social Change and the 1983 Political Elite in Turkey," Boğazçi University, April, photocopy.

ARE (Arab Republic of Egypt), Presidency (1980), *The Public Sector: Its Obstacles and Evolution,* National Specialized Committees, Cairo (in Arabic).

Arian, Asher (1985), *Politics in Israel: The Second Generation,* Chatham, N.J., Chatham House Pub.

Aricanli, Tosun (1985), "Agricultural Labor Responses to Population Growth and Agrotechnical Intervention: The Gezira Scheme," in Shorter and Zurayk (1985), 96–114.

―――― (1986), "Agrarian Relations in Turkey: A Historical Sketch," in Richards (1986b).

Arjomand, Said (1981), "Shi'ite Islam and the Revolution in Iran," *Government and Opposition* 16, 3 (Summer), 293–316.

―――― (1982), "À la recherche de la conscience collective: Durkheim's Ideological Impact in Turkey and Iran," *American Sociologist* 17, 2 (May), 94–102.

―――― (1984), "The Significance of the Islamic Revolution in Iran," photocopy.

―――― (1986), "Iran's Islamic Revolution in Comparative Perspective," *World Politics* 38, 3 (April), 383–414.

Ashraf, A., and Banuazizi, A. (1985), "The State, Classes, and Modes of Mobilization in the Iranian Revolution," *State, Culture and Society* 1, 3, 3–40

Ashraf, Ahmad (1970), "Historical Obstacles to the Development of a Bourgeoisie in Iran," in M. A. Cook, ed., *Studies in the Economic History of the Middle East,* London, Oxford University Press, 308–32.

―――― (1984), "State and Class: The Pahlavids and the Ulama in the Making of Modern Iran," photocopy.

―――― (1986), "State and Agrarian Relations Before and After the Revolution in Iran," photocopy.

Askari, Hossein al-, and Cummings, John (1978), "Land Reform in the Middle East," *IJMES* 8, 4 (October), 580–608.

Askari, Hossein al-, Cummings, John, and Glova, Michael (1982), *Taxation and Tax Policies in the Middle East,* Boston, Butterworth Scientific.

Assaad, Ragui (1989), "The Employment Crisis in Egypt: Trends and Issues," American University in Cairo, January, typescript.

Awad, Mohamed Hashim (1970), "Government Policy Toward Private Industry in the Sudan," *L'Egypte Contemporaine* 61, 181–200.

―――― , ed. (1983), *Socio-economic Change in the Sudan,* Khartoum, Khartoum University Press.

Ayoubi, N. (1981), "The Administrative Apparatus and Its Leadership," in Saad al-Din Ibrahim, ed., *Egypt in the Quarter Century, 1952–1977,* Beirut, 86–119 (in Arabic).

Ayoubi, Nazih (1982), "Organization for Development: The Politico-Administrative Framework of Economic Activity in Egypt under Sadat," *Public Administration and Development* 2, 4, 279–94.

―――― (1985), "Arab Bureaucracies: Expanding Size, Changing Roles," Politics Dept., University of Exeter, England, photocopy.

―――― (1986), "Bureaucratization as Development: Administrative Development and Development Administration in the Arab World," *International Review of Administration Sciences* 52, 201–22.

Ayres, Ron (1983), "Arms Production as a Form of Import Substituting Industrialization: The Turkish Case," *World Development* 11, 9, 813–23.

Baduel, Pierre-Robert (1983), "Le VIe Plan Tunisien: 1982–86," *Grand Maghreb*, March 21, 1983, 54–57.

Baer, Gabriel (1962), *A History of Landownership in Modern Egypt, 1800–1950*, London, Oxford University Press.

Baer, Werner, et al. (1976), "On State Capitalism in Brazil: Some New Issues and Questions," *Inter-American Economic Affairs* 30, Winter, 69–96.

Bakhash, Shaul (1984), *The Reign of the Ayatollahs*, New York, Basic Books.

Ball, Nicole (1983), "Defense and Development: A Critique of the Benoit Study," *Economic Development and Cultural Change* 31, 4 (July), 507–24.

Barnett, Tony (1977), *The Gezira Scheme—An Illusion of Development*, London, Frank Cass.

Batatu, Hanna (1978), *The Old Social Classes and the Revolutionary Movements of Iraq*, Princeton, N.J., Princeton University Press.

———— (1979), "Class Analysis and Iraqi Society," *Peuples Mediterranéens*, No. 8 (July-Sept.), 101–16.

Bates, D., and Rassam, A. (1983), *Peoples and Cultures of the Middle East*, Englewood, N.J., Prentice-Hall.

Bates, Robert (1981), *Markets and States in Tropical Africa*, Berkeley, University of California Press.

Bauer, P. T. (1973), *Dissent on Development*, Delhi, Vikas.

Beblawi, Hazem (1984), *The Arab Gulf Economy in a Turbulent Age*, London, Croom Helm.

Benachenhou, A. (1975), "Réflexions sur la politique des revenues en Algérie," *Revue Algérienne* 12, Mar. 1.

Ben-Dor, Gabriel (1983), *State and Conflict in the Middle East*, New York, Praeger.

Benhoutia, Tahar (1980), *L'Economie de l'Algérie*, Paris, François Maspéro.

Benissad, M. E. (1982), *Economie du Developpement de l'Algerie*, Paris, Economica.

Bennoune, Mahfoud (1988), *The Making of Contemporary Algeria, 1830–1987*, Cambridge, Cambridge Universiuty Press.

Benoit, Emile (1973), *Defense and Economic Growth in Developing Countries*, Lexington, Mass., Lexington Books.

Ben-Porath, Yoram (1972), "Fertility in Israel, an Economist's Interpretation: Differentials and Trends, 1950–1970," in Cooper and Alexander (1972), 502–41.

Ben Romdane, M. (1981), "L'accumulation du capital et les classes sociales en Tunisie depuis l'indépendance," Doct. d'Etat de Science Economique, University de Tunis, mimeo.

———— (1982), "Mutations économiques et sociales et mouvement ouvrier en Tunisie de 1956–1980," *Annuaire de l'Afrique de Nord* 21, 259–84.

Berar-Awad, Azita (1984), *Employment Planning in the Sudan: An Overview of Selected Issues*, Geneva, ILO.

Berberoğlu, Berch (1981), "Turkey: The Crisis of the Neo-Colonial System," *Race and Class* 22, 3, 277–91.

Berger, Morroe (1964), *The Arab World Today*, New York, Doubleday.

Bernard, Chantale (1984), "Economies maghrébines: à la redécouverte des vertus de la PMI," *Grand Maghreb*, No. 28 (Feb. 6), 42–44; No. 29 (March 19), 45–48.

Berrada, A. (1979), "Politique budgétaire et financement du grand capital privé au Maroc," *Revue juridique, politique et economique du Maroc*, No. 5, 95–122.

Berrada, Abdelkader (1984), "Les dépenses publiques du personnel au Maroc," *Al-Asas,* No. 61.

Berry, R. Albert, and Cline, William (1979), *Agrarian Structural and Productivity in Developing Countries,* Baltimore, Johns Hopkins University Press.

Bianchi, Robert (1984), *Interest Groups and Political Development in Turkey,* Princeton, N.J., Princeton University Press.

—— (1985), "Businessmen's Associations in Egypt and Turkey," *American Academy of Political and Social Science, Annals,* No. 482 (Nov.), 147–59.

—— (1986), "The Corporatization of the Egyptian Labor Movement," *MEJ* 4, 3 (Summer), 429–44.

Bienen, Henry S. (1983), "Armed Forces and National Modernization: Continuing the Debate," *Comparative Politics* 16 (Oct.), 1–16.

Bienen, Henry S., and Gersovitz, M. (1985), "Economic Stabilization Conditionality and Political Stability," *International Organization* 39, 4 (Autumn), 729–54.

Bienen, Henry S., and Moore, J. (1987), "The Sudan: Military Economic Corporations," *Armed Forces and Society* 13, 4, 489–516.

Bill, James A. (1972a), "Class Analysis and the Dialectics of Modernization in the Middle East," *IJMES* 3, 417–34.

—— (1972b), *The Politics of Iran,* Columbus, O., Charles Merrill.

Bill, James A., and Leiden, C. (1984), *Politics in the Middle East,* Boston, Little, Brown.

Binder, Leonard (1957), "Prolegomena to the Comparative Study of Middle East Governments," *American Political Science Review* 51, 3, 651–68.

—— (1978) *In a Moment of Enthusiasm,* Chicago, Chicago University Press.

Binswanger, Hans (1986), *Agricultural Mechanization: Issues and Policies,* Washington, D.C., World Bank, Report No. 64-70 (Oct. 30).

Birks, J. S., and Sinclair, C. A. (1979), "Egypt: A Frustrated Labor Exporter?" *MEJ* 33, 3, 288–303.

—— (1980a), *Arab Manpower,* London, Croom Helm.

—— (1980b), *International Migration and Development in the Arab Region,* Geneva, ILO.

—— (1984), "Libya: Problems of a Rentier State," in Lawless and Findlay (1984), 241–75.

Blair, John M. (1976), *The Control of Oil,* New York, Vintage Books.

Blake, Gerald, Dewdney, John, and Mitchell, Jonathan (1987), *The Cambridge Atlas of the Middle East and North Africa,* Cambridge, Cambridge University Press.

Bohi, Douglas R., and Quandt, William B. (1984), *Energy Security in the 1980's: Economic and Political Perspectives,* Washington, D.C., Brookings Institution.

Bonnenfant, Paul (1982) *La Péninsule arabique d'aujourd'hui,* Tome 1, Paris, Editions du CNRS.

Boratav, Korkut (1981), "Kemalist economic policies and étatism," in Kazancigil and Özbudun (1981).

—— (1986), "Import-Substitution and Income Distribution under a Populist Regime: The Case of Turkey," *Development Policy Review* 4, 117–39.

Bourdieu, Pierre, and Sayad, Abdelmalek (1964), *Le déracinement: la crise de l'agriculture traditionnelle en Algérie,* Paris, Editions de Minuit.

Brahimi, Abdelhamid (1977), *Dimensions et Perspectives du Monde Arabe,* Paris, Economica.

Brien, Jay O. (1985), "Sowing the Seeds of Famine: The Political Economy of Food Deficits in Sudan," *Review of African Political Economy* 33, Aug., 23–32.

Brown, L. C. (1984), *International Politics and the Middle East: Old Rules, Dangerous Games,* Princeton, N.J., Princeton University Press.

Brown, L. C., and Itzkowitz, N., eds. (1977), *Psychological Dimensions of Near Eastern Studies,* Princeton, N.J., Darwin Press.

Brown, Lester R. (1974), *By Bread Alone,* New York, Praeger Pub.

Buitzer, Karl (1976), *Early Hydraulic Civilization in Egypt,* Chicago, University of Chicago Press.

Bujra, A. S. (1971), *The Politics of Stratification: A Study of Political Change in a South Arabian Town,* Oxford, Clarendon Press.

Burns, W. J. (1985), *Economic Aid and American Foreign Policy toward Egypt:1955–1981,* Albany, N.Y., SUNY Press.

Caldwell, John C. (1986), "Routes to Low Mortality in Poor Countries," *Population and Development Review* 12, 2 (June), 171–220.

Camau, Michel (1984), "L'Etat tunisien: de la tutelle au désengagement," *Maghreb-Machrek,* No. 103 (Jan.-March), 8–38.

Cardoso, F. H. (1979), "On the Characterization of Authoritarian Regimes in Latin America," in Collier (1979), 33–60.

Carrère d'Encausse, Hélène (1975), *La Politique Soviétique au Moyen-Orient, 1955–1975,* Paris, Presses de la FNSP (Fondation Nationale des Sciences Politiques).

Celasun, Merih (1983), *Sources of Industrial Growth and Structural Change: The Case of Turkey,* Washington, D.C., World Bank Staff Working Papers, No. 641.

———— (1986), "Comment: Income Distribution and Domestic Terms of Trade in Turkey," *METU Studies in Development* 13, 1-2, 193–216.

Chambers, Richard (1964), "The Civil Bureaucracy: Turkey," in Ward and Rustow (1964), 301–27.

Charmes, Jacques (1986), *Emploi et Revenues dans le Secteur Non-Structuré des Pays du Maghreb et du Machrek,* New York, Social Science Research Council (SSRC).

Chatelus, Michel (1980), "La croissance économique: mutation des structures et dynamisme de déséquilibre," in Raymond (1980).

———— (1981), "A propos du développement industriel au Moyen-orient," *Maghreb-Machrek,* No. 92 (April-June), 63–73.

———— (1982), "De la rente pétrolière au développement économique: perspectives et contradictions de l'évolution économique dans la péninsule," in Bonnenfant (1982), 75–154.

———— (1984), "Attitudes Toward Public Sector Management and Reassertion of the Private Sector in the Arab World," paper presented at the MESA annual meeting, San Francisco, Nov. 28–Dec. 1.

Chatelus, Michel, and Schmeil, Yves (1984), "Toward a New Political Economy of State Industrialization in the Arab Middle East," *IJMES* 16, 251–65.

Chayanov, A. V. (1966), *The Theory of Peasant Economy,* New York, Richard D Irwin, Inc.

Chenery, Hollis, and Syrquin, Moshe (1975), *Patterns of Development, 1950–70,* London, Oxford University Press.

Choucri, Nazli (1986), "The Hidden Economy: A New View of Remittances in the Arab World," *World Development* 14, 6, 697–712.

Claisse, A. (1977), "Les entreprises publiques au Maroc," *Revue Française d'Administration Publique,* No. 4 (Oct.-Dec.), 877–97.

Cleaver, Kevin M. (1982), *The Agricultural Development Experience of Algeria, Morocco, and Tunisia,* World Bank Staff Working Papers, No. 552.

Clément, J. F. (1986), "Les révoltes urbaines de Janvier 1984 au Maroc," *Bulletin du Réseau Villes Monde Arabe,* No. 5 (Nov.), 3–46.

Cohen, John M., et al. (1981), "Development From Below: Local Development Associations in the Yemen Arab Republic," *World Development* 9, 11/12, 1039–61.

Colclough, Christopher (1982), "The Impact of Primary Schooling on Economic Development: A Review of the Evidence," *World Development* 10, 2/3, 1018–35.

Collier, David, ed. (1979), *The New Authoritarianism in Latin America,* Princeton, Princeton University Press.

Commander, Simon, and Burgess, Simon (1988), "Labor Markets in N. Africa and the Near East: A Survey of Developments since 1970," Aleppo, Syria, International Center for Agricultural Research in Dry Areas (ICARDA).

Coon, Carlton (1958), *Caravan: The Story of the Middle East,* New York, Henry Holt.

Cooper, C., and Alexander, S., eds. (1972), *The Economic Development and Population Growth in the Middle East,* New York, American Elsevier.

Cottam, Richard (1964), *Nationalism in Iran,* Pittsburgh, University of Pittsburgh Press.

Courière, Yves (1968), *Les Fils de Toussaint,* Paris, Fayard.

———— (1969), *Le Temps des Léopards,* Paris, Fayard.

———— (1970), *L'Heure des Colonels,* Paris, Fayard.

———— (1971), *Les Feux du Desespoir,* Paris, Fayard.

Crusoe, Jonathan (1986), "Economic Outlook: Guns and Butter: Phase Two," in Frederick W. Axelgard, ed., *Iraq in Transition: A Political Economic and Strategic Perspective,* Boulder, Colo., Westview Press, 33–58.

Dalrymple, Dana G. (1986), *Development and Spread of High Yielding Wheat Varieties in Developing Countries,* Washington, D.C., USAID.

Danielson, Albert L. (1982), *The Evolution of OPEC,* New York, Harcourt Brace Jovanovich.

Danielson, Michael, and Keleş, Rusen (1980), "Urbanization and Income Distribution in Turkey," in Özbudun and Ulusan (1980), 269–310.

———— (1985), *The Politics of Rapid Urbanization: Government and Growth in Modern Turkey,* New York, Holmes and Meier.

Dann, Uriel (1969), *Iraq Under Qassem: A Political History, 1958–1963,* Jerusalem, Israel Universities Press.

Davies, Stephen, et al. (1984), *Small Enterprises in Egypt: A Study of Two Governorates,* Working Paper No. 16, MSU International Development Papers, Dept. of Agricultural Economy, Michigan State University, E. Lansing, Mich.

Davis, Eric (1983), *Challenging Colonialism: Bank Misr and Egyptian Industrialization, 1920–1941,* Princeton, N.J., Princeton University Press.

Davis, J. (1982), "Qaddafi's Theory and Practice of Non-Representative Government," *Government and Opposition* 17, 1 (Winter), 61–78.

de Janvry, Alain (1981), *The Agrarian Question and Reformism in Latin America,* Baltimore, Johns Hopkins University Press.

Dekmejian, Hrair (1971), *Egypt Under Nasir: A Study in Political Dynamics,* Albany, N.Y., SUNY Press.

DERSA (1981), *L'Algérie en débat,* Paris, Maspéro.

Derviş, Kemal, and Robinson, Sherman (1980), "The Structure of Income Inequality in Turkey, 1950–1973," in Özbudun and Ulusan (1980), 83–122.

Destanne de Bernis, G. (1963), *Problèmes de l'Algérie indépendante,* Paris, Tiers Monde.

———— (1971), "Industries industrialisantes et options algériennes," *Tiers Monde,* No. 47, 545–63.

de Thier, Jean-Jacques (1987), "Agricultural Prices in Egypt: Issues, Policies and Perspectives," FAO (mimeo).

Deutsch, K., and Foltz, W., eds. (1966), *Nation-Building,* New York, Atherton Press.

Dib, M.A.M. el-, Ismail, S. M., and Gad, Osman (1984), "Economic Motivations and Impacts of External Migration of Agricultural Workers in an Egyptian Village," *Population Studies* 11, 68, 27–46 (in Arabic).

Din, Ajmed Safi el- (1983), "A Survey of the Sudanese Economy," in Awad (1983), 11–38.

Divine, Donna R. (1979), "Political Legitimacy in Israel: How Important is the State?" *IJMES,* No. 10.

Dixon, Ruth B. (1971), "Explaining Cross-Cultural Variations in Age at Marriage and Proportions Never Marrying," *Population Studies* 25, 2 (July), 215–33.

———— (1980), "Women in Agriculture: Counting the Labor Force in Developing Countries," *Population and Development Review* 8, 3 (Sept.), 539–66.

Djilas, Milovan (1957), *The New Class,* London, Thames and Hudson.

Doeringer, Peter, and Piore, Michael J. (1970), *Internal Labor Markets and Manpower Analysis,* Lexington, Mass: Heath, Lexington Books.

Drysdale, Alasdair (1982), "The Asad Regime and Its Troubles," *MERIP Reports,* No. 110 (Nov.-Dec.), 3–11.

Drysdale, Alasdair, and Blake, Gerald (1985), *The Middle East: A Political Geography,* London and New York, Oxford University Press.

Duchac, René, ed. (1973), *La formation des élites politiques maghrébines,* Paris, Librairie Générale de Droit et de Jurisprudence.

Duwidar, Muhammed (1980), *The Egyptian Economy between Backwardness and Evolution,* Dar al-Jama'at Alexandria (in Arabic).

Eckaus, R., McCarthy, D., and Mohie el-Din, A. (1978), "Multi-Sector General Equilibrium Policy Models for Egypt," Cairo University and Massachusetts Institute of Technology, mimeo.

Economic and Social Commission for Western Asia (1986), "Study on Impacts of Returning Migration in Selected Countries of the ECWA Region," DPDI/86/14, United Nations, March (in Arabic).

Economist Intelligence Unit (1987a), *Algeria,* London, The Economist, Ltd., No. 1.

———— (1987b), *Tunisia,* London, The Economist, Ltd., No. 1.

Edirisinghe, Nevelle (1987), *The Food Stamp Scheme in Sri Lanka: Costs, Benefits and Options for Modification,* Washington, D.C., IFPRI, Research Report No. 58.

Egyptian Ministry of Labor (1984), *Meeting on Organizational Structure of Egyptian Labor,* Cairo (Arabic).

Ehrlich, Paul (1968), *The Population Bomb,* New York, Ballantine.

Eickelman, D. F. (1981), *The Middle East: An Anthropological Approach,* Englewood, N.J., Prentice-Hall.

Emerson, Rupert (1960), *From Empire to Nation,* Boston, Beacon Press.

Entelis, John P. (1980), *Comparative Politics of North Africa,* Syracuse, N.Y., Syracuse University Press.

———— (1986), *Algeria: The Revolution Institutionalized,* Boulder, Colo., Westview Press.

Etienne, Bruno (1977), *L'Algérie: Cultures et Révolution,* Paris, Editions du Seuil.

FAO (1983), "Agricultural Price Policies in the Near East: Lessons and Experience," 16th FAO Regional Conference for the Near East, Aden, PDRY, 11–15 March.

―――― (1984), "Strategies for Agricultural Investment in the Near East," 17th FAO Regional Conference for the Near East, PDRY, 11–15 March.

―――― (1986), "World-Wide Estimates and Projections of the Agricultural and Non-Agricultural Population Segments, 1950–2025," Statistical Div., Economic and Social Policy Dept., Rome, Dec. *FAO Production Yearbook,* Rome, FAO, various years.

Farid, S. (1970), *Top Management in Egypt: Its Structure, Quality and Problems,* Santa Monica, Calif., Rand Corp.

Farques, Philippe (1982), "Présentation démographique des pays de la péninsule Arabique," in Bonnenfant (1982), 155–90.

Farsoun, Karen (1975), "State Capitalism in Algeria," *MERIP Reports,* No. 35, Feb.

Fathaly, Omar, and Palmer, Monte (1980), *Political Development and Social Change in Libya,* Lexington, Mass., Lexington Books.

Fattah, Zeki (1979), "Development and Structural Change in the Iraqi Economy and Manufacturial Industry: 1960–1970," *World Development* 7, 8, 813–23.

Fergany, Nader (1988), "Some Aspects of Return Migration in Egypt," Unpublished, April, typescript.

Fikry, Mona (1983), "Appendix C: Social Implications of the Wheat Development Program (Project Blé) for the Impact Evaluation (Tunisia)," in USAID (1983).

Findlay, Alan (1984), "Tunisia: the Vicissitudes of Economic Development," in Lawless and Findlay (1984), 217–40.

Findlay, Anne (1984), "The Moroccan Economy in the 1970s," in Lawless and Findlay (1984), 191–216.

First, Ruth (1974), *Libya: The Elusive Revolution,* Harmondsworth, UK, Penguin.

Fischer, Michael (1982), "Islam and the Revolt of the Petit Bourgeoisie," *Daedalus* 3, 1, 101–25.

Fitzgerald, E.V.K. (1977), "On State Accumulation in Latin America," in E.V.K. Fitzgerald et al., eds., *The State and Economic Development in Latin America,* Cambridge, Cambridge University Press.

―――― (1979), *The Political Economy of Peru,* London, Cambridge University Press.

Floyd, Robert H. (1984), "Some Topical Issues Concerning Public Enterprises," in Floyd, Gray, and Short (1984), 1–35.

Floyd, Robert, Gray, Clive S. and Short, R. P. (1984), *Public Enterprise in Mixed Economies: Some Macroeconomic Aspects,* Washington, D.C., IMF.

Fredriksen, P. C., and Looney, R. E. (1983), "Defense Expenditures and Economic Growth in Developing Countries," *Armed Forces and Society* 9, 4, 633–45.

Gabay, Rony (1978), *Communism and Agrarian Reform in Iraq,* London, Croom Helm.

Geertz, Clifford (1971), "In Search of North Africa," *New York Review of Books,* April 22, 10.

Gellner, E., and Micaud, C., eds. (1972), *Arabs and Berbers,* London, Duckworth.

Ghiles, Francis (1986), "Algeria Faces the Moment of Truth," *Financial Times,* April 9.

Ghonemy, M. Riad el- (1984), "Economic Growth, Income Distribution and Rural Poverty in the Near East," Rome, FAO.

Ghosh, Joyati (1984), "Urban Labour Markets," in *Labour Markets in the Sudan,* Geneva, ILO.

Ghun'aim, 'Adil (1968), "Concerning the Case of the New Class in Egypt," *al-Tali'a,* No. 4, 82–93 (in Arabic).

Gibb, H.A.R. (1960), "Politics and Prospects in the Arab Middle East," in Douglas Grant, ed., *The Islamic Near East,* Toronto, University of Toronto Press, 168–80.

Gillis, Malcolm, et al. (1987), *Economics of Development,* 2d ed., New York, Norton.

Glavanis, Pandeli (1984), "State and Labour in Libya," in Lawless and Findlay (1984), 120–49.

Gotheil, Fred (1981), "Iraqi and Syrian Socialism: An Economic Appraisal," *World Development* 9, 9/10 (Sept./Oct.), 825–38.

Griffin, James, and Teece, David J. (1982), *OPEC Behavior and World Oil Prices,* London, George Allen and Unwin.

Griffin, Keith (1974), *The Political Economy of Agrarian Change,* Cambridge, Mass., Harvard University Press.

Grindle, Merilee (1986), *State and Countryside: Development Policy and Agrarian Politics in Latin America,* Baltimore, Johns Hopkins University Press.

Gunter, Karl (1986), "The Informal Sector in the YAR," paper presented to the SSRC Conference on the Informal Sector in the Middle East, Tutzing, West Germany, July.

Gutmann, E., and Landau, J. (1985), "The Political Elite and National Leadership in Israel," in G. Lenczowski, ed., *Political Elites in the Middle East,* Washington, D.C., American Enterprise Institute (AEI), 163–200.

Hale, William (1981), *The Political and Economic Development of Modern Turkey,* London, Croom Helm.

Halliday, Fred (1979), *Iran: Dictatorship and Development,* Harmondsworth, UK, Penguin.

Halpern, Manfred (1963), *The Politics of Social Change in the Middle East and North Africa,* Princeton, Princeton Universtiy Press.

Handoussa, Heba (1986), "Speculation on the Industrial Public Sector in the Years of the Five Year Plan, 1987/88–1991/92," paper presented at the 11th Annual Conference of Egyptian Economists, Cairo (in Arabic).

———— (1988), "The Burden of Public Sector Employment and Remuneration: A Case Study of Egypt," Cairo, September, typescript (for the ILO).

Hannoyer, Jean (1980), "Le Monde Rural Avant les Reformes," in Raymond (1980).

———— (1985), "Grands projets hydrauliques en Syrie," *Maghreb-Machrek,* No. 109 (July-Sept.), 24–42.

Hannoyer, Jean, and Seurat, Michel (1979), *Etat et Secteur Public Industriel en Syrie,* Lyon, Centre des etudes et des recherches sur le Moyen Orient Contemporain (CERMOC), Presses Universitaires de Lyon.

Hansen, Bent (1985), "The Egyptian Labor Market: An Overview," World Bank Discussion Paper, Report No. DRD/60.

Hansen, Bent, and Nashashibi, Karim (1975), *Foreign Trade and Economic Development: Egypt,* New York, Columbia University Press for the National Bureau of Economic Research (NBER).

Hansen, Bent, and Radwan, Samir (1982), *Employment Opportunities and Equity in Egypt,* Geneva, ILO.

Harberger, A. C. (1971), "On Measuring the Social Opportunity Cost of Labor," *International Labor Review,* June.

Harik, Ilya (1974), *The Political Mobilization of Peasants: A Study of an Egyptian Community,* Bloomington, Indiana University Press.

Hassan, Ali-Mohamed el-, ed. (1976), *An Introduction to the Sudan Economy,* Khartoum, Khartoum University Press.

Helms, Christina (1981), *The Cohesion of Saudi Arabia,* Baltimore, Johns Hopkins University Press.

———— (1984), *Iraq: Eastern Flank of the Arab World,* Washington, D.C., Brookings Institution.

Hemphill, Paul (1979), "The Formation of the Iraqi Army: 1921–23," in Kelidar (1979), 88–110.

Heper, Metin (1985), *The State Tradition in Turkey,* London, Eothen Press.

Hermassi, Elbaki (1972), *Leadership and National Development in North Africa,* Berkeley, University of California Press.

Hershlag, Z. Y. (1968), *Turkey: The Challenge of Growth,* Leiden, E. J. Brill.

Hinnebusch, Raymond (1979), "Party and Peasant in Syria," *Cairo Papers in Social Science* 3, 1 (Nov.).

—— (1985), *Egyptian Politics under Sadat,* Cambridge, Cambridge University Press.

Hirschman, Albert (1963), *Journeys Toward Progress: Studies of Economic Policy-Making in Latin America,* New York, Twentieth Century Fund.

—— (1968), "The Political Economy of Import-Substituting Industrialization," *Quarterly Journal of Economics* 82, 1–32.

Hodgkin, Thomas (1980), "The Revolutionary Tradition in Islam," *Race and Class* 21, 3, 221–37.

Hodgson, Marshall G.S. (1974a), *The Venture of Islam,* Vol. 2: *The Expansion of Islam in the Middle Period,* Chicago, University of Chicago Press.

—— (1974b), *The Venture of Islam,* Vol.3: *The Gunpowder Empire and Modern Times,* Chicago, University of Chicago Press.

Hooglund, Eric (1980), "Rural Participation in the Revolution," *MERIP Reports,* No. 87 (May), 3–6.

—— (1982), *Land and Revolution in Iran: 1960–1980,* Austin, University of Texas Press.

—— (1987), "Iran and the Gulf War," *MERIP Reports,* No. 148 (Sept.-Oct.), 11–18.

Hopkins, Nicholas (1977), "The Emergence of Class in a Tunisian Town," *IJMES* 8, 453–91.

—— (1983), "Social Aspects of Mechanization," in Richards and Martin (1983), 181-98.

Horne, Alistair (1978), *A Savage War of Peace: Algeria 1954-62,* New York, Viking.

Hudson, Michael (1968), *The Precarious Republic: Modernization in Lebanon,* New York, Random House.

—— (1977), *Arab Politics,* New Haven, Yale University Press.

—— (1983), "The Islamic Factor in Syrian and Iraqi Politics," in Piscatori (1983), 73–97.

Huntington, Samuel (1968), *Political Order in Changing Societies,* New Haven, Yale University Press.

Hussein, 'Adil (1977), *The Bureaucratic Bourgeoisie: Between the Marxist Understanding and Marxising Slogans,* Beirut (in Arabic).

—— (1982), *The Egyptian Economy from Independence to Dependency: 1974-1979,* 2 vols., Cairo, Dar al-Mustaqbal al-'Arabi (in Arabic).

Hussein, Mahmoud (1971), *La lutte de classes en Egypte, 1945-70,* Paris, Maspéro.

Huvespian, Nubar, et al. (1985), *Turkey: Between the Bureaucratic Elite and Military Rule,* Beirut, Arab Studies Foundation (in Arabic).

Ibrahim, Fouad N. (1984), *Ecological Imbalance in the Republic of the Sudan—with Reference to Desertification in Darfur,* Bayreuth: Druckhaus Bayreuth Verlagsgesellschaft.

Ibrahim, Ibrahim, ed. (1983), *Arab Resources,* London, Croom Helm, for the Center for Contemporary Arab Studies, Washington, D.C.

Ibrahim, Saad Eddin (1980), "Anatomy of Egypt's Militant Islamic Groups: Methodological Note and Preliminary Findings," *IJMES* 12, 4, 423–53.

———— (1982a), *The New Arab Social Order*, London, Croom Helm.

———— (1982b), "Social Mobility and Income Distribution in Egypt, 1952–77," in Abdel-Khaleq and Tignor (1982), 375–434.

ICARDA (1979), *An Introduction to Agriculture Within the Syrian Economy*, Aleppo, ICARDA.

IFAD (International Fund for Agricultural Development).(1985), *Report of the Special Programming Mission to the P.D.R.Y.*, Rome, IFAD.

———— (1987), *Report of the Special Programming Mission of IFAD to the Republic of Sudan*, Rome.

IFID (1987), *Balance des Paiements et Mécanismes d'Ajustement dans les Pays du Maghreb*, Tunis.

Ikram, Khalid (1980), *Egypt: Economic Management in a Period of Transition*, Baltimore, Johns Hopkins Press.

Ilchman, W. F., and Uphoff, N. T. (1969), *The Political Economy of Change*, Berkeley, University of California Press.

ILO, Republic of Sudan (1985), *After the Famine: A Programme of Action to Strengthen the Survival Strategies of Affected Populations*, Geneva, ILO.

IMF (1987), *International Financial Statistics*, Washington, D.C., IMF.

International Institute for Environment and Development, *World Resources, 1986*, New York, Basic Books.

Islami, A. Reza, and Kavoussi, R. M. (1984), *The Political Economy of Saudi Arabia*, Near Eastern Studies, No. 1, University of Washington, Seattle.

Islamoğlu, Huri Inan, and Keyder, Çağlar (1977), "Agenda for Ottoman History," *Review* 1, Summer, 31–55.

Ismael, Tareq, ed. (1970), *Governments and Politics of the Contemporary Middle East*, Homewood, Ill., Dorsey Press.

Issa, Shakir M. (1979), "The Distribution of Income in Iraq, 1971," in Kelidar (1979), 123–34.

Issawi, Charles (1956), "Economic and Social Foundations of Democracy in the Middle East," *International Affairs*, Jan., 27–42.

———— (1963), *Egypt in Revolution*, Oxford, Oxford University Press.

———— (1969), "Economic Change and Urbanization in the Middle East," in Ira M. Lapidus, ed., *Middle Eastern Cities*, Berkeley, University of California Press, 102–21.

———— (1978), "The Iranian Economy 1925–1975: Fifty Years of Economic Development," in G. Lenczowski, ed., *Iran Under the Pahlevis*, Stanford, Calif., Hoover Institution, 129–66.

———— (1982), *An Economic History of the Middle East and North Africa*, New York, Columbia University Press.

Jaubert, Ronald (1983), "Sedentary Agriculture in the Drier Areas of Syria: Development Problems and Implications for ICARDA," Aleppo, ICARDA, Feb.

Johnson, Paul (1988), "The Impact of the Islamic Revolution on the State/Private Sector Symbiosis," SSRC (mimeo).

Johnston, Bruce, and Kilby, Peter (1975), *Agriculture and Structural Transformation: Economic Strategies in Late-Developing Countries*, New York, Oxford University Press.

Johnston, Bruce, and Mellor, John W. (1961), "The Role of Agriculture in Economic Development," *American Economic Review* 51, Sept., 566–93.

Jones, Leroy P. (1975), *Public Enterprise and Economic Development: The Korean Case,* Seoul, Korea Development Institute.

――――, ed. (1982), *Public Enterprise in Less-Developed Countries,* New York, Cambridge University Press.

Kalecki, Michael (1972), *Selected Essays on the Economic Growth of the Socialist and the Mixed Economy,* Cambridge, Cambridge University Press, 1972.

――――(1976), "Observations on Social and Economic Aspects of Intermediate Regimes," *Essays in Developing Economies,* Atlantic Highlands, N.J., Humanities Press, 30–37.

Karaspan, Omer (1987), "Turkey's Armaments Industries," *MERIP Reports,* Jan.-Feb., 27–31.

Karpat, Kemal (1959), *Turkey's Politics,* Princeton, Princeton University Press.

――――(1976), *The Gecekondu: Rural Migration and Urbanization,* Cambridge, Cambridge University Press.

Kasfir, Nelson (1979), "Explaining Ethnic Political Participation," *World Politics* 31, 3, 365–88.

Katanani, Ahmad K. (1981), "Economic Alternatives to Migration," paper presented to the Conference on International Migration in the Arab World, United Nations Economic Commission for West Africa (UNECWA), Nicosia, Cyprus, May.

Katouzian, Homa (1981), *The Political Economy of Modern Iran: Despotism and Pseudo-Modernism, 1926–79,* New York, New York University Press.

Kavalsky, Basil (1980), "Poverty and Human Development in the Middle East and North Africa," in *Poverty and the Development of Human Resources: Regional Perspectives,* World Bank Staff Working Papers, No. 406.

Kazancigil, Ali, and Özbudun, Ergun, eds. (1981), *Atatürk: Founder of a Modern State,* Hamden, Conn., Archon Books.

Kazemi, F., and Abrahamian, E. (1978), "The Non-Revolutionary Peasantry of Modern Iran," *Iranian Studies* 11, 259–308.

Kazemi, Farhad (1980a), *Poverty and Revolution in Iran: The Migrant Poor, Urban Marginality and Politics,* New York, New York University Press.

――――(1980b), "Urban Migrants and the Revolution," *Iranian Studies* 13, 1–4, 257–78.

Keddie, Nikki R. (1981), *Roots of Revolution: An Interpretive History of Modern Iran,* New Haven, Yale University Press.

Keilany, Z. (1973), "Socialism and Economic Change in Syria," *Middle Eastern Studies,* 11, January.

――――(1980), "Land Reform in Syria," *Middle Eastern Studies,* Oct.

Kelidar, Abbas, ed. (1979), *The Integration of Modern Iraq,* London, Croom Helm.

Kelley, Allen C., Khalifa, Atef M., and El-Khorazaty, M. Nabil (1982), *Population and Development in Rural Egypt,* Durham, N.C., Duke University Press.

Kelley, C., and Williamson, Jeffrey (1984a), "Population Growth, Industrial Revolutions, and the Urban Transition," *Population and Development Review* 10, 3 (Sept.).

――――(1984b), *What Drives Third World City Growth?,* Princeton, Princeton University Press.

Kenz, Ali el- (1987), *Le complexe sidérurgique d'El-Hadjar,* Paris, Editions CNRS.

Kepel, Gilles (1986), *Muslim Extremism in Egypt: The Prophet and the Pharoah,* Berkeley, University of California Press.

Kerr, Malcolm (1963), "Arab Radical Notions of Democracy," St. Anthony's Papers, No. 16.

———— (1965), "Egypt," in James Coleman, ed., *Education and Political Development*, Princeton, N.J., Princeton University Press, 169–94.

Kerr, Malcolm, and Yassin, Sayed el-, eds. (1982), *Rich and Poor States in the Middle East*, Boulder, Colo., Westview Press/American University in Cairo.

Kerwin, Robert (1951), "Private Enterprise in Turkish Industrial Development," *MEJ* 5, Winter, 23–38.

———— (1959), "Etatism in Turkey; 1933–50," in Hugh Aitken, ed., *The State and Economic Growth*, New York, Social Science Research Council.

Keyder, Çağlar (1979), "The Political Economy of Turkish Democracy," *New Left Review*, No. 115 (May-June), 3–45.

———— (1987), *State and Class in Turkey: A Study in Capitalist Development*, London, New York, Verso.

Khadduri, Majid (1963), *Modern Libya: A Study in Political Development*, Baltimore, Johns Hopkins University Press.

Khader, Bichara, and Badran, Adnan, eds. (1987), *The Economic Development of Jordan*, London, Croom Helm.

Khafaji, 'Issam al- (1983), *The State and the Evolution of Capitalism in Iraq: 1968–1978*, Cairo, Dar al-Mustaqbal al-Arabi (in Arabic).

Khalaf, Samir (1987), *Lebanon's Predicament*, New York, Columbia University Press.

Khaldi, Nabil (1984), *Evolving Food Gaps in the Middle East/North Africa: Prospects and Policy Implications*, Washington, D.C., IFPRI, Research Report No.47.

Khalid, Mansour (1985), *Nimeiri and the Revolution of Dis-May*, London, KPI Press.

Khoury, Philip (1983a), "Islamic Revival and the Crisis of the Secular State in the Arab World: an Historical Appraisal," in Ibrahim (1983), 213–36.

———— (1983b), *Urban Notables and Arab Nationalism, The Politics of Damascus 1860–1920*, New York, Columbia University Press.

Kienle, Eberhard (1985), "The Conflict between the Baath Regimes of Syria and Iraq prior to their Consolidation," Ethnizität and Gesellschaft Occasional Paper, No. 5, Berlin, Free University.

Kimmerling, Baruch (1983), *Zionism and Economy*, Cambridge, Mass., Schenkman Pub. Co.

King, Russell (1977), *Land Reform, A World Survey*, London, G. Bell and Sons, Ltd.

Koo, Hagen (1984), "The Political Economy of Income Distribution in South Korea," *World Development* 12, 10, 1029–37.

Kopits, George (1987), *Structural Reform, Stabilization and Growth in Turkey*, Washington, D.C., IMF.

Kravis, Irving, Heston, Alan, and Summers, Robert (1978), *International Comparisons of Real Product and Purchasing Power*, Baltimore, Johns Hopkins University Press.

Krishna, Raj (1982), "Some Aspects of Agricultural Growth, Price Policy and Equity," *Food Research Institute Studies* 18, 3, 1–43.

Krueger, Anne (1974), *Foreign Trade Regimes and Economic Development: Turkey*, New York, National Bureau of Economic Research (NBER).

Kubursi, Afif (1984), *Oil, Industrialization and Development in the Arab Gulf States*, London, Croom Helm.

Kuran, Timur (1980), "Internal Migration: The Unorganized Urban Sector and Income Distribution in Turkey, 1963–73," in Özbudun and Ulusan (1980), 349–78.

Kuznets, Simon (1966), *Modern Economic Growth: Rate, Structure and Spread*, New Haven, Yale University Press.

"Labour Immigration in the Gulf States: Patterns, Trends, and Prospects," in *Quarterly Review of the Intergovernmental Committee for Migration* (1986), Jan.

Lackner, Helen (1978), *A House Built on Sand: A Political Economy of Saudi Arabia,* London, Ithaca Press.

Lal, Deepak (1987), "The Political Economy of Economic Liberalization," *World Bank Economic Review* 1, 2 (Jan.), 273–300.

Landes, David (1958), *Bankers and Pashas,* Cambridge, Harvard University Press.

Langley, K. (1961), *The Industrialization of Iraq,* Cambridge, Harvard University Press.

La Palombara, J., and Weiner, M. (1966), *Political Parties and Political Development,* Princeton, Princeton University Press.

Lapham, R. J. (1983), "Background Notes and Illustrative Tables on Populations in the Middle East," for Conference on Population and Political Stability in the NESA Region March 1983, Washington, D.C.

Launay, Michel (1963), *Paysans Algériens: la Terre, la Vigne, et les Hommes,* Paris, Editions du Seuil.

Lawless, R., and Findlay, A., eds. (1984), *North Africa: Contemporary Politics and Economic Development,* London, Croom Helm.

Lawless, Richard (1984), "Algeria: The Contradictions of Rapid Industrialization," in Lawless and Findlay (1984), 153–90.

Lawson, F. H. (1985), "Social Origins of Inflation in Contemporary Egypt," *Arab Studies Quarterly* 7, 1, 36–57.

Lazreg, Marnia (1976a), "Bureaucracy and Class: the Algerian Dialectic," *Dialectical Anthropology* 1, 4 (Sept.), 295–305.

——— (1976b), *The Emergence of Classes in Algeria,* Boulder, Colo., Westview Press.

Leca, Jean (1975), "Algerian Socialism: Nationalism, Industrialization and State-building," in Helen Desfosses and Jacques Levesque, eds., *Socialism in the Third World,* New York, Praeger.

——— (1986), "Social Structure and Political Stability: Comparative Evidence from the Algerian, Syrian and Iraqi Cases," Paris, Presses de la Fondation Nationale des Sciences Politiques (FNSP) (photocopy).

Leca, Jean, and Grimaud, Nicole (1986), "Le secteur privé en Algérie," *Maghreb-Machrek,* No. 113 (July-Sept.), 102–19.

Leca, Jean, and Vatin, J.-C. (1975), *L'Algérie politique, institutions et régime,* Paris, Presses de la Fondation Nationale des Sciences Politiques (FNSP).

Lerner, Daniel (1959), *The Passing of Traditional Society,* Glencoe, Ill., The Free Press.

Lesch, Ann Mosely (1985), "Egyptian Labor Migration: Economic Trends and Government Policies," *UFSI Reports,* No. 38.

——— (1986), "Party Politics in the Sudan," *UFSI Reports,* Africa Series, No. 9.

Leveau, Rémy (1985), *Le Fellah marocain: défenseur du trone,* Paris, Presses de la Fondation Nationale des Sciences Politiques.

Lewis, Bernard (1961), *The Emergence of Modern Turkey,* Oxford, Oxford University Press.

Lewis, W. Arthur (1954), "Economic Development with Unlimited Supplies of Labour," *Manchester School of Economic and Social Studies* 22, 139–91.

Lipton, Michael (1977), *Why Poor People Stay Poor: Urban Bias in World Development,* Cambridge, Harvard University Press.

Little, Arthur D. (1978), *An Assessment of Egypt's Industrial Sector,* Report to Interagency Task Force Reviewing Assistance to Egypt, Boston, Jan.

Little, I.M.D., Scitovsky, Tibor, and Scott, Maurice (1970), *Industry and Trade in Some Developing Countries,* London, Oxford University Press.

Longuenesse, Elisabeth (1978), "Bourgeoisie, Petite-Bourgeoisie et Couches Moyennes en Syrie," *Peuples Méditerranéens,* No. 4 (July-Sept.), 21–43.

——— (1979), "The Class Nature of the State in Syria," *MERIP Reports* 9, 4, (May), 3–11.

——— (1985a), "The Syrian Working Class Today," *MERIP Reports* 15, 6 (July-Aug.), 17–25.

——— (1985b), "Syrie, secteur public industriel," *Maghreb-Machrek,* No. 109 (July-Sept.), 5–24.

McClelland, David (1963), "National Character and Economic Growth in Turkey and Iran," in Lucian Pye, ed., *Communications and Political Development,* Princeton, Princeton University Press, 152–81.

McLachlan, Keith (1979), "Iraq: Problems of Regional Development," in Kelidar (1979), 135–49.

Mahfouz, Afaf (1972), *Socialisme et Pouvoir en Egypte,* Paris, Librairie Générale de Droit.

Mahmoud, Fatima Babika (1984), *The Sudanese Bourgeoisie: Vanguard of Development?* London, Khartoum University Press/Zed Press.

Majd, Mohammad G. (1987), "Land Reform Policies in Iran," *American Journal of Agricultural Economics* 69, 4 (Nov.), 843–48.

Malki, Habib el- (1980), "Capitalisme d'Etat, Développement de la bourgeoisie et problématique de la transition—le cas du Maroc," *Revue juridique, politique et économique du Maroc,* No. 8, 207–28.

——— (1982), *L'économie marocaine: bilan d'une décennie, 1970–1980,* Paris, Editions CNRS.

Mamdani, Mahmood (1972), *The Myth of Population Control: Family Caste and Class in an Indian Village,* New York, Monthly Review Press.

Mann, Charles K. (1980), "The Effects of Government Policy on Income Distribution: A Case Study of Wheat Production in Turkey since World War II," in Özbudun and Ulusan (1980), 197–246.

Margulies, Ronnie, and Yildizoğlu, Ergin (1984), "Trade Unions and Turkey's Working Class," *MERIP Reports,* February, 15–30, 31.

Marshall, S. E., and Stokes, R. G. (1981), "Tradition and the Veil: Female Status in Tunisia and Algeria," *Journal of Modern African Studies* 19, 4, 625–46.

Mazur, Michael P. (1979), *Economic Growth and Development in Jordan,* Boulder, Colo., Westview Press.

Meillasoux, Claude (1981), *Maidens, Meal, and Money,* Cambridge, Cambridge University Press.

Mellor, John (1976), *The New Economics of Growth: A Strategy for India and the Developing World,* Ithaca, Cornell University Press.

——— (1983), "Food Prospects for the Developing Countries," *American Economic Review* 73, 2, 239–43.

Mernissi, Fatima (1987), *Beyond the Veil,* Bloomington, Indiana University Press.

Mesmoudi, Tahar el- (1982), *Le Crédit agricole et le développement de l'agriculture au Maroc,* Rabat, Société des Editeurs Réunis.

Métral, F. (1984), "State and Peasants in Syria," *Peasant Studies* 11, 2 (Winter).

——— (1985), "Etat et paysans dans le Ghab en Syrie," *Maghreb-Machrek,* No. 109 (July-Sept.), 43–63.

Métral, François (1980), "Le Monde Rural Syrien à l'ère des réformes," in Raymond (1980), 297–326.

Meyer, Gunter (1986), "The Impact of Migration and Social Co-operation on the Development of the Informal Sector in the Urban Centers of the YAR," paper presented to the SSRC Conference on the Informal Sector in the Middle East, Tutzing, West Germany, July.

Michel, Hubert (1973), "Algérie," in Duchac (1973).

Midaoui, Ahmed el- (1981), *Les entreprises publiques au Maroc et leur participation au développement*, Casablanca, Editions Afrique-Orient.

Migdal, Joel (1977), "Urbanization and Political Change: The Impact of Foreign Rule," *Comparative Studies in Society and History* 19, July, 328–49.

―――― (1987), "Strong States, Weak States: Power and Accomodation," in M. Weiner and S. P. Huntington, eds., *Understanding Political Development*, Boston, Little, Brown, 391–436.

Moghadem, Fatemeh Etemad (1982), "Farm Size, Management and Productivity: A Study of Four Iranian Villages," *Oxford Bulletin of Economics and Statistics* 44, 4 (Nov.), 357–79.

Mohie el-Din, Amr (1982), *Income Distribution and Basic Needs in Urban Egypt*, Cairo Papers in Social Science, Vol. 5, Monog. 3, Nov.

Mohie el-Din, Amr, and Ibrahim, Saad-Eddin (1981), "State Socialism and Economic Growth," in Saad Eddin Ibrahim,ed., *Egypt in the Quarter Century, 1952–1977*, Beirut, 302–34 (in Arabic).

Moore, Barrington (1967), *Social Origins of Dictatorship and Democracy*, London, Allen Lane/Penguin Press.

Moore, C. H. (1965), *Tunisia since Independence*, Berkeley, University of California Press.

―――― (1970), *Politics in North Africa*, Boston, Little, Brown.

―――― (1977), "Clientelist Ideology and Political Change: Fictitious Networks in Egypt and Tunisia," in Ernest Gellner and John Waterbury, eds., *Patrons and Clients in Mediterranean Societies*, London, Duckworth, 255–74.

―――― (1980), *Images of Development: Egyptian Engineers in Search of Industry*, Cambridge, MIT Press.

―――― (1985), "Egyptian Financial Infitah: Toward a Privatized Arab Order?" paper presented at MESA, Nov. 22–25, New Orleans.

Moore, C. H., and Hochschild, A. (1968), "Student Unions in North African Politics," *Daedalus* 97, 1, 21–50.

Mosk, Carl (1983) *Patriarchy and Fertility: Japan and Sweden, 1880–1960*, New York, Academic Press.

Mosley, Leonard (1974), *Power Play: Oil in the Middle East*, London, Penguin.

Mubarrak, Husni (1987), "Charter for National Action in the Second Presidency," *al-Ahram al-Iqtisadi*, Oct. 19 (in Arabic).

Mullen, T. W. (1984), "Will Saddam Outlast the Iran-Iraq War?" *Middle East Insight* 3, 4, 30–37.

Mumcuoğlu, Maksut (1980), "Political Activities of Trade Unions and Income Distribution," in Özbudun and Ulusan (1980), 379–408.

Mu'nis, Hussain (1984), *Pashas and Super Pashas*, Cairo, al-Zahra lil 'Allam al Arabi (in Arabic).

Mursi, Fu'ad (1976), *This Is the Economic Open-Door Policy*, Cairo, Dar al-Thiqafa (in Arabic).

Mutin, G. (1980), "Agriculture et dépendance alimentaire en Algérie," *Maghreb-Machrek*, No. 90.

Myint, Hla (1959), "The 'Classical Theory' of International Trade and the Under-developed Countries," *Economic Journal* 68, 2, 317–37.

Mynti, Cynthia (1985), "Women, Work, Population and Development in YAR," in Julinda Abunasr, Nabil F. Khoury, and Henry T. Ayyam, eds., *Women, Employment and Development in the Arab World,* Berlin, Mouton.

Najmabadi, Afsaneh (1987), *Land Reform and Social Change in Iran,* Salt Lake City, University of Utah Press.

Nasr, Salim (1981), "Les travailleurs de l'industrie manufacturière au Machrek," *Maghreb-Machrek,* No. 92 (April, May, June), 7–24.

———— (1985), "Roots of the Shi'i Movement," *MERIP Reports,* June, 10–16.

National Academy of Sciences (1982a), *The Estimation of Recent Trends in Fertility and Mortality in Egypt,* Washington, D.C., National Academy Press.

———— (1982b), *Trends in Fertility and Mortality in Turkey, 1935–1975,* Washington, D.C., National Academy Press.

National Research Council (1986), *Population Growth and Economic Development: Policy Questions,* Washington, D.C., National Academy Press.

Nattagh, Nina (1986), *Agricultural and Regional Development in Iran, 1962–1978,* Cambridgeshire, Middle East and North African Studies Press, Ltd.

Nellis, John (1977), "Socialist Management in Algeria," *Journal of Modern African Studies* 15, 4, 529–44.

———— (1980a), "Algerian Socialism and its Critics," *Canadian Journal of Political Science,* 13, 2 (Sept.), 481–507.

———— (1980b), "Maladministration: Cause or Result of Underdevelopment?: The Algerian Example," *Canadian Journal of African Studies* 13, 3, 407–22.

———— (1983), "A Comparative Assessment of the Development Performances of Algeria and Tunisia," *MEJ* 37, 3, 370–93.

Nelson, Harold D., ed. (1979), *Tunisia: A Country Study,* Washington, D.C., Area Handbook Series, American University Press.

————, ed. (1985a), *Algeria: A Country Study,* Washington D.C., Area Handbook Series, American University Press.

————, ed. (1985b), *Morocco: A Country Study,* Washington, D.C., Area Handbook Series, American University Press.

Nelson, Joan (1979), *Access to Power: Politics and the Urban Poor in Developing Nations,* Princeton, N.J., Princeton University Press.

———— (1984), "The Political Economy of Stabilization Commitment, Capacity and Public Response," *World Development* 12, 10, 983–1006.

———— (1985), "Short-Run Public Reactions to Food Subsidy Cuts in Selected Sub-Saharan and North African Countries," Washington, D.C., USAID.

Nerfin, Marc (1974), *Entretiens avec Ahmed Ben Salah,* Paris, Maspéro.

Nettl, J. P. (1968), "The State as a Conceptual Variable," *World Politics* 20, July, 559–92.

Niblock, Tim, ed. (1982a), *Iraq: The Contemporary State,* London, Croom Helm.

————, ed. (1982b), *State, Society and Economy in Saudi Arabia,* London, Croom Helm.

Nimeiri, Sayed (1976), "Industry in the Sudan," in Ali Mohamed el-Hassan (1976), 76–101.

North, Douglas, and Thomas, Robert (1980), *The Rise of the Western World: A New Economic History,* Cambridge, Cambridge University Press.

Nouschi, André (1970), "North Africa in the Period of Colonization," *Cambridge History of Islam,* Vol.1: *The Further Islamic Lands—Islamic Society and Civilization,* Cambridge, Cambridge University Press, 299–326.

Nove, Alec (1969), *An Economic History of the U.S.S.R.,* New York, Penguin.

Nowshirvani, Vahid (1987), "The Yellow Brick Rood: Self-Sufficiency or Self-Enrichment in Saudi Agriculture?" *MERIP Reports* 17, 2 (March-April).

Nyrop, Richard F., ed. (1982), *Egypt: A Country Study,* Washington D.C., Area Handbook Series, American University Press.

O'Brien, Patrick (1966), *The Revolution in Egypt's Economic System,* New York, Oxford University Press.

_____ (1985), "Sowing the Seeds of Famine: The Political Economy of Food Deficits in the Sudan," *Review of African Political Economy* 33, 23–32.

O'Donnell, Guillermo (1978), "Reflections on the Patterns of Change in the Bureaucratic-Authoritarian State," *Latin American Research Review* 12, 1, 3–38.

Olson, Robert W. (1982), *The Ba'th and Syria, 1947–1982,* Princeton, N.J., Kingston Press Inc.

Öncü, Ayşe (1980), "Chambers of Industry in Turkey: An Inquiry into State-Industry Relations as a Distributive Domain," in Özbudun and Ulusan (1980), 455–63.

Ouhichi K., and Riad, A. (1984), "Armées et armements au Maghreb," *Grand Maghreb,* No. 30 (April), 39–41; No. 31 (June), 39–42.

Owen, Roger (1981), *The Middle East in the World Economy, 1800–1914,* London, New York, Methuen.

_____ (1985), *Migrant Workers in the Gulf,* London, Minority Rights Group Report, No.68, Sept.

_____ (1986), "Large Landowners, Agricultural Progress and the State in Egypt, 1800–1970: An Overview," in Richards (1986b), 69–96.

Özbudun, Ergun (1981), "The Nature of the Kemalist Political Regime" in Kazancigil and Özbudun (1981), 79–102.

Özbudun, Ergun, and Ulusan, Aydin (1980), *The Political Economy of Income Distribution in Turkey,* New York, Holmes and Meier.

Özgediz, Selçuk (1980), "Education and Income Distribution in Turkey," in Özbudun and Ulusan (1980), 501–24.

Palloix, C. (1980), "Le financement de l'industrialization," *Tiers Monde* 21, 83 (July-Sept).

Pamuk, Şevket (1981), "Political Economy of Industrialization in Turkey," *MERIP Reports,* No. 93 (Jan.), 26–30.

Paulino, Leonardo (1986), *Food in the Third World: Past Trends and Projections to 2000,* IFPRI, Research Report No. 52 (June).

Peneff, Jean (1981), *Industriels Algériens,* Centre des recherches et des études sur les sociétés mediterranéen (CRESM), CNRS, Paris.

Penrose, Edith, and Penrose, E. F. (1978), *Iraq: International Relations and National Development,* Boulder, Colo., Ernest Benn/Westview Press.

Peretz, Don (1988), *The Middle East Today, 5th ed.* New York, Praeger.

Pfeifer, Karen (1985), *Agrarian Reform Under State Capitalism in Algeria,* Boulder, Colo., Westview Press.

Picard, E. (1981), "Clivages et consensus au sein du commandement militaire Baathists Syrien (1970–79)," in Alain Rouquie, ed., *La politique de Mars,* Paris, Le Sycomore, 198–219.

Piscatori, James, ed. (1983), *Islam in the Political Process,* Cambridge, Cambridge University Press.

Presidency of Egypt, National Specialized Committees, National Committee for Production and Economic Affairs (1980), *The Public Sector: Its Obstacles and Evolution,* Cairo.

Psacharopoulos, G. (1980), "Returns to Education: An Updated International Comparison," in *Education and Income,* World Bank Staff Working Papers, No. 402, 75–109.

Quandt, William B. (1969), *Revolution and Political Leadership: Algeria, 1954–1968*, Cambridge, MIT Press.

_____ (1981), *Saudi Arabia in the 1980's: Foreign Policy, Security, and Oil*, Washington, D.C., The Brookings Institution.

Rabinovich, I., and Reinharz J., eds. (1984), *Israel in the Middle East*, Oxford and New York, Oxford University Press.

Radwan, S., and Lee, E. (1986), *Agrarian Change in Egypt: An Anatomy of Rural Poverty*, London, Croom Helm.

Radwan, Samir (1977), *Agrarian Reform and Rural Poverty: Egypt, 1952–1975*, Geneva, ILO.

Raffinot, Marc, and Jacquemot, Pierre (1977), *Le capitalisme d'état algérien*, Paris, Maspéro.

Ranis, Gustav (1984), "Growth and Equity in Development: An Overview," in Allen Maunder and Kazushi Ohkawa, eds., *Growth and Equity in Agricultural Development*, Oxford, Gower.

Rawls, John (1971), *A Theory of Justice*, Cambridge, Harvard University Press.

Raymond, A., ed. (1980), *La Syrie d'aujourd'hui*, Paris, CNRS.

Razavi, H., and Vakil, F. (1984), *The Political Environment of Economic Planning in Iran, 1971–1983*, Boulder, Colo., Westview Press.

Reich, B., and Long, D., eds. (1986), *The Government and Politics of the Middle East and North Africa*, Boulder, Colo., Westview Press.

Reutlinger, Shlomo, and Selowsky, Marcelo (1976), *Malnutrition and Poverty: Magnitude and Policy Options*, World Bank Staff Occasional Paper No. 23, Baltimore, Md., Johns Hopkins University Press.

Reynolds, Lloyd G. (1985), *Economic Growth in the Third World, 1950–1980*, New Haven, Yale University Press.

Riad, Hassan (1964), *L'Egypte Nassérienne*, Paris, Editions de Minuit.

Richards, Alan (1982), *Egypt's Agricultural Development, 1800–1980: Technical and Social Change*, Boulder, Colo., Westview Press.

_____ (1986a), *Development and Modes of Production in Marxist Economics: A Critical Evaluation*, Chur and New York, Harwood Academic Publishers.

_____ ed. (1986b), *Food States and Peasants: Analyses of the Agrarian Question in the Middle East*, Boulder, Colo., Westview Press.

_____ (1987), "Routes to Low Mortality in Low-Income Countries: Comment," UCSC (University of California, Santa Cruz) Applied Economics Working Paper No.43.

Richards, Alan, and Martin, Philip, eds. (1983), *Migration, Mechanization and Agricultural Labor Markets in Egypt*, Boulder, Colo. and Cairo, Westview Press/American University at Cairo.

Rivier, Francois (1980), *Croissance industrielle dans une économie assistée: le cas Jordanien*, Lyon, CERMOC, Presses Universitaires de Lyon.

_____ (1981), "Politiques industrielles en Egypte," *Maghreb-Machrek*, No. 92, April-June.

Rivlin, Paul (1985), *The Dynamics of Economic Policy Making in Egypt*, New York, Praeger.

Roberts, Hugh (1982), "The Unforeseen Development of the Kabyle Question in Contemporary Algeria," *Government and Opposition* 17, 3, 312–34.

_____ (1983), "The Economics of Berberism: The Kabyle Question in Contemporary Algeria," *Government and Opposition* 18, 2, 218–35.

_____ (1984), "The Politics of Algerian Socialism," in Lawless and Findlay (1984), 5–49.

Roos, Leslie, and Roos, Noralou (1971), *Managers of Modernization: Organization and Elites in Turkey (1950–1969)*, Cambridge, Harvard University Press.

Rosenfeld, H., and Carmi, S. (1976), "The Privatization of Public Means, the State-Made Middle Class, and the Realization of Family Value in Israel," in J. G. Peristiany, ed., *Kinship and Modernization in Mediterranean Society*, Rome, American Universities Field Staff, 131–53.

Roy, Delwin (1975), "Development Administration in the Middle East," *International Review of Administration Sciences* 41, 2.

——— (1980), "An Examination of Legal Instrumentalism in Public Enterprise Development in the Middle East," *Georgia Journal of International and Comparative Law* 10, 2 (Summer), 271–300.

Rugh, William (1973), "The Emergence of a New Middle Class in Saudi Arabia," *MEJ* 27, 1, 7–20.

Rustow, Dankwart A., and Mugno, John F. (1976), *OPEC: Success and Prospects*, New York, New York University Press.

Ruttan, Vernon (1977), "The Green Revolution: Seven Generalizations," *International Development Review* 19, 4, 16–23.

Saab, Edward (1968), *La Syrie ou la révolution dans la rancoeur*, Paris, Julliard.

Sabri-Abdalla, Ismail, et al. (1983), *Images of the Arab Future*, New York, St. Martin's Press.

Sader, Makram (1981), "Le développement industriel de l'Irak," *Maghreb-Machrek*, No. 92, April-June.

Sadowski, Yahya (1985), "Cadres, Guns and Money: The Eighth Regional Congress of the Syrian Ba'th," *MERIP Reports*, No. 134 (July-Aug.), 3–8.

Said, Rifa'at (1979), *Nasserist Expectations, Dar al-Tali'a*, Cairo, Dar al-Tali'a (in Arabic).

Sa'id, Samia (1985), "The Social Origins of the Elite of the Economic Open-Door in Egyptian Society, 1974–80," MA Thesis, Faculty of Economics and Political Science, Cairo Univ. (in Arabic).

——— (1986), *Who Owns Egypt? An Analytic Study of the Social Origins of the Economic Open-Door Elite in Egyptian Society*, Dar al-Mustaqbal al-Arabi, Cairo (in Arabic).

Said-Amer (1978), *L'industrialization en Algérie*, Paris, Editions Anthropos, 59.

Salmanyadeh, Cyrus (1980), *Agricultural Change and Rural Society in Southern Iran*, Cambridge, UK, Middle East and North African Studies Press.

Samān, Ahmad Hamdullah al- (1985), "Those who gained and those who lost from infitah," *al-Ahram al-Iqtisadi*, No. 871, 34–35 (in Arabic).

Sampson, Anthony (1975), *The Seven Sisters: The Great Oil Companies and the World They Shaped*, New York, Bantam Books.

Santucci, J. C. (1983), "Le plan quinquennal marocain: 1981–85," *Grand Maghreb*, No. 22 (June), 40–44.

Schmitter, P. C. (1974), "Still the Century of Corporatism?" *Review of Politics* 36, 85–132.

Schneider, Steven A. (1983), *The Oil Price Revolution*, Baltimore, Johns Hopkins University Press.

Schultz, T. Paul (1972), "Fertility Patterns and Their Determinants in the Arab Middle East," in Cooper and Alexander (1972), 400–501.

———, ed. (1978), *Distortions of Agricultural Incentives*, Bloomington, Indiana University Press.

——— (1981), *Economics of Population*, Reading, Mass., Addison-Wesley Pub. Co.

Schultz, T. W. (1981), *Investing in People: The Economics of Population Quality,* Berkeley, University of California Press.

Scobie, Grant (1981), *Government Policy and Food Imports: The Case of Wheat in Egypt,* Washington, D.C., IFPRI Research Report, No. 29, Dec.

Scott, James C. (1985), *Weapons of the Weak: Everyday Forms of Peasant Resistance,* New Haven, Yale University Press.

Scoville, J. G. (1985), "The Labor Market in Prerevolutionary Iran," *World Development* 34, 1 (Oct.), 143–51.

Seitz, John (1980), "The Failure of US Technical Assistance in Public Administration: The Iranian Case," *Public Administration Review* 40, 5 (Sept.-Oct.).

Semmoud, B. (1982), "Croissance du Secteur industriel privé en Algérie dans ses rélations avec le secteur national," *Revue Canadienne des Etudes Africaines,* No. 2.

Sen, Amartya (1981a), *Poverty and Famines: An Essay on Entitlement and Deprivation,* Oxford, Oxford University Press.

———— (1981b), "Public Action and the Quality of Life in Developing Countries," *Oxford Bulletin of Economics and Statistics* 43, 4 (Nov.), 287–319.

Sethuramen, S. V., ed. (1981), *The Urban Informal Sector in Developing Countries: Employment, Poverty and Environment,* Geneva, ILO.

Sharabi, Hisham (1962), *Government and Politics of the Middle East in the Twentieth Century,* Princeton, N.J., Van Nostrand Co.

Sharkansky, Ira (1984), "Religion and State in Begin's Israel," *Jerusalem Quarterly* 31, Spring, 31–49.

Shaw, J., and Long, David (1982), *Saudi Arabian Modernization,* New York, Praeger.

Shaw, R. Paul (1983), *Mobilizing Human Resources in the Arab World,* London, Routledge and Kegan Paul.

Sherbiny, Naiem A. (1984a), "Expatriate Labor Flows to the Arab Oil Countries in the 1980's," *MEJ* 38, 4 (Autumn), 643–67.

———— (1984b), "Expatriate Labor in Arab Oil Producing Countries," *Finance and Development* 21, 4 (Dec.), 34–37.

Short, R. P. (1984), "The Role of Public Enterprises: An International Statistical Comparison," in Floyd, Gray, and Short (1984), 109–45.

Shorter, F. C., and Zurayk, Huda, eds. (1985), *Population Factors in Development Planning in the Middle East,* New York, Population Council.

Shorter, Frederic C. (1985), "Demographical Measures of Inequality and Development," in Shorter and Zurayk (1985).

Signoles, P., and Ben Romdane, M. (1983), "Les formes récentes de l'industrialisation tunisiènne, 1979–1980," in GRESMO, *L'industrialisation du Bassin Méditerranéen,* Grenoble, Presses Universitaires de Grenoble, 109–50.

Simon, Julian (1982), *The Ultimate Resource,* Princeton, N.J., Princeton University Press.

Simpson, M. C. (1978), *Alternative Strategies for Agricultural Development in the Central Rainlands of the Sudan with Special Reference to Damazin Area,* Rural Development Studies No.3, University of Leeds.

Sivan, Emmanuel (1985), *Radical Islam: Medieval Theology and Modern Politics,* New Haven, Yale University Press.

Sklar, Richard (1979), "The Nature of Class Domination in Africa," *Journal of Modern Africa Studies* 17, 531–52.

Skocpol, Theda (1982), "Rentier State and Shi'a Islam in the Iranian Revolution," *Theory and Society* 2, 3, 265–304.

────── (1983), *States and Social Revolutions,* Cambridge, Cambridge University Press.

Sluglett, Marian Farouk, and Sluglett, Peter (1987), *Iraq Since 1958: From Revolution to Dictatorship,* London and New York, KPI.

Sluglett, Peter, and Sluglett, Marion Farouk (1984), "Modern Morocco: Political Immobilism, Economic Dependence," in Lawless and Findlay (1984), 50–100.

Smith, Tony (1975), "The Political and Economic Ambitions of Algerian Land Reform, 1962–1974," *MEJ* 29, 3 (Summer).

Smock, David, and Smock, Audry (1975), *The Politics of Pluralism: A Comparative Study of Lebanon and Ghana,* New York, Elsevier.

Soffer, Arnon (1986), "Lebanon—Where Demography is the Core of Politics and Life," *Middle Eastern Studies* 22, 2 (April), 192–205.

Somel, Kutlu (1986), "Agricultural Support Policies in Turkey, 1950–1980: An Overview," in Richards (1986b), 97–130.

Souali, M., and Merrouni, M. (1981), "Question de l'Enseignement au Maroc," *Bullétin Economique et Social du Maroc,* No. 5, 143–46.

Sousa, Alya (1982), "Eradication of Illiteracy in Iraq," in Niblock (1982a).

Springborg, Robert (1977), "New Patterns of Agrarian Reform in the Middle East and North Africa," *MEJ,* Spring, 127–42.

────── (1981), "Baathism in Practice: Agriculture, Politics and Political Culture in Syria and Iraq," *Middle Eastern Studies* 17, 2 (April), 191–209.

────── (1982), *Family, Power, and Politics in Egypt,* Philadelphia, University of Pennsyvania Press.

────── (1986), "Iraq's Agrarian *Infitah,*" *MEJ* 40, 1, Winter, 33–52.

────── (1987), "The President and the Field Marshal," *MERIP Reports* 17, 4 (July-Aug.), 4–16.

Stark, Oded (1983), "A Note on Labor Migration Functions," *Journal of Development Studies* 19, 4 (July), 539–43.

Stauffer, Thomas R. (with Frank H. Lennox) (1984), *Accounting for "Wasting Assets": Income Measurement for Oil and Mineral-Exporting Rentier States,* Vienna, OPEC Fund for International Development (Nov.)

Stepan, Alfred (1978), *The State and Society: Peru in Comparative Perspective,* Princeton, N.J., Princeton University Press.

Stobaugh, Robert, and Yergin, Daniel (1979), *Energy Future,* New York, Random House.

Stookey, Robert, ed. (1984), *The Arabian Peninsula: Zone of Ferment,* Stanford, Calif., Hoover Institution Press.

Stork, Joe (1975), *Middle East Oil and the Energy Crisis,* New York, Monthly Review Press.

────── (1979), "Oil and the Penetration of Capitalism in Iraq: An Interpretation," *Peuples Mediterranéens,* No. 9, Oct.-Dec., 125–52.

────── (1982), "State Power and Economic Structure: Class Determination and State Formation in Contemporary Iraq," in Niblock (1982a), 27–46.

────── (1987), "Arms Industries of the Middle East," *MERIP Reports,* No. 144 (Jan.-Feb.), 12–16.

Sudanese Government Task Force, assisted by World Bank Consultants (1978), *Public Corporations in Sudan,* Khartoum, Feb.

Sugar, Peter (1964), "Economic and Political Modernization: Turkey," in Ward and Rustow (1964), 146–75.

Sunar, I., and Toprak, B. (1983), "Islam in Politics: The Case of Turkey," *Government and Opposition* 18, 4 (Autumn), 421–41.

Sunar, Ilkay, and Sayari, Sabri (1986), "Democracy in Turkey: Problems and Prospects," in Guillermo O'Donnell, et al., eds., *Transitions from Authoritarian Rule: Prospects for Democracy,* Baltimore, Johns Hopkins University Press, 165–86.

Sutton, Keith (1984), "Algeria's Socialist Villages—A Reassessment," *Journal of Modern African Studies* 22, 2, 223–48.

Swanson, Jon C. (1979), *Emigration and Economic Development: The Case of the YAR,* Boulder, Colo., Westview Press.

Swearingen, Will D. (1987) *Moroccan Mirages: Agrarian Dreams and Deceptions, 1912–1986,* Princeton, N.J., Princeton University Press.

Tachau, Frank, and Heper, Metin (1983), "The State, Politics, and the Military in Turkey," in *Comparative Politics* 16 (October), 17–33.

Taylor-Awny, E. (1984), "Peasants or Proletarians: The Transformation of Agrarian Production Relations in Egypt," in H. Finch and B. Munslow, eds., *Proletarianisation in the Third World,* London, Croom Helm.

Tessler, Mark (1984), "Continuity and Change in Moroccan Politics," Parts 1 and 2, *UFSI Reports.*

Thiery, Simon Pierre (1982), *La crise du système productif algérien,* Services du reproduction des Theses, Université de Grenoble.

Tignor, Robert L. (1984), *State, Private Enterprise and Economic Change in Egypt, 1918–1952,* Princeton, N.J., Princeton University Press.

Tilly, Charles, ed. (1975), *The Formation of National States in Europe,* Princeton, N.J., Princeton University Press.

Timmer, C. Peter, Falcon, Walter P., and Pearson, Scott (1983), *Food Policy Analysis,* Baltimore and London, Johns Hopkins University Press.

Tlemcani, R. (1986), *State and Revolution in Algeria,* Boulder, Colo., Westview Press.

Todaro, Michael P. (1969), "A Model of Labor Migration and Urban Unemployment in Less Developed Countries," *American Economic Review* 59, 1, 138–48.

———— (1984), "Urbanization in Developing Nations: Trends, Prospects and Policies," in Pradip K. Ghosh, ed. *Urban Development in the Third World,* Westport, Conn., Greenwood.

Townsend, John (1982), "Industrial Development and the Decision-Making Process," in Niblock (1982a).

Trimberger, Ellen Kay (1978), *Revolution from Above: Military Bureaucrats and Development in Japan, Turkey, Egypt, and Peru,* New Brunswick, N.J., Transaction Books.

Tully, Dennis (1986), "Rainfed Farming Systems of the Near East Region," Aleppo, ICARDA, April, mimeo.

Tuma, Elias (1978), "Bottlenecks and Constraints in Agrarian Reform in the Near East," Background Paper for the World Conference on Agrarian Reform and Rural Institutions, FAO, Rome.

———— (1987), *Economic and Political Change in the Middle East,* Palo Alto, Calif., Pacific Books.

Tunisia, Republic of (1982), *Indicateurs Socio-Economiques Permettant de Surveiller et d'évaluer la Reforme Agraire et le Développement Rural,* Institut Nationale de la Statistique.

Turner, John C. (1969), "Uncontrolled Urban Settlement: Problems and Policies," in Gerald Breese, ed., *The City in Newly Developing Countries,* Englewood Cliffs, N.J., Prentice Hall, 507–34.

Ulman, A. H., and Tachau, F. (1965), "Turkish Politics: The Attempt to Reconcile Rapid Modernization with Democracy," *MEJ* 19, 153–68.

Uner, Sunday (1986), "Migration and Labor Transformation in Rural Turkey," in Richards (1986b), 265–82.

UNESCO, *Statistical Yearbook,* Paris, UNESCO, various years.

UNICEF (1986), *The State of the World's Children, 1984,* New York, Oxford University Press.

UNIDO (United Nations Industrial Development Organization) (1987), *Industry and Development: Global Report, 1987,* Vienna.

USAID (1983), "Tunisia: The Wheat Development Program," PN-AAL-022, Oct.

———— (1986), "Morocco Country Development Strategy Statement," Agency for International Development.

USDA (U.S. Department of Agriculture) (1987), *Middle East and North Africa: Situation and Outlook Report,* Washington, D.C., Economic Research Service.

U.S. Institute of Medicine (1979), "Health in Egypt: Recommendations for U.S. Assistance," Washington, D.C., Prepared for USAID, Jan.

Van Dam, N. (1981), *The Struggle for Power in Syria: Sectarianism, Regionalism and Tribalism, 1961–1978,* rev. ed., London, Croom Helm.

van der Kloet, Hendrik (1975), *Inégalités dans les Milieux Ruraux: Possibilités et Problèmes de la Modernisation Agricole au Maroc,* Geneva, United Nations Research on International Social Development (UNRISD).

Vandewalle, Dirk (1985), "Domestic Structure in International Political Economy: State Capitalism in Algeria and Libya," paper prepared for APSA annual meetings, Aug. 29–Sept. 1, New Orleans.

———— (1986), "Libya's Revolution Revisited," *MERIP Reports,* Nov.-Dec., 30–35.

Viratelle (1970), *L'Algérie Algérienne,* Paris, Editions économie et humanisme.

Volkan, V. D., and Itzkowitz, N. (1984), *The Immortal Atatürk,* Chicago, University of Chicago Press.

Walstedt, Bertil (1980), *State Manufacturing Enterprise in a Mixed Economy: The Turkish Case,* Baltimore and London, World Bank/Johns Hopkins Press.

Walt, Stephen (1987), *The Origins of Alliances,* Ithaca, N.Y., Cornell University Press.

Ward, R. E., and Rustow, D., eds. (1964) *Political Modernization in Japan and Turkey,* Princeton, N.J., Princeton University Press.

Warriner, Dorreen (1948), *Land and Poverty in the Middle East,* London, Royal Institute of International Affairs (RIIA).

———— (1962), *Land Reform and Development in the Middle East,* London, RIIA.

Waterbury, John (1970), *The Commander of the Faithful: The Moroccan Political Elite: A Study in Segmented Politics,* New York, Columbia University Press.

———— (1973a), "Land, Man, and Development in Algeria: Part II, Population, Employment and Emigration," *AUFS Reports,* North Africa Series, Vol. 17, No. 2.

———— (1973b), "Land, Man, and Development in Algeria: Part III, The Four Year Plan," *AUFS Reports,* North Africa Series, Vol. 17, No. 3.

———— (1978), *Egypt: Burdens of the Past, Options for the Future,* Bloomington, Indiana University Press.

———— (1979), *Hydropolitics of the Nile Valley,* Syracuse, Syracuse University Press

———— (1982), "Patterns of Urban Growth and Income Distribution in Egypt," in Abdel-Khalek and Tignor (1982), 307–50.

———— (1983), *The Egypt of Nasser and Sadat: The Political Economy of Two Regimes,* Princeton, N.J., Princeton University Press.

—— (1985), "The 'Soft State' and the Open Door: Egypt's Experience with Economic Liberalization, 1974–1984," *Comparative Politics* 18, 1 (October), 65–84.

Weulerrse, Jacques (1946), *Paysans de Syrie et du Proche Orient,* Paris, Gallimard.

Wickwar, W. Hardy (1963), *The Modernization of Administration in the Middle East,* Beirut, Khayat.

Wikan, Unni (1980), *Life Among the Poor in Cairo,* London, Tavistock.

Wittfogel, Karl (1964), *Oriental Despotism,* 5th ed., New Haven, Conn., Yale University Press.

Wolf, Eric (1968), *Peasant Wars of the Twentieth Century,* New York, Harper and Row.

World Bank (1979), *Yemen Arab Republic: Development of a Traditional Economy,* Washington, D.C., World Bank.

—— (1981), *Morocco: Economic and Social Development Report,* Washington, D.C., Oct.

—— (1982), *Turkey: Industrialization and Trade Strategy,* Washington, D.C., A World Bank Country Study.

—— (1983a), *Arab Republic of Egypt: Issues of Trade Strategy and Investment Planning,* Washington, D.C., World Bank.

—— (1983b), *World Development Report,* New York, Oxford University Press.

—— (1984), *World Development Report,* New York, Oxford University Press.

—— (1985), *Sudan: Prospects for Rehabilitation of the Sudanese Economy,* Report No. 5496-SU, Oct. 7.

—— (1986a), *Jordan: Issues of Employment and Labor Market Imbalances,* Report No. 5117-JO, May.

—— (1986b), *Poverty and Hunger,* Washington, D.C.

—— (1986c), *YAR: Agricultural Strategy Paper,* Report No. 5574-YAR, May.

—— (1987), *World Development Report,* New York, Oxford University Press.

World Resources Institute (1986), *World Resources, 1986: An Assessment of the Resource Base that Supports the Global Economy,* Washington, D.C., Worldwatch.

Wright, John (1970), *Libya,* New York, Praeger.

Wrigley, E., and Schofield, R. (1981), *The Population History of England, 1541–1871: A Reconstruction,* Cambridge, Harvard University Press.

Yalpat, Altan (1984), "Turkey's Economy under the Generals," *MERIP Reports,* No. 43 (March/April), 16–24.

Yotopoulos, Pan A., and Nugent, Jeffrey B. (1973), "A Balanced-Growth Version of the Linkage Hypothesis: A Test," *Quarterly Journal of Economics* 87, 4, 157–71.

Youngblood, Curtis E., et al. (1983), *Consumption Effects of Agricultural Policies: Bread Prices in the Sudan,* Raleigh, N.C., for Ministry of Finance and Economic Planning, Sudan, and USAID.

Zartman, I. W. (1975), "Algeria: A Post-Revolutionary Elite," in Frank Tachau, ed., *Political Elites and Political Development,* New York, Schenkmen-Wiley, 255–91.

——, ed. (1987) *The Political Economy of Morocco,* New York, Praeger.

Zartman, I. W., et al. (1982), *Political Elites in Arab North Africa,* New York, Longman.

Zghal, Abdelkader (1977), "Pourquoi la Réforme Agraire Ne Mobilise-t-elle Pas les Paysans, Maghrébins?" in Bruno Etiènne, ed., *Problèmes Agraires au Maghreb,* Paris, CNRS, 295–312.

Zonis, Marvin (1971), *The Political Elite of Iran,* Princeton, N.J., Princeton University Press.

Zureik, Elia (1981), "Theoretical Considerations for a Sociological Study of the Arab State," *Arab Studies Quarterly* 3, 3, 229–57.

# INDEX